FILM THEORY AND CRITICISM

FILM THEORY
AND
CRITICISM

Introductory Readings

Gerald Mast
Marshall Cohen

New York
OXFORD UNIVERSITY PRESS
London   1974   Toronto

Selections from works by the following authors were made possible by the kind permission of these publishers, representatives, and authors:

Joe Adamson: "Suspended Animation" is here published for the first time by arrangement with the author.

James Agee: *Agee on Film: Volume I.* Copyright © 1946, 1949, 1958 by The James Agee Trust. Reprinted by permission of Grosset & Dunlap, Inc. and Peter Owen Ltd., London.

Rudolf Arnheim: *Film as Art.* Originally published by the University of California Press. Reprinted by permission of The Regents of the University of California.

Béla Balázs: *Theory of the Film,* 1952. Reprinted by permission of Dover Publications Inc. and Dennis Dobson Publishers.

Charles Barr: *Film Quarterly,* Volume 16, Number 4. Copyright © 1963 by The Regents of the University of California. Reprinted by permission of The Regents and Charles Barr.

Richard Meran Barsam: *Nonfiction Film: A Critical History.* Copyright © 1973 by Richard Meran Barsam. Published by E. P. Dutton & Co., Inc., and used with their permission.

Roland Barthes: *Mythologies,* translated from the French *Mythologies.* Copyright

PREFACE

This collection of readings gathers together under one cover the most significant theories and theorists of film. Given the youth of the film art, the variety of its possibilities, and the fact that it incorporates so many other arts, it is not surprising that the general pattern of film theory is one of disagreement and diversity. Theorists have responded in many different ways to the fact that film has been both silent and with sound, in color and black-and-white, short and long, plotted and plotless, realistic and fantastic, logical and irrational, two- and three-dimensional, in wide and narrow screen, fictional and factual, live and animated, entertaining and educational.

In order to give some shape to this complexity, the book organizes its selections around seven topics which have emerged as the basic subjects of film theory. In the first section, Film and Reality, the collection examines the relationship between the motion picture and the reality which it photographs. In the second, Film Image and Film Language, the theorists examine the syntax and structure of the film itself. They ask how it generates "meaning." The third section, The Film Medium, considers the term "cinematic" and asks what qualities, if any, make the film art unique. The fourth section, Film, Theater, and Literature, continues this line of questioning and asks, in particular, how the film is related to those literary arts with which it has so much in common and from which it yet differs so greatly. The fifth section, Kinds of Film, analyzes some of the main genres of film and discusses the difficulties that arise in attempting to categorize films in these ways. The sixth section, The Film Artist, investigates the question of who, if anyone, ought to be called the artist in the collaborative endeavor of filmmaking. The seventh section, The Film Audience, asks what kind of experience film provides for its audience and what kind of experience it ought to provide.

Film theory is of importance not only for its own sake but also for the contribution it can make to film criticism. Each section therefore includes, in addition to the more theoretical articles, critical essays which show how the more general issues arise in connection with specific films and filmmakers. It is our hope that this anthology will contribute to the growing interest in film theory and to the practice of a more rigorous criticism than that which prevails at the present time.

We wish to thank Dudley Andrew, Hannah Arendt, Richard Balkin, Stanley Kauffmann, Harriet Serenkin, and John Wright for their helpful advice and comments.

CONTENTS

xi

CONTENTS

xii

CONTENTS

Shakespeare and Film

V

KINDS OF FILM

353

xiii

CONTENTS

VI
THE FILM ARTIST
489

VII
THE FILM AUDIENCE
575

xiv

CONTENTS

xv

I

Film and Reality

The main tradition of Western aesthetics, deriving from Aristotle's *Poetics*, adopts the view that art "imitates" nature or, in Hamlet's phrase, holds "the mirror up to nature." Painting, from the early Renaissance to the late nineteenth century, from Giotto to Manet and the impressionists, pursued this ideal with ever-increasing success. Later the novels of Balzac and Tolstoy achieved a more accurate representation of nature and society than anything literature had previously known, and the plays of Ibsen and Chekhov seemed to carry Hamlet's ideal of the theater to its limit. All these achievements were eclipsed, however, by the invention of photography. For the camera, and especially the motion picture camera, was unique in its ability to represent nature. If the ideal of art is to create an illusion of reality, the motion picture made it possible to achieve this ideal in an unprecedented way.

But is the aim of art to imitate nature at all? And if it is, what role remains for the other arts when film achieves it so simply and perfectly? An anti-realist tradition therefore denies that the goal of art is the imitation of nature. It has argued that to create a work of art is not simply to copy the world but to add another, and very special, object to the world. This object may be valuable because it offers an interpretation or idealization of the world, or even because it creates another, wholly autonomous, world. Others in this anti-realist tradition argue that the value of such an object may be that it expresses the feelings and emotions of its creator, or that the artist manages to impose a beautiful or a significant form on the

1

materials with which he works. The artist's feelings may be expressed abstractly, and the resulting form may be purely imaginative. The work of art may not allude to nature at all.

For example, theorists of modern painting have argued that painting should not even attempt to provide a three-dimensional representation of reality but acknowledge, instead, that it is essentially the application of pigments to a two-dimensional surface. This modernist view assumes that painting cannot and should not compete with film in attempting to mirror reality. Painting must renounce that task altogether. Others have argued, however, that film cannot reproduce reality either. And, even if it could, it ought not to try. According to this anti-realist view, film, like any other art form, must offer an interpretation of the world or, by the manipulation of the camera, create an alternative world. Just as painting must acknowledge that it is not really a mirror but pigments on canvas, cinema must acknowledge that it is simply projected images on a screen. To claim that these images ought to be images of physical reality—as opposed to any other kinds of images—is pure dogma. Why should these images not liberate the imagination from the tedium of reality, introducing us to the world of abstractions or of dreams instead?

Siegfried Kracauer, the German-born film historian and aesthetician, is a leading exponent of the realist view of cinema. In his book, *Theory of Film*, Kracauer argues that because film literally photographs reality it alone is capable of holding the mirror up to nature. Film actually reproduces the raw material of the physical world within the work of art. This makes it impossible for a film to be a "pure" expression of the artist's formative intentions or an abstract, imaginative expression of his emotions. Kracauer insists that it is the clear obligation and the special privilege of film (a descendant of still photography) to record and reveal, and thereby redeem, physical reality.

Kracauer's attitude is a response to the common complaint that the abstractions and categorizations of modern science and technology make it impossible for us to appreciate the concrete world in which we live—what John Crowe Ransom called "the world's body." The distinct function of art (especially of poetic imagery) might well be to help us possess the concrete world once more. Kracauer believes that the film art actually does this; it "literally redeems this world from its dormant state, its state of virtual non-existence, by endeavoring to experience it through the camera." For Kracauer film delivers us from technology by technology.

In his earlier work, *From Caligari to Hitler*, a study of the German cinema from 1919 to 1933, Kracauer traces the decline of German political culture as reflected in the history of its cinema. His view is that the German film's concern for artistic design and its dedication to purely formal values actually prepared the way for Hitler's rise by subtly diverting the audience from a serious appraisal of social realities. This era of German film, usually considered one of the great periods in the history of cinema, is for Kracauer an example of all that cinema must avoid. By ignoring the claims of camera reality the German cinema achieved the damnation, not the redemption, of German life.

André Bazin, who also insists on the unique realism of cinema, does so, however, from a markedly different viewpoint. Bazin, a French critic who founded the influential journal, *Cahiers du Cinéma*, in the late 1940s and whose practicing disciples include Jean-Luc Godard, François Truffaut, and Claude Chabrol, is perhaps the most important theorist of the "second" film generation, a generation for whom the experience of the silent film was no longer decisive. Unlike Kracauer, Bazin views the film's realism as an expression of the mythic, not of the scientific, spirit and believes that its function is not to redeem physical reality but to exempt us from our physical destiny. This magical aim finds expression in the "myth of total cinema," the ideal of a complete recreation of the world in its own image. Bazin welcomes the sound film as a necessary step toward this ideal. For similar reasons, he believes that *mise-en-scène* (arranging the elements of the scene and the camera's relationship to them so as to preserve their physical reality) is a more natural technique than *montage*.

But Bazin's conception of total cinema also leads to interesting questions—particularly in view of the most recent decade (the "third" generation) of film technology and film style. Would he have welcomed the widespread use of color and the advent of holography and of three-dimensional cinema, as his principles seem to indicate? And what would his attitude have been to the self-consciousness and self-referential tendencies of the film in the last decade? Devices such as slow motion, the freeze frame, the split screen, and color tinting call attention to the screen itself, rather than treating it as a simple window on the world. Although Bazin put his trust in the mechanical representation of uninterpreted reality, many of his followers have insisted on the artifice of the cinematic image.

Rudolph Arnheim, the psychologist and film aesthetician, is a leading "first generation" exponent of the anti-realist tradition in film theory. For Arnheim, if cinema were the mere mechanical reproduction of real life it could not be an art at all. Arnheim acknowledges the existence of a primitive desire to get material objects into one's power by creating them afresh, but he believes that this primitive impulse must be distinguished from the impulse to create art. The "wax museum" ideal may satisfy our primitive impulse, but it fails to satisfy the true artistic urge—not simply to copy, but to originate, to interpret, and to mold. The very properties that keep photography from reproducing reality perfectly must be exploited by the film artist, for they alone provide the possibilities for a film art. Bazin's myth of "total" cinema is nothing more than Arnheim's fallacy of the "complete" film. The pursuit of an ever more complete realism through the use of sound, color, and stereoscopic vision is simply a prescription for undermining the achievement of film art, which must respect, even welcome, the inherent limitations of the art.

For William Earle, a contemporary philosopher in the existentialist and phenomenological tradition, film art is not anti-realist by definition, but the medium is peculiarly apt for expressing an anti-realist sensibility. By severing the connection between sensations and perceptions, by divorcing things from their scientific connotations, and by calling attention to the film image itself, the anti-realist tradition expresses its attitude toward an all too "boring" reality. For anti-realists the attempt of realists to record and reveal physical reality is not only naïve; it is an inauthentic attempt to allay man's anxiety about the reality of physical existence. For Earle, the realist ideal is simply an invitation to spiritual death.

Parker Tyler, one of the most influential American critics and theorists who has recently achieved fame as the Socrates of Gore Vidal's *Myra Breckenridge*, sets his discussion of Bergman's *Persona* and Antonioni's *Blow-Up* against the background of the debate over realism in the cinema. He suggests that these masterpieces show the inadequacy of theorists like Kracauer, who insist that film must confine itself to recording physical reality, as well as of theorists like Susanne Langer, who argue that film narrative operates in the "dream-mode." We learn with the photographer in *Blow-Up* that Kracauer is wrong—photography affords only a limited access to reality; but we must also reject what Tyler takes to be Susanne Langer's assumption that film deals only with phenomena like the hallucinations of the nurse in *Persona*. In Tyler's view, psychic realities "inflect" and even transform the world, just as the artist's imagination does. It is precisely this active, imaginative power that expresses itself in film and prevents film from having to choose between the realism of Kracauer and Earle's revolt against it.

SIEGFRIED KRACAUER
FROM THEORY OF FILM

BASIC CONCEPTS

Like the embryo in the womb, photographic film developed from distinctly separate components. Its birth came about from a combination of instantaneous photography, as used by Muybridge and Marey, with the older devices of the magic lantern and the phenakistoscope. Added to this later were the contributions of other nonphotographic elements, such as editing and sound. Nevertheless photography, especially instantaneous photography, has a legitimate claim to top priority among these elements, for it undeniably is and remains the decisive factor in establishing film content. The nature of photography survives in that of film.

Originally, film was expected to bring the evolution of photography to an end—satisfying at last the age-old desire to picture things moving. This desire already accounted for major developments within the photographic medium itself. As far back as 1839, when the first daguerreotypes and talbotypes appeared, admiration mingled with disappointment about their deserted streets and blurred landscapes. And in the 'fifties, long before the innovation of the hand camera, successful attempts were made to photograph subjects in motion. The very impulses which thus led from time exposure to snapshot engendered dreams of a further extension of photography in the same direction—dreams, that is, of film. About 1860, Cook and Bonnelli, who had developed a device called a photobioscope, predicted a "complete revolution of photographic art. . . . We will see . . . landscapes," they announced, "in which the trees bow to the whims of the wind, the leaves ripple and glitter in the rays of the sun."

Along with the familiar photographic leitmotif of the leaves, such kindred subjects as undulating waves, moving clouds, and changing facial expressions ranked high in early prophecies. All of them conveyed the longing for an instrument which would capture the slightest incidents of the world about us — scenes that often would involve crowds, whose incalculable movements resemble, somehow, those of waves or leaves. In a memorable statement published before the emergence of instantaneous photography, Sir John Herschel not only predicted the basic features of the film camera but assigned to it a task which it has never since disowned: "the vivid and lifelike reproduction and handing down to the latest posterity of any transaction in real life — a battle, a debate, a public solemnity, a pugilistic conflict." Ducos du Hauron and other forerunners also looked forward to what we have come to label newsreels and documentaries — films devoted to the rendering of real-life events. This insistence on recording went hand in hand with the expectation that motion pictures could acquaint us with normally imperceptible or otherwise induplicable movements — flashlike transformations of matter, the slow growth of plants, etc. All in all, it was taken for granted that film would continue along the lines of photography. . . .

PROPERTIES OF THE MEDIUM

The properties of film can be divided into basic and technical properties.

The basic properties are identical with the properties of photography. Film, in other words, is uniquely equipped to record and reveal physical reality and, hence, gravitates toward it.

Now there are different visible worlds. Take a stage performance or a painting: they too are real and can be perceived. But the only reality we are concerned with is actually existing physical reality — the transitory world we live in. (Physical reality will also be called "material reality," or "physical existence," or "actuality," or loosely just "nature." Another fitting term might be "camera-reality.") . . . The other visible worlds reach into this world without, however, really forming a part of it. A theatrical play, for instance, suggests a universe of its own which would immediately crumble were it related to its real-life environment.

As a reproductive medium, film is of course justified in reproducing memorable ballets, operas, and the like. Yet even assuming that such reproductions try to do justice to the specific requirements of the screen, they basically amount to little more than "canning," and are of no interest to us here. Preservation of performances which lie outside physical reality proper is at best a sideline of a medium so particularly suited to explore that reality. This is not to deny that reproductions, say, of stage production numbers may be put to good cinematic use in certain feature films and film genres.

Of all the technical properties of film the most general and indispensable is editing. It serves to establish a meaningful continuity of shots and is therefore unthinkable in photography. (Photomontage is a graphic art rather than a specifically photographic genre.) Among the more special cinematic techniques are some which have been taken over from photography—e.g. the close-up, soft-focus pictures, the use of negatives, double or multiple exposure, etc. Others, such as the lap-dissolve, slow and quick motion, the reversal of time, certain "special effects," and so forth, are for obvious reasons exclusively peculiar to film.

These scanty hints will suffice. It is not necessary to elaborate on technical matters which have been dealt with in most previous theoretical writings on film. Unlike these, which invariably devote a great deal of space to editing devices, modes of lighting, various effects of the close-up, etc., the present book concerns itself with cinematic techniques only to the extent to which they bear on the nature of film, as defined by its basic properties and their various implications. The interest lies not with editing in itself, regardless of the purposes it serves, but with editing as a means of implementing—or defying, which amounts to the same—such potentialities of the medium as are in accordance with its substantive characteristics. In other words, the task is not to survey all possible methods of editing for their own sake; rather, it is to determine the contributions which editing may make to cinematically significant achievements. Problems of film technique will not be neglected; however, they will be discussed only if issues going beyond technical considerations call for their investigation.

This remark on procedures implies what is fairly obvious anyway: that the basic and technical properties differ substantially from each other. As a rule the former take precedence over the latter in the sense that they are responsible for the cinematic quality of a film. Imagine a film which, in keeping with the basic properties, records interesting aspects of physical reality but does so in a technically imperfect manner; perhaps the lighting is awkward or the editing uninspired. Nevertheless such a film is more specifically a film than one which utilizes brilliantly all the cinematic devices and tricks to produce a statement disregarding camera-reality. Yet this should not lead one to underestimate the influence of the technical properties. It will be seen that in certain cases the knowing use of a variety of techniques may endow otherwise nonrealistic films with a cinematic flavor.

THE TWO MAIN TENDENCIES

If film grows out of photography, the realistic and formative tendencies must be operative in it also. Is it by sheer accident that the two tendencies manifested themselves side by side immediately after the rise of the medium? As if to encompass the whole range of cinematic endeavors at the outset, each went the limit in exhausting its own possibilities. Their prototypes were Lumière, a strict realist, and Méliès, who gave free rein to his artistic imagination. The films they made embody, so to speak, thesis and antithesis in a Hegelian sense.

Lumière and Méliès

Lumière's films contained a true innovation, as compared with the repertoire of the zootropes or Edison's peep boxes: they pictured everyday life after the manner of photographs. Some of his early pictures, such as *Baby's Breakfast (Le Déjeuner de bébé)* or *The Card Players (La Partie d'écarté)*, testify to the amateur photographers's delight in family idyls and genre scenes. And there was *Teasing the Gardener (L'Arroseur arrosé)*, which enjoyed immense popularity because it elicited from the flow of everyday life a proper story with a funny climax to boot. A gardener is watering flowers and, as he unsuspectingly proceeds, an impish boy steps on the hose, releasing it at the very moment when his perplexed victim examines the dried-up nozzle. Water squirts out and hits the gardener smack in the face. The denouement is true to style, with the gardener chasing and spanking the boy. This film, the germ cell and archetype of all film comedies to come, represented an imaginative attempt on the part of Lumière to develop photography into a means of story telling. Yet the story was just a real-life incident. And it was precisely its photographic veracity which made Maxim Gorki undergo a shock-like experience. "You think," he wrote about *Teasing the Gardener*, "the spray is going to hit you too, and instinctively shrink back."

On the whole, Lumière seems to have realized that story telling was none of his business; it involved problems with which he apparently did not care to cope. Whatever story-telling films he, or his company, made—some more comedies in the vein of his first one, tiny historical scenes, etc.—are not characteristic of his production. The bulk of his films recorded the world about us for no other purpose than to present it. This is in any case what Mesguich, one of Lumière's "ace" cameramen, felt to be their message. At a time when the talkies were already in full swing he epitomized the work of the master as follows: "As I see it, the Lumière Brothers had established the true domain of the cinema in the right manner. The novel, the theater, suffice for the study of the human heart. The cinema is the dynamism of life, of nature and its manifestations, of the crowd and its eddies. All that asserts itself through movement depends on it. Its lens opens on the world."

Lumière's lens did open on the world in this sense. Take his immortal first reels *Lunch Hour at the Lumière Factory (Sortie des usines Lumière), Arrival of a Train (L'Arrivée d'un train), La Place des Cordeliers à Lyon:* their themes were public places, with throngs of people moving in diverse directions. The crowded streets captured by the stereographic photographs of the late 'fifties thus reappeared on the primitive screen. It was life at its least controllable and most unconscious moments, a jumble of transient, forever dissolving patterns accessible only to the camera. The much-imitated shot of the railway station, with its emphasis on the confusion of arrival and departure, effectively illustrated the fortuity of these patterns; and their fragmentary character was exemplified by the clouds of smoke which leisurely drifted upward. Significantly, Lumière used the motif of smoke on several occasions. And he seemed anxious to avoid any personal interference with the given data. Detached records, his shots resembled the imaginary shot of the grandmother which Proust contrasts with the memory image of her.

Contemporaries praised these films for the very qualities which the prophets and forerunners had singled out in their visions of the medium. It is inevitable that, in the comments on Lumière, "the ripple of leaves stirred by the wind" should be referred to enthusiastically. The Paris journalist Henri de Parville, who used the image of the trembling leaves, also identified Lumière's over-all theme as "nature caught in the act." Others pointed to the benefits which science would derive from Lumière's invention. In America his camera-realism defeated Edison's kinetoscope with its staged subjects.

Lumière's hold on the masses was ephemeral. In 1897, not more than two years after he had begun to make films, his popularity subsided. The sensation had worn off; the heyday was over. Lack of interest caused Lumière to reduce his production.

Georges Méliès took over where Lumière left off, renewing and intensifying the medium's waning appeal. This is not to say that he did not occasionally follow the latter's example. In his beginnings he too treated the audience to sightseeing tours; or he dramatized, in the fashion of the period, realistically staged topical events. But his main contribution to the cinema lay in substituting staged illusion for unstaged reality, and contrived plots for everyday incidents.

The two pioneers were aware of the radical differences in their approach. Lumière told Méliès that he considered film nothing more than a "scientific curiosity," thereby implying that his cinematograph could not possibly serve artistic purposes. In 1897, Méliès on his part published a prospectus which took issue with Lumière: "Messrs. Méliès and Reulos specialize mainly in fantastic or artistic scenes, reproductions of theatrical scenes, etc. . . . thus creating a special genre which differs entirely from the customary views supplied by the cinematograph—street scenes or scenes of everyday life."

Méliès's tremendous success would seem to indicate that he

catered to demands left unsatisfied by Lumière's photographic realism. Lumière appealed to the sense of observation, the curiosity about "nature caught in the act"; Méliès ignored the workings of nature out of the artist's delight in sheer fantasy. The train in *Arrival of a Train* is the real thing, whereas its counterpart in Méliès's *An Impossible Voyage (Voyage à travers l'impossible)* is a toy train as unreal as the scenery through which it is moving. Instead of picturing the random movements of phenomena, Méliès freely interlinked imagined events according to the requirements of his charming fairy-tale plots. Had not media very close to film offered similar gratifications? The artist-photographers preferred what they considered aesthetically attractive compositions to searching explorations of nature. And immediately before the arrival of the motion picture camera, magic lantern performances indulged in the projection of religious themes, Walter Scott novels, and Shakespearean dramas.

Yet even though Méliès did not take advantage of the camera's ability to record and reveal the physical world, he increasingly created his illusions with the aid of techniques peculiar to the medium. Some he found by accident. When taking shots of the Paris Place de l'Opéra, he had to discontinue the shooting because the celluloid strip did not move as it should; the surprising result was a film in which, for no reason at all, a bus abruptly transformed itself into a hearse. True, Lumière also was not disinclined to have a sequence of events unfold in reverse, but Méliès was the first to exploit cinematic devices systematically. Drawing on both photography and the stage, he innovated many techniques which were to play an enormous role in the future—among them the use of masks, multiple exposure, superimposition as a means of summoning ghosts, the lap-dissolve, etc. And through his ingenuity in using these techniques he added a touch of cinema to his playful narratives and magic tricks. Stage traps ceased to be indispensable; sleights-of-hand yielded to incredible metamorphoses which film alone was able to accomplish. Illusion produced in this climate depended on another kind of craftsmanship than the magician's. It was cinematic illusion, and as such went far beyond theatrical make-believe. Méliès's *The Haunted Castle (Le Manoir du diable)* "is conceivable only in the cinema and due to the cinema," says

Henri Langlois, one of the best connoisseurs of the primitive era.

Notwithstanding his film sense, however, Méliès still remained the theater director he had been. He used photography in a pre-photographic spirit—for the reproduction of a papier-maché universe inspired by stage traditions. In one of his greatest films, *A Trip to the Moon (Le Voyage dans la lune)*, the moon harbors a grimacing man in the moon and the stars are bull's-eyes studded with the pretty faces of music hall girls. By the same token, his actors bowed to the audience, as if they performed on the stage. Much as his films differed from the theater on a technical plane, they failed to transcend its scope by incorporating genuinely cinematic subjects. This also explains why Méliès, for all his inventiveness, never thought of moving his camera; the stationary camera perpetuated the spectator's relation to the stage. His ideal spectator was the traditional theatergoer, child or adult. There seems to be some truth in the observation that, as people grow older, they instinctively withdraw to the positions from which they set out to struggle and conquer. In his later years Méliès more and more turned from theatrical film to filmed theater, producing *féeries* which recalled the Paris Châtelet pageants.

The Realistic Tendency

In following the realistic tendency, films go beyond photography in two respects. First, they picture movement itself, not only one or another of its phases. But what kinds of movements do they picture? In the primitive era when the camera was fixed to the ground, it was natural for film makers to concentrate on moving material phenomena; life on the screen was life only if it manifested itself through external, or "objective," motion. As cinematic techniques developed, films increasingly drew on camera mobility and editing devices to deliver their messages. Although their strength still lay in the rendering of movements inaccessible to other media, these movements were no longer necessarily objective. In the technically mature film "subjective" movements—movements, that is, which the spectator is invited to execute—constantly compete with objective ones. The spectator may have to identify himself with a tilting, panning, or traveling camera which insists on bringing motionless

14

as well as moving objects to his attention. Or an appropriate arrangement of shots may rush the audience through vast expanses of time and/or space so as to make it witness, almost simultaneously, events in different periods and places.

Nevertheless the emphasis is now as before on objective movement; the medium seems to be partial to it. As René Clair puts it: "If there is an aesthetics of the cinema . . . it can be summarized in one word: 'movement.' The external movement of the objects perceived by the eye, to which we are today adding the inner movement of the action." The fact that he assigns a dominant role to external movement reflects, on a theoretical plane, a marked feature of his own earlier films—the ballet-like evolutions of their characters.

Second, films may seize upon physical reality with all its manifold movements by means of an intermediary procedure which would seem to be less indispensable in photography—staging. In order to narrate an intrigue, the film maker is often obliged to stage not only the action but the surroundings as well. Now this recourse to staging is most certainly legitimate if the staged world is made to appear as a faithful reproduction of the real one. The important thing is that studio-built settings convey the impression of actuality, so that the spectator feels he is watching events which might have occurred in real life and have been photographed on the spot.

Falling prey to an interesting misconception, Emile Vuillermoz champions, for the sake of "realism," settings which represent reality as seen by a perceptive painter. To his mind they are more real than real-life shots because they impart the essence of what such shots are showing. Yet from the cinematic point of view these allegedly realistic settings are no less stagy than would be, say, a cubist or abstract composition. Instead of staging the given raw material itself, they offer, so to speak, the gist of it. In other words, they suppress the very camera-reality which film aims at incorporating. For this reason, the sensitive moviegoer will feel disturbed by them. (The problems posed by films of fantasy which, as such, show little concern for physical reality will be considered later on.)

Strangely enough, it is entirely possible that a staged real-life event evokes a stronger illusion of reality on the screen than would the original event if it had been captured directly by the camera.

15

The late Ernö Metzner who devised the settings for the studio-made mining disaster in Pabst's *Kameradschaft*—an episode with the ring of stark authenticity—insisted that candid shots of a real mining disaster would hardly have produced the same convincing effect.

One may ask, on the other hand, whether reality can be staged so accurately that the camera-eye will not detect any difference between the original and the copy. Blaise Cendrars touches on this issue in a neat hypothetical experiment. He imagines two film scenes which are completely identical except for the fact that one has been shot on the Mont Blanc (the highest mountain of Europe) while the other was staged in the studio. His contention is that the former has a quality not found in the latter. There are on the mountain, says he, certain "emanations, luminous or otherwise, which have worked on the film and given it a soul." Presumably large parts of our environment, natural or man-made, resist duplication.

The Formative Tendency

The film maker's formative faculties are offered opportunities far exceeding those offered the photographer. The reason is that film extends into dimensions which photography does not cover. These differ from each other according to area and composition. With respect to areas, film makers have never confined themselves to exploring only physical reality in front of the camera but, from the outset, persistently tried to penetrate the realms of history and fantasy. Remember Méliès. Even the realistic-minded Lumière yielded to the popular demand for historical scenes. As for composition, the two most general types are the story film and the non-story film. The latter can be broken down into the experimental film and the film of fact, which on its part comprises, partially or totally, such subgenres as the film on art, the newsreel, and the documentary proper.

It is easy to see that some of these dimensions are more likely than others to prompt the film maker to express his formative aspirations at the expense of the realistic tendency. As for areas, consider that of fantasy: movie directors have at all times rendered dreams or visions with the aid of settings which are anything but realistic. Thus in *Red Shoes* Moira Shearer dances, in a somnambulistic trance, through fantastic worlds avowedly intended to project her unconscious mind — agglomerates of landscape-like forms, near-abstract shapes, and luscious color schemes which have all the traits of stage imagery. Disengaged creativity thus drifts away from the basic concerns of the medium. Several dimensions of composition favor the same preferences. Most experimental films are not even designed to focus on physical existence; and practically all films following the lines of a theatrical story evolve narratives whose significance overshadows that of the raw material of nature used for their implementation. For the rest, the film maker's formative endeavors may also impinge on his realistic loyalities in dimensions which, because of their emphasis on physical reality, do not normally invite such encroachments; there are enough documentaries with real-life shots which merely serve to illustrate some self-contained oral commentary.

Clashes Between the Two Tendencies

Films which combine two or more dimensions are very frequent; for instance, many a movie featuring an everyday-life incident includes a dream sequence or a documentary passage. Some such combinations may lead to overt clashes between the realistic and formative tendencies. This happens whenever a film maker bent on creating an imaginary universe from freely staged material also feels under an obligation to draw on camera-reality. In his *Hamlet* Laurence Olivier has the cast move about in a studio-built, conspicuously stagy Elsinore, whose labyrinthine architecture seems calculated to reflect Hamlet's unfathomable being. Shut off from our real-life environment, this bizarre structure would spread over the whole of the film were it not for a small, otherwise insignificant scene in which the real ocean outside that dream orbit is shown. But no sooner does the photographed ocean appear than the spectator experiences something like a shock. He cannot help recognizing that this little scene is an outright intrusion; that it abruptly introduces an element incompatible with the rest of the imagery. How he then reacts to it depends upon his sensibilities. Those indifferent to the peculiarities of the medium, and therefore unquestioningly accepting the staged Elsinore, are likely to resent the unexpected

17

emergence of crude nature as a letdown, while those more sensitive to the properties of film will in a flash realize the make-believe character of the castle's mythical splendor. Another case in point is Renato Castellani's *Romeo and Juliet*. This attempt to stage Shakespeare in natural surroundings obviously rests upon the belief that camera-reality and the poetic reality of Shakespeare verse can be made to fuse into each other. Yet the dialogue as well as the intrigue establish a universe so remote from the chance world of real Verona streets and ramparts that all the scenes in which the two disparate worlds are seen merging tend to affect one as an unnatural alliance between conflicting forces.

Actually collisions of this kind are by no means the rule. Rather, there is ample evidence to suggest that the two tendencies which sway the medium may be interrelated in various other ways. Since some of these relationships between realistic and formative efforts can be assumed to be aesthetically more gratifying than the rest, the next step is to try to define them.

THE CINEMATIC APPROACH

It follows from what has been said . . . that films may claim aesthetic validity if they build from their basic properties; like photographs, that is, they must record and reveal physical reality. . . . One might argue that too exclusive an emphasis on the medium's primary relation to physical reality tends to put film in a strait jacket. This objection finds support in the many existing films which are completely unconcerned about the representation of nature. There is the abstract experimental film. There is an unending succession of "photoplays" or theatrical films which do not picture real-life material for its own sake but use it to build up action after the manner of the stage. And there are the many films of fantasy which neglect the external world in freely composed dreams or visions. The old German expressionist films went far in this direction; one of their champions, the German art critic Herman G. Scheffauer, even eulogizes expressionism on the screen for its remoteness from photographic life.

Why, then, should these genres be called less "cinematic" than films concentrating on physical existence? The answer is of course that it is the latter alone which afford insight and enjoyment other-

wise unattainable. True, in view of all the genres which do not cultivate outer reality and yet are here to stay, this answer sounds somewhat dogmatic. But perhaps it will be found more justifiable in the
light of the following two considerations.

First, favorable response to a genre need not depend upon its ade-
quacy to the medium from which it issues. As a matter of fact,
many a genre has a hold on the audience because it caters to widespread social and cultural demands; it is and remains popular for
reasons which do not involve questions of aesthetic legitimacy.
Thus the photoplay has succeeded in perpetuating itself even
though most responsible critics are agreed that it goes against the
grain of film. Yet the public which feels attracted, for instance, by
the screen version of *Death of a Salesman*, likes this version for the
very virtues which made the Broadway play a hit and does not in
the least care whether or not it has any specifically cinematic
merits.

Second, let us for the sake of argument assume that my definition of aesthetic validity is actually one-sided; that it results from a
bias for one particular, if important, type of cinematic activities and
hence is unlikely to take into account, say, the possibility of hybrid
genres or the influence of the medium's nonphotographic components. But this does not necessarily speak against the propriety of
that definition. In a strategic interest it is often more advisable to
loosen up initial one-sidedness—provided it is well founded—than
to start from all too catholic premises and then try to make them
specific. The latter alternative runs the risk of blurring differences
between the media because it rarely leads far enough away from the
generalities postulated at the outset; its danger is that it tends to entail a confusion of the arts. When Eisenstein, the theoretician, began
to stress the similarities between the cinema and the traditional
art media, identifying film as their ultimate fulfillment, Eisenstein,
the artist, increasingly trespassed the boundaries that separate
film from elaborate theatrical spectacles: think of his *Alexander
Nevsky* and the operatic aspects of his *Ivan the Terrible*.

In strict analogy to the term "photographic approach" the film
maker's approach is called "cinematic" if it acknowledges the basic
aesthetic principle. It is evident that the cinematic approach materializes in all films which follow the realistic tendency. This implies
that even films almost devoid of creative aspirations, such as news-

reels, scientific or educational films, artless documentaries, etc., are tenable propositions from an aesthetic point of view—presumably more so than films which for all their artistry pay little attention to the given outer world. But as with photographic reportage, newsreels and the like meet only the minimum requirement.

What is of the essence in film no less than photography is the intervention of the film maker's formative energies in all the dimensions which the medium has come to cover. He may feature his impressions of this or that segment of physical existence in documentary fashion, transfer hallucinations and mental images to the screen, indulge in the rendering of rhythmical patterns, narrate a human-interest story, etc. All these creative efforts are in keeping with the cinematic approach as long as they benefit, in some way or other, the medium's substantive concern with our visible world. As in photography, everything depends on the "right" balance between the realistic tendency and the formative tendency; and the two tendencies are well balanced if the latter does not try to overwhelm the former but eventually follows its lead.

THE ISSUE OF ART

When calling the cinema an art medium, people usually think of films which resemble the traditional works of art in that they are free creations rather than explorations of nature. These films organize the raw material to which they resort into some self-sufficient composition instead of accepting it as an element in its own right. In other words, their underlying formative impulses are so strong that they defeat the cinematic approach with its concern for camera-reality. Among the film types customarily considered art are, for instance, the above-mentioned German expressionist films of the years after World War I; conceived in a painterly spirit, they seem to implement the formula of Hermann Warm, one of the designers of *The Cabinet of Dr. Caligari* settings, who claimed that "films must be drawings brought to life." Here also belongs many an experimental film; all in all, films of this type are not only intended as autonomous wholes but frequently ignore physical reality or exploit it for purposes alien to photographic veracity. By the same token, there is an inclination to classify as works of art feature films which combine forceful artistic composition with devotion to significant subjects and values. This would apply to a number of adaptations of great stage plays and other literary works.

Yet such a usage of the term "art" in the traditional sense is misleading. It lends support to the belief that artistic qualities must be attributed precisely to films which neglect the medium's recording obligations in an attempt to rival achievements in the fields of the fine arts, the theater, or literature. In consequence, this usage tends to obscure the aesthetic value of films which are really true to the medium. If the term "art" is reserved for productions like *Hamlet* or *Death of a Salesman*, one will find it difficult indeed to appreciate properly the large amount of creativity that goes into many a documentary capturing material phenomena for their own sake. Take Ivens's *Rain* or Flaherty's *Nanook*, documentaries saturated with formative intentions: like any selective photographer, their creators have all the traits of the imaginative reader and curious explorer; and their readings and discoveries result from full absorption in the given material and significant choices. Add to this that some of the crafts needed in the cinematic process—especially editing—represent tasks with which the photographer is not confronted. And they too lay claim to the film maker's creative powers.

This leads straight to a terminological dilemma. Due to its fixed meaning, the concept of art does not, and cannot, cover truly "cinematic" films—films, that is, which incorporate aspects of physical reality with a view to making us experience them. And yet it is they, not the films reminiscent of traditional art works, which are valid aesthetically. If film is an art at all, it certainly should not be confused with the established arts. There may be some justification in loosely applying this fragile concept to such films as *Nanook*, or *Paisan*, or *Potemkin* which are deeply steeped in camera-life. But in defining them as art, it must always be kept in mind that even the most creative film maker is much less independent of nature in the raw than the painter or poet; that his creativity manifests itself in letting nature in and penetrating it.

ANDRÉ BAZIN
FROM WHAT IS CINEMA?

THE MYTH OF TOTAL CINEMA

Paradoxically enough, the impression left on the reader by Georges Sadoul's admirable book on the origins of the cinema is of a reversal, in spite of the author's Marxist views, of the relations between an economic and technical evolution and the imagination of those carrying on the search. The way things happened seems to call for a reversal of the historical order of causality, which goes from the economic infrastructure to the ideological superstructure, and for us to consider the basic technical discoveries as fortunate accidents but essentially second in importance to the preconceived ideas of the inventors. The cinema is an idealistic phenomenon. The concept men had of it existed so to speak fully armed in their minds, as if in some platonic heaven, and what strikes us most of all is the obstinate resistance of matter to ideas rather than of any help offered by techniques to the imagination of the researchers.

Furthermore, the cinema owes virtually nothing to the scientific spirit. Its begetters are in no sense savants, except for Marey, but it is significant that he was only interested in analyzing movement and not in reconstructing it. Even Edison is basically only a do-it-yourself man of genius, a giant of the *concours Lépine*. Niepce, Muybridge, Leroy, Joly, Demeny, even Louis Lumière himself, are all monomaniacs, men driven by an impulse, do-it-yourself men or at best ingenious industrialists. As for the wonderful, the sublime E. Reynaud, who can deny that his animated drawings are the result of an unremitting pursuit of an *idée fixe*? Any account of the cinema that was drawn merely from the technical inventions that made it possible would be a poor one indeed. On the contrary, an approximate and complicated visualization of an idea invariably precedes the industrial discovery which alone can open the way to its practical use. Thus if it is evident to us today that the cinema even at its most elementary stage needed a transparent, flexible, and resistant base and a dry sensitive emulsion capable of receiving an image instantly—everything else being a matter of setting in order a mechanism far less complicated than an eighteenth-century clock—it is clear that all the definitive stages of the invention of the cinema had been reached before the requisite conditions had been fulfilled. In 1877 and 1880, Muybridge, thanks to the imaginative generosity of a horse-lover, managed to construct a large complex device which enabled him to make from the image of a galloping horse the first series of cinematographic pictures. However to get this result he had to be satisfied with wet collodion on a glass plate, that is to say, with just one of the three necessary elements—namely instantaneity, dry emulsion, flexible base. After the discovery of gelatino-bromide of silver but before the appearance on the market of the first celluloid reels, Marey had made a genuine camera which used glass plates. Even after the appearance of celluloid strips Lumière tried to use paper film.

Once more let us consider here only the final and complete form of the photographic cinema. The synthesis of simple movements studied scientifically by Plateau had no need to wait upon the industrial and economic developments of the nineteenth century. As Sadoul correctly points out, nothing had stood in the way, from antiquity, of the manufacture of a phenakistoscope or a zootrope. It is true that here the labors of that genuine savant Plateau were at the origin of the many inventions that made the popular use of his discovery possible. But while, with the photographic cinema, we have cause for some astonishment that the discovery somehow precedes the technical conditions necessary to its existence, we must here explain, on the other hand, how it was that the invention took so long to emerge, since all the prerequisites had been assembled and the persistence of the image on the retina had been known for a long time. It might be of some use to point out that although the two were not necessarily connected scientifically, the efforts of Plateau are pretty well contemporary with those of Nicéphore Niepce, as if the attention of researchers had waited to concern itself with synthesizing movement until chemistry quite independently of optics had become concerned, on its part, with the automatic fixing of the image.

I emphasize the fact that this historical coincidence can apparently in no way be explained on grounds of scientific, economic, or industrial evolution. The photographic cinema could just as well have grafted itself onto a phenakistoscope foreseen as long ago as the sixteenth century. The delay in the invention of the latter is as disturbing a phenomenon as the existence of the precursors of the former.

But if we examine their work more closely, the direction of their research is manifest in the instruments themselves, and, even more undeniably, in their writings and commentaries we see that these precursors were indeed more like prophets. Hurrying past the various stopping places, the very first of which materially speaking should have halted them, it was at the very height and summit that most of them were aiming. In their imaginations they saw the cinema as a total and complete representation of reality; they saw in a trice the reconstruction of a perfect illusion of the outside world in sound, color, and relief.

As for the latter, the film historian P. Potoniée has even felt justified in maintaining that it was not the discovery of photography but of stereoscopy, which came onto the market just slightly before the first attempts at animated photography in 1851, that opened the eyes of the researchers. Seeing people immobile in space, the photographers realized that what they needed was movement if their photographs were to become a picture of life and a faithful copy of nature. In any case, there was not a single inventor who did not try to combine sound and relief with animation of the image—whether it be Edison with his kinetoscope made to be attached to a phonograph, or Demenay and his talking portraits, or even Nadar who shortly before producing the first photographic interview, on Chevreul, had written, "My dream is to see the photograph register the bodily movements and the facial expressions of a speaker while the phonograph is recording his speech" (February, 1887). If color had not yet appeared it was because the first experiments with the three-color process were slower in coming. But E. Reynaud had been painting his little figurines for some time and the first films of Méliès are colored by stencilling. There are numberless writings, all of them more or less wildly enthusiastic, in which inventors conjure up nothing less than a total cinema that is to provide that complete illusion of life which is still a long way away. Many are familiar with that passage from *L'Éve Future* in which Villiers de l'Isle-Adam, two years before Edison had begun his researches on animated photography, puts into the inventor's mouth the following description of a fantastic achievement: ". . . the vision, its transparent flesh miraculously photographed in color and wearing a spangled costume, danced a kind of popular Mexican dance. Her movements had the flow of life itself, thanks to the process of successive photography which can retain six minutes of movement on microscopic glass, which is subsequently reflected by means of a powerful lampascope. Suddenly was heard a flat and unnatural voice, dull-sounding and harsh. The dancer was singing the *alza* and the *olé* that went with her *fandango*."

The guiding myth, then, inspiring the invention of cinema, is the accomplishment of that which dominated in a more or less vague fashion all the techniques of the mechanical reproduction of reality in the nineteenth century, from photography to the phonograph, namely an integral realism, a recreation of the world in its own image, an image unburdened by the freedom of interpretation of the artist or the irreversibility of time. If cinema in its cradle lacked all the attributes of the cinema to come, it was with reluctance and because its fairy guardians were unable to provide them however much they would have liked to.

If the origins of an art reveal something of its nature, then one may legitimately consider the silent and the sound film as stages of a technical development that little by little made a reality out of the original "myth." It is understandable from this point of view that it would be absurd to take the silent film as a state of primal perfection which has gradually been forsaken by the realism of sound and color. The primacy of the image is both historically and technically accidental. The nostalgia that some still feel for the silent screen does not go far enough back into the childhood of the seventh art. The real primitives of the cinema, existing only in the imaginations of a few men of the nineteenth century, are in complete imitation of nature. Every new development added to the cinema must, paradoxically, take it nearer and nearer to its origins. In short, cinema has not yet been invented!

It would be a reversal then of the concrete order of causality, at least psychologically, to place the scientific discoveries or the industrial techniques that have loomed so large in its development at the source of the cinema's invention. Those who had the least confidence in the future of the cinema were precisely the two industrialists Edison and Lumière. Edison was satisfied with just his kinetoscope and if Lumière judiciously refused to sell his patent to Méliès it was undoubtedly because he hoped to make a large profit out of it for himself, but only as a plaything of which the public would soon tire. As for the real savants such as Marey, they were only of indirect assistance to the cinema. They had a specific purpose in mind and were satisfied when they had accomplished it. The fanatics, the madmen, the disinterested pioneers, capable, as was Berard Palissy, of burning their furniture for a few seconds of shaky images, are neither industrialists nor savants, just men obsessed by their own imaginings. The cinema was born from the converging of these various obsessions, that is to say, out of a myth, the myth of total cinema. This likewise adequately explains the delay of Plateau in applying the optical principle of the persistence of the image on the retina, as also the continuous progress of the syntheses of movement as compared with the state of photographic techniques. The fact is that each alike was dominated by the imagination of the century. Undoubtedly there are other examples in the history of techniques and inventions of the convergence of research, but one must distinguish between those which come as a result precisely of scientific evolution and industrial or military requirements and those which quite clearly precede them. Thus, the myth of Icarus had to wait on the internal combustion engine before descending from the platonic heavens. But it had dwelt in the soul of everyman since he first thought about birds. To some extent, one could say the same thing about the myth of cinema, but its forerunners prior to the nineteenth century have only a remote connection with the myth which we share today and which has prompted the appearance of the mechanical arts that characterize today's world.

RUDOLF ARNHEIM
FROM FILM AS ART

THE COMPLETE FILM

The technical development of the motion picture will soon carry the mechanical imitation of nature to an extreme. The addition of sound was the first obvious step in this direction. The introduction of sound film must be considered as the imposition of a technical novelty that did not lie on the path the best film artists were pursuing. They were engaged in working out an explicit and pure style of silent film, using its restrictions to transform the peep show into an art. The introduction of sound film smashed many of the forms that the film artists were using in favor of the inartistic demand for the greatest possible "naturalness" (in the most superficial sense of the word). By sheer good luck, sound film is not only destructive but also offers artistic potentialities of its own. Owing to this accident alone the majority of art-lovers still do not realize the pitfalls in the road pursued by the movie producers. They do not see that the film is on its way to the victory of wax museum ideals over creative art.

The development of the silent film was arrested possibly forever when it had hardly begun to produce good results; but it has left us with a few splendidly mature films. In the future, no doubt, "progress" will be faster. We shall have color films and stereoscopic films, and the artistic potentialities of the sound film will be crushed at an even earlier stage of their development.

What will the color film have to offer when it reaches technical perfection? We know what we shall lose artistically by abandoning the black-and-white film. Will color ever allow us to achieve a similar compositional precision, a similar independence of "reality"?

The masterpieces of painting prove that color provides wider possibilities than black-and-white and at the same time permits of a very exact and genuine style. But can painting and color photography be compared? Whereas the painter has a perfectly free hand with color and form in presenting nature, photography is obliged to record mechanically the light values of physical reality. In achromatic photography the reduction of everything to the gray scale resulted in an art medium that was sufficiently independent and divergent from nature. There is not much likelihood of any such transpositon of reality into a qualitatively different range of colors in color film. To be sure, one can eliminate individual colors—one may, for example, cut out all blues, or, vice versa, one may cut out everything except the blues. Probably it is possible also to change one or more color tones qualitatively—for example, give all reds a cast of orange or make all the yellows greenish—or let colors change places with one another—turn all blues to red and all reds to blue—but all this would be, so to speak, only transposition of reality, mechanical shifts, whose usefulness as a formative medium may be doubted. Hence there remains only the possibility of controlling the color by clever choice of what is to be photographed. All kinds of fine procedures are conceivable, especially in the montage of colored pictures, but it must not be overlooked that in this way the subjective formative virtues of the camera, which are so distinctive a characteristic of film, will be more and more restricted, and the artistic part of the work will be more and more focused upon what is set up and enacted *before* the camera. The camera is thereby increasingly relegated to the position of a mere mechanical recording machine.

Above all, it is hardly realistic to speculate on the artistic possibilities of the color film without keeping in mind that at the same time we are likely to be presented with the three-dimensional film and the wide screen. Efforts in these directions are in progress. The illusion of reality will thereby have been increased to such a degree that the spectator will not be able to appreciate certain artistic color effects even if they should be feasible technically. It is quite conceivable that by a careful choice and arrangement of objects it might be possible to use the color on the projection surface artistically and harmoniously. But if the film image becomes stereoscopic there is no longer a plane surface within the confines of the screen, and therefore there can be no composition of that surface; what remains will be effects that are also possible on the stage. The increased size of the screen will render any two-dimensional or three-dimensional composition less compelling; and formative devices such as montage and changing camera angles will become unusable if the illusion of reality is so enormously strengthened. Obviously, montage will seem an intolerable accumulation of heterogeneous settings if the illusion of reality is very strong. Obviously also a change in the position of the camera will now be felt as an actual displacement within the space of the picture. The camera will have to become an immobile recording machine, every cut in the film strip will be mutilation. Scenes will have to be taken in their entire length and with a stationary camera, and they will have to be shown as they are. The artistic potentialities of this form of film will be exactly those of the stage. Film will no longer be able in any sense to be considered as a separate art. It will be thrown back to before its first beginnings—for it was with a fixed camera and an uncut strip that film started. The only difference will be that instead of having all before it film will have nothing to look forward to.

This curious development signifies to some extent the climax of that striving after likeness to nature which has hitherto permeated the whole history of the visual arts. Among the strivings that make human beings create faithful images is the primitive desire to get material objects into one's power by creating them afresh. Imitation also permits people to cope with significant experiences; it provides release, and makes for a kind of reciprocity between the self and the world. At the same time a reproduction that is true to nature provides the thrill that by the hand of man an image has been created which is astoundingly like some natural object. Nevertheless, various countertendencies—some of them purely perceptual—have prevented mechanically faithful imitation from being achieved hundreds of years ago. Apart from rare exceptions, only our modern age has succeeded in approaching this dangerous goal. In practice, there has always been the artistic urge not simply to copy but to originate, to interpret, to mold. We may, however, say that aesthetic theory has rarely sanctioned such activities.

FILM AND REALITY

Even for artists like Leonardo da Vinci the demand for being as
true to nature as possible was a matter of course when he talked
theory, and Plato's attack on artists, in which he charged them
with achieving nothing but reproductions of physical objects,
is far from the general attitude.

To this very day some artists cherish this doctrine, and the
general public does so to an even greater extent. In painting and
sculpture it is only in recent decades that works have been appearing which show that their creators have broken with this
principle intellectually and not merely practically. If a man considers that the artist should imitate nature, he may possibly paint
like Van Gogh, but certainly not like Paul Klee. We know that the
very powerful and widespread rejection of modern art is almost
entirely supported by the argument that it is not true to nature.
The development of film shows clearly how all-powerful this ideal
still is.

Photography and its offspring, film, are art media so near to
nature that the general public looks upon them as superior to such
old-fashioned and imperfect imitative techniques as drawing and
painting. Since on economic grounds film is much more dependent
on the general public than any other form of art, the "artistic"
preferences of the public sweep everything before them. Some
work of good quality can be smuggled in but it does not compensate for the more fundamental defeats of film art. The complete
film is the fulfillment of the age-old striving for the complete
illusion. The attempt to make the two-dimensional picture as
nearly as possible like its solid model succeeds; original and copy
become practically indistinguishable. Thereby all formative potentialities which were based on the differences between model
and copy are eliminated and only what is inherent in the original
in the way of significant form remains to art.

H. Baer in a remarkable little essay in the *Kunstblatt* has pointed
out that color film represents the accomplishment of tendencies
which have long been present in graphic art.

"Graphic art (he says)—of which photography is one branch—
has always striven after color. The oldest woodcuts, the block-
books, were finished off by being handpainted. Later, a second,
colored, plate was added to the black-and-white—as in Dürer's
portrait of 'Ulrich Varnbühler.' A magnificent picture of a knight

30

in armor in black, silver, and gold, exists by Burgmair. In the eighteenth century multicolored etchings were produced. In the nineteenth the lithographs of Daumier and Gavarni are colored in mass production. . . . Color invaded the graphic arts as an increased attraction for the eye. Uncivilized man is not as a rule satisfied with black-and-white. Children, peasants and primitive peoples demand the highest degree of bright coloring. It is the primitives of the great cities who congregate before the film screen. Therefore film calls in the aid of bright colors. It is a fresh stimulus."

In itself, the perfection of the "complete" film need not be a catastrophe—if silent film, sound film, and colored sound film were allowed to exist alongside it. There is no objection to the "complete" film as an alternative to the stage—it might help to take into remote places fine performances of good works, as also of operas, musical comedies, ballets, the dance. Moreover, by its very existence it would probably have an excellent influence on the other—the real—film forms, by forcing them to advance along their own lines. Silent film, for example, would no longer provide dialogue in its titles, because then the absence of the spoken word would be felt as artificial and disturbing. In sound film, too, any vague intermediate form between it and the stage would be avoided. Just as the stage will feel itself obliged by the very existence of film to emphasize its own characteristic—the predominance of dramatic speech—so the "complete" film could relegate the true film forms to their own sphere.

The fact is, however, that whereas aesthetically these categories of film could and should exist along with mechanically complete reproduction, they are inferior to it in the capacity to imitate nature. Therefore the "complete" film is certain to be considered an advance upon the preceding film forms, and will supplant them all.

WILLIAM EARLE
REVOLT AGAINST REALISM
IN THE FILMS

Let us call *realist* a certain sensibility which feels most at home living among familiar things in their familiar places, or among persons with recognizable characters acting or suffering in comprehensible ways. I shall presently return to these adjectives, *familiar, recognizable,* and *comprehensible,* to define reality. Meanwhile, unquestionably there is some such sensibility; unquestionably its pleasures are genuine and widespread—why, otherwise, would most commercial films address themselves to it?—but equally unquestionably, there is another sensibility which finds any such *reality* the very home of the boring and a serious invitation to spiritual death. For its life consists not so much in revisiting the familiar, recognizing what had been seen before, or comprehending the familiar under generalizable concepts, as in encountering something never seen before, in the primary cognition of novel singularities which can not be comprehended under the universal, in short, in a primordial disclosure of what can only be called, in our present terms, *unreal.* For pleasure let each sensibility look at the films of its choice; but philosophically the two sensibilities and their respective arts are not exactly on such an equal footing. The realist satisfaction in seeing variations on what had already been seen and in the reconfirmation of its conviction in an eternal, known moral order by seeing things "come out right" is clearly of a *derived* order. Nothing can become familiar unless previously encountered originally; and a moral order can not be reconfirmed unless it has been threatened. Existentially, the satisfactions of realist art almost seem to be created precisely in order to extinguish the lurking anxiety that the real world is nothing in the first place but a delusive fiction. Any such contention must be supported by plausible evidence; so I will now turn to the general question, what is realism? in order to show its range and pervasiveness, and then consider three alternatives to it, sensory, surrealist, and ironic art. In this discussion, we shall try to keep our eyes on what might be pertinent to movies.

I. REALISM

If *realism* is taken simply as one aesthetic manner in painting, literature, and movies, an option, among others, like naturalism, expressionism, symbolism, etc., open to the artist's taste and defining a school, perhaps we shall be dealing only with certain ambiguous by-products which, whatever their use, hardly enable us to get at origins. In the case of realism, the simple truth is that it is hardly a peculiar aesthetic style at all. Every human being is already and forever *realist*; he has other potentialities but those other potentialities are necessarily rooted in a basic realism: *perception itself* is inherently realist, and *reality* is inherently defined in terms of possible perception. The simplest definition of a reality is obviously, "that which we can perceive," a definition not meant as a philosophical contention opposed, let us say, to Plato, Plotinus, Spinoza, or Hegel, who define an ultimate reality otherwise. It is a simple stipulation of meaning, and one which will, I hope, be useful to a consideration of realism as pertinent to movies. In a word, in everyday life we count something as a reality if we can perceive it; otherwise it has a dubious mode of being, best left to the philosophers. And *perception*, what does it mean? For the moment, it is enough if we consider it any continuing act of the senses, or better, all of them cooperatively, which grasps something individual. Hence the real world is composed of those things we can see, hear, touch, feel, bump into. Let us call all of this *perception*; and since movies are primarily seen and heard, the *real* for movies then will be what can be seen and heard. To this somewhat sterile beginning, I will add a few pages from the phenomenology of perception to define a little more clearly what any such perceptible reality must be. A definition is necessary since it is far from obvious what these ordinary perceptible realities are; by defining them, perhaps, we can see eventually what some radically different alternatives are to that realism which inherently adheres to perception. In short, by systematically altering every feature of perception, we can at the same time make sense of some of the origins of alternative sensibilities in contemporary cinema.

What then are some central features of perception and the real world? I will discuss them under three titles: A. The *referential* character of perception; B. its *public* character; C. the *meanings* of real things.

A. The Referential Character of Perception

Sensation, first of all, must be distinguished from *perception;* or, in the whole perceptual act, that aspect of it which is purely private to me, which is a literal part of my own flowing perceptual consciousness I call *sensation*, but insofar as these same sensations are taken by me as *referring* to something beyond myself, they are *perceptions* of that thing. Only I *sense* the ache of my tooth; yet, if I take that ache as issuing from my tooth, as "perceptive" of the tooth, then the sensation refers to a tooth which my dentist can also see. Or, as the phenomenologists say, perception "intends" a perceptual *object* which lies in a world open to all perceivers. It refers to identities beyond the sheer privacy of my own sensation.

Precisely how a stream of sensation can refer to or intend these identities beyond itself is a subtle and delicate problem, but for our purposes we can summarize some central features. The question is pertinent to movies since the realities which constitute the home of the realist sensibility are none other than these perceptual identities, things and people. And briefly, sensations will be interpreted by the perceiver as perceptions of an identity when in fact they exhibit a certain order or when they are bound together by a systematic repeatability. And so, if indeed I am perceiving a chair, then my sensations of it will change as I move nearer or farther away, but change systematically, following what we later call the *laws of perspective* but which operate informally in the very act of perception itself. Thus, if I should move closer to the chair, and my sensation of it got progressively smaller, or abruptly and nonsystematically changed at every instant, I should not then take my sensations as the perceptions of anything but rather as mere sensations, a dizziness in me. Or if every time I blinked my eye, what I saw absolutely changed in every one of its sensed qualities, I would not take my sensations as referential at all; and no real identities would be constituted in the process. A perceptual reality, therefore, can change very rapidly indeed; but every appearance of it can not be *wholly* disconnected from my previous perceptions or no reality would appear at all. My sensations would not refer to any identity and would therefore collapse into non-referential and purely subjective sensings. In a word, real identities must be constituted through repeatability and familiarity; they are automatically built-up through recognition. If I perceive a man walking out of the door, an inherent part of that perception is the belief that *that same man could* walk back through, whether in fact he does or does not. And if he does not, then indeed he must be somewhere else, and not simply nowhere by virtue of his disappearance from my sensation.

A second aspect of perception and its world of realities is, namely, that these real identities are always taken by perception to be *in a world*. And, for perception, this world is not so much a sum total of things nor an infinite container, as it is a horizon which itself can never be perceived but which expresses the sense in perception that its realities are always somewhere even when not seen by me; that there could be other perceivers besides myself who could see the same things; and that things and persons themselves have perceptible properties even when those properties are not being actually perceived.

A reality then for perception is a recognizable identity with its own place in a world of similar identities.

B. *Public Availability of Perceptual Realities*

Closely connected with the above, a reality for my perception has the inherent meaning of something there *for other senses and other perceivers too*. Therefore, if I *see* something, I should in general be able to touch it, too; if these and the other senses do not yield coherent sensations, I doubt the *reality* of the thing; but also, if only *I* can perceive the thing, and no one else in my place could see it, I begin to doubt the reality of my perception. It was only a subjective sensation or perhaps a mere illusion. All the properties which I ascribe as "real properties" to the real thing must similarly be publicly available. If the public sees it as red and I see it as grey, its real property is red and I am color-blind.

C. The Meanings of Things

Finally, our whole description is hopelessly oversimplified. No one *merely* perceives things and persons. Philosophers as other-wise diverse as Dewey and Heidegger have shown the vacuity of mere perception if not its theoretical impossibility. Nietzsche called it "immaculate perception." All realities we encounter have a meaning for us, a significance which is not in the least reducible to mere perception. Automobiles, pencils, buildings, streets, and above all persons, are hardly to be understood as compositions of colors, shapes, sounds, etc. They are rather things and persons we are already living with, whose very essence is *what they are for us:* what we can do with them, what they can do to us, how we feel about them, in short, their role in our complete active emotional and not merely perceptual *life.* They are structured with values, if you like; their meaning for us is not experienced as something superadded to bare perception but inherent in that perception from the start. Some aestheticians like to think of this aspect as though it were a literary association; but there is nothing literary about it, nor is it necessarily an association brought to mere things from without; the identities in the first place are invariably things and persons for us, with that meaning already there. And that meaning implicates again a public world, where such things are already in their places. And their places in the world are their already familiar relations to other things and people, where those meanings emerge. The hammer is for hammering and its place is its proximity to the hand and the hammerable, or else it is displaced. A hammer flying from tree to tree loses its sense of hammer. Or it becomes a bird-hammer.

In summary then, perception is inherently realist; it constitutes its real things out of its own order, things which are in a world, related to their proper places, and in such a way that this real world of real things is there in more or less the same way for everyone. It is *necessarily* familiar, recognizable, comprehensible. A revolt in the cinema against realism would take each of these features and by its radical removal be in a position to exhibit what can never be realistically perceived, the unreal. From our present point of view, there would be two directions. One would proceed to remove system from sensation so that it *could* not constitute real identities: this I shall call sub-realist, sensory, or, following Marcel Duchamp, "retinal art." A second, moving in the opposite direction, would retain identities, but by *dislocation*, or removing them from their proper places, constitute an unreal world, no longer comprehensible in any realist sense, and, as André Breton said, would disclose the marvellous.

II. SENSORY OR RETINAL ART

Movies are in an excellent position to accomplish the first destruction of realism; for obviously, since the realities in question are given only through a medium in the form of images, by removing the imagistic character of the medium, we can easily in the same blow remove any possibility of perceiving real identities through them. Nothing need be done except reverse every excellence in the realist camera: if lens makers have finally designed optics with virtually no sensible distortion at all, we will use cracked lenses, lenses out of focus, smeared with vaseline, or covered with filters and screens; or if a zoom lens is best used for exact framing, by moving too close, or looking at the object from an odd angle, all trace of recognizability can be removed; or if the film transport of camera and projector are designed for perfect synchronization, we can easily run them so far out of synch that motions can be arrested or wholly altered, and so on through the usual bag of camera tricks. Triple and quadruple exposure can quickly reverse any world or obliterate foreground and background relationships. Editing can be so abrupt and quick that no recognizability, familiarity, or comprehensibility can occur. Briefly, what for the realist perception was an *image*, now loses that function and what is left approximates *sensation without perception;* we suffer perhaps for the first time a continuing experience of what some philosophers used to call "sense-data." LSD films move in this direction and, compared with them, dreams and hallucinations are hopelessly organized and significant of a world.

The senses, by themselves, of course quickly tire; they come alive only in change to such an extent that some animals can see nothing at all unless it moves. Sensation dies when stopped; it is perfectly natural that having deprived perception of the conditions of its operation, the sensation remaining must go faster and faster. Twenty-four absolutely diverse and unrelated frames per second seems far too slow for some; a number of projectors can, therefore, be brought to bear on the same or different screens. And if the senses left to themselves love speed, they also have an obvious longing for the *violent*; gentle changes of intensity will pass unnoticed, until the violence of light and sound approaches an assault on their very physiological limits. A friend of mine who makes films in this vein recently remarked that his ideal was a film that would "punch the audience squarely in the eyes"; oddly enough he felt that this was the best way to "teach people how to see," forgetting in his enthusiasm that no one either can or needs to be *taught* how to see: at very least, would we not have first to see the teacher who was to teach us how to see? What *can* be taught or induced by filmic conditions is *how not to see in order to sense;* and this surely is what the films presently under discussion aim at through the systematic defeat of every built-in expectation of perception.

Many of the same considerations must apply *mutatis mutandi* to the sound of sensory movies. There is a marked preference for electronic and aleatoric sound, and for *musique concrète*. For just as in realist perception, colors and shapes are the appearances of *something*, and sounds are the sounds and voices *of* things and persons, disclosing their qualities and character. Even in performance, the sounds are always the sounds of a violin, piano, singer, a real something or other giving out these sounds. If now the thing sounding or person speaking is suppressed or becomes unrecognizable, then something like a sounding which is not taken to be the sound *of anything* emerges, an aural sense-datum. Further, if all comprehensible pattern is removed, as in chance sound, then the result at last means nothing, announces nothing, expresses no one personality; we now have the perfect sound track for a sensory film.

III. SURREALISM

The revolt against realism can take an opposite direction, that of surrealism, and that surrealism and retinal or sensory art are indeed opposite directions was clear even in the twenties; surrealism was never friendly to purely abstract or non-representational painting. That the familiar and prefabricated perceptual reality is not the final horizon in which men must live can be shown best not by removing the conditions for all genuine perception, and thereby plunging the spirit into pure sensation, but rather by offering it what Breton repeatedly called the "marvellous." And, for Breton, the marvellous was never regarded as simply a new aesthetic style or excitement, but rather as a necessary means of liberating the spirit from any final engrossment in what passes for the real, what offers itself to perception and to comprehension. Against that world it offers another, the surreal, within which the real world is seen as but one minor variation, a variation moreover constructed by and correlative to our least admirable desires, the desire not to be oneself but rather a member of the public, the very public which defines reality.

Surrealism then is primarily an effort to effect a spiritual re-orientation; its theater of operations was never exclusively in works of art but rather in that very public reality which it wished to undermine: hence the necessity for its jokes, outrages, scandals, manifestoes, demonstrations, its temporary flirtation with revolutionary communism, and its love for gratuitous scandals such as Benjamin Peret's penchant for spitting at priests. Overflowing from this particular sentiment was its aesthetic, a sensibility directed to the irrational and magical.

The surreal world, unlike that of sensory art, is indeed a world and is populated by identities; its world is composed of things drawn from the real world but now de- or sur-realized; they are set free from their public or scientific connections and places in order to live a life of their own. Perhaps the most general name for such a freeing is dislocation; for if the very meanings of the things and persons we encounter derive from their relations to their proper places, a dislocation will show that object in a new light. The bringing together of distant realities can then strike off new sparks; the surrealists never tired of repeating from Lautréamont the "beauty of the chance encounter of a sewing machine and an umbrella on a dissecting table." The displacement of things and persons from their own space and own time, from their own relative dimensions and public values is designed to offer the spirit a world closer to its own desire. Its own desire was from the beginning understood in Freudian terms; it was the subconscious, where contraries were identified, which knew nothing of the world as redefined by science, which was at home in the magical, and whose desires must be liberated from the expected, the public, the predictable, the morality of public safety.

The techniques are well-known: automatic writing and free association to eliminate reflection; collective works, where many worked on a single object, no one knowing what the other was doing, the so-called "exquisite corpse"; random trips around Paris; coincidences through chance street encounters; found objects, collage, frottage, the primitive, the insane, the erotic, the criminal, the violent; each form of subjectivity disclosed its own domain of the surreal, a world not accessible to ordinary action, perception, or reason, and appearing to those faculties as marvellous and magical.

To return to films, it is almost as though they were predestined to be an excellent surrealist medium. For if we are already accustomed to the liberties which language and painting can take with reality, moving pictures almost automatically make us expect some sort of true camera reality; films remain a form of photography, and while everyone *knows* the camera can lie, we do not look initially at photographs as though they were lies. And so the force of movies to wrench us out of our habitual realism is particularly great. Further, the conditions of viewing a movie, in a darkened room, are particularly conducive to a form of dreamy participation where the marvellous would not appear simply as wrong, silly, or outrageous. Similarly the liberties which can be taken in editing and arranging, and the very same camera tricks which are used for a wholly different effect by sensory art, can now serve surrealist purposes admirably.

If the one real world and its reflection in movies provide us with the satisfactions of recognizability and comprehension, the worlds of surrealism are inherently private, plural, organizable into no whole, and invariably either strange, marvellous, or funny. If reality is not so much funny as serious, the systematic *disruption* of the expectations generated by familiarity could be, if not serious in their damage, hilarious, for example, in René Clair's *Entr'acte*. And the surrealists always regarded humor, particularly black humor, as especially liberating. Or, when serious, as in the early Buñuel films, evocative of the revolutionary sentiment of indigna- tion, as Buñuel says, in the "conviction that this is NOT the best of all possible worlds"; or magical, as in some of Man Ray's films, where the bringing together of distant realities constructs a world closer to the hidden desires of the heart than the public reality could provide. These sentiments, obviously, are modifications of the sentiments appropriate to perceptual public reality; nothing can be strange unless measured against the familiar, or have the unexpectedness of a joke unless there were expectations to be de- feated. And yet the final intent of these surrealist worlds is not to be a mere derivation of the real public world so much as the dis- closure of the domain of the possible, in the middle of which the real, public world is finally seen to be just as mysterious and arbi- trary as any other possibility. The real perceptual world then could be finally experienced as a surrealist poem imagined by the *public in each of us*. At this point, realism and surrealism join hands in a poetic realism; but that particular meeting is only possible after the detour into the imaginary of surrealism and not before. It is here that the late Siegfried Kracauer's view of film as the "redemption of physical reality" might find its place.

IV. IRONIC FILMS

There remains from our present perspective one more alternative to realism in the film. Realist films of course do not offer us realities themselves, but rather *images of them*. If sensory art destroys images in their function of presenting us something else of which they are images, and if surrealism retains that function of present- ing something else, but profoundly alters the character of the some- thing else presented, a remaining alternative would be to develop films which *called attention* to the image, while still employing it as an image. Here, our experience would be an ironic one, doubly aware both of the scene passing before our eyes and of our seeing it through images. In a purely realist film, every effort is devoted

41

to making the audience unaware of the camera, unaware that they are seeing only a reflected reality. The camera moves rarely, the sequences of what is shown agree with the order of showing it; everything is shown as we would see it if we were there in person. On the other hand, in ironic films we have the double awareness of seeing some action as it is refracted through an artificial medium. Now the camera will be hand held, so its jiggle will remind the audience that they are indeed looking at a movie; sometimes processing perforations are shown, and the trailers and leaders of film as they come back from the developer; sometimes the actors ham it up so we are aware they are acting. Or, as in the case of Jean-Luc Godard, the film will make references to other films, reminding the audience that this is a film, making a commentary on or spoofing other films. Sometimes the film or film-making itself becomes the subject of the action, as in *8½*, *Muriel*, or *Blow-Up*. Insofar as there is any suggestion in these ironic films that there is no public, stable reality at all, but only imaginary or *filmic versions* of it, they fall within the general revolt against any acquiescence to the real. Alain Resnais' films also proceed to dissolve any assurance in a public reality by demonstrating the ambiguity of the meaning of the present through its dependence on the past, a past moreover which is itself ambiguous through its significance for the present. Memory here becomes the artist whose materials are always on the verge of losing any independent reality whatsoever. But this carries us into other problems.

Finally, it should be understood that realism, sensory, surrealist, and ironic are only ideal types. No film perfectly exemplifies them, or could exemplify them. Not that this is the fault of the films or of the types; in any closer consideration, we should certainly find that each film most closely exemplified nothing but its own type, that is, no type at all. Each is what it is and asks not so much to be typed as simply seen.

PARKER TYLER
MASTERPIECES
BY ANTONIONI AND BERGMAN

It is useless to pretend that the film is not still the Cinderella of the arts. Insofar as this is true, the other arts (without themselves wishing it) take on the look of ugly stepsisters whose affability and condescension tend to caricature them. Rather self-consciously, well-known novelists have undertaken to analyze the spell cast on them by this vulgar medium or to point out, dutifully, why the disadvantaged "movies" can never, never rate with the medium whose practice *they* so obviously enjoy. Serious-minded specialists of the film have written respectable, even intelligent books on the craft, the aesthetics and the theory of the brave medium. But these books, despite enduring circulation, remain peculiarly isolated. From the viewpoint of universal schooling, they afford an orthodox branch of instruction in the arts; from the viewpoint of critical practice (film reviewing and so on) they are nevertheless oddly removed from the specific problem of deciding how good a given film is. I consider, and I am not alone in the opinion, that Bergman's *Persona* and Antonioni's *Blow-Up* are especially fine films, quite exceptional among recent works; so highly exceptional that, in view of the separation between film theory and the practice of film criticism, their ways of utilizing the technical nature of film to express attitudes toward human experience should come to the widest notice as major advances in the film's artistic sophistication. In brief, they are masterpieces.

Yet from the casual reviews of them I have read, I don't think that the particular eloquence they share has been thoroughly assessed or even identified; thus the applause given them lacks persuasive cogency. A few critics are serious enough to have recognized the allegorical character of *Blow-Up* as an irony involved with the widespread naïve belief in the photograph as conclusive testimony to the existence of "reality" as distinct from the existence of "illusion" (or art). It was historically inevitable that, once invented, photography would take supreme place as witness to the world of things, to "things as they are." The gullible sentimentality of this myth of convenience has been punctured hundreds of times in hundreds of ways and yet it persists. *Blow-Up* punctures it creatively on a level far above the average. Our society's materialistic and statistical structure, all conscientious objections to one side, has preserved the truth-telling myth of photography as an indispensable feature of the larger myth of science's super-efficiency. The very point that so much fictional fudge is passed off in the film medium draws between "fact" and "fancy" a disconcertingly evident line with a false validity.

Making films and thinking about them on almost any level, in any economic sphere, is far too sophisticated in the trivial sense; so sophisticated that Bergman's and Antonioni's originality in creating two anti-science legends may pass in general for arty-smartiness. This would be a true pity. Back of much hostility to film "trickiness" is the sodden documentary cult, opposed to creating "illusions" with the medium and forever attacking imaginative work by pressing the claims of the camera as the sole true eye of truth. Hence a tangible embarrassment to those committed to the creative faculty of film was the late Siegfried Kracauer's *Theory of Film: the Redemption of Physical Reality.* Unquestionably a scholarly work, it kept implying with an unpardonable ambiguity that film "can be an art" but, in effect, it borrows art for an occasion, like a costume concealing its actual identity. Amid mercilessly massed evidence, we learn that film is a visual medium whose overwhelmingly ideal function is reporting the boundless facts of the physical world.

The existence of such a theory can be explained only by the curious if involuntary isolation endured today by all criticism on the subject of film art. Certainly, Kracauer knew a ready-made audience awaited his book and would hail a formidable thesis reassuring everyone dedicated to the idea that truth-telling in film means what both science and the newspapers call documenting the facts. Yet why, one may go on asking, could such a theory register so convincingly (his book has become standard since it was first published in 1960) when a sizeable array of books elevating film as an art in its own right is also on library shelves, and when the validity of the photograph as statistical evidence of the truth has so often been called in question and refuted? The facile answer is that Kracauer's book is very informative as a technical inquiry; that is, it goes to much trouble to demonstrate the catholic resourcefulness of film: its ability to show both how an artist may develop a pictorial idea and how, without surgery, the inmost sanctums of the live body may be visited; so, in sum, photography is a leading aid in the study of art as of science. Indeed, if Kracauer were alive, his reaction to *Blow-Up* might be that it is an ingeniously simple fiction illustrating his own thesis with highly impressive point.

This, I say, is the *facile* answer and, in its way, irrefutable. Why, I feel bound to object, such a patently split view of film as an art and film as relentless investigator and ingenious reporter? Why, furthermore, the constant effort on the part of certain film enthusiasts to downgrade film as an art—a tactic which is tantamount to isolating the creative faculty of film as mere popular entertainment? Among hardcore intellectuals, one regularly runs up against an automatic condescension, a reflex of sheer suspicion, consigning creative film to a small corner where it must be heavily screened by the most sceptical experts to earn the nominal title of art. If we scrutinize the practice of film criticism, even in superior places, we find the better fiction films frequently reviewed as if they were novels cast in sequences of pictorial and aural illustrations. Naturally, critics don't always consciously commit themselves to an inevitable parallelism of film with literature and the stage. Yet the truth becomes plain when a novel or a play has been turned into a film and the issue is broached on the basis of film as a pyrotechnic art of translation—an interpretive, rather than a creative, art. A whole book has been written by a well-meaning and cultivated scholar about the methods by which film converts a novel into its own technical idiom.* But the value of end-judgements (just how

---

*George Bluestone, *Novels into Film*, University of California Press, 1961.

good an independent work of art a given film may be) remains in curious suspense despite all the lip service rendered, even in literary quarterlies, to film *as* film. Overconscientious film critics may become so attentive to technical quantities as never to decide just what a given film says. By its own dynamic reflex, the film art is to be observed inveterately trying to disengage itself from the debris of confusions caused by its reputation as a synthetic medium with the emphasis on the *non-creative* side. Filmic and semi-filmic photographic experiments shown at Expo 67, the World's Fair at Montreal, were bald exploitations of technique (multiple screen and "environmental" photography) having only a token implication for serious artistic use.

Film's unique position as a quasi-art is mainly due to a reversible Janus-faced situation. The historic idea on which Kracauer based his book, and which compasses an enormous tacit prejudice about film, is that the photograph is rightly only a mirror of the optically apprehensible world, no matter what degree of materiality its subjects have. This becomes a crucial point when in some fiction film a ghost is supposed to materialize or when dreams (those optically unverifiable facts!) are projected as if their figures had material existence. In Bergman's *Persona* a psychiatric nurse, isolated with her female patient as an experiment, develops acute neurotic symptoms that can be regarded only as hallucinations; meanwhile her patient would be doing nicely were it not for the nurse's growingly violent hysteria. Since this film has no supernatural atmosphere, we have to consider the nurse's hallucinations as simple projections of the mind expressed through an optical medium. Bergman has been astute in devising a scene with three participants, all of whom have the usual physical aspect of photographed persons but only two of whom (the patient and her nurse) are supposed to be present: the third is the patient's physically absent husband. In other words, as in Surrealist films where the imagined action is dreamlike, the physical world is here photographed out of natural context in a purely psychic dimension. It is exactly this creation of a non-objective world with objects (here, people) that the physical-reality dogmatists most deplore as foreign to the film medium.

Persona is thoroughly involved with a clinical situation. In the psychiatric clinic (where the main action of the film begins) the general condition is for the stuff of dreams to be tangible, for dream narratives to be treated between analyst and patient as if they were "live action"—as actually taking place. To the analyst, as to the poet and all visionary artists, the mind is as much a place as the world, with laws that derive from those of the physical world without being the very same laws; accordingly, the dreamer himself and those perceived in dream seldom obey gravity and material bounds strictly; they fade in and out as material bodies may do in film; they come "on stage" and go off as arbitrarily as if in some Expresionist or Surrealist film work. It could have been due only to the position of dreams in the context of psychoanalysis that another scholarly theorist of film, the philosopher, Suzanne K. Langer, should have ventured, however cursorily, to define the narrative action of film as "dream mode." The harmony and discrepancy between Kracauer's and Professor Langer's specializing theories form, as it happens, the Janus-face to which I alluded above.

According to one of these theories, the moving photograph is properly a guarantee of the physical world in which we live and the way this world behaves; according to the other, the film properly guarantees just the opposite, contravening the laws of daily physical behavior so as to reproduce the image of the same world in its dream mode. Yet of Professor Langer's theory I ask: why doesn't it specify the filmic "mode" as the psychology of spontaneous association—a stream of consciousness like, for instance, Molly Bloom's, conscious but irrational, flitting about in time and space with no responsibility to chronological narrative or any other convention? It is interesting that in the mediocre, quite uninspired film made from the text of Joyce's *Ulysses*, Molly's interior monologue is done in vocalized excerpts accompanied by illustrating passages of film. Indeed the whole film is a visual/aural excerpt from the original work. The point of our awkward, Janus-faced pair of theories is that *both* assume that the film's dominant function is *reportorial*; one reports the physical aspect of life, the other reports a special mental aspect—or, if you will, seeks to duplicate its "mode." The only difference between Langer's dream-mode film, on one hand, and certain types of poetry and prose fantasy, such as Molly Bloom's, on the other, is that the former alone depends absolutely, it is supposed, on the nature of its communicative medium (the film); in fact, according to the theory, it is *strictly limited* by that medium.

Yet why, one bluntly asks, should this be so? The novel, one may grant, is made of words (a "communication medium") but there is nothing in the nature of language to restrict it to the uses of the novel form, or lyric poetry or the dramatic form. Language can absorb a great variety of formal modulations. So why should there by anything self-limiting about film to restrict it to the statistical form of physical documentation (Kracauer) or the mental form of dream mode (Langer)?—especially when, by juxtaposing the two theories as Janus-faced, they become diametric contradictions establishing themselves exclusively on the same territory? Sophisticated film artists such as Antonioni and Bergman, fortunately, are not incommoded by these heavily scholastic theories; quite the reverse: for in these films of theirs, both theories might be viewed as pompous shadows lurking back of the film-maker's serious playfulness, which tacitly, with a sort of impertinence, involves the scholarly delusions as themes for irony and parody.

Let us go even deeper. Back of most published discourse on film is the reactionary human impulse to make of everything—from metaphysical philosophy to common dreams and daydreams—one of science's matter-of-fact attributes. The nineteenth-century phenomenon of the photograph was seized by this same reactionary impulse and developed as a supreme weapon to attack the higher functions of the mind. This is clear if we consider that the appearance of ghosts and ectoplasm from mediums in trance were, at one time, to be "proven" or "disproven" by resorting to photographing them. For the Kracauer and Langer theories, the moving photograph has become willy-nilly a symptom of the degeneration of classic philosophic postulates into a quasi-scientific metaphysics. Typically this is an obsession with reality as process, method and passing aspect rather than as a domain of permanent or total truths. Two such degenerate postulates are Kracauer's "flow of life" and "open end," which he proposes as criteria for the true filmic function. But here his theory, not surprisingly, is found facing the same way as Professor Langer's. Her dream-mode film also implies the "open end" and "flow of life" as necessary traits of a disorderly, uncontrolled world without true climax, sustained rhythm or firm spatial orientation. The obvious difference seems that Kracauer has assumed what every rationalist assumes: the physicality of life exists under a variegated, containing and efficient *order*—social, economic, political, etc.; in short, logical; otherwise, as irrational, as irresponsible to mental logic and objective order, the world of things as reflected by the mind would perforce overflow into the absolute fantasy of Langer's shapeless, unmanageable dream mode. Hence psychiatry, as a modern phenomenon, appears as another instrument of the aim of science to press the free-association aspect of imagination (of which dream is the unconscious function) into a quarantine of statutory disorder. Professor Langer thinks, if less obviously, as much within a framework of scientific logic as Kracauer does. Without being rude enough to use the terminology of the mental clinic, she assumes that film is the technical medium expressing directly and purely the content dealt with indirectly and rationally by dream-analyst and psychiatrist. Professor Langer is generous enough not to take a view of her dogma as correctional or inhibitive, and in this respect her companion theorist is equally magnanimous. Their liberalism is their strategy: she is as willing to let the dream mode flow recklessly on in the film as he is willing to let this medium of "physical redemption" simulate at will the imaginative tactics of the other arts.

The practical point, nevertheless, is that film does not "simulate" or "assimilate" fiction and fantasy any more than the dictionary simulates or assimilates the novel, the poem and the play. In positive terms, there is no common basic fact about exposed film except the camera mechanism that makes possible an optical result (the photograph) just as there is no common basic fact about the literary medium except that it is composed of the vocabulary. There is, indeed, as experts have stressed a "vocabulary" of the film, or (as one scholar has expressly put it) a grammar; thus, film has no given moral or aesthetic function, no absolute principle or technical limit, aside from precisely the sort of instruments given language by style, rhetoric and grammar. To assume anything else of film to be *parti-pris* without the smallest justification except the dogmatic obsession of science cults to win dominion over all "reality." The general label for the science cult of film is Documentary. The only question is whether film shall "document" the disorderly flow of life (free mental association) or the orderly flow of life (mirror reflections of the objective world of matter "as it is").

49

I trust I do not seem to overemphasize the importance of theoretic background in approaching the excellences of the two films I wish to praise. The empiric situation in criticism is such that I believe such considerations very vital—indeed integral with just what *Persona* and *Blow-Up* have particularly to tell us. *Persona*, I repeat, deals with a psychiatric situation in recognizable terms of the clinic. *Blow-Up* deals (seen in the same superficial light) with the documentary, quasi-legalistic validity of the photograph. Yet each film gives its theme a profound and specific modulation. *Persona* has turned ordinary plot order and meaning-content inside out; first, by encasing the main action in a kind of amnion of visual irrationality, and second, by sending the course of regular psychiatric therapy utterly off its track. The film's opening sequence introduces the spectator without ceremony to a shockingly irrational set of briefly held images; that is, the sequence begins, minus any credits, without the least token explanation of why these particular images are shown or why they have the sequence they do; in themselves, they are only obscurely "associational."

Their shots of action are overquick in pace (one is from a very dated film farce with an actor in skeleton masquerade); antithetically, their shots of inertia approach the quality of stills. In fact, when the animated cartoon of a little fat woman doing setting-up exercises on her back suddenly "freezes," we have a probable satiric reference (becoming more certain later on) to the current film mannerism of suddenly introducing frozen single frames into the cinematic flow to accentuate a climax or sub-climax. Here the "climax" is accidental and might be due (as a literal shot of the film strip slipping from a whirring reel suggests) to some technical mishap that stops film during its projection. Another apparent technical mishap is a shot of objects momentarily so much out of focus that they assume abstract form. There are also random shots of quiet natural scenery, the palm of a human hand pierced by a nail, profiles of dead, sleeping or anaesthetized persons. Finally, when a nude boy, his thin prostrate body draped with a sheet to his neck, awakes at the sound of a bell, turns on his stomach and starts reading a book, we suddenly realize that the preceding potpourri is more than some spliced film clips gathered from the cutting-room floor. They have been "plays" upon the faculty of the film deliberately and accidentally to animate and deanimate as well as to "report" animacy and inanimacy and to identify things through optical concentration—to *focus on* them; the demonstrated process of optically focusing and unfocusing implies that extreme relaxation of mental attention which drains all meaning from objects that technically are still in clear optical register. While reporting live movement, this prelude to *Persona* says, cinema may impose on such movement an artificial quietus (the frozen frame) that in one sense is a parody of death and in another only the conventional superspeed still of a person in live movement; cinema (as we find when the awakened boy sees on the wall next to him the huge head of a woman going in and out of focus) may also conceal, reveal or transform the identities and qualities of the objects it mirrors. Here is the camera's *active* faculty as opposed to its *passive* faculty of simple reporting.

Bergman, in effect, is whimsically parodying the Langerian dream mode, but not in order to make a Surrealist construct; rather, to inflect the meaning of the ordinary world of "physical reality" which he now proceeds, paradoxically, to report. The catch is that this world, as he further reveals, is typically compromised by mental phenomena that tend to transform normal appearances and reorient normal behavior. I have already mentioned one incident in the action that follows now: the imagined materiality of an absent person. There is not one facet in the film's little prelude which does not have its place in an orbit of metaphors about a master metaphor. The latter is presented immediately after the ensuing credits and it is the crux of Bergman's psychiatric theme. An actress (who may be playing in a film or on the stage) "goes dry" during a speech in *Electra*—which *Electra* the narratage does not say— stares awestruck into space, then gives a suppressed giggle. She never willingly, during the entire film, speaks again except for two parrot-like words she is induced to murmur by her nurse: "No, nothing."

The terrible blank she has drawn in the midst of the tragic speech has been parodied by the open, unmoored and enigmatic antics of the prelude: particularly the freeze of the little female clown doing setting up exercises and a swift, inexplicable interlude of "white leader"—the unsensitized film at both ends of a reel which the audience does not see, or glimpses only subliminally, but which here is a briefly sustained light flash dazzling us from a blank screen. We also recall that during the prelude the awakened boy (who may be the son the actress has abandoned) has seen a woman's face going in and out of focus, a face whose features he begins caressing. In line with the close-ups of objects so out of focus as to be abstractions, the actress's mental blackout may pass for the model of the whole opening series of metaphors that arbitrarily identify, or fail to identify, familiar objects. Thus it is the world itself, her private and professional life, everything about her past and her present, which the actress fails to identify (i.e., focus on mentally) when she forgets her lines and is immobilized for an instant.

After apologizing for ruining the scene, the actress presumably goes home and from there, as we find next, to a hospital room where she stays as an unusual "withdrawal" case. The female psychiatrist in charge is a mature, hardbitten number who crisply, suavely informs the mute actress that doubtless catatonia is a new "role" for her and that eventually she will tire of it as she seems to have tired of her stage roles. The actress, Elizabeth Vogler, has abandoned a loving husband as well as a loving child and she has steadfastly refused to see either since the incident which has fatally isolated her. However, the presiding psychiatrist tries an experiment by sending her patient off to her own cottage by the sea in the company of the attractive young nurse who has been assigned to the case.

Here the two young women begin living in pleased contentment the simplest rustic life although the actress responds to her nurse's one-sided running conversation only by a smile or a casual, apparently "innocent" caress. We soon witness, as the nurse develops hysterical symptoms, the kind of narration characteristic of Surrealist and other fantasy films: abrupt transitions of mood, leap editing, and scenes involving the nurse, the patient and the latter's absent husband as performers of a sort of psychodrama automatically projected, it would seem, by the nurse, not the patient. I say "automatically." Yet, since she duly snaps out of each breakdown or episodic trance, returning to her rational personality, we may wonder how genuine these hallucinative fits are. Speaking psychiatrically, the nurse may have stumbled on a method by which she hopes to provoke the other into responses that will lead her out of her speechless withdrawal. But the nurse's hallucinations seem too spontaneous and private to relate to a conscious psychiatric manoeuvre. Each of the women reads books and Alma, the nurse, sometimes reads to her patient; the actress is calm until she is forced to react to Alma's increasingly unsuppressed agitation, which might well be Lesbian in impulse.

By the time the nurse has a chance to read a letter from Elizabeth to her psychiatrist, disclosing that she takes Alma objectively and lightly, it is clear that Bergman has been indulging in ambiguity by offering a version of a case history whose true depths lie in the imaginative domain, not in the statistical realms favored by either of the simplistic schools of film thinking: Kracauer's or Langer's. Of the greatest aesthetic importance is the impression one may get, toward the film's end, that the prelude has been a parody of the well-known pastime of dial-twisting on TV and radio. This conclusion crystallizes by way of two similar incidents. In the early stage of her withdrawal, Elizabeth, having a small TV set in her hospital room, is willing for the nurse to turn it on; once, however, when some romantic drama is being broadcast, she repeats the crucial giggle and the nurse turns the set off. And again, quite alone, she is nervously pacing the room when a TV newscast, which she has been ignoring, flashes on one of the ghastly self-immolations of Buddhist priests in Vietnam. The newscaster's hortatory voice has that provocative tonality that some of us condemn as blatant sensationalism. Now *all* voices, to this withdrawn actress, have a repellently blatant urgency.

News photographers, of course, have been on hand when the priest set himself afire. Past the seated figure enveloped with flame, TV watchers are seeing still other photographers snapping pictures and aiming film cameras. The world of suffering, violence and grief has become an awful intrusion into Elizabeth Vogler's consciousness while, in the view of millions of other inhabitants of the world, this intrusion is not only welcome, but craved. For countless numbers, turning on or off the sight and sound of life's "tragedies" is simply a matter of dial-twisting, an obsessive distraction entirely frivolous even as it flatters the twister's power-fantasy. Perhaps, as Elizabeth shrinks away from the vision in horror, there was never a more stringent satire on the way modern society untragically and amorally regards its own woes and sorriest scandals. To the actress what is modishly called "electric circuitry" has

53

brought back in objective, for-true form the grim image of human disaster for which classic tragedy provides a traditional catharsis —that catharsis which was interrupted when without warning she "ran dry" in the midst of a speech. . . .

Whatever the technical cause, Elizabeth had been victimized by a *retroactive* function of the tragic catharsis; in the light of modernity we may say that, for her, the *cleansing* tragic madness has turned into the *defiling* communication madness. Art, we might also infer, has failed this actress in a great private crisis. Just why does not matter in face of her utter abnegation of the persona of social consciousness. The further action of the film implies that the collective issue has overtaken and replaced the strictly private one. Elizabeth Vogler may have given up the world's life; the world's life has not given itself up, or her, and the therapy of the psychodrama now taking place proves this. By some strange twist, the nurse is now the willing patient, the actress the unwilling doctor-psychiatrist.

For Alma either will not give up the idea of her patient's cure or, what seems more likely, is seeking a cure for her own suddenly exposed dilemma. After having confessed her own erotic excesses (technically heterosexual) and gone through her hallucinations, the nurse proceeds methodically to impose on her "patient" in verbal form a psychodrama that is supposedly the actress's but that well may be a product of the nurse's imagination. Bergman's plastic use of film leaves the truth ambiguous. During the pseudo-clinical session, Alma's monologue is repeated in toto, the camera on Elizabeth's face the first time around, on Alma's the second. The schizoid dimension has been anticipated by the visual, seemingly "physical," accident of splitting Alma's image in two at a crucial moment when she identifies with Elizabeth, who has stepped with naked foot on a broken glass and given an outcry. During the invented case history, Elizabeth's face has shown signs of dismay and guilt; is it her story or the nurse's? The question is resolved, rather than answered, by a plastic device. Suddenly the screen fills with a still photograph of a woman's face: one side Alma's, the other Elizabeth's. The thrilling effect is that of a mask and the classic calm of catharsis seems to close the agony.

But has there been true catharsis?—for either: both? The nature of modern experience seems to suspend any certainty and the remaining action is only tantalizing. The "mask" has reminded us of the also colossal, but vaguer, woman's face that appeared to the reading boy of the prelude. Actually the affair resumes its turmoil to reach a kind of catastrophe: the electric circuitry of modern life permits catastrophe but not catharsis—not, that is to say, *consciousness*. The plot itself draws a blank. Goaded by Elizabeth's stalwart resistance, the frantic nurse has traded slaps with her, threatened her with boiling water and at last vindictively cries that she loathes her. Therapeutic psychodrama has exhausted itself trying to replace cathartic tragedy. The end is redundancy. Alma simply resumes her professional face and matter-of-factly, as Elizabeth too, starts packing for departure. It is clear the actress will not forgive her last insult. We then see nothing more of Elizabeth; we see only Alma closing up the cottage and taking her packed suitcases to board a bus . . . and the boy, caressing the huge enigmatic face, returns. That is all.

Persona and *Blow-Up* are brilliant tours-de-force illuminated by a special negative dimension that functions as lucid irony. If Bergman's film demonstrates the absurdity of the dream-mode theory of film unless there be some intellectual framework to sustain it as a creative entity, Antonioni's vividly projected adventure of a very young fashion photographer is a devastating sarcasm indirectly commenting on the just as naïve physical-redemption theory of film. We perceive, if we detect the true meaning of Antonioni's device, how vain would be Kracauer's protest that *Blow-Up* vindicates his conception of the photograph as self-sufficient chronicler of reality. The young photographer's smartness consists in having converted the profession of fashion photography into high-camp fantasy. His studio work is deliberately campy, no involuntary parody of chic but as close to the real thing as its fine satiric edge allows. A great point is scored soon as a rapidfire series of still shots he is making with a posh model ends bang! with her on the floor and him straddling her in accidental mimicry of coitus. The neurotic state of his relations with his craft is shown up by a real, and quite funny, orgy that later takes place with two young novices who have been pestering him for a job. There are strong indications he is fed up both professionally and sexually.

Yet passionate photographers have a nervous reflex so long as a camera be slung from one shoulder: they can't resist a fresh subject. Owing to a subject encountered by chance while the armed photographer is strolling in a park, *Blow-Up* proceeds to give us a real fantasy experience as psychodramatically compelling as *Persona's*, though not so complex. He has gotten on the track of an adult couple seeking enough privacy, it might be, for love-making and succeeds in taking a whole suite of shots of their progress, which ends in a deep embrace during which the woman detects the photographer's presence. He beats a retreat, but she, leaving her partner, overtakes him and demands the films. Partly because she seems unduly concerned, partly because she is good-looking, the photographer (never named in the film) asks her to his studio for solemn parley. When she arrives, there is some flirtatious verbal sparring. Without much ado, she goes to bed with him on the tacit assurance that, when up, she will get the film rolls. When she is dressed again, the photographer is as good as his supposed word, but what he hands her is a substitute for the films she expects.

Scenting something peculiar in the whole business, he has clung to his interest in what the prints will show. Developing them, he is much arrested by one, of which he feverishly starts making blow-ups: it shows the woman gazing about in alarm as her partner's face is buried in her neck. Is it because she has seen him—the photographer? Every blow-up of sectional details of this shot, getting bigger and bigger, excites the photographer more and more: he is looking for a *visible* clue that will better explain the woman's anxiety to obtain the photographs. Suddenly a convincing explanation materializes. It is nothing less than evidence of an intended crime. The mightiest blow-up of all discloses the blurred image of a man aiming a revolver at the embracing couple from the nearby shrubbery. Now it is night-time and the photographer rushes back to the park. There he finds the prostrate corpse of the man who was making love. A crime *has* been committed.

So it would seem. Having an impulse to act, the alarmed and bewildered photographer rushes back to his studio where he finds, indeed, he has made a decisive error. The betraying blow-ups he has left tacked to his wall have disappeared and so have all the original negatives. The woman and her accomplice, acting too quickly for him, have made off with the evidence. Panicked, he goes back to the park and as he has feared, of course, the corpse has also vanished. The case of retributive justice—the whole position of righteous, vigilant society—has drawn a blank and it is the fault of his own negligence. He seems to reproach himself like a good Kracauerian. He does not seem to apprehend the mere technical and tentative role of the photograph he has taken; it is merely the first entry into a complex human mystery: murder and its skein of motives. Statistically, to be sure, it is of obvious importance; without it, the law must take a wide-open, very handicapped course; the police themselves could not move without a shred of material evidence.

Subjective consciousness, alas! is not a camera and neither is physically unsupported verbal allegation. To the film-conscious, on the other hand, the frustrated plight of things is brought home with a poignant throb. Photography, the mythic all-seeing eye, has been embarrassingly balked. The precise position of our hero as a *still* photographer is especially pathetic. Only one instantaneous segment of reality and the road to the truth would stand wide open! The series of blow-ups should remind the film-conscious that a melodramatic filmic technique of telling a story by a rapidly paced series of stills has entered the scene: the brief film *La Jetée* (The Jetty) is an excellent example. In a cinema age, this exciting film looks like a well-edited excerpt from a normally made film: a close-knit succession of dramatic highpoints that individually are merely frozen frames. The possibility of the same technique is cleverly insinuated by the progressive blow-ups developed by Antonioni's photographer.

Now, in sick confusion, the young man visits a painter friend to ask his advice—or rather, just to communicate his sense of frustration. With rather facile philosophy, the painter points to one of his canvases and indicating a detail remarks: "That's the clue." One reflects that this painting, whatever its visible/invisible mysteries of meaning, is a finished work, a total object. Otherwise it is not a true painting. Yet the "work" the photographer is now imagining ⊙ not only highly indeterminate: it entirely lacks optical documentation. It is a floating wispy idea in his head whose irony, as if in "negative," seems to gather about his person in space. Thus his painter friend's assurance can only be humiliating. He wanders back disconsolately, camera slung on his shoulder, to the fatal park. . . . There he encounters by a tennis court a fantastic group of people he has casually run into earlier the same day. They have painted themselves up and dressed like clowns and apparently are on a binge which has taken the form of crowding in an open, much dated auto and driving all night around the city.

Their deliberately theatrical fantasy is no "stranger" than his own work with fashion models, no more "bizarre" than the crime and the way he has encountered it. He sees the car stop by the tennis court and its boisterous occupants pile out. Two, a man and a woman, immediately take the court and begin a mimic tennis game without balls or racquets. Theirs is the art of Marcel Marceau, and as we see, with the photographer, a very skilled and persuasive example. The simple overwhelming truth is that the tennis players are imagining the existence of an absent element of the physical world (tennis balls and racquets) which are not only invisible but imponderable. In brief, they are as absent as Elizabeth Vogler's husband in the psychodramatized fantasy of the nurse in *Persona;* if there is optical evidence of *him* for the sake of perfect clarity, it is only because the situation in Bergman's film is much more specific and complex than the clowns' tennis game. The appearance or non-appearance of tennis ball and man would be equally *conventional* in the imaginative sense.

As silent movies show, and as Elizabeth Vogler's muteness shows, speech in film is equally conventional. Speechlessness in *Persona,* however, has a symbolic role: it signifies total moral abnegation of the world and makes, together with all the other technical stoppages Bergman has introduced in the prelude, a galaxy of automatic discontinuities in reality. But the clowns' mimic tennis game is calculated and positive, not involuntary and negative. It knits up the ravelled sleeve of the film art. The physical presence which it pretends is true is likewise symbolic. No matter how many frames a film may have, no matter how tightly continuous its flow, the very nature of its formal statement guarantees the essential importance, the virtual presence, of what lies beyond any single frame or the sum of all the frames. The image of reality I mean is psychic consciousness, which cannot be photographed in an instant of vision or an infinity of instants, for tacitly it is, even in a painting, an *invisible* totality.

The wise clowns in *Blow-Up* have an inspired impulse to involve this moody bystander who has been interested in their game, for now, his interest ebbing, he has sauntered away. They pretend the ball has been knocked out of court and frantically plead, in pantomime, for its return; supposedly, it has rolled in his direction. At first the photographer seems reluctant or vague; then he stoops toward his feet and pretends to heave it back. The moment is drenched with high filmic splendor. Now, in a conventional *envoi*, the camera begins receding from his still disconsolate-seeming figure till he is quite distant. Before we leave him, however, he suddenly fades out, leaving empty the vista of the greensward. . . . It is another film convention given a sharp fillip like some device from *Persona*. There is a weight of sovereign irony behind it and it gives a knockout punch to the physical-redemption theory of film. Like painting, film is imagery and has nothing whatever to do with the existence of physical bodies as such. Film, being a time art, requires a much bigger, more complex unit of psychic consciousness to support it than does the still photograph. It is this purely psychic force—the totality of *Blow-Up*—that possesses the "empty" greensward and, the photographer's figure gone, endows space with supreme meaning.

II
Film Image
and
Film Language

The art of music did not arise as soon as man learned how to create pleasing sounds. It was necessary to arrange those sounds into scales, to organize them into harmonic systems, and to devise appropriate musical forms for them. Similarly, the art of poetry required more than the mere existence of a list of words. These words had to be arranged according to rules of grammar and organized into intelligible literary structures. When the poet writes an epic, his words must be capable of telling a story, and when he writes a sonnet, they must fall into specific rhyme schemes and structural patterns.

The great Soviet filmmakers, Sergei Eisenstein and Vsevolod Pudovkin, thought about the art of the cinema in a similar way. This art required more than the mere ability to take moving pictures of reality, and, therefore, it required more than the discovery of photography. But what more? What is it that transformed a new technical ability into a great new art? The answer was montage, the art of combining pieces of film or shots (film's "sounds" or "words") into larger units—first, the scene, then, the sequence, and, finally, the complete film. D. W. Griffith, the great American director of *The Birth of a Nation* and *Intolerance*, to whom the Soviet directors acknowledged a great debt, was not important because he took better pictures than anybody else. He was important for having discovered montage, the fluid integration of the camera's total range of shots, from extreme close-up to distant panorama, so as to produce the most coherent narrative sequence, the most systematic meaning, and the most effective rhythmic pattern. In doing so, Griffith had, they thought, contributed to the development of a cinematic language and invented the distinctive art of the film.

The career of Sergei M. Eisenstein, the most brilliant figure in Soviet cinema, began as a stage director. The youthful Eisenstein then made four films in five years: *Strike* (1924), *Potemkin* (1925), *October* (1927), and *Old and New* (1928). In the 1930s and 1940s (until his death in 1948) Eisenstein worked primarily as a theorist and teacher, completing only *Alexander Nevsky* and *Ivan the Terrible, Parts I and II*. Eisenstein's conversion from an artist to a theorist is to be explained in part by political realities, for his emphasis on cinematic "form" was uncongenial to his government's official aesthetics. But it is equally true that his conception of montage did not easily accomodate itself to the use of synchronized dialogue and, therefore, to the kind of film which prevailed in the 1930s.

Eisenstein viewed montage as a kind of collision or conflict, especially between a shot and its successor. Two shots could conflict in their emotional content (happy versus sad), in their use of light (dark versus light), in their rhythms (slow versus fast), in their objects (large versus small), in their directions of movement (right versus left), or in any combination thereof. In his films, this conflict produced the tense, violent rhythms that became an Eisenstein trademark. Conflict was also important to Eisenstein because he took it to be an expression, in the realm of images, of the Marxist's dialectical principle. Indeed, Eisenstein maintained that just as the meaning of a sentence arises from the interaction of its individual words, cinematic meaning is the result of the dialectical interplay of shots. His emphasis on the conflict of shots, as distinct from a mere linking of shots, distinguishes his conception from that of his colleague, Pudovkin. Pudovkin's view of montage as a method of building, of adding one thing to another, is not merely of theoretical interest. His theory produced his more realistic narratives *(Mother, Storm over Asia)*, with their more deliberate, calmer pace.

Eisenstein, like most of the "first" generation theorists, was uncomfortable with the addition of synchronized dialogue. Because "silent" films had always used asynchronous sound effects and music, Eisenstein believed that the sound film could use these tools with even greater precision and complexity. But he positively rejected dialogue as being incompatible with the proper use of montage. By contrast André Bazin, a theorist of the "second" generation, while assenting to the incompatibility of dialogue and montage, regards synchronized speech as a necessary and proper development. For Bazin, dialogue returns film to the rightful path from which montage and silence diverted it. According to him, the film image ought to reveal nature whole, not present reality by cutting it into tiny bits. The cinematic method Bazin endorses, which combines composing with the camera and staging an action in front of it, has, like montage, come to be known by a French term, mise-en-scène.

In Bazin's view the montage theorists did not in fact speak for all of the silent film, and he discerns in the work of von Stroheim, Murnau, and Flaherty an alternative, mise-en-scène tradition. Bazin sees this tradition as emphasizing not the ordering, but the content of images. The film's effect and meaning is not the product of a juxtaposition of images, but is inherent in the visual images themselves. For Bazin, the montage theorists' emphasis on the analogy between word and shot is false, and he rejects it along with their reluctance to employ sound as a source of cinematic meaning. Bazin argues that the mise-en-scène tradition within silent film actually looked toward the incorporation of synchronous sound as a fulfillment, not as a violation, of the film's destiny.

In the 1930s and '40s Bazin sees German expressionism and Russian symbolism as having been superseded by a form of editing more appropriate to the dialogue film. This "analytic" editing, which characteristically manifests itself in the dramatic technique of shot and reverse-shot, was an important innovation. Still more important, however, was the development of the shot-in-depth by Orson Welles and William Wyler in the early 1940s (anticipated in the 1930s by Jean Renoir), which made even the use of "analytic" montage unnecessary. Entire scenes could now be covered in one take, the camera remaining motionless. For Bazin, the shot-in-depth, like the use of synchronous sound, constituted a crucial advance toward total cinema.

Christian Metz, a contemporary French theorist sympathetic to Bazin's ideas, concentrates his attention on the possible application of modern linguistic theory to the cinema. In doing so, he represents a very important tendency in contemporary film theory. If film is a system of communication, the methods, and perhaps even the concepts, of semiology (the theory of how "language" systems, including non-verbal "languages" like cinema, generate intelligible meanings) must somehow be applicable to it. Many theorists feel that considering film as a semiological system will permit film criticism, which suffers (in the opinion of many besides semiologists) from impressionism, subjectivity, and vagueness, to attain a scientific precision and rigor. Like Bazin, Metz is critical of the claim that the shot plays the role in cinema language that the word does in verbal language. He believes that the shot is a form of assertion and therefore closer to the statement than to the word.

Despite his skepticism about the analogy of word and shot, Metz believes that as cinema mastered the art of narrative it did in fact develop a distinctive language. The central problem of a semiology of the cinema is to explain the procedures by which cinema indicates such narrative phenomena as succession, priority, temporal breaks, causal relations, and spatial continuity. As he shows in his analysis of what he calls the alternating *syntagma*, the order in which the signifying images occur may or may not be the same as that in which the realities they signify occur. The student of the language of cinema must therefore account for the processes and mechanisms which make it possible for the viewer to interpret them correctly. For Metz, the film does not simply reveal reality; it describes it in a language whose features we are only beginning to understand.

Charles Barr, a contemporary English critic also sympathetic to Bazin's ideas, defends the development of CinemaScope against those who reject it as a desecration of cinematic art. He notes the similarity of the attacks on the wide screen to those earlier attacks on synchronized sound, and he believes that both attacks are corollaries of the assumptions of the montage theorists. Barr therefore expands Bazin's attacks on montage theory, questioning even more vigorously the alleged analogy between word and shot. He also disputes Eisenstein's claim that associative montage gives a viewer the freedom to participate actively in the aesthetic experience. Barr finds it no accident that the rhetorical and coercive montage of Eisenstein, admittedly designed to serve propagandistic purposes, can now most frequently be found in television commercials. Barr in effect brings Bazin into the 1960s by viewing the wide screen as a refinement of the shot-in-deptn method that Bazin endorsed and an advance in the representation of "nature whole" that "total" cinema seeks.

VSEVOLOD PUDOVKIN
FROM FILM TECHNIQUE

[ON EDITING]

METHODS OF TREATMENT OF THE MATERIAL

(Structural Editing)

A cinematograph film, and consequently also a scenario, is always divided into a great number of separate pieces (more correctly, it is built out of these pieces). The sum of the shooting-script is divided into sequences, each sequence into scenes, and, finally, the scenes themselves are constructed from a whole series of pieces (script-scenes) shot from various angles. An actual scenario, ready for use in shooting, must take into account this basic property of the film. The scenarist must be able to write his material on paper exactly as it will appear upon the screen, thus giving exactly the content of each shot as well as its position in sequence. The construction of a scene from pieces, a sequence from scenes, and reel from sequences, and so forth, is called *editing*. Editing is one of the most significant instruments of effect possessed by the film technician and, therefore, by the scenarist also. Let us now become acquainted with its methods one by one.

Editing of the Scene

Everyone familiar with a film is familiar with the expression "close-up." The alternating representation of the faces of the characters during a dialogue; the representation of hands, or feet, filling the whole screen—all this is familiar to everyone. But in order to know how properly to use the close-up, one must understand its significance, which is as follows: the close-up directs the attention of the spectator to that detail which is, at the moment, important to the course of the action. For instance, three persons are taking part in a scene. Suppose the significance of this scene consist in the *general* course of the action (if, for example, all three are lifting some heavy object), then they are taken simultaneously in a *general* view, the so-called long-shot. But suppose any one of them change to an independent action having significance in the scenario (for example, separating himself from the others, he draws a revolver cautiously from his pocket), then the camera is directed on him alone. His action is recorded separately.

What is said above applies not only to persons, but also to separate parts of a person, and objects. Let us suppose a man is to be taken apparently listening calmly to the conversation of someone else, but actually restraining his anger with difficulty. The man crushes the cigarette he holds in his hand, a gesture unnoticed by the other. This hand will always be shown on the screen separately, in close-up, otherwise the spectator will not notice it and a characteristic detail will be missed. The view formerly obtained (and is still held by some) that the close-up is an "interruption" of the long-shot. This idea is entirely false. It is no sort of interruption. It represents a proper form of construction.

In order to make clear to oneself the nature of the process of editing a scene, one may draw the following analogy. Imagine yourself observing a scene unfolded in front of you, thus: a man stands near the wall of a house and turns his head to the left; there appears another man slinking cautiously through the gate. The two are fairly widely distant from one another—they stop. The first takes some object and shows it to the other, mocking him. The latter clenches his fists in a rage and throws himself at the former. At this moment a woman looks out of a window on the third floor and calls, "Police!" The antagonists run off in opposite directions. Now, how would this have been observed?

1. The observer looks at the first man. He turns his head.

2. What is he looking at? The observer turns his glance in the same direction and sees the man entering the gate. The latter stops.

3. How does the first react to the appearance on the scene of the second? A new turn by the observer; the first takes out an object and mocks the second.

4. How does the second react? Another turn; he clenches his fists and throws himself on his opponent.

5. The observer draws aside to watch how both opponents roll about fighting.

6. A shout from above. The observer raises his head and sees the woman shouting at the window.

7. The observer lowers his head and sees the result of her warning—the antagonists running off in opposite directions.

The observer happened to be standing near and saw every detail, saw it clearly, but to do so he had to turn his head, first left, then right, then upwards, whithersoever his attention was attracted by the interest of observation and the sequence of the developing scene. Suppose he had been standing farther away from the action, taking in the two persons and the window on the third floor simultaneously, he would have received only a general impression, without being able to look separately at the first, the second, or the woman. Here we have approached closely the basic significance of editing. Its object is the showing of the development of the scene in relief, as it were, by guiding the attention of the spectator now to one, now to the other separate element. The lens of the camera replaces the eye of the observer, and the changes of angle of the camera—directed now on one person, now on another, now on one detail, now on another—must be subject to the same conditions as those of the eyes of the observer. The film technician, in order to secure the greatest clarity, emphasis, and vividness, shoots the scene in separate pieces and, joining them and showing them, directs the attention of the spectator to the separate elements, compelling him to see as the attentive observer saw. From the above is clear the manner in which editing can even work upon the emotions. Imagine to yourself the excited observer of some rapidly developing scene. His agitated glance is thrown rapidly from one spot to another. If we imitate this glance with the camera we get a series of pictures, rapidly alternating pieces, creating a *stirring scenario editing-construction.* The reverse would be long pieces changing by mixes, conditioning a calm and slow editing-construction (as one may shoot, for example, a herd of cattle wandering along a road, taken from the viewpoint of a pedestrian on the same road).

We have established, by these instances, the basic significance of the constructive editing of scenes. It builds the scenes from separate pieces, of which each concentrates the attention of the spectator only on that element important to the action. The sequence of these pieces must not be uncontrolled, but must correspond to the natural transference of attention of an imaginary observer (who, in the end, is represented by the spectator). In this sequence must be expressed a special logic that will be apparent only if each shot contain an impulse towards transference of the attention to the next. For example (1) A man turns his head and looks; (2) What he looks at is shown.

Editing of the Sequence

The guidance of the attention of the spectator to different elements of the developing action in succession is, in general, characteristic of the film. It is its basic method. We have seen that the separate scene, and often even the movement of one man, is built up upon the screen from separate pieces. Now, the film is not simply a collection of different scenes. Just as the pieces are built up into scenes endowed, as it were, with a connected action, so the separate scenes are assembled into groups forming whole sequences. The sequence is constructed (edited) from scenes. Let us suppose ourselves faced with the task of constructing the following sequence: two spies are creeping forward to blow up a powder magazine; on the way one of them loses a letter with instructions. Someone else finds the letter and warns the guard, who appears in time to arrest the spies and save the magazine. Here the scenarist has to deal with simultaneity of various actions in several different places. While the spies are crawling towards the magazine, someone else finds the letter and hastens to warn the guard. The spies have nearly reached their objective; the guards are warned and rushing towards the magazine. The spies have completed their preparations; the guard arrives in time. If we pursue the previous analogy between the camera and an observer, we now not only have to turn it from side to side, but also to move it from place to place. The observer (the camera) is now on the road shadowing the spies, now in the guardroom recording the confusion, now back at the magazine showing the spies at work, and so forth. But, in combination of the separate scenes (editing), the former law of sequence succession remains in force. A consecutive sequence will appear upon the screen only if the attention of the spectator be transferred correctly from scene to scene. And this correctness is conditioned as follows: the spectator sees the creeping spies, the loss of the letter, and finally the person who finds the letter. The person with the letter rushes for help. The spectator is seized with inevitable excitement—Will the man who found the letter be able to forestall the explosion? The scenarist immediately answers by showing the spies nearing the magazine—his answer has the effect of a warning "Time is short." The excitement of the spectator—Will they be in time?—continues; the scenarist shows the guard turning out. Time is very short—the spies are shown beginning their work. Thus, transferring attention now to the rescuers, now to the spies, the scenarist answers with actual impulses to increase of the spectator's interest, and the construction (editing) of the sequence is correctly achieved.

There is a law in psychology that lays it down that if an emotion give birth to a certain movement, by imitation of this movement the corresponding emotion can be called forth. If the scenarist can effect in even rhythm the transference of interest of the intent spectator, if he can so construct the elements of increasing interest that the question, "What is happening at the other place?" arises and at the same moment the spectator is transferred whither he wishes to go, then the editing thus created can really excite the spectator. One must learn to understand that editing is in actual fact a compulsory and deliberate guidance of the thoughts and associations of the spectator. If the editing be merely an uncontrolled combination of the various pieces, the spectator will understand (apprehend) nothing from it; but if it be co-ordinated according to a definitely selected course of events or conceptual line, either agitated or calm, it will either excite or soothe the spectator.

Editing of the Scenario

The film is divided into reels. The reels are usually equal in length, on an average from 900 to 1,200 feet long. The combination of the reels forms the picture. The usual length of a picture should not be more than from 6,500 to 7,500 feet. This length, as yet, involves no unnecessary exhaustion of the spectator. The film is usually divided into from six to eight reels. It should be noted here, as a practical hint, that the average length of a piece (remember the editing of scenes) is from 6 to 10 feet, and consequently from

100 to 150 pieces go to a reel. By orientating himself on these figures, the scenarist can visualise how much material can be fitted into the scenario. The scenario is composed of a series of sequences. In discussing the construction (editing) of the scenario from sequences, we introduce a new element into the scenarist's work— the element of so-called dramatic continuity of action that was discussed at the beginning of this sketch. The continuity of the separate sequences when joined together depends not merely upon the simple transference of attention from one place to another, but is conditioned by the development of the action forming the foundation of the scenario. It is important, however, to remind the scenarist of the following point: a scenario has always in its development a moment of greatest tension, found nearly always at the end of the film. To prepare the spectator, or, more correctly, preserve him, for this final tension, it is especially important to see that he is not affected by unnecessary exhaustion during the course of the film. A method . . . that the scenarist can employ to this end is the careful distribution of the titles (which always distract the spectator), securing compression of the greater quantity of them into the first reels, and leaving the last one for uninterrupted action.

Thus, first is worked out the action of the scenario, the action is then worked out into sequences, the sequences into scenes, and these constructed by editing from the pieces, each corresponding to a camera angle.

EDITING AS AN INSTRUMENT OF IMPRESSION

(Relational Editing)

We have already mentioned, in the section on editing of sequences, that editing is not merely a method of the junction of separate scenes or pieces, but is a method that controls the "psychological guidance" of the spectator. We should now acquaint ourselves with the main special editing methods having as their aim the impression of the spectator.

Contrast.—Suppose it be our task to tell of the miserable situation of a starving man; the story will impress the more vividly if associated with mention of the senseless gluttony of a well-to-do man.

72

On just such a simple contrast relation is based the corresponding editing method. On the screen the impression of this contrast is yet increased, for it is possible not only to relate the starving sequence to the gluttony sequence, but also to relate separate scenes and even separate shots of the scenes to one another, thus, as it were, forcing the spectator to compare the two actions all the time, one strengthening the other. The editing of contrast is one of the most effective, but also one of the commonest and most standardised, of methods, and so care should be taken not to overdo it.

Parallelism. — This method resembles contrast, but is considerably wider. Its substance can be explained more clearly by an example. In a scenario as yet unproduced a section occurs as follows: a working man, one of the leaders of a strike, is condemned to death; the execution is fixed for 5 a.m. The sequence is edited thus: a factory-owner, employer of the condemned man, is leaving a restaurant drunk, he looks at his wrist-watch: 4 o'clock. The accused is shown — he is being made ready to be led out. Again the manufacturer, he rings a door-bell to ask the time: 4.30. The prison waggon drives along the street under heavy guard. The maid who opens the door — the wife of the condemned — is subjected to a sudden senseless assault. The drunken factory-owner snores on a bed, his leg with trouser-end upturned, his hand hanging down with wrist-watch visible, the hands of the watch crawl slowly to 5 o'clock. The workman is being hanged. In this instance two thematically unconnected incidents develop in parallel by means of the watch that tells of the approaching execution. The watch on the wrist of the callous brute, as it were connects him with the chief protagonist of the approaching tragic *dénouement*, thus ever present in the consciousness of the spectator. This is undoubtedly an interesting method, capable of considerable development.

Symbolism. — In the final scenes of the film *Strike* the shooting down of workmen is punctuated by shots of the slaughter of a bull in a stockyard. The scenarist, as it were, desires to say: just as a butcher fells a bull with the swing of a pole-axe, so, cruelly and in cold blood, were shot down the workers. This method is especially interesting because, by means of editing, it introduces an abstract concept into the consciousness of the spectator without use of a title.

Simultaneity. — In American films the final section is constructed from the simultaneous rapid development of two actions, in which the outcome of one depends on the outcome of the other. The end of the present-day section of *Intolerance* . . . is thus constructed. The whole aim of this method is to create in the spectator a maximum tension of excitement by the constant forcing of a question, such as, in this case: Will they be in time?—will they be in time?

The method is a purely emotional one, and nowadays overdone almost to the point of boredom, but it cannot be denied that of all the methods of constructing the end hitherto devised it is the most effective.

Leit-motif (reiteration of theme).—Often it is interesting for the scenarist especially to emphasise the basic theme of the scenario. For this purpose exists the method of reiteration. Its nature can easily be demonstrated by an example. In an anti-religious scenario that aimed at exposing the cruelty and hypocrisy of the Church in employ of the Tsarist régime the same shot was several times repeated: a church-bell slowly ringing and, superimposed on it, the title: "The sound of bells sends into the world a message of patience and love." This piece appeared whenever the scenarist desired to emphasise the stupidity of patience, or the hypocrisy of the love thus preached.

The little that has been said above of relational editing naturally by no means exhausts the whole abundance of its methods. It has merely been important to show that constructional editing, a method specifically and peculiarly filmic, is, in the hands of the scenarist, an important instrument of impression. Careful study of its use in pictures, combined with talent, will undoubtedly lead to the discovery of new possibilities and, in conjunction with them, to the creation of new forms.

SERGEI EISENSTEIN
FROM FILM FORM

[MONTAGE AND CONFLICT]

A shot, A single piece of celluloid. A tiny rectangular frame in which there is, organized in some way, a piece of an event.

"Cemented together, these shots form montage. When this is done in an appropriate rhythm, *of course!*"

This, roughly, is what is taught by the old, old school of film-making, that sang:

"Screw by screw,
Brick by brick . . ."

Kuleshov, for example, even writes with a brick:

If you have an idea-phrase, a particle of the story, a link in the whole dramatic chain, then that idea is to be expressed and accumulated from shot-ciphers, just like bricks.

"The shot is an element of montage. Montage is an assembly of these elements." This is a most pernicious make-shift analysis. . . .

The shot is by no means an *element* of montage.

The shot is a montage *cell.*

Just as cells in their division form a phenomenon of another order, the organism or embryo, so, on the other side of the dialectical leap from the shot, there is montage.

By what, then, is montage characterized and, consequently, its cell—the shot?

By collision. By the conflict of two pieces in opposition to each other. By conflict. By collision.

In front of me lies a crumpled yellowed sheet of paper. On it is a mysterious note:

"Linkage—P" and "Collision—E."

This is a substantial trace of a heated bout on the subject of montage between P (Pudovkin) and E (myself).

This has become a habit. At regular intervals he visits me late at night and behind closed doors we wrangle over matters of principle. A graduate of the Kuleshov school, he loudly defends an understanding of montage as a *linkage* of pieces. Into a chain. Again, "bricks." Bricks, arranged in series to *expound* an idea.

I confronted him with my viewpoint on montage as a *collision*. A view that from the collision of two given factors *arises* a concept.

From my point of view, linkage is merely a possible *special* case.

Recall what an infinite number of combinations is known in physics to be capable of arising from the impact (collision) of spheres. Depending on whether the spheres be resilient, non-resilient, or mingled. Amongst all these combinations there is one in which the impact is so weak that the collision is degraded to an even movement of both in the same direction.

This is the one combination which would correspond with Pudovkin's view.

Not long ago we had another talk. Today he agrees with my point of view. True, during the interval he took the opportunity to acquaint himself with the series of lectures I gave during that period at the State Cinema Institute. . . .

So, montage is conflict.

As the basis of every art is conflict (an "imagist" transformation of the dialectical principle). The shot appears as the *cell* of montage. Therefore it also must be considered from the viewpoint of *conflict*.

Conflict within the shot is potential montage, in the development of its intensity shattering the quadrilateral cage of the shot and exploding its conflict into montage impulses *between* the montage pieces. As, in a zigzag of mimicry, the *mise-en-scène* splashes out into a spatial zigzag with the *same* shattering. As the slogan, "All obstacles are vain before Russians," bursts out in the multitude of incident of *War and Peace.*

MONTAGE AND CONFLICT

If montage is to be compared with something, then a phalanx of montage pieces, of shots, should be compared to the series of explosions of an internal combustion engine, driving forward its automobile or tractor: for, similarly, the dynamics of montage serve as impulses driving forward the total film.

Conflict within the frame. This can be very varied in character: it even can be a conflict in—the story. As in that "prehistoric" period in films (although there are plenty of instances in the present, as well), when entire scenes would be photographed in a single, uncut shot. This, however, is outside the strict jurisdiction of the film-form.

These are the "cinematographic" conflicts within the frame:

Conflict of graphic directions.

> *(Lines—either static or dynamic)*

Conflict of scales.
Conflict of volumes.
Conflict of masses.

> *(Volumes filled with various intensities of light)*

Conflict of depths.

And the following conflicts, requiring only one further impulse of intensification before flying into antagonistic pairs of pieces:

Close shots and long shots.

Pieces of graphically varied directions. Pieces resolved in volume, with pieces resolved in area.

Pieces of darkness and pieces of lightness.

And, lastly, there are such unexpected conflicts as:

Conflicts between an object and its dimension—and conflicts between an event and its duration.

These may sound strange, but both are familiar to us. The first is accomplished by an optically distorted lens, and the second by stop-motion or slow-motion.

The compression of all cinematographic factors and properties within a single dialectical formula of conflict is no empty rhetorical diversion.

We are now seeking a unified system for methods of cinematographic expressiveness that shall hold good for all its elements. The assembly of these into series of common indications will solve the task as a whole.

Experience in the separate elements of the cinema cannot be absolutely measured.

Whereas we know a good deal about montage, in the theory of the shot we are still floundering about amidst the most academic attitudes, some vague tentatives, and the sort of harsh radicalism that sets one's teeth on edge.

To regard the frame as a particular, as it were, molecular case of montage makes possible the direct application of montage practice to the theory of the shot.

And similarly with the theory of lighting. To sense this as a collision between a stream of light and an obstacle, like the impact of a stream from a fire-hose striking a concrete object, or of the wind buffeting a human figure, must result in a usage of light entirely different in comprehension from that employed in playing with various combinations of "gauzes" and "spots."

Thus far we have one such significant principle of conflict: *the principle of optical counterpoint.*

And let us not now forget that soon we shall face another and less simple problem in counterpoint: *the conflict in the sound film of acoustics and optics.* . . .

Within cinema, and characterizing it, occurs what may be described as:

visual counterpoint

In applying this concept to the film, we gain several leads to the problem of film grammar. As well as a *syntax* of film manifestations, in which visual counterpoint may determine a whole new system of forms of manifestation. . . .

For all this, the *basic premise* is:

The shot is by no means an element of montage.

The shot is a montage cell (or molecule).

In this formulation the dualistic division of

Sub-title and shot

and

Shot and montage

leaps forward in analysis to a dialectic consideration as three different phases of one homogeneous task of expression, its homogeneous characteristics determining the homogeneity of their structural laws.

78

INTER-RELATION OF THE THREE PHASES:

Conflict within a thesis (an abstract idea)—*formulates* itself in the dialectics of the sub-title—*forms* itself spatially in the conflict within the shot—and *explodes* with increasing intensity in montage-conflict among the separate shots.

This is fully analogous to human, psychological expression. This is a conflict of motives, which can also be comprehended in three phases:

1. Purely verbal utterance. Without intonation—expression in speech.

2. Gesticulatory (mimic-intonational) expression. Projection of the conflict onto the whole expressive bodily system of man. Gesture of bodily movement and gesture of intonation.

3. Projection of the conflict into space. With an intensification of motives, the zigzag of mimic expression is propelled into the surrounding space following the same formula of distortion. A zigzag of expression arising from the spatial division caused by man moving in space. *Mise-en-scène.*

This gives us the basis for an entirely new understanding of the problem of film form.

We can list, as examples of types of conflicts within the form—characteristic for the conflict within the shot, as well as for the conflict between colliding shots, or, montage:

1. Graphic conflict.　　　　4. Spatial conflict.
2. Conflict of planes.　　　 5. Light conflict.
3. Conflict of volumes.　　　6. Tempo conflict, and so on.

Nota bene.—This list is of principal features, of *dominants*. It is naturally understood that they occur chiefly as complexes.

For a transition to montage, it will be sufficient to divide any example into two independent primary pieces, as in the case of graphic conflict, although all other cases can be similarly divided:

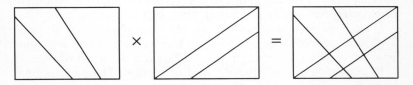

SOME FURTHER EXAMPLES:

7. Conflict between matter and viewpoint (achieved by spatial distortion through camera-angle).
8. Conflict between matter and its spatial nature (achieved by *optical distortion* by the lens).
9. Conflict between an event and its temporal nature (achieved by *slow-motion* and *stop-motion*)
   and finally
10. Conflict between the whole *optical* complex and a quite different sphere.

Thus does conflict between optical and acoustical experience produce:

sound-film,

which is capable of being realized as

audio-visual counterpoint.

Formulation and investigation of the phenomenon of cinema as forms of conflict yield the first possibility of devising a homogeneous system of *visual dramaturgy* for all general and particular cases of the film problem.

Of devising a *dramaturgy of the visual film-form* as regulated and precise as the existing *dramaturgy of the film-story.*

From this viewpoint on the film medium, the following forms and potentialities of style may be summed up as a film syntax, or it may be more exact to describe the following as:

a tentative film-syntax.

We shall list here a number of potentialities of dialectical development to be derived from this proposition: The concept of the moving (time-consuming) image arises from the superimposition — or counterpoint — of two differing immobile images.

I. Each *moving fragment of montage.* Each photographed piece. Technical definition of the phenomenon of movement. *No composition as yet.* (A running man. A rifle fired. A splash of water.)

II. *An artificially produced image of motion.* The basic optical element is used for deliberate compositions:

80

A. *Logical*

Example 1 (from *October*): a montage rendition of a machine-gun being fired, by cross-cutting details of the firing.

> *Combination A:* a brightly lit machine-gun. A different shot in a low key. Double burst: graphic burst + light burst. Close-up of machine-gunner.

> *Combination B:* Effect almost of double exposure achieved by *clatter* montage effect. Length of montage pieces — two frames each.

Example 2 (from *Potemkin*): an illustration of instantaneous action. Woman with pince-nez. Followed immediately — without transition — by the same woman with shattered pince-nez and bleeding eye: impression of a shot hitting the eye.

B. *Illogical*

Example 3 (from *Potemkin*): the same device used for pictorial symbolism. In the thunder of the *Potemkin*'s guns, a marble lion leaps up, in protest against the bloodshed on the Odessa steps. Composed of three shots of three stationary marble lions at the Alupka Palace in the Crimea: a sleeping lion, an awakening lion, a rising lion. The effect is achieved by a correct calculation of the length of the second shot. Its superimposition on the first shot produces the first action. This establishes time to impress the second position on the mind. Superimposition of the third position on the second produces the second action: the lion finally rises.

Example 4 (from *October*): Example 1 showed how the firing was manufactured symbolically from elements outside the process of firing itself. In illustrating the monarchist *putsch* attempted by General Kornilov, it occurred to me that his militarist *tendency* could be shown in a montage that would employ religious details for its material. For Kornilov had revealed his intention in the guise of a peculiar "Crusade" of Moslems (!), his Caucasian "Wild Division," together with some Christians, against the Bolsheviki. So we intercut shots of a Baroque Christ (apparently exploding in the radiant beams of his halo) with shots of an egg-shaped mask of Uzume, Goddess of Mirth, completely self-contained. The temporal conflict between the closed egg-form and the graphic star-form produced the effect of an instantaneous *burst* — of a bomb, or shrapnel. . . .

81

Thus far the examples have shown *primitive-physiological* cases
—employing superimposition of optical motion *exclusively.*

III. *Emotional* combinations, not only with the visible elements
of the shots, but chiefly with chains of psychological associations.
Association montage. As a means for pointing up a situation
emotionally.

In Example 1, we had two successive shots A and B, identical
in subject. However, they were not identical in respect to the
position of the subject within the frame:

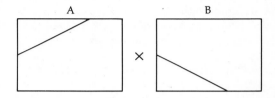

producing *dynamization in space*—an impression of spatial dynamics:

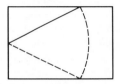

The degree of difference between the positions A and B determines
the tension of the movement.

For a new case, let us suppose that the subjects of Shots A and
B are not *identical.* Although the associations of the two shots
are identical, that is, associatively identical.

This *dynamization of the subject,* not in the field of space but
of psychology, i.e., *emotion,* thus produces:

emotional dynamization.

Example 1 (in *Strike*): the montage of the killing of the
workers is actually a cross montage of this carnage with the
butchering of a bull in an abattoir. Though the subjects are
different, "butchering" is the associative link. This made for

a powerful emotional intensification of the scene. As a matter of fact, homogeneity of gesture plays an important part in this case in achieving the effect—both the movement of the dynamic gesture within the frame, and the static gesture dividing the frame graphically.

This is a principle subsequently used by Pudovkin in *The End of St. Petersburg*, in his powerful sequence intercutting shots of stock exchange and battlefield. His previous film, *Mother*, had a similar sequence: the ice-break on the river, paralleled with the workers' demonstration.

Such a means may decay pathologically if the essential viewpoint —emotional dynamization of the subject—is lost. As soon as the film-maker loses sight of this essence the means ossifies into lifeless literary symbolism and stylistic mannerism. Two examples of such hollow use of this means occur to me:

Example 2 (in *October*): the sugary chants of compromise by the Mensheviki at the Second Congress of Soviets—during the storming of the Winter Palace—are intercut with hands playing harps. This was a purely literary parallelism that by no means dynamized the subject matter. Similarly in Otzep's *Living Corpse*, church spires (in imitation of those in *October*) and lyrical landscapes are intercut with the courtroom speeches of the prosecutor and defense lawyer. This error was the same as in the "harp" sequence.

On the other hand, a majority of *purely dynamic* effects can produce positive results:

Example 3 (in *October*): the dramatic moment of the union of the Motorcycle Battalion with the Congress of Soviets was dynamized by shots of abstractly spinning bicycle wheels, in association with the entrance of the new delegates. In this way the large-scale emotional content of the event was transformed into actual dynamics.

This same principle—giving birth to concepts, to emotions, by juxtaposing two disparate events—led to:

83

IV. *Liberation of the whole action from the definition of time and space.* My first attempts at this were in *October*.

Example 1: a trench crowded with soldiers appears to be crushed by an enormous gun-base that comes down inexorably. As an anti-militarist symbol seen from the viewpoint of subject alone, the effect is achieved by an apparent bringing together of an independently existing trench and an overwhelming military product, just as physically independent.

Example 2: in the scene of Kornilov's *putsch*, which puts an end to Kerensky's Bonapartist dreams. Here one of Kornilov's tanks climbs up and crushes a plaster-of-Paris Napoleon standing on Kerensky's desk in the Winter Palace, a juxtaposition of purely symbolic significance.

This method has now been used by Dovzhenko in *Arsenal* to shape whole sequences, as well as by Esther Schub in her use of library footage in *The Russia of Nikolai II and Lev Tolstoy*.

I wish to offer another example of this method, to upset the traditional ways of handling plot—although it has not yet been put into practice.

In 1924–1925 I was mulling over the idea of a filmic portrait of *actual* man. At that time, there prevailed a tendency to show actual man in films only in *long* uncut dramatic scenes. It was believed that cutting (montage) would destroy the idea of actual man. Abram Room established something of a record in this respect when he used in *The Death Ship* uncut dramatic shots as long as 40 meters or 135 feet. I considered (and still do) such a concept to be utterly unfilmic.

Very well—what would be a linguistically accurate characterization of a man?

His raven-black hair . . .

The waves of his hair . . .

His eyes radiating azure beams . . .

His steely muscles . . .

Even in a less exaggerated description, any verbal account of a person is bound to find itself employing an assortment of waterfalls, lightning-rods, landscapes, birds, etc.

Now why should the cinema follow the forms of theater and painting rather than the methodology of language, which allows wholly new concepts of ideas to arise from the combination of two concrete denotations of two concrete objects? Language is much closer to film than painting is. For example, in painting the form arises from *abstract* elements of line and color, while in cinema the material *concreteness* of the image within the frame presents — as an element — the greatest difficulty in manipulation. So why not rather lean towards the system of language, which is forced to use the same mechanics in inventing words and word-complexes?

On the other hand, why is it that montage cannot be dispensed with in orthodox films?

The differentiation in montage-pieces lies in their lack of existence as single units. Each piece can evoke no more than a certain association. The accumulation of such associations can achieve the same effect as is provided for the spectator by purely physiological means in the plot of a realistically produced play.

For instance, murder on the stage has a purely physiological effect. Photographed in *one* montage-piece, it can function simply as *information*, as a sub-title. *Emotional* effect begins only with the reconstruction of the event in montage fragments, each of which will summon a certain association — the sum of which will be an all-embracing complex of emotional feeling. Traditionally:

1. A hand lifts a knife.
2. The eyes of the victim open suddenly.
3. His hands clutch the table.
4. The knife is jerked up.
5. The eyes blink involuntarily.
6. Blood gushes.
7. A mouth shrieks.
8. Something drips onto a shoe . . .

and similar film clichés. Nevertheless, in regard to the *action as a whole, each fragment-piece* is almost *abstract*. The more differentiated they are the more abstract they become, provoking no more than a certain association.

Quite logically the thought occurs: could not the same thing be accomplished more productively by not following the plot so slavishly, but by materializing the idea, the impression, of *Murder* through a free accumulation of associative matter? For the most

85

important task is still to establish the idea of murder—the feeling of murder, as such. The plot is no more than a device without which one isn't yet capable of telling something to the spectator! In any case, effort in this direction would certainly produce the most interesting variety of forms.

Someone should try, at least! Since this thought occurred to me, I have not had time to make this experiment. And today I am more concerned with quite different problems. But, returning to the main line of our syntax, something there may bring us closer to these tasks.

While, with I, II, and III, tension was calculated for purely physiological effect—from the purely optical to the emotional, we must mention here also the case of the same conflict-tension serving the ends of new concepts—of new attitudes, that is, of purely intellectual aims.

Example 1 (in *October*): Kerensky's rise to power and dictatorship after the July uprising of 1917. A comic effect was gained by sub-titles indicating regular ascending ranks (*"Dictator"—"Generalissimo"—"Minister of Navy—and of Army"*—etc.) climbing higher and higher—cut into five or six shots of Kerensky, climbing the stairs of the Winter Palace, all with exactly the *same* pace. Here a conflict between the flummery of the ascending ranks and the "hero's" trotting up the same unchanging flight of stairs yields an intellectual result: Kerensky's essential nonentity is shown satirically. We have the counterpoint of a literally expressed conventional idea with the *pictured* action of a particular person who is unequal to his swiftly increasing duties. The incongruence of these two factors results in the spectator's purely *intellectual* decision at the expense of this particular person. Intellectual dynamization.

Example 2 (in *October*): Kornilov's march on Petrograd was under the banner of "In the Name of God and Country." Here we attempted to reveal the religious significance of this episode in a rationalistic way. A number of religious images, from a magnificent Baroque Christ to an Eskimo idol, were cut together. The conflict in this case was between the concept and the symbolization of God. While idea and image appear to accord completely in the first statue shown, the two elements move further from each other with each successive image. Maintaining the denotation of "God," the images increasingly disagree with our concept of God, inevitably leading to individual conclusions about the true nature of all deities. In this case, too, a chain of images attempted to achieve a purely intellectual resolution, resulting from a conflict between a preconception and a *gradual discrediting of it in purposeful steps.*

Step by step, by a process of comparing each new image with the common denotation, power is accumulated behind a process that can be formally identified with that of logical deduction. The decision to release these ideas, as well as the method used, is already *intellectually* conceived.

The conventional *descriptive* form for film leads to the formal possibility of a kind of filmic reasoning. While the conventional film directs the *emotions*, this suggests an opportunity to encourage and direct the whole *thought process*, as well.

These two particular sequences of experiment were very much opposed by the majority of critics. Because they were understood as purely political. I would not attempt to deny that *this form is most suitable for the expression of ideologically pointed theses,* but it is a pity that the critics completely overlooked the purely filmic potentialities of this approach.

ANDRÉ BAZIN
FROM WHAT IS CINEMA ?

THE EVOLUTION
OF THE LANGUAGE OF CINEMA

By 1928 the silent film had reached its artistic peak. The despair of its elite as they witnessed the dismantling of this ideal city, while it may not have been justified, is at least understandable. As they followed their chosen aesthetic path it seemed to them that the cinema had developed into an art most perfectly accommodated to the "exquisite embarrassment" of silence and that the realism that sound would bring could only mean a surrender to chaos.

In point of fact, now that sound has given proof that it came not to destroy but to fulfill the Old Testament of the cinema, we may most properly ask if the technical revolution created by the sound track was in any sense an aesthetic revolution. In other words, did the years from 1928 to 1930 actually witness the birth of a new cinema? Certainly, as regards editing, history does not actually show as wide a breach as might be expected between the silent and the sound film. On the contrary there is discernible evidence of a close relationship between certain directors of 1925 and 1935 and especially of the 1940's through the 1950's. Compare for example Erich von Stroheim and Jean Renoir or Orson Welles, or again Carl Theodore Dreyer and Robert Bresson. These more or less clear-cut affinities demonstrate first of all that the gap separating the 1920's and the 1930's can be bridged, and secondly that certain cinematic values actually carry over from the silent to the sound film and, above all, that it is less a matter of setting silence over against sound than of contrasting certain families of styles, certain basically different concepts of cinematographic expression.

Aware as I am that the limitations imposed on this study restrict me to a simplified and to that extent enfeebled presentation of my argument, and holding it to be less an objective statement than a working hypothesis, I will distinguish, in the cinema between 1920 and 1940, between two broad and opposing trends: those directors who put their faith in the image and those who put their faith in reality. By "image" I here mean, very broadly speaking, everything that the representation on the screen adds to the object there represented. This is a complex inheritance but it can be reduced essentially to two categories: those that relate to the plastics of the image and those that relate to the resources of montage, which after all, is simply the ordering of images in time.

Under the heading "plastics" must be included the style of the sets, of the make-up, and, up to a point, even of the performance, to which we naturally add the lighting and, finally, the framing of the shot which gives us its composition. As regards montage, derived initially as we all know from the masterpieces of Griffith, we have the statement of Malraux in his *Psychologie du cinéma* that it was montage that gave birth to film as an art, setting it apart from mere animated photography, in short, creating a language.

The use of montage can be "invisible" and this was generally the case in the prewar classics of the American screen. Scenes were broken down just for one purpose, namely, to analyze an episode according to the material or dramatic logic of the scene. It is this logic which conceals the fact of the analysis, the mind of the spectator quite naturally accepting the viewpoints of the director which are justified by the geography of the action or the shifting emphasis of dramatic interest.

But the neutral quality of this "invisible" editing fails to make use of the full potential of montage. On the other hand these potentialities are clearly evident from the three processes generally known as parallel montage, accelerated montage, montage by attraction. In creating parallel montage, Griffith succeeded in conveying a sense of the simultaneity of two actions taking place at a geographical distance by means of alternating shots from each. In *La Roue* Abel Gance created the illusion of the steadily increasing speed of a locomotive without actually using any images of speed (indeed the wheel could have been turning on one spot) simply by a multiplicity of shots of ever-decreasing length.

Finally there is "montage by attraction," the creation of S. M. Eisenstein, and not so easily described as the others, but which may be roughly defined as the reenforcing of the meaning of one image by association with another image not necessarily part of the same episode—for example the fireworks display in *The General Line* following the image of the bull. In this extreme form, montage by attraction was rarely used even by its creator but one may consider as very near to it in principle the more commonly used ellipsis, comparison, or metaphor, examples of which are the throwing of stockings onto a chair at the foot of a bed, or the milk overflowing in H.G. Clouzot's *Quai des orfèvres*. There are of course a variety of possible combinations of these three processes.

Whatever these may be, one can say that they share that trait in common which constitutes the very definition of montage, namely, the creation of a sense or meaning not proper to the images themselves but derived exclusively from their juxtaposition. The well-known experiment of Kuleshov with the shot of Mozhukhin in which a smile was seen to change its significance according to the image that preceded it, sums up perfectly the properties of montage.

Montage as used by Kuleshov, Eisenstein, or Gance did not give us the event; it alluded to it. Undoubtedly they derived at least the greater part of the constituent elements from the reality they were describing but the final significance of the film was found to reside in the ordering of these elements much more than in their objective content.

The matter under recital, whatever the realism of the individual image, is born essentially from these relationships—Mozhukhin plus dead child equal pity—that is to say an abstract result, none of the concrete elements of which are to be found in the premises; maidens plus appletrees in bloom equal hope. The combinations are infinite. But the only thing they have in common is the fact that they suggest an idea by means of a metaphor or by an association of ideas. Thus between the scenario properly so-called, the ultimate object of the recital, and the image pure and simple, there is a relay station, a sort of aesthetic "transformer." The meaning is not in the image, it is in the shadow of the image projected by montage onto the field of consciousness of the spectator.

Let us sum up. Through the contents of the image and the re-sources of montage, the cinema has at its disposal a whole arsenal of means whereby to impose its interpretation of an event on the spectator. By the end of the silent film we can consider this arsenal to have been full. On the one side the Soviet cinema carried to its ultimate consequences the theory and practice of montage while the German school did every kind of violence to the plastics of the image by way of sets and lighting. Other cinemas count too besides the Russian and German, but whether in France or Sweden or the United States, it does not appear that the language of cinema was at a loss for ways of saying what it wanted to say.

If the art of cinema consists in everything that plastics and montage can add to a given reality, the silent film was an art on its own. Sound could only play at best a subordinate and supple-mentary role: a counterpoint to the visual image. But this possible enhancement—at best only a minor one—is likely not to weigh much in comparison with the additional bargain-rate reality intro-duced at the same time by sound.

Thus far we have put forward the view that expressionism of montage and image constitute the essence of cinema. And it is precisely on this generally accepted notion that directors from silent days, such as Erich von Stroheim, F.W. Murnau, and Robert Flaherty, have by implication cast a doubt. In their films, montage plays no part, unless it be the negative one of inevitable elimina-tion where reality superabounds. The camera cannot see everything at once but it makes sure not to lose any part of what it chooses to see. What matters to Flaherty, confronted with Nanook hunting the seal, is the relation between Nanook and the animal; the actual length of the waiting period. Montage could suggest the time involved. Flaherty however confines himself to showing the actual waiting period; the length of the hunt is the very substance of the image, its true object. Thus in the film this episode requires one set-up. Will anyone deny that it is thereby much more moving than a montage by attraction?

Murnau is interested not so much in time as in the reality of dramatic space. Montage plays no more of a decisive part in *Nosferatu* than in *Sunrise*. One might be inclined to think that the plastics of his image are impressionistic. But this would be a superficial view. The composition of his image is in no sense pictorial. It adds nothing to the reality, it does not deform it, it forces it to reveal its structural depth, to bring out the preexisting relations which become constitutive of the drama. For example, in *Tabu*, the arrival of a ship from left screen gives an immediate sense of destiny at work so that Murnau has no need to cheat in any way on the uncompromising realism of a film whose settings are completely natural.

But it is most of all Stroheim who rejects photographic expressionism and the tricks of montage. In his films reality lays itself bare like a suspect confessing under the relentless examination of the commissioner of police. He has one simple rule for direction. Take a close look at the world, keep on doing so, and in the end it will lay bare for you all its cruelty and its ugliness. One could easily imagine as a matter of fact a film by Stroheim composed of a single shot as long-lasting and as close-up as you like. These three directors do not exhaust the possibilities. We would undoubtedly find scattered among the works of others elements of nonexpressionistic cinema in which montage plays no part—even including Griffith. But these examples suffice to reveal, at the very heart of the silent film, a cinematographic art the very opposite of that which has been identified as *"cinéma par excellence,"* a language the semantic and syntactical unit of which is in no sense the Shot; in which the image is evaluated not according to what it adds to reality but what it reveals of it. In the latter art the silence of the screen was a drawback, that is to say, it deprived reality of one of its elements. *Greed*, like Dreyer's *Jeanne d' Arc*, is already virtually a talking film. The moment that you cease to maintain that montage and the plastic composition of the image are the very essence of the language of cinema, sound is no longer the aesthetic crevasse dividing two radically different aspects of the seventh art. The cinema that is believed to have died of the soundtrack is in no sense *"the* cinema." The real dividing line is elsewhere. It was operative in the past and continues to be through thirty-five years of the history of the language of the film.

Having challenged the aesthetic unity of the silent film and divided it off into two opposing tendencies, now let us take a look at the history of the last twenty years.

THE EVOLUTION OF THE LANGUAGE OF CINEMA

From 1930 to 1940 there seems to have grown up in the world, originating largely in the United States, a common form of cinematic language. It was the triumph in Hollywood, during that time, of five or six major kinds of film that gave it its overwhelming superiority: (1) American comedy (*Mr. Smith Goes to Washington*, 1936); (2) The burlesque film (The Marx Brothers); (3) The dance and vaudeville film (Fred Astaire and Ginger Rogers and the Ziegfield Follies); (4) The crime and gangster film *(Scarface, I Am a Fugitive from a Chain Gang, The Informer);* (5) Psychological and social dramas *(Back Street, Jezebel);* (6) Horror or fantasy films *(Dr. Jekyll and Mr. Hyde, The Invisible Man, Frankenstein);* (7) The western *(Stagecoach, 1939).* During that time the French cinema undoubtedly ranked next. Its superiority was gradually manifested by way of a trend towards what might be roughly called stark somber realism, or poetic realism, in which four names stand out: Jacques Feyder, Jean Renoir, Marcel Carné, and Julien Duvivier. My intention not being to draw up a list of prize-winners, there is little use in dwelling on the Soviet, British, German, or Italian films for which these years were less significant than the ten that were to follow. In any case, American and French production sufficiently clearly indicate that the sound film, prior to World War II, had reached a well-balanced stage of maturity.

First as to content: Major varieties with clearly defined rules capable of pleasing a worldwide public, as well as a cultured elite, provided it was not inherently hostile to the cinema.

Secondly as to form: well-defined styles of photography and editing perfectly adapted to their subject matter; a complete harmony of image and sound. In seeing again today such films as *Jezebel* by William Wyler, *Stagecoach* by John Ford, or *Le Jour se lève* by Marcel Carné, one has the feeling that in them an art has found its perfect balance, its ideal form of expression, and reciprocally one admires them for dramatic and moral themes to which the cinema, while it may not have created them, has given a grandeur, an artistic effectiveness, that they would not otherwise have had. In short, here are all the characteristics of the ripeness of a classical art.

I am quite aware that one can justifiably argue that the originality of the postwar cinema as compared with that of 1938 derives from the growth of certain national schools, in particular the dazzling display of the Italian cinema and of a native English cinema freed

93

from the influence of Hollywood. From this one might conclude that the really important phenomenon of the years 1940–1950 is the introduction of new blood, of hitherto unexplored themes. That is to say, the real revolution took place more on the level of subject matter than of style. Is not neorealism primarily a kind of humanism and only secondarily a style of film-making? Then as to the style itself, is it not essentially a form of self-effacement before reality?

Our intention is certainly not to preach the glory of form over content. Art for art's sake is just as heretical in cinema as elsewhere, probably more so. On the other hand, a new subject matter demands new form, and as good a way as any towards understanding what a film is trying to say to us is to know how it is saying it.

Thus by 1938 or 1939 the talking film, particularly in France and in the United States, had reached a level of classical perfection as a result, on the one hand, of the maturing of different kinds of drama developed in part over the past ten years and in part inherited from the silent film, and, on the other, of the stabilization of technical progress. The 1930's were the years, at once, of sound and of panchromatic film. Undoubtedly studio equipment had continued to improve but only in matters of detail, none of them opening up new, radical possibilities for direction. The only changes in this situation since 1940 have been in photography, thanks to the increased sensitivity of the film stock. Panchromatic stock turned visual values upside down, ultrasensitive emulsions have made a modification in their structure possible. Free to shoot in the studio with a much smaller aperture, the operator could, when necessary, eliminate the soft-focus background once considered essential. Still there are a number of examples of the prior use of deep focus, for example in the work of Jean Renoir. This had always been possible on exteriors, and given a measure of skill, even in the studios. Anyone could do it who really wanted to. So that it is less a question basically of a technical problem, the solution of which has admittedly been made easier, than of a search after a style—a point to which we will come back. In short, with panchromatic stock in common use, with an understanding of the potentials of the microphone, and with the crane as standard studio equipment, one can really say that since 1930 all the technical requirements for the art of cinema have been available.

Since the determining technical factors were practically eliminated, we must look elsewhere for the signs and principles of the evolution of film language, that is to say by challenging the subject matter and as a consequence the styles necessary for its expression.

By 1939 the cinema had arrived at what geographers call the equilibrium-profile of a river. By this is meant that ideal mathematical curve which results from the requisite amount of erosion. Having reached this equilibrium-profile, the river flows effortlessly from its source to its mouth without further deepening of its bed. But if any geological movement occurs which raises the erosion level and modifies the height of the source, the water sets to work again, seeps into the surrounding land, goes deeper, burrowing and digging. Sometimes when it is a chalk bed, a new pattern is dug across the plain, almost invisible but found to be complex and winding, if one follows the flow of the water.

THE EVOLUTION OF EDITING SINCE THE ADVENT OF SOUND

In 1938 there was an almost universal standard pattern of editing. If, somewhat conventionally, we call the kind of silent films based on the plastics of the image and the artifices of montage, "expressionist" or "symbolistic," we can describe the new form of storytelling "analytic" and "dramatic." Let us suppose, by way of reviewing one of the elements of the experiment of Kuleshov, that we have a table covered with food and a hungry tramp. One can imagine that in 1936 it would have been edited as follows:

(1) Full shot of the actor and the table.
(2) Camera moves forward into a close-up of a face expressing a mixture of amazement and longing.
(3) Series of close-ups of food.
(4) Back to full shot of person who starts slowly towards the camera.
(5) Camera pulls slowly back to a three-quarter shot of the actor seizing a chicken wing.

Whatever variants one could think of for this scene, they would all have certain points in common:

(1) The verisimilitude of space in which the position of the actor

is always determined, even when a close-up eliminates the decor.

(2) The purpose and the effects of the cutting are exclusively dramatic or psychological.

In other words, if the scene were played on a stage and seen from a seat in the orchestra, it would have the same meaning, the episode would continue to exist objectively. The changes of point of view provided by the camera would add nothing. They would present the reality a little more forcefully, first by allowing a better view and then by putting the emphasis where it belongs.

It is true that the stage director like the film director has at his disposal a margin within which he is free to vary the interpretation of the action but it is only a margin and allows for no modification of the inner logic of the event. Now, by way of contrast, let us take the montage of the stone lions in *The End of St. Petersburg*. By skillful juxtaposition a group of sculptured lions are made to look like a single lion getting to its feet, a symbol of the aroused masses. This clever device would be unthinkable in any film after 1932. As late as 1935 Fritz Lang, in *Fury*, followed a series of shots of women dancing the can-can with shots of clucking chickens in a farmyard. This relic of associative montage came as a shock even at the time, and today seems entirely out of keeping with the rest of the film. However decisive the art of Marcel Carné, for example, in our estimate of the respective values of *Quai des Brumes* or of *Le Jour se lève* his editing remains on the level of the reality he is analyzing. There is only one proper way of looking at it. That is why we are witnessing the almost complete disappearance of optical effects such as superimpositions, and even, especially in the United States, of the close-up, the too violent impact of which would make the audience conscious of the cutting. In the typical American comedy the director returns as often as he can to a shot of the characters from the knees up, which is said to be best suited to catch the spontaneous attention of the viewer—the natural point of balance of his mental adjustment.

Actually this use of montage originated with the silent movies. This is more or less the part it plays in Griffith's films, for example in *Broken Blossoms*, because with *Intolerance* he had already introduced that synthetic concept of montage which the Soviet cinema was to carry to its ultimate conclusion and which is to be found again, although less exclusively, at the end of the silent era. It is understandable, as a matter of fact, that the sound image, far less flexible than the visual image, would carry montage in the direction of realism, increasingly eliminating both plastic impressionism and the symbolic relation between images.

Thus around 1938 films were edited, almost without exception, according to the same principle. The story was unfolded in a series of set-ups numbering as a rule about 600. The characteristic procedure was by shot-reverse-shot, that is to say, in a dialogue scene, the camera followed the order of the text, alternating the character shown with each speech.

It was this fashion of editing, so admirably suitable for the best films made between 1930 and 1939, that was challenged by the shot in depth introduced by Orson Welles and William Wyler. *Citizen Kane* can never be too highly praised. Thanks to the depth of field, whole scenes are covered in one take, the camera remaining motionless. Dramatic effects for which we had formerly relied on montage were created out of the movements of the actors within a fixed framework. Of course Welles did not invent the in-depth shot any more than Griffith invented the close-up. All the pioneers used it and for a very good reason. Soft focus only appeared with montage. It was not only a technical must consequent upon the use of images in juxtaposition, it was a logical consequence of montage, its plastic equivalent. If at a given moment in the action the director, as in the scene imagined above, goes to a close-up of a bowl of fruit, it follows naturally that he also isolates it in space through the focusing of the lens. The soft focus of the background confirms therefore the effect of montage, that is to say, while it is of the essence of the storytelling, it is only an accessory of the style of the photography. Jean Renoir had already clearly understood this, as we see from a statement of his made in 1938 just after he had made *La Bête humaine* and *La Grande illusion* and just prior to *La Règle du jeu*: "The more I learn about my trade the more I incline to direction in depth relative to the screen. The better it works, the less I use the kind of set-up that shows two actors facing the camera, like two well-behaved subjects posing for a still portrait." The truth of the matter is, that if you are looking for the precursor of Orson Welles, it is not Louis Lumière or Zecca, but rather Jean Renoir. In his films, the search after composition in depth is, in effect, a partial replacement of montage by frequent panning shots and entrances. It is based on a respect for the continuity of dramatic space and, of course, of its duration.

To anybody with eyes in his head, it is quite evident that the sequence of shots used by Welles in *The Magnificent Ambersons* is in no sense the purely passive recording of an action shot within the same framing. On the contrary, his refusal to break up the action, to analyze the dramatic field in time, is a positive action the results of which are far superior to anything that could be achieved by the classical "cut."

All you need to do is compare two frames shot in depth, one from 1910, the other from a film by Wyler or Welles, to understand just by looking at the image, even apart from the context of the film, how different their functions are. The framing in the 1910 film is intended, to all intents and purposes, as a substitute for the missing fourth wall of the theatrical stage, or at least in exterior shots, for the best vantage point to view the action, whereas in the second case the setting, the lighting, and the camera angles give an entirely different reading. Between them, director and cameraman have converted the screen into a dramatic checkerboard, planned down to the last detail. The clearest if not the most original examples of this are to be found in *The Little Foxes* where the *mise-en-scène* takes on the severity of a working drawing. Welles' pictures are more difficult to analyze because of his overfondness for the baroque. Objects and characters are related in such a fashion that it is impossible for the spectator to miss the significance of the scene. To get the same results by way of montage would have necessitated a detailed succession of shots.

What we are saying then is that the sequence of shots "in depth" of the contemporary director does not exclude the use of montage —how could he, without reverting to a primitive babbling?—he makes it an integral part of his "plastic." The storytelling of Welles or Wyler is no less explicit that John Ford's but theirs has the advantage over his that it does not sacrifice the specific effects that can be derived from unity of image in space and time. Whether an episode is analyzed bit by bit or presented in its physical entirety cannot surely remain a matter of indifference, at least in a work with some pretensions to style. It would obviously be absurd to deny that montage has added considerably to the progress of film language, but this has happened at the cost of other values, no less definitely cinematic.

This is why depth of field is not just a stock in trade of the cameraman like the use of a series of filters or of such-and-such a style of lighting, it is a capital gain in the field of direction—a dialectical step forward in the history of film language.

Nor is it just a formal step forward. Well used, shooting in depth is not just a more economical, a simpler, and at the same time a more subtle way of getting the most out of a scene. In addition to affecting the structure of film language, it also affects the relationships of the minds of the spectators to the image, and in consequence it influences the interpretation of the spectacle.

It would lie outside the scope of this article to analyze the psychological modalities of these relations, as also their aesthetic consequences, but it might be enough here to note, in general terms:

(1) That depth of focus brings the spectator into a relation with the image closer to that which he enjoys with reality. Therefore it is correct to say that, independently of the contents of the image, its structure is more realistic;

(2) That it implies, consequently, both a more active mental attitude on the part of the spectator and a more positive contribution on his part to the action in progress. While analytical montage only calls for him to follow his guide, to let his attention follow along smoothly with that of the director who will choose what he should see, here he is called upon to exercise at least a minimum of personal choice. It is from his attention and his will that the meaning of the image in part derives.

(3) From the two preceding propositions, which belong to the realm of psychology, there follows a third which may be described as metaphysical. In analyzing reality, montage presupposes of its very nature the unity of meaning of the dramatic event. Some other form of analysis is undoubtedly possible but then it would be another film. In short, montage by its very nature rules out ambiguity of expression. Kuleshov's experiment proves this *per absurdum* in giving on each occasion a precise meaning to the expression on a face, the ambiguity of which alone makes the three successively exclusive expressions possible.

On the other hand, depth of focus reintroduced ambiguity into the structure of the image if not of necessity—Wyler's films are never ambiguous—at least as a possibility. Hence it is no exaggeration to say that *Citizen Kane* is unthinkable shot in any other way but in depth. The uncertainty in which we find ourselves as to the spiritual key or the interpretation we should put on the film is built into the very design of the image.

It is not that Welles denies himself any recourse whatsoever to the expressionistic procedures of montage, but just that their use from time to time in between sequences of shots in depth gives them a new meaning. Formerly montage was the very stuff of cinema, the texture of the scenario. In *Citizen Kane* a series of superimpositions is contrasted with a scene presented in a single take, constituting another and deliberately abstract mode of story-telling. Accelerated montage played tricks with time and space while that of Welles, on the other hand, is not trying to deceive us; it offers us a contrast, condensing time, and hence is the equivalent for example of the French imperfect or the English frequentative tense. Like accelerated montage and montage of attractions these superimpositions, which the talking film had not used for ten years, rediscovered a possible use related to temporal realism in a film without montage.

If we have dwelt at some length on Orson Welles it is because the date of his appearance in the filmic firmament (1941) marks more or less the beginning of a new period and also because his case is the most spectacular and, by virtue of his very excesses, the most significant.

Yet *Citizen Kane* is part of a general movement, of a vast stirring of the geological bed of cinema, confirming that everywhere up to a point there had been a revolution in the language of the screen.

I could show the same to be true, although by different methods, of the Italian cinema. In Roberto Rossellini's *Paisà* and *Allemania Anno Zero* and Vittorio de Sica's *Ladri de Biciclette*, Italian neorealism contrasts with previous forms of film realism in its stripping away of all expressionism and in particular in the total absence of the effects of montage. As in the films of Welles and in spite of conflicts of style, neorealism tends to give back to the cinema a sense of the ambiguity of reality. The preoccupation of Rossellini when dealing with the face of the child in *Allemania Anno Zero* is the exact opposite of that of Kuleshov with the close-up of Mozhukhin. Rossellini is concerned to preserve its mystery. We should not be misled by the fact that the evolution of neorealism is not manifest, as in the United States, in any form of revolution in editing. They are both aiming at the same results by different methods. The means used by Rossellini and de Sica are less spectacular but they are no less determined to do away with montage and to transfer to the screen the *continuum* of reality. The dream of Zavattini is just to make a ninety-minute film of the life of a man to whom nothing ever happens. The most "aesthetic" of the neorealists, Luchino Visconti, gives just as clear a picture as Welles of the basic aim of his directorial art in *La Terra Trema*, a film almost entirely composed of one-shot sequences, thus clearly showing his concern to cover the entire action in interminable deep-focus panning shots.

However we cannot pass in review all the films that have shared in this revolution in film language since 1940. Now is the moment to attempt a synthesis of our reflections on the subject.

It seems to us that the decade from 1940 to 1950 marks a decisive step forward in the development of the language of the film. If we have appeared since 1930 to have lost sight of the trend of the silent film as illustrated particularly by Stroheim, F. W. Murnau, Robert Flaherty, and Dreyer, it is for a purpose. It is not that this trend seems to us to have been halted by the talking film. On the contrary, we believe that it represented the richest vein of the so-called silent film and, precisely because it was not aesthetically tied to montage, but was indeed the only tendency that looked to the realism of sound as a natural development. On the other hand it is a fact that the talking film between 1930 and 1940 owes it virtually nothing save for the glorious and retrospectively prophetic exception of Jean Renoir. He alone in his searchings as a director prior to *La Règle du jeu* forced himself to look back beyond the resources provided by montage and so uncovered the secret of a film form that would permit everything to be said without chopping the world up into little fragments, that would reveal the hidden meanings in people and things without disturbing the unity natural to them.

It is not a question of thereby belittling the films of 1930 to 1940, a criticism that would not stand up in the face of the number of masterpieces, it is simply an attempt to establish the notion of a dialectic progress, the highest expression of which was found in the films of the 1940's. Undoubtedly, the talkie sounded the knell of a certain aesthetic of the language of film, but only wherever it had turned its back on its vocation in the service of realism. The sound film nevertheless did preserve the essentials of montage, namely discontinuous description and the dramatic analysis of action. What it turned its back on was metaphor and symbol in exchange for the illusion of objective presentation. The expressionism of montage has virtually disappeared but the relative realism of the kind of cutting that flourished around 1937 implied a congenital limitation which escaped us so long as it was perfectly suited to its subject matter. Thus American comedy reached its peak within the framework of a form of editing in which the realism of the time played no part. Dependent on logic for its effects, like vaudeville and plays on words, entirely conventional in its moral and sociological content, American comedy had everything to gain, in strict line-by-line progression, from the rhythmic resources of classical editing.

Undoubtedly it is primarily with the Stroheim-Murnau trend—almost totally eclipsed from 1930 to 1940—that the cinema has more or less consciously linked up once more over the last ten years. But it has no intention of limiting itself simply to keeping this trend alive. It draws from it the secret of the regeneration of realism in storytelling and thus of becoming capable once more of bringing together real time, in which things exist, along with the duration of the action, for which classical editing had insidiously substituted mental and abstract time. On the other hand, so far from wiping out once and for all the conquests of montage, this reborn realism gives them a body of reference and a meaning. It is only an increased realism of the image that can support the abstraction of montage. The stylistic repertory of a director such as Hitchcock, for example, ranged from the power inherent in the basic document as such, to superimpositions, to large close-ups. But the close-ups of Hitchcock are not the same as those of C. B. de Mille in *The Cheat* [1915]. They are just one type of figure, among others, of his style. In other words, in the silent days, montage evoked what the director wanted to say; in the editing of 1938, it described it. Today we can say that at last the director writes in film. The image—its plastic composition and the way it is set in time, because it is founded on a much higher degree of realism—has at its disposal more means of manipulating reality and of modifying it from within. The film-maker is no longer the competitor of the painter and the playwright, he is, at last, the equal of the novelist.

102

CHRISTIAN METZ
FROM FILM LANGUAGE

SOME POINTS
IN THE SEMIOTICS
OF THE CINEMA

The purpose of this text is to examine some of the problems and difficulties confronting the person who wants to begin undertaking, in the field of "cinematographic language," de Saussure's project of a general semiotics: to study the ordering and functionings of the main signifying units used in the filmic message. Semiotics, as de Saussure conceived it, is still in its childhood, but any work bearing on one of the nonverbal "languages," provided that it assumes a resolutely semiological relevance and does not remain satisfied with vague considerations of "substance," brings its contribution, whether modest or important, to that great enterprise, the general study of significations.

The very term "cinematographic *language*" already poses the whole problem of the semiotics of film. It would require a long justification, and strictly speaking it should be used only after the in-depth study of the semiological mechanisms at work in the filmic message had been fairly well advanced. Convenience, however, makes us retain, right from the start, that frozen syntagma—"language"—which has gradually assumed a place in the special vocabulary of film theoreticians and aestheticians. Even from a strictly semiological point of view, one can perhaps at this time give a preliminary justification for the expression "cinematographic language" (not to be confused with "cinematographic *langue*" (language system), which does not seem to me acceptable)—a justification that, in the present state of semiological investigations, can only be very general. I hope to outline it in this essay. . . .

CINEMA AND NARRATIVITY

A first choice confronts the "film semiologist": Is the corpus to be made up of feature films *(narrative films)* or, on the contrary, of short films, documentaries, technological, pedagogical, or advertising films, etc.? It could be answered that it depends simply on what one wants to study—that the cinema possesses various "dialects," and that each one of these "dialects" can become the subject of a specific analysis. This is undoubtedly true. Nevertheless, there is a hierarchy of concerns (or, better yet, a methodological urgency) that favors—in the beginning at least—the study of the narrative film. We know that, in the few years immediately before and after the Lumière brothers' invention in 1895, critics, journalists, and the pioneer cinematographers disagreed considerably among themselves as to the *social function* that they attributed to, or predicted for, the new machine: whether it was a means of preservation or of making archives, whether it was an auxiliary technography for research and teaching in sciences like botany or surgery, whether it was a new form of journalism, or an instrument of sentimental devotion, either private or public, which could perpetuate the living image of the dear departed one, and so on. That, over all these possibilities, the cinema could evolve into a machine for telling stories had never been really considered. From the very beginnings of the cinematograph there were various indications and statements that suggested such an evolution, but they had no common measure with the magnitude that the narrative phenomenon was to assume. The merging of the cinema and of narrativity was a great fact, which was by no means predestined—nor was it strictly fortuitous. It was a historical and social fact, a fact of civilization (to use a formula dear to the sociologist Marcel Mauss), a fact that in turn conditioned the later evolution of the film as a semiological reality, somewhat in the same way—indirect and general,* though effective —that "external" linguistic events (conquests, colonizations, transformations of language) influence the "internal" functioning of idioms. In the realm of the cinema, all nonnarrative genres—the documentary, the technical film, etc.—have become marginal

---

*Except, of course, for specific lexical facts.

provinces, border regions so to speak, while the *feature-length film of novelistic fiction*, which is simply called a "film" — the usage is significant† — has traced more and more clearly the king's highway of filmic expression.

This purely numerical and social superiority is not the only fact concerned. Added to it is a more "internal" consideration: Nonnarrative films for the most part are distinguished from "real" films by their social purpose and by their content much more than by their "language processes." The basic figures of the semiotics of the cinema — montage, camera movements, scale of the shots, relationships between the image and speech, sequences, and other large syntagmatic units — are on the whole the same in "small" films and in "big" films. It is by no means certain that an independent semiotics of the various nonnarrative genres is possible other than in the form of a series of discontinuous remarks on the points of difference between these films and "ordinary" films. To examine fiction films is to proceed more directly and more rapidly to the heart of the problem.

There is, moreover, an encouraging diachronic consideration. We know, since the observations of Béla Balázs, André Malraux, Edgar Morin, Jean Mitry, and many others, that the cinema was not a specific "language" from its inception. Before becoming the means of expression familiar to us, it was a simple means of mechanical recording, preserving, and reproducing moving visual spectacles — whether of life, of the theater, or even of small *mises-en-scène*, which were specially prepared and which, in the final analysis, remained theatrical — in short, a "means of reproduction," to use André Malraux's term. Now, *it was precisely to the extent that the cinema confronted the problems of narration* that, in the course of successive gropings, it came to produce a body of specific signifying procedures. Historians of the cinema generally agree in dating the beginning of the "cinema" as we know it in the period 1910–15. Films like *Enoch Arden, Life for the Czar, Quo Vadis?, Fantômas, Cabiria, The Golem, The Battle of Gettysburg*, and above all *Birth of a Nation* were among the first films, in the acceptation we now give this word when we use it without a determinant: Narration of

---

†As in statements like "The short was terrible, but the film was great" or "What are they showing tonight? a series of shorts or a film?" etc.

a certain magnitude based on procedures that are supposed to be specifically cinematographic. It so happens that these procedures were perfected in the wake of the narrative endeavor. The pioneers of "cinematographic language"—Méliès, Porter, Griffith—couldn't care less about "formal" research conducted for its own sake; what is more (except for occasional naïve and confused attempts), they cared little about the symbolic, philosophical or human "message" of their films. Men of denotation rather than of connotation, they wanted above all to tell a story; they were not content unless they could subject the continuous, analogical material of photographic duplication to the *articulations*—however rudimentary—of a narrative discourse. Georges Sadoul has indeed shown how Méliès, in his story-teller's naïveté, was led to invent double exposure, the device of multiple exposures with a mask and a dark backdrop, the dissolve and the fade-in, and the pan shot. Jean Mitry, who has written a very precise synthesis of these problems, examines the first occurrences of a certain number of procedures of filmic language—the close-up, the pan shot, the tracking shot, parallel montage, and interlaced, or alternate, montage—among the film primitives. I will summarize the conclusions he reaches: The principal "inventions" are credited to the Frenchmen Méliès and Promio, to the Englishmen G. A. Smith and J. Williamson, and to the American E. S. Porter; it was Griffith's role to define and to stabilize—we would say, to codify—the *function* of these different procedures in relation to the filmic *narrative*, and thereby unify them up to a certain point in a coherent "syntax" (note that it would be better to use the term *syntagmatic category;* Jean Mitry himself avoids the word syntax). Between 1911 and 1915, Griffith made a whole series of films having, more or less consciously, the value of experimental probings, and *Birth of a Nation*, released in 1915, appears as the crowning work, the sum and the public demonstration of investigations that, however naïve they may have been, were nonetheless systematic and fundamental. Thus, it was in a single motion that the cinema became narrative and took over some of the attributes of a language.

Today, still, the so-called filmic procedures are in fact filmic-narrative. This, to my mind, justifies the priority of the narrative film in the filmosemiological enterprise—a priority that must not of course become an exclusivity.

STUDIES OF DENOTATION AND STUDIES OF CONNOTATION IN THE SEMIOTICS OF THE CINEMA

The facts I have just reviewed lead to another consequence. The semiotics of the cinema can be conceived of either as a semiotics of connotation or as a semiotics of denotation. Both directions are interesting, and it is obvious that on the day when the semiological study of film makes some progress and begins to form a body of knowledge, it will have considered connotative and denotative significations together. The study of connotation brings us closer to the notion of the cinema as an art (the "seventh art"). As I have indicated elsewhere in more detail, the art of film is located on the same semiological "plane" as literary art: The properly aesthetic orderings and constraints—versification, composition, and tropes in the first case; framing, camera movements, and light "effects" in the second—serve as the connoted instance, which is superimposed over the denoted meaning. In literature, the latter appears as the purely linguistic signification, which is linked, in the employed idiom, to the units used by the author. In the cinema, it is represented by the literal (that is, perceptual) meaning of the spectacle reproduced in the image, or of the sounds duplicated by the sound-track. As for connotation, which plays a major role in all aesthetic languages,* its significate is the literary or cinematographic "style," "genre" (the epic, the western, etc.), "symbol" (philosophical, humanitarian, ideological, and so on), or "poetic atmosphere"— and its signifier is the whole denotated semiological material, whether signified or signifying. In American gangster movies, where, for example, the slick pavement of the waterfront distills an impression of anxiety and hardness (significate of the connotation), the scene represented (dimly lit, deserted wharves, with stacks of crates and overhead cranes, the significate of denotation), and the technique of the shooting, which is dependent on the effects of lighting in order to produce a certain *picture* of the docks (signifier of denotation), converge to form the signifier of connotation. The

---

* Aesthetic language practices a kind of promotion of connotation, but connotation occurs as well in various phenomena of expressiveness proper to ordinary language, like those studied by Charles Bally (*Le Langage et la vie*, Geneva, Payot, 1926).

same scene filmed in a different light would produce a different impression; and so would the same technique used on a different subject (for example, a child's smiling face). Film aestheticians have often remarked that filmic effects must not be "gratuitous," but must remain "subordinate to the plot." This is another way of saying that the significate of connotation can establish itself only when the corresponding signifier brings into play *both* the signifier and the significate of denotation.

The study of the cinema as an art—the study of cinematographic expressiveness—can therefore be conducted according to methods derived from linguistics. For instance, there is no doubt that films are amenable to analyses comparable *(mutatis mutandis)* to those Thomas A. Sebeok has applied to Cheremis songs, or to those Samuel R. Levin has proposed. But there is another task that requires the careful attention of the film semiologist. For also, and even first of all, through its procedures of *denotation*, the cinema is a specific language. The concept of *diegesis* is as important for the film semiologist as the idea of art. The word is derived from the Greek διήγησις, "narration" and was used particularly to designate one of the obligatory parts of judiciary discourse, the recital of facts. The term was introduced into the framework of the cinema by Étienne Souriau. It designates the film's *represented* instance (which Mikel Dufrenne contrasts to the expressed, properly aesthetic, instance)—that is to say, the sum of a film's denotation: the narration itself, but also the fictional space and time dimensions implied in and by the narrative, and consequently the characters, the landscapes, the events, and other narrative elements, in so far as they are considered in their denoted aspect. How does the cinema indicate successivity, precession, temporal breaks, causality, adversative relationships, consequence, spatial proximity, or distance, etc.? These are central questions to the semiotics of the cinema.

One must not indeed forget that, from the semiological point of view, the cinema is very different from still photography whence its technique is derived. In photography, as Roland Barthes has clearly shown, the denoted meaning is secured entirely through the automatic process of photochemical reproduction; denotation is a visual transfer,* which is not codified and has no inherent organiza-

---

*I am speaking here as a semiologist and not as a psychologist. Comparative studies of visual perception, both in "real" and in filmic conditions, have indeed isolated all the optical distortions that differentiate between the photograph and the

tion. Human intervention, which carries some elements of a proper semiotics, affects only the level of connotation (lighting, camera angle, "photographic effects," and so on). And, in point of fact, there is no specifically photographic procedure for designating the significate "house" in its denotated aspect, unless it is by showing a house. In the cinema, on the other hand, a whole semiotics of denotation is possible and necessary, for a film is composed of *many* photographs (the concept of montage, with its myriad consequences)—photographs that give us mostly only partial views of the diegetic referent. In film a "house" would be a shot of a staircase, a shot of one of the walls taken from the outside, a close-up of a window, a brief establishing shot of the building,† etc. Thus a kind of filmic *articulation* appears, which has no equivalent in photography: It is the denotation itself that is being constructed, organized, and to a certain extent codified (*codified*, not necessarily *encoded*). Lacking absolute laws, filmic intelligibility nevertheless depends on a certain number of dominant habits: A film put together haphazardly would not be understood.

I return to my initial observations: "Cinematographic language" is first of all the literalness of a plot. Artistic effects, even when they are substantially inseparable from the semic act by which the film tells us its story, nevertheless constitute another level of signification, which from the methodological point of view must come "later."

PARADIGMATIC AND SYNTAGMATIC CATEGORIES

There is a danger that the semiotics of the cinema will tend to develop along the syntagmatic rather than along the paradigmatic

---

object. But these transformations, which obey the laws of optical physics, of the chemistry of emulsions and of retinal physiology, do not constitute a signifying system.

†Even if this over-all view is the only one shown us in the film, it is still the result of a choice. We know that the modern cinema has partially abandoned the practices of visual fragmentation and excessive montage in favor of the continuous shot (cf. the famous "shot-sequence" controversy). This condition *modifies* to the same extent the semiotics of filmic denotation, but it in no way dismisses it. Simply, cinematographic language, like other languages, has a diachronic side. A single "shot" itself contains several elements (example: switching from one view to another through a camera movement, and without montage).

axis. It is not that there is no filmic paradigm: At specific points along the chain of images the number of units liable to occur is limited, so that, in these circumstances, the unit that does appear derives its meaning in relation to the other members of the paradigm. This is the case with the "fade-dissolve" duality within the framework of the "conjunction of two sequences":* a simple commutation, which the users—that is to say, the spectators—perform spontaneously, makes it possible to isolate the corresponding significates: a spatiotemporal break with the establishing of an underlying transitive link (dissolve), and a straightforward spatiotemporal break (fade). But in most of the *positions* of the filmic chain, the number of units liable to appear is very much open (though not infinite). Much more open, in any case, than the series of lexemes that, by their nonfinite nature, are nonetheless opposed to the series of grammatical monemes in linguistics. For, despite the difficulty, already emphasized by Joseph Vendryes in *Le Langage*, of accurately enumerating the words of an idiom, it is at least possible to indicate the maximum and minimum limits, thus arriving at the approximate order of magnitude (for example, in French the lexeme *"lav-"* exists, but the lexeme *"patouf"* does not†). The case is different in the cinema, where the number of images is indefinite. Several times indefinite, one should say. For the "pro-filmic" spectacles‡ are themselves unlimited in number; the exact nature of lighting can be varied infinitely and by quantities that are nondiscrete; the same applies to the axial distance between the subject and the camera (in variations which are said to be scalar—that is, scale of the shot),§ to the camera angle, to the properties of the film and

---

*Fades, or dissolves, can also occur in other settings, especially at the center of sequences. In such cases, their value is different.

†The lexemic unit *"lav-"* corresponds to *"wash-"* in English; *"patouf"* is no more of a lexeme in English than it is in French.—TRANSLATOR.

‡As defined by Étienne Souriau. The "profilmic" spectacle is whatever is placed in front of the camera, or whatever one places the camera in front of, in order to "shoot" it.

§In *Le Langage cinématographique* (Paris, 1962), Francois Chevassu maintains (p. 14) that the "scale of shots" is coded. I would say instead that it is the technical terminology ("close-up," "thirty-degree angle shot," "medium shot," etc.) that is coded. The actual scale of the shots constitutes a continuous gradation, from the closest to the furthest shot. Codification intervenes at the metalinguistic level (studio jargon) in this case, and not on that of the language object (that is, cinematographic language).

110

the focal length of the lens, and to the exact trajectory of the camera movements (including the stationary shot, which represents zero degree in this case). It suffices to vary one of these elements by a perceptible quantity to obtain *another* image. The shot is therefore not comparable to the word in a lexicon; rather it resembles a complete statement (of one or more sentences), in that it is already the result of an essentially free combination, a "speech" arrangement. On the other hand the word is a syntagma that is precast by code— a "vertical" syntagma, as R. F. Mikus would say. Let us note in this connection that there is another similarity between the image and the statement: Both are actualized units, whereas the word in itself is a purely potential unit of code. The image is almost always assertive—and assertion is one of the great "modalities" of actualization, of the semic act. It appears therefore that the paradigmatic category in film is condemned to remain partial and fragmentary, at least as long as one tries to isolate it on the level of the *image*. This is naturally derived from the fact that *creation* plays a larger role in cinematographic language than it does in the handling of idioms: To "speak" a language is to use it, but to "speak" cinematographic language is to a certain extent to invent it. The speakers of ordinary language constitute a group of users; film-makers are a group of creators. On the other hand, movie *spectators* in turn constitute a group of users. That is why the semiotics of the cinema must frequently consider things from the point of view of the spectator rather than of the film-maker. Étienne Souriau's distinction between the filmic point of view and the *"cinéastique,"* or film-making, point of view is a very useful concept; film semiotics is mainly a *filmic* study. The situation has a rough equivalent in linguistics: Some linguists connect the speaker with the message, while the listener in some way "represents" the code, since he requires it to understand what is being said to him, while the speaker is presumed to know beforehand what he wants to say.

But, more than paradigmatic studies, it is the syntagmatic considerations that are at the center of the problems of filmic denotation. Although each image is a free creation, the arrangement of these images into an intelligible sequence—cutting and montage— brings us to the heart of the semiological dimension of film. It is a rather paradoxical situation: Those proliferating (and not very discrete!) units—the *images*—when it is a matter of composing a film, suddenly accept with reasonably good grace the constraint of a few large syntagmatic structures. While no image ever entirely resembles another image, the great majority of narrative films resemble each other in their principal syntagmatic figures. *Filmic narrativity*—since it has again crossed our path—by becoming stable through convention and repetition over innumerable films, has gradually shaped itself into forms that are more or less fixed, but certainly not immutable. These forms represent a synchronic "state" (that of the present cinema), but if they were to change, it could only be through a complete positive evolution, liable to be challenged—like those that, in spoken languages, produce diachronic transformations in the distribution of aspects and tenses. Applying de Saussure's thought to the cinema, one could say that the large syntagmatic category of the narrative film *can change*, but that no single person can make it change over night.* A failure of intellection among the viewers would be the automatic sanctioning of a purely individual innovation, which the system would refuse to confirm. The originality of creative artists consists, here as elsewhere, in tricking the code, or at least in *using* it ingeniously, rather than in attacking it directly or in violating it—and still less in ignoring it.

AN EXAMPLE: THE ALTERNATING SYNTAGMA

It is not within the scope of this paper to analyze the principal types of *large* filmic *syntagma*. Instead, as an example, I will simply indicate some of the characteristics of one type, the *alternating syntagma* (for example, image of a mother-image of her daughter-image of the mother, etc.). The alternating syntagma rests on the principle of alternating distribution of two or more diegetic elements. The images thus fall into two or more *series*, each one of which, if shown continuously, would constitute a normal sequence. The alternating syntagma is, precisely, a rejection of the grouping by continuous series (which remains potential), for reasons of connotation—the search for a certain "construction" or a certain "effect." This type of syntagma apparently made its first appearance in 1901 in England, in a film by Williamson, *Attack on a*

---

* But then, I should have added, by the same token, that this syntagmatic category contains a paradigmatic category, and consequently I should have shown less skepticism as to the possibilities of a paradigmatic category in the cinema.

Mission in China, one of those "re-enacted news reels" that were popular at the time. In it, one saw images of a mission surrounded by Boxers (during the rebellion of that name) alternating with shots of marines coming to the rescue.* Subsequently the procedure becomes more or less usual.

The alternation defines the form of the signifier, but not necessarily, as we shall see, that of the significate—which amounts to saying that the relationship between the signifier and the significate is not always analogous in the alternating syntagma. If one takes the nature of the *significate of temporal denotation* as a relevant basis, one can distinguish three cases of alternating syntagma. In the first case (which might be called the *alternator*), the alternation of the signifiers refers to a parallel alternation of the significates (analogous relationship). Example: two tennis players framed alternately, at the moment each one is returning the ball. In the second case (which would be the *alternate syntagma*), the alternating of the signifiers corresponds to a simultaneity of the significates. Example: the pursuers and the pursued. Every spectator understands that he is seeing two chronological series which are contemporaneous at each instant, and that, while he is seeing the pursued galloping away (locus of the signifier, on the screen), the pursuers are nonetheless continuing the chase (locus of the signifier, in the diegesis). Thus the semiotic *nexus*—alternating simultaneity—is no longer analogous. But it does not become "arbitrary" because of that: It remains motivated (remember that analogy is one of the forms of motivation), and the understanding of this kind of syntagma by the viewer is relatively "natural." The motivation must be explained by the spontaneous psychological mechanisms of filmic perception. Anne Souriau has shown that sequences of the "pursued-pursuing" variety are readily understood, with little previous exposure, by the spectator (on the condition, only, that the rhythm of the alternation not be too slow), for he "interpolates spontaneously" the visual material that the film presents. He guesses that series 1 continues to unfold in the plot while he is seeing series 2 in the image. The third case could be called *parallel syntagma*: Two series of events are mixed together through montage without having any relevant temporal relationships on the level

---

*"Alternation" means simultaneity here. It pertains therefore to the *alternate syntagma*, as I am about to define that term.

of the significate (diegesis), at least with respect to denotation. It is this variety of syntagma that film theoreticians sometimes refer to with expressions like "neutral temporal relationships." Example: a sinister urban landscape at night, alternating with a sunny pastoral view. There is nothing to indicate whether the two scenes are simultaneous or not (and if not, which precedes and which follows). It is simply a matter of two motifs brought together for "symbolic" reasons by montage (the rich and the poor, life and death, reaction and revolution, etc.) and without their literal location in time as a pertinent factor. It is as if the denoted temporal relationship had yielded to the rich, multiple values of connotation, which depend on the context as well as on the substance of the significate.

The three varieties of alternating syntagma constitute a small system whose internal configuration recalls somewhat the structure of verbal grammatical persons as conceived by Émile Benveniste. A first correlation (presence or absence of relevant temporal denotation)allows us to distribute parallel montage to one side (absence), and alternate and alternator montage to the other (presence). Within the second term, another correlation (nature of the significate of temporal denotation) distinguishes between the alternate (significate equals simultaneity) and the alternator (significate equals alternation).*

---

* I have retained this passage because it gives a simple example of what commutation can be in the filmic corpus, but the factual conclusions presented here no longer correspond to the current state of my investigations of the considered point. First of all, the study of various passages of films has made it appear that the "alternator" cannot always be distinguished from the "alternate" syntagma (or, in rarer cases, from the parallel syntagma) by any really probing difference: In the example of the tennis players, it can also be considered that the two partners are both supposed to be engaged in action continuously and simultaneously (i.e., alternate syntagma). Thus—and although certain cases seem to subsist where the alternate syntagma appears, more clearly than in other cases, as a *variant* similar to what I have called here the "alternator"—I have not retained the alternator as a separate type or sub-type. Then, there are cases where the alternating of images on the screen corresponds to temporal relationships not mentioned in this article: For example, one finds "alternating syntagmas" that interweave a "present" series with a "past" series (a kind of alternating flashback), and in which consequently the relationship of the two series can be defined neither by simultaneity nor by the term "neutral temporal relationship." One will note also that the concept of "alternating syntagma" has a certain obscure correspondence to that of the "frequentative syntagma." . . . In the final analysis, however, the reason I have dropped the "alternator" *as a general category*

OTHER PROBLEMS

These very brief remarks provided an example of what the syntagmatic study of filmic denotation could be. There are important differences between the semiotics of the cinema and linguistics itself. Without repeating those mentioned elsewhere, let me recall some of the main points: Film contains nothing corresponding to the purely distinctive units of the second articulation; all of its units—even the simplest, like the dissolve and the wipe—are directly significant (and moreover, as I have already pointed out, they only occur in the actualized state). The commutations and other manipuations by which the semiotics of the cinema proceeds therefore affect the large significatory units. The "laws" of cinematographic language call for *statements* within a narrative, and not monemes within a statement, or still less phonemes within a moneme.

Contrary to what many of the theoreticians of the silent film declared or suggested ("*Ciné langue,*" "visual Esperanto," etc.), the cinema is certainly not a language system *(langue)*. It can, however, be considered as a *language*, to the extent that it orders signifying elements within ordered arrangements different from those of spoken idioms—and to the extent that these elements are not traced on the perceptual configurations of reality itself (which does not tell stories). Filmic manipulation transforms what might have been a mere visual transfer of reality into discourse. Derived from a kind of signification that is purely analogous and continuous —animated photography, cinematography—the cinema gradually shaped, in the course of its diachronic maturation, some elements of a proper semiotics, which remain scattered and fragmentary within the open field of simple visual duplication.*

---

of classification is less because of the drawbacks I have just pointed out (and which various adjustments could suppress) than because of an over-all *reformulation* of the table of the main types of filmic arrangement. Taken separately, the analysis developed above remains partially valid.

* But I should have added here that the significations that analogy and mechanical duplication yield—although they do not pertain to *cinematographic* language as a specific system—nevertheless do have the effect of bringing structures and elements that belong to *other* systems which are also cultural, which also carry meaning and which are also more or less organized, into the cinema (as a whole).

115

The "shot"—an already complex unit, which must be studied—remains an indispensable reference for the time being, in somewhat the same way that the "word" was during a period of linguistic research. It might be somewhat adventurous to compare the shot to the *taxeme*, in Louis Hjelmslev's sense, but one can consider that it constitutes the largest *minimum segment* (the expression is borrowed from André Martinet), since at least one shot is required to make a film, or part of a film—in the same way, a linguistic statement must be made up of at least one phoneme. To isolate several shots from a sequence is still, perhaps, to analyze the sequence; to remove several frames from a shot is to destroy the shot. If the shot is not the smallest unit of filmic *signification* (for a single shot may convey several informational elements), it is at least the smallest unit of the filmic chain.*

One cannot conclude, however, that every minimum filmic segment is a shot. Besides shots, there are other minimum segments, *optical devices*—various dissolves, wipes, and so on—that can be defined as visual but not photographic elements. Whereas images have the objects of reality as referents, optical procedures, which do not represent anything, have images as referents (those contiguous in the syntagma). The relationship of these procedures to the actual shooting of the film is somewhat like that of morphemes to lexemes; depending on the context, they have two main functions: as "trick" devices (in this instance, they are sorts of semiological exponents influencing contiguous images), or as "punctuation." The expression "filmic punctuation," which use has ratified, must not make us forget that optical procedures separate large, complex statements and thus correspond to the articulations of the literary narrative (with its pages and paragraphs, for example), whereas actual punctuation—that is to say, typographical punctuation—separates sentences (period, exclamation mark, question mark, semicolon), and clauses (comma, semicolon, dash), possibly even "verbal bases," with or without characteristics (apostrophe, or dash, between two "words," and so on).

---

* Similarly, the phoneme is not the minimum distinctive unit, since the latter is the "feature," but it is the minimum element of the spoken *sequence*, the threshold below which an order of consecutiveness yields to an order of simultaneity.

IN CONCLUSION

The concepts of linguistics can be applied to the semiotics of the cinema only with the greatest caution. On the other hand, the methods of linguistics—commutation, analytical breakdown, strict distinction between the significate and the signifier, between substance and form, between the relevant and the irrelevant, etc.—provide the semiotics of the cinema with a constant and precious aid in establishing units that, though they are still very approximate, are liable over time (and, one hopes, through the work of many scholars) to become progressively refined. . . .

THE CINEMA AS SUCH HAS NOTHING CORRESPONDING TO THE DOUBLE ARTICULATION OF VERBAL LANGUAGES

Let us note first that the cinema has no *distinctive* units (I mean distinctive units of its own).* It does not have anything corresponding to the phoneme or to the relevant phonic feature on the level of expression, nor, on the level of content, does it have anything equivalent to the seme in Algirdas Julien Greimas's sense, or in Bernard Pottier's sense.

Even with respect to the signifying units, the cinema is initially deprived of discrete elements. It proceeds by whole "blocks of reality," which are actualized with their total meaning in the discourse. These blocks are the "shots." The discrete units identifiable in the filmic discourse on another level—for, as we shall see, there is

---

* I mean to say that cinematographic language as such lacks distinctive units. For, as a totality, the cinema contains various other signifying systems, each one of which behaves differently in relation to the problem of articulations.

The most obvious example—there are others less apparent—of the superposition of codes within the total cinematographic institution (superpositions that complicate the problem of the articulations of the cinema) is provided by the occurrence of the *verbal element* in talking films: The effect of its intervention is to integrate the doubly articulated significations into the global message of the film, but not into the specific language of the "cinema."

117

another level—are not equivalent to the first articulation of spoken languages.

Certainly, it is true that montage is in a sense an analysis, a sort of articulation of the reality shown on the screen. Instead of showing us an entire landscape, a film-maker will show us successively a number of partial views, which are broken down and ordered according to a very precise intention. It is well known that the nature of the cinema is to transform the world into discourse.

But this kind of articulation is not a true articulation in the linguistic sense. Even the most partial and fragmentary "shot" (what film people call the close-up) still presents a complete segment of reality. The close-up is only a shot taken closer than other shots.

It is true that the film *sequence* is a real unit—that is to say, a sort of coherent *syntagma* within which the "shots" react (semantically) to each other. This phenomenon recalls up to a certain point the manner in which words react to each other within a sentence, and that is why the first theoreticians of the cinema often spoke of the shot as a word, and the sequence as a sentence. But these were highly erroneous identifications, and one can easily list five radical differences between the filmic "shot" and the linguistic word:

(1) Shots are infinite in number, contrary to words, but like statements, which can be formulated in a verbal language.

(2) Shots are the creations of the film-maker, unlike words (which pre-exist in lexicons), but similar to statements (which are in principal the invention of the speaker).

(3) The shot presents the receiver with a quantity of undefined information, contrary to the word. From this point of view, the shot is not even equivalent to the sentence. Rather, it is like the complex statement of undefined length (how is one to describe a film shot completely by means of natural language?).

(4) The shot is an actualized unit, a unit of discourse, an assertion, unlike the word (which is a purely virtual lexical unit), but like the statement, which always refers to reality or a reality (even when it is interrogative or jussive). The image of a house does not signify "house," but "Here is a house"; the image contains a sort of index of actualization, by the mere fact that it occurs in a film.

(5) Only to a small extent does a shot assume its meaning in paradigmatic contrast to the other shots that might have occurred

at the same point along the filmic chain (since the other possible shots are infinite in number), whereas a word is always a part of at least one more or less organized semantic field. The important linguistic phenomenon of the clarification of present units by absent units hardly comes into play in the cinema. Semiologically, this confirms what the aestheticians of the cinema have frequently observed: namely, that the cinema is an "art of presence" (the dominance of the image, which "shuts out" everything external to itself).

The filmic "shot" therefore resembles the statement rather than the word. Nevertheless, it would be wrong to say that it is equivalent to the statement. For there are still great differences between the shot and the linguistic statement. Even the most complex statement is reducible, in the final analysis, to discrete elements (words, morphemes, phonemes, relevant features), which are fixed in number and in nature.

To be sure, the filmic shot is also the result of an ordering of several elements (for example, the different visual elements in the image—what is sometimes called the *interior montage*), but these elements are indefinite in number and undefined in nature, like the shot itself. The analysis of a shot consists in progressing from a nondiscrete whole to smaller nondiscrete wholes: One can decompose a shot, but one cannot reduce it.

All that can be affirmed, therefore, is that a shot is less unlike a statement than a word, but it does not necessarily resemble a statement.

CHARLES BARR
CINEMASCOPE:
BEFORE AND AFTER

CinemaScope was introduced by 20th Century-Fox in 1953. It confused a lot of people, and has continued to do so. It was assumed that its value was purely a sensational one, that it was self-evidently "inartistic," and that once the novelty wore off the companies would be forced to drop it as abruptly as they had dropped 3-D, Hollywood's previous answer to the Television Menace. A decade later, however, the CinemaScope revolution is a fait accompli. Not only are a large proportion of Hollywood films in CinemaScope or similar processes, but other countries too make Scope films in increasing numbers. Most theaters have been adapted for Scope projection without changing the old pattern of exhibition, as it had been forecast they would have to. Cinema-Scope scarcely makes an impact any longer for its own sake: most of the really big pictures today are made on 70mm film or in Cinerama. It is even possible now to be disappointed when a blockbuster *(The Guns of Navarone, The Longest Day)* is "only" in CinemaScope.

I will assume that the technical details are familiar. Since Fox holds the rights to CinemaScope itself, other companies have preferred to develop their own variants, some of which use different methods, and are arguably superior but which are similar in essentials, with an aspect ratio (height to width) of 1:2.35. All of these can be classed together, as indeed they usually are, as "CinemaScope" or just as "Scope."

CinemaScope has had a more general indirect influence: although non-Scope productions still use 35mm nonanamorphic film, very few of them are still designed for projection in the old 1:1.33 ratio. Instead, the top and bottom are masked off, and the image thrown over a wider area. This ratio is, it seems, becoming settled at 1:1.85. Thus all films, with the occasional foreign-language exception, are now widescreen films; this format will clearly share, in a minor way, some of the characteristics of CinemaScope, and normally when I talk of the effects of the "CinemaScope" ratio this can be taken to mean something like "Scope; and even more so the 70mm systems; and to a lesser extent the wide screen."

The commercial survival of Cinemascope has disconcerted critics, especially English-speaking ones. So far as I can see, all of them had condemned it from the start as a medium for anything other than the spectacular and the trivial. Its shape was apparently wrong for "serious" or "intimate" drama, for the kind of film and the kind of effects which a sensitive director aims at. Now Cinema-Scope was, obviously, a commercial innovation designed purely to save the finances of Fox, whose executives were evasive and hypocritical in their pretense that they were doing this for Art's sake. Most of the early Scope films were indeed crude. Fox was enlightened neither in choice of subjects nor of directors: among those who made the first of these films were Koster, Dunne, Johnson, Dmytryk, and Negulesco. However, since then a great number of serious and or intimate films have been made in Scope, too many to catalogue, and too many for it to be worth remarking on any longer, when each comes out. The early ones included *A Star is Born* (Cukor), *East of Eden* (Kazan), and *River of No Return* (Preminger); then, among others, all Truffaut's features; *La Dolce Vita, The Island, Trials of Oscar Wilde, Lola, Lola Montes, Rebel Without a Cause, Bitter Victory, Tarnished Angels, Man of the West, The Tall Men, Some Came Running, The Courtship of Eddie's Father* . . . not forgetting *L'Année Dernière à Marienbad* and, on 70 mm film, *Lawrence of Arabia* and *Exodus*.

The cycle of events has been very close to that which followed the introduction of sound. That too was a commercial move, designed to save Warner Brothers, and it led to a comparable, temporary chaos. Most commentators were misled into thinking that sound must be in itself inartistic, and a betrayal of "pure" cinema, but gradually it became accepted as a useful development, and one could say that Scope too is coming, tacitly, to be accepted, because there is really no alternative. . . .

The point is this: the rejection of CinemaScope was, and is, based on certain familiar, but in fact highly disputable, assumptions, the fundamental one being that the film image consists of a *frame* into which a number of things are successively *fitted*, and that a film is made by sticking such images together in a creative way. The old 1:1.33 ratio screen was compatible with this aesthetic, and the CinemaScope screen is not, but instead of considering afresh whether these preconceptions were valid the critics simply used them to make an a priori condemnation of a format which is, one admits, manifestly unsuitable for "framing" things.

One can call this the "traditional" aesthetic: it is the one which is found in books. It puts the emphasis on framing, the close-up, camera angles, and montage. Montage is only the French word for editing, and is clearly indispensable to any director; the difference is that here this stage is made into the crucial one in a process which consists of selecting details and "showing them one by one" (Pudovkin in *Film Technique*).

I believe this aesthetic was always misguided, at least in the dogmatic form in which it was applied, and that the most valuable and forward-looking films at any time have been made to some extent outside it. Ideally, Scope could have been the occasion for its ceremonial abandonment. It was no longer workable, but then it was no longer necessary. It is a hangover from the silent cinema, but people still try to muddle through using it as an implicit basis for their judgment even of Scope films: it is not surprising if they can't cope. You still get films evaluated according to whether the "set-ups" are "imaginative" or not, and a film which uses long takes and few close-ups is liable to be dismissed automatically as unfilmic or as visually dull. Any summary of the development of style is bound to be schematic, but if one bears in mind that there can be no clear-cut division between sound and silent, and between post- and pre-Scope, I think it is useful to go back and estimate how this "traditional" aesthetic was established, and became ingrained.

There were four main factors:

(1) The image was narrow and unaccompanied by sound; it was therefore difficult to make a full impact within a single shot, and

without cutting. Naturally, this objection applies less and less after the introduction of, in turn, the moving camera, sound, composition in depth, and CinemaScope.

The film was a new and bewildering medium; this aesthetic made it easy to assimilate to the pattern of other arts, notably painting and literature:

(2) It played down the film's basis in "reality," which was felt to be incompatible with art.

(3) It took the shot as a "unit," like the ideogram or the word: this made it more easily manageable and gave it the prestige of a "language" of its own.*

Finally, (4) it was formulated and applied chiefly by certain Russian directors; theirs is one kind of film, and of temperament, which it really suits.

These points merge into one another, and need to be elaborated more fully.

The first films were straightforward records of everyday reality. As such, they gave audiences a big thrill. Lumière set up his camera to take a scene in a single, static shot: workers leaving a factory, a train entering a station, a family eating out of doors, etc. The spectators' first instinct was to scramble out of the way of the approaching train, and in the background of the shot of the family eating *(Bébé Mange sa Soupe)* they noticed the detail of leaves blowing in the wind, and called out excitedly.

However, once the novelty of such shots wore off, it became apparent that the impact of a single image was limited. You do not, in fact, get a very strong sense of actuality from a narrow, silent image; it is too much of an abstraction, the picture too remote. For the same reason, there is not much scope for the integration of background detail. It was difficult to cover a scene of any complexity, as film-makers discovered when they began to extend their range and to tell stories. Few of them thought to move the camera, or to move and group people with any precision, within the frame. The usual solution would be to photograph the action in long shot, in order to get it all in, or to huddle actors and décor unrealistically

---

* "In the silent cinema, montage had a precise meaning, because it represented language. From the silent cinema we have inherited this myth of montage, though it has lost most of its meaning."

—Roberto Rossellini

close together. Then came montage, and the close-up, and this was of course a great advance. But although Griffith is associated with their development, he was already very skillful in controlling, when appropriate, all the elements of a scene within the same shot; indeed, the most striking thing today about *Birth of a Nation* is the number of scenes which are played in a remarkably modern, integral style (for instance: the scenes in the hospital; at the Camerons' home; in Lincoln's office). To judge from the few films of his that I have seen, and particularly *The Coward* (1915), Thomas Ince was working in the same way.

Meanwhile, however, pundits had decided that the film could not be art if it confined itself to recording "reality," and they extended this to mean that an uncut piece of film was nothing, that montage was all. Now "reality" is a word which has to be handled carefully. Nabokov nicely describes it as "one of the few words which mean nothing without quotes."

Both the still and the movie camera make a record of "reality" in the sense that they record, objectively, what is put in front of them. As Helmut Gernsheim (*Creative Photography*, 1960) expresses it: "The camera intercepts images, the paintbrush reconstructs them." This worried theorists from the start. No other art presented this problem, and no other art, furthermore, had ever been suddenly invented like this, rootless, instead of evolving slowly, and evolving a function as it did so. A decision had to be made. One interpretation was this: the camera records reality, but reality is not art, therefore photography cannot be art. And later: the cinema cannot be art. The second interpretation arises from this and is complementary to it: agreed, reality is not art, but we improve upon it by treating it in a creative way. In practice, this meant getting as far away as possible from objectivity, and it produced, in the first decades of photography, some quite ludicrous results, prints being posed and processed and stuck together in a form of "montage" in such a way as to be indistinguishable from painting. The "masterpieces" of this art look grotesque today, and I think warn us against dismissing as irrelevant the objective basis of the cinema. Gernsheim *(op. cit.)* puts this phase into perspective: "The mistaken ambition to compete with painting drove a minority to artificial picture-making alien to the nature of photography . . . to appreciate photography requires above all understanding of the qualities and limitations peculiar to it."

This is what André Bazin—the Gernsheim of the cinema—means when he says "Les virtualités esthétiques de la photographie résident dans la révélation du réel." In this essay* Bazin makes a far more useful analysis of the nature of film and its implications for film style, than Kracauer does in the whole of his book.

The film image is taken direct from "reality" and the spectator perceives and "recognizes" it direct; there is no intermediate process as there is when the writer "translates" his material into words which are in turn translated back by the imagination of the reader. This is a major difference which conditions the whole of the respective media, and the attempt to draw literal analogies between the two (for instance between the word and the shot) is as much of a dead end as the attempt to assimilate photography to the rules of painting.

However, to say that the camera records "reality" is not to advocate that the cinema should remain at the level of Lumière. The experience of seeing even a film like *Exodus*, which is about the furthest the cinema has gone in the direction of "reality"—70mm film, long static takes, complete surface authenticity—is not something we get each day when we go out into the street. It is *a* reality, organized by the director; and in any case a record of reality is not the same thing as reality itself. The director selects or stages his "reality," and photographs it; we perceive the image, on the screen, in the course of the film. This process *in itself* means that the experience belongs to the "imaginative" as opposed to the "actual" life to use the categories distinguished by the art critic Roger Fry (*An Essay in Aesthetics*, 1909). Fry was talking about differences in our perception of life and of paintings, but the distinction applies equally to film, and he did in fact cite the examples of the elementary newsreel-type films of his time to illustrate how even a "transparent" recording of an everyday scene was perceived in a radically different way from actuality. This distinction, which is basic to our responses to any art, is summed up thus by I. A. Richards *(Principles of Literary Criticism)*: "In ordinary life a thousand considerations prohibit for most of us any complete working-out of our response; the range and complexity of the impulse-systems involved is less; the need for action, the comparative uncertainty and vagueness of the situation, the intrusion of accidental irrelevancies, in-

---

*"Ontology of the Photographic Image," *What is Cinema?*

convenient temporal spacing—the action being too slow or too fast
—all these obscure the issue and prevent the full development of
the experience. But in the "imaginative experience" these obstacles
are removed. . . . As a chemist's balance to a grocer's scales, so is
the mind in the imaginative moment to the mind engaged in ordinary intercourse or in practical affairs."

The crucial point is that in the cinema this distinction operates
before the montage stage, and independently of it.

Art does indeed involve organization, but this is just as possible
within a complex image as in a montage sequence: it can in many
ways be more subtle. I will analyze these possibilities more specifically later on. For a number of reasons, as I say, they had not been
explored very fully in the early days of the cinema. The cutting
together of separate shots is a more obviously "creative" method,
and a more straightforward one.

Even if it's true, as I think it is, that those who first imagined and
developed the cinematograph thought in terms of a *total* illusion,
with sound, color and depth† and that the restricted form it temporarily took was in this sense accidental, it is still possible to see
the history of the cinema as a nicely arranged series of advances,
each one coming when directors, and audiences, were ready for it.
First they learned to cope with the camera alone, then gradually
with more and more of the ingredients of reality: they could hardly
have controlled all of them at once, from the start, without practice or precedent, any more than primitive musicians would have
been able to cope immediately with a symphony orchestra—or
audiences to respond to it. The greater density of the sound-Scope-
color image requires a more precise control than the simple "unit"
image does. One has to ascend by stages. The idea of predetermined
advance should not be applied too rigidly, for the immediate instrument of each advance has after all been financial pressure, and
Warners' crisis, and therefore their introduction of the sound film,
could have come a few years earlier or later; similarly with Fox
and the introduction of CinemaScope. But this does not make the
whole thing fortuitous, as Macgowan seems to imply when he says
that we might easily have had Todd-AO thirty years ago, at the

---

† Cf. Bazin's essay "The Myth of Total Cinema," also published in the first volume
of *What is Cinema?*

same time as sound, only support was withheld. The cinema evolves by a form of Natural Selection: technicians and financiers provide the "mutations," and their survival depends upon whether they can be usefully assimilated at the time.

Often when "use of CinemaScope" is picked out by a critic it indicates an obtrusive style, with the director striving to "compensate" for the openness of the frame, or indulging in flashy compositional effects—as in, say, Kurosawa's *The Hidden Fortress*, or *Vera-Cruz*, the first half-hour of which Robert Aldrich makes into an absolute orgy of formalism, composing frames within frames, and blocking up the sides of the image with rocks, trees, etc. In general, what they say about the camera makes a good working rule for Scope: if you notice it, it's bad. Or, more reasonably: you don't have to notice it for it to be good. This is not to forbid the critic the phrase "use of Scope," which may be useful to avoid periphrasis, provided that it's not made into a criterion in itself, unrelated to the work as a whole.

In their book *Hitchcock*, Chabrol and Rohmer mention that in CinemaScope "the extreme edges of the screen are virtually unusable": that the edges are by no means useless, but that they will not be used for the placing of details meaningful for their own sake.

While the chief advantage of Scope is, as they maintain, its opening-up of the frame, the greater sense it gives us of a continuous space—and this is where it relates to the film they are discussing here, namely *Rope*—this is a slight over-simplification. Sometimes people can be placed at the extreme edges for perfectly legitimate effect: as in *The Tall Men* (Walsh, 1955): Jane Russell and Clark Gable play a long, intimate scene together; it ends in a fight, and they retire sulking to opposite corners of the room—and of the Scope frame, leaving a great gulf between them. A different effect: near the end of *The True Story of Jesse James* (Nicholas Ray, 1957) Jesse decides to retire: he goes out into the garden to play with his children: a green and white image, Jesse on the right: a man walks past, glimpsed on the extreme left of the frame, and calls out a greeting: the strong "horizontal" effect here reinforces the feeling of a new freedom. In *Spartacus* Kubrick uses a similar technique for the shots of Crassus and his entourage visiting the training camp; the contrast between this openness and the cooped-up images showing the gladiators' existence helps express the general contrast between luxury and oppression.

But it is not only the horizontal line which is emphasized in CinemaScope (this was implied by critics who concentrated on the *shape* of the frame qua shape—as though it were the frame of a painting—and concluded that the format was suitable only for showing/framing horizontal things like crocodiles and processions). The more open the frame, the greater the impression of depth: the image is more vivid, and involves us more directly. The most striking effect in Cinerama is the roller-coaster shot, which gives us a very strong sensation of movement forward. Even though at the crucial moment we may be focussing only on the very center of the image, i.e., the area of track directly in front of the roller-coaster— an area, in fact, no larger than the standard frame—the rest of the image is not useless. We may not be conscious of what exactly is there, but we are marginally aware of the objects and the space on either side. It is this peripheral vision which orients us and makes the experience so vivid. Similar effects were tried in the early films in Todd-AO (roller-coaster; train ride) and CinemaScope (the shots from the nose of the plane in *How to Marry a Millionaire*). In Scope the involvement is less strong, but it is still considerable: so are its implications. Although the shots quoted aim at nothing more than a circus effect, *physical* sensation of this kind can be dramatically useful (elementary form-and-content). This power was there even in the 1:1.33 image, but for the most part (after Lumière's train) remàined latent. But there are classic examples of movement in this plane in Renoir's *Partie de Campagne:* the long-held shot at the end, taken from the stern of the boat being rowed home; rain on the water: an overwhelming sense of nostalgia conveyed by the movement. And in Wyler's *The Best Years of Our Lives*, the shots from the nose of the plane in which the three servicemen are returning home. The movement gives us a direct insight into their sensations and through this into "what it is like" generally for them.

Scope automatically gives images like these more "weight," and it also of course enhances the effect of lateral movement.

In *Rebel Without a Cause* (Ray, 1956) a shot of extraordinary beauty comes after the first twenty minutes of the film, during which the surroundings have been uniformly cramped and depressing, the images physically cluttered-up and dominated by blacks and browns. Now, James Dean is about to set out for school; he looks out of the window. He recognizes a girl (Natalie Wood) walking past in the distance. Cut to the first day/exterior shot, the first bright one, the first "horizontal" one. A close shot of Natalie Wood, in a light-green cardigan, against a background of green bushes. As she walks the camera moves laterally with her. This makes a direct, sensual impression which gives us an insight into Dean's experience, while at the same time remaining completely natural and unforced. On the small screen, such an image could not conceivably have had a comparable weight.

One of the climaxes of *Jesse James* is Jesse's revenge killing of a farmer. This is important to the story because it ruins Jesse's chance of an amnesty, and it is equally important to the understanding of his character in that it illustrates his pride, and his thoughtlessness. The crucial shot here has the farmer ploughing his land. Jesse rides up behind him, stops, and lifts his rifle. The man starts to run but Jesse keeps with him. The camera tracks back with them, holding this composition—the farmer in the foreground, running into the camera, Jesse inexorably behind, aiming—until finally Jesse shoots him dead. This is over in a moment but has a hypnotic, almost a slow-motion impact, which again is the result of the greater physical involvement achieved by Scope, its more vivid sense of space. The impact is direct, and there is no need to emphasize it by putting it into literal slow-motion, or making a significant "pattern."

Rudolf Arnheim, in *Film as Art*, claims that any such sensation of depth will be undesirable: compositional patterns which in the more abstract image would come across as being deliberate will, if the image is more vivid, seem natural, even accidental, so that the spectator may fail to note their symbolic force.*

From this point of view, an even more relevant Scope scene is

---

* Arnheim also wrote, and I am not making it up: "Silent laughter is often more effective than if the sound is actually heard. The gaping of the open mouth gives a vivid, highly artistic interpretation of the phenomenon 'laughter.' If, however, the sound is also heard, the opening of the mouth appears obvious and its value as a means of expression is almost entirely lost." But I don't know that this argument against sound is any more unconvincing than that against Scope—the logic is identical.

this one from *River of No Return*, analyzed by V. F. Perkins in *Movie*. I think the narrative is clear enough from his description:

"As Harry lifts Kay from the raft, she drops the bundle which contains most of her 'things' into the water. Kay's gradual loss of the physical tokens of her way of life has great symbolic significance. But Preminger is not over-impressed. The bundle simply floats away off-screen while Harry brings Kay ashore. It would be wrong to describe this as understatement. The symbolism is in the event, not in the visual pattern, so the director presents the action clearly and leaves the interpretation to the spectator."

Arnheim would no doubt regard this as a reductio ad absurdum. His attitude, which is shared, deep down, by most critics, is based on his phobia of using the camera as a "recording machine" (reality is not art). It further reflects an unwillingness to leave the spectator any freedom to interpret action or behavior, or to make connections. This concept of "freedom" has been distorted as much as that of "reality." It's taken to be absurd that a director should allow a viewer any freedom of interpretation, for he may then notice things that he isn't meant to, or fail to notice things that he should; he may get the wrong point altogether. This is in line with the idea that the test of a good film is whether it "makes statements."

Now in this scene from *River of No Return*, the spectator is "free" to notice the bundle, and, when he does so, free to interpret it as significant. But there is nothing random about the shot. The detail is placed in the background of the shot, and integrated naturally, so that we have to make a positive act of interpreting, of "reading," the shot. The act of interpreting the visual field—and through that the action—is in itself valuable. The significance of the detail is not announced, it is allowed to speak for itself. An alert spectator will notice the bundle, and "follow" it as it floats off screen.

The traditional method would be to make its significance unmistakable by cutting in close-ups. In this case we would gather that the bundle is meaningful *because* it is picked out for us. In Preminger's film, the process is reversed: we pick it out *because* it is meaningful. The emphasis arises organically out of the whole action; it is not imposed.

"The symbolism is in the event, not in the visual pattern." Before Scope, it was difficult to show the "event" lucidly, with each detail given its appropriate weight. It wasn't impossible: many Renoir films, as well as Mizoguchi's *Ugetsu Monogatari*, are superlative examples of the "opening-up" of the 1:1.33 frame to achieve this kind of fluidity. But on the whole the tendency was to split up the event into its component parts, and to impose, whether deliberately or not, a "visual pattern," a pattern of montage and/or of obtrusively "composed" images. And a *visual* pattern involves a pattern of motivation, a pattern of significance, which in certain films is appropriate, but is more often damagingly crude.

At this stage one can hardly avoid talking of "participation," which is another much-abused word. Everyone agrees, in principle, that art should not so much state as reveal, and that we should not just register its meaning but understand it. Our experience of a work should involve active participation more than passive assimilation.

The Russians, in their theoretical work, appropriated this idea, and applied it in a somewhat outrageous way; but critics, even intelligent ones, have continued to accept what they said. The confusion rests on a misunderstanding of the relation between film and the other arts, notably literature. Eisenstein said that "participation" took place in the association of successive images (as in the association of juxtaposed images in poetry)—that it depended purely on montage. In *October* he had intercut shots of Kerensky with ironic titles, and then with shots of a peacock preening itself. These images in themselves are fairly neutral, but the spectator fuses them together freely, he "participates," and arrives at an "intellectual decision" at the expense of Kerensky. In *Strike* we are shown, alternately, shots of workmen being massacred and of bulls being slaughtered: again, the two sets of images are independent of each other and we have to make the imaginative link between the two. Commenting recently on passages like these, an English critic said, "Thus, Eisenstein's 'intellectual cinema' proves itself a superior means of communication by demanding the co-operation of the spectator in consideration of the conflicting ideologies that Eisenstein chose to convey."

This seems to me so much solemn nonsense. The whole is more than the sum of its parts; but then the whole is *always* more than the sum of its parts. The spectator "interprets" but there is no genuine freedom of association. A montage link of this kind re-

131

minds one of the children's puzzle which consists of a series of numbered dots: when they are joined together correctly, the outline of an animal appears. We participate in solving these, but only in a mechanical way, and there is only one correct solution. The very last thing Eisenstein really wants us to do is to evaluate for ourselves, or even experience for ourselves, what we are shown. He does not show us heroic actions — which we can recognize or judge to be heroic — he shows actions (not even that, but only *bits* of actions) and tells us that they are heroic (or alternatively brutal). Vakoulintchouk, in *Potemkin*, is "defined" by the shots which are intercut with shots of his dead body: close-ups of weeping women, sympathetic titles. Similarly we are *told* how to react to Kerensky and to the killing of the workmen — told obliquely, it is true, by a form of visual code, but still told; nothing is in any useful sense communicated. It is revealing that the whole meaning of these films can be reversed, as happened apparently in places with *Potemkin*, by merely re-arranging certain shots and titles, just as one can reverse the meaning of a slogan by replacing one name with another. (This would be inconceivable with *Birth of a Nation*.)

What is in question is not Eisenstein's artistry, within his chosen field, but rather the way his technique has been rationalized, by him and by others, and a universal validity claimed for it. The style is appropriate to what he was aiming to do, namely to make propaganda. He was not interested (in the silent films) in characterization or in shades of meaning, nor did he want to leave the spectator any freedom of response. The struggle of authority against revolution, and of Old against New, is one of Black and White. Andrew Sarris, in an excellent article on Rossellini in the *New York Film Bulletin*, contrasts this extreme montage style — "Eisenstein's conceptual editing extracts a truth from the collision of two mechanistic forces in history" — with "Rossellini's visual conception of a unified cosmos undivided by the conceptual detail of montage," and he implies one should accept each on its own terms. I think it's legitimate to say that, even if the style reflects the vision accurately, the vision is crude, and the style, although powerful, crude likewise. The words Eisenstein and his contemporaries use in describing it are significant: impact, collision, clash, the juxtaposition of "concepts"; the approach is essentially a rhetorical one. What is obvious anyway from this is that Eisenstein is a special case, that few directors see things his way, and that few subjects are amenable to this treatment. Drama is not normally reducible to concepts, clashes and collisions. (This is quite apart from the implications of the change to the sound film, after which the technique becomes still less relevant.)

People complain sometimes that Eisenstein's methods of intellectual and ideological montage have been forgotten, as have the associative techniques of Pudovkin's *Mother*, and imply that directors today must be deficient in imagination: but insofar as they reject these techniques they are more subtle. And a field where they do notably survive is that of the filmed commercial. The product may not in itself look very special (a "dead object") but it takes on associations when intercut with a smiling mother holding a smiling baby. The montage-unit style no doubt sells products, and puts over propaganda, more effectively than would a more fluid one, and there are other films too for which it is perfectly appropriate: educational work, certain documentaries, anything which aims to put over a message concisely. One would not advocate CinemaScope for these.

Jean Mitry, in his interesting book *Eisenstein* criticizes him for at times indulging in arbitrary symbolism (the slaughterhouse in *Strike*), but he accepts Eisenstein's analogies between the interpretation of film and poetic images: the film-maker juxtaposing unrelated images by montage is like the poet juxtaposing words. But the reader genuinely "participates" in the associations he makes from the words, in building them up into a fused whole: words are allusive whereas the film image is concrete. Film images follow each other in rigid sequence, which we cannot vary; the interaction of words is much more flexible. The more one goes into the differences between word and shot, and between the literary and filmic sequences of description, the more shaky do all the analogies made by the Russians seem.

There is no literary equivalent for "getting things in the same shot." This seems never to have struck them. Both Eisenstein and Pudovkin made laborious comparisons between the word or ideogram and the individual shot, and between the sentence and the montage-sequence. This seems fantastically naïve. How else can you translate "the cat sat on the mat" into film except in a single shot? Disciples tend to admit that these theories went a bit far—

after all, they never went quite so far in their films—but without realizing that the rest of their aesthetic, which sounds more plausible, is in fact equally shaky, and for similar reasons.

For instance: a writer has to describe details successively, even though they may exist together. In this case he will aim, by his description, to evoke a "total" simultaneous reality in the reader's mind. Because of the indirect, allusive quality of language this is not really a handicap. Thackeray, in his *Irish Sketchbook*, gives a description of a mountain scene, evoking it by a series of details and of comparisons: he adds, "Printer's ink cannot give these wonderful hues, and *the reader will make his picture at his leisure*" (my italics). But the film image is direct, it *shows* things.

In *Lolita* (the book) there is a scene which, had it been presented without comment, might have seemed a perfect vindication of the rules laid down by Pudovkin in *Film Technique*, in that it consists of a series of details, which Nabokov describes successively, and which Pudovkin would have filmed successively ("showing them one by one, just as we would describe them in separate sequence in literary work"). It is the scene of the death of Humbert's wife: "I rushed out. The far side of our steep little street presented a peculiar sight. . . . *I have to put the impact of an instantaneous vision into a sequence of words; their physical accumulation on the page impairs the actual flash, the sharp unity of impression.* Rug-heap, old-man doll, Miss O's nurse running with a rustle back to the screened porch . . ." (my italics).

It's naïve to suppose that even the most fragmented lines—"ships, towers, domes, theatres and temples lie/open unto the fields and to the sky"—can be given an exact cinematic equivalent by a montage of ships, towers, domes, and so on. Eisenstein makes much of the fragmentary narrative of Dickens; this is fair enough in that a change of scene would correspond to a cut in film, but it does not hold for the *texture* of a narrative. Thomas Hardy makes a useful reference here, and at the risk of seeming repetitive I'd like to consider some passages from his novels.

Often he will introduce a character by, as it were, discovering him within a landscape. Being a writer, he describes things one by one, but they all contribute to the creation of a broad, total environment. His protagonists emerge from this, and are in turn absorbed into it; they are never detached; we retain a mental picture of them as a part of it. The film equivalent is to *show* them as a part of it, to engulf them in it. Boetticher's *Ride Lonesome* and Ray's *The Savage Innocents* are two films which portray people dominated by, almost defined by, their natural environment, and this connection is perfectly conveyed in their first images. In *Ride Lonesome*, the camera is held on a shot of a vast plain, stretching away to mountains in the distance; then it tilts down slowly and we become aware of a rider coming toward us from deep among the rocks below. *The Savage Innocents* has a long, empty snowscape: the camera is still: a sledge enters frame left, deep within the shot, and is drawn gradually toward us. One can contrast this with the opening of *Scott of the Antarctic:* a montage of snow vistas, evocative music. We look *at* the scene instead of being involved in it, as we are in *The Savage Innocents;* and we accept, intellectually, for the purposes of the narrative, that the characters are there, instead of genuinely feeling it. Both Boetticher's and Ray's films are in Scope, and this helps enormously: it increases the involvement of the spectator and the physical integration of the characters.

It might be said that these are "landscape" films, that Scope is suitable for them but not for more confined drama. But the same principles hold; the dichotomy often expressed between interior and exterior drama is a false one.

Consider this passage from *Tess of the d'Urbervilles*. On her wedding night, Tess confesses to her husband about the child she had by Alec:

"Her narrative had ended; even its reassertions and secondary explanations were done. Tess's voice throughout had hardly risen higher than its opening tone; there had been no exculpatory phrase of any kind, and she had not wept.

"But the complexion even of external things seemed to suffer transmutation as her announcement proceeded. The fire in the grate looked impish—demoniacally funny, as if it did not care in the least about her strait. The fender grinned idly, as if it too did not care. The light from the water-bottle was merely engaged in a chromatic problem. All material objects around announced their irresponsibility with terrible iteration. And yet nothing had changed since the moments when he had been kissing her; or rather, nothing in the substance of things. But the essence of things had changed."

The Russians, again, might interpret this their own way: fragmentation, subjectivity, justifying a similar technique for film. But in film everything is concrete. Film shows the substance, it cannot *show* the essence, but it can *suggest* the essence by *showing* the substance. It suggests inner reality by showing outer reality with the greatest possible intensity. The writer has to build up a scene by description and allusion: images and metaphors, however fanciful, can help to strengthen our *objective* picture of the scene, whereas if transposed to film they would distract, and distort (imagine a close-up of the fender, grinning idly). For filming this passage from *Tess* I can't imagine a better method than to keep both of them in the frame the whole time, with the "material objects" around and between them, and to have her explanation, and then his silence, and reactions, in a single take, without any overt emphasis from the camera. Ideally, in CinemaScope, which makes the surroundings more palpable, and enables you to get close to one or both of the characters without shutting out the rest of the scene. The more precisely the camera charts the substance of things, the external movement of words, expressions, gestures, the more subtly can it express the internal movement: the essence of things.

Such a sequence would be condemned a priori by Arnheim ("immobile recording machine") and by Eisenstein, who laid down that *any* scene where a transition in feeling was observed, without a cut, was "theatrical." Need one point out that you can get a far greater control, on film, of all the elements of the scene, and of how each spectator sees them? And that the division of change into before and after can often be crudely mechanical? There could be no more eloquent illustration of this danger than the scene which Eisenstein holds up as an example of how to handle such a change in feeling: the cream-separator episode from the *The General Line*.

A great comfort to upholders of the "traditional" aesthetic has always been the Kuleshov/Pudovkin experiment (three neutral CUs of an actor, Mosjoukine, intercut with three different shots, to give the impression of three different emotions). This was felt to define the cinema for all time, and to establish that its essence was montage. If the same effect was difficult to achieve with sound, and then CinemaScope, that must prove that they were a bad thing. I do not honestly think that the effect on spectators of these sequences, presented as Pudovkin relates, can have been quite so overwhelming as he claims (is there any evidence, I wonder, that the experiment was done, and does not represent wishful thinking?), but one can accept that they do, up to a point, work: we understand what is being depicted, we complete the equations. Later experiments by psychologists have confirmed that one expression abstracted from its context looks very much like another. But this can far more reasonably be seen, I think, as an argument for not abstracting it in the first place.

The experiment illustrates that each act of perception automatically conditions succeeding ones; this is something which applies continuously, to life as well as to art, and which any intelligent artist will have taken into account in working out a style—not, however, to the extent of making it the cornerstone of his method. Pudovkin here reminds one of the bakers who first extract the nourishing parts of the flour, process it, and then put some back as "extra goodness": the result may be eatable, but it is hardly the only way to make bread, and one can criticize it for being unnecessary and "synthetic." Indeed one could extend the culinary analogy and say that the experience put over by the traditional aesthetic is essentially a *predigested* one. These two epithets have in ordinary usage a literal meaning and, by extension, a metaphorical one, applied pejoratively; the same correlation is valid here.

Writers like Manvell, Reisz, and Lindgren (all of whom base their aesthetic more or less closely on the Russians') advocate a method which gives us a *digest* of what we might see, in real life, if we were experiencing a given scene. Lindgren, in *The Art of the Film*, goes into this in most detail. He makes the usual comparisons with literary fragmentation, and then between what we see in life and in films. Sometimes we consciously see things as a whole, in their interrelationship (general shot). Sometimes we look round (pan) or walk (tracking shot). Normally we focus on one thing at a time (close-up or close-shot) and we look from one thing to another (cutting). Now it should be clear that the correspondence is by no means exact. In a film we sit facing the same direction all the time, looking at a screen which is set at a finite distance. In life we are oriented in our surroundings and our perception of them is continuous—continuous in time and space. But Lindgren claims that "in so far as the film is photographic and reproduces movement, it can give us a lifelike semblance of what we see; in so far as it employs editing, it can exactly [sic] reproduce the *manner* in which we see it."

At any time we see "central" things and "marginal" things; of the latter we may be aware, or half-aware, or they may serve merely to orient us. The traditional aesthetic separates out the central things: the marginal ones it either omits as inessential and distracting, or intercuts in close shot—in which case they are no longer marginal but central.

So an alternative method, a more strictly realistic one, which Lindgren and company pass over, is to present a complex image organized in such a way that we are induced to interpret it for ourselves. This is where genuine participation comes in, as in the sequence quoted from *River of No Return*.

Manvell *(The Film and the Public)* writes that "the comparatively narrow bounds of the normal screen shape sharpen perception by closing it in, giving the director full control of every detail which the audience should perceive." Conversely in CinemaScope "the sharpened perception of the normal film will be lost." In his aesthetic, we either see a thing or we don't. If a detail is important, the director singles it out for us; if there is a symbol or a meaningful connection to be noted, the director again does it for us, emphasizing it by close-ups. (Cf. Eisenstein's criticism of Dovshenko's *Earth*, on the grounds that he had not made the symbolism explicit enough —i.e., he had not brought the symbolic detail into close-up but had left it integrated, so that it might appear accidental.) We do not have to bother about noticing it for ourselves, or estimating whether it is significant. On the other hand when the image is complex we *have* to be alert to interpret it and the details within it. The difference between the Preminger method cited from *River of No Return* and the explicit close-up/montage style which he could have used, but didn't, corresponds to the difference between reading the meaning for ourselves and having it spelled out for us.*

"I don't think CinemaScope is a good medium. It's good only for showing great masses of movement. For other things, it's dis-

---

*Cf. also in *Citizen Kane* Welles's extremely subtle handling of the Rosebud/snow-glass paperweight imagery, which he often leaves naturally in the background of the shot for us to notice, and to make the connections. Pages could be written on this.

tracting, it's hard to focus attention, and it's very difficult to cut. Some people just go ahead and cut it and let people's eyes jump around and find what they want to find. It's very hard for an audience to focus—they have too much to look at—they can't see the whole thing." (Howard Hawks in an interview with Peter Bogdanovich.)

This is the danger; it was more worrying at the introduction of Scope, when audiences did apparently have to get used to "exploring" the more open image, but this I think was temporary. If a Scope image is decently organized the eyes will not just "jump around and find what they want to find," purely at random— they can be led to focus on detail, and to look from one thing to another within the frame with the emphasis which the director intends: that is, if the spectator is alert. Hawks may not like Scope (he had an apparently traumatic experience using it for *Land of the Pharaohs*, perhaps his worst film), but he approves of the 1:1.85 screen, and his style has always been one which allows the spectator freedom; in this sense he does not need Scope. One of the best of all examples of the alternative style to Lindgren's is from his *Hatari!* (wide screen). General shot of a bedroom: right of frame, in bed, waiting for her supper, Elsa Martinelli (back to camera); on the bed, John Wayne. Centre of frame, background, a tame cheetah. Left of frame, enter Red Buttons, carrying a tray; he trips over the cheetah's tail and the supper lands on Wayne, Martinelli, and the floor. Typically, Hawks takes this (exceedingly funny) scene in one static shot. It is done with a beautiful directness and lucidity, and without any of the usual look-this-is-funny comedy emphasis. The scene exists autonomously, action and reaction being integrated: Martinelli suddenly collapses with the giggles but we can only just see her at the edge of the frame. The nicest thing of all is the cheetah's reaction. He is obviously quite bewildered by the whole episode. We can see him in the background, looking up in pained manner at Red Buttons, and Hawks leaves him there, fading out the scene after a brief moment. Contrast the almost invariable procedure in other films for handling animal performers: that of extracting a certain laugh by cutting in their cute reactions in close-up. We are left "free" to interpret the scene visually, and this means we are free to respond. Our responses are not "signposted" by successive close-ups—foot tripping over tail, result, various reactions. No single reading of the scene is imposed. One could put it another way: the scene, as directed, is at once more subtle and more *authentic*. The reason why animals' reactions are normally cut in separately is not only that they thus get a surer laugh but that it's difficult to direct an animal so that it genuinely does what it is represented to be doing. It is sometimes held to be the chief glory of the cinema that you can, by montage, "create" an event like this which never happened. But the result (leaving aside certain kinds of film where the convention obviously allows this) is mechanical.*

The same applies in a less obvious way to other details of action and acting. It is much easier to put together a complex scene synthetically out of separate details—especially when you have an incompetent actor, or a child—than to organize and film the scene in its integrity. But you sacrifice the possibility of real conviction, of real subtlety.

The advantage of Scope over even the wide screen of *Hatari!* is that it enables complex scenes to be covered even more naturally: detail can be integrated, and therefore perceived, in a still more realistic way. If I had to sum up its implications I would say that it gives a greater range for *gradation of emphasis*. George Kaplan wrote in *Scene* that "there is no room for subtlety on 70mm film"; on the contrary, there is twice as much room, as is clear both from arithmetic and from *Exodus*. The 1:1.33 screen is too much of an abstraction, compared with the way we normally see things, to admit easily the detail which can only be really effective if it is perceived *qua* casual detail. There are innumerable applications of this (the whole question of significant imagery is affected by it): one quite common one is the scene where two people talk, and a third watches, or just appears in the background unobtrusively— he might be a person who is relevant to the others in some way, or who is affected by what they say, and it is useful for us to be "reminded" of his presence. The simple cutaway shot coarsens the effect by being too obvious a directorial aside (Look who's watching) and on the smaller screen it's difficult to play off foreground and background within the frame: the detail tends to look too obviously planted. The frame is so closed-in that any detail which

---

*Bazin analyzed this issue—the existence of which no one before him seems to have realized—in another definitive essay, "The Virtues and Limitations of Montage."

is placed there *must* be deliberate—at some level we both feel this and know it intellectually.* Greater flexibility was achieved long before Scope by certain directors using depth of focus and the moving camera (one of whose main advantages, as Dai Vaughan pointed out in *Definition* 1, is that it allows points to be made literally "in passing"). Scope as always does not create a new method, it encourages, and refines, an old one. The most beautiful example of this "gradation of emphasis" point is I think *The Courtship of Eddie's Father*; others include *The True Story of Jesse James, Ride the High Country* (all Scope) and *Exodus* (70mm). This is not something which can be isolated from the excellence of the films as a whole, nor can it be satisfactorily documented—one just has to sit in front of the films and see how space and décor and relationships are organized, and the eye led from one point to another within the image; how connections are made, and characters introduced, not being "added on" to the rest of the context but developing *out of* it.

Few of the films like these which I'd regard as being the richest of all are liked by critics; to praise Ray, Preminger, Hawks, or Minnelli makes one liable to the charge of subscribing to a "cult," a common defense mechanism which enables critics to avoid any challenge to their preconceptions. While it's possible, of course, to reject any of these films in the last analysis, I think the disagreement is more basic than this. Mainstream critics have been conditioned to recognize only a style based on montage and the close-up, and on "signposting" of effects, as valid, and may be in effect physically unable to respond to a film which requires an active interpretation on every level. I mean by this that, as we become more sophisticated and get more familiar with ideas and concepts, we tend to interpret films in literary terms, and our visual acuteness

---

*In Antonioni's *Il Grido* there is a shot taken from inside a house: a woman goes out of the door and walks away. The door stays slightly ajar and through this very narrow aperture we continue to see her walking in a dead straight line away from the camera. This is a far too neat continued effect, and audiences groan. It is too good to be true that she should have walked along exactly the one line which would have kept her visible. On the other hand if the aperture had been wider, she would have been "free" to deviate, and even if she had in fact taken precisely the same path the shot would have been more acceptable—not in spite of but *because* of the "frame" of the door "fitting" her less well. I don't think it is fanciful to compare the door that frames her with the frame of the film image in general.

atrophies. Norman Fruchter, conducting a Film Appreciation course for unsophisticated teenagers, found that "the cadets' visual responses were far more acute than anyone might have given them credit for. I had to watch a film at least three times to see as much as they caught in a single viewing. They rarely missed detail. . . ." (*Sight and Sound*, Autumn, 1962). Now the traditional aesthetic allows for, and encourages, our more sophisticated tendencies by, as I described, "predigesting" a scene and serving it up in separate units, each one of which we can read like a sign. Critics who are conditioned by this will keep on (consciously or subconsciously) trying to separate out the "subject" of each shot, the "content" of each sequence, even when the film is made in a denser and more fluid style which does not admit this kind of treatment. They resent, or more commonly fail to understand, directors who give them too much work to do, and they naturally resent CinemaScope, which automatically makes for a more open, complex image.

The specific objections made to CinemaScope now, I hope, fall into place: they are really no objections at all. Sidney Lumet in an interview (*Film Quarterly*, Winter, 1960) was asked about the new screen processes and answered "I think they're ridiculous, I think they're pointless, I think they're typical Hollywood products. And typical Hollywood mentality, because the essence of any dramatic piece is people, and it is symptomatic that Hollywood finds a way of photographing people directly opposite to the way they are built. CinemaScope makes no sense until people are fatter than they are taller."

This is about as logical as to say that a book should be the shape of what it's about. If the screen is to correspond exactly to the human build then we should have vertical CinemaScope. If to the human face, it should be square (if not oval), and the most common criticism of Scope was, indeed, that it made the close-up impossible: it no longer "fits" the screen. As Gavin Lambert said, "A face squashed across a concave screen is clearly an unedifying prospect." (In CinemaScope, unlike Cinerama, the screen is seldom noticeably curved, and clearly the objection is more to the dimensions than to the curvature itself.)

The argument is effectively a circular one. I think one can sum up the development of the close-up roughly like this: the natural subject for the film is man-in-a-situation. But the frame was too narrow for this to be shown comfortably: also, it was difficult to organize from scratch, without some experience of the cinema and what could be done with it. So man-in-situation came to be conveyed by man + situation: close-up of a face, intercut with shots defining his experience and/or surroundings.

Certain film-makers welcomed this because it was more manageable and also more clearly "creative." At the same time, the process was rejected by others as being mechanical. One can look at this first from the point of view of actor and director. There is a loss of spontaneity, which is reflected in the film. "If you isolate a detail, that means that you have to take it up again from cold, to resuscitate the emotion" (Vincente Minnelli). "The close-up in the cinema is essentially a reconstruction, something pre-fabricated, carefully worked up" (Jean Renoir).

This in turn affects the spectator, who has to take on trust the connection between the close-up and the rest of the scene; man + situation tends to become a formula, a cruder digest of a reality which is continuous and complex. "If I were to throw in ten more details, everything in my films would suddenly become extremely clear. But those ten details are just what I don't want to add. Nothing could be easier than to take a close-up; I don't take any, lest I be tempted to use them" (Roberto Rossellini).

Directors like these worked out a more integral style presenting man-*in*-situation. This involved compensating for the narrowness of the frame by moving the camera laterally and composing the scene in depth. If the actors were brought close to the camera they would fill the screen, and blot out the background; therefore they were seldom brought close. This style is associated mainly with Renoir, who in 1938 wrote: "The more I advance in my craft, the more I feel it necessary to have the scene set in depth in relation to the screen; and the less can I stand actors placed carefully before the camera, as if they were posing for their photograph. It suits me rather to set my actors freely at different distances from the camera, to make them move about." This can be traced back to *Boudu Sauvé des Eaux* (1932) and even to his silent films; and there are others in the 'thirties like Hawks and Ophuls who, while not applying any formal principle of composition in depth, concentrate on the organization of the space within the image, and avoid the detached close-up — see especially *The Criminal Code* and *Liebelei*.

These, together with *Boudu*, make up a marvelous trio of early sound films, which if one relied upon historians one would scarcely know existed, for according to most theories they oughtn't to.

The most spectacular application of these ideas is undoubtedly Antonioni's *Le Amiche* (made in 1955 but in the 1:1.33 ratio), of which he said: "I wanted to show my characters in their context, not to separate them, by montage, from their daily environment. You will find no cross-cutting whatever in *Le Amiche:* this technique expresses nothing." There are no close-ups in this film, and the average length of shot is 30 seconds, which is a lot. Antonioni realizes, and demonstrates, that the interaction of people with each other and with their surroundings is much more subtly expressed by showing them simultaneously. To dissociate them by montage tends to dissociate them altogether. The difference is not one of degree but of kind.

How does this relate to CinemaScope? Many of the directors who thus "anticipate" it do not in fact use it; partly this is chance, partly that they can get along without. But while I would not quite agree with the magazine *Présence du Cinéma*, which states that everything is automatically better in Scope, I think that, other things being equal, Scope refines this style. The director can now afford to bring a character closer to the lens without shutting out the context, and this flexibility is useful. He can have two faces in close shot together, instead of having to cut from one to the other, or to squeeze them in unnaturally close together. (Antonioni, although he has not worked in Scope, has taken advantage of the 1:1.85 screen in this way. Ian Cameron discusses this apropos of *L'Avventura* in *Film Quarterly*, Fall, 1962).

In CinemaScope the close-up, so far from being impossible, is for the first time fully acceptable: it *cannot* be a mechanical, all-purpose CU like the one of Mosjoukine, and it cannot be detached, it must include a genuine and not just a token background. I say "cannot": at least, if it is done this way, it is patently absurd. The image is too open, its space too palpable, to accommodate the "dead object" and give it spurious life. A lifeless film is twice as lifeless in Scope, as certain directors continue to demonstrate by building up scenes in the cutting-room out of the most perfunctory of component-shots. The most grotesque example is *The Lion*, but *The Left Hand of God, The Barbarian and the Geisha, Bus*

Stop, and *The Deep Blue Sea* are also instructively inept. (I don't suggest that Scope *makes* them bad; they would have been anyway, but Scope shows them up more clearly. Over-all, and with certain clear exceptions like the didactic and the animated film, Scope makes the bad film worse and the good film better: it should gradually separate the sheep among directors from the goats.)

Look at the Scope close-up, as before, from both angles, how it is shot, and how we see it. If it is to pass, it must be analytic rather than synthetic: instead of taking an insert CU, then, against a neutral background, the director will have to recreate the ambience of the whole, and this helps the actor. The actor at the same time is freer to move within the frame, and thus within his surroundings, instead of being "placed carefully before the camera". Mariette Hartley, the girl in *Ride the High Country*, stands at the window of her house, talking to a boy: Scope close-up: she moves around nervously while she talks, and the director (Sam Peckinpah) doesn't have to worry about keeping her fixed to any chalk-marks because there is room enough within the frame; the effect is marvelously spontaneous.

Kazan's *Wild River* (about the evacuation of a remote community by the Tennessee Valley Authority) is a film where environment, and its effect on different people, is as significant as in *Le Amiche* and *The Magnificent Ambersons*. Because it is in Scope it doesn't matter that it is full of close-ups and crosscut sequences. Antonioni's reservations no longer apply; Kazan can concentrate on a single face without dissociating it from its context and "dislocating" the spectator.

Finally, a not unusual CinemaScope scene (from Ray's *Bitter Victory*) which contradicts most of the facile generalizations about Scope, made alike by those against and those in favor. The three main characters sit around a table, talking. The atmosphere is important—a military club in Africa, during the war, a nervous, falsely cheerful environment. The scene is taken in a series of full or medium close-ups, each of the three in turn, as they talk, sometimes two together. The normal theoretical attitude is that this would be fine on the old-ratio screen but clumsy if not impossible in Scope. If anything, the reverse is true, and it works brilliantly *because* it is in Scope: the cutting does not disorient us, the close-ups do not wholly isolate the characters, we know where we are all through. At the edges of the frame there is décor and space and perhaps some casual detail; thus when the camera is on one of the men, Richard Burton, we can see a couple dancing, and an Arab guard, and a general background of the room; we are completely situated at each moment, and accept the scene as real, while getting the full concentration on each face which Ray intends. So far from distracting this awareness of environment and of the characters' relation in space is necessary.

In talking about the close-ups in *Bitter Victory* I am talking about the montage. The two have always been lumped together, by people condemning Scope ("the close-up and montage become impossible") and by those welcoming it ("but montage and the close-up are not essential anyway"); the implications of Scope are identical for both. Montage is at once less necessary and more acceptable. Bazin and Roger Leenhardt, two of the few who approved of Scope from the start, imagined it would come to eliminate cutting within a sequence, and that this was no bad thing, but fortunately the medium is more flexible: some directors cut more in Scope, some less. There is no need to fragment reality, but there is less harm in fragmenting it because the different bits can be fitted together more satisfactorily. . . .

III
The Film Medium

Film theory and film criticism have been largely concerned with one central issue: What is "cinematic?" Which paths should the cinema follow? Which should it reject? Attempts to answer this question inevitably take their lead from Lessing's classic essay, *Laocoon*, in which the eighteenth century German dramatist and essayist attempted to demonstrate that the visual arts organize their materials spatially while the poetic arts organize their materials temporally. The materials, procedures, subjects, and effects of these two different forms (or "media") of artistic organization are therefore necessarily different. In this spirit, film theorists have attempted to discover the characteristics of the film medium, declaring those subjects, materials, procedures, and effects that "exploit" the characteristics of the medium proper, legitimate, and truly cinematic and those subjects, materials, procedures, and effects that "violate" the characteristics of the medium barren, misleading and fundamentally uncinematic.

The concept of a medium is, of course, a difficult one. Is the medium to be defined in purely physical terms (that is, the projection of images at twenty-four frames per second on a screen) or rather in terms of an artistic language (angle and distance of shots, rhythms and patterns of editing, and so forth)? Does it include the main structural features of the art (such as plot) and its main historical conventions (say, its genres)? And how are we to determine which possibilities of the medium are legitimate? Is it legitimate to pursue any possibility inherent in the medium, or only those for

147

which the medium has a special affinity? And how are we to judge what those special affinities are? May two different artistic media share those affinities or must an art confine itself, as certain purists urge, to realizing only those possibilities that it shares with no other art?

Erwin Panofsky, the great art historian who was a contemporary of both Arnheim and Kracauer, has written the most influential discussion of the subject. He argues that an art ought to exploit the "unique and specific" possibilities of its medium; and in the film medium these can be defined as the "dynamization of space" and the "spatialization of time." Both these features are visual ones, and Panofsky's primarily visual conception of the film medium is vulnerable to the objection that it accords an undue priority to the silent film, placing unwise restrictions on the use of speech in films. According to Panofsky's principle of "co-expressibility," "the sound, articulate or not, cannot express any more than is expressed, at the same time, by visible movement." Panofsky claims that the Shavian dialogue in the film version of Shaw's *Pygmalion* falls flat and suggests that Olivier's monologues in *Henry V* are successful only to the extent that Olivier's face becomes "a huge field of action" in oblique "close-up." But those who admire the brilliant Hollywood "dialogue" comedies of the 30s and early 40s and who recall that Olivier does not deliver the "St. Crispin's Day" speech in *Henry V* in close-up will receive these views with a measure of skepticism. Indeed, Panofsky modified them in the revised version of his essay that appears in this anthology.

Siegfried Kracauer acknowledges the difficulty of defining the film medium but believes, nevertheless, that cinema has certain "inherent affinities." There are, in particular, certain subjects in the physical world that may be termed "cinematic" because they exert a peculiar attraction on the medium. Kracauer argues that cinema is predestined and even eager to exhibit them. Like Panofsky, Kracauer accepts the use of sound in films only under certain very restrictive conditions, and he especially dislikes the development of the "theatrical" film: "What even the most theatrical minded silent film could not incorporate—pointed controversies, Shavian witticisms, Hamlet's soliloquies—has been annexed to the screen." But Kracauer finds this annexation unfortunate; it in no way proves that such theatrical speeches are legitimate possibilities of the cinematic medium, for "popularity," in Kracauer's view, has no bearing on questions of aesthetic legitimacy.

Kracauer calls the comedies of Frank Capra and Preston Sturges border-line cases, but only on the ground that their witty dialogue is "complemented and compensated for" by "visuals of independent interest" (he means that they include slapstick sequences). Just as witty dialogue violates the visual requirements of the medium and requires "compensation," surrealistic projections of inner realities, expressionist dreams and visions, and experimental abstractions violate the realist requirements of the medium. On the other hand, certain types of movement—the chase and dancing—and certain types of objects—those that are normally too big or too small to be seen—are peculiarly appropriate subjects of cinema. But does the dance really have a greater affinity for the film than it does for the stage? Must the film avoid what is normally seen simply because it is the subject matter of other arts? One can agree with Kracauer that the close-up is a peculiarly cinematic technique, and even with the influential Hungarian theorist, scenarist, and film-maker, Béla Balázs, that the close-up is responsible for the "discovery of the human face," without supposing that the film must devote itself exclusively to the exploitation of these "unique" potentialities.

Rudolph Arnheim shares Panofsky's and Kracauer's view that the film ought to stress the peculiar possibilities of the cinematic medium. But he feels obligated to refute the view that cinema is a mere mechanical reproduction of physical reality. If it were, it would not be an art. Arnheim therefore insists on the various discrepancies between the film image and the standard perception of physical reality. The film image suffers a reduction of depth, a distortion of perspective, an accentuation of perspective overlapping and, in the past, an absence of color and articulate speech. Arnheim asserts that the true task of cinema is to exploit these very "defects" and turn them to an advantage, just as painting exploits the fact that it is a two-dimensional, enclosed object. There can be no doubt that a great art can be devised that confines itself to exploiting these defects (the silent film was such an art), but can we accept the suggestion that film must avoid exploiting the affinities with physical reality that Kracauer mentions, just because they conform to, rather than deviate from, reality? And should we regret the fact that we can remedy some of the "defects" of a medium rather than exploit them? Should we regret the development of sound, as all three of these theorists do?

Robert Warshow, an important American critic of the era just after World War II, tries to show that Carl Dreyer's basic problem as an artist is one that almost inevitably confronts the self-conscious creator of "art" films. Warshow defines an art film as one that attempts to exploit only the visual or the formal properties of the cinematic medium, often because this exploitation is thought to be the proper way to realize the cinema's peculiar affinity for pure movement. But, Warshow argues, in showing human beings in movement, one cannot divorce movement from content, form from document, or spectacle from drama. The inherent realism of the medium asserts itself, upsetting the artist's intention and making inevitable a profound incoherence of style. These are the practical consequences of violating the conditions of the medium, which demand attention to physical reality, narrative coherence, psychological observation, and historical accuracy.

Finally, Francis Sparshott, a contemporary philosopher and aesthetician, challenges the assumptions of the Lessing tradition to which all these writers subscribe. Sparshott regards many of the views expressed by Panofsky, Kracauer, and Arnheim as dogmas. "Whatever can be done with a medium is among its possibilities and hence 'true to' it in a sense that has yet to be shown to be illegitimate." Sparshott offers an account of the film medium which indicates both its great range and its special features—its unique way of representing space, time, and motion. This analysis provides the foundation for his conclusion: "Film is unique in its capacity for visual recording and analysis, in its ability to convey the unique present reality of things, in its ability to reveal the qualities of lives; but also in its formal freedom, its capacity for realizing fantasy and developing abstract forms." Sparshott's essay implies that a definition of the film medium ought not to be some simple assertion of dogma or a naked attempt to establish as law the dictates of individual taste or the surmises of personal experience.

ERWIN PANOFSKY
STYLE AND MEDIUM
IN THE MOTION PICTURES

Film art is the only art the development of which men now living have witnessed from the very beginnings; and this development is all the more interesting as it took place under conditions contrary to precedent. It was not an artistic urge that gave rise to the discovery and gradual perfection of a new technique; it was a technical invention that gave rise to the discovery and gradual perfection of a new art.

From this we understand two fundamental facts. First, that the primordial basis of the enjoyment of moving pictures was not an objective interest in a specific subject matter, much less an aesthetic interest in the formal presentation of subject matter, but the sheer delight in the fact that things seemed to move, no matter what things they were. Second, that films—first exhibited in "kinetoscopes," viz., cinematographic peep shows, but projectable to a screen since as early as 1894—are, originally, a product of genuine folk art (whereas, as a rule, folk art derives from what is known as "higher art"). At the very beginning of things we find the simple recording of movements: galloping horses, railroad trains, fire engines, sporting events, street scenes. And when it had come to the making of narrative films these were produced by photographers who were anything but "producers" or "directors," performed by people who were anything but actors, and enjoyed by people who would have been much offended had anyone called them "art lovers."

The casts of these archaic films were usually collected in a "café" where unemployed supers or ordinary citizens possessed of a suitable exterior were wont to assemble at a given hour. An enterprising photographer would walk in, hire four or five convenient characters and make the picture while carefully instructing them what to do: "Now, you pretend to hit this lady over the head"; and (to the lady): "And you pretend to fall down in a heap." Productions like these were shown, together with those purely factual recordings of "movement for movement's sake," in a few small and dingy cinemas mostly frequented by the "lower classes" and a sprinkling of youngsters in quest of adventure (about 1905, I happen to remember, there was only one obscure and faintly disreputable *kino* in the whole city of Berlin, bearing, for some unfathomable reason, the English name of "The Meeting Room"). Small wonder that the "better classes," when they slowly began to venture into these early picture theaters, did so, not by way of seeking normal and possibly serious entertainment, but with that characteristic sensation of self-conscious condescension with which we may plunge, in gay company, into the folkloristic depths of Coney Island or a European kermis; even a few years ago it was the regulation attitude of the socially or intellectually prominent that one could confess to enjoying such austerely educational films as *The Sex Life of the Starfish* or films with "beautiful scenery," but never to a serious liking for narratives.

Today there is no denying that narrative films are not only "art" —not often good art, to be sure, but this applies to other media as well—but also, besides architecture, cartooning and "commercial design," the only visual art entirely alive. The "movies" have reestablished that dynamic contact between art production and art consumption which, for reasons too complex to be considered here, is sorely attenuated, if not entirely interrupted, in many other fields of artistic endeavor. Whether we like it or not, it is the movies that mold, more than any other single force, the opinions, the taste, the language, the dress, the behavior, and even the physical appearance of a public comprising more than 60 per cent of the population of the earth. If all the serious lyrical poets, composers, painters and sculptors were forced by law to stop their activities, a rather small fraction of the general public would become aware of the fact and a still smaller fraction would seriously regret it. If the same thing were to happen with the movies the social consequences would be catastrophic.

152

In the beginning, then, there were the straight recordings of movement no matter what moved, viz., the prehistoric ancestors of our "documentaries"; and, soon after, the early narratives, viz., the prehistoric ancestors of our "feature films." The craving for a narrative element could be satisfied only by borrowing from older arts, and one should expect that the natural thing would have been to borrow from the theater, a theater play being apparently the *genus proximum* to a narrative film in that it consists of a narrative enacted by persons that move. But in reality the imitation of stage performances was a comparatively late and thoroughly frustrated development. What happened at the start was a very different thing. Instead of imitating a theatrical performance already endowed with a certain amount of motion, the earliest films added movement to works of art originally stationary, so that the dazzling technical invention might achieve a triumph of its own without intruding upon the sphere of higher culture. The living language, which is always right, has endorsed this sensible choice when it still speaks of a "moving picture" or, simply, a "picture," instead of accepting the pretentious and fundamentally erroneous "screen play."

The stationary works enlivened in the earliest movies were indeed pictures: bad nineteenth-century paintings and postcards (or waxworks à la Madame Tussaud's), supplemented by the comic strips—a most important root of cinematic art—and the subject matter of popular songs, pulp magazines and dime novels; and the films descending from this ancestry appealed directly and very intensely to a folk art mentality. They gratified—often simultaneously—first, a primitive sense of justice and decorum when virtue and industry were rewarded while vice and laziness were punished; second, plain sentimentality when "the thin trickle of a fictive love interest" took its course "through somewhat serpentine channels," or when Father, dear Father returned from the saloon to find his child dying of diphtheria; third, a primordial instinct for bloodshed and cruelty when Andreas Hofer faced the firing squad, or when (in a film of 1893–94) the head of Mary Queen of Scots actually came off; fourth, a taste for mild pornography (I remember with great pleasure a French film of *ca.* 1900 wherein a seemingly but not really well-rounded lady as well as a seemingly but not really slender one were shown changing to bathing suits—an honest, straightforward *porcheria* much less objectionable than the

153

now extinct Betty Boop films and, I am sorry to say, some of the more recent Walt Disney productions); and, finally, that crude sense of humor, graphically described as "slapstick," which feeds upon the sadistic and the pornographic instinct, either singly or in combination.

Not until as late as *ca.* 1905 was a film adaptation of *Faust* ventured upon (cast still "unknown," characteristically enough), and not until 1911 did Sarah Bernhardt lend her prestige to an unbelievably funny film tragedy, *Queen Elizabeth of England.* These films represent the first conscious attempt at transplanting the movies from the folk art level to that of "real art"; but they also bear witness to the fact that this commendable goal could not be reached in so simple a manner. It was soon realized that the imitation of a theater performance with a set stage, fixed entries and exits, and distinctly literary ambitions is the one thing the film must avoid.

The legitimate paths of evolution were opened, not by running away from the folk art character of the primitive film but by developing it within the limits of its own possibilities. Those primordial archetypes of film productions on the folk art level—success or retribution, sentiment, sensation, pornography, and crude humor—could blossom forth into genuine history, tragedy and romance, crime and adventure, and comedy, as soon as it was realized that they could be transfigured—not by an artificial injection of literary values but by the exploitation of the unique and specific possibilities of the new medium. Significantly, the beginnings of this legitimate development antedate the attempts at endowing the film with higher values of a foreign order (the crucial period being the years from 1902 to *ca.* 1905), and the decisive steps were taken by people who were laymen or outsiders from the viewpoint of the serious stage.

These unique and specific possibilities can be defined as *dynamization of space* and, accordingly, *spatialization of time.* This statement is self-evident to the point of triviality but it belongs to that kind of truths which, just because of their triviality, are easily forgotten or neglected.

In a theater, space is static, that is, the space represented on the stage, as well as the spatial relation of the beholder to the spectacle, is unalterably fixed. The spectator cannot leave his seat, and the setting of the stage cannot change, during one act (except for such incidentals as rising moons or gathering clouds and such illegitimate reborrowings from the film as turning wings or gliding backdrops). But, in return for this restriction, the theater has the advantage that time, the medium of emotion and thought conveyable by speech, is free and independent of anything that may happen in visible space. Hamlet may deliver his famous monologue lying on a couch in the middle distance, doing nothing and only dimly discernible to the spectator and listener, and yet by his mere words enthrall him with a feeling of intensest emotional action.

With the movies the situation is reversed. Here, too, the spectator occupies a fixed seat, but only physically, not as the subject of an aesthetic experience. Aesthetically, he is in permanent motion as his eye identifies itself with the lens of the camera, which permanently shifts in distance and direction. And as movable as the spectator is, as movable is, for the same reason, the space presented to him. Not only bodies move in space, but space itself does, approaching, receding, turning, dissolving and recrystallizing as it appears through the controlled locomotion and focusing of the camera and through the cutting and editing of the various shots — not to mention such special effects as visions, transformations, disappearances, slow-motion and fast-motion shots, reversals and trick films. This opens up a world of possibilities of which the stage can never dream. Quite apart from such photographic tricks as the participation of disembodied spirits in the action of the *Topper* series, or the more effective wonders wrought by Roland Young in *The Man Who Could Work Miracles*, there is, on the purely factual level, an untold wealth of themes as inaccessible to the "legitimate" stage as a fog or a snowstorm is to the sculptor; all sorts of violent elemental phenomena and, conversely, events too microscopic to be visible under normal conditions (such as the life-saving injection with the serum flown in at the very last moment, or the fatal bite of the yellow-fever mosquito); full-scale battle scenes; all kinds of operations, not only in the surgical sense but also in the sense of any actual construction, destruction or experimentation, as in *Louis Pasteur* or *Madame Curie*; a really grand party, moving through many rooms of a mansion or a palace. Features like these, even the mere shifting of the scene from one place to another by means of a car perilously negotiating heavy traffic or a motorboat steered through a nocturnal harbor, will not only always retain their primitive cinematic appeal but also remain enormously effective as a means of stirring the emotions and creating suspense. In addition, the movies have the power, entirely denied to the theater, to convey psychological experiences by directly projecting their content to the screen, substituting, as it were, the eye of the beholder for the consciousness of the character (as when the imaginings and hallucinations of the drunkard in the otherwise overrated *Lost Weekend* appear as stark realities instead of being described by mere words). But any attempt to convey thought and feelings exclusively, or even primarily, by speech leaves us with a feeling of embarrassment, boredom, or both.

What I mean by thoughts and feelings "conveyed exclusively, or even primarily, by speech" is simply this: Contrary to naïve expectation, the invention of the sound track in 1928 has been unable to change the basic fact that a moving picture, even when it has learned to talk, remains a picture that moves and does not convert itself into a piece of writing that is enacted. Its substance remains a series of visual sequences held together by an uninterrupted flow of movement in space (except, of course, for such checks and pauses as have the same compositional value as a rest in music), and not a sustained study in human character and destiny transmitted by effective, let alone "beautiful," diction. I cannot remember a more misleading statement about the movies than Mr. Eric Russell Bentley's in the spring number of the *Kenyon Review*, 1945: "The potentialities of the talking screen differ from those of the silent screen in adding the dimension of dialogue—which could be poetry." I would suggest: "The potentialities of the talking screen differ from those of the silent screen in integrating visible movement with dialogue which, therefore, had better not be poetry."

All of us, if we are old enough to remember the period prior to 1928, recall the old-time pianist who, with his eyes glued on the screen, would accompany the events with music adapted to their mood and rhythm; and we also recall the weird and spectral feeling overtaking us when this pianist left his post for a few minutes and the film was allowed to run by itself, the darkness haunted by the monotonous rattle of the machinery. Even the silent film, then, was never mute. The visible spectacle always required, and received, an audible accompaniment which, from the very beginning, distinguished the film from simple pantomime and rather classed it — *mutatis mutandis* — with the ballet. The advent of the talkie meant not so much an "addition" as a transformation: the transformation of musical sound into articulate speech and, therefore, of quasi pantomime into an entirely new species of spectacle which differs from the ballet, and agrees with the stage play, in that its acoustic component consists of intelligible words, but differs from the stage play and agrees with the ballet in that this acoustic component is not detachable from the visual. In a film, that which we hear remains, for good or worse, inextricably fused with that which we see; the sound, articulate or not, cannot express any more than is expressed, at the same time, by visible movement; and in a good film it does not even attempt to do so. To put it briefly, the play — or, as it is very properly called, the "script" — of a moving picture is subject to what might be termed the *principle of coexpressibility*.

Empirical proof of this principle is furnished by the fact that, wherever the dialogical or monological element gains temporary prominence, there appears, with the inevitability of a natural law, the "close-up." What does the close-up achieve? In showing us, in magnification, either the face of the speaker or the face of the listeners or both in alternation, the camera transforms the human physiognomy into a huge field of action where — given the qualification of the performers — every subtle movement of the features, almost imperceptible from a natural distance, becomes an expressive event in visible space and thereby completely integrates itself with the expressive content of the spoken word; whereas, on the stage, the spoken word makes a stronger rather than a weaker impression if we are not permitted to count the hairs in Romeo's mustache.

This does not mean that the scenario is a negligible factor in the making of a moving picture. It only means that its artistic intention differs in kind from that of a stage play, and much more from that of a novel or a piece of poetry. As the success of a Gothic jamb figure depends not only upon its quality as a piece of sculpture but also, or even more so, upon its integrability with the architecture of the portal, so does the success of a movie script — not unlike that of an opera libretto — depend, not only upon its quality as a piece

157

of literature but also, or even more so, upon its integrability with the events on the screen.

As a result—another empirical proof of the coexpressibility principle—good movie scripts are unlikely to make good reading and have seldom been published in book form; whereas, conversely, good stage plays have to be severely altered, cut, and, on the other hand, enriched by interpolations to make good movie scripts. In Shaw's *Pygmalion*, for instance, the actual process of Eliza's phonetic education and, still more important, her final triumph at the grand party, are wisely omitted; we see—or, rather, hear—some samples of her gradual linguistic improvement and finally encounter her, upon her return from the reception, victorious and splendidly arrayed but deeply hurt for want of recognition and sympathy. In the film adaptation, precisely these two scenes are not only supplied but also strongly emphasized; we witness the fascinating activities in the laboratory with its array of spinning disks and mirrors, organ pipes and dancing flames, and we participate in the ambassadorial party, with many moments of impending catastrophe and a little counterintrigue thrown in for suspense. Unquestionably these two scenes, entirely absent from the play, and indeed unachievable upon the stage, were the highlights of the film; whereas the Shavian dialogue, however severely cut, turned out to fall a little flat in certain moments. And wherever, as in so many other films, a poetic emotion, a musical outburst, or a literary conceit (even, I am grieved to say, some of the wisecracks of Groucho Marx) entirely lose contact with visible movement, they strike the sensitive spectator as, literally, out of place. It is certainly terrible when a soft-boiled he-man, after the suicide of his mistress, casts a twelve-foot glance upon her photograph and says something less-than-coexpressible to the effect that he will never forget her. But when he recites, instead, a piece of poetry as sublimely more-than-coexpressible as Romeo's monologue at the bier of Juliet, it is still worse. Reinhardt's *Midsummer Night's Dream* is probably the most unfortunate major film ever produced; and Olivier's *Henry V* owes its comparative success, apart from the all but providential adaptability of this particular play, to so many *tours de force* that it will, God willing, remain an exception rather than set a pattern. It combines "judicious pruning" with the interpolation of pageantry, nonverbal comedy and melodrama;

it uses a device perhaps best designated as "oblique close-up" (Mr. Olivier's beautiful face inwardly listening to but not pronouncing the great soliloquy); and, most notably, it shifts between three levels of archaeological reality: a reconstruction of Elizabethan London, a reconstruction of the events of 1415 as laid down in Shakespeare's play, and the reconstruction of a performance of this play on Shakespeare's own stage. All this is perfectly legitimate; but, even so, the highest praise of the film will always come from those who, like the critic of the *New Yorker*, are not quite in sympathy with either the movies *au naturel* or Shakespeare *au naturel*.

As the writings of Conan Doyle potentially contain all modern mystery stories (except for the tough specimens of the Dashiell Hammett school), so do the films produced between 1900 and 1910 pre-establish the subject matter and methods of the moving picture as we know it. This period produced the incunabula of the Western and the crime film (Edwin S. Porter's amazing *Great Train Robbery* of 1903) from which developed the modern gangster, adventure, and mystery pictures (the latter, if well done, is still one of the most honest and genuine forms of film entertainment, space being doubly charged with time as the beholder asks himself not only "What is going to happen?" but also "What has happened before?"). The same period saw the emergence of the fantastically imaginative film (Méliès) which was to lead to the expressionist and surrealist experiments (*The Cabinet of Dr. Caligari, Sang d'un Poète*, etc.), on the one hand, and to the more superficial and spectacular fairy tales à la Arabian Nights, on the other. Comedy, later to triumph in Charlie Chaplin, the still insufficiently appreciated Buster Keaton, the Marx Brothers and the pre-Hollywood creations of René Clair, reached a respectable level in Max Linder and others. In historical and melodramatic films the foundations were laid for movie iconography and movie symbolism, and in the early work of D. W. Griffith we find, not only remarkable attempts at psychological analysis *(Edgar Allan Poe)* and social criticism *(A Corner in Wheat)* but also such basic technical innovations as the long shot, the flashback and the close-up. And modest trick films and cartoons paved the way to Felix the Cat, Popeye the Sailor, and Felix's prodigious offspring, Mickey Mouse.

Within their self-imposed limitations the earlier Disney films, and certain sequences in the later ones,* represent, as it were, a chemically pure distillation of cinematic possibilities. They retain the most important folkloristic elements—sadism, pornography, the humor engendered by both, and moral justice—almost without dilution and often fuse these elements into a variation on the primitive and inexhaustible David-and-Goliath motif, the triumph of the seemingly weak over the seemingly strong; and their fantastic independence of the natural laws gives them the power to integrate space with time to such perfection that the spatial and temporal experiences of sight and hearing come to be almost interconvertible. A series of soap bubbles, successively punctured, emits a series of sounds exactly corresponding in pitch and volume to the size of the bubbles; the three uvulae of Willie the Whale—small, large and medium—vibrate in consonance with tenor, bass and baritone notes; and the very concept of stationary existence is completely

---

*I make this distinction because it was, in my opinion, a fall from grace when *Snow White* introduced the human figure and when *Fantasia* attempted to picturalize The World's Great Music. The very virtue of the animated cartoon is to animate, that is to say endow lifeless things with life, or living things with a different kind of life. It effects a metamorphosis, and such a metamorphosis is wonderfully present in Disney's animals, plants, thunderclouds and railroad trains. Whereas his dwarfs, glamourized princesses, hillbillies, baseball players, rouged centaurs and *amigos* from South America are not transformations but caricatures at best, and fakes or vulgarities at worst. Concerning music, however, it should be borne in mind that its cinematic use is no less predicated upon the principle of coexpressibility than is the cinematic use of the spoken word. There is music permitting or even requiring the accompaniment of visible action (such as dances, ballet music and any kind of operatic compositions) and music of which the opposite is true; and this is, again, not a question of quality (most of us rightly prefer a waltz by Johann Strauss to a symphony by Sibelius) but one of intention. In *Fantasia* the hippopotamus ballet was wonderful, and the Pastoral Symphony and "Ave Maria" sequences were deplorable, not because the cartooning in the first case was infinitely better than in the two others (*cf.* above), and certainly not because Beethoven and Schubert are too sacred for picturalization, but simply because Ponchielli's "Dance of the Hours" is coexpressible while the Pastoral Symphony and the "Ave Maria" are not. In cases like these even the best imaginable music and the best imaginable cartoon will impair rather than enhance each other's effectiveness.

Experimental proof of all this was furnished by Disney's recent *Make Mine Music* where The World's Great Music was fortunately restricted to Prokofieff. Even among the other sequences the most successful ones were those in which the human element was either absent or reduced to a minimum; Willie the Whale, the Ballad of Johnny Fedora and Alice Blue-Bonnet, and, above all, the truly magnificent Goodman Quartet.

abolished. No object in creation, whether it be a house, a piano, a tree or an alarm clock, lacks the faculties of organic, in fact anthropomorphic, movement, facial expression and phonetic articulation. Incidentally, even in normal, "realistic" films the inanimate object, provided that it is dynamizable, can play the role of a leading character as do the ancient railroad engines in Buster Keaton's *General* and *Niagara Falls*. How the earlier Russian films exploited the possibility of heroizing all sorts of machinery lives in everybody's memory; and it is perhaps more than an accident that the two films which will go down in history as the great comical and the great serious masterpiece of the silent period bear the names and immortalize the personalities of two big ships: Keaton's *Navigator* (1924) and Eisenstein's *Potemkin* (1925).

The evolution from the jerky beginnings to this grand climax offers the fascinating spectacle of a new artistic medium gradually becoming conscious of its legitimate, that is, exclusive, possibilities and limitations—a spectacle not unlike the development of the mosaic, which started out with transposing illusionistic genre pictures into a more durable material and culminated in the hieratic supernaturalism of Ravenna; or the development of line engraving, which started out as a cheap and handy substitute for book illumination and culminated in the purely "graphic" style of Dürer.

Just so the silent movies developed a definite style of their own, adapted to the specific conditions of the medium. A hitherto unknown language was forced upon a public not yet capable of reading it, and the more proficient the public became the more refinement could develop in the language. For a Saxon peasant of around 800 it was not easy to understand the meaning of a picture showing a man as he pours water over the head of another man, and even later many people found it difficult to grasp the significance of two ladies standing behind the throne of an emperor. For the public of around 1910 it was no less difficult to understand the meaning of the speechless action in a moving picture, and the producers employed means of clarification similar to those we find in medieval art. One of these were printed titles or letters, striking equivalents of the medieval *tituli* and scrolls (at a still earlier date there even used to be explainers who would say, *viva voce*, "Now he thinks his wife is dead but she isn't" or "I don't wish to offend the ladies in the audience but I doubt that any of them would have done that

161

much for her child"). Another, less obtrusive method of explanation was the introduction of a fixed iconography which from the outset informed the spectator about the basic facts and characters, much as the two ladies behind the emperor, when carrying a sword and a cross respectively, were uniquely determined as Fortitude and Faith. There arose, identifiable by standardized appearance, behavior and attributes, the well-remembered types of the Vamp and the Straight Girl (perhaps the most convincing modern equivalents of the medieval personifications of the Vices and Virtues), the Family Man, and the Villain, the latter marked by a black mustache and walking stick. Nocturnal scenes were printed on blue or green film. A checkered tablecloth meant, once for all, a "poor but honest" milieu; a happy marriage, soon to be endangered by the shadows from the past, was symbolized by the young wife's pouring the breakfast coffee for her husband; the first kiss was invariably announced by the lady's gently playing with her partner's necktie and was invariably accompanied by her kicking out with her left foot. The conduct of the characters was predetermined accordingly. The poor but honest laborer who, after leaving his little house with the checkered tablecloth, came upon an abandoned baby could not but take it to his home and bring it up as best he could; the Family Man could not but yield, however temporarily, to the temptations of the Vamp. As a result these early melodramas had a highly gratifying and soothing quality in that events took shape, without the complications of individual psychology, according to a pure Aristotelian logic so badly missed in real life.

Devices like these became gradually less necessary as the public grew accustomed to interpret the action by itself and were virtually abolished by the invention of the talking film. But even now there survive—quite legitimately, I think—the remnants of a "fixed attitude and attribute" principle and, more basic, a primitive or folkloristic concept of plot construction. Even today we take it for granted that the diphtheria of a baby tends to occur when the parents are out and, having occurred, solves all their matrimonial problems. Even today we demand of a decent mystery film that the butler, though he may be anything from an agent of the British Secret Service to the real father of the daughter of the house, must not turn out to be the murderer. Even today we love to see Pasteur, Zola or Ehrlich win out against stupidity and wickedness, with their respective wives trusting and trusting all the time. Even today we much prefer a happy finale to a gloomy one and insist, at the very least, on the observance of the Aristotelian rule that the story have a beginning, a middle and an ending—a rule the abrogation of which has done so much to estrange the general public from the more elevated spheres of modern writing. Primitive symbolism, too, survives in such amusing details as the last sequence of *Casablanca* where the delightfully crooked and right-minded *préfet de police* casts an empty bottle of Vichy water into the wastepaper basket; and in such telling symbols of the supernatural as Sir Cedric Hardwicke's Death in the guise of a "gentleman in a dustcoat trying" *(On Borrowed Time)* or Claude Rains's Hermes Psychopompos in the striped trousers of an airline manager *(Here Comes Mister Jordan)*.

The most conspicuous advances were made in directing, lighting, camera work, cutting and acting proper. But while in most of these fields the evolution proceeded continuously—though, of course, not without detours, breakdowns and archaic relapses—the development of acting suffered a sudden interruption by the invention of the talking film; so that the style of acting in the silents can already be evaluated in retrospect, as a lost art not unlike the painting technique of Jan van Eyck or, to take up our previous simile, the burin technique of Dürer. It was soon realized that acting in a silent film neither meant a pantomimic exaggeration of stage acting (as was generally and erroneously assumed by professional stage actors who more and more frequently condescended to perform in the movies), nor could dispense with stylization altogether; a man photographed while walking down a gangway in ordinary, everyday-life fashion looked like anything but a man walking down a gangway when the result appeared on the screen. If the picture was to look both natural and meaningful the acting had to be done in a manner equally different from the style of the stage and the reality of ordinary life; speech had to be made dispensable by establishing an organic relation between the acting and the technical procedure of cinephotography—much as in Dürer's prints color had been made dispensable by establishing an organic relation between the design and the technical procedure of line engraving. This was precisely what the great actors of the silent period accomplished, and it is a significant fact that the best of them did not come from the stage, whose crystallized tradition prevented Duse's only film, *Cenere*, from being more than a priceless record of Duse. They came instead from the circus or the variety, as was the case of Chaplin, Keaton and Will Rogers; from nothing in particular, as was the case of Theda Bara, of her greater European parallel, the Danish actress Asta Nielsen, and of Garbo; or from everything under the sun, as was the case of Douglas Fairbanks. The style of these "old masters" was indeed comparable to the style of line engraving in that it was, and had to be, exaggerated in comparison with stage acting (just as the sharply incised and vigorously curved *tailles* of the burin are exaggerated in comparison with pencil strokes or brushwork), but richer, subtler and infinitely more precise. The advent of the talkies, reducing if not abolishing this difference between screen acting and stage acting, thus confronted the actors and actresses of the silent screen with a serious problem. Buster Keaton yielded to temptation and fell. Chaplin first tried to stand his ground and to remain an exquisite archaist but finally gave in, with only moderate success *(The Great Dictator)*. Only the glorious Harpo has thus far successfully refused to utter a single articulate sound; and only Greta Garbo succeeded, in a measure, in transforming her style in principle. But even in her case one cannot help feeling that her first talking picture, *Anna Christie*, where she could ensconce herself, most of the time, in mute or monosyllabic sullenness, was better than her later performances; and in the second, talking version of *Anna Karenina*, the weakest moment is certainly when she delivers a big Ibsenian speech to her husband, and the strongest when she silently moves along the platform of the railroad station while her despair takes shape in the consonance of her movement (and expression) with the movement of the nocturnal space around her, filled with the real noises of the trains and the imaginary sound of the "little men with the iron hammers" that drives her, relentlessly and almost without her realizing it, under the wheels.

Small wonder that there is sometimes felt a kind of nostalgia for the silent period and that devices have been worked out to combine the virtues of sound and speech with those of silent acting, such as the "oblique close-up" already mentioned in connection with *Henry V*; the dance behind glass doors in *Sous les Toits de Paris*; or, in the

Histoire d'un Tricheur, Sacha Guitry's recital of the events of his youth while the events themselves are "silently" enacted on the screen. However, this nostalgic feeling is no argument against the talkies as such. Their evolution has shown that, in art, every gain entails a certain loss on the other side of the ledger; but that the gain remains a gain, provided that the basic nature of the medium is realized and respected. One can imagine that, when the cavemen of Altamira began to paint their buffaloes in natural colors instead of merely incising the contours, the more conservative cavemen foretold the end of paleolithic art. But paleolithic art went on, and so will the movies. New technical inventions always tend to dwarf the values already attained, especially in a medium that owes its very existence to technical experimentation. The earliest talkies were infinitely inferior to the then mature silents, and most of the present technicolor films are still inferior to the now mature talkies in black and white. But even if Aldous Huxley's nightmare should come true and the experiences of taste, smell and touch should be added to those of sight and hearing, even then we may say with the Apostle, as we have said when first confronted with the sound track and the technicolor film, "We are troubled on every side, yet not distressed; we are perplexed, but not in despair."

From the law of time-charged space and space-bound time, there follows the fact that the screenplay, in contrast to the theater play, *has no aesthetic existence independent of its performance, and that its characters have no aesthetic existence outside the actors.*

The playwright writes in the fond hope that his work will be an imperishable jewel in the treasure house of civilization and will be presented in hundreds of performances that are but transient variations on a "work" that is constant. The script-writer, on the other hand, writes for one producer, one director and one cast. Their work achieves the same degree of permanence as does his; and should the same or a similar scenario ever be filmed by a different director and a different cast there will result an altogether different "play."

Othello or Nora are definite, substantial figures created by the playwright. They can be played well or badly, and they can be "interpreted" in one way or another; but they most definitely exist, no matter who plays them or even whether they are played at all. The character in a film, however, lives and dies with the actor.

165

It is not the entity "Othello" interpreted by Robeson or the entity "Nora" interpreted by Duse; it is the entity "Greta Garbo" incarnate in a figure called Anna Christie or the entity "Robert Montgomery" incarnate in a murderer who, for all we know or care to know, may forever remain anonymous but will never cease to haunt our memories. Even when the names of the characters happen to be Henry VIII or Anna Karenina, the king who ruled England from 1509 to 1547 and the woman created by Tolstoy, they do not exist outside the being of Garbo and Laughton. They are but empty and incorporeal outlines like the shadows in Homer's Hades, assuming the character of reality only when filled with the lifeblood of an actor. Conversely, if a movie role is badly played there remains literally nothing of it, no matter how interesting the character's psychology or how elaborate the words.

What applies to the actor applies, *mutatis mutandis*, to most of the other artists, or artisans, who contribute to the making of a film: the director, the sound man, the enormously important cameraman, even the make-up man. A stage production is rehearsed until everything is ready, and then it is repeatedly performed in three consecutive hours. At each performance everybody has to be on hand and does his work; and afterward he goes home and to bed. The work of the stage actor may thus be likened to that of a musician, and that of the stage director to that of a conductor. Like these, they have a certain repertoire which they have studied and present in a number of complete but transitory performances, be it *Hamlet* today and *Ghosts* tomorrow, or *Life with Father per saecula saeculorum*. The activities of the film actor and the film director, however, are comparable, respectively, to those of the plastic artist and the architect, rather than to those of the musician and the conductor. Stage work is continuous but transitory; film work is discontinuous but permanent. Individual sequences are done piecemeal and out of order according to the most efficient use of sets and personnel. Each bit is done over and over again until it stands; and when the whole has been cut and composed everyone is through with it forever. Needless to say that this very procedure cannot but emphasize the curious consubstantiality that exists between the person of the movie actor and his role. Coming into existence piece by piece, regardless of the natural sequence of events, the "character" can grow into a unified whole only if the

166

actor manages to be, not merely to play, Henry VIII or Anna Karenina throughout the entire wearisome period of shooting. I have it on the best of authorities that Laughton was really difficult to live with in the particular six or eight weeks during which he was doing—or rather being—Captain Bligh.

It might be said that a film, called into being by a co-operative effort in which all contributions have the same degree of permanence, is the nearest modern equivalent of a medieval cathedral; the role of the producer corresponding, more or less, to that of the bishop or archbishop; that of the director to that of the architect in chief; that of the scenario writers to that of the scholastic advisers establishing the iconographical program; and that of the actors, cameramen, cutters, sound men, make-up men and the divers technicians to that of those whose work provided the physical entity of the finished product, from the sculptors, glass painters, bronze casters, carpenters and skilled masons down to the quarry men and woodsmen. And if you speak to any one of these collaborators he will tell you, with perfect *bona fides*, that his is really the most important job—which is quite true to the extent that it is indispensable.

This comparison may seem sacrilegious, not only because there are, proportionally, fewer good films than there are good cathedrals, but also because the movies are commercial. However, if commercial art be defined as all art not primarily produced in order to gratify the creative urge of its maker but primarily intended to meet the requirements of a patron or a buying public, it must be said that noncommercial art is the exception rather than the rule, and a fairly recent and not always felicitous exception at that. While it is true that commercial art is always in danger of ending up as a prostitute, it is equally true that noncommercial art is always in danger of ending up as an old maid. Noncommercial art has given us Seurat's "Grande Jatte" and Shakespeare's sonnets, but also much that is esoteric to the point of incommunicability. Conversely, commercial art has given us much that is vulgar or snobbish (two aspects of the same thing) to the point of loathsomeness, but also Dürer's prints and Shakespeare's plays. For, we must not forget that Dürer's prints were partly made on commission and partly intended to be sold in the open market; and that Shakespeare's plays—in contrast to the earlier masques and intermezzi which were produced at court by aristocratic amateurs and could afford to be so incomprehensible that even those who described them in printed monographs occasionally failed to grasp their intended significance—were meant to appeal, and did appeal, not only to the select few but also to everyone who was prepared to pay a shilling for admission.

It is this requirement of communicability that makes commercial art more vital than noncommercial, and therefore potentially much more effective for better or for worse. The commercial producer can both educate and pervert the general public, and can allow the general public—or rather his idea of the general public—both to educate and to pervert himself. As is demonstrated by a number of excellent films that proved to be great box office successes, the public does not refuse to accept good products if it gets them. That it does not get them very often is caused not so much by commercialism as such as by too little discernment and, paradoxical though it may seem, too much timidity in its application. Hollywood believes that it must produce "what the public wants" while the public would take whatever Hollywood produces. If Hollywood were to decide for itself what it wants it would get away with it—even if it should decide to "depart from evil and do good." For, to revert to whence we started, in modern life the movies are what most other forms of art have ceased to be, not an adornment but a necessity.

That this should be so is understandable, not only from a sociological but also from an art-historical point of view. The processes of all the earlier representational arts conform, in a higher or lesser degree, to an idealistic conception of the world. These arts operate from top to bottom, so to speak, and not from bottom to top; they start with an idea to be projected into shapeless matter and not with the objects that constitute the physical world. The painter works on a blank wall or canvas which he organizes into a likeness of things and persons according to his idea (however much this idea may have been nourished by reality); he does not work with the things and persons themselves even if he works "from the model." The same is true of the sculptor with his shapeless mass of clay or his untooled block of stone or wood; of the writer with his sheet of paper or his dictaphone; and even of the stage designer with his empty and sorely limited section of space. It is the movies, and only the movies, that do justice to that materialistic interpretation of the universe which, whether we like it or not, pervades contemporary civilization. Excepting the very special case of the animated cartoon, the movies organize material things and persons, not a neutral medium, into a composition that receives its style, and may even become fantastic or pretervoluntarily symbolic, not so much by an interpretation in the artist's mind as by the actual manipulation of physical objects and recording machinery. The medium of the movies is physical reality as such: the physical reality of eighteenth-century Versailles—no matter whether it be the original or a Hollywood facsimile indistinguishable therefrom for all aesthetic intents and purposes—or of a suburban home in Westchester; the physical reality of the Rue de Lappe in Paris or of the Gobi Desert, of Paul Ehrlich's apartment in Frankfurt or of the streets of New York in the rain; the physical reality of engines and animals, of Edward G. Robinson and Jimmy Cagney. All these objects and persons must be organized into a work of art. They can be arranged in all sorts of ways ("arrangement" comprising, of course, such things as make-up, lighting and camera work); but there is no running away from them. From this point of view it becomes evident that an attempt at subjecting the world to artistic prestylization, as in the expressionist settings of *The Cabinet of Dr. Caligari* (1919), could be no more than an exciting experiment that could exert but little influence upon the general course of events. To prestylize reality prior to tackling it amounts to dodging the problem. The problem is to manipulate and shoot unstylized reality in such a way that the result has style. This is a proposition no less legitimate and no less difficult than any proposition in the older arts.

SIEGFRIED KRACAUER
FROM THEORY OF FILM

THE ESTABLISHMENT OF PHYSICAL EXISTENCE

In establishing physical existence, films differ from photographs in two respects: they represent reality as it evolves in time; and they do so with the aid of cinematic techniques and devices.

Consequently, the recording and revealing duties of the two kindred media coincide only in part. And what do they imply for film in particular? The hunting ground of the motion picture camera is in principle unlimited; it is the external world expanding in all directions. Yet there are certain subjects within that world which may be termed "cinematic" because they seem to exert a peculiar attraction on the medium. It is as if the medium were predestined (and eager) to exhibit them. The following pages are devoted to a close examination of these cinematic subjects. Several lie, so to speak, on the surface; they will be dealt with under the title "recording functions." Others would hardly come to our attention or be perceptible were it not for the film camera and/or the intervention of cinematic techniques; they will be discussed in the subsequent section "revealing functions." To be sure, any camera revelation involves recording, but recording on its part need not be revealing.

RECORDING FUNCTIONS

Movement

At least two groups of quite common external phenomena are naturals for the screen. As might be expected, one is made up of all kinds of movements, these being cinematic because only the motion picture camera is able to record them. Among them are three types which can be considered cinematic subjects par excellence.

The Chase

"The chase," says Hitchcock, "seems to me the final expression of the motion picture medium." This complex of interrelated movements is motion at its extreme, one might almost say, motion as such—and of course it is immensely serviceable for establishing a continuity of suspenseful physical action. Hence the fascination the chase has held since the beginning of the century. The primitive French comedies availed themselves of it to frame their space-devouring adventures. Gendarmes pursued a dog who eventually turned the tables on them *(Course des sergeants de ville);* pumpkins gliding from a cart were chased by the grocer, his donkey, and passers-by through sewers and over roofs (*La Course des potirons, 1907;* English title: *The Pumpkin Race*). For any Keystone comedy to forgo the chase would have been an unpardonable crime. It was the climax of the whole, its orgiastic finale—a pandemonium, with onrushing trains telescoping into automobiles and narrow escapes down ropes that dangled above a lion's den.

But perhaps nothing reveals the cinematic significance of this reveling in speed more drastically than D. W. Griffith's determination to transfer, at the end of all his great films, the action from the ideological plane to that of his famous "last-minute rescue," which was a chase pure and simple. Or should one say, a race? In any case, the rescuers rush ahead to overwhelm the villains or free their victims at the very last moment, while simultaneously the inner emotion which the dramatic conflict has aroused yields to a state of acute physiological suspense called forth by exuberant physical motion and its immediate implications. Nor is a genuine Western imaginable without a pursuit or a race on horseback. As Flaherty put it, Westerns are popular "because people never get tired of seeing a horse gallop across the plains." Its gallop seems still to gain momentum by contrast with the immense tranquility of the far-away horizon.

Dancing

The second type of specifically cinematic movement is dancing. This does not apply, of course, to the stage ballet which evolves in a space-time outside actuality proper. Interestingly enough, all

attempts at "canning" it adequately have so far failed. Screen reproductions of theatrical dancing either indulge in a completeness
which is boring or offer a selection of attractive details which confuse in that they dismember rather than preserve the original. Dancing attains to cinematic eminence only if it is part and parcel of
physical reality. René Clair's early sound films have judiciously
been called ballets. True, they are, but the performers are real-life
Parisians who just cannot help executing dance movements when
going about their love adventures and minor quarrels. With infinite
subtlety Clair guides them along the divide between the real and
unreal. Sometimes it appears as though these delivery boys, taxi
drivers, girls, clerks, shopkeepers, and nondescript figures are mari-
onettes banding together and parting from each other according to
designs as delicate as lacework; and then again they are made to
look and behave like ordinary people in Paris streets and bistros.
And the latter impression prevails. For, even granted that they are
drawn into an imaginary universe, this universe itself reflects
throughout our real world in stylizing it. What dancing there is,
seems to occur on the spur of the moment; it is the vicissitudes of
life from which these ballets issue.

Fred Astaire too prefers apparent impromptu performances to
stage choreography; he is quite aware that this type of performance
is appropriate to the medium. "Each dance," says he, "ought to
spring somehow out of character or situation, otherwise it is simply
a vaudeville act." This does not mean that he would dispense with
theatrical production numbers. But no sooner does he perform in
vaudeville fashion than he breaks out of the prison of prearranged
stage patterns and, with a genius for improvisation, dances over
tables and gravel paths into the everyday world. It is a one-way
route which invariably leads from the footlights to the heart of
camera-reality. Astaire's consummate dancing is meant to belong
among the real-life events with which he toys in his musicals; and
it is so organized that it imperceptibly emerges from, and disappears, in the flow of these happenings. . . .

Nascent Motion

The third type of motion which offers special interest cinematically is not just another group of interrelated movements but movement as contrasted with motionlessness. In focusing upon this contrast, films strikingly demonstrate that objective movement—any

movement, for that matter—is one of their choice subjects. Alexander Dovzhenko in both *Arsenal* and *Earth* frequently stops the action to resume it after a short lull. The first phase of this procedure—characters or parts of them abruptly ceasing to move—produces a shock effect, as if all of a sudden we found ourselves in a vacuum. The immediate consequence is that we acutely realize the significance of movement as an integral element of the external world as well as film.

But this is only part of the story. Even though the moving images on the screen come to a standstill, the thrust of their movement is too powerful to be discontinued simultaneously. Accordingly, when the people in *Arsenal* or *Earth* are shown in the form of stills, the suspended movement nevertheless perpetuates itself by changing from outer motion into inner motion. Dovzhenko has known how to make this metamorphosis benefit his penetrations of reality. The immobile lovers in *Earth* become transparent; the deep happiness which is moving them turns inside out. And the spectator on his part grasps their inward agitation because the cessation of external motion moves him all the more intensely to commune with them. Yet despite these rewarding experiences he cannot help feeling a certain relief when eventually the characters take on life again —an event which marks the second and final phase of the procedure. It is a return to the world of film, whose inherent motion alone renders possible such excursions into the whirlpool of the motionless. . . .

Inanimate Objects

Since the inanimate is featured in many paintings, one might question the legitimacy of characterizing it as a cinematic subject. Yet it is a painter—Fernand Léger—who judiciously insists that only film is equipped to sensitize us, by way of big close-ups, to the possibilities that lie dormant in a hat, a chair, a hand, and a foot. Similarly Cohen-Séat: "And I? says the leaf which is falling.—And we? say the orange peel, the gust of wind. . . . Film, whether intentionally or not, is their mouthpiece." Nor should it be forgotten that the camera's ability to single out and record the orange peel or the hand marks a decisive difference between screen and stage, so close to each other in some respects. Stage imagery inevitably centers on the actor, whereas film is free to dwell on parts of his appearance and detail the objects about him. In using its freedom to bring the inanimate to the fore and make it a carrier of action, film only protests its peculiar requirement to explore all of physical existence, human or nonhuman. Within this context it is of interest that in the early 'twenties, when the French cinema was swamped with theatrical adaptations and stage-minded dramas, Louis Delluc tried to put the medium on its own feet by stressing the tremendous importance of objects. If they are assigned the role due to them, he argued, the actor too "is no more than a detail, a fragment of the matter of the world."

Actually, the urge to raise hats and chairs to the status of full-fledged actors has never completely atrophied. From the malicious escalators, the unruly Murphy beds, and the mad automobiles in silent comedy to the cruiser Potemkin, the oil derrick in *Louisiana Story* and the dilapidated kitchen in *Umberto D.*, a long procession of unforgettable objects has passed across the screen—objects which stand out as protagonists and all but overshadow the rest of the cast. Or remember the powerful presence of environmental influences in *The Grapes of Wrath*, the part played by nocturnal Coney Island in *Little Fugitive*, the interaction between the marshland and the guerilla fighters in the last episode of *Paisan*. Of course, the reverse holds true also: films in which the inanimate merely serves as a background to self-contained dialogue and the closed circuit of human relationships are essentially uncinematic.

REVEALING FUNCTIONS

"I ask that a film *discover* something for me" declares Luis Buñuel, who is himself a fiery pathfinder of the screen. And what are films likely to discover? The evidence available suggests that they assume three kinds of revealing functions. They tend to reveal things normally unseen; phenomena overwhelming consciousness; and certain aspects of the outer world which may be called "special modes of reality."

Things Normally Unseen

The many material phenomena which elude observation under normal circumstances can be divided into three groups. The first includes objects too small to be readily noticed or even perceived by the naked eye and objects so big that they will not be fully taken in either.

The Small and the Big

The small. The small is conveyed in the form of close-ups. D. W. Griffith was among the first to realize that they are indispensable for cinematic narration. He initiated their use, as we now know it, in *After Many Years* (1908), an adaptation of Tennyson's *Enoch Arden*. There his memorable first close-up appeared within contexts which Lewis Jacobs describes as follows: "Going further than he had ventured before, in a scene showing Annie Lee brooding and waiting for her husband's return, Griffith daringly used a large close-up of her face. . . . He had another surprise, even more radical, to offer. Immediately following the close-up of Annie, he inserted a picture of the object of her thoughts—her husband cast away on a desert isle."

On the surface, this succession of shots seems simply designed to lure the spectator into the dimension of her intimate preoccupations. He first watches Annie from a distance and then approaches her so closely that he sees only her face; if he moves on in the same direction, as the film invites him to do, it is logical that he should penetrate Annie's appearance and land inside her mind. Granting the validity of this interpretation, the close-up of her face is not an end in itself; rather, along with the subsequent shots, it serves to suggest what is going on behind that face—Annie's longing for reunion with her husband. A knowingly chosen detail of her physique thus would help establish the whole of her being in a dramatic interest.

The same obviously holds true of another famous Griffith close-up: Mae Marsh's clasped hands in the trial episode of *Intolerance*. It almost looks as if her huge hands with the convulsively moving fingers were inserted for the sole purpose of illustrating eloquently her anguish at the most crucial moment of the trial; as if, generally speaking, the function of any such detail exhausted itself in intensifying our participation in the total situation. This is how Eisenstein conceives of the close-up. Its main function, says he, is "not so much to *show* or to *present* as to *signify*, to *give meaning*, to *designate*." To designate what? Evidently something of importance to the narrative. And montage-minded as he is, he immediately adds that the significance of the close-up for the plot accrues to it less from its own content than from the manner in which it is juxtaposed with the surrounding shots. According to him, the close-up is primarily a montage unit.

But is this really its only function? Consider again the combination of shots with the close-up of Annie's face: the place assigned to the latter in the sequence intimates that Griffith wanted us also to absorb the face for its own sake instead of just passing through and beyond it; the face appears before the desires and emotions to which it refers have been completely defined, thus tempting us to get lost in its puzzling indeterminacy. Annie's face is also an end in itself. And so is the image of Mae Marsh's hands. No doubt it is to impress upon us her inner condition, but besides making us experience what we would in a measure have experienced anyway because of our familiarity with the characters involved, this close-up contributes something momentous and unique—it reveals how her hands behave under the impact of utter despair.

Eisenstein criticizes the close-ups in Griffith films precisely for their relative independence of the contexts in which they occur. He calls them isolated units which tend "to show or to present"; and he insists that to the extent that they indulge in isolation they fail to yield the meanings which the interweaving processes of montage may elicit from them. Had Eisenstein been less possessed with the magic powers of montage he would certainly have acknowledged the cinematic superiority of the Griffith close-up. To Griffith such huge images of small material phenomena are not only integral components of the narrative but disclosures of new aspects of physical reality. In representing them the way he does, he seems to have been guided by the conviction that the cinema is all the more cinematic if it acquaints us with the physical origins, ramifications, and connotations of all the emotional and intellectual events which comprise the plot; that it cannot adequately account for these inner developments unless it leads us through the thicket of material life from which they emerge and in which they are embedded. . . .

The big. Among the large objects, such as vast plains or panoramas of any kind, one deserves special attention: the masses. No doubt imperial Rome already teemed with them. But masses of people in the modern sense entered the historical scene only in the wake of the industrial revolution. Then they became a social force of first magnitude. Warring nations resorted to levies on an unheard-of scale and identifiable groups yielded to the anonymous multitude which filled the big cities in the form of amorphous crowds. Walter Benjamin observes that in the period marked by the rise of photography the daily sight of moving crowds was still a spectacle to which eyes and nerves had to get adjusted. The testimony of sensitive contemporaries would seem to corroborate this sagacious observation: The Paris crowds omnipresent in Baudelaire's *Les Fleurs du mal* function as stimuli which call forth irritating kaleidoscopic sensations; the jostling and shoving passers-by who, in Poe's *Man of the Crowd*, throng gas-lit London provoke a succession of electric shocks.

At the time of its emergence the mass, this giant animal, was a new and upsetting experience. As might be expected, the traditional arts proved unable to encompass and render it. Where they failed, photography easily succeeded; it was technically equipped to portray crowds as the accidental agglomerations they are. Yet only film, the fulfillment of photography in a sense, was equal to the task of capturing them in motion. In this case the instrument of reproduction came into being almost simultaneously with one of its main subjects. Hence the attraction which masses exerted on still and motion picture cameras from the outset. It is certainly more than sheer coincidence that the very first Lumière films featured a crowd of workers and the confusion of arrival and departure at a railway station. Early Italian films elaborated upon the theme; and D. W. Griffith, inspired by them, showed how masses can be represented cinematically. The Russians absorbed his lesson, applying it in ways of their own. . . .

The Transient

The second group of things normally unseen comprises the transient. Here belong, first, fleeting impressions—"the shadow of a cloud passing across the plain, a leaf which yields to the wind." Evanescent, like dream elements, such impressions may haunt the moviegoer long after the story they are called upon to implement has sunk into oblivion. The manes of the galloping horses— flying threads or streamers rather than manes—in the chariot race episode of Fred Niblo's *Ben Hur* are as unforgettable as the fiery

177

traces of the projectiles that tear the night in *Desert Victory*. The motion picture camera seems to be partial to the least permanent components of our environment. It may be anticipated that the street in the broadest sense of the word is a place where impressions of this kind are bound to occur. "The cinema," says Aragon, delighting in its snapshot-like predilection for the ephemeral, "has taught us more about man in a few years than centuries of painting have taught: fugitive expressions, attitudes scarcely credible yet real, charm and hideousness"

Second, there are movements of so transitory a nature that they would be imperceptible were it not for two cinematic techniques: accelerated-motion, which condenses extremely slow and, hence, unobservable developments, such as the growth of plants, and slow-motion, which expands movements too fast to be registered. Like the big close-up, these correlated techniques lead straight into "reality of another dimension." Pictures of stalks piercing the soil in the process of growing open up imaginary areas, and racing legs shown in slow-motion do not just slow down but change in appearance and perform bizarre evolutions—patterns remote from reality as we know it. Slow-motion shots parallel the regular close-ups; they are, so to speak, temporal close-ups achieving in time what the close-up proper is achieving in space. That, unlike the latter, they are used rather infrequently, may be traced to the fact that the enlargement of spatial phenomena, as effected by the close-up, seems more "natural" to us than the expansion of a given time interval. (On the other hand, it appears that film makers draw more readily on slow-motion than on the reverse technique— perhaps simply because it does not require so lengthy preparations.)

As contrived-reality pictures, the deviant images gained by both techniques, especially slow-motion, may well figure in nonrealistic experimental films. Yet they live up to the cinematic approach only if they are made to fulfill a revealing function within contexts focusing on physical existence. The late Jean Epstein, who felt so immensely attracted by "reality of another dimension," considered this their true destination. Referring to waves in slow-motion and clouds in accelerated-motion, he declared that for all their "startling physics and strange mechanics" they "are but a portrait—seen in a certain perspective—of the world in which we live."

178

Blind Spots of the Mind

The third and last group of things normally unseen consists of phenomena which figure among the blind spots of the mind; habit and prejudice prevent us from noticing them. The role which cultural standards and traditions may play in these processes of elimination is drastically illustrated by a report on the reactions of African natives to a film made on the spot. After the screening the spectators, all of them still unacquainted with the medium, talked volubly about a chicken they allegedly had seen picking food in the mud. The film maker himself, entirely unaware of its presence, attended several performances without being able to detect it. Had it been dreamed up by the natives? Only by scanning his film foot by foot did he eventually succeed in tracing the chicken: it appeared for a fleeting moment somewhere in a corner of a picture and then vanished forever.

The following types of objects are cinematic because they stubbornly escape our attention in everyday life.

Unconventional complexes. Film may bare real-life complexes which the conventional figure-ground patterns usually conceal from view. Imagine a man in a room: accustomed as we are to visualize the human figure as a whole, it would take us an enormous effort to perceive instead of the whole man a pictorial unit consisting, say, of his right shoulder and arm, fragments of furniture and a section of the wall. But this is exactly what photography and, more powerfully, film may make us see. The motion picture camera has a way of disintegrating familiar objects and bringing to the fore—often just in moving about—previously invisible interrelationships between parts of them. These newly arising complexes lurk behind the things known and cut across their easily identifiable contexts. *Jazz Dance*, for instance, abounds with shots of ensembles built from human torsos, clothes, scattered legs, and what not—shapes which are almost anonymous. In rendering physical existence, film tends to reveal configurations of semi-abstract phenomena. Sometimes these textures take on an ornamental character. In the Nazi propaganda film *Triumph of the Will* moving banners fuse into a very beautiful pattern at the moment when they begin to fill the screen.

The refuse. Many objects remain unnoticed simply because it never occurs to us to look their way. Most people turn their backs on garbage cans, the dirt underfoot, the waste they leave behind. Films have no such inhibitions; on the contrary, what we ordinarily prefer to ignore proves attractive to them precisely because of this common neglect. Ruttmann's *Berlin* includes a wealth of sewer grates, gutters, and streets littered with rubbish; and Cavalcanti in his *Rien que les heures* is hardly less garbage-minded. To be sure, shots in this vein may be required by the action, but intrigues inspired by a sense of the medium are often so devised that they offer the camera ample opportunity to satisfy its inborn curiosity and function as a rag-picker; think of the old silent comedies — e.g. Chaplin's *A Dog's Life* — or pictures which involve crime, war, or misery. Since sights of refuse are particularly impressive after spectacles extolling the joy of living, film makers have repeatedly capitalized on the contrast between glamorous festivities and their dreary aftermath. You see a banquet on the screen and then, when everybody has gone, you are made to linger for a moment and stare at the crumpled tablecloth, the half-emptied glasses, and the unappetizing dishes. The classical American gangster films indulged in this effect. *Scarface* opens on a restaurant at dawn, with the remnants of the nocturnal orgy strewn over floors and tables; and after the gangsters' ball in Sternberg's *Underworld* Bancroft totters through a maze of confetti and streamers left over from the feast.

The familiar. Nor do we perceive the familiar. It is not as if we shrank from it, as we do in the case of refuse; we just take it for granted without giving it a thought. Intimate faces, streets we walk day by day, the house we live in — all these things are part of us like our skin, and because we know them by heart we do not know them with the eye. Once integrated into our existence, they cease to be objects of perception, goals to be attained. In fact, we would be immobilized if we focused on them. This is confirmed by a common experience. A man entering his room will immediately feel disturbed if during his absence something has been changed in it. But in order to find out about the cause of his uneasiness he must discontinue his routine occupations; only in deliberately scrutinizing, and thus estranging, the room will he be able to discover what it actually is that has been changed. Proust's narrator is acutely aware of this very estrangement when he suddenly sees his grandmother not as he always believed her to be but as she really is or at least as she would appear to a stranger—a snapshot likeness severed from his dreams and memories.

Films make us undergo similar experiences a thousand times. They alienate our environment in exposing it. One ever-recurrent film scene runs as follows: Two or more people are conversing with each other. In the middle of their talk the camera, as if entirely indifferent to it, slowly pans through the room, inviting us to watch the faces of the listeners and various furniture pieces in a detached spirit. Whatever this may mean within the given context, it invariably dissolves a well-known total situation and thereby confronts the spectator with isolated phenomena which he previously neglected or overlooked as matter-of-course components of that situation. As the camera pans, curtains become eloquent and eyes tell a story of their own. The way leads toward the unfamiliar in the familiar. How often do we not come across shots of street corners, buildings, and landscapes with which we were acquainted all our life; we naturally recognize them and yet it is as if they were virgin impressions emerging from the abyss of nearness. The opening sequence of Vigo's *Zéro de conduite* shows two boys traveling back to school by train. Is it just an ordinary night trip? Vigo manages to transform a familiar railway compartment into a magic wigwam in which the two, drunk from their boasts and pranks, are floating through the air.

This transformation is partly achieved with the aid of a device, both photographic and cinematic, which deserves some attention— the use of uncommon camera angles. Vigo occasionally represents the railway compartment slantwise and from below so that the whole room seems to drift along in the haze from the cigars which the high-strung schoolboys are smoking, while little toy balloons hover to and fro before their pale faces. Proust knew about the alienating effect of this device. After having mentioned that certain photographs of scenery and towns are called "admirable," he continues: "If we press for a definition of what their admirers mean by that epithet, we shall find that it is generally applied to some unusual picture of a familar object, a picture different from those that we are accustomed to see, unusual and yet true to nature, and for that reason doubly impressive because it startles us, makes us emerge from our habits, and at the same time brings us back to ourselves by recalling to us an earlier impression." And to concretize

181

this definition, he refers to the picture of a cathedral which does not render it as it is normally seen—namely, in the middle of the town—but is taken from a point of view from which the building "will appear thirty times the height of the houses." . . .

Phenomena Overwhelming Consciousness

Elemental catastrophes, the atrocities of war, acts of violence and terror, sexual debauchery, and death are events which tend to overwhelm consciousness. In any case, they call forth excitements and agonies bound to thwart detached observation. No one witnessing such an event, let alone playing an active part in it, should therefore be expected accurately to account for what he has seen. Since these manifestations of crude nature, human or otherwise, fall into the area of physical reality, they range all the more among the cinematic subjects. Only the camera is able to represent them without distortion.

Actually the medium has always shown a predilection for events of this type. There is practically no newsreel that would not indulge in the ravages of an inundation, a hurricane, an airplane crash, or whatever catastrophe happens to be at hand. The same applies to feature films. One of the first film strips ever made was *The Execution of Mary Queen of Scots* (1895); the executioner cuts off her head and then holds it in his uplifted hand so that no spectator can possibly avoid looking at the frightful exhibit. Pornographic motifs also emerged at a very early date. The path of the cinema is beset with films reveling in disasters and nightmarish incidents. Suffice it to pick out, at random, the war horrors in Dovzhenko's *Arsenal* and Pabst's *Westfront 1918;* the terrible execution sequence at the end of *Thunder over Mexico*, a film based on Eisenstein's Mexican material; the earthquake in *San Francisco;* the torture episode in Rossellini's *Open City;* the depiction of a Polish Nazi concentration camp in *The Last Stop;* the scene with the young hoodlums wantonly mistreating a blind man in Buñuel's *Los Olvidados*.

Because of its sustained concern with all that is dreadful and off limits, the medium has frequently been accused of a penchant for cheap sensationalism. What lends support to this verdict is the indisputable fact that films have a habit of dwelling on the sensational much longer than any moral purpose would seem to justify;

182

it often is as if that purpose served merely as a pretext for rendering a savage murder or the like.

In defense of the medium one might argue that it would not be the mass medium it is if it failed to provide stunning sensations; and that, in offering them, it only follows a venerable tradition. Since time immemorial, people have craved spectacles permitting them vicariously to experience the fury of conflagrations, the excesses of cruelty and suffering, and unspeakable lusts—spectacles which shock the shuddering and delighted onlooker into unseeing participation.

Yet this argument misses the point. The point is, rather, that the cinema does not simply imitate and continue the ancient gladiator fights or the *Grand Guignol* but adds something new and momentous: it insists on rendering visible what is commonly drowned in inner agitation. Of course, such revelations conform all the more to the cinematic approach if they bear on actual catastrophes and horrors. In deliberately detailing feats of sadism in their films, Rossellini and Buñuel force the spectator to take in these appalling sights and at the same time impress them on him as real-life events recorded by the imperturbable camera. Similarly, besides trying to put across their propaganda messages, the Russian films of the 'twenties convey to us the paroxysmal upheavals of real masses which, because of their emotional *and* spatial enormity, depend doubly upon cinematic treatment to be perceptible.

The cinema, then, aims at transforming the agitated witness into a conscious observer. Nothing could be more legitimate than its lack of inhibitions in picturing spectacles which upset the mind. Thus it keeps us from shutting our eyes to the "blind drive of things."

Special Modes of Reality

Finally films may expose physical reality as it appears to individuals in extreme states of mind generated by such events as we have mentioned, mental disturbances, or any other external or internal causes. Supposing such a state of mind is provoked by an act of violence, then the camera often aspires to render the images which an emotionally upset witness or participant will form of it. These images also belong among the cinematic subjects. They are distorted from the viewpoint of a detached observer; and they differ from each other according to the varying states of mind in which they originate.

In his *Ten Days That Shook the World*, for instance, Eisenstein composes a physical universe reflecting exultation. This episode runs as follows: At the beginning of the October Revolution, worker delegates succeed in bringing a contingent of Cossacks over to their side; the Cossacks put their half-drawn swords with the ornamented pommels back into their sheaths, and then the two groups boisterously fraternize in a state of euphoria. The ensuing dance scene is represented in the form of an accelerated montage sequence which pictures the world as experienced by the overjoyed. In their great joy, dancers and onlookers who constantly mingle cannot help perceiving incoherent pieces of their immediate environment in motion. It is a whirling agglomerate of fragments that surrounds them. And Eisenstein captures this jumble to perfection by having follow each other — in a succession which becomes ever faster with the growing ecstasy — shots of Cossack boots executing the *krakoviak*, worker legs dancing through a puddle, clapping hands, and faces inordinately broadened by laughter.

In the world of a panic-stricken individual laughter yields to grimacing and dazzling confusion to fearful rigidity. At any rate, this is how Ernö Metzner conceived of that world in his *Ueberfall*. Its "hero" is a wretched little fellow who gets a lucky break thanks to a coin he furtively picks up in the street and then stakes in a crap game. As he walks away with his wallet stuffed, a thug follows him at a steadily diminishing distance. The man is scared. No sooner does he take to his heels than all the objects about him make common cause with his pursuer. The dark railway underpass turns into a sinister trap; frozen threats, the dilapidated slum houses close ranks and stare at him. (It is noteworthy that these effects are largely due to accomplished photography.) Temporarily saved by a streetwalker, who puts him up in her room, the man knows that the thug continues to lie in wait for him down in the street. The curtain moves, and he feels that the room itself harbors dangers. There is no escape wherever he looks. He looks into the mirror: what shines out of it are distorted reflections of his mask-like features.

BÉLA BALÁZS
FROM THEORY OF THE FILM

THE CLOSE-UP

THE FACE OF THINGS

The first new world discovered by the film camera in the days of the silent film was the world of very small things visible only from very short distances, the hidden life of little things. By this the camera showed us not only hitherto unknown objects and events: the adventures of beetles in a wilderness of blades of grass, the tragedies of day-old chicks in a corner of the poultry-run, the erotic battles of flowers and the poetry of miniature landscapes. It brought us not only new themes. By means of the close-up the camera in the days of the silent film revealed also the hidden mainsprings of a life which we had thought we already knew so well. Blurred outlines are mostly the result of our insensitive shortsightedness and superficiality. We skim over the teeming substance of life. The camera has uncovered that cell-life of the vital issues in which all great events are ultimately conceived; for the greatest landslide is only the aggregate of the movements of single particles. A multitude of close-ups can show us the very instant in which the general is transformed into the particular. The close-up has not only widened our vision of life, it has also deepened it. In the days of the silent film it not only revealed new things, but showed us the meaning of the old.

VISUAL LIFE

The close-up can show us a quality in a gesture of the hand we never noticed before when we saw that hand stroke or strike something, a quality which is often more expressive than any play of the features. The close-up shows your shadow on the wall with which you have lived all your life and which you scarcely knew; it shows the speechless face and fate of the dumb objects that live with you in your room and whose fate is bound up with your own. Before this you looked at your life as a concert-goer ignorant of music listens to an orchestra playing a symphony. All he hears is the leading melody, all the rest is blurred into a general murmur. Only those can really understand and enjoy the music who can hear the contrapuntal architecture of each part in the score. This is how we see life: only its leading melody meets the eye. But a good film with its close-ups reveals the most hidden parts in our polyphonous life, and teaches us to see the intricate visual details of life as one reads an orchestral score.

LYRICAL CHARM OF THE CLOSE-UP

The close-up may sometimes give the impression of a mere naturalist preoccupation with detail. But good close-ups radiate a tender human attitude in the contemplation of hidden things, a delicate solicitude, a gentle bending over the intimacies of life-in-the-miniature, a warm sensibility. Good close-ups are lyrical; it is the heart, not the eye, that has perceived them.

Close-ups are often dramatic revelations of what is really happening under the surface of appearances. You may see a medium shot of someone sitting and conducting a conversation with icy calm. The close-up will show trembling fingers nervously fumbling a small object—sign of an internal storm. Among pictures of a comfortable house breathing a sunny security, we suddenly see the evil grin of a vicious head on the carved mantelpiece or the menacing grimace of a door opening into darkness. Like the *leitmotif* of impending fate in an opera, the shadow of some impending disaster falls across the cheerful scene.

Close-ups are the pictures expressing the poetic sensibility of the director. They show the faces of things and those expressions on them which are significant because they are reflected expressions of our own subconscious feeling. Herein lies the art of the true cameraman.

In a very old American film I saw this dramatic scene: the bride at the altar suddenly runs away from the bridegroom whom she

186

detests, who is rich and who has been forced on her. As she rushes away she must pass through a large room full of wedding presents. Beautiful things, good things, useful things, things radiating plenty and security smile at her and lean towards her with expressive faces. And there are the presents given by the bridegroom: faces of things radiating touching attention, consideration, tenderness, love— and they all seem to be looking at the fleeing bride, because she looks at them; all seem to stretch out hands towards her, because she feels they do so. There are ever more of them—they crowd the room and block her path—her flight slows down more and more, then she stops and finally turns back. . . .

Having discovered the soul of things in the close-up, the silent film undeniably overrated their importance and sometimes succumbed to the temptation of showing "the hidden little life" as an end in itself, divorced from human destinies; it strayed away from the dramatic plot and presented the "poetry of things" instead of human beings. But what Lessing said in his *Laokoon* about Homer—that he never depicted anything but human actions and always described objects only inasmuch as they took part in the action—should to this day serve as a model for all epic and dramatic art as long as it centres around the presentation of man.

THE FACE OF MAN

Every art always deals with human beings, it is a human manifestation and presents human beings. To paraphrase Marx: "The root of all art is man." When the film close-up strips the veil of our imperceptiveness and insensitivity from the hidden little things and shows us the face of objects, it still shows us man, for what makes objects expressive are the human expressions projected on to them. The objects only reflect our own selves, and this is what distinguished art from scientific knowledge (although even the latter is to a great extent subjectively determined). When we see the face of things, we do what the ancients did in creating *gods* in man's image and breathing a human soul into them. The close-ups of the film are the creative instruments of this mighty visual anthropomorphism.

What was more important, however, than the discovery of the

physiognomy of things, was the discovery of the human face. Facial expression is the most subjective manifestation of man, more subjective even than speech, for vocabulary and grammar are subject to more or less universally valid rules and conventions, while the play of features, as has already been said, is a manifestation not governed by objective canons, even though it is largely a matter of imitation. This most subjective and individual of human manifestations is rendered objective in the close-up.

A NEW DIMENSION

If the close-up lifts some object or some part of an object out of its surroundings, we nevertheless perceive it as existing in space; we do not for an instant forget that the hand, say, which is shown by the close-up, belongs to some human being. It is precisely this connection which lends meaning to its every movement. But when Griffith's genius and daring first projected gigantic "severed heads" on to the cinema screen, he not only brought the human face closer to us in space, he also transposed it from space into another dimension. We do not mean, of course, the cinema screen and the patches of light and shadow moving across it, which being visible things, can be conceived only in space; we mean the expression on the face as revealed by the close-up. We have said that the isolated hand would lose its meaning, its expression, if we did not know and imagine its connection with some human being. The facial expression on a face is complete and comprehensible in itself and therefore we need not think of it as existing in space and time. Even if we had just seen the same face in the middle of a crowd and the close-up merely separated it from the others, we would still feel that we have suddenly been left alone with this one face to the exclusion of the rest of the world. Even if we have just seen the owner of the face in a long shot, when we look into the eyes in a close-up, we no longer think of that wide space, because the expression and significance of the face has no relation to space and no connection with it. Facing an isolated face takes us out of space, our consciousness of space is cut out and we find ourselves in another dimension: that of physiognomy. The fact that the features of the face can be seen side by side, i.e. in space—that the eyes are at the top, the ears at the sides and the mouth lower down—loses all reference to space when we see, not a figure of flesh and bone, but an expression, or in other words when we see emotions, moods, intentions and thoughts, things which although our eyes can see them, are not in space. For feelings, emotions, moods, intentions, thoughts are not themselves things pertaining to space, even if they are rendered visible by means which are.

MELODY AND PHYSIOGNOMY

We will be helped in understanding this peculiar dimension by Henri Bergson's analysis of time and duration. A melody, said Bergson, is composed of single notes which follow each other in sequence, i.e. in time. Nevertheless a melody has no dimension in time, because the first note is made an element of the melody only because it refers to the next note and because it stands in a definite relation to all other notes down to the last. Hence the last note, which may not be played for some time, is yet already present in the first note as a melody-creating element. And the last note completes the melody only because we hear the first note along with it. The notes sound one after the other in a time-sequence, hence they have a real duration, but the coherent line of melody has no dimension in time; the relation of the notes to each other is not a phenomenon occurring in time. The melody is not born gradually in the course of time but is already in existence as a complete entity as soon as the first note is played. How else would we know that a melody is begun? The single notes have duration in time, but their relation to each other, which gives meaning to the individual sounds, is outside time. A logical deduction also has its sequence, but premise and conclusion do not follow one another in time. The process of thinking as a psychological process may have duration; but the logical forms, like melodies, do not belong to the dimension of time.

Now facial expression, physiognomy, has a relation to space similar to the relation of melody to time. The single features, of course, appear in space; but the significance of their relation to one another is not a phenomenon pertaining to space, no more than are the emotions, thoughts and ideas which are manifested in the facial expressions we see. They are picture-like and yet they seem outside space; such is the psychological effect of facial expression.

189

SILENT SOLILOQUY

The modern stage no longer uses the spoken soliloquy, although without it the characters are silenced just when they are the most sincere, the least hampered by convention: when they are alone. The public of to-day will not tolerate the spoken soliloquy, allegedly because it is "unnatural." Now the film has brought us the silent soliloquy, in which a face can speak with the subtlest shades of meaning without appearing unnatural and arousing the distaste of the spectators. In this silent monologue the solitary human soul can find a tongue more candid and uninhibited than in any spoken soliloquy, for it speaks instinctively, subconsciously. The language of the face cannot be suppressed or controlled. However disciplined and practisedly hypocritical a face may be, in the enlarging close-up we see even that it is concealing something, that it is looking a lie. For such things have their own specific expressions superposed on the feigned one. It is much easier to lie in words than with the face and the film has proved it beyond doubt.

In the film the mute soliloquy of the face speaks even when the hero is not alone, and herein lies a new great opportunity for depicting man. The poetic significance of the soliloquy is that it is a manifestation of mental, not physical, loneliness. Nevertheless, on the stage a character can speak a monologue only when there is no one else there, even though a character might feel a thousand times more lonely if alone among a large crowd. The monologue of loneliness may raise its voice within him a hundred times even while he is audibly talking to someone. Hence the most deep-felt human soliloquies could not find expression on the stage. Only the film can offer the possibility of such expression, for the close-up can lift a character out of the heart of the greatest crowd and show how solitary it is in reality and what it feels in this crowded solitude.

The film, especially the sound film, can separate the words of a character talking to others from the mute play of features by means of which, in the middle of such a conversation, we are made to overhear a mute soliloquy and realize the difference between this soliloquy and the audible conversation. What a flesh-and-blood actor can show on the real stage is at most that his words are insincere and it is a mere convention that the partner in such a conversation is blind to what every spectator can see. But in the isolated close-up of the film we can see to the bottom of a soul by means of such tiny movements of facial muscles which even the most observant partner would never perceive.

A novelist can, of course, write a dialogue so as to weave into it what the speakers think to themselves while they are talking. But by so doing he splits up the sometimes comic, sometimes tragic, but always awe-inspiring, unity between spoken word and hidden thought with which this contradiction is rendered manifest in the human face and which the film was the first to show us in all its dazzling variety.

"POLYPHONIC" PLAY OF FEATURES

The film first made possible what, for lack of a better description, I call the "polyphonic" play of features. By it I mean the appearance on the same face of contradictory expressions. In a sort of physiognomic chord a variety of feelings, passions and thoughts are synthesized in the play of the features as an adequate expression of the multiplicity of the human soul.

Asta Nielsen once played a woman hired to seduce a rich young man. The man who hired her is watching the results from behind a curtain. Knowing that she is under observation, Asta Nielsen feigns love. She does it convincingly: the whole gamut of appropriate emotion is displayed in her face. Nevertheless we are aware that it is only play-acting, that it is a sham, a mask. But in the course of the scene Asta Nielsen really falls in love with the young man. Her facial expression shows little change; she had been "registering" love all the time and done it well. How else could she now show that this time she was really in love? Her expression changes only by a scarcely perceptible and yet immediately obvious nuance— and what a few minutes before was a sham is now the sincere expression of a deep emotion. Then Asta Nielsen suddenly remembers that she is under observation. The man behind the curtain must not be allowed to read her face and learn that she is now no longer feigning, but really feeling love. So Asta now pretends to be pretending. Her face shows a new, by this time threefold, change. First she feigns love, then she genuinely shows love, and as she is not permitted to be in love in good earnest, her face again registers a sham, a pretence of love. But now it is this pretence that is a lie. Now she is lying that she is lying. And we can see all this clearly in her face, over which she has drawn two different masks. At such times an invisible face appears in front of the real one, just as spoken words can by association of ideas conjure up things unspoken and unseen, perceived only by those to whom they are addressed.

In the early days of the silent film Griffith showed a scene of this character. The hero of the film is a Chinese merchant. Lillian Gish, playing a beggar-girl who is being pursued by enemies, collapses at his door. The Chinese merchant finds her, carries her into his house and looks after the sick girl. The girl slowly recovers, but her face remains stone-like in its sorrow. "Can't you smile?" the Chinese asks the frightened child who is only just beginning to trust him. "I'll try," says Lillian Gish, picks up a mirror and goes through the motions of a smile, aiding her face muscles with her fingers. The result is a painful, even horrible mask which the girl now turns towards the Chinese merchant. But his kindly friendly eyes bring a real smile to her face. The face itself does not change; but a warm emotion lights it up from inside and an intangible nuance turns the grimace into a real expression.

In the days of the silent film such a close-up provided an entire scene. A good idea of the director and a fine performance on the part of the actor gave as a result an interesting, moving, new experience for the audience.

MICROPHYSIOGNOMY

In the silent film facial expression, isolated from its surroundings, seemed to penetrate to a strange new dimension of the soul. It revealed to us a new world—the world of microphysiognomy which could not otherwise be seen with the naked eye or in everyday life. In the sound film the part played by this 'microphysiognomy' has greatly diminished because it is now apparently possible to express in words much of what facial expression apparently showed. But it is never the same—many profound emotional experiences can never be expressed in words at all.

Not even the greatest writer, the most consummate artist of the pen, could tell in words what Asta Nielsen tells with her face in close-up as she sits down to her mirror and tries to make up for the last time her aged, wrinkled face, raddled with poverty, misery, disease and prostitution, when she is expecting her lover, released after ten years in jail; a lover who has retained his youth in captivity because life could not touch him there.

ASTA AT THE MIRROR

She looks into the mirror, her face pale and deadly earnest. It expresses anxiety and unspeakable horror. She is like a general who, hopelessly encircled with his whole army, bends once more, for the last time, over his maps to search for a way out and finds there is no escape. Then she begins to work feverishly, attacking that disgustingly raddled face with a trembling hand. She holds her lipstick as Michelangelo might have held his chisel on the last night of his life. It is a life-and-death struggle. The spectator watches with bated breath as this woman paints her face in front of her mirror. The mirror is cracked and dull, and from it the last convulsions of a tortured soul look out on you. She tries to save her life with a little rouge! No good! She wipes it off with a dirty rag. She tries again. And again. Then she shrugs her shoulders and wipes it all off with a movement which clearly shows that she has now wiped off her life. She throws the rag away. A close-up shows the dirty rag falling on the floor and after it has fallen, sinking down a little more. This movement of the rag is also quite easy to understand— it is the last convulsion of a death agony.

In this close-up "microphysiognomy" showed a deeply moving human tragedy with the greatest economy of expression. It was a great new form of art. The sound film offers much fewer opportunities for this kind of thing, but by no means excludes it and it would be a pity if such opportunities were to be neglected, unnecessarily making us all the poorer. . . .

MUTE DIALOGUES

In the last years of the silent film the human face had grown more and more visible, that is, more and more expressive. Not only had "microphysiognomy" developed but together with it the faculty of understanding its meaning. In the last years of the silent film we saw not only masterpieces of silent monologue but of mute dialogue as well. We saw conversations between the facial expressions of two human beings who understood the movements of each others' faces better than each others' words and could perceive shades of meaning too subtle to be conveyed in words.

A necessary result of this was . . . that the more space and time in the film was taken up by the inner drama revealed in the "microphysiognomic" close-up, the less was left of the predetermined 8,000 feet of film for all the external happenings. The silent film could thus dive into the depths—it was given the possibility of presenting a passionate life-and-death struggle almost exclusively by close-ups of faces.

Dreyer's film *Jeanne d'Arc* provided a convincing example of this in the powerful, lengthy, moving scene of the Maid's examination. Fifty men are sitting in the same place all the time in this scene. Several hundred feet of film show nothing but big close-ups of heads, of faces. We move in the spiritual dimension of facial expression alone. We neither see nor feel the space in which the scene is in reality enacted. Here no riders gallop, no boxers exchange blows. Fierce passions, thoughts, emotions, convictions battle here, but their struggle is not in space. Nevertheless this series of duels between looks and frowns, duels in which eyes clash instead of swords, can hold the attention of an audience for ninety minutes without flagging. We can follow every attack and riposte of these duels on the faces of the combatants; the play of their features indicates every stratagem, every sudden onslaught. The silent film has here brought an attempt to present a drama of the spirit closer to realization than any stage play has ever been able to do. . . .

194

RUDOLF ARNHEIM
FROM FILM AS ART

FILM AND REALITY

Film resembles painting, music, literature, and the dance in this respect—it is a medium that may, but need not, be used to produce artistic results. Colored picture post cards, for instance, are not art and are not intended to be. Neither are a military march, a true confessions story, or a strip tease. And the movies are not necessarily film art.

There are still many educated people who stoutly deny the possibility that film might be art. They say, in effect: "Film cannot be art, for it does nothing but reproduce reality mechanically." Those who defend this point of view are reasoning from the analogy of painting. In painting, the way from reality to the picture lies via the artist's eye and nervous system, his hand and, finally, the brush that puts strokes on canvas. The process is not mechanical as that of photography, in which the light rays reflected from the object are collected by a system of lenses and are then directed onto a sensitive plate where they produce chemical changes. Does this state of affairs justify our denying photography and film a place in the temple of the Muses?

It is worth while to refute thoroughly and systematically the charge that photography and film are only mechanical reproductions and that they therefore have no connection with art—for this is an excellent method of getting to understand the nature of film art.

With this end in view, the basic elements of the film medium will be examined separately and compared with the corresponding characteristics of what we perceive "in reality." It will be seen how fundamentally different the two kinds of image are; and that it is just these differences that provide film with its artistic resources. We shall thus come at the same time to understand the working principles of film art.

THE PROJECTION OF SOLIDS
UPON A PLANE SURFACE

Let us consider the visual reality of some definite object such as a cube. If this cube is standing on a table in front of me, its position determines whether I can realize its shape properly. If I see, for example, merely the four sides of a square, I have no means of knowing that a cube is before me, I see only a square surface. The human eye, and equally the photographic lens, acts from a particular position and from there can take in only such portions of the field of vision as are not hidden by things in front. As the cube is now placed, five of its faces are screened by the sixth, and therefore this last only is visible. But since this face might equally well conceal something quite different—since it might be the base of a pyramid or one side of a sheet of paper, for instance—our view of the cube has not been selected characteristically.

We have, therefore, already established one important principle: If I wish to photograph a cube, it is not enough for me to bring the object within range of my camera. It is rather a question of my position relative to the object, or of where I place it. The aspect chosen above gives very little information as to the shape of the cube. One, however, that reveals three surfaces of the cube and their relation to one another, shows enough to make it fairly unmistakable what the object is supposed to be. Since our field of vision is full of solid objects, but our eye (like the camera) sees this field from only one station point at any given moment, and since the eye can perceive the rays of light that are reflected from the object only by projecting them onto a plane surface—the retina—the reproduction of even a perfectly simple object is not a mechanical process but can be set about well or badly.

The second aspect gives a much truer picture of the cube than the first. The reason for this is that the second shows more than the first—three faces instead of only one. As a rule, however, truth does not depend on quantity. If it were merely a matter of finding

196

which aspect shows the greatest amount of surface, the best point of view could be arrived at by purely mechanical calculation. There is no formula to help one choose the most characteristic aspect: it is a question of feeling. Whether a particular person is "more himself" in profile than full face, whether the palm or the outside of the hand is more expressive, whether a particular mountain is better taken from the north or the west cannot be ascertained mathematically—they are matters of delicate sensibility.

Thus, as a preliminary, people who contemptuously refer to the camera as an automatic recording machine must be made to realize that even in the simplest photographic reproduction of a perfectly simple object, a feeling for its nature is required which is quite beyond any mechanical operation. We shall see later, by the way, that in artistic photography and film, those aspects that best show the characteristics of a particular object are not by any means always chosen; others are often selected deliberately for the sake of achieving specific effects.

REDUCTION OF DEPTH

How do our eyes succeed in giving us three-dimensional impressions even though the flat retinae can receive only two-dimensional images? Depth perception relies mainly on the distance between the two eyes, which makes for two slightly different images. The fusion of these two pictures into one image gives the three-dimensional impression. As is well known, the same principle is used in the stereoscope, for which two photographs are taken at once, about the same distance apart as the human eyes. This process cannot be used for film without recourse to awkward devices, such as colored spectacles, when more than one person is to watch the projection. For a single spectator it would be easy to make a stereoscopic film. It would only mean taking two simultaneous shots of the same incident a couple of inches apart and then showing one of them to each eye. For display to a larger number of spectators, however, the problem of stereoscopic film has not yet been solved satisfactorily—and hence the sense of depth in film pictures is extraordinarily small. The movement of people or objects from front to back makes a certain depth evident—but it is only necessary to glance into a stereoscope, which makes everything stand out most realistically, to recognize how flat the film picture is. This is another example of the fundamental difference between visual reality and film.

The effect of film is neither absolutely two-dimensional nor absolutely three-dimensional, but something between. Film pictures are at once plane and solid. In Ruttmann's film *Berlin* there is a scene of two subway trains passing each other in opposite directions. The shot is taken looking down from above onto the two trains. Anyone watching this scene realizes, first of all, that one train is coming toward him and the other going away from him (three-dimensional image). He will then also see that one is moving from the lower margin of the screen toward the upper and the other from the upper toward the lower (plane image). This second impression results from the projection of the three-dimensional movement onto the screen surface, which, of course, gives different directions of motion.

The obliteration of the three-dimensional impression has as a second result a stronger accentuation of perspective overlapping. In real life or in a stereoscope, overlapping is accepted as due merely to the accidental arrangement of objects, but very marked cuts result from superimpositions in a plane image. If a man is holding up a newspaper so that one corner comes across his face, this corner seems almost to have been cut out of his face, so sharp are the edges. Moreover, when the three-dimensional impression is lost, other phenomena, known to psychologists as the constancies of size and shape, disappear. Physically, the image thrown onto the retina of the eye by any object in the field of vision diminishes in proportion to the square of the distance. If an object a yard distant is moved away another yard, the area of the image on the retina is diminished to one-quarter of that of the first image. Every photographic plate reacts similarly. Hence in a photograph of someone sitting with his feet stretched out far in front of him the subject comes out with enormous feet and much too small a head. Curiously enough, however, we do not in real life get impressions to accord with the images on the retina. If a man is standing three feet away and another equally tall six feet away, the area of the image of the second does not appear to be only a quarter of that of the first. Nor if a man stretches out his hand toward one does it look disproportionately large. One sees the two men as equal in size and the hand as normal. This phenomenon is known as the constancy of size. It is impossible for most people—excepting those accustomed to drawing and painting, that is, artificially trained— to see according to the image on the retina. This fact, incidentally, is one of the reasons the average person has trouble copying things "correctly." Now an essential for the functioning of the constancy of size is a clear three-dimensional impression; it works excellently in a stereoscope with an ordinary photograph, but hardly at all in a film picture. Thus, in a film picture, if one man is twice as far from the camera as another, the one in front looks very considerably the taller and broader.

It is the same with the constancy of shape. The retinal image of a table top is like the photograph of it; the front edge, being nearer to the spectator, appears much wider than the back; the rectangular surface becomes a trapezoid in the image. As far as the average person is concerned, however, this again does not hold good in practice: he *sees* the surface as rectangular and draws it that way too. Thus the perspective changes taking place in any object that extends in depth are not observed but are compensated unconsciously. That is what is meant by the constancy of form. In a film picture it is hardly operative at all—a table top, especially if it is near the camera, looks very wide in front and very narrow at the back.

These phenomena, as a matter of fact, are due not only to the reduction of three-dimensionality but also to the unreality of the film picture altogether—an unreality due just as much to the absence of color, the delimitation of the screen, and so forth. The result of all this is that sizes and shapes do not appear on the screen in their true proportions but distorted in perspective. . . .

THE MAKING OF A FILM

It has been shown above that the images we receive of the physical world differ from those on the movie screen. This was done in order to refute the assertion that film is nothing but the feeble mechanical reproduction of real life. The analysis has furnished us with the data from which we can hope to derive now the principles of film art.

By its very nature, of course, the motion picture tends to satisfy the desire for faithful reports about curious, characteristic, exciting things going on in this world of ours. The first sensation provided by film in its early music-hall days was to depict everyday things in a lifelike fashion on the screen. People were greatly thrilled by the sight of a locomotive approaching at top speed or the emperor in person riding down *Unter den Linden*. In those days, the pleasure given by film derived almost entirely from the subject matter. A film art developed only gradually when the movie makers began consciously or unconsciously to cultivate the peculiar possibilities of cinematographic technique and to apply them toward the creation of artistic productions. To what extent the use of these means of expression affects the large audiences remains a moot question. Certainly box-office success depends even now much more on what is shown than on whether it is shown artistically.

The film producer himself is influenced by the strong resemblance of his photographic material to reality. As distinguished from the tools of the sculptor and the painter, which by themselves produce nothing resembling nature, the camera starts to turn and a likeness of the real world results mechanically. There is serious danger that the film maker will rest content with such shapeless reproduction. In order that the film artist may create a work of art it is important that he consciously stress the peculiarities of his medium. This, however, should be done in such a manner that the character of the objects represented should not thereby be destroyed but rather strengthened, concentrated, and interpreted. . . .

People who did not understand anything of the art of film used to cite silence as one of its most serious drawbacks. These people regard the introduction of sound as an improvement or completion of silent film. This opinion is just as senseless as if the invention of three-dimensional oil painting were hailed as an advance on the hitherto known principles of painting.

From its very silence film received the impetus as well as the power to achieve excellent artistic effects. Charles Chaplin wrote somewhere that in all his films there was not a single scene where he "spoke," that is, moved his lips. Hundreds of the most various situations in human relationships are shown in his films, and yet he did not feel the need to make use of such an ordinary faculty as speech. And nobody has missed it. The spoken word in Chaplin's films is as a rule replaced by pantomime. He does not *say* that he is pleased that some pretty girls are coming to see him, but performs the silent dance, in which two bread rolls stuck on forks act as dancing feet on the table *(The Gold Rush)*. He does not argue, he fights. He avows his love by smiling, swaying his shoulders, and moving his hat. When he is in the pulpit he does not preach in words, but acts the story of David and Goliath *(The Pilgrim)*. When he is sorry for a poor girl, he stuffs money into her handbag. He shows renunciation by simply walking away (finale of *The Circus*). The incredible visual concreteness of every one of his scenes makes for a great part of Chaplin's art; and this should not be forgotten when it is said—as is often done and of course not without foundation—that his films are not really "filmic" (because his camera serves mainly as a recording machine).

Mention has already been made of the scene from Sternberg's *The Docks of New York* in which a revolver shot is illustrated by the rising of a flock of birds. Such an effect is not just a contrivance on the part of a director to deal with the evil of silence by using an indirect visual method of explaining to the audience that there has been a bang. On the contrary, a positive artistic effect results from the paraphrase. Such indirect representation of an event in a material that is strange to it, or giving not the action itself but only its consequences, is a favorite method in all art. To take an example at random: when Francesca da Rimini tells how she fell in love with the man with whom she was in the habit of reading, and only says "We read no more that day," Dante thereby indicates indirectly, simply by giving the consequences, that on this day they kissed each other. And this indirectness is shockingly impressive.

In the same way, the rising of the birds is particularly effective, and probably more so than if the actual sound of the pistol shot were heard. And then another factor comes in: the spectator does not simply *infer* that a shot has been fired, but he actually *sees* something of the quality of the noise—the suddenness, the abruptness of the rising birds, give visually the exact quality that the shot possesses acoustically. In Jacques Feyder's *Les Nouveaux Messieurs* a political meeting becomes very uproarious, and in order to calm the rising emotions Suzanne puts a coin into a mechanical piano. Immediately the hall is lit up by hundreds of electric bulbs, and now the music chimes in with the agitative speech. The music is not heard: it is a silent film. But Feyder shows the audience excitedly listening to the speaker; and suddenly the faces soften and relax; all the heads begin quite gently to sway in time to the music. The rhythm grows more pronounced until at last the spirit of the dance has seized them all; and they swing their bodies gaily from side to side as if to an unheard word of command. The speaker has to give way to the music. Much more clearly than if the music were actually heard, this shows the power that suddenly unites all these discontented people, puts them into the same merry mood; and indicates as well the character of the music itself, its sway and rhythm. What is particularly noteworthy in such a scene is not merely how easily and cleverly the director makes visible something that is not visual, but by so doing, actually strengthens its effect. If the music were really heard, the spectator might simply realize that music was sounding, but by this indirect method, the particular point, the important part of this music—its rhythm, its power to unite and "move" men—is conspicuously brought out. Only these special attributes of the music are given, and appear as the music itself. Similarly the fact that a pistol shot is sudden, explosive, startling, becomes doubly impressive by transposition into the visible, because only these particular attributes and not the shot itself are given. Thus silent film derives definite artistic potentialities from its silence. What it wishes particularly to emphasize in an audible occurrence is transposed into something visual; and thus instead of giving the occurrence "itself," it gives only some of its telling characteristics, and thereby shapes and interprets it.

Owing to its insubstantiality silent film does not in any way give the effect of being dumb pantomime. Its silence is not noticed, unless the action happens to culminate in something acoustic for which nothing can be substituted, and which is therefore felt as missing—or unless one is accustomed to sound film. Because of sound film, in the future it will be possible only with great difficulty to show speech in a silent way. Yet this is a most effective artistic device. For if a man is heard speaking, his gestures and facial expression only appear as an accompaniment to underline the sense of what is said. But if one does not hear what is said, the meaning becomes indirectly clear and is artistically interpreted by muscles of the face, of the limbs, of the body. The emotional quality of the conversation is made obvious with a clarity and definiteness which are hardly possible in the medium of actual speech. Moreover, the divergence between reality and dumb show gives the actor and his director plenty of leeway for artistic invention. (The creative power of the artist can only come into play where reality and the medium of representation do not coincide.)

Dialogue in silent film is not simply the visible part of a real spoken dialogue. If a real dialogue is shown without the sound, the spectator will often fail to grasp what it is all about; he will find the facial expression and the gestures unintelligible. In silent film, the lips are no longer word-forming physical organs but a means of visual expression—the distortion of an excited mouth or the fast chatter of lips are not mere by-products of talking; they are communications in their own right. Silent laughter is often more effective than if the sound is actually heard. The gaping of the open mouth gives a vivid, highly artistic interpretation of the phenomenon "laughter." If, however, the sound is also heard, the opening of the mouth appears obvious and its value as a means of expression is almost entirely lost. This opportunity of the silent film was once used by the Russians in a most unusual and effective manner. A shot of a soldier who had gone mad in the course of a battle and was laughing hideously with his mouth wide open was joined with a shot of the body of a soldier who had died of poison gas, and whose mouth was fixed in death in a ghastly, rigid grin.

The absence of the spoken word concentrates the spectator's attention more closely on the visible aspect of behavior, and thus the whole event draws particular interest to itself. Hence it is that very ordinary shots are often so impressive in silent films—such as a documentary shot of an itinerant hawker crying his wares with grandiose gestures. If his words could be heard the effect of the gestures would not be half as great, and the whole episode might attract very little attention. If, however, the words are omitted, the spectator surrenders entirely to the expressive power of the gestures. Thus by merely robbing the real event of something—the sound—the appeal of such an episode is greatly heightened. . . .

ROBERT WARSHOW
DAY OF WRATH:
THE ENCLOSED IMAGE

Carl Dreyer's basic problem as an artist is one that seems almost inevitably to confront the self-conscious creator of "art" films: the conflict between a love for the purely visual and the tendencies of a medium that is not only visual but also dramatic. The principle that the film is a medium based on movement has often been used to justify a complete preoccupation with visual patterns, as if the ideal film would be one that succeeded in divorcing movement from content, but it is this principle itself that raises the problem, for the presentation of human beings in movement necessarily leads to the creation of drama; thus the maker of "art" films, unless he limits himself to complete abstraction or to generalized poetic symbolism, tends to raise aesthetic demands that he cannot satisfy within the framework he has set. Only in the earlier parts of *Day of Wrath* can Dreyer be said to have solved this problem. And the solution, though brilliant, is essentially unstable; the weaknesses of the film's later parts grow out of the virtues of its beginning.

The film opens with the playing of "Dies Irae," a dreadful, insistent hymn prolonged to the point where it comes to seem a kind of outrage; it is music that does not aim at the listener's pleasure or require his consent. In effect, this music establishes the existence of a world whose graces pretend to no connection with the needs of human beings, a world that may find it proper in the realization of its designs to burn a woman alive for being a witch.

There is only the most unemphatic indication that such a world is supposed to have existed in Denmark early in the seventeenth century. It is not a historical world—though it exemplifies certain historical ideas—and the primary tendency of Dreyer's direction is to keep it from becoming historical, to preserve it self-enclosed and static. Everything leading up to the execution of the witch Marthe is presented like a pageant: each movement is graceful and dignified, each figure in some particular fashion beautiful, each shot "composed"; and the camera focuses always on the leading figures of the pageant itself, following their slow and predetermined movement with an entranced solemnity that permits no glance at the actuality which has brought them into being. Not a single shot is spent on documentation, and though the whole "issue" is between good and evil, these concepts, too, exist only as parts of the spectacle: "evil" is the figure of an old woman whose function is to be thrown upon a fire after completing certain movements of flight, suffering, struggle, and despair; "good" is the process by which this ceremony is carried out.

No dramatic conflict surrounds the witch herself—her one mistaken effort to bargain for life remains no more than an expected stage in her destruction—and there is only the barest beginning of the drama that is to take place after her death. Her very sufferings are given an explicit quality of formality: three screams mark the three decisive moments—capture, confession, death; when she lies bound to the ladder and impotently shaking her fist, one's attention is drawn to a pattern of leaf-shadows that moves across her face. And all problematical aspects of the subject—questions of justice and authority, the reality of witchcraft, the existence of God and the Devil—are avoided or postponed: it is shown, for example, that the pastor Absalon, who is the leading figure in the witch's condemnation, is himself in an ambiguous situation, but this is not permitted to become a dramatic problem until after her death; and the activities that constitute the witch's crime, though formally indicated, remain vague—only later on is it shown that she might have been regarded as actually dangerous.

Yet this formalized and narrow spectacle creates a degree of excitement beyond anything one experiences during the later, more dramatic portions of the film; by the time the witch falls screaming upon the fire, the tension has come close to a point at which it might be reasonable to leave the theater. The chief source of this tension seems to be in the interplay between Dreyer's general approach to art and certain of the specific tendencies of his medium.

Dreyer's initial impulse, in his deliberate exclusion of the historical and dramatic, is to deprive events of the quality of reality; it is this, indeed, which accounts for his concern with the past: since the past can be contemplated but not changed, it exists from one point of view as an aesthetic object ready-made—one can experience it "pure." But he practices his aestheticism on events that possess *a priori* an unusual emotional importance, and in one of the most realistic of all mediums. In the screen's absolute clarity, where all objects are brought close and defined unambiguously, the "reality" of an event can be made to inhere simply in its visible presence; so long as the internal structure of a film remains consistent, all its elements are in these terms equally "real"—that is, completely visible. Thus at his best—which means, in this film, when he is creating his own images and not imitating the creations of seventeenth-century painting—Dreyer is able to give his aestheticized vision of the past all the force of reality without impairing its aesthetic autonomy; in the absence of a historical-dramatic reality, the purely visible dominates and is sufficient: the witch is an object of art, but she is also—and just as fully—a human being (she is *there*), and she is burnt; the burning is so to speak accomplished by the camera, which can see the witch without having to "interpret" her.

The effect is something like a direct experience of the tension between art and life. In a sense, the image *as* image becomes a dramatic force: the issue is not, after all, good against evil or God against Satan, but flesh against form; stripped as it is of all historical or social reference, the spectacle is of a woman burnt to serve beauty. It is a spectacle not to be understood—the image itself is all the meaning—but to be endured; and the enormous excitement that surrounds it, the sense almost of a prolonged assault on one's feelings, results largely from the exclusion of all that might be used to create an appearance of understanding. Even to see the witch as a victim of injustice would provide a certain relief by placing the events on the screen within some "normal" frame of response. But no such opportunity appears, nothing *in* the film is allowed to speak for the audience or to the audience (two of the characters cannot bear to watch the burning, but this is not what is wanted: it is merely a sign of their weakness). It is as if the director, in his refusal to acknowledge that physical movement implies dramatic movement, were denying the relevance of the spectator's feelings; one is left with no secure means of connecting the witch with reality, and yet she is real in herself and must be responded to; as responses are blocked, the tension increases.

In this blocking of responses, it is again important that Dreyer's aestheticism leads him to the past. The historical past, being real, embodies a multitude of possibilities; the aesthetic past is created by eliminating all possibilities but one, and that is the accomplished one. Thus time becomes fate: the image is distant and untouchable because its form was fixed long before we come to see it; the witch *will* be burnt because witches *were* burnt. The feelings of the spectator really are in a way irrelevant: he is watching what has ceased to exist, and there is no one to "care" what he feels. He has his feelings nevertheless.

In the later parts of the film, in order to relieve the tension that has been established, it became necessary to permit a reassertion of those historical-dramatic elements which have been so rigidly suppressed. But the basic style of the film is already fixed, and this need to introduce new elements results in incongruities, passages of boredom, and dramatic incoherence.

The dramatic plot which begins to work itself out after the witch's death concerns the adultery of the pastor's young wife Anne and his son Martin; Anne becomes a witch, ensnaring her lover and later killing her husband by the power of evil. The ambiguity of the pastor's position, too, is involved with witchcraft: his sin was to conceal the fact that Anne's mother was a witch. Thus witchcraft is no longer pure image, it is a way of behaving, and the question of its reality is no longer to be avoided. A psychological answer is impossible: Dreyer is already committed to keeping the past *in* the past. But the supernatural answer, which is the one he chooses (and with a hesitation that only makes matters worse), is just as bad: once the question of witchcraft is raised, no one can be expected to believe in its reality.

The attempt to impose belief by purely aesthetic means is inevitably a failure, both dramatically and visually. There is a scene in which the pastor walks home at night through an "evil" storm that is the height of visual banality; then his wife, at home with her lover, is shown saying, "If he were dead—"; then back to the pastor, who suddenly straightens up in the howling wind and says to his companion, "I felt as if Death had brushed me by." And there is a continual effort to use the camera for symbolic comment that eventually becomes clear enough but is never convincing: when Anne first tries her "power" in order to call Martin to her side, Dreyer repeats on her face the shifting pattern of leaves that appeared on the face of the old witch before she was burnt; when the lovers walk in the fields, the camera keeps turning upward to the trees above their heads. In general, there is an attempt to equate the outdoors, the world of nature, with evil (the pastor's mother, who is the one firm moral pillar, is never seen outside the rigidly ordered household she controls); but the camera cannot create a religious system.

The purely dramatic failure is most obvious in the film's conclusion, when Martin turns against Anne and thus leads her to confess her witchcraft. Martin's defection is not made to seem an adequate reason for Anne's confession, and Martin's action itself is entirely without motivation: the very skill with which the director now tries to transmute visual patterns into drama (as earlier he had tried to make dramatic patterns purely visual) becomes a kind of irrelevancy. But even in this later section of the film there is still much that is successful. When Anne resolves to kill her husband, a virtual transformation of character is accomplished by the manipulation of lighting. And whenever the aesthetic image does not come into direct conflict with the dramatic structure, it can still take on some of the purity and completeness of the earlier scenes—for example, in the procession of choir boys at the pastor's funeral—except that now the image is felt as an interruption of the action.

At bottom, the film is an aesthetic paradox: out of the pure and enclosed image Dreyer creates a sort of "pure drama," in which the point of conflict is precisely the exclusion of drama; but this in turn creates a tension that the image alone cannot resolve; the dramatic nature of the medium must reassert itself in the later portions of the film, and Dreyer is involved again in the initial contradiction.

F. E. SPARSHOTT
BASIC FILM AESTHETICS

The basic aesthetics of film as of any other art must be descriptive and analytic, giving an account of the relevant variables and their means of variation. And any such account must be rooted in some notion, however imprecise, of what a work of the art in question is. What, then, is a film? It seems to be characteristic of the art that acceptable definitions need to specify not only the nature of the work itself but also the means essential to its production and its characteristic effects. A sample definition might go like this: "A film is a series of motionless images projected onto a screen so fast as to create in the mind of anyone watching the screen an impression of continuous motion, such images being projected by a light shining through a corresponding series of images arranged on a continuous band of flexible material." Much variation in detail and in emphasis is possible, but no definition can dispense with two important features: a succinct description of at least the basic features of the *mechanism* employed, and an allusion to the creation of an *illusion* of motion. Let us consider these necessary features in turn.

MECHANISM

More than any other art, film is technologically determined. Music, dance, drawing, painting, sculpture, poetry, even architecture need for their original and rudimentary forms either no materials or materials lying everywhere at hand, but cinematography cannot begin without laboriously invented and precisely constructed equipment. The history of film is the history of the invention of its means. Aestheticians of the cinema may often be differentiated by how they react to various aspects of its technology: the properties of lenses and emulsions, the conditions of production and display. Thus the most notorious dogmas about how films ought to be made are demands for truth to the supposed tendencies of some aspect of the medium: to the clarity and convincingness of photographic images, or to the impartial receptivity of a film camera to whatever may be put before it, or to the camera's way of reducing whatever is put before it to a homogeneous image, or to the ease with which assorted scraps of film may be so cemented as to suggest a common provenance, and so on. It is characteristic of such dogmas that they fasten on one such aspect and tendency and ignore the rest. All of them ignore one very important factor: just because the means of cinema are so complex, anyone who has mastered them (and, equally rare and difficult, who has regular access to them) will naturally use them to convey whatever message or vision he may wish to convey, whether or not it is "cinematic" by any plausible definition. People use their languages to say what they wish to say, not what the language makes it easy to say. Most theorists of cinema insist that the outcome of this natural tendency is bound to be a bad film, but one hardly sees why. Whatever can be done with a medium is among its possibilities and hence "true to" it in a sense that has yet to be shown to be illegitimate. A person may become (or may train himself to be) sensitive to the degree in which films exploit or ignore some possibility of the medium, and then may govern his taste or regulate his critical judgment accordingly, but one does not see why such arbitrary selective systems should be imposed on those who would reject them. It is one thing to show that it is almost impossible to make a good film by photographing a stage performance of a play, by enumerating the probable sources of boredom and irritation; it is quite another to declare that all filmed plays are necessarily nonfilmic and on that account bad films.

ILLUSION

The second necessary feature of our sample definition was its reference to an illusion. Perhaps alone among the arts, and certainly in a way quite different from any of the other major arts, film is necessarily an art of illusion from the very beginning; and illusion, like technology, serves as a focal point around which aesthetic disputes arrange themselves. On the one hand, it may be taken as an opportunity to be exploited. Both by fabricating the images to be projected and by manipulating the speed and sequence of their projection, films can and do revel in the creation of the most elaborate illusions. On the other hand, illusion may be seen as the temptation to be resisted. The motion on the screen has to be unreal, but can and should faithfully portray a motion that really took place just so in the real world. Both tendencies go back to the earliest days of cinema, in the work of the realist Lumière and the fantasist Méliès. But that does not mean that film-makers have to choose between embracing and eschewing illusion: quite usually, and in the films of at least some acknowledged masters, fantasy is put at the service of realism (e.g. the stone lions in *Potemkin*) or realism at the service of fantasy (e.g. the homecoming in *Ugetsu*).

To speak broadly of "illusion" as we have done is misleading. While the basic illusion of motion is an automatic and unavoidable function of the mechanism of human vision, what I shall call the "secondary illusions" constructed upon it, to the effect that an event or movement of a certain sort is taking place, are not automatic but depend on the filmgoer's knowledge and his ability or willingness to acquiesce in a pretense. Writers on film often mention a scene in which an Indian villager is pursued by a tiger. The pursuit is shown entirely by intercut shots of scared man and slavering beast until, at the very end, pursuer and pursued at last appear together in a single shot. For Bazin, this saves the scene: previously one had assumed that the propinquity of man and beast was an illusion created by cutting, now one suddenly sees that it was not. For Montagu, it is stupid: the effect was created by the cutting, the concluding two-shot is a banal assertion. And of course on reflection one realizes that either it was a tame tiger or we are being served another trick shot. It seems obvious that different audiences will differ in their susceptibilities to such effects; trying to decide the proprieties (as both writers do) by invoking ultimate principles is surely a waste of time.

THE BIAS OF EXPOSITION

As the example we have just given shows, the secondary illusions of film relate not to what is projected on the screen but to the supposed provenance of the image. No more than when attending a stage play does anyone at the movies feel as if an event were really taking place before his eyes. But why should there be illusions of provenance? The answer seems to lie in the complex relations between cinematography and photography, and the peculiar nature of photographic images themselves. A clue to these relations may be found in the fact that all but one of the demands of "truth to the medium" that we used as examples mentioned some aspect of photography, although our sample definition of a film made no allusion to photography at all.

The images whose successive projection makes a film are most easily produced by photography; but they can be drawn directly on the film stock. A photograph to represent an object is most easily made by aiming a camera at an object of the appropriate kind; but what is photographed may also be a model or a drawing or even another photograph made for the purpose. A photograph of an event or happening is most easily made by finding one and photographing it; but scenes may be enacted and scenery constructed for the purpose. The required succession of images is most easily produced by using a device that will take a lot of photographs in rapid succession and fix them in the right order; but it can be (and in animated cartoons is) drawn or photographed frame by frame. And the obvious way to work the film camera (though not necessarily the easiest; rather it is synchronization that requires care) is to run it at the same speed as you will run your projector; but it can be run faster or slower. Film thus has a bias, quite strong though readily resistible, towards its simplest form, that in which the projector repeats a camera event; and one tends if not on one's guard to assume, wherever nothing in the film suggests the contrary, that what is shown on the screen represents such a repetition, as if the projector copied a camera that enacted the spectator's eye.

An eye is not a camera, and a photographic image does not show what eyes see. As you look around you, your eye constantly adjusts its iris as brightness changes and alters its focus as depth changes. The parallax effect of the use of two eyes gives everything you see a shifting and unstable character, since everything not focused on at the moment yields a vague doubled image. The eye in nature is therefore restless; in looking at a photograph, all in one plane and with a relatively small range of luminosity, the eye

212

is spared much of its labor. However, though a photographic image is not at all like the visible world, it does have precisely the quality that old theorists used to ascribe to that venerable phantom of optics, the retinal image. A photographic image represents a sort of ideal projection, the way we normalize in imagination what we see. What the invention of photography did was not to reproduce vision but to achieve a dream of ideal vision. A photographic image is not so much a true one as a convincing one. Photographs tend to carry an irresistible sense of authenticity. Looking at a good photograph is not like looking at the photographed thing (this is so far from being the case that Peter Ustinov's famous remark, that he made *Billy Budd* in black-and-white because it was more realistic than color, hardly seems paradoxical); it is like looking at a faithful record.

The basic illusion of movement by itself gives an impression not of reality but of a sort of unattributable vivacity. This becomes evident when one watches an animated cartoon. Verisimilitude adds nothing to the lifelikeness of such films, and the elaborate devices used by Disney in his later years to suggest a third dimension have been abandoned as futile (as well as expensive). The sense of reality elicited by such films is akin to that of painting: we attribute the actions we see neither to the real world nor to the screen image, but to Donald Duck and the cartoon world created for him. It is not the illusion of movement, then, that moves us to attribute what we see to the world of experience; rather it is the photographic character of the image that lends films their characteristic bias of exposition, and to the extent that it is present and uncontradicted by the nature of what is presented encourages us to take what we see as the record of something that took place as we see it taking place. The viewer tends to normalize in this sense his perception of films made in the most diverse ways.

Many theories about how films ought to be made represent attitudes to the bias of exposition just described. The Soviet filmmakers of the twenties claimed that the whole art of film lay in exploiting its tendency by the use of montage or associative cutting, joining strips of photographed film in such a way as to synthesize in the spectator's mind an experiential reality that went beyond the images shown. Siegfried Kracauer urged on the contrary that the best use of film is an honest reliance on its capacity to convey authenticity, to preserve and celebrate the sense of reality. His argument was not that a film should actually be a record or chronicle, but that it should celebrate and "redeem," as no other medium can, the radiant actuality of the physical world, eschewing alike fantasies and superimposed formal arrangements. Other critics, noting that film bestows verisimilitude on the deserving and the undeserving alike, urge that film includes among its unique capacities that of making "dreams come true." Only film can *show* the impossible happening and thus make fantasy convincing. In the opposite direction, some exponents of contemporary "underground" film go beyond Kracauer (and beyond Rossellini and the Italian neorealists) in urging that to cut film at all is to falsify: the finished film should consist of all that the camera took in the order it was taken in, and if this means that some shots are out-of-focus, ill-exposed or irrelevant, they will thereby only be truer to the film experience. On this view, a film records not what happened in front of the camera but what happened to the film *in* the camera. And finally, some extremists might urge that the only honest way to make a film is to set a camera up somewhere and let it just run, taking in whatever may happen along. But at that point the urge to honesty would surely defeat itself by suggesting a standard it cannot fulfill. Films are not natural events, and it is pointless to prevaricate about the selective intervention of the film-maker.

FILM SPACE

That the realism of film is that of a graphic record and not that of an illusive actuality is apparent in the peculiar nature of film space, the actual and suggested spatial relations between elements of the film and between film and spectator. Many writers imply that a film-goer ordinarily feels himself to be in the same relation to the filmed scene as the camera was (or purports to have been). On this basis such trick shots as those showing a room through the flames of a fire in the fireplace are condemned on the ground that the audience know that nobody would be in that position. But this seems to be mistaken. Spectators seem to identify themselves with the camera viewpoint only when some such process as Cinerama is used which makes the screen approximate to the total visual environment. Otherwise, shots taken looking straight downward do not give one a sense of vertigo (though they may do to persons extremely susceptible in this regard), and even the most rapid changes in camera position do not produce in an experienced film-goer any sense of nausea or disorientation. If one really accepted a change in camera position as a change in one's personal view-point, rapid intercutting between different viewpoints would ob-viously be intolerable. There is certainly a sense in which one has a feeling of spatial presence at the filmed scene (which is not to be confused with psychological involvement in the action), construing the scene as a three-dimensional space in which one is involved and has a viewpoint. This depth and inclusiveness of cinema space owes much to parallax, the differential motion and occlusion of dis-tant objects as the viewpoint changes. It follows that when, as often happens nowadays, action is interrupted by stop-motion, the whole nature of the space in which the action takes place is instantly transformed (a striking instance is the concluding scene of *The Strawberry Statement*). This little-noted factor is important. With-out such a change in spatiality, stop-motion might give the impres-sion that the world had suddenly come to a halt; as it is, it confronts us rather with a transition to a different mode of representation, and hence perhaps a different mode of being.

The more one reflects on one's sense of cinema space, the more it seems to be one peculiar to cinema. The use of a zoom lens in-creasing the (objective) size of the image does have the effect of bringing the action nearer; but walking towards the screen, though it produces a (subjectively) larger image and does bring the screen nearer, does not bring the action nearer at all. One's sense of spatial involvement in a scene does not depend on one's occupying any particular seat, but only on one's being neither too close nor too far to see the screen properly. Similar considerations apply to all the distortions of space that result from the use of various lenses. The resulting plasticity of space relations is accepted as a narrative device or as an invitation to an imaginary viewpoint, it does not disorient the audience. The use of a deep-focus lens for Miss Havi-sham's room in *Great Expectations* certainly has a "magnifying" effect, but a curious one: we do not feel that we are in a big room, but that "this is how it must have seemed to Pip." Again, in the scene where the girl runs toward the airplane in *Zabriskie Point* the scale-relations between girl and low horizon are such that for a second or two we accept what we see as an ordinary medium-shot; then we notice that for all her running the girl is not receding much, and realize that it is a typical telephoto shot. But the effect of this realization on me was not to alter my feeling of where I was in relation to the scene, but to change my interpretation of that relation. In fact, a telephoto shot answers to no possible real spatial relationship between spectator and event: there is a viewing angle, but no possible viewpoint. Yet this never disturbs anyone.

Phenomena of the sort we have been mentioning suggest that one's sense of space in film is somehow bracketed or held in suspense: one is aware of one's implied position and accepts it, but is not existentially committed to it. A simple explanation of this is that most of the time one is simultaneously aware of a film (as one is of a painting) both as a two-dimensional arrangement on the screen and as a three-dimensional scene, so that neither aspect dominates the mind except in moments of excitement or disaffection. A subtler explanation is that cinema vision is alienated vision. A man's sense of where he is depends largely on his sense of balance and his muscular senses, and all a filmgoer's sensory cues other than those of vision and hearing relate firmly to the theater and seat in which he sits. In the scene with the epileptic doctor in *Carnet du Bal*, which is taken with a consistently tilted camera, what one sees on the screen insists that one is off balance, but one's body insists that it is not; and the effect on me is the one Duvivier surely intended, a feeling of malaise accompanied by a sense of *vicarious* disorientation on behalf of the protagonist.

Some of the spatial ambiguity of film is shared with still photography. No matter how one moves a photograph around in relation to oneself, it continues to function as a faithful record implying a viewpoint from which it was taken: and there is a sense in which one continues to be "at" this viewpoint no matter what angle the photograph is inspected from. What differentiates film from still photography is not only the sense of vivacity and hence spatial reality that motion imparts, but also the great size and contrasting illumination of the film image in the darkened theater, whereby it comes much closer to dominating the visual sense, and the relatively invariant relation between screen and spectator.* The di-

---

*Note that in being transferred to the domestic television screen a film loses all three characteristics: size, luminosity, and audience immobility. It becomes an object rather than an experience.

rector determines the audience's spatial relation to his films, but what he determines remains an imaginary space; we are within the film's space but not part of its world; we observe from a viewpoint at which we are not situated.

It is the alienation of the visual sense in cinema space that makes possible many of the uses and special effects of film that work against its function as record. Being deprived of so many sensory cues, the spectator loses all sense of absolute scale, so that back-projections and painted backgrounds may wear a convincing air of reality, and the apparent size of any object may be varied by placing it in a magnified or diminished setting, or simply (as when storms and wrecks are shot using models in tanks) by trading on the spectator's narrative assumptions.

FILM AND DREAM

Unique as it is, the alienated spatiality of film, in which the spectator participates without contact, and which he observes from a viewpoint that contrives to be both definite and equivocal or impossible, presents striking analogies to the space of dreams. Or perhaps, since different people seem to have widely varying dream perceptions, I should limit myself to saying that my own spatial relation to my dream worlds is like nothing in waking reality so much as it is like my relation to film worlds. In my dreams, too, I see from where I am not, and move helplessly in a space whose very nature is inconstant, and may see beside me the being whose perceptions I share. There are indeed many ways in which film-going is like dreaming; but the likeness is always qualified. Films are like dreams in involving one in a world whose course one cannot control, but unlike them in that their world does not incorporate the dream of effort and participation. Filmed reality shares with dreamed reality (as nothing else does) its tolerance of limit-lessly inconsequent transitions and transformations; but it lacks that curious conceptual continuity of dreams in which what is a raven may become a writing-desk or may simultaneously *be* a writing-desk, and in which one *knows* that what looks like one person is really a quite different person. The conceptual equivalences essayed by film-makers (e.g. Eisenstein's equation of Kerensky with a peacock in *October*), which usually proceed by intercutting shots of the two entities to be equated, seem rather to be the visual equivalent of similes or metaphors than equivalents of the dream carryover, which depends on a dream-interpretation imposed on the dream-percept and not (as must be the case in film) on an interpretation suggested by the percept itself.

The dreamlikeness of film has often been noted. Usually the recognition takes the form of a loose analogy with daydreaming (which is quite different), but Susanne Langer for one has made the formal analogy with dreaming the basis of her account of the nature of film. The analogy must not be pushed too far. A quite fundamental difference between a filmgoer and a dreamer is that the former remains in control of his faculties, capable of sustained and critical attention. A dream-like inconsequentiality is thus far from typical of film, though it remains among filmic possibilities and the filmgoing public at large acquiesces in a degree of cheerful incoherence (as in *Casino Royale*) that in other arts is acceptable only to the sophisticate.

To the extent that the analogy between film and dream is taken seriously, it seems to invite Freudians to apply their methods of symbolic interpretation with even more confidence than they do to other arts. But they seem not to have accepted the invitation (except in so far as Freudian methodology lies behind the auteur theory of criticism), perhaps because not enough film-makers are safely dead yet. In any case, before we reach that level of interpretation we have to complete our survey of the basic attributes of the film world.

FILM TIME AND FILM REALITY

The same confusion between an actual event and a convincing record that has made critics write of the camera as a surrogate for the spectator's eye leads them to say that film time is present time, that in watching a film one seems to see things happening *now*, as though one were present not at the film but at the filmed event. But this contention is vulnerable to the same sort of objection that refutes the doctrine of the camera eye. In one sense it is true but trivial: of course what one sees is always here and now, because "here" and "now" are defined by one's presence. In any other sense it is false, or we should not be able to take in our stride the flashbacks and flash-forwards, the accelerations and decelerations, that are part of film's stock in trade. Rather, it is as though we were spectators of the temporality of the films we see. Film time has a quality analogous to that dreamlike floating between participation and observation, between definite and indeterminate relationships, that gives film space its pervasive character. Granted, the fundamental illusion of motion combines with the convincingness of a photographic record to ensure that we ordinarily do read the presented motion as continuous and as taking just as much time to happen as it takes us to observe it; but this supposition is readily defeated by any counterindication. D. W. Griffith, challenged on his early use of spatiotemporal discontinuities, justified himself by appealing to the example of Dickens, and surely he was right to do so. The time of a novel is filmic, as its space is not. Events can be filmed, as they can be narrated, with equal facility in any order, at any speed, with any degree of minuteness. Unlike the novelist, however, the film-maker has no language proper to his medium in which to specify temporal relations. He may use titles, trick dissolves, a narrator's voice, or datable visual clues to establish his temporal relations; but some directors seem to feel that such devices are clumsy or vulgar, and prefer to trust the public's acumen or simply to leave the relations indeterminate.

The dream-relationships of film space and the narrative nature of film time combine to encourage an ambiguity that may be fruitful or merely irritating. One often does not know whether one is seeing what in the film's terms is real, or only what is passing through the mind of one of the film's characters. This ambiguity becomes acute whenever there is a temporal jump, for time (as Kant observed) is the form of subjectivity. A flash-back may represent a character's memory, or may simply be a narrative device; a flash-forward may stand for a character's premonition, or simply an anticipation by the film-maker,* and, where the temporally displaced scene is recalled or foreseen, it may stand either for the event as it was or would be, or for the way it is (perhaps falsely) conjured up. The

---

*The terms "flash-back" and "flash-forward" are often used in such a way as to suggest that every film has a normal time from which all sequences assignable to other times are to be regarded as deviations. But why should this be so? The terms are better taken as marking temporal discontinuities rather than displacements.

status of film events thus becomes equivocal, and such uncertainty may pervade an entire film. Thus in *8½* some scenes are remembered, some dreamed, some imagined, and some belong to the reality of the film's story. There are many scenes whose status is unclear at the time, and some whose status never becomes clear. Does the opening scene of the closed car in the traffic jam show a seizure which makes the cure necessary (as Arnheim seems to think), or is it a dream of a patient already undergoing treatment (as most critics suppose)? Nothing in the version of the film I saw determined either answer. A more striking equivocation occurs in *Easy Rider*, when a brief glimpse of an unexplained roadside fire is identified at the end of the film as the burning of the hero's motorcycle. Was that first glimpse a premonition of the hero's (and if so, just what did he foresee?), or a *memento mori* by the director, or just a pointless interjection to which no meaning can be assigned? In such a self-indulgent piece of hokum, who can say? In general, the tolerability of such unresolved ambiguities is likely to depend partly on the handling of "reality" in the film as a whole, partly on one's confidence in the director's control over his medium, and partly on one's own tolerance of ambiguity. In any case, one must not suppose that such questions as we have just posed need have a single "right" answer (perhaps what the director "meant"). All the director has done is to splice celluloid, and if he has not provided enough clues to determine a reading then no meaning is determined. What the director may have had in mind is not the same as what he put on film, and directors sometimes have nothing at all in mind. The flexibility of film technique is a standing invitation to meaningless trickery, and the complexities of production involve endless risks of inadvertent nonsense.

As the apparent time of the action changes, then, so changes the subjectivity/objectivity rating of what we see; and so too may vary our degree of confidence in our ability to assign a rating. Nor are such ambiguities the prerogative of highbrow excursions like *Last Year at Marienbad*. They occur quite naturally in unsophisticated films. For example, in Jerry Lewis's Jekyll-and-Hyde fantasy *The Nutty Professor* the transformation scene in the laboratory slips onto a plane of witty extravagance quite removed from the surface naturalism of the rest of the film. Are we witnessing the event or a metaphor for the event? Who knows? One could spend a long time figuring out possible meanings for it, but in fact it comes across as just a happy episode and the popcorn-grinding jaws do not miss a beat.

FILM MOTION

The ambiguities of space and time combine to give film motion an endless complexity that we have no space to explore here. Let us confine our attention to some additional complications. In the earliest movies, each scene was taken with a fixed camera, so that the motion shown took place within a fixed frame and against an unchanging background. A scene in a modern film is likely to be enriched or muddled with three different kinds of camera motion. The camera may be shifted from place to place, turned horizontally or vertically to alter its field of reception, or modified by changing the focal length of its lens so as to take in a greater or smaller area. This third kind of camera shot is often dismissed as the equivalent of a tracking shot, moving the camera viewpoint toward or away from the scene, but it is not; it retains much of the sense of getting a different view from the same position. A camera can also be rotated on its focal axis, or joggled and steadied, but these can be set aside for now as occasional effects.

Even a shot of immobile objects taken with an immobile camera need not be devoid of movement, for there is also movement of light: illumination may change in direction, in intensity, in color, in sharpness. And even when the light remains unchanged, the much-used prints that most audiences see have a sort of constant surface shimmer, a vibrant presence derived from the random stains and lesions hard use imparts, that has a good deal to do with the "film experience" and is exploited by some film-makers in much the same spirit that furniture-makers fake a "distressed finish." The free combinations of all the kinds of film motion can impart to a single scene a plastic, balletic quality, a unique kind of formal beauty that is at once abstract and realistic and has no parallel in any other medium.

The mobility of the frame combines with the camera's typical neglect of natural boundaries to produce a marked contrast between the actions of theater and cinema. The stage world is a closed world; an actor who goes offstage loses all determinate existence for the audience; but the edge of a cinema screen functions like a window frame through which we glimpse part of a world to which we attribute infinite continuity. This sense of infinity adds an implicit freedom of movement to the actual freedom that the camera's mobility affords.

Because film space and time are observed rather than lived, film motion can be speeded up or slowed down within scenes in a way denied to theater, in which events take their proper time. (Conversely, theater has a way of achieving temporal plasticity denied to film, by exploiting the stage-unreality of the offstage world: in theater, but not in film, offstage actions are often performed in the course of a scene in an incongruously short time.) The effects of such variations in time depend on context, in a way that becomes easier to understand when we reflect that motion photography was invented to serve not one realistic purpose but two: not only to observe and record movements, but also to study and examine them. And of course very fast movements are best studied by slowing down their representation, very slow ones by speeding it up. Nature films are quite regularly made at unnatural speeds, accelerating plant growth and decelerating bird flight, and replays of crucial movements in sport are usually in slow motion. In this context of study the spectator has no sense of unreality at all: he feels simply that he is getting a better look. But in narrative contexts things are different. Acceleration was early discovered to have a reliably comic effect. But deceleration is more variable, for it may produce an impression of joy, or unreality, or obsessiveness, or solemnity, or inevitability. Its effects often evade description, but directors find them reliable enough for regular use, and they have hardened into more than one cliché. One such is the flash-back reverie, where the slow motion seems to work by suggesting weightlessness and hence ethereality (as in *The Pawnbroker*). Another is the use of weightlessness as a metaphor for lightheartedness (as in many TV commercials). A third is the slow-motion death by shooting (as in *Bonnie and Clyde*), partly an appeal to voyeurism but partly a symbolization of death through the transposition of the action into another key of reality.

One can think of acceleration and deceleration as a sort of pre-editing, the equivalent of adding or subtracting frames in a film taken at projector speed. It is basic to film that editing can produce an impression of motion by intercutting suitably spaced shots of the same object in different positions (as by successive still photographs). The impression does not depend on the basic illusion of continuity: provided that the mind can supply a possible trajectory, all that is needed is that the object should appear to be the same and that its position in successive shots should appear to be different. But beyond this, the effect of *any* sustainedly rapid cutting is to produce an impression of rapid motion, even if the intercut shots have no common content and one cannot say what (apart from "things") is moving. An intermediate sort of effect produced by editing is a two-dimensional movement of light, where the continuity of light and dark areas in successive shots is enough to entice the mind to complete a *Gestalt;* but this effect is of limited application, in that it draws attention away from the filmed world to the screen surface.

Cinema's repertory of motions both presented and psychologically suggested is so extensive and so essential that one might think that what film shares with still photography is unimportant, and specifically that two-dimensional composition within the frame can play no significant part in film at all. But that would be going too far. Not only does the awareness of the screen and its flat pattern play an essential part in grounding the ambiguous nature of film space, but directors in practice often do envisage their scenes statically. They make sketches for their key scenes beforehand, and use viewfinders to compose a scene before shooting it. A film no less than a play may proceed from tableau to tableau. Nonetheless, the tableau is insidiously misleading in more than one way. The more one reads about films the more clearly one sees how each film is invariably illustrated by a handful of constantly recurring still shots: *Potemkin* comes to be represented by half a dozen stills, *Caligari* by two, *Nosferatu* by one. Most of these are not even frames taken from the actual film, but photographs taken on a still camera before or after shooting. And they are chosen for their pictorial qualities. What I most vividly recall from *Bicycle Thieves* is the mountain of bundled clothing in the pawnshop, but that image would be nothing without the camera's movement and the action of adding one's own bundle to the mountain; and what the stills show me is a pretty, pathetic picture of the hero and his son sitting on the sidewalk. Thus in time one's recollection of what a film was like becomes distorted.

223

SOUND

We have been discussing film in visual terms. But for rather more than half its history film has been fully an art of sound as well as sight in the sense that the associated sound has been determined by the same celluloid strip that carries the image. The justification of our procedure is that sight remains primary. It is the requirements of the visual image that call for the elaboration of equipment and the circumstances of display that are fundamental to cinema. Film sound has no distinctive qualities in itself, and can be meaningfully discussed only as an adjunct to the visual.

Though a sound track for a film can be made directly at the time of shooting simply by hanging microphones near the action and recording on the film whatever they pick up, this is neither necessary nor usual. The sound track is usually made separately and combined with the visual film later. The resulting complexities for sound film are theoretically immense, though in practice the technology is not intimidating. The use of magnetic tape has made the recording, inventing, blending, splicing and modification of sounds easy and inexpensive as the analogous procedures for visual film can never be.

The fundamental classification of film sounds is that enunciated by Kracauer. A sound may belong to the world of the film (e.g. the dialogue of its characters) or it may be extraneous (e.g. background music or a commentary). In the former case, it may belong to the very scene being shown on the screen or it may not (you may hear what is happening elsewhere from what you see, or be reminded by the sound track of a previous scene; as a marginal case, what you hear may be a sound remembered by one of the characters). If the sound does belong to the scene being shown, its provenance may be on or off camera (as you hear someone talk, you may see him, or the person he is addressing, or someone who overhears him, or an opening door that he fails to notice). Thus sound may (and in a slackly made film often does) merely duplicate or reinforce what is visible, but it may play an independent structural or narrative role, and may affect the interpretation or emotional tone of what is seen. For example, distortions, fadings, and swellings of voices can be used to overcome one of the difficulties of film narrative, that of economically revealing to the audience a state of mind that someone is successfully hiding from those around him. Background music may supply an ironic comment, as when the refueling of aircraft in *Dr. Strangelove* is accompanied by a love song — a Russian film of the silent days would have made the point by intercutting shots of animals mating, and what a bore it would have been. One can even try to use a musical score to supplement narrative deficiencies, or even to contradict the apparent tendency of what is seen to be happening, though such techniques have some notorious fiascos to their credit.

When determinate sound was first introduced, many film-lovers were opposed to it. In principle, the objection was invalid, for films had never been shown without accompanying (and would-be relevant) sound (a "silent" film shown in silence is a curiosity rather than a significant experience), and in principle the change only guaranteed that from now on the sound would indeed be relevant. But in practice what was feared was the "talking film," in which the sound track merely enabled the audience to hear what they could already see. And the use of sound does indeed make sloppy and mindless film-making easier. But sound can be and properly is used not merely to add another dimension to the film experience but to add an extra perspective to the visual experience itself.

As an alternative to the mindless use of attached sound that they dreaded, the Russian theorists of the late twenties proposed that their favorite device of associative or metaphorical montage should be extended to sound: intercut images should form a counterpoint against intercut sounds. This did not happen. For one thing, auditory comprehension has a much slower tempo than visual; for another, sounds tend to blend whereas images contrast. The proposed contrapuntal montage would have been impossibly overloaded, if not unintelligible. What montage requires from sound, it turns out, is not a contrapuntal pattern but a chordal backing for its visual melody, a continuous equivalent for or commentary on the character of the whole episode. In any case, the possibility of using sound effects as commentary on the visual images has made elaborate visual montage an obsolete device. This can be thought of as a catastrophic and uncompensated loss to the art of film, but the matter is open to question. Although Eisenstein and others made the use of associative intercutting into a Marxist aesthetic dogma (inasmuch as the conflict of contrasting shots forms a "dialectic" from which the realist truth is synthesized), others have pointed out that the device endears itself to totalitarian regimes by lending itself to lying propaganda: the associations it creates are entirely irrational. Partly, too, the reliance on cutting was enforced by the use of heavy and inflexible camera equipment. Conversely, the decreasing reliance on editing in scene construction is partly due to the introduction of ever more mobile and flexible equipment, partly to the familiarity of multicamera television procedures, partly to difficulties in synchronizing dialogue, but partly also to the fact that commercial directors tend not to do their own cutting anyway, losing effective control over their films as soon as shooting stops.

STRUCTURE

We have been dealing with the materials of film. To make a movie, the materials must somehow be organized. A film can be made simply by linking images and sounds in abstract rhythmic concatenation (as in McLaren's films), or by loosely arranging them around a theme (as in travelogues). But these straightforward methods, though in some ways they represent an ideal of pure cinema, seem to work well only for quite short films, and (especially since the decline of vaudeville) the staple of film production is the "feature," long enough to give the cash customers their money's worth. There are no theoretical limits to the length of a clearly articulated pattern of imagery, but most abstract films are short. The closest actual approximation to an abstract or purely formal method of organizing images is to associate them with extended musical forms, since the latter constitute long formal sequences of a kind that audiences already know and accept; but Disney's *Fantasia*, though often and lucratively revived, has not aroused emulation and in any case supplemented the musical structure with at least an illusion of parallel narrative form. More usually, coherence is sought through the organization of the subject matter of the imagery: by exploring a problem, or an object, or a place, or a situation, or an event (documentary), or, commonest of all, by constructing a fictitious or historical story. The contrast between documentary and the regular "feature" is not so much that between fact

226

and fiction, for features may be factual and most documentaries have fictional aspects, as between exploratory and narrative methods of organization. The reason for the dominance of the narrative feature lies partly in the flexibility of the film medium, which makes it especially suitable for a free-running narrative whose closest affinities are with novels and biographies, but partly in the assumption that the "mass audience" will associate exploration with instruction and hence with tedium. Now that the mass audience is safely shut away with its TV set things may change: *Woodstock* is a portent. Meanwhile, writers on cinema are bound to assume that the narrative feature remains the norm.

It is from the normal narrative form that the customary description of the articulation of film is derived. In a sense, and from the editor's viewpoint, the unit is the frame, but this does not exist for perception. Aesthetically, a film consists of shots organized into scenes which are themselves articulated into sequences. This structure corresponds, very roughly, to an analysis of activity into movements (shots), actions (scenes), and episodes (sequences). Accordingly, shots cohere into scenes through relevance, each shot being experienced as relevant to expectations aroused earlier in the scene (ideally, I suppose, by the preceding shot). Scenes are divided by jump-cuts or dissolves marking a change of subject; sequences are divided by such more emphatic punctuation as fade-out and fade-in. But (as with novel and theater) no rules or firm conventions demand such articulation: the determining changes are discontinuities of place, time, participants or activities (in abstract films, changes in the kind of image or movement; in documentaries, changes of aspect or style). The film-maker's use of punctuating devices is merely incidental to these. Actually, the very concept of a "shot" becomes nebulous and archaic as cameras become more mobile: the distinction between scene and shot takes on a vagueness such as infects the distinction between an action and its constituent movements.

The plasticity of camera viewpoint is such that films, like novels and unlike plays, can focus one's attention precisely. Only what is irreducibly relevant to the story need to be shown. A raised eyebrow can fill the screen. In theater, perception follows attention: one looks at the relevant part of what is visible on stage and ignores the rest. In film, attention follows perception: whatever is not rele-

227

vant is either not screened or thrown into shadow or out of focus. Hence, film storytelling can and sometimes does achieve great elegance and economy. Styles change, however. The introduction of the wide screen has made the use of close-ups to isolate relevant detail seem rather blatant, and encourages a more fluid and relaxed style of presentation in which more use is made of the simultaneous presence on the screen of more than one focus for attention.

The focusing habit of the camera and the necessary priority of the visual might make one think that the most filmic and hence the best film story was one in which the *precise* content of each shot set up the story through its dynamic connection with the next. One might further infer from this that tragedy with its overriding architectonic goes against the grain of film, which has a special affinity for such episodic forms as picaresque comedy. There is something in that, but we warned at the start against the facile assumption that the best works in any medium are those which take its most obvious opportunities as procedural rules, and an overly filmic film might have the mechanized aggressiveness of a "well-made play." One could more reasonably infer that the least filmic and hence dullest films would be those in which the dialogue carried the story and the camera just coasted along. And yet that is how most films seem to be made. One can see why. Many films are adapted from literary works in which the dialogue alone can be borrowed without alteration. But in any case the logistics of making a full-scale film are such that it more or less has to be constructed from a detailed shooting-script. Films are largely *written* before they are shot. But writers are bound to be word-oriented. Besides, dialogue is the only part of the script that contributes directly to determining the actual quality of the finished film: specifications of visual images cannot include what will differentiate the effective from the flat, the fine from the clumsy. Perhaps most important, to throw responsibility for the story onto the dialogue is to play safe and easy. So long as the actors mouth the lines the story will somehow come through, and the director can content himself with the most perfunctory and generalized camera work. If the story depends on what can be seen, much greater care must be taken over exactly what is shown, and that will add to the shooting time which is the variable on which the cost of a film chiefly depends.

228

ART, COMMERCE, AND CRITICISM

Now the cat is out of the bag. Films are traditionally about money, and film as most people know it is commercial film. Film did not begin as high art or as folk art, but as the offspring of technological curiosity and showmanship. It got into the public eye by way of peep-show and vaudeville, and its first exponents did not think of themselves as artists. The structural analogies between film and novel, and the superficial likenesses between film and drama, suggest affiliations that took some time to develop. A glance at the advertisements in your local newspaper should convince you that film has yet to free itself from the hectic world and accent of the fairground.

Though cheap and flexible sound and camera equipment has done much to effect what Andrew Sarris has called "demystifying the medium," the financial structure of the film industry has still some claim to be considered as part of the technological conditions that we have recognized to be paramount in cinema. The decisive factors here are that the initial costs of making even a cheap film are high, but the printing, distribution, and exhibition costs are low. So the costs can be recovered if enough people are willing to see the film—which they will be able to do only if enough people are willing to show it. Nor is this a consequence of the sickness of western bourgeois society. No one, socialist or capitalist, is going to be allowed to tie up so much of other people's labor and equipment unless there is some reasonable assurance that there will be something to show for it: if not money, then prestige or the approved performance of some supposed social function. By the same token, the complexities of the arrangements for distributing or showing films are almost certain to deprive the director of control over the final condition and destiny of his work. A film critic is seldom commenting on the work of an individual or a cohesive group so much as on the upshot of a loosely connected series of independent decisions. He may thus succumb to feelings of irrelevance.

There are three plausible lines a critic can take here. One is to confine his attention to noncommercial films. Of course, these are atypical, but the critic can say (as Parker Tyler says) that it is not typical for a film to be a work of art. Most drawings, to take a parallel case, are not works of art but advertisements or sources of technical information or doodles, and no one expects a critic to waste his time on such objects.

A second critical line is to accept that most films, both commercial and "underground," are junk, to be greeted with silence or a dismissive gesture, but that any kind of interest or excellence may turn up in any sort of film. Such a rejection of all commitments to styles and cultural traditions is in the line of twentieth-century critical orthodoxy, but may find it hard to steer between the Scylla of an empty formalistic aestheticism and the Charybdis of a relativism that accepts everything equally because everything succeeds in being what it is.

A third critical line is to accept cinema as a demotic art and devise a critical system appropriate to such an art. George Orwell has shown the way. His exemplary study of Frank Richards devoted itself to describing the "world" depicted or implied by the ensemble of Richard's work, and exploring the repertory of mannerisms which gave that world a facile coherence. Students of Jung and Frye have enlarged this critical armory by showing how to expose the underlying mythical archetypes and patterns in popular fiction. These methods have been applied to Hollywood films in what is misnamed the "auteur theory" of criticism (which is a policy rather than a theory). Whatever a studio does to a film, a strong-minded director can impregnate it indelibly with his own basic textures, his view of human relationships, his favorite narrative devices, and obsessive images. In fact, the measure of a director's stature may be the extent to which he can retain these elements of his own style when working on an uncongenial assignment from his studio. And by comparing a director's different films, which taken in isolation had been thought undistinguished if no worse, one can educe a complex world full of ironies and unexpected insights.

Some auteur critics seem to assume that any director whose work is susceptible to their methods is thereby proved to be an artist, and his films shown to be good films. This is a strange assumption. Critics of other arts are far from supposing that to show that a work is recognizable and typical of its author has any tendency to show that it is a good work. In fact, the analogue in other arts is a form of criticism specifically devised for handling material incapable of yielding anything of interest to a more searching critique. Auteur criticism may work best as a heuristic device: armed with his comparisons and with his trained eye for manners and genres, a critic can show us meaning where we saw none; but when we have been shown we must be able to see for ourselves. In other arts we accept that one may not understand any work by an innovating artist until one has familiarized oneself with his style; but it is strange to have a similar esoteric status claimed for the output of a studio work-horse. The paradox of auteur criticism is that while its methods are devised to handle cinema as a demotic art, it relies on a view of that art which is inaccessible to most of its normal public. How many people are going to get to see a Raoul Walsh festival?

In so far as the normal film is about human affairs, it is susceptible to criticism on the same basis as literary or dramatic works or figurative paintings, in terms of its verisimilitude, psychological richness, moral maturity, social significance, political viability, relations to the divine and the unconscious and so on. The fact that such topics are not specific to film does not make them trivial or irrelevant*: on the contrary, most actual serious discussion of films centers on this human side, and so it should. But we need say nothing about such criticism here. In practice we all know what we want to say; in theory the basic moves are familiar from discussions of criticism in the older arts. From this point of view, the art of film criticism would lie in knowledge of and sensitivity to the ways in which such human qualities can be conveyed by such cinematic means as we have been discussing.

The salient feature of film is the enormous range of its specific effects. Film is unique in its capacity for visual recording and analysis, in its ability to convey the unique present reality of things, in its ability to reveal the qualities of lives; but also in its formal freedom, its capacity for realizing fantasy and developing abstract forms. In view of this inexhaustible flexibility of the medium, it is ludicrous to lay down general principles as to what is a good film.

---

*It has become fashionable among practitioners of the visual arts to apply the term "literary" to all humanistic or nonformal aspects of works of art, thus suggesting that in being a picture *of* something a work is somehow untrue of the visual. This implies that seeing or hearing something happen is an indirect way of reading about it. In fact, of course, scenes convey meaning as naturally and directly as words.

Those critics who do so are in most cases obviously fixated on the kind of film that was around when they were first moved by movies. A judicious critic will equip himself with the most exhaustive possible grasp of the variables and variations accessible to filmmakers, and note just which of these the director is exploiting and how he is doing it. So much can be done in a film that it requires close attention and knowledge to discern what is actually being done. Technical assessment and appreciation can almost be read off from the roll of specific opportunities opened up by the director's initial options and then seized or missed: take care of the facts and the values will take care of themselves. Beyond that, the moral and cultural side of a critique must depend on the maturity and sensitivity of the critic's social and moral awareness. If you could teach someone to be a critic, you could teach him to be a man.

IV

Film, Theater, and Literature

Theorists have often attempted to discover the characteristics of the film medium by comparing it with other media. Panofsky, for example, contrasts the theater's static use of space and its independence of the principle of co-expressibility with cinema's more dynamic use of space and its rigorous subjection to that principle. For Panofsky, this difference explains why film adaptations of plays are so unlikely to succeed. Any attempt to transfer theater's essentially verbal resources to the cinema violates the principle that no more should be expressed verbally than can be expressed visually. The cinema's business is not the photographing of theatrical decor, a prestylized reality, but the photographing of actual physical reality so that it has style. Panofsky finds cinema the only medium that does justice to the materialistic interpretation of the universe which pervades contemporary civilization.

Like Panofsky, Hugo Munsterberg, the Harvard psychologist and philosopher who was a colleague of both William James and George Santayana, attempted in 1916 to delineate the features of the silent "photoplay" by contrasting it with the theater. For Munsterberg, the representation of physical reality is the concern not of cinema, but of theater. In true cinema, "the massive outer world has lost its weight, it has been freed from space, time and causality, and it has been clothed in the forms of our consciousness." Theater is bound by the same laws that govern nature, but the cinema is free to be shaped by the inner movements of the mind. Theater therefore trespasses on the realm of cinema when it employs any analogue of the close-up or the flash-back, and Münsterberg is as harsh a critic of "cinematified" theater as Panofsky is of "theatricalized" film.

For Münsterberg the true function of the close-up is not to provide a closer view of nature but to reproduce the mental act of attention. Similarly, the cut-back provides a cinematic equivalent of human memory and is alien to theater, which is bound by the laws of nature and the necessities of temporal succession. In the theater, "men of flesh and blood with really plastic bodies stand before us. They move like any moving body in our surroundings. Moreover, those happenings on the stage, just like events in life, are independent of our subjective attention and memory and imagination. They go their objective course." If it were the object of cinema, then, to "imitate" nature, film could hardly compete with theater. "The color of the world has disappeared, the persons are dumb, no sound reaches our ears. The depth of the scene appears unreal, the motion has lost its natural character. Worst of all, the objective course of events is falsified . . ." The genius of cinema is not, then, to "imitate" nature; rather it is to display the triumph of mind over matter.

The essay by Susan Sontag, the influential American writer and director, may be read as a critique of both Panofsky and Münsterberg. Despite their many and important differences, both "insist on a single model for film" and for theater, too. Their conception of the stage derives from notions of realism based on Ibsen and the French well-made play more than it does on the epic use of the stage by Shakespeare, the Russian constructivists, or Brecht. Similarly, their views of film display a strong prejudice in favor of the methods of the silent film. They are all too ready to confine cinema within rigid boundaries and to insist on maintaining artistic "purity," a separation of the various arts. Although Sontag understands the impulse to purity, she also understands a contrasting artistic ideal, one descending from Wagner rather than Lessing, which takes as its ideal a comprehensive "mixed-media" art form in the tradition of Greek theater and the Wagnerian music-drama. She does not choose between puristic and anti-puristic conceptions of the cinema or of the theater, but suggests awaiting future developments without prejudice.

Sontag accepts both the fact that many successful films have been "adapted" from plays and the fact that cinematic effects have been employed successfully in the theater. Béla Balázs also agrees that adaptation is possible. Indeed, he notes that many of the greatest masterpieces of the Greeks and of Shakespeare are themselves adaptations. He nevertheless agrees with those who argue that it is impossible to transfer "themes" or "content" from one artistic form to another, for each content requires its own form. He resolves the conflict between the possibility of adaptation and the impossibility of transferring content to an alien form, by arguing that in a successful adaptation the artist does not simply transfer content.

In Balázs's view, the artist goes back to the original work and selects from its "materials" those elements that are appropriate to the cinematic form (whether those "materials" are the events, characters, and dialogue contained in the work the artist is adapting or the "naked" realities from which those elements were themselves derived is not entirely clear). In effect, these selected "materials" become a new content for the film's new form, so that the inseparability of form and content is as applicable to a cinematic adaptation as to any other art.

André Bazin, too, insists on the value of adaptations. He thinks that Cocteau's *Les Parents Terrible* and Olivier's *Henry V* are superb films. But he does not agree with Balázs that one selects from the original "material" in order to make a successful adaptation. Rather, "a good adaptation should result in a restoration of the essence and spirit" of the original play. Indeed, in films like Cocteau's and Olivier's, one is "no longer adapting, one is staging a play by means of cinema."

Bazin realizes that if the living actor's presence were essential to the effects of theater, the successful staging of a play by means of cinema would be impossible. He therefore argues that there is a sense in which the actor is present on the screen just as a person is "present" in a mirror. Although Bazin's refutation of the importance of presence is not very convincing (Stanley Cavell treats the issue much more systematically in *The World Viewed*), it allows him to assert that the primary difference between stage and screen is not one of living beings but of architecture. Bazin thinks that theatrical speech often fails in a film not because it was written for living speakers but because it was written to be uttered in a particular kind of world. The problem of filming a play is to find a decor that preserves the closed, microcosmic qualities of theatrical architecture for which the dialogue was written and which at the same time preserves the natural realism of the screen. The screen is not a world in itself but a window on the world which consistently dwarfs and dissipates theatrical speech. Bazin believes this problem is worth solving, for even if original film scripts are preferable to adaptations, truly distinguished ones are rare. The cinema cannot afford to ignore its theatrical heritage, any more than the drama can afford the loss of the audiences that film can bring it.

Eisenstein too insists on the cultural heritage of cinema. He argues that Griffith even learned montage, which Eisenstein considers the essence of film, from the pages of Dickens. Eisenstein plainly sees no theoretical bar to adapting novels successfully to the screen, as proved by his own attempt to adapt Drieser's *An American Tragedy*. Indeed, it is not implausible to argue, as Bazin and Sontag have, that the film's deepest affinities are with the novel, not with the play. The novel is "cinematic" in its fluid handling of time and space, in its "focused" narrative control, in its ability to alternate description with dialogue, and even in the privacy and isolation of its audiences. The film has adapted more fiction than drama.

In contrast, George Bluestone, a contemporary American scholar, argues that film and novel are fundamentally different. The novel (like the stage in Panofsky's view) is fundamentally a linguistic medium, while the film is primarily visual. Although both D. W. Griffith and Joseph Conrad state that their purpose is to make us "see," Bluestone contends that while we literally "see" films (we perceive the images themselves), we do not literally see anything in a sentence except the words (which we apprehend conceptually). The film, therefore, "necessarily leaves behind those characteristic contents of thought which only language can approximate: tropes, dreams, memories, conceptual consciousness." The adapter must, as Balázs has suggested, treat the novel merely as raw material and create for the film its own form and content, which will be sensual and perceptual, rather than conceptual and discursive as was the original novel.

Perhaps no films more clearly illuminate the tensions between cinema and literature than the attempts to adapt Shakespeare to the screen. Not surprisingly, critical discussions of those specific attempts reflect the general, theoretical issues. Peter Brook, the British stage and film director, examines the problem of transferring Shakespeare's verse and imagery to film, a medium he finds less fluid than the Elizabethan stage (this observation is in sharp contrast to Panofsky's claims about the static stage space). Frank Kermode, the English literary critic, assesses Brook's subsequent attempt to solve these problems when he brought *King Lear* to the screen. James Agee, the most celebrated American film critic of the last generation, records his admiration for Olivier's *Henry V*, arguing that it is more successful than all but the rarest stage productions in communicating Shakespeare's language. André Bazin appeals to his own theory of the relation between theater and cinema to explain how Welles, in his *Othello*, also succeeds in transferring Shakespeare's language to the screen. J. Blumenthal, a British critic, shares Peter Brook's great admiration for Kurosawa's *Throne of Blood* but casts doubt on Brook's search for a way to translate Shakespeare's poetry into an alien medium. Blumenthal believes that Kurosawa's brilliant success is due to his objectification of Macbeth's thoughts in physical terms; he thinks that words and especially poetry have "no place in any film."

HUGO MUNSTERBERG
FROM THE FILM:
A PSYCHOLOGICAL STUDY

THE MEANS OF THE PHOTOPLAY

We have now reached the point at which we can knot together all our threads, the psychological and the esthetic ones. If we do so, we come to the true thesis of this whole book. Our esthetic discussion showed us that it is the aim of art to isolate a significant part of our experience in such a way that it is separate from our practical life and is in complete agreement within itself. Our esthetic satisfaction results from this inner agreement and harmony, but in order that we may feel such agreement of the parts we must enter with our own impulses into the will of every element, into the meaning of every line and color and form, every word and tone and note. Only if everything is full of such inner movement can we really enjoy the harmonious coöperation of the parts. The means of the various arts, we saw, are the forms and methods by which this aim is fulfilled. They must be different for every material. Moreover the same material may allow very different methods of isolation and elimination of the insignificant and reënforcement of that which contributes to the harmony. If we ask now what are the characteristic means by which the photoplay succeeds in overcoming reality, in isolating a significant dramatic story and in presenting it so that we enter into it and yet keep it away from our practical life and enjoy the harmony of the parts, we must remember all the results to which our psychological discussion in the first part of the book has led us.

We recognized there that the photoplay, incomparable in this respect with the drama, gave us a view of dramatic events which was completely shaped by the inner movements of the mind. To be sure, the events in the photoplay happen in the real space with its depth. But the spectator feels that they are not presented in the three dimensions of the outer world, that they are flat pictures which only the mind molds into plastic things. Again the events are seen in continuous movement; and yet the pictures break up the movement into a rapid succession of instantaneous impressions. We do not see the objective reality, but a product of our own mind which binds the pictures together. But much stronger differences came to light when we turned to the processes of attention, of memory, of imagination, of suggestion, of division of interest and of emotion. The attention turns to detailed points in the outer world and ignores everything else: the photoplay is doing exactly this when in the close-up a detail is enlarged and everything else disappears. Memory breaks into present events by bringing up pictures of the past: the photoplay is doing this by its frequent cutbacks, when pictures of events long past flit between those of the present. The imagination anticipates the future or overcomes reality by fancies and dreams; the photoplay is doing all this more richly than any chance imagination would succeed in doing. But chiefly, through our division of interest our mind is drawn hither and thither. We think of events which run parallel in different places. The photoplay can show in intertwined scenes everything which our mind embraces. Events in three or four or five regions of the world can be woven together into one complex action. Finally, we saw that every shade of feeling and emotion which fills the spectator's mind can mold the scenes in the photoplay until they appear the embodiment of our feelings. In every one of these aspects the photoplay succeeds in doing what the drama of the theater does not attempt.

If this is the outcome of esthetic analysis on the one side, of psychological research on the other, we need only combine the results of both into a unified principle: *the photoplay tells us the human story by overcoming the forms of the outer world, namely, space, time, and causality, and by adjusting the events to the forms of the inner world, namely, attention, memory, imagination, and emotion.*

We shall gain our orientation most directly if once more, under this point of view, we compare the photoplay with the performance on the theater stage. We shall not enter into a discussion of the character of the regular theater and its drama. We take this for granted. Everybody knows that highest art form which the Greeks created and which from Greece has spread over Asia, Europe, and America. In tragedy and in comedy from ancient times to Ibsen, Rostand, Hauptmann, and Shaw we recognize one common purpose and one common form for which no further commentary is needed. How does the photoplay differ from a theater performance? We insisted that every work of art must be somehow separated from our sphere of practical interests. The theater is no exception. The structure of the theater itself, the framelike form of the stage, the difference of light between stage and house, the stage setting and costuming, all inhibit in the audience the possibility of taking the action on the stage to be real life. Stage managers have sometimes tried the experiment of reducing those differences, for instance, keeping the audience also in a fully lighted hall, and they always had to discover how much the dramatic effect was reduced because the feeling of distance from reality was weakened. The photoplay and the theater in this respect are evidently alike. The screen too suggests from the very start the complete unreality of the events.

But each further step leads us to remarkable differences between the stage play and the film play. In every respect the film play is further away from the physical reality than the drama and in every respect this greater distance from the physical world brings it nearer to the mental world. The stage shows us living men. It is not the real Romeo and not the real Juliet; and yet the actor and the actress have the ringing voices of true people, breathe like them, have living colors like them, and fill physical space like them. What is left in the photoplay? The voice has been stilled: the photoplay is a dumb show. Yet we must not forget that this alone is a step away from reality which has often been taken in the midst of the dramatic world. Whoever knows the history of the theater is aware of the tremendous rôle which the pantomime has played in the development of mankind. From the old half-religious pantomimic and suggestive dances out of which the beginnings of the real drama grew to the fully religious pantomimes of medieval ages and, further on, to many silent mimic elements in modern performances, we find a continuity of conventions which make the pantomime almost the real background of all dramatic development. We know how popular the pantomimes were among the Greeks, and how they stood in the foreground in the imperial period of Rome. Old

241

Rome cherished the mimic clowns, but still more the tragic panto-mimics. "Their very nod speaks, their hands talk and their fingers have a voice." After the fall of the Roman empire the church used the pantomime for the portrayal of sacred history, and later centuries enjoyed very unsacred histories in the pantomimes of their ballets. Even complex artistic tragedies without words have triumphed on our present-day stage. *L'Enfant Prodigue* which came from Paris, *Sumurun* which came from Berlin, *Petroushka* which came from Petrograd, conquered the American stage; and surely the loss of speech, while it increased the remoteness from reality, by no means destroyed the continuous consciousness of the bodily existence of the actors.

Moreover the student of a modern pantomime cannot overlook a characteristic difference between the speechless performance on the stage and that of the actors of a photoplay. The expression of the inner states, the whole system of gestures, is decidedly different: and here we might say that the photoplay stands nearer to life than the pantomime. Of course, the photoplayer must somewhat exaggerate the natural expression. The whole rhythm and intensity of his gestures must be more marked than it would be with actors who accompany their movements by spoken words and who express the meaning of their thoughts and feelings by the content of what they say. Nevertheless the photoplayer uses the regular channels of mental discharge. He acts simply as a very emotional person might act. But the actor who plays in a pantomime cannot be satisfied with that. He is expected to add something which is entirely unnatural, namely a kind of artificial demonstration of his emotions. He must not only behave like an angry man, but he must behave like a man who is consciously interested in his anger and wants to demonstrate it to others. He exhibits his emotions for the spectators. He really acts theatrically for the benefit of the by-standers. If he did not try to do so, his means of conveying a rich story and a real conflict of human passions would be too meager. The photoplayer, with the rapid changes of scenes, has other possibilities of conveying his intentions. He must not yield to the temptation to play a pantomime on the screen, or he will seriously injure the artistic quality of the reel.

The really decisive distance from bodily reality, however, is created by the substitution of the actor's picture for the actor himself. Lights and shades replace the manifoldness of color effects and mere perspective must furnish the suggestion of depth. We traced it when we discussed the psychology of kinematoscopic perception. But we must not put the emphasis on the wrong point. The natural tendency might be to lay the chief stress on the fact that those people in the photoplay do not stand before us in flesh and blood. The essential point is rather that we are conscious of the flatness of the picture. If we were to see the actors of the stage in a mirror, it would also be a reflected image which we perceive. We should not really have the actors themselves in our straight line of vision; and yet this image would appear to us equivalent to the actors themselves, because it would contain all the depth of the real stage. The process which leads from the living men to the screen is more complex than a mere reflection in a mirror, but in spite of the complexity in the transmission we do, after all, see the real actor in the picture. The photograph is absolutely different from those pictures which a clever draughtsman has sketched. In the photoplay we see the actors themselves and the decisive factor which makes the impression different from seeing real men is not that we see the living persons through the medium of photographic reproduction but that this reproduction shows them in a flat form. The bodily space has been eliminated. We said once before that stereoscopic arrangements could reproduce somewhat this plastic form also. Yet this would seriously interfere with the character of the photoplay. We need there this overcoming of the depth, we want to have it as a picture only and yet as a picture which strongly suggests to us the actual depth of the real world. We want to keep the interest in the plastic world and want to be aware of the depth in which the persons move, but our direct object of perception must be without the depth. That idea of space which forces on us most strongly the idea of heaviness, solidity and substantiality must be replaced by the light flitting immateriality.

But the photoplay sacrifices not only the space values of the real theater; it disregards no less its order of time. The theater presents its plot in the time order of reality. It may interrupt the continuous flow of time without neglecting the conditions of the dramatic art. There may be twenty years between the third and the fourth act, inasmuch as the dramatic writer must select those elements spread over space and time which are significant for the development of

243

his story. But he is bound by the fundamental principle of real time, that it can move only forward and not backward. Whatever the theater shows us now must come later in the story than that which it showed us in any previous moment. The strict classical demand for complete unity of time does not fit every drama, but a drama would give up its mission if it told us in the third act something which happened before the second act. Of course, there may be a play within a play, and the players on the stage which is set on the stage may play events of old Roman history before the king of France. But this is an enclosure of the past in the present, which corresponds exactly to the actual order of events. The photoplay, on the other hand, does not and must not respect this temporal structure of the physical universe. At any point the photoplay interrupts the series and brings us back to the past. We studied this unique feature of the film art when we spoke of the psychology of memory and imagination. With the full freedom of our fancy, with the whole mobility of our association of ideas, pictures of the past flit through the scenes of the present. Time is left behind. Man becomes boy; today is interwoven with the day before yesterday. The freedom of the mind has triumphed over the unalterable law of the outer world.

It is interesting to watch how playwrights nowadays try to steal the thunder of the photoplay and experiment with time reversals on the legitimate stage. We are esthetically on the borderland when a grandfather tells his grandchild the story of his own youth as a warning, and instead of the spoken words the events of his early years come before our eyes. This is, after all, quite similar to a play within a play. A very different experiment is tried in *Under Cover*. The third act, which plays on the second floor of the house, ends with an explosion. The fourth act, which plays downstairs, begins a quarter of an hour before the explosion. Here we have a real denial of a fundamental condition of the theater. Or if we stick to recent products of the American stage, we may think of *On Trial*, a play which perhaps comes nearest to a dramatic usurpation of the rights of the photoplay. We see the court scene and as one witness after another begins to give his testimony the courtroom is replaced by the scenes of the actions about which the witness is to report. Another clever play, *Between the Lines*, ends the first act with a postman bringing three letters from the three children of the house.

The second, third, and fourth acts lead us to the three different homes from which the letters came and the action in the three places not only precedes the writing of the letters, but goes on at the same time. The last act, finally, begins with the arrival of the letters which tell the ending of those events in the three homes. Such experiments are very suggestive but they are not any longer pure dramatic art. It is always possible to mix arts. An Italian painter produces very striking effects by putting pieces of glass and stone and rope into his paintings, but they are no longer pure paintings. The drama in which the later event comes before the earlier is an esthetic barbarism which is entertaining as a clever trick in a graceful superficial play, but intolerable in ambitious dramatic art. It is not only tolerable but perfectly natural in any photoplay. The pictorial reflection of the world is not bound by the rigid mechanism of time. Our mind is here and there, our mind turns to the present and then to the past: the photoplay can equal it in its freedom from the bondage of the material world.

But the theater is bound not only by space and time. Whatever it shows is controlled by the same laws of causality which govern nature. This involves a complete continuity of the physical events: no cause without following effect, no effect without preceding cause. This whole natural course is left behind in the play on the screen. The deviation from reality begins with that resolution of the continuous movement which we studied in our psychological discussions. We saw that the impression of movement results from an activity of the mind which binds the separate pictures together. What we actually see is a composite; it is like the movement of a fountain in which every jet is resolved into numberless drops. We feel the play of those drops in their sparkling haste as one continuous stream of water, and yet are conscious of the myriads of drops, each one separate from the others. This fountainlike spray of pictures has completely overcome the causal world.

In an entirely different form this triumph over causality appears in the interruption of the events by pictures which belong to another series. We find this whenever the scene suddenly changes. The processes are not carried to their natural consequences. A movement is started, but before the cause brings its results another scene has taken its place. What this new scene brings may be an effect for which we saw no causes. But not only the processes are interrupted. The intertwining of the scenes which we have traced in detail is itself such a contrast to causality. It is as if different objects could fill the same space at the same time. It is as if the resistance of the material world had disappeared and the substances could penetrate one another. In the interlacing of our ideas we experience this superiority to all physical laws. The theater would not have even the technical means to give us such impressions, but if it had, it would have no right to make use of them, as it would destroy the basis on which the drama is built. We have only another case of the same type in those series of pictures which aim to force a suggestion on our mind. We have spoken of them. A certain effect is prepared by a chain of causes and yet when the causal result is to appear the film is cut off. We have the causes without the effect. The villain thrusts with his dagger—but a miracle has snatched away his victim.

While the moving pictures are lifted above the world of space and time and causality and are freed from its bounds, they are certainly not without law. We said before that the freedom with which the pictures replace one another is to a large degree comparable to the sparkling and streaming of the musical tones. The yielding to the play of the mental energies, to the attention and emotion, which is felt in the film pictures, is still more complete in the musical melodies and harmonies in which the tones themselves are merely the expressions of the ideas and feelings and will impulses of the mind. Their harmonies and disharmonies, their fusing and blending, is not controlled by any outer necessity, but by the inner agreement and disagreement of our free impulses. And yet in this world of musical freedom, everything is completely controlled by esthetic necessities. No sphere of practical life stands under such rigid rules as the realm of the composer. However bold the musical genius may be he cannot emancipate himself from the iron rule that his work must show complete unity in itself. All the separate prescriptions which the musical student has to learn are ultimately only the consequences of this central demand which music, the freest of the arts, shares with all the others. In the case of the film, too, the freedom from the physical forms of space, time, and causality does not mean any liberation from this esthetic bondage either. On the contrary, just as music is surrounded by more technical rules than literature, the photoplay must be held together by the esthetic demands still more firmly than is the drama. The arts which are subordinated to the conditions of space, time, and causality find a certain firmness of structure in these material forms which contain an element of outer connectedness. But where these forms are given up and where the freedom of mental play replaces their outer necessity, everything would fall asunder if the esthetic unity were disregarded.

This unity is, first of all, the unity of action. The demand for it is the same which we know from the drama. The temptation to neglect it is nowhere greater than in the photoplay where outside matter can so easily be introduced or independent interests developed. It is certainly true for the photoplay, as for every work of art, that nothing has the right to existence in its midst which is not internally needed for the unfolding of the unified action. Wherever two plots are given to us, we receive less by far than if we had only one plot. We leave the sphere of valuable art entirely when a unified action is ruined by mixing it with declamation, and propaganda which is not organically interwoven with the action itself. It may be still fresh in memory what an esthetically intolerable helter-skelter performance was offered to the public in *The Battle-cry of Peace.* Nothing can be more injurious to the esthetic cultivation of the people than such performances which hold the attention of the spectators by ambitious detail and yet destroy their esthetic sensibility by a complete disregard of the fundamental principle of art, the demand for unity. But we recognized also that this unity involves complete isolation. We annihilate beauty when we link the artistic creation with practical interests and transform the spectator into a selfishly interested bystander. The scenic background of the play is not presented in order that we decide whether we want to spend our next vacation there. The interior decoration of the rooms is not exhibited as a display for a department store. The men and women who carry out the action of the plot must not be people whom we may meet tomorrow on the street. All the threads of the play must be knotted together in the play itself and none should be connected with our outside interests. A good photoplay must be isolated and complete in itself like a beautiful melody. It is not an advertisement for the newest fashions.

This unity of action involves unity of characters. It has too often been maintained by those who theorize on the photoplay that the development of character is the special task of the drama, while the photoplay, which lacks words, must be satisfied with types. Probably this is only a reflection of the crude state which most photoplays of today have not outgrown. Internally, there is no reason why the means of the photoplay should not allow a rather subtle depicting of complex character. But the chief demand is that the characters remain consistent, that the action be developed according to inner necessity and that the characters themselves be in harmony with the central idea of the plot. However, as soon as we insist on unity we have no right to think only of the action which gives the content of the play. We cannot make light of the form. As in music the melody and rhythms belong together, as in painting not every color combination suits every subject, and as in poetry not every stanza would agree with every idea, so the photoplay must bring action and pictorial expression into perfect harmony. But this demand repeats itself in every single picture. We take it for granted that the painter balances perfectly the forms in his painting, groups them so that an internal symmetry can be felt and that the lines and curves and colors blend into a unity. Every single picture of the sixteen thousand which are shown to us in one reel ought to be treated with this respect of the pictorial artist for the unity of the forms.

The photoplay shows us a significant conflict of human actions in moving pictures which, freed from the physical forms of space, time, and causality, are adjusted to the free play of our mental experiences and which reach complete isolation from the practical world through the perfect unity of plot and pictorial appearance.

SUSAN SONTAG
FILM AND THEATRE

The big question is whether there is an unbridgeable division, even opposition, between the two arts. Is there something genuinely "cinematic"?

Almost all opinion holds that there is. A commonplace of discussion has it that film and theatre are distinct and even antithetical arts, each giving rise to its own standards of judgment and canons of form. Thus Erwin Panofsky argues, in his celebrated essay "Style and Medium in the Motion Pictures" (1934, rewritten in 1946), that one of the criteria for evaluating a movie is its freedom from the impurities of theatricality. To talk about film, one must first define "the basic nature of the medium." Those who think prescriptively about the nature of live drama, less confident in the future of their art than the *cinéphiles* in theirs, rarely take a comparably exclusivist line.

The history of cinema is often treated as the history of its emancipation from theatrical models. First of all from theatrical "frontality" (the unmoving camera reproducing the situation of the spectator of a play fixed in his seat), then from theatrical acting (gestures needlessly stylized, exaggerated—needlessly, because now the actor could be seen "close up"), then from theatrical furnishings (unnecessary "distancing" of the audience's emotions, disregarding the opportunity to immerse the audience in reality). Movies are regarded as advancing from theatrical stasis to cinematic fluidity, from theatrical artificiality to cinematic naturalness and immediacy. But this view is far too simple.

Such over-simplification testifies to the ambiguous scope of the camera eye. Because the camera *can* be used to project a relatively

249

passive, unselective kind of vision—as well as the highly selective ("edited") vision generally associated with movies—cinema is a "medium" as well as an art, in the sense that it can encapsulate any of the performing arts and render it in a film transcription. (This "medium" or non-art aspect of film attained its routine incarnation with the advent of television. There, movies themselves became another performing art to be transcribed, miniaturized on film.) One *can* film a play or ballet or opera or sporting event in such a way that film becomes, relatively speaking, a transparency, and it seems correct to say that one is seeing the event filmed. But theatre is never a "medium." Thus, because one can make a movie "of" a play but not a play "of" a movie, cinema had an early but, I should argue, fortuitous connection with the stage. Some of the earliest films were filmed plays. Duse and Bernhardt and Barrymore are on film—marooned in time, absurd, touching; there is a 1913 British film of Forbes-Robertson playing Hamlet, a 1923 German film of *Othello* starring Emil Jannings. More recently, the camera has "preserved" Helene Weigel's performance of *Mother Courage* with the Berliner Ensemble, the Living Theatre production of *The Brig* (filmed by the Mekas brothers), and Peter Brook's staging of Weiss's *Marat/Sade*.

But from the beginning, even within the confines of the notion of film as a "medium" and the camera as a "recording" instrument, a great deal other than what occurred in theatres was taken down. As with still photography, some of the events captured on moving photographs were staged but others were valued precisely because they were *not* staged—the camera being the witness, the invisible spectator, the invulnerable voyeuristic eye. (Perhaps public happenings, "news," constitute an intermediate case between staged and unstaged events; but film as "newsreel" generally amounts to using film as a "medium.") To create on film a *document* of a transient reality is a conception quite unrelated to the purposes of theatre. It only appears related when the "real event" being recorded is a theatrical performance. And the first use of the motion picture camera was to make a documentary record of unstaged, casual reality: Louis Lumière's films of crowd-scenes in Paris and New York made in the 1890's antedate any use of film in the service of plays.

The other paradigmatic non-theatrical use of film, which dates from the earliest activity of the motion-picture camera, is for the creation of *illusion*, the construction of fantasy. The pioneer figure here is, of course, Georges Méliès. To be sure, Méliès (like many directors after him) conceived of the rectangle of the screen on analogy with the proscenium stage. And not only were the events staged; they were the very stuff of invention: imaginary journeys, imaginary objects, physical metamorphoses. But this, even adding the fact that Méliès situated his camera "in front of" the action and hardly moved it, does not make his films theatrical in an invidious sense. In their treatment of persons as things (physical objects) and in their disjunctive presentation of time and space, Méliès' films are quintessentially "cinematic"—so far as there is such a thing.

The contrast between theatre and films is usually taken to lie in the materials represented or depicted. But exactly where does the difference lie? It's tempting to draw a crude boundary. Theatre deploys artifice while cinema is committed to reality, indeed to an ultimately physical reality which is "redeemed," to use Siegfried Kracauer's striking word, by the camera. The aesthetic judgment that follows this bit of intellectual map-making is that films shot in real-life settings are better (*i.e.*, more cinematic) than those shot in a studio (where one can detect the difference). Obviously, if Flaherty and Italian neo-realism and the *cinema verité* of Vertov, Rouch, Marker, and Ruspoli are the preferred models, one would judge rather harshly the period of 100% studio-made films inaugurated around 1920 by *The Cabinet of Dr. Caligari*, films with ostentatiously artificial landscapes and decor, and deem the right direction to be that taken at the same period in Sweden, where many films with strenuous natural settings were being shot "on location." Thus, Panofsky attacks *Dr. Caligari* for "prestylizing reality," and urges upon cinema "the problem of manipulating and shooting unstylized reality in such a way that the result has style."

But there is no reason to insist on a single model for film. And it is helpful to notice that, for the most part, the apotheosis of realism, the prestige of "unstylized reality," in cinema is actually a covert political-moral position. Films have been rather too often acclaimed as the democratic art, the art of mass society. Once one takes this description very seriously, one tends (like Panofsky and Kracauer) to want movies to continue to reflect their origins in a vulgar level of the arts, to remain loyal to their vast uneducated audience. Thus, a vaguely Marxist orientation jibes with a fundamental tenet of romanticism. Cinema, at once high art and popular art, is cast as the art of the authentic. Theatre, by contrast, means dressing up, pretense, lies. It smacks of aristocratic taste and the class society. Behind the objection of critics to the stagy sets of *Dr. Caligari,* the improbable costumes and florid acting of Renoir's *Nana,* the talkiness of Dreyer's *Gertrud,* as "theatrical," lay the feeling that such films were false, that they exhibited a sensibility both pretentious and reactionary which was out-of-step with the democratic and more mundane sensibility of modern life.

Anyway, whether aesthetic defect or not in the particular case, the synthetic look in films is not necessarily a misplaced theatricalism. From the beginning of film history, there were painters and sculptors who claimed that cinema's true future resided in artifice, construction. It lay not in figurative narration or story-telling of any kind (either in a relatively realistic or in a "surrealistic" vein), but in abstraction. Thus, Theo van Doesburg in his essay of 1929, "Film as Pure Form," envisages film as the vehicle of "optical poetry," "dynamic light architecture," "the creation of a moving ornament." Films will realize "Bach's dream of finding an optical equivalent for the temporal structure of a musical composition." Today, a few film-makers—for example, Robert Breer—continue to pursue this conception of film, and who is to say it is not cinematic?

Could anything be farther from the scope of theatre than such a degree of abstraction? It's important not to answer that question too quickly.

Some locate the division between theatre and film as the difference between the play and the filmscript. Panofsky derives this difference from what he takes to be the most profound one: the difference between the *formal* conditions of seeing a play and those of seeing a movie. In the theatre, says Panofsky, "space is static, that is, the space represented on the stage, as well as the spatial relation of the beholder to the spectacle, is unalterably fixed," while in the cinema "the spectator occupies a fixed seat, but only physically, not as the subject of an aesthetic experience." In the cinema, the spectator is "aesthetically . . . in permanent motion as his eye identifies with the lens of the camera, which permanently shifts in distance and direction."

True enough. But the observation does not warrant a radical dissociation of theatre from film. Like many critics, Panofsky is assuming a "literary" conception of theatre. To a theatre which is conceived of basically as dramatized literature, texts, words, he contrasts cinema which is, according to the received phrase, primarily "a visual experience." In effect, we are being asked to acknowledge tacitly the period of silent films as definitive of cinematic art and to identify theatre with "plays," from Shakespeare to Tennessee Williams. But many of the most interesting movies today are not adequately described as images with sound added. And what if theatre is conceived of as more than, or something different from, plays?

Panofsky may be over-simplifying when he decries the theatrical taint in movies, but he is sound when he argues that, historically, theatre is only one of the arts that feeds into cinema. As he remarks, it is apt that films came to be known popularly as moving *pictures* rather than as "photoplays" or "screen plays." Movies derive less from the theatre, from a performance art, an art that already moves, than they do from works of art which were stationary. Bad nineteenth-century paintings and postcards, wax-works à la Madame Tussaud, and comic strips are the sources Panofsky cites. What is surprising is that he doesn't connect movies with earlier narrative uses of still photography—like the family photo-album. The narrative techniques developed by certain nineteenth-century novelists, as Eisenstein pointed out in his brilliant essay on Dickens, supplied still another prototype for cinema.

Movies are images (usually photographs) that move, to be sure. But the distinctive unit of films is not the image but the principle of connection between the images, the relation of a "shot" to the one that preceded it and the one that comes after. There is no peculiarly "cinematic" as opposed to "theatrical" mode of linking images.

Panofsky tries to hold the line against the infiltration of theatre by cinema, as well as vice versa. In the theatre, not only can the spectator not change his angle of vision but, unlike movies, "the settings of the stage cannot change during one act (except for such incidentals as rising moons or gathering clouds and such illegitimate reborrowings from film as turning wings or gliding backdrops)." Were we to assent to this, the ideal play would be *No Exit*, the ideal set a realistic living room or a blank stage.

No less dogmatic is the complementary dictum about what is illegitimate in films—according to which, since films are "a visual experience," all components must be demonstrably subordinate to the image. Thus, Panofsky asserts: "Wherever a poetic emotion, a musical outburst, or a literary conceit (even, I am grieved to say, some of the wisecracks of Groucho Marx) entirely lose contact with visible movement, they strike the sensitive spectator as, literally, out of place." What, then, of the films of Bresson and Godard, with their allusive, densely thoughtful texts and their characteristic refusal to be visually beautiful? How could one explain the extraordinary rightness of Ozu's relatively immobilized camera?

The decline in average quality of films in the early sound period (compared with the level reached by films in the 1920's) is undeniable. Although it would be facile to call the sheer uninterestingness of most films of this period simply a regression to theatre, it is a fact that film-makers did turn more frequently to plays in the 1930's than they had in the preceding decade. Countless stage successes like *Outward Bound, Dinner at Eight, Blithe Spirit, Faisons un Rêve, Twentieth Century, Boudu Sauvé des Eaux, She Done Him Wrong, Anna Christie, Marius, Animal Crackers, The Petrified Forest,* were filmed. The success of movie versions of plays is measured by the extent to which the script rearranges and displaces the action and deals less than respectfully with the spoken text—as do certain films of plays by Wilde and Shaw, the Olivier Shakespeare films (at least *Henry V*), and Sjöberg's *Miss Julie.* But the basic disapproval of films which betray their origins in plays remains. A recent example: the outright hostility which greeted Dreyer's latest film, *Gertrud.* Not only does *Gertrud,* which I believe to be a minor masterpiece, follow a turn-of-the-century play that has characters conversing at length and quite formally, but it is filmed almost entirely in middle-shot.

Some of the films I have just mentioned are negligible as art; several are first-rate. (The same for the plays, though no correlation between the merits of the movies and those of the "original" plays can be established.) However, their virtues and faults cannot be sorted out as a cinematic versus a theatrical element. Whether derived from plays or not, films with complex or formal dialogue, films in which the camera is static or in which the action stays indoors, are not necessarily theatrical. *Per contra,* it is no more part of the putative "essence" of movies that the camera must rove over a large physical area, than it is that movies ought to be silent.

Though most of the action of Kurosawa's *The Lower Depths*, a fairly faithful transcription of Gorki's play, is confined to one large room, it is as cinematic as the same director's *Throne of Blood*, a very free and laconic adaptation of *Macbeth*. The quality of Melville's claustrophobic *Les Enfants Terribles* is as peculiar to the movies as Ford's *The Searchers* or a train journey in Cinerama.

What does make a film theatrical in an invidious sense is when the narration becomes coy or self-conscious: compare Autant-Lara's *Occupe-Toi d'Amélie*, a brilliant cinematic use of the conventions and materials of theatricality, with Ophuls' clumsy use of similar conventions and materials in *La Ronde*.

Allardyce Nicoll, in his book *Film and Theatre* (1936), argues that the difference may be understood as a difference in kinds of characters. "Practically all effectively drawn stage characters are types [while] in the cinema we demand individualization and impute greater power of independent life to the figures on the screen." (Panofsky, it might be mentioned, makes exactly the opposite point: that the nature of films, in contrast to plays, requires flat or stock characters.)

Nicoll's thesis is not as arbitrary as it may at first appear. I would relate it to the fact that often the indelible moments of a film, and the most potent elements of characterization, are precisely the "irrelevant" or unfunctional details. (A random example: the ping-pong ball the schoolmaster toys with in Ivory's *Shakespeare Wallah*.) Movies thrive on the narrative equivalent of a technique familiar from painting and photography, off-centering. It is this that creates the pleasing disunity of fragmentariness (what Nicoll means by "individualization"?) of the characters of many of the greatest films. In contrast, linear "coherence" of detail (the gun on the wall in the first act that must go off by the end of the third) is the rule in Occidental narrative theatre, and gives rise to the sense of the unity of the characters (a unity that may appear like the statement of a "type").

But even with these adjustments, Nicoll's thesis seems less than appealing when one perceives that it rests on the idea that "When we go to the theatre, we expect theatre and nothing else." What is this theatre-and-nothing-else? It is the old notion of artifice. (As if art were ever anything else. As if some arts were artificial but others not.) According to Nicoll, when we are in a theatre "in every way the 'falsity' of a theatrical production is borne in upon us, so that we are prepared to demand nothing save a theatrical truth." In the cinema, however, every member of the audience, no matter how sophisticated, is on essentially the same level; we all believe that the camera cannot lie. As the film actor and his role are identical, so the image cannot be dissociated from what is imaged. Cinema, therefore, gives us what is experienced as the truth of life.

Couldn't theatre dissolve the distinction between the truth of artifice and the truth of life? Isn't that just what the theatre as ritual seeks to do? Isn't that what is being sought when theatre is conceived as an *exchange* with an audience?—something that films can never be.

If an irreducible distinction between theatre and cinema does exist, it may be this. Theatre is confined to a logical or *continuous* use of space. Cinema (through editing, that is, through the change of shot—which is the basic unit of film construction) has access to an alogical or *discontinuous* use of space. In the theatre, people are either in the stage space or "off." When "on," they are always visible or visualizable in contiguity with each other. In the cinema, no such relation is necessarily visible or even visualizable. (Example: the last shot of Paradjanov's *In the Shadows of Our Ancestors*.) Some films considered objectionably theatrical are those which seem to emphasize spatial continuities, like Hitchcock's virtuoso *Rope* or the daringly anachronistic *Gertrud*. But closer analysis of both these films would show how complex their treatment of space is. The longer and longer "takes" toward which sound films have been moving are, in themselves, neither more nor less cinematic than the short "takes" characteristic of silents.

Thus, cinematic virtue does not reside in the fluidity of the positioning of the camera nor in the mere frequency of the change of shot. It consists in the arrangement of screen images and (now) of sounds. Méliès, for example, though he didn't get beyond the static positioning of his camera, had a very striking conception of how to link screen images. He grasped that editing offered an equivalent to the magician's sleight of hand—thereby suggesting that one of the features of film (as distinct from theatre) is that *anything* can happen, that there is nothing that can't be represented convincingly.

256

Through editing, Méliès presents discontinuities of physical substance and behavior. In his films, the discontinuities are, so to
speak, practical, functional; they accomplish a transformation of
ordinary reality. But the continuous *re*invention of space (as well
as the option of temporal indeterminacy) peculiar to film narration
does not pertain only to the cinema's ability to fabricate "visions,"
to show us a radically altered world. The most "realistic" use of the
motion-picture camera also involves a discontinuous account of
space.

Film narration has a "syntax," composed of the rhythm of associations and disjunctions. As Cocteau has written, "My primary
concern in a film is to prevent the images from flowing, to oppose
them to each other, to anchor them and join them without destroying their relief." (But does such a conception of film syntax entail,
as Cocteau thinks, our disavowal of movies as "mere entertainment
instead of a vehicle for thought"?)

In drawing a line of demarcation between theatre and films, the
issue of the continuity of space seems to me more fundamental than
the difference that might be pointed out between theatre as an
organization of movement in three-dimensional space (like dance)
versus cinema as an organization of plane space (like painting).
The theatre's capacities for manipulating space and time are,
simply, much cruder and more labored than film's. Theatre cannot
equal the cinema's facilities for the strictly-controlled repetition of
images, for the duplication or matching of word and image, and for
the juxtaposition and over-lapping of images. (Through advanced
lighting techniques, one can now "dissolve" on the stage. But as yet
there is no equivalent, not even through the most adept use of
scrim, of the "lap dissolve.")

Theatre has been described as a mediated art, presumably because it usually consists of a pre-existent play mediated by a particular performance which offers one of many possible interpretations
of the play. Film, in contrast, is regarded as unmediated—because
of its larger-than-life scale and more unrefusable impact on the eye,
and because (in Panofsky's words) "the medium of the movies is
physical reality as such" and the characters in a movie "have no
aesthetic existence outside the actors." But there is an equally valid
sense which shows movies to be the mediated art and theatre the
unmediated one. We see what happens on the stage with our own

257

eyes. We see on the screen what the camera sees. In the cinema, narration proceeds by ellipsis (the "cut" or change of shot); the camera eye is a unified point of view that continually displaces itself. But the change of shot can provoke questions, the simplest of which is: from *whose* point of view is the shot seen? And the ambiguity of point of view latent in all cinematic narration has no equivalent in the theatre.

Indeed, one should not neglect to emphasize the aesthetically positive role of disorientation in the cinema. Examples: Busby Berkeley dollying back from an ordinary-looking stage already established as some thirty feet deep to disclose a stage area three hundred feet square. Resnais planning from character X's point of view a full 360°, to come to rest upon X's face.

Much may be made of the fact that, in its concrete existence, cinema is an *object* (a *product*, even) while theatre is a *performance*. Is this so important? In a way, no. Whether objects (like films or paintings) or performances (like music or theatre), all art is first a mental act, a fact of consciousness. The object aspect of film, the performance aspect of theatre are merely means — means to the experience, which is not only "of" but "through" the film and the theatre-event. Each subject of an aesthetic experience shapes it to his own measure. With respect to any *single* experience, it hardly matters that a film is usually identical from one projection of it to another while theatre performances are highly mutable.

The difference between object-art and performance-art lies behind Panofsky's observation that "the screenplay, in contrast to the theatre play, has no aesthetic existence independent of its performance," and characters in movies *are* the stars who enact them. It is because the film is an object, a totality that is set, that movie roles are identical with the actors' performances; while in the theatre (in the West, an additive rather than an organic art?) only the written play is "fixed," an object and therefore existing apart from any staging of it. Yet this dichotomy is not beyond dispute. Just as movies needn't necessarily be designed to be shown in theatres at all (they can be intended for more continuous and casual looking), a movie *may* be altered from one projection to the next. Harry Smith, when he runs off his own films, makes each projection an unrepeatable performance. And, again, it is not true that all theatre is only about

258

written plays which may be given a good or a bad production. In Happenings and other recent theatre-events, we are precisely being offered "plays" identical with their productions in the same sense as the screenplay is identical with the film.

Yet, a difference remains. Because the film is an object, it is totally manipulable, totally calculable. A film is like a book, another portable art-object; making a film, like writing a book, means constructing an inanimate thing, every element of which is determinate. Indeed, in films, this determinacy has or can have a quasi-mathematical form, like music. (A shot lasts a certain number of seconds, a change of angle of so many degrees is required to "match" two shots.) Given the total determinacy of the result on celluloid (whatever the extent of the director's conscious intervention), it was inevitable that some film directors would want to devise schemas to make their intentions more exact. Thus, it was neither perverse nor primitive of Busby Berkeley to have used only one camera to shoot the whole of each of his mammoth dance numbers. Every "set-up" was designed to be shot from only one exactly calculated angle. Bresson, working on a far more self-conscious level of artistry, has declared that, for him, the director's task is to find the single correct way of doing each shot. An image cannot be justified in itself, according to Bresson; it has an exactly specifiable relation to the temporally adjacent images, which relation constitutes its "meaning."

But the theatre allows only the loosest approximation to this sort of formal concern. (And responsibility. Justly, French critics speak of the director of a film as its "author.") Because they are performances, something always "live," theatre-events are not subject to a comparable degree of control, do not admit a comparably exact integration of effects.

It would be foolish to conclude that the best films are those which arise from the greatest amount of conscious planning; the plan may be faulty; and with some directors, instinct works better than any plan. Besides, there is an impressive body of "improvised" cinema. (To be distinguished from the work of some film-makers, notably Godard, who have become fascinated with the "look" of improvised cinema.) Nevertheless, it seems indisputable that cinema, not only potentially but by its nature, is a more rigorous art than theatre.

Thus, not merely a failure of nerve accounts for the fact that theatre, this seasoned art, occupied since antiquity with all sorts of local offices—enacting sacred rites, reinforcing communal loyalty, guiding morals, provoking the therapeutic discharge of violent emotions, conferring social status, giving practical instruction, affording entertainment, dignifying celebrations, subverting established authority—is now on the defensive before movies, this brash art with its huge, amorphous, passive audience. Meanwhile, movies continue to maintain their astonishing pace of formal articulation. (Take the commercial cinema of Europe, Japan, and the United States simply since 1960, and consider what audiences have become habituated to in the way of increasingly elliptical story-telling and visualization.)

But note: this youngest of the arts is also the one most heavily burdened with memory. Cinema is a time machine. Movies preserve the past, while theatres—no matter how devoted to the classics, to old plays—can only "modernize." Movies resurrect the beautiful dead; present intact vanished or ruined environments; employ, without irony, styles and fashions that seem funny today; solemnly ponder irrelevant or naïve problems. The historical flavor of anything registered on celluloid is so vivid that practically all films older than two years or so are saturated with a kind of pathos. (The pathos I am describing, which overtakes animated cartoons and drawn, abstract films as well as ordinary movies, is not simply that of old photographs.) Films age (being objects) as no theatre-event does (being always new). There is no pathos of mortality in theatre's "reality" as such, nothing in our response to a good performance of a Mayakovsky play comparable to the aesthetic role the emotion of nostalgia has when we see a film by Pudovkin.

Also worth noting: compared with the theatre, innovations in cinema seem to be assimilated more efficiently, seem altogether to be more shareable—and not only because new films are quickly and widely circulated. Also, partly because virtually the entire body of accomplishment in film can be consulted in the present, most film-makers are more knowledgeable about the history of their art than most theatre directors are about the recent past of theirs.

The key word in many discussions of cinema is "possibility." A merely classifying use of the word occurs, as in Panofsky's engaging judgment that, "within their self-imposed limitations the earlier Disney films . . . represent, as it were, a chemically pure distillation of cinematic possibilities." But behind this relatively neutral sense lurks a more polemical sense of cinema's "possibility." What is regularly intimated is the obsolescence of theatre, its supercession by films.

Thus, Panofsky describes the mediation of the camera eye as opening "up a world of possibility of which the stage can never dream." Artaud, earlier, thought that motion pictures may have made the theatre obsolete. Movies "possess a sort of virtual power which probes into the mind and uncovers undreamt of possibilities. . . . When this art's exhilaration has been blended in the right proportions with the psychic ingredient it commands, it will leave the theatre far behind and we will relegate the latter to the attic of our memories."

Meyerhold, facing the challenge head on, thought the only hope for theatre lay in a wholesale emulation of the cinema. "Let us 'cinematify' the theatre," he urged. The staging of plays must be "industrialized," theatres must accommodate audiences in the tens of thousands rather than in the hundreds, etc. Meyerhold also seemed to find some relief in the idea that the coming of sound signalled the downfall of movies. Believing that their international appeal depended entirely on the fact that screen actors didn't speak any particular language, he couldn't imagine in 1930 that, even if that were so, technology (dubbing, sub-titling) could solve the problem.

Is cinema the successor, the rival, or the revivifier of the theatre?

Art forms *have* been abandoned. (Whether because they became obsolete is another question.) One can't be sure that theatre is not in a state of irremediable decline, spurts of local vitality notwithstanding. But why should it be rendered obsolete by movies? It's worth remembering that predictions of obsolescence amount to declaring that a something has one peculiar task (which another something may do as well or better). Has theatre one peculiar task or aptitude?

Those who predict the demise of the theatre, assuming that cinema has engulfed its function, tend to impute a relation between films and theatre reminiscent of what was once said about photography and painting. If the painter's job had been no more than fabricating likenesses, the invention of the camera might indeed have made painting obsolete. But painting is hardly just "pictures," any more than cinema is just theatre for the masses, available in portable standard units.

In the naïve tale of photography and painting, painting was reprieved when it claimed a new task, abstraction. As the superior realism of photography was supposed to have liberated painting, allowing it to go abstract, cinema's superior power to represent (not merely to stimulate) the imagination may appear to have emboldened the theatre in a similar fashion, inviting the gradual obliteration of the conventional "plot."

Actually, painting and photography evidence parallel developments rather than a rivalry or a supercession. And, at least in principle, so have theatre and film. The possibilities for theatre that lie in going beyond psychological realism, in seeking greater abstractness, are not less germane to the future of narrative films. Conversely, the notion of movies as witness to real life, testimony rather than invention, the treatment of collective situations rather than the depiction of personal "dramas," is equally relevant to the stage. Not surprisingly, what follows some years after the rise of *cinema verité*, the sophisticated heir of documentary films, is a documentary theatre, the "theatre of fact." (Cf. Hochhuth, Weiss's *The Investigation*, recent projects of the Royal Shakespeare Company in London.)

The influence of the theatre upon films in the early years is well known. According to Kracauer, the distinctive lighting of *Dr. Caligari* (and of many subsequent German silents) can be traced to an experiment with lighting Max Reinhardt made shortly before, in his production of Sorge's play, *The Beggar*. Even in this period, however, the impact was reciprocal. The accomplishments of the "Expressionist film" were immediately absorbed by the Expressionist theatre. Stimulated by the cinematic technique of the "iris-in," stage lighting took to singling out a lone player, or some segment of the scene, masking out the rest of the stage. Rotating sets tried to approximate the instantaneous displacement of the camera eye. (More recently, reports have come of ingenious lighting techniques used by the Gorki Theatre in Leningrad, directed since 1956 by Georgi Tovstonogov, which allow for incredibly rapid scene changes taking place behind a horizontal curtain of light.)

Today traffic seems, with few exceptions, entirely one way: film to theatre. Particularly in France and in Central and Eastern Europe, the staging of many plays is inspired by the movies. The aim of adapting neo-cinematic devices for the stage (I exclude the outright use of films within the theatre production) seems mainly to tighten up the theatrical experience, to approximate the cinema's absolute control of the flow and location of the audience's attention. But the conception can be even more directly cinematic. Example: Josef Svoboda's production of *The Insect Play* by the Capek brothers at the Czech National Theatre in Prague (recently seen in London) which frankly attempted to install a mediated vision upon the stage, equivalent to the discontinuous intensifications of the camera eye. According to a London critic's account, "the set consisted of two huge, faceted mirrors slung at an angle to the stage, so that they reflect whatever happens there defracted as if through a decanter stopper or the colossally magnified eye of a fly. Any figure placed at the base of their angle becomes multiplied from floor to proscenium; farther out, and you find yourself viewing it not only face to face but from overhead, the vantage point of a camera slung to a bird or a helicopter."

Perhaps the first to propose the use of film itself as *one* element in a theatre experience was Marinetti. Writing between 1910 and 1914, he envisaged the theatre as a final synthesis of all the arts; and as such it had to use the newest art form movies. No doubt the cinema also recommended itself for inclusion because of the priority Marinetti gave to the use of existing forms of popular entertainment, such as the variety theatre and the *café-chantant*. (He called his projected art form "the Futurist Variety Theatre.") And cinema, at that time, was not considered as anything other than a vulgar art.

Soon after, the idea begins to occur frequently. In the total-theatre projects of the Bauhaus group in the 1920's (Gropius, Piscator, etc.), film had a regular place. Meyerhold insisted on its use in the theatre. (He described his program as fulfilling Wagner's once "wholly utopian" proposals to "use all means available from the other arts.") Film's actual employment has by now a fairly long history, which includes "the living newspaper," "epic theatre," and "happenings." This year marked the introduction of a film sequence into Broadway-type theatre. In two highly successful musicals, London's *Come Spy with Me* and New York's *Superman*, both parodic in tone, the action is interrupted to lower a screen and run off a movie showing the pop-art hero's exploits.

Thus far, the use of film within live theatre-events has tended to be stereotyped. Film is employed as *document*, supportive of or redundant to the live stage events (as in Brecht's productions in East Berlin). Or else it is employed as *hallucinant;* recent examples are Bob Whitman's Happenings, and a new kind of nightclub situation, the mixed-media discothèque (Andy Warhol's The Plastic Inevitable, Murray the K's World). The interpolation of film into the theatre-experience may be enlarging from the point of view of theatre. But in terms of what film is capable of, it seems a reductive, monotonous use of film.

Every interesting aesthetic tendency now is a species of radicalism. The question each artist must ask is: What is *my* radicalism, the one dictated by *my* gifts and temperament? This doesn't mean all contemporary artists believe that art progresses. A radical position isn't necessarily a forward-looking position.

Consider the two principal radical positions in the arts today. One recommends the breaking down of distinctions between genres: the arts would eventuate in one art, consisting of many different kinds of behavior going on at the same time, a vast behavioral magma or synaesthesis. The other position recommends the maintaining and clarifying of barriers between the arts, by the intensification of what each art distinctively is; painting must use only those means which pertain to painting, music only those which are musical, novels those which pertain to the novel and to no other literary form, etc.

The two positions are, in a sense, irreconcilable. Except that both are invoked to support a perennial modern quest—the quest for the definitive art form. An art may be proposed as definitive because it is considered the most rigorous, or most fundamental. For these reasons, Schopenhauer suggested and Pater asserted that all art aspires to the condition of music. More recently, the thesis that all the arts are leading toward one art has been advanced by enthusiasts of the cinema. The candidacy of film is founded on its being so exact and, potentially, so complex—a rigorous combination of music, literature, and the image.

Or, an art may be proposed as definitive because it is the most inclusive. This is the basis of the destiny for theatre held out by Wagner, Marinetti, Artaud, John Cage—all of whom envisage theatre as nothing less than a total art, potentially conscripting all the arts into its service. And as the ideas of synaesthesia continue to proliferate among painters, sculptors, architects, and composers, theatre remains the favored candidate for the role of summative art. So conceived, of course, theatre's claims do contradict those of cinema. Partisans of theatre would argue that while music, painting, dance, cinema, the speaking of words, etc. can all converge on a "stage," the film-object can only become bigger (multiple screens, 360° projection, etc.) or longer in duration or more internally articulated and complex. Theatre can be anything, everything; in the end, films can only be more of what they specifically (that is to say, cinematically) are.

Underlying the competing apocalyptic expectations for both arts, one detects a common animus. In 1923 Béla Balázs, anticipating in great detail the thesis of Marshall McLuhan, described movies as the herald of a new "visual culture" that will give us back our bodies, and particularly our faces, which have been rendered illegible, soulless, unexpressive by the centuries-old ascendancy of "print." An animus against literature, against "the printing press" and its "culture of concepts," also informs most of the interesting thinking about the theatre in our time.

What's important is that no definition or characterization of theatre and cinema, even the most self-evident, be taken for granted.

For instance: both cinema and theatre are temporal arts. Like music (and unlike painting), everything is *not* present all at once.

Could this be modified? The allure of mixed-media forms in theatre suggests not only a more elongated and more complex "drama" (like Wagnerian opera) but also a more compact theatre-experience which approaches the condition of painting. This prospect of increased compactness is broached by Marinetti; he calls it simultaneity, a leading idea of Futurist aesthetics. In becoming a final synthesis of all the arts, says Marinetti, theatre "would use the new twentieth-century devices of electricity and the cinema; this would enable plays to be extremely short, since all these technical means would enable the theatrical synthesis to be achieved in the shortest possible space of time, as all the elements could be presented simultaneously."

A pervasive notion in both advanced cinema and theatre is the idea of art as an act of violence. Its source is to be found in the aesthetics of Futurism and of Surrealism; its principal "texts" are, for theatre, the writings of Artaud and, for cinema, the two classic films of Luis Buñuel, *L'Age d'Or* and *Un Chien Andalou*. (More recent examples: the early plays of Ionesco, at least as conceived; the "cinema of cruelty" of Hitchcock, Clouzot, Franju, Robert Aldrich, Polanski; work by the Living Theatre; some of the neo-cinematic lighting techniques used in experimental theatres; the sound of late Cage and LaMonte Young.) The relation of art to an audience understood to be passive, inert, surfeited, can only be assault. Art becomes identical with aggression.

This theory of art as assault on the audience—like the complementary notion of art as ritual—is understandable, and precious. Still, one must not neglect to question it, particularly in the theatre. For it can become as much a convention as anything else; and end, like all theatrical conventions, by reinforcing the deadness of the audience. (As Wagner's ideology of a total theatre played its role in confirming the stupidity and bestiality of German culture.)

Moreover, the depth of the assault must be assessed honestly. In the theatre, this entails not "diluting" Artaud. Artaud's writings represent the demand for a totally open (therefore, flayed, self-cruel) consciousness of which theatre would be *one* adjunct or instrument. No work in the theatre has yet amounted to this. Thus, Peter Brook has astutely and forthrightly disclaimed that his company's work in London in the "Theatre of Cruelty," which culminated in his celebrated production of Weiss's *Marat/Sade*, is genuinely Artaudian. It is Artaudian, he says, in a trivial sense only. (Trivial from Artaud's point of view, not from ours.)

266

For some time, all useful ideas in art have been extremely sophisticated. Like the idea that everything is what it is, and not another thing. A painting is a painting. Sculpture is sculpture. A poem is a poem, not prose. Etcetera. And the complementary idea: a painting can be "literary" or sculptural, a poem can be prose, theatre can emulate and incorporate cinema, cinema can be theatrical.

We need a new idea. It will probably be a very simple one. Will we be able to recognize it?

BÉLA BALÁZS
FROM THEORY OF THE FILM

ART FORM AND MATERIAL

It is an accepted practice that we adapt novels and plays for the film; sometimes because we think their stories "filmic," sometimes because the popularity they have gained as novels or plays is to be exploited in the film market. Original film stories are very few and far between, a circumstance which undoubtedly points to the undeveloped state and imperfections of script-writing.

There is little point in discussing the practical aspects of this question. Shall we demand original film stories when even all the adaptations taken together are insufficient to satisfy the demand? In practice the law of supply and demand decides the issue. If there were a greater supply of good original film stories, there would probably be less adaptations from other forms.

We however are at the present moment interested in the laws of art and not the law of supply and demand. The method of adapting novels or plays may obey the latter law—but does it not contravene the laws of art? Must not such pandering to a practical demand necessarily be detrimental to the interests of art and the aesthetic culture of the public?

"Necessarily" is the key word here, because on it depends whether the problem is one of principle. For if such adaptations can be good *in principle* then it is for the film critics to decide in each case whether they are well or ill done and there is no theoretical problem.

There is, however, an old—one could almost say classic—aesthetic viewpoint which rejects on principle all adaptations on the grounds that they are necessarily inartistic. Here is a problem that is of the greatest interest for the theory of art because, although the opponents of adaptations base themselves on an undoubtedly correct thesis, they are nevertheless wrong. The history of literature is full of classic masterpieces which are adaptations of other works.

The theoretical reason on which the opposition to adaptations is based is that there is an organic connection between form and content in every art and that a certain art form always offers the most adequate expression for a certain content. Thus the adaptation of a content to a different art form can only be detrimental to a work of art, if that work of art was good. In other words, one may perhaps make a good film out of a bad novel, but never out of a good one.

This theoretically impeccable thesis is contradicted by such realities as these: Shakespeare took the stories of some of his very good plays from certain very good old Italian tales and the plots of the Greek classical drama were also derived from older epics.

Most of the classical dramas used the material of the old epics and if we turn the pages of Lessing's *Hamburgische Dramaturgie* we will find that the very first three reviews in it deal with plays adapted from novels. It should be mentioned that the author of the immortal art philosophy contained in *Laokoon*, whose concern was precisely to find the specific laws governing each form of art, found much to criticize in the plays which he reviewed, but had no objection to their being the adaptations of novels. On the contrary, he proffered much good advice as to how such adaptations could be more skilfully done.

The contradiction appears so obvious that one must wonder why no learned aestheticist ever bothered to clear up this problem. For if the objection on principle to adaptations were merely a theoretical error, the matter would be simple. But it is not an error; it is a logical conclusion from the undeniably correct thesis about the connection between content and form.

It is obvious that the contradiction here is only apparent—an undialectic nailing-down of partial truths. It may be worth while to probe deeper for the source of the error.

To accept the thesis that the content or material determines the form and with it the art form, and nevertheless to admit the possibility of putting the same material into a different form, is thinkable only if the terms used are used loosely, that is if the terms "content" and "form" do not exactly cover what we are accustomed to call material, action, plot, story, subject, etc. on the one hand, and "art form" on the other. There can be no doubt that it is possible to take the subject, the story, the plot of a novel, turn it into a play or a film and yet produce perfect works of art in each case—the form being in each case adequate to the content. How is this possible? It is possible because, while the subject, or story, of both works is identical, their *content* is nevertheless different. It is this different *content* that is adequately expressed in the changed form resulting from the adaptation.

The unsophisticated and naïve believe that life itself provides the writer with ready-made dramas and novels. According to this view every event has an *a priori*, immanent affinity to a certain form of art; that life itself determines what happenings are suitable for a play, for a novel or for a film; the writer is given, as it were, a pre-determined material as a definite subject susceptible of being used in only one way, in only one art form. If a certain subject takes his fancy, he cannot use the art form he pleases—that has been already decided by the artistic predetermination inherent in reality itself.

The world outside us, however, has an objective reality which is independent of our consciousness and hence independent of our artistic ideas. Reality has colours, shapes and sounds but it can have no immanent affinity to painting, sculpture or music, for these are specifically human activities. Reality does not of itself curdle into any art form, not even into subjects suitable for definite art forms, and waiting like ripe apples for some artist to pick them. Art and its forms are not *a priori* inherent in reality but are methods of human approach to it, although of course this approach and its methods are also elements of reality as a whole.

These methods of approach are naturally neither arbitrary nor is their number unlimited. In the cultural sphere of civilized humanity several such methods of approach (or art forms) have evolved as historically given objective forms of culture, and although they are merely subjective forms by means of which human consciousness approaches reality, they nevertheless appear to the individual as being objectively given. The parallel of the dialectic interaction of river and river-bed could again be quoted here as the model for the mutual relationship of material and art form.

Hence, if there is a "dramatic" theme or subject which appears specific because it already shows the peculiar characteristics of the dramatic art form, then it is already *content* (which really determines the form it can take) and no longer mere "material" i.e. merely the raw material of living reality, which cannot as yet determine its art form and could be the content of any of them not yet being content in its own right.

Such specific themes (or contents) are no longer mere fragments of reality—they are an approach to reality from the viewpoint of a certain form of art. One might call them "semifashioned" for they are already prepared to fit into a certain art form. If we call them "themes" "subjects" or "stories," we are already using a correlative term which cannot be conceived in itself, but only as the theme of something, e.g. a drama, as the subject of a novel, as the story on which a film is based. Such can be found only in a reality already regarded from the angle of one or the other of the forms of art.

What is the conclusion from this? That the raw material of reality can be fashioned into many different art forms. But a "content," which determines the form, is no longer such raw material.

Are there not writers who write nothing but plays or nothing but novels? They, too, regard the entire reality of life, but only from the viewpoint of their own form of art, which has become an organic part of their approach. There are others who work in more than one art form; writers who regard life now with the eye of the novelist, now with the eye of the dramatist. So it may happen that they see the same bit of reality more than once; perhaps once as a drama and once as a film. But if this does happen, they would not be adapting their own drama for the screen. They would have gone back to their own basic experience and formed the same raw material once as a play, once as a film. It is quite certain that there are few outstanding events in history which have not served as material for ballads, plays, epics or novels. But a historical event is in itself only material, not theme. Material can still be regarded from the angle of various art forms. But a theme is already something regarded from the viewpoint of one or the other art form, lifted out of a multiform reality and developed into a dominant *motif*. Such themes can be adequately expressed in only one art form; they determine their art form, for they have themselves been determined by it. Such a theme, such a reality, such a material is already "content" and determines its form.

271

Take a portrait. The reality of the model is as yet only raw material. It can be painted or drawn in black-and-white or modelled in clay. But if a true painter looks at the model, he will see colours in the first place, the colours will be the dominant characteristic and once this has happened the colours will no longer be raw material — they will be a theme for a painter, a content which determines the form, which is the art form, which is painting. A black-and-white artist will see the lines of the same model. Here, the same material will provide a different artistic theme, and this theme will be the content determining the art form, which will be drawing or etching or some other line technique. A sculptor may see the same model, and yet not the same model, for in his case it will be a model for a sculpture. The same material will provide for him a theme of plastic shapes, and thereby determine the adequate art form, sculpture.

The same applies to the literary forms. One writer may feel the atmosphere, the fleeting moods in a subject and take that for his theme; probably he will make it a short story. Another will see in the same subject a central conflict, an inexorable problem which demands a dramatic approach. The raw material of life may be the same, but the themes of the two writers will be different. And the different themes will give rise to different contents and demand different art forms. A third writer might come across the same event and see in it not the event itself but the inner adventures of human beings interacting with one another and showing the web of their destinies like a multicoloured carpet of life. This third writer would probably write a novel. Thus the same event as raw material regarded from three different angles can result in three themes, three contents, three forms of art. What mostly happens, however, is that a subject already used in one form of art is adapted to another form — in other words, it would not be the same model sitting to three different artists but rather a drawing made after a painting, or a sculpture after a drawing. This is much more problematic than the other case.

If, however, the artist is a true artist and not a botcher, the dramatist dramatizing a novel or a film-script writer adapting a play may use the existing work of art merely as raw material, regard it from the specific angle of his own art form as if it were raw reality, and pay no attention to the form once already given to the material. The playwright, Shakespeare, reading a story by Bandello, saw in it not the artistic form of a masterpiece of story-telling but merely the naked event narrated in it. He saw it isolated from the story form, as raw life-material with all its dramatic possibilities, i.e. possibilities which Bandello could never have expressed in a *novella*.

Thus although it is the raw material of a Bandello story that was given new form in a Shakespeare play, there is no trace of the main content of the play in the Bandello story. In that story Shakespeare saw a totally different theme and therefore the content that determined the art form of his play was also totally different.

I would like to mention here a less well-known adaptation, for the reason that the poet who was its author was at the same time an accomplished theoretician who could explain how and why the adaptation was made. Friedrich Hebbel, the German playwright, wrote plays based on the mighty epic material of the Nibelung saga. It would be quite impossible to accuse Hebbel of insufficient respect for the eternal greatness of the Germanic epic and its peerless formal perfection. Hebbel had no intention of improving on the Nibelung saga, nor can any intention of a popularization for money-making purposes be ascribed to this very serious writer. What then were his motives and his purpose in undertaking such an adaptation?

Hebbel himself gives the reason in his famous diary: "It seems to me that on the foundation of the Nibelung saga one could build a purely human tragedy which would be quite natural in its motivation."

What, then, did Hebbel do? He kept the mythical foundation, that is the skeleton of the story. But he gave it a different interpretation. The actions and events remained largely the same, but were given other motives and explanations.

Thus the same event, being given quite different emphasis, was turned into a different theme. The theme and content of Hebbel's Nibelung trilogy is not identical with that of the Nibelung saga. For although in Hebbel's drama Hagen kills Siegfried, as he does in the saga, he does so from entirely different motives and Kriemhild's vengeance, as depicted in Hebbel's drama, is a tragedy of a quite different order than the same event in the Germanic epic.

Nearly every artistically serious and intelligent adaptation is such a re-interpretation. The same external action has quite different inner motives, and it is these inner motives which throw light on the hearts of the characters and determine the content which determines the form. The material, that is the external events, serve merely as clues, and clues can be interpreted in many ways—as we know from the detective stories.

It often happens that a writer uses a second time, in another art form, the material he himself has once already used in a certain art form. We know that nowadays, especially when it is a question of adapting novels or plays for the films, this is mostly done for financial reasons. A successful novel can be adapted first as a play and then as a film, and thus make money for its author several times over. But sometimes such adaptations are made with quite serious artistic intentions.

Let us take a case in which no suspicion of financial motives can arise. We know that Goethe wanted to make a play out of his very interesting story "The man of fifty," which is a part of his *Wilhelm Meister*. The plan of this play has been preserved—it gives, already divided into acts and scenes, the content of the projected play, which is the content of the story, only told in a different way. This different way very instructively shows why Goethe felt the need of re-writing in another art form the material once already used. We can see in detail how in the projected play he stresses aspects which are scarcely or not at all perceptible in the short story, how he tries to bring to the surface a totally different layer of reality. The course of events is similar, but their significance is different and it contains a quite different inner experience. The reality from which he borrowed his material included this inner experience; but when he shaped his material into a short story, he had to pass by this inner experience; it was for this reason that he felt the urge of dipping once more into the depths of the same life-material by means of another art form.

It may at first sound paradoxical to say that it is often a respect for the laws of style that govern the various art forms which makes adaptations justifiable and even necessary. The severe style of the drama, for instance, demands the omission of the multiple colours and changing moods of real life. The drama is the art form suited to great conflicts and the wealth of detail which a novel may contain finds no room in its severe structure. But sometimes the author is loath to let all the wealth of mood and detail go to waste and so he puts it into a novel rather than impair the pure style of the drama. And if an author wants to pour into a film the colours of life which are barred by the severe style of the drama, he does so not because he does not respect the style of the various art forms, but because he respects them absolutely.

ANDRÉ BAZIN
FROM WHAT IS CINEMA

THEATER AND CINEMA

The leitmotiv of those who despise filmed theater, their final and apparently insuperable argument, continues to be the unparalleled pleasure that accompanies the presence of the actor. "What is specific to theater," writes Henri Gouhier, in *The Essence of Theater*, "is the impossibility of separating off action and actor." Elsewhere he says "the stage welcomes every illusion except that of presence; the actor is there in disguise, with the soul and voice of another, but he is nevertheless there and by the same token space calls out for him and for the solidity of his presence. On the other hand and inversely, the cinema accommodates every form of reality save one —the physical presence of the actor." If it is here that the essence of theater lies then undoubtedly the cinema can in no way pretend to any parallel with it. If the writing, the style, and the dramatic structure are, as they should be, rigorously conceived as the receptacle for the soul and being of the flesh-and-blood actor, any attempt to substitute the shadow and reflection of a man on the screen for the man himself is a completely vain enterprise. There is no answer to this argument. The successes of Laurence Olivier, of Welles, or of Cocteau can only be challenged—here you need to be in bad faith—or considered inexplicable. They are a challenge both to critics and philosophers. Alternatively one can only explain them by casting doubts on that commonplace of theatrical criticism "the irreplaceable presence of the actor."

THE CONCEPT OF PRESENCE

At this point certain comments seem called for concerning the concept of "presence," since it would appear that it is this concept,

276

as understood prior to the appearance of photography, that the cinema challenges.

Can the photographic image, especially the cinematographic image, be likened to other images and in common with them be regarded as having an existence distinct from the object? Presence, naturally, is defined in terms of time and space. "To be in the presence of someone" is to recognize him as existing contemporaneously with us and to note that he comes within the actual range of our senses—in the case of cinema of our sight and in radio of our hearing. Before the arrival of photography and later of cinema, the plastic arts (especially portraiture) were the only intermediaries between actual physical presence and absence. Their justification was their resemblance which stirs the imagination and helps the memory. But photography is something else again. In no sense is it the image of an object or person, more correctly it is its tracing. Its automatic genesis distinguishes it radically from the other techniques of reproduction. The photograph proceeds by means of the lens to the taking of a veritable luminous impression in light—to a mold. As such it carries with it more than mere resemblance, namely a kind of identity—the card we call by that name being only conceivable in an age of photography. But photography is a feeble technique in the sense that its instantaneity compels it to capture time only piecemeal. The cinema does something strangely paradoxical. It makes a molding of the object as it exists in time and, furthermore, makes an imprint of the duration of the object.

The nineteenth century with its objective techniques of visual and sound reproduction gave birth to a new category of images, the relation of which to the reality from which they proceed requires very strict definition. Even apart from the fact that the resulting aesthetic problems cannot be satisfactorily raised without this introductory philosophical inquiry, it would not be sound to treat the old aesthetic questions as if the categories with which they deal had in no way been modified by the appearance of completely new phenomena. Common sense—perhaps the best philosophical guide in this case—has clearly understood this and has invented an expression for the presence of an actor, by adding to the placards announcing his appearance the phrase "in flesh and blood." This means that for the man in the street the word "presence," today, can be ambiguous, and thus an apparent redundancy is not out of place in this age of cinema. Hence it is no longer as certain as it was that there is no middle stage between presence and absence. It is likewise at the ontological level that the effectiveness of the cinema has its source. It is false to say that the screen is incapable of putting us "in the presence of" the actor. It does so in the same way as a mirror—one must agree that the mirror relays the presence of the person reflected in it—but it is a mirror with a delayed reflection, the tin foil of which retains the image.* It is true that in the theater Molière can die on the stage and that we have the privilege of living in the biographical time of the actor. In the film about Manolete however we are present at the actual death of the famous matador and while our emotion may not be as deep as if we were actually present in the arena at that historic moment, its nature is the same. What we lose by way of direct witness do we not recapture thanks to the artificial proximity provided by photographic enlargement? Everything takes place as if in the time-space perimeter which is the definition of presence. The cinema offers us effectively only a measure of duration, reduced but not to zero, while the increase in the space factor reestablishes the equilibrium of the psychological equation.

OPPOSITION AND IDENTIFICATION

An honest appraisal of the respective pleasures derived from theater and cinema, at least as to what is less intellectual and more direct about them, forces us to admit that the delight we experience

---

*Television naturally adds a new variant to the "pseudopresences" resulting from the scientific techniques for reproduction created by photography. On the little screen during live television the actor is actually present in space and time. But the reciprocal actor-spectator relationship is incomplete in one direction. The spectator sees without being seen. There is no return flow. Televised theater, therefore, seems to share something both of theater and of cinema: of theater because the actor is present to the viewer, of cinema because the spectator is not present to the actor. Nevertheless, this state of not being present is not truly an absence. The television actor has a sense of the millions of ears and eyes virtually present and represented by the electronic camera. This abstract presence is most noticeable when the actor fluffs his lines. Painful enough in the theater, it is intolerable on television since the spectator who can do nothing to help him is aware of the unnatural solitude of the actor. In the theater in similar circumstances a sort of understanding exists with the audience, which is a help to an actor in trouble. This kind of reciprocal relationship is impossible on television.

at the end of a play has a more uplifting, a nobler, one might perhaps say a more moral, effect than the satisfaction which follows
a good film. We seem to come away with a better conscience. In a
certain sense it is as if for the man in the audience all theater is
"Corneillian." From this point of view one could say that in the best
films something is missing. It is as if a certain inevitable lowering
of the voltage, some mysterious aesthetic short circuit, deprived
us in the cinema of a certain tension which is a definite part of
theater. No matter how slight this difference it undoubtedly exists,
even between the worst charity production in the theater and the
most brilliant of Olivier's film adaptations. There is nothing banal
about this observation and the survival of the theater after fifty
years of cinema, and the prophecies of Marcel Pagnol, is practical
proof enough. At the source of the disenchantment which follows
the film one could doubtless detect a process of depersonalization
of the spectator. As Rosenkrantz wrote in 1937, in *Esprit*, in an
article profoundly original for its period, "The characters on the
screen are quite naturally objects of identification, while those on
the stage are, rather, objects of mental opposition because their
real presence gives them an objective reality and to transpose them
into beings in an imaginary world the will of the spectator has to
intervene actively, that is to say, to will to transform their physical
reality into an abstraction. This abstraction being the result of a
process of the intelligence that we can only ask of a person who is
fully conscious." A member of a film audience tends to identify
himself with the film's hero by a psychological process, the result
of which is to turn the audience into a "mass" and to render emotion uniform. Just as in algebra if two numbers equal a third, then
they are equal to one another, so here we can say, if two individuals identify themselves with a third, they identify themselves with
one another. Let us compare chorus girls on the stage and on the
screen. On the screen they satisfy an unconscious sexual desire and
when the hero joins them he satisfies the desire of the spectator in
the proportion to which the latter has identified himself with the
hero. On the stage the girls excite the onlooker as they would in
real life. The result is that there is no identification with the hero.
He becomes instead an object of jealousy and envy. In other words,
Tarzan is only possible on the screen. The cinema calms the spectator, the theater excites him. Even when it appeals to the lowest

279

instincts, the theater up to a certain point stands in the way of the creation of a mass mentality.* It stands in the way of any collective representation in the psychological sense, since theater calls for an active individual consciousness while the film requires only a passive adhesion.

These views shed a new light on the problem of the actor. They transfer him from the ontological to the psychological level. It is to the extent to which the cinema encourages identification with the hero that it conflicts with the theater. Put this way the problem is no longer basically insoluble, for it is a fact that the cinema has at its disposal means which favor a passive position or on the other hand, means which to a greater or lesser degree stimulate the consciousness of the spectator. Inversely the theater can find ways of lessening the psychological tension between spectator and actor. Thus theater and cinema will no longer be separated off by an unbridgeable aesthetic moat, they would simply tend to give rise to two attitudes of mind over which the director maintains a wide control.

Examined at close quarters, the pleasure derived from the theater not only differs from that of the cinema but also from that of the novel. The reader of a novel, physically alone like the man in the dark movie house, identifies himself with the character. That is why after reading for a long while he also feels the same intoxication of an illusory intimacy with the hero. Incontestably, there is in the pleasure derived from cinema and novel a self-satisfaction, a concession to solitude, a sort of betrayal of action by a refusal of social responsibility.

The analysis of this phenomenon might indeed be undertaken from a psychoanalytic point of view. Is it not significant that the psychiatrists took the term catharsis from Aristotle? Modern pedagogic research on psychodrama seems to have provided fruitful insights into the cathartic process of theater. The ambiguity existing in the child's mind between play and reality is used to get him to free himself by way of improvised theater from the repressions from which he suffers. This technique amounts to creating a kind of vague theater in which the play is of a serious nature and the

---

*Crowd and solitude are not antinomies: the audience in a movie house is made up of solitary individuals. Crowd should be taken here to mean the opposite of an organic community freely assembled.

actor is his own audience. The action that develops on these occasions is not one that is divided off by footlights, which are undoubtedly the architectural symbol of the censor that separates us from the stage. We delegate Oedipus to act in our guise and place him on the other side of a wall of fire—that fiery frontier between fantasy and reality which gives rein to Dionysiac monsters while protecting us from them. These sacred beasts will not cross this barrier of light beyond which they seem out of place and even sacrilegious—witness the disturbing atmosphere of awe which surrounds an actor still made up, like a phosphorescent light, when we visit him in his dressing room. There is no point to the argument that the theater did not always have footlights. These are only a symbol and there were others before them from the cothurnus and mask onwards. In the seventeenth century the fact that young nobles sat up on the stage is no denial of the role of the footlights, on the contrary, it confirms it, by way of a privileged violation so to speak, just as when today Orson Welles scatters actors around the auditorium to fire on the audience with revolvers. He does not do away with the footlights, he just crosses them. The rules of the game are also made to be broken. One expects some players to cheat.* With regard to the objection based on presence and on that alone, the theater and the cinema are not basically in conflict. What is really in dispute are two psychological modalities of a performance. The theater is indeed based on the reciprocal awareness of the presence of audience and actor, but only as related to a performance. The theater acts on us by virtue of our participation in a theatrical action across the footlights and as it were under the protection of their censorship. The opposite is true in the cinema.

---

*Here is a final example proving that presence does not constitute theater except in so far as it is a matter of a performance. Everyone either at his own or someone else's expense has known the embarrassment of being watched without knowing it or in spite of knowing it. Lovers who kiss on public benches offer a spectacle to the passerby, but they do not care. My concierge who has a feeling for the *mot juste* says, when she sees them, that it is like being at the movies. Each of us has sometimes found himself forced to his annoyance to do something absurd before other people. On those occasions we experience a sense of angry shame which is the very opposite of theatrical exhibitionism. Someone who looks through a keyhole is not at the theater; Cocteau has rightly demonstrated in *Le sang d'un poète* that he was already at the cinema. And nevertheless there are such things as "shows," when the protagonists are present to us in flesh and blood but one of the two parties is ignorant of the fact or goes through with it reluctantly. This is not "play" in the theatrical sense.

281

Alone, hidden in a dark room, we watch through half-open blinds a spectacle that is unaware of our existence and which is part of the universe. There is nothing to prevent us from identifying ourselves in imagination with the moving world before us, which becomes *the* world. It is no longer on the phenomenon of the actor as a person physically present that we should concentrate our analysis, but rather on the ensemble of conditions that constitute the theatrical play and deprive the spectator of active participation. We shall see that it is much less a question of actor and presence than of man and his relation to the decor.

BEHIND THE DECOR

The human being is all-important in the theater. The drama on the screen can exist without actors. A banging door, a leaf in the wind, waves beating on the shore can heighten the dramatic effect. Some film masterpieces use man only as an accessory, like an extra, or in counterpoint to nature which is the true leading character. Even when, as in *Nanook* and *Man of Aran*, the subject is man's struggle with nature, it cannot be compared to a theatrical action. The mainspring of the action is not in man but nature. As Jean-Paul Sartre, I think it was, said, in the theater the drama proceeds from the actor, in the cinema it goes from the decor to man. This reversal of the dramatic flow is of decisive importance. It is bound up with the very essence of the *mise-en-scène*. One must see here one of the consequences of photographic realism. Obviously, if the cinema makes use of nature it is because it is able to. The camera puts at the disposal of the director all the resources of the telescope and the microscope. The last strand of a rope about to snap or an entire army making an assault on a hill are within our reach. Dramatic causes and effects have no longer any material limits to the eye of the camera. Drama is freed by the camera from all contingencies of time and space. But this freeing of tangible dramatic powers is still only a secondary aesthetic cause, and does not basically explain the reversal of value between the actor and the decor. For sometimes it actually happens that the cinema deliberately deprives itself of the use of setting and of exterior nature—we have already seen a perfect instance of this in *Les Parents terribles*—while the theater in contrast uses a complex machinery to give a feeling of ubiquity to the audience. Is *La Passion de Jeanne d'Arc* by Carl Dreyer, shot entirely in close-up, in the virtually invisible and in fact theatrical settings by Jean Hugo, less cinematic than *Stagecoach?* It seems to me that quantity has nothing to do with it, nor the resemblance to certain theater techniques. The ideas of an art director for a room in *Les Dames aux camélias* would not noticeably differ whether for a film or a play. It's true that on the screen you would doubtless have some close-ups of the blood-stained handkerchief, but a skillful stage production would also know how to make some play with the cough and the handkerchief. All the close-ups in *Les Parents terribles* are taken directly from the theater where our attention would spontaneously isolate them. If film direction only differed from theater direction because it allows us a closer view of the scenery and makes a more reasonable use of it, there would really be no reason to continue with the theater and Pagnol would be a true prophet. For it is obvious that the few square yards of the decor of Vilar's *La Danse de la mort* contributed as much to the drama as the island on which Marcel Cravene shot his excellent film. The fact is that the problem lies not in the decor itself but in its nature and function. We must therefore throw some light on an essentially theatrical notion, that of the dramatic place.

There can be no theater without architecture, whether it be the cathedral square, the arena of Nîmes, the palace of the Popes, the trestle stage on a fairground, the semicircle of the theater of Vicenza that looks as if it were decorated by Bérard in a delirium, or the rococo amphitheaters of the boulevard houses. Whether as a performance or a celebration, theater of its very essence must not be confused with nature under penalty of being absorbed by her and ceasing to be. Founded on the reciprocal awareness of those taking part and present to one another, it must be in contrast to the rest of the world in the same way that play and reality are opposed, or concern and indifference, or liturgy and the common use of things. Costume, mask, or make-up, the style of the language, the footlights, all contribute to this distinction, but the clearest sign of all is the stage, the architecture of which has varied from time to time without ever ceasing to mark out a privileged spot actually or virtually distinct from nature. It is precisely in virtue of this *locus dramaticus* that decor exists. It serves in greater or less degree to set the place apart, to specify. Whatever it is, the decor constitutes the walls of this three-sided box opening onto the auditorium, which we call the stage. These false perspectives, these façades, these arbors, have another side which is cloth and nails and wood. Everyone knows that when the actor "retires to his apartment" from the yard or from the garden, he is actually going to his dressing room to take off his make-up. These few square feet of light and illusion are surrounded by machinery and flanked by wings, the hidden labyrinths of which do not interfere one bit with the pleasure of the spectator who is playing the game of theater. Because it is only part of the architecture of the stage, the decor of the theater is thus an area materially enclosed, limited, circumscribed, the only discoveries of which are those of our collusive imagination.

Its appearances are turned inward facing the public and the footlights. It exists by virtue of its reverse side and of anything beyond, as the painting exists by virtue of its frame. Just as the picture is not to be confounded with the scene it represents and is not a window in a wall. The stage and the decor where the action unfolds constitute an aesthetic microcosm inserted perforce into the universe but essentially distinct from the Nature which surrounds it.

It is not the same with cinema, the basic principle of which is a denial of any frontiers to action.

The idea of a *locus dramaticus* is not only alien to, it is essentially a contradiction of the concept of the screen. The screen is not a frame like that of a picture but a mask which allows only a part of the action to be seen. When a character moves off screen, we accept the fact that he is out of sight, but he continues to exist in his own capacity at some other place in the decor which is hidden from us. There are no wings to the screen. There could not be without destroying its specific illusion, which is to make of a revolver or of a face the very center of the universe. In contrast to the stage the space of the screen is centrifugal. It is because that infinity which the theater demands cannot be spatial that its area can be none other than the human soul. Enclosed in this space the actor is at the focus of a two-fold concave mirror. From the auditorium and from the decor there converge on him the dim lights of conscious human beings and of the footlights themselves. But the fire with which he burns is at once that of his inner passion and of that focal point at which he stands. He lights up in each member of his audience an accomplice flame. Like the ocean in a sea shell the dramatic infinities of the human heart moan and beat between the enclosing walls of the theatrical sphere. This is why this dramaturgy is in its essence human. Man is at once its cause and its subject.

On the screen man is no longer the focus of the drama, but will become eventually the center of the universe. The impact of his action may there set in motion an infinitude of waves. The decor that surrounds him is part of the solidity of the world. For this reason the actor as such can be absent from it, because man in the world enjoys no a priori privilege over animals and things. However there is no reason why he should not be the mainspring of the drama, as in Dreyer's *Jeanne d'Arc*, and in this respect the cinema may very well impose itself upon the theater. As actions *Phèdre* or *King Lear* are no less cinematographic than theatrical, and the visible death of a rabbit in *La Règle du jeu* affects us just as deeply as that of Agnès' little cat about which we are merely told.

But if Racine, Shakespeare, or Molière cannot be brought to the cinema by just placing them before the camera and the microphone, it is because the handling of the action and the style of the dialogue were conceived as echoing through the architecture of the auditorium. What is specifically theatrical about these tragedies is not their action so much as the human, that is to say the verbal, priority given to their dramatic structure. The problem of filmed theater at least where the classics are concerned does not consist so much in transposing an action from the stage to the screen as in transposing a text written for one dramaturgical system into another while at the same time retaining its effectiveness. It is not therefore essentially the action of a play which resists film adaptation, but above and beyond the phases of the intrigue (which it would be easy enough to adapt to the realism of the screen) it is the verbal form which aesthetic contingencies or cultural prejudices oblige us to respect. It is this which refuses to let itself be captured in the window of the screen. "The theater," says Baudelaire, "is a crystal chandelier." If one were called upon to offer in comparison a symbol other than this artificial crystal-like object, brilliant, intricate, and circular, which refracts the light which plays around its center and holds us prisoners of its aureole, we might say of the cinema that it is the little flashlight of the usher, moving like an uncertain comet across the night of our waking dream, the diffuse space without shape or frontiers that surrounds the screen.

The story of the failures and recent successes of theater on film will be found to be that of the ability of directors to retain the dramatic force of the play in a medium that reflects it or, at least, the ability to give this dramatic force enough resonance to permit a film audience to perceive it. In other words, it is a matter of an aesthetic that is not concerned with the actor but with decor and editing. Henceforth it is clear that filmed theater is basically destined to fail whenever it tends in any manner to become simply the photographing of scenic representation even and perhaps most of all when the camera is used to try and make us forget the footlights and the backstage area. The dramatic force of the text, instead of being gathered up in the actor, dissolves without echo into the cinematic ether. This is why a filmed play can show due respect to the text, be well acted in likely settings, and yet be completely worthless. This is what happened, to take a convenient example, to *Le Voyageur sans baggages*. The play lies there before us apparently true to itself yet drained of every ounce of energy, like a battery dead from an unknown short. But over and beyond the aesthetic of the decor we see clearly both on the screen and on the stage that in the last analysis the problem before us is that of realism. This is the problem we always end up with when we are dealing with cinema.

THE SCREEN AND THE REALISM OF SPACE

The realism of the cinema follows directly from its photographic nature. Not only does some marvel or some fantastic thing on the screen not undermine the reality of the image, on the contrary it is its most valid justification. Illusion in the cinema is not based as it is in the theater on convention tacitly accepted by the general public; rather, contrariwise, it is based on the inalienable realism of that which is shown. All trick work must be perfect in all material respects on the screen. The "invisible man" must wear pyjamas and smoke a cigarette.

Must we conclude from this that the cinema is dedicated entirely to the representation if not of natural reality at least of a plausible reality of which the spectator admits the identity with nature as he knows it? The comparative failure of German expressionism would seem to confirm this hypothesis, since it is evident that *Caligari* attempted to depart from realistic decor under the influence of the theater and painting. But this would be to offer an oversimplified explanation for a problem that calls for more subtle answers. We are prepared to admit that the screen opens upon an artificial world provided there exists a common denominator between the cinematographic image and the world we live in. Our experience of space is the structural basis for our concept of the universe. We may say in fact, adapting Henri Gouhier's formula, "The stage welcomes every illusion except the illusion of presence," that "the cinematographic image can be emptied of all reality save one—the reality of space."

It is perhaps an overstatement to say "all reality" because it is difficult to imagine a reconstruction of space devoid of all reference to nature. The world of the screen and our world cannot be juxtaposed. The screen of necessity substitutes for it since the very concept of universe is spatially exclusive. For a time, a film is the Universe, the world, or if you like, Nature. We will see how the films that have attempted to substitute a fabricated nature and an artificial world for the world of experience have not all equally succeeded. Admitting the failure of *Caligari* and *Die Nibelungen* we then ask ourselves how we explain the undoubted success of *Nosferatu* and *La Passion de Jeanne d'Arc*, the criterion of success being that these films have never aged. Yet it would seem at first sight that the methods of direction belong to the same aesthetic family, and that viewing the varieties of temperament and period, one could group these four films together as expressionist as distinct from realist. However, if we examine them more closely we see that there are certain basic differences between them. It is clear in the case of R. Wiene and Murnau. *Nosferatu* plays, for the greater part of the time, against natural settings whereas the fantastic qualities of *Caligari* are derived from deformities of lighting and decor. The case of Dreyer's *Jeanne d'Arc* is a little more subtle since at first sight nature plays a nonexistent role. To put it more directly, the decor by Jean Hugo is no whit less artificial and theatrical than the settings of *Caligari*; the systematic use of close-ups and unusual angles is well calculated to destroy any sense of space. Regular cinéclub goers know that the film is unfailingly introduced with the famous story of how the hair of Falconetti was actually cut in the interest of the film and likewise, the actors, we are told, wore no make-up. These references to history ordinarily have no more than gossip value. In this case, they seem to me to hold the aesthetic secret of the film; the very thing to which it owes its continued survival. It is precisely because of them that the work of Dreyer ceases to have anything in common with the theater, and indeed one might say, with man. The greater recourse Dreyer has exclusively to the human "expression," the more he has to reconvert it again into Nature. Let there be no mistake, that prodigious fresco of heads is the very opposite of an actor's film. It is a documentary of faces. It is not important how well the actors play, whereas the pockmarks on Bishop Cauchon's face and the red patches of Jean d'Yd are an integral part of the action. In this drama-through-the-microscope the whole of nature palpitates beneath every pore. The movement of a wrinkle, the pursing of a lip are seismic shocks and the flow of tides, the flux and reflux of this human epidermis. But for me Dreyer's brilliant sense of cinema is evidenced in the exterior scene which every other director would assuredly have shot in the studio. The decor as built evoked a Middle Ages of the theater and of miniatures. In one sense, nothing is less realistic than this tribunal in the cemetery or this drawbridge, but the whole is lit by the light of the sun and the gravedigger throws a spadeful of real earth into the hole.*

It is these "secondary" details, apparently aesthetically at odds with the rest of the work, which give it its truly cinematic quality.

If the paradox of the cinema is rooted in the dialectic of concrete and abstract, if cinema is committed to communicate only by way of what is real, it becomes all the more important to discern those elements in filming which confirm our sense of natural reality and those which destroy that feeling. On the other hand, it certainly argues a lack of perception to derive one's sense of reality from these accumulations of factual detail. It is possible to argue that *Les Dames du Bois de Boulogne* is an eminently realistic film, though

---

*This is why I consider the graveyard scene in *Hamlet* and the death of Ophelia bad mistakes on Olivier's part. He had here a chance to introduce sun and soil by way of counterpoint to the setting of Elsinore. Does the actual shot of the sea during the soliloquy of Hamlet show that he had sensed the need for this? The idea, excellent in itself, is not well handled technically.

everything about it is stylized. Everything, except for the rarely noticeable sound of a windshield-wiper, the murmur of a waterfall, or the rushing sound of soil escaping from a broken vase. These are the noises, chosen precisely for their "indifference" to the action, that guarantee its reality.

The cinema being of its essence a dramaturgy of Nature, there can be no cinema without the setting up of an open space in place of the universe rather than as part of it. The screen cannot give us the illusion of this feeling of space without calling on certain natural guarantees. But it is less a question of set construction or of architecture or of immensity than of isolating the aesthetic catalyst, which it is sufficient to introduce in an infinitesimal dose, to have it immediately take on the reality of nature.

The concrete forest of *Die Nibelungen* may well pretend to be an infinite expanse. We do not believe it to be so, whereas the trembling of just one branch in the wind, and the sunlight, would be enough to conjure up all the forests of the world.

If this analysis be well founded, then we see that the basic aesthetic problem of filmed theater is indeed that of the decor. The trump card that the director must hold is the reconversion into a window onto the world of a space oriented toward an interior dimension only, namely the closed and conventional area of the theatrical play.

It is not in Laurence Olivier's *Hamlet* that the text seems to be rendered superfluous or its strength diminished by directorial interpretations, still less in Welles' *Macbeth*, but paradoxically in the stage productions of Gaston Baty, to the precise extent that they go out of their way to create a cinematographic space on the stage; to deny that the settings have a reverse side, thus reducing the sonority of the text simply to the vibration of the voice of the actor who is left without his "resonance box" like a violin that is nothing else but strings. One would never deny that the essential thing in the theater is the text. The latter conceived for the anthropocentric expression proper to the stage and having as its function to bring nature to it cannot, without losing its raison d'être, be used in a space transparent as glass. The problem then that faces the film-maker is to give his decor a dramatic opaqueness while at the same time reflecting its natural realism. Once this paradox of space has been dealt with, the director, so far from hesitating to bring theatrical conventions and faithfulness to the text to the screen will find himself now, on the contrary, completely free to rely on them. From that point on it is no longer a matter of running away from those things which "make theater" but in the long run to acknowledge their existence by rejecting the resources of the cinema, as Cocteau did in *Les Parents terribles* and Welles in *Macbeth*, or by putting them in quotation marks as Laurence Olivier did in *Henry V*. The evidence of a return to filmed theater that we have had during the last ten years belongs essentially to the history of decor and editing. It is a conquest of realism—not, certainly, the realism of subject matter or realism of expression but that realism of space without which moving pictures do not constitute cinema.

GEORGE BLUESTONE
FROM NOVELS INTO FILM

LIMITS OF THE NOVEL
AND THE FILM

THE MODES OF CONSCIOUSNESS

It is a commonplace by now that the novel has tended to retreat more and more from external action to internal thought, from plot to character, from social to psychological realities. Although these conflicting tendencies were already present in the polarity of Fielding and Sterne, it was only recently that the tradition of *Tristram Shandy* superseded the tradition of *Tom Jones*. It is this reduction of the novel to experiences which can be verified in the immediate consciousness of the novelist that Mendilow has called modern "inwardness" and E. M. Forster the "hidden life." Forster suggests the difference when he says that "The hidden life is, by definition, hidden. The hidden life that appears in external signs is hidden no longer, has entered the realm of action. And it is the function of the novelist to reveal the hidden life at its source." But if the hidden life has become the domain of the novel, it has introduced unusual problems.

In a recent review of Leon Edel's *The Psychological Novel: 1900–1950*, Howard Mumford Jones sums up the central problems which have plagued the modern novelist: the verbal limitations of nonverbal experience; the dilemma of autobiographical fiction in which the novelist must at once evoke a unique consciousness and yet communicate it to others; the difficulty of catching the flux of time in static language. The summary is acutely concise in picking out the nerve centers of an increasingly subjective novel where

291

"after images fished out of the stream of past time . . . substitute a kind of smoldering dialectic for the clean impact of drama."

Béla Balázs has shown us how seriously we tend to underestimate the power of the human face to convey subjective emotions and to suggest thoughts. But the film, being a presentational medium (except for its use of dialogue), cannot have direct access to the power of discursive forms. Where the novel discourses, the film must picture. From this we ought not to conclude like J. P. Mayer that "our eye is weaker than our mind" because it does not "*hold* sight impressions as our imagination does." For sense impressions, like word symbols, may be appropriated into the common fund of memory. Perceptual knowledge is not necessarily different in strength; it *is* necessarily different in kind.

The rendition of mental states—memory, dream, imagination— cannot be as adequately represented by film as by language. If the film has difficulty presenting streams of consciousness, it has even more difficulty presenting states of mind which are defined precisely by the absence in them of the visible world. Conceptual imaging, by definition, has no existence in space. However, once I cognize the signs of a sentence through the conceptual screen, my consciousness is indistinguishable from nonverbal thought. Assuming here a difference between *kinds* of images—between images of things, feelings, concepts, words—we may observe that conceptual images evoked by verbal stimuli can scarcely be distinguished in the end from those evoked by nonverbal stimuli. The stimuli, whether they be the signs of language or the sense data of the physical world, lose their spatial characteristics and become components of the total ensemble which is consciousness.

On the other hand, the film image, being externalized in space, cannot be similarly converted through the conceptual screen. We have already seen how alien to the screen is the compacted luxuriance of the trope. For the same reasons, dreams and memories, which exist nowhere but in the individual consciousness, cannot be adequately represented in spatial terms. Or rather, the film, having only arrangements of space to work with, cannot render thought, for the moment thought is externalized it is no longer thought. The film, by arranging external signs for our visual perception, or by presenting us with dialogue, can lead us to *infer* thought. But it cannot show us thought directly. It can show us characters thinking, feeling, and speaking, but it cannot show us their thoughts and feelings. A film is not thought; it is perceived.

That is why pictorial representations of dreams or memory on the screen are almost always disappointing. The dreams and memories of *Holiday for Henrietta* and *Rashomon* are spatial referents to dreams and memories, not precise renditions. To show a memory or dream, one must balloon a separate image into the frame (Gypo remembering good times with Frankie in *The Informer*); or superimpose an image (Gypo daydreaming about an ocean voyage with Katie); or clear the frame entirely for the visual equivalent (in *Wuthering Heights*, Ellen's face dissolving to the house as it was years ago). Such spatial devices are always to some degree dissatisfying. Acting upon us perceptually, they cannot render the conceptual feel of dreams and memories. The realistic tug of the film is too strong. If, in an effort to bridge the gap between spatial representation and nonspatial experience, we accept such devices at all, we accept them as cinematic conventions, not as renditions of conceptual consciousness.

Given the contrasting abilities of film and novel to render conceptual consciousness, we may explore further the media's handling of time. . . .

PSYCHOLOGICAL TIME: THE TIME-FLUX

As soon as we enter the realm of time-in-flux, we not only broach all but insoluble problems for the novel but we also find a sharp divergence between prose and cinema. The transient, sequential, and irreversible character of language is no longer adequate for this type of time experience. For in the flux, past and present lose their identity as discrete sections of time. The present becomes "specious" because on second glance it is seen as fused with the past, obliterating the line between them.

Discussing its essential modernity, Mendilow lends support to the idea that the whole of experience is implicit in every moment of the present by drawing from Sturt's *Psychology of Time*. For Sturt tries to work out the sense in which we are caught by a perpetual present permeated by the past:

One of the reasons for the feeling of pastness is that we are familiar with the things or events that we recognize as past. But it remains true that this feeling of familiarity is a *present* experience, and therefore logically should not arouse a concept of the past. On the other hand, a present impression (or memory) of something which is past is different from a present impression of something which is present but familiar from the past.

How this seeming contradiction operates in practice may be seen when we attempt to determine precisely which of two past events is prior, and in what manner the distinction between the memory of a past thing and the impression of a present thing is to be made. At first glance, we seem perfectly able to deduce which of two remembered events is prior. For example, on the way to the store this morning, I met a group of children going to school. I also mailed my letter just as the postman came by. I know that ordinarily the children go to school at nine o'clock and the postman comes by at eleven. Therefore, I deduce that I went to the store *before* I mailed my letter. Although I have not been able to give the act of my going to the store an exact location in the past, I have been able to establish its priority.

On second thought, however, it seems as if (apart from the deductions one makes by deliberate attention to relationships) the memory of a past event comes to me with its pastness already intended. The image I have of my friend *includes* the information that this is the way he looked the year before he died. Similarly, if I have a mental image of myself on a train to Kabul, then summon up an image of myself eating chestnuts, I know that the first is an image of a past thing and the second an image of a present thing because the image of myself on the train includes the information that the event took place last year. At the same time, I know that I am eating chestnuts right now. Here the perceptual witnessing of my present action checks and defines my mental images, confirming both the priority of the train ride and the presentness of the eating.

But suppose I bring my attention to bear on an object which is present now and which was also present yesterday at the same time, in the same place, in the same light. If, for example, I look at the lamp in my room, which fulfills all these requirements, then close my eyes and behold the mental image, how am I to know if that image refers to the lamp which was there yesterday or to the lamp which is there today? In this instance, which is tantamount to fusing a thing's past with its present, my present image, for all practical purposes, no longer respects the distinction between past and present. It offers me no way of knowing the exact location of its temporal existence.

This obliteration between past and present is precisely the problem which faces the novelist who wishes to catch the flux in language. If he is faced with the presentness of consciousness on the one hand, and the obliteration of the discrete character of past and present on the other, how is he to express these phenomena in a language which relies on tenses?

Whether we look at William James' "stream of consciousness," Ford Madox Ford's "chronological looping," or Bergson's "durée," we find the theorists pondering the same problem: language, consisting as it does of bounded, discrete units cannot satisfactorily represent the unbounded and continuous. We have a sign to cover the concept of a thing's "becoming"; and one to cover the concept of a thing's "having become." But "becoming" is a *present* participle, "become" a *past* participle, and our language has thus far offered no way of showing the continuity between them.

So elusive has been the *durée* that the novelist has submitted to the steady temptation of trying to escape time entirely. But here, too, the failure has served to dramatize the medium's limitations. Speaking of Gertrude Stein's attempt to emancipate fiction from the tyranny of time, E. M. Forster notes the impasse: "She fails, because as soon as fiction is completely delivered from time it cannot express anything at all."

To be sure, there seem to be intuitive moments of illumination in Proust and Wolfe during which a forgotten incident floats up from oblivion in its pristine form and seems thereby to become free of time. Proust's involuntary memory fuses the experience of his mother's madeleine cake with the former experience of Aunt Léonie's, and the intervening time seems, for the moment, obliterated. But it is the precise point of Proust's agonizing effort that—despite our ability, through involuntary memory, to experience simultaneously events "with countless intervening days between"—there is always a sense in which these events remain "widely separated from one another in Time." The recognition of this conflict helps us understand why every formulation which attempts to define a "timeless" quality in a novel seems unsatisfactory, why Mendilow's attempt to find an "ideal time" in Kafka seems to say little more than that Kafka was not plagued by the problem. In the end, the phrase "timeless moment" poses an insuperable contradiction in terms.

We can see the problem exemplified concretely in a passage from Thomas Wolfe's *The Hills Beyond*. The passage describes Eugene Gant's visit to the house in St. Louis where his family had lived thirty years before. Eugene can remember the sights, shapes, sounds, and smells of thirty years ago, but something is missing— a sense of absence, the absence of his brother Grover, of his family away at the fair:

> And he felt that if he could sit there on the stairs once more, in solitude and absence in the afternoon, he would be able to get it back again. Then would he be able to remember all that he had seen and been—that brief sum of himself, the universe of his four years, with all the light of Time upon it—that universe which was so short to measure, and yet so far, so endless, to remember. Then would he be able to see his own small face again, pooled in the dark mirror of the hall, and discover there in his quiet three years' self the lone integrity of "I," knowing: "Here is the House, and here House listening; here is Absence, Absence in the afternoon; and here in this House, this Absence, is my core, my kernel—here am I!"

The passage shows the characteristic, almost obsessive longing of the modern novel to escape the passage of time by memory; the recognition that the jump, the obliteration, cannot be made; the appropriation of non-space as a reality in the novel—not the feeling of absence alone, but the absence of absence.

We arrive here at the novel's farthest and most logical remove from the film. For it is hard to see how any satisfactory film equivalents can be found for such a paragraph. We can show Eugene waiting in the house, then superimpose an image of the boy as he might have looked thirty years before, catch him watching a door as if waiting for Grover to return. But as in all cinematic attempts to render thought, such projection would inevitably fail. How are we to capture that combination of past absence and present longing, if both are conditions contrary to spatial fact?

The film-maker, in his own and perhaps more acute way, also

faces the problem of how to render the flux of time. "Pictures have no tenses," says Balázs. Unfolding in a perpetual present, like visual perception itself, they cannot express either a past or a future. One may argue that the use of dialogue and music provides a door through which a sense of past and future may enter. Dialogue, after all, is language, and language does have referential tenses. A character whose face appears before us may *talk* about his past and thereby permeate his presence with a kind of pastness. Similarly, as we saw in our discussion of sound in editing, music may be used to counterpoint a present image (as in *High Noon* and *Alexander Nevsky*) and suggest a future event. In this way, apparently, a succession of present images may be suffused with a quality of past or future.

At best, however, sound is a secondary advantage which does not seriously threaten the primacy of the spatial image. When Ellen, the housekeeper, her withered face illumined by the fire, begins telling her story to Lockwood in *Wuthering Heights*, we do sense a certain tension between story-teller and story. But in the film we can never fully shake our attention loose from the teller. The image of her face has priority over the sound of her voice. When Terry Malone tells Edie about his childhood in *On the Waterfront*, the present image of his face so floods our consciousness that his words have the thinnest substance only. The scars around his eyes tell us more about his past than any halting explanation. This phenomenon is essentially what Panofsky calls the "principle of coexpressibility," according to which a moving picture—even when it has learned to talk—remains a picture that moves, and does not convert itself into a piece of writing that is enacted. That is why Shakesperian films which fail to adapt the fixed space of the stage to cinematic space so often seem static and talky.

In the novel, the line of dialogue stands naked and alone; in the film, the spoken word is attached to its spatial image. If we try to convert Marlon Brando's words into our own thought, we leave for a moment the visual drama of his face, much as we turn away from a book. The difference is that, whereas in the book we miss nothing, in the film Brando's face has continued to act, and the moment we miss may be crucial. In a film, according to Panofsky, "that which we hear remains, for good or worse, inextricably fused with that which we see." In that fusion, our seeing (and therefore our sense of the present) remains primary.

If, however, dialogue and music are inadequate to the task of capturing the flux, the spatial image itself reveals two characteristics which at least permit the film to make a tentative approach. The first is the quality of familiarity which attaches itself to the perceptual image of a thing after our first acquaintance. When I first see Gelsomina in *La Strada*, I see her as a stranger, as a girl with a certain physical disposition, but without a name or a known history. However, once I identify her as a character with a particular relationship to other characters, I am able to include information about her past in the familiar figure which now appears before me. I do not have to renew my acquaintance at every moment. Familiarity, then, becomes a means of referring to the past, and this past reference fuses into the ensemble which is the present Gelsomina. The spatial image of Gelsomina which I see toward the end of the film includes, in its total structure, the knowledge that she has talked to the Fool and returned to Zampano. In a referential sense, the pastness is built in.

That the film is in constant motion suggests the second qualification of film for approximating the time-flux. At first glance, the film seems bound by discrete sections, much as the novel is bound by discrete words. At the film's outer limit stands the frame; and within the frame appear the distinct outlines of projected objects, each one cut as by a razor's edge. But the effect of running off the frames is startlingly different from the effect of running off the sentence. For whether the words in a novel come to me as nonverbal images or as verbal meanings, I can still detect the discrete units of subject and predicate. If I say, "The top spins on the table," my mind assembles first the top, then the spinning, then the table. (Unless, of course, I am capable of absorbing the sentence all at once, in which case the process may be extended to a paragraph composed of discrete sentences.) But on the screen, I simply perceive a shot of a top spinning on a table, in which subject and predicate appear to me as *fused*. Not only is the top indistinguishable from its spinning, but at every moment the motion of the top seems to contain the history of its past motion. It is true that the top-image stimulated in my mind by the sentence resembles the top-image stimulated by the film in the sense that both contain the illusion of continuous motion. Yet this resemblance does not appear in the *process* of cognition. It appears only after the fact, as it were, only after the component words have been assembled. Although the mental and filmic images do meet in rendering the top's continuity of motion, it is in the mode of apprehending them that we find the qualitative difference.

In the cinema, for better or worse, we are bound by the forward looping of the celluloid through the projector. In that relentless unfolding, each frame is blurred in a total progression. Keeping in mind Sturt's analysis of the presentness of our conceptions, a presentness permeated by a past and therefore hardly ruled by tense at all, we note that the motion in the film's *present* is unique. Montage depends for its effects on instantaneous successions of different spatial entities which are constantly exploding against each other. But a succession of such variables would quickly become incomprehensible without a constant to stabilize them. In the film, that constant is motion. No matter how diverse the moving spaces which explode against each other, movement itself pours over from shot to shot, binding as it blurs them, reinforcing the relentless unrolling of the celluloid.

Lindgren advances Abercrombie's contention that completeness in art has no counterpart in real life, since natural events are never complete: "In nature nothing at any assignable point begins and nothing at any assignable point comes to an end: all is perfect continuity." But Abercrombie overlooks both our ability to perceive spatial discreteness in natural events and the film's ability to achieve "perfect continuity." So powerful is this continuity, regardless of the *direction* of the motion, that at times we tend to forget the boundaries of both frame and projected object. We attend to the motion only. In those moments when motion alone floods our attention and spatial attributes seem forgotten, we suddenly come as close as the film is able to fulfilling one essential requirement of the time-flux—the boundaries are no longer perceptible. The transience of the shot falls away before the sweeping permanence of its motion. Past and present seem fused, and we have accomplished before us a kind of spatial analogue for the flux of time.

If the film is incapable of maintaining the illusion for very long, if its spatial attributes, being primary, presently assert themselves, if the film's spatial appeal to the eye overwhelms its temporal appeal to the mind, it is still true that the film, above all other nonverbal arts, comes closest to rendering the time-flux. The combination of familiarity, the film's linear progression, and what Panofsky calls the "Dynamization of Space" permits us to intuit the *durée* insofar as it can, in spatial art, be intuited at all.

The film, then, cannot render the attributes of thought (metaphor, dream, memory); but it can find adequate equivalents for the kind of psychological time which is characterized by variations in rate (distension, compression; speed-up, *ralenti*); and it approaches, but ultimately fails, like the novel, to render what Bergson means by the time-flux. The failure of both media ultimately reverts to root differences between the structures of art and consciousness.

Our analysis, however, permits a usable distinction between the two media. Both novel and film are time arts, but whereas the formative principle in the novel is time, the formative principle in the film is space. Where the novel takes its space for granted and forms its narrative in a complex of time values, the film takes its time for granted and forms its narrative in arrangements of space. Both film and novel create the illusion of psychologically distorted time and space, but neither destroys time or space. The novel renders the illusion of space by going from point to point in time; the film renders time by going from point to point in space. The novel tends to abide by, yet explore, the possibilities of psychological law; the film tends to abide by, yet explore, the possibilities of physical law.

Where the twentieth-century novel has achieved the shock of novelty by explosions of words, the twentieth-century film has achieved a comparable shock by explosions of visual images. And it is a phenomenon which invites detailed investigation that the rise of the film, which preëmpted the picturing of bodies in nature, coincides almost exactly with the rise of the modern novel which preëmpted the rendition of human consciousness.

Finally, to discover distinct formative principles in our two media is not to forget that time and space are, for artistic purposes, ultimately inseparable. To say that an element is contingent is not to say that it is irrelevant. Clearly, spatial effects in the film would be impossible without concepts of time, just as temporal effects

300

in the novel would be impossible without concepts of space. We are merely trying to state the case for a system of priority and emphasis. And our central claim—namely that time is prior in the novel, and space prior in the film—is supported rather than challenged by our reservations.

SERGEI EISENSTEIN
FROM DICKENS, GRIFFITH, AND THE FILM TODAY

The most thrilling figure was Griffith, for it was in his works that the cinema made itself felt as more than an entertainment or pastime. The brilliant new methods of the American cinema were united in him with a profound emotion of story, with human acting, with laughter and tears, and all this was done with an astonishing ability to preserve all that gleam of a filmically dynamic holiday, which had been captured in *The Gray Shadow* and *The Mark of Zorro* and *The House of Hate*. That the cinema could be incomparably greater, and that this was to be the basic task of the budding Soviet cinema—these were sketched for us in Griffith's creative work, and found ever new confirmation in his films.

Our heightened curiosity of those years in *construction and method* swiftly discerned wherein lay the most powerful affective factors in this great American's films. This was in a hitherto unfamiliar province, bearing a name that was familiar to us, not in the field of art, but in that of engineering and electrical apparatus, first touching art in its most advanced section—in cinematography. This province, this method, this principle of building and construction was *montage*.

This was the montage whose foundations had been laid by American film-culture, but whose full, completed, conscious use and world recognition was established by our films. Montage, the rise of which will be forever linked with the name of Griffith. Montage, which played a most vital rôle in the creative work of Griffith and brought him his most glorious successes.

Griffith arrived at it through the method of parallel action. And, essentially, it was on this that he came to a standstill. But we mustn't run ahead. Let us examine the question of how montage came to Griffith or—how Griffith came to montage.

Griffith arrived at montage through the method of parallel action, and he was led to the idea of parallel action by—Dickens! . . .

What were the novels of Dickens for his contemporaries, for his readers? There is one answer: they bore the same relation to them that the film bears to the same strata in our time. They compelled the reader to live with the same passions. They appealed to the same good and sentimental elements as does the film (at least on the surface); they alike shudder before vice, they alike mill the extraordinary, the unusual, the fantastic, from boring, prosaic and everyday existence. And they clothe this common and prosaic existence in their special vision.

Illumined by this light, refracted from the land of fiction back to life, this commonness took on a romantic air, and bored people were grateful to the author for giving them the countenances of potentially romantic figures.

This partially accounts for the close attachment to the novels of Dickens and, similarly, to films. . . .

Perhaps the secret lies in Dickens's (as well as cinema's) creation of an extraordinary plasticity. The observation in the novels is extraordinary—as is their optical quality. The characters of Dickens are rounded with means as plastic and slightly exaggerated as are the screen heroes of today. The screen's heroes are engraved on the senses of the spectator with clearly visible traits, its villains are remembered by certain facial expressions, and all are saturated in the peculiar, slightly unnatural radiant gleam thrown over them by the screen.

It is absolutely thus that Dickens draws his characters—this is the faultlessly plastically grasped and pitilessly sharply sketched gallery of immortal Pickwicks, Dombeys, Fagins, Tackletons, and others. . . .

Analogies and resemblances cannot be pursued too far—they lose conviction and charm. They begin to take on the air of machination or card-tricks. I should be very sorry to lose the conviction of the affinity between Dickens and Griffith, allowing this abundance of common traits to slide into a game of anecdotal semblance of tokens.

All the more that such a gleaning from Dickens goes beyond the limits of interest in Griffith's individual cinematic craftsmanship and widens into a concern with film-craftsmanship in general. This is why I dig more and more deeply into the film-indications of Dickens, revealing them through Griffith—for the use of future film-exponents. So I must be excused, in leafing through Dickens, for having found in him even—a "dissolve." . . .

However, let us turn to the basic montage structure, whose rudiment in Dickens's work was developed into the elements of film composition in Griffith's work. Lifting a corner of the veil over these riches, these hitherto unused experiences, let us look into *Oliver Twist*. Open it at the twenty-first chapter. Let's read its beginning:

CHAPTER XXI*

1. It was a cheerless morning when they got into the street; blowing and raining hard; and the clouds looking dull and stormy.

The night had been very wet: for large pools of water had collected in the road: and the kennels were overflowing.

There was a faint glimmering of the coming day in the sky; but it rather aggravated than relieved the gloom of the scene: the sombre light only serving to pale that which the street lamps afforded, without shedding any warmer or brighter tints upon the wet housetops, and dreary streets.

There appeared to be nobody stirring in that quarter of the town; for the windows of the houses were all closely shut; and the streets through which they passed, were noiseless and empty.

2. By the time they had turned into the Bethnal Green Road, the day had fairly begun to break. Many of the lamps were already extinguished;

a few country waggons were slowly toiling on, towards London;

and now and then, a stage-coach, covered with mud, rattled briskly by:

the driver bestowing, as he passed, an admonitory lash upon the heavy waggoner who, by keeping on the wrong side of the road, had endangered his arriving at the office, a quarter of a minute after his time.

---

*For demonstration purposes I have broken this beginning of the chapter into smaller pieces than did its author; the numbering is, of course, also mine.

The public-houses, with gas-lights burning inside, were already open.

By degrees, other shops began to be unclosed; and a few scattered people were met with.

Then, came straggling groups of labourers going to their work;
then, men and women with fish-baskets on their heads:
donkey-carts laden with vegetables;
chaise-carts filled with live-stock or whole carcasses of meat;
milk-women with pails;
and an unbroken concourse of people, trudging out with various supplies to the eastern suburbs of the town.

3. As they approached the City, the noise and traffic gradually increased;
and when they threaded the streets between Shoreditch and Smithfield, it had swelled into a roar of sound and bustle.

It was as light as it was likely to be, till night came on again; and the busy morning of half the London population had begun. . . .

4. It was market-morning.
The ground was covered, nearly ankle-deep, with filth and mire;
and a thick steam, perpetually rising from the reeking bodies of the cattle,
and mingling with the fog,
which seemed to rest upon the chimney-tops, hung heavily above.
. . .
Countrymen,
butchers,
drovers,
hawkers,
boys,
thieves,
idlers,
and vagabonds of every low grade,
were mingled together in a dense mass;

5. the whistling of drovers,
the barking of dogs,
the bellowing and plunging of oxen,
the bleating of sheep,
the grunting and squeaking of pigs;
the cries of hawkers,
the shouts, oaths and quarrelling on all sides;

305

the ringing of bells
and roar of voices, that issued from every public-house;
the crowding, pushing, driving, beating,
whooping and yelling;
the hideous and discordant din that resounded from every corner
of the market;
and the unwashed, unshaven, squalid, and dirty figures constantly
running to and fro, and bursting in and out of the throng; rendered
it a stunning and bewildering scene, which quite confounded the
senses.

How often have we encountered just such a structure in the work
of Griffith? This austere accumulation and quickening tempo, this
gradual play of light: from burning street-lamps, to their being
extinguished; from night, to dawn; from dawn, to the full radiance
of day (*It was as light as it was likely to be, till night came on
again*); this calculated transition from purely visual elements to an
interweaving of them with aural elements: at first as an indefinite
rumble, coming from afar at the second stage of increasing light,
so that the rumble may grow into a roar, transferring us to a purely
aural structure, now concrete and objective (section 5 of our breakdown); with such scenes, picked up *en passant*, and intercut into the
whole—like the driver, hastening towards his office; and, finally,
these magnificently typical details, the reeking bodies of the cattle,
from which the steam rises and mingles with the over-all cloud of
morning fog, or the close-up of the legs in the almost ankle-deep
filth and mire, all this gives the fullest cinematic sensation of the
panorama of a market. . . .

If in the above-cited examples we have encountered prototypes
of characteristics for Griffith's *montage exposition*, then it would
pay us to read further in *Oliver Twist*, where we can find another
montage method typical for Griffith—the method of a *montage
progression of parallel scenes, intercut into each other*.

For this let us turn to that group of scenes in which is set forth
the familiar episode of how Mr. Brownlow, to show faith in Oliver
in spite of his pick-pocket reputation, sends him to return books
to the book-seller, and of how Oliver again falls into the clutches
of the thief Sikes, his sweetheart Nancy, and old Fagin.

These scenes are unrolled absolutely à la Griffith: both in their
inner emotional line, as well as in the unusual sculptural relief and

306

delineation of the characters; in the uncommon full-bloodedness of the dramatic as well as the humorous traits in them; finally, also in the typical Griffith-esque montage of parallel interlocking of all the links of the separate episodes. Let us give particular attention to this last peculiarity, just as unexpected, one would think, in Dickens, as it is characteristic for Griffith!

CHAPTER XIV

COMPRISING FURTHER PARTICULARS OF OLIVER'S STAY AT MR. BROWNLOW'S, WITH THE REMARKABLE PREDICTION WHICH ONE MR. GRIMWIG UTTERED CONCERNING HIM, WHEN HE WENT OUT ON AN ERRAND.

. . . "Dear me, I am very sorry for that," exclaimed Mr. Brownlow; "I particularly wished those books to be returned tonight."

"Send Oliver with them," said Mr. Grimwig, with an ironical smile; "he will be sure to deliver them safely, you know."

"Yes; do let me take them, if you please, Sir," said Oliver. "I'll run all the way, Sir."

The old gentleman was just going to say that Oliver should not go out on any account; when a most malicious cough from Mr. Grimwig determined him that he should; and that, by his prompt discharge of the commission, he should prove to him the injustice of his suspicions: on this head at least: at once.

[Oliver is prepared for the errand to the bookstall-keeper.]

"I won't be ten minutes, Sir," replied Oliver, eagerly.

[Mrs. Bedwin, Mr. Brownlow's housekeeper, gives Oliver the directions, and sends him off.]

"Bless his sweet face!" said the old lady, looking after him. "I can't bear, somehow, to let him go out of my sight."

At this moment, Oliver looked gaily round, and nodded before he turned the corner. The old lady smilingly returned his salutation, and, closing the door, went back to her own room.

"Let me see; he'll be back in twenty minutes, at the longest," said Mr. Brownlow, pulling out his watch, and placing it on the table. "It will be dark by that time."

"Oh! you really expect him to come back, do you?" inquired Mr. Grimwig.

"Don't you?" asked Mr. Brownlow, smiling.

The spirit of contradiction was strong in Mr. Grimwig's breast, at the moment; and it was rendered stronger by his friend's confident smile.

"No," he said, smiting the table with his fist, "I do not. The boy has a new suit of clothes on his back; a set of valuable books under his arm; and a five-pound note in his pocket. He'll join his old friends the thieves, and laugh at you. If ever that boy returns to this house, Sir, I'll eat my head."

With these words he drew his chair closer to the table; and there the two friends sat, in silent expectation, with the watch between them.

This is followed by a short "interruption" in the form of a digression:

> It is worthy of remark, as illustrating the importance we attach to our own judgments, and the pride with which we put forth our most rash and hasty conclusions, that, although Mr. Grimwig was not by any means a bad-hearted man, and though he would have been unfeignedly sorry to see his respected friend duped and deceived, he really did most earnestly and strongly hope, at that moment, that Oliver Twist might not come back.

And again a return to the two old gentlemen:

> It grew so dark, that the figures on the dial-plate were scarcely discernible; but there the two old gentlemen continued to sit, in silence: with the watch between them.

Twilight shows that only a little time has passed, but the *close-up* of the watch, *already twice* shown lying between the old gentlemen, says that a great deal of time has passed already. But just then, as in the game of "will he come? won't he come?", involving not only the two old men, but also the kind-hearted reader, the worst fears and vague forebodings of the old housekeeper are justified by the cut to the new scene—Chapter XV. This begins with a short scene in the public-house, with the bandit Sikes and his dog, old Fagin and Miss Nancy, who has been obliged to discover the whereabouts of Oliver.

> "You are on the scent, are you, Nancy?" inquired Sikes, proffering the glass.
> "Yes, I am, Bill," replied the young lady, disposing of its contents; "and tired enough of it I am, too. . . ."

Then, one of the best scenes in the whole novel—at least one that since childhood has been perfectly preserved, along with the evil figure of Fagin—the scene in which Oliver, marching along with the books, is suddenly

> startled by a young woman screaming out very loud, "Oh, my dear brother!" And he had hardly looked up, to see what the matter was, when he was stopped by having a pair of arms thrown tight round his neck.

With this cunning maneuver Nancy, with the sympathies of the whole street, takes the desperately pulling Oliver, as her "prodigal brother," back into the bosom of Fagin's gang of thieves. This fifteenth chapter closes on the now familiar montage phrase:

> The gas-lamps were lighted; Mrs. Bedwin was waiting anxiously at the open door; the servant had run up the street twenty times to see if there were any traces of Oliver; and still the two old gentlemen sat, perseveringly, in the dark parlour: with the watch between them.

In Chapter XVI Oliver, once again in the clutches of the gang, is subjected to mockery. Nancy rescues him from a beating:

> "I won't stand by and see it done, Fagin," cried the girl. "You've got the boy, and what more would you have? Let him be—let him be, or I shall put that mark on some of you, that will bring me to the gallows before my time."

By the way, it is characteristic for both Dickens and Griffith to have these sudden flashes of goodness in "morally degraded" characters and, though these sentimental images verge on hokum, they are so faultlessly done that they work on the most skeptical readers and spectators!

At the end of this chapter, Oliver, sick and weary, falls "sound asleep." Here the physical time unity is interrupted—an evening and night, crowded with events; but the montage unity of the episode is not interrupted, tying Oliver to Mr. Brownlow on one side, and to Fagin's gang on the other.

Following, in Chapter XVIII, is the arrival of the parish beadle, Mr. Bumble, in response to an inquiry about the lost boy, and the appearance of Bumble at Mr. Brownlow's, again in Grimwig's company. The content and reason for their conversation is revealed by the very title of the chapter: OLIVER'S DESTINY CONTINUING UNPROPITIOUS, BRINGS A GREAT MAN TO LONDON TO INJURE HIS REPUTATION . . .

"I fear it is all too true," said the old gentleman sorrowfully, after looking over the papers. "This is not much for your intelligence; but I would gladly have given you treble the money, if it had been favourable to the boy."

It is not at all improbable that if Mr. Bumble had been possessed of this information at an earlier period of the interview, he might have imparted a very different coloring to his little history. It was too late to do it now, however; so he shook his head gravely; and, pocketing the five guineas, withdrew. . . .

"Mrs. Bedwin," said Mr. Brownlow, when the housekeeper appeared; "that boy, Oliver, is an impostor."

"It can't be, Sir. It cannot be," said the old lady energetically. . . . "I never will believe it, Sir. . . . Never!"

"You old women never believe anything but quack-doctors, and lying story-books," growled Mr. Grimwig. "I knew it all along. . . ."

"He is a dear, grateful, gentle child, Sir," retorted Mrs. Bedwin, indignantly. "I know what children are, Sir; and have done these forty years; and people who can't say the same, shouldn't say anything about them. That's my opinion!"

This was a hard hit at Mr. Grimwig, who was a bachelor. As it extorted nothing from that gentleman but a smile, the old lady tossed her head, and smoothed down her apron preparatory to another speech, when she was stopped by Mr. Brownlow.

"Silence!" said the old gentleman, feigning an anger he was far from feeling. "Never let me hear the boy's name again. I rang to tell you that. Never. Never, on any pretence, mind! You may leave the room, Mrs. Bedwin. Remember! I am in earnest."

And the entire intricate montage complex of this episode is concluded with the sentence:

There were sad hearts in Mr. Brownlow's that night.

It was not by accident that I have allowed myself such full extracts, in regard not only to the composition of the scenes, but also to the delineation of the characters, for in their very modeling, in their characteristics, in their behavior, there is much typical of Griffith's manner. This equally concerns also his "Dickens-esque" distressed, defenseless creatures (recalling Lillian Gish and Richard Barthelmess in *Broken Blossoms* or the Gish sisters in *Orphans of the Storm*), and is no less typical for his characters like the two old gentlemen and Mrs. Bedwin; and finally, it is entirely characteristic of him to have such figures as are in the gang of "the merry old Jew" Fagin.

In regard to the immediate task of our example of Dickens's montage progression of the story composition, we can present the results of it in the following table:

1. *The old gentlemen.*
2. Departure of Oliver.
3. *The old gentlemen and the watch. It is still light.*
4. Digression on the character of Mr. Grimwig.
5. *The old gentlemen and the watch. Gathering twilight.*
6. Fagin, Sikes and Nancy in the public-house.
7. Scene on the street.
8. *The old gentlemen and the watch. The gas-lamps have been lit.*
9. Oliver is dragged back to Fagin.
10. Digression at the beginning of Chapter XVII.
11. The journey of Mr. Bumble.
12. *The old gentlemen* and Mr. Brownlow's command to forget Oliver forever.

As we can see, we have before us a typical and, for Griffith, a model of parallel montage of two story lines, where one (the waiting gentlemen) emotionally heightens the tension and drama of the other (the capture of Oliver). It is in "rescuers" rushing along to save the "suffering heroine" that Griffith has, with the aid of parallel montage, earned his most glorious laurels!

Most curious of all is that in the *very center* of our breakdown of the episode, is wedged another "interruption"—a whole digression at the beginning of Chapter XVII, on which we have been purposely silent. What is remarkable about this digression? It is Dickens's own "treatise" on the principles of this montage construction of the story which he carries out so fascinatingly, and which passed into the style of Griffith. Here it is:

> It is the custom on the stage, in all good murderous melodramas, to present the tragic and the comic scenes, in as regular alternation, as the layers of red and white in a side of streaky well-cured bacon. The hero sinks upon his straw bed, weighed down by fetters and misfortunes; and, in the next scene, his faithful but unconscious squire regales the audience with a comic song. We behold, with throbbing bosoms, the heroine in the grasp of a proud and ruthless baron: her virtue and her life alike in danger; drawing forth her dagger to preserve the one at the cost of the other; and just as our expectations are wrought up to the highest pitch, a whistle is heard: and we are straightway transported to the great hall of the castle: where a grey-headed seneschal sings a funny chorus with a funnier body of vassals, who are free of all sorts of places from church vaults to palaces, and roam about in company, carolling perpetually.
>
> Such changes appear absurd; but they are not so unnatural as they would seem at first sight. The transitions in real life from well-spread boards to death-beds, and from mourning-weeds to holiday garments, are not a whit less startling; only, there, we are busy actors, instead of passive lookers-on; which makes a vast difference. The actors in the mimic life of the theatre, are blind to violent transitions and abrupt impulses of passion of feeling, which, presented before the eyes of mere spectators, are at once condemned as outrageous and preposterous.
>
> As sudden shiftings of the scene, and rapid changes of time and place, are not only sanctioned in books by long usage, but are by many considered as the great art of authorship: an author's skill in his craft being, by such critics, chiefly estimated with relation to the dilemmas in which he leaves his characters at the end of every chapter: this brief introduction to the present one may perhaps be deemed unnecessary. . . .

There is another interesting thing in this treatise: in his own words, Dickens (a life-long amateur actor) defines his direct relation to the theater melodrama. This is as if Dickens had placed himself in the position of a connecting link between the future, unforeseen art of the cinema, and the not so distant (for Dickens) past—the traditions of "good murderous melodramas."

This "treatise," of course, could not have escaped the eye of the patriarch of the American film, and very often his structure seems to follow the wise advice, handed down to the great film-maker of the twentieth century by the great novelist of the nineteenth. And Griffith, hiding nothing, has more than once acknowledged his debt to Dickens's memory. . . .

I don't know how my readers feel about this, but for me personally it is always pleasing to recognize again and again the fact that our cinema is not altogether without parents and without pedigree, without a past, without the traditions and rich cultural heritage of the past epochs. It is only very thoughtless and presumptous people who can erect laws and an esthetic for cinema, proceeding from premises of some incredible virgin-birth of this art!

Let Dickens and the whole ancestral array, going back as far as the Greeks and Shakespeare, be superfluous reminders that both Griffith and our cinema prove our origins to be not solely as of Edison and his fellow inventors, but as based on an enormous cultured past; each part of this past in its own moment of world history has moved forward the great art of cinematography. Let this past be a reproach to those thoughtless people who have displayed arrogance in reference to literature, which has contributed so much to this apparently unprecedented art and is, in the first and most important place: the art of viewing—not only the *eye*, but *viewing*—both meanings being embraced in this term. . . .

Shakespeare and Film

GEOFFREY REEVES
FINDING SHAKESPEARE
ON FILM:
FROM AN INTERVIEW
WITH PETER BROOK

There are two Shakespeare films which warrant special attention, the Soviet *Hamlet* by Kozintsev (1964) and Kurosawa's *Throne of Blood* (*Macbeth*, 1957) which is a great masterpiece, perhaps the only true masterpiece inspired by Shakespeare, but it cannot properly be considered Shakespeare because it doesn't use the text. Kurosawa follows the plot very closely, but by transposing it into the Japan of the Middle Ages and making Macbeth a Samurai, he is doing another *Seven Samurai*. Where the story comes from doesn't matter; he is doing what every film-maker has always done—constructing a film from an idea and using appropriate dialogue. So that what may be the best Shakespearean film doesn't help us with the problems of filming Shakespeare.

The Russian *Hamlet* has been criticized for being academic, and it is: however, it has one gigantic merit—everything in it is related to the director's search for the sense of the play—his structure is inseparable from his meaning. The strength of the film is in Kozintsev's ability to realize his own conception with clarity. This is the first Shakespeare film to reflect this form of directorial approach: a search for over-all meaning as opposed to the many and varied, sometimes dazzling, attempts to capture on the screen the actor-manager's view of the play as imagery, theatricality, passion, color, effects.

Hamlet is a firm piece of work; Kozintsev knows where he stands politically and socially. He knows what bars and wood and stone and fire mean to him; he knows the relationship of black to white, of full screen to empty screen, *in terms of content*. Moreover, Kozintsev managed to get away from the Russian tradition of operatic theater by using the new Pasternak translation, which is colder, quicker, and more realistic than the nineteenth-century version, and by avoiding conventional theater actors. But the limitation lies in its style; when all is said and done, the Soviet *Hamlet* is post-Eisenstein realistic—thus, super-romantic—thus, a far cry from essential Shakespeare—which is neither epic, nor barbaric, nor colorful, nor abstract, nor realistic in any of our uses of the words. The Elizabethan theater had a very complicated yet marvellously free technique, a use of words that was most sophisticated; its blank verse slides in and out of prose, producing texts which continually change gear. If you could extract the mental impression made by the Shakespearean strategy of images, you would get a piece of pop collage. The effect is like a word whose letters are written across three overlapping pictures in the mind. You see the actor as a man standing in the distance and you also see his face, very close to you—perhaps his profile and the back of his head at the same time—and you also see the background. When Hamlet is doing any one of his soliloquies, the background that Shakespeare can conjure in one line evaporates in the next and new images take over. I think that the freedom of the Elizabethan theater is still only partially understood, people having got used to talking in clichés about the non-localized stage. What people do not fully face is that the non-localized stage means that every single thing under the sun is possible, not only quick changes of location: a man can turn into twins, change sex, be his past, his present, his future, be a comic version of himself and a tragic version of himself, and be none of them, *all at the same time*.

Kott's great essay on Gloucester's suicide points out that the act of jumping off an imaginary cliff only takes on its full meaning when performed on a bare stage. Then it becomes a character doing a meaningless jump, and also an actor doing a meaningful jump—both, with full implications both concrete and imaginary, at the same moment. In the cinema, at least in all the films of Shakespeare we have seen, a Gloucester would be forced to stand on a windy heath of some description, although fifty per cent of the extra-ordinariness of the powerful image is that this is happening on a pretended heath, on the boards of nowhere. A meaning is released by the double nature of the act, a meaning which isn't there if you isolate one aspect of it. A leap on a bare stage can be done by anyone, and a leap on a heath is just as simple. But *Lear* gives you both at once in the theater. So the result is like the idea itself striking you in its purest form. On the other hand, in Kozintsev's *Hamlet* its style is eventually its prison. The film creates a plausible world in which the action can reasonably unfold, but the price we pay for this plausible world is that the complexities I have been talking about cannot be encompassed and demonstrated. That is, the problem of filming Shakespeare is one of finding ways of shifting gears, style and conventions as lightly and deftly on the screen as within the mental processes reflected by Elizabethan blank verse onto the screen of the mind. The ponderousness of film is that everything about it tends towards consistency within each single image. And we once thought the cinema mobile!

The effect that the invention of sound had on film in general, and on this problem especially, is curious and crucial. Sound stopped the cinema right in its tracks. People thought that sound would deprive the camera of mobility, and so it did—but only for a short time. Then the crane began swinging and gibbing—and for years everyone fondly imagined that the cinema was mobile again. Mobility of *thought*, which the silent film had, is only now being recaptured in post-Godard techniques. In experiment (if not in actual subject matter) Godard is the most important director today. Continually he liberates the picture from its own consistency. At one moment, you are genuinely looking at a photograph of two people in a bar, then you are half alienated, then you are three-quarters alienated, then you are looking at it as a film-maker, then you are reminded that it is made by actors, and then you are thrown right back into believing it. This relates to alienation in the theater and directly with the free theater-free cinema that the original Elizabethan Shakespeare must have been.

A man being objectively recorded sitting in front of a camera does not constitute an objective reality. This particular *cul de sac* has been with us for a number of years. Gradually, we are coming to realize that photography is not objective, is not realistic—the reality of the cinema exists at the time of the projection, at the moment when an image is projected on the screen—if there is a spectator, then the interplay of image and spectator is the only reality. The reality of six weeks or six months before—a man sitting in a room—is no longer real; there is no *virtue* in the so-called "naturalism" of the photographic process. It *would* be real if it gave you total information, but simple recording cannot begin to do that.

We did a very interesting exercise in this connection in the Stratford studio. I seated one of the actors in front of the group and asked him to think up an elaborate situation for himself and then to live, as an actor, all he could of the inner conditions of this situation. Then the group questioned him to find out what was going on. He was not allowed to answer them. This, of course, created a completely absurd situation. One saw a man who was going through something in his mind. That was all. Eventually he revealed his inner novelette—that he was waiting for his girl-friend to see a doctor to discover if she was pregnant, which would mean an abortion and finding the money, and possibly his wife discovering, etc., but of course none of this could possibly be indicated. The exercise simply drove home the fact that what the eye sees is often of no narrative value whatsoever. The actor stayed motionless, deadpan; interpretations of his state varied from the idea that he was waiting for the dentist, to all kinds of wild interpretations. Frustration built as the group couldn't reach the actor and the silent immobile actor couldn't reach them; so, they realized that surface appearances are non-communicative.

It is this realization which leads, to take extremes, both Antonioni and Godard to their (very different) ways of working. Antonioni accepts the stability of the shot and then employs a variety of devices in the attempt to capture the invisible. Godard attacks the stability of the shot, and tries to capture a multiplicity of aspects. What both of them are rejecting is the notion that the frame, by itself or in temporal juxtaposition, carries the meaning— that a single frame is a full unit. The classic theory of cutting, based on the belief that you are juxtaposing units, which in themselves have a certain completeness—the shot is a unit, the shot is a word, the shot is a brick—is false. *Moderato Cantabile* was a personal experiment to discover whether it is possible to photograph an almost invisible reality, whether it is possible in photographing nothing but a surface to get under that surface.

My premise is a greedy one: in the theater, and especially in the cinema, I want to capture all possible information. This leads me to suspect the self-imposed consistency of any consistent style, because this precludes one learning something one might want to know. If you have a purely intimate story about two people, then one wants to know the social reference; if it is an epic subject, one wants to know something of the inner life. It is only in Shakespeare that you find the balance: nothing is sacrificed, nothing is made less. There is no watering down for the sake of cohesion; all aspects are there in full strength without neutralizing each other.

Putting the Gloucester suicide on film would seem to me to involve the use of alienation. Alienation provides infinite possibilities, and is the only device which leads us back to the possibilities of blank verse. The verse image repeatedly puts objects and ideas into fresh perspective, and so does alienation. The freeze frame, caption, sub-title, etc., are all crude examples of filmic alienation. But meeting Shakespeare's requirements poses a problem very different in scope. Godard's films may be leading a search for a new style, but this style cannot cope with the huge resources, the scale and range of action which Shakespeare demands.

A technique with great potential for Shakespeare was used in Francis Thompson's lyrical documentary for Johnson's Wax at the New York World's Fair. People fought to get to see this little study of boys growing up in different parts of the world. The film brilliantly uses the old Abel Gance multiple-screen technique, and shows its extraordinary possibilities. There are three screens side by side, three simultaneous projections. This gives an area as great as a Cinerama screen, but whereas Cinerama pretends that it is all one huge image, one vast window on the world, Thompson's technique is more Brechtian. The thin black gaps between his screens never let you forget that you are looking at three separate frames. Sometimes the screens are used as one, as in the great canoeing sequences on enormous landscapes, the canoes shooting across, jumping the break—it is like sitting behind a pillar in an old movie-house. But those breaks are there as constant reminders that the instant the director no longer needs or wants a full Cinerama scale, he can cut to something quite different. And that is Thompson's strategy: one minute the three screens show traffic flowing in America, a wedding in Italy, an African landscape; then the juxtaposition splinters and one screen shows an African boy while the other two are still in New York; next, there may be three different views of the same thing; next, identical closeups; then, one screen may keep the same view while the others show different angles and aspects, and so on. This is not aesthetically wrenching: Thompson's film makes no greater demands of imaginative effort than standard film-making, but he can make his audience shift from three screens saying the same thing to three saying different things as a natural part of his language, a language potentially as flexible as verse.

The great advantage of this device is that it breaks into the inner consistency of each frame, by opening the range of endless possible permutations. You can show Hamlet in the battlements of Elsinore on the right-hand screen, and the other two screens may just show a rampart and the sea. Or, to return to Gloucester, you can have a heath, and the moment that a soliloquy begins you can drop the heath out of your picture and concentrate on different views of Gloucester. If you like, you can suddenly open one of your screens to a caption, write a line, write a sub-title. If you want, in the middle of a realistic action in color you could have another or the same in black and white, and the third captioned. You could have statistics, or a cartoon parodying the photographic action. This is a film technique which has exactly the possibilities of a Brechtian stage and an Elizabethan one. I believe that this multiple-screen technique is a real opening, a way that Shakespeare might be found on film. But this is just a hunch, and economically hard to realize.

The only thing that matters today is to define the problem. The filmed picture of an actor on a bare stage is a more cramped and constipated statement than the simple face of an actor on a bare stage. But at the start bare stage and blank screen are equal. How can the screen free itself of its own consistencies so as to reflect the mobility of thought that blank verse demands?

FRANK KERMODE
SHAKESPEARE IN THE MOVIES

Antony and Cleopatra
directed by Charlton Heston.

Macbeth
directed by Roman Polanski.

King Lear
directed by Peter Brook.

Piety, as we've all discovered by now, won't get us anywhere.
If Shakespeare has a right to attention, that right must be established again and again. The authority that establishes it has itself
to be proved by demonstration, not by the old appeal to the dead,
the sanctity of what has been accepted always, everywhere, and
by everybody. Some of the men who direct his plays on stage or
on film are intensely aware of this, and of the fact that their giant,
if he is to live at all, must live in change. There was a time, in the
history of the movies, when a man might make a version of a
Shakespeare play and expect it to last for many years. That time
has passed, not only because television can exhaust the movie
almost at one shot (as it did Olivier's *Richard III*) but because the
very concept of the "classic" performance has withered.

Shakespeare is a willing but restless collaborator; his fidelity
is to next year's language. He has never, like true classical drama,
required that if rapport is to be kept up, the whole culture must
hold itself in a position of fidelity. He can be made new in far more

322

possible ways than Racine or the Japanese Nō play. Obviously the cinema has advantages as a setting for the wrestling match between this angel and the bold director.

Roger Manvell, in his useful and well-illustrated survey of the history of filmed Shakespeare,* makes the point that the cinema can, much better than the modern theater, match the fluidity of action on the Shakespearean stage. This is too obvious to dwell on, since the forty-odd scenes of *Antony and Cleopatra* or the arrival of a forest at Macbeth's castle, or of a ghost at his banquet, present no real difficulty to the movies, and though modern stage directors have found how to do most of these things there are still problems, as the sad stage history of *Macbeth* demonstrates. And as Manvell rightly remarks, much more is required than fluidity. He emphasizes the problem (peculiar of course to English versions) of ensuring that what we see endorses rather than replaces the text, "points" rather than usurps it. As George Bernard Shaw observed in 1936, "It is extraordinary how much can be spoiled if you let the photographer . . . get the upper hand. There is the human voice; you have the verse and the lines. They may be deliberately distorted for some reason, but you have to be careful."

Some of these difficulties are primarily technical—Manvell reprints an interesting conversation with Peter Hall that explores them—but others go deeper. It's still harder to get an actor to say the lines right than to bring Birnam Wood to Dunsinane, and it's harder still to rethink imaginatively the text of the play without falling into fanciful perversity. Granted, any archaeological reproduction of a Shakespeare play will certainly be a dead thing, the rethinking has to be done and the risk taken. But it's asking a lot of the average director.

Consider what he has to do. Certain plays—the three discussed below are among them—are commonly regarded as very great works. But common consent is not only not enough, it is in this situation a danger. The new maker has got to feel that the true nature of their greatness has eluded *him*, at any rate; that the testimony of others is mostly irrelevant; and that what he does with

---

*Shakespeare and the Film by Roger Manvell. Praeger, 184 pp., $10.00. (Contains a filmography of the principal—not all—Shakespeare movies since 1929.)

it must show what he found in it—not everything, but something—that confirmed his intuition that it was worth doing, and so at once justifies his authority and establishes that of the play.

This requirement immediately rules out the modish tinkerer, the director with ingenious theories that interest him more than any laborious encounter with the words will ever do. But it also rules out the dull man who leaves everything to the text. Of the three directors whose work is discussed here one is capable of the extraordinary effort, not to speak of the intelligence and imagination, needed to reduce his whole text to chaos and recompose it. Keats spoke of *King Lear* as a text he had to *burn through*. Peter Brook has done something like that to the same play. The others have simply not understood the need.

There is no need to waste much time on Charlton Heston's *Antony and Cleopatra*, a work of no imagination. During the negotiations for Antony's marriage to Octavia two gladiators thump one another in the arena below. As one impales the other with his trident the negotiations conclude, and Octavius gives a thumbs-up sign at the words "the power of Caesar." This bright idea is so tediously executed, cutting back and forth from the arena to the politicians, that one dreads the bright ideas to follow. However, there are very few. The disastrous Cleopatra of Hildegarde Neil has neither presence (when she speaks of her majesty, as she often does, we take it as a kind of in-joke) nor sexuality.

Every actress I have seen play Cleopatra (Edith Evans, Vivien Leigh, Peggy Ashcroft) has done something—though Vivien Leigh didn't do much—to make the part new: it is primarily a question of discovering the verse. Miss Neil has no voice and no skill, and the pain of listening to her grows literally unbearable; I left after "O withered is the garland of the war," shirking the remainder. Heston is a conscientious Antony, large, generous, cruel, and so on, but inexpressive and clumsy with the verse. Some good performances in the smaller parts (notably John Castle's Octavius) and good stuff in the battle scenes on shore and afloat cannot save this expensive disaster. The screenplay is not willful or stupid, but totally uninspired; the whole thing comes down, sadly, to dull reproduction—the degree of superficial fidelity achieved simply enhances its spuriousness.

324

The film of *Macbeth* is much more interesting. A lot of intelligence and skill have gone into it, not of the highest kind, but they should always be noticed; and it has an odd quality of getting better as it goes along, as if some of the real work—the work of de-creation and re-imagining—suggested itself, and got started, in the course of shooting. The provenance of this movie—financing by *Playboy*, adaptation by Tynan and Polanski, direction by Polanski—is not such as to inspire in me, at any rate, great trust in the outcome. But this is a more than competent and often a beautiful film, vastly more so, in obvious ways, than Peter Brook's *Lear*.

The parts of the film made on location in Northumberland and Wales are often splendid. Birnam Wood does indeed come convincingly to Dunsinane, the young, little known players perform creditably, and the fights are fantastic. At one moment, when a warrior struck another a thudding blow between the legs with one of those spiky balls on the end of a chain, I winced. The Thane of Cawdor suffers an exotic on-stage execution; the murder of Lady Macduff and her children is elaborately horrible. The weird sisters run a full-scale spine-chilling sabbath, and we get a screenful of horrific dugs.

But it isn't sweated out, re-imagined. It's powerful, vulgar, and vain by turns, and a great Shakespeare film might well be all these things; but this isn't a great one. The first thing a director has to learn about *Macbeth* is that it is written in a peculiar dialect. Its language and rhythms are quite different from those of the other major tragedies, and up to the murder of Duncan it is especially strange and strained. It allows a narrative to go forward while, by miming crisis and criminal choice, the language insists on a scarcely tolerable degree of attention to one point in time, the present. The future is in this endless instant. And on this moment everything turns, the whole either/or of the thing: lost and won, fair and foul, present grace and great prediction, which grain will grow and which will not.

For Macbeth "function/is smothered in surmise and nothing is/ But what is not"; he is subject to a supernatural soliciting that "cannot be ill, cannot be good." This dreadful cooperation of language with our sense of a world in the balance continues in Lady Macbeth's first vertiginous speech: "What thou wouldst highly/ That wouldst thou holily." Macbeth's crucial soliloquy trembles with this disease of language: surcease-success, be-all, end-all.

Now this really is the crux of the matter. As Bernard Shaw and Peter Hall realized, the film we see mustn't spoil such astonishing effects of language. In Polanski's movie these are lost. Only after the murder is the playing, the direction, and the editing acceptable at all. In the crucial first movement neither of the principals gives the slightest indication of awareness of what is being so uniquely achieved in the text. The great soliloquy is a director's disaster. Spoken voice-over as Macbeth sits at table with his royal guest, it drags drearily on, canceling the nerve-rending rhythms; it is interrupted by the entertainments laid on for the diners, including a rendering by Fleance of the song "Your eyen two will slay me suddenly," written not for a court such as this, admirably displaying what the publicity men describe as "eleventh-century ruggedness," but by Chaucer for the court of Richard II three hundred years later, and in another country. Anachronisms are not important in themselves, but this one is not only absurd in view of the stated aims of the makers but an inexcusably camp intrusion which will be felt as such by people who have no idea of the origin of the piece.

The eleventh-century world of this *Macbeth* is modishly cruel and desperate; a world of treacherous feudal chieftains, in which one political murder will be certainly followed by another. Even as Malcolm is crowned his brother Donalbain rides off, uncanonically, to consult the weird sisters. There are three kings in play and film; in the film alone all of them are hailed as such by Ross. For Ross has turned out to be a traitor. This fits the scheme of universal treachery, and I suppose Polanski or Tynan got the idea from the old chestnut about who was the Third Murderer—the unknown who turns up to help the two originally commissioned by Macbeth to murder Banquo. Why not Ross? And if so, why not make Ross not the friend but the betrayer of Lady Macduff? It will make it a little harder to manage the scene where Ross informs Macduff of the murder of his family; but that matters little compared with the advantages that accrue. For here is a brand-new character, his importance disguised in the original—a Machiavellian, a good guy who is really a traitor.

326

It's some kind of an achievement, and a characteristic one. For whereas Shakespeare's text seems to be about the purgation of a state—a country once happy but suffering a horrible infliction of evil—the film says that it's always this way, whatever you try to do about it. In Shakespeare Macduff kills Macbeth, comes in saying, "The time is free," and hails the new king Malcolm. In Polanski Ross hails Malcolm, and Donalbain rides off to the witches. In Shakespeare Duncan is a good, even a holy man, like his contemporary Edward the Confessor, whom Shakespeare also drags in. Here he happens merely to be the current boss, whose murder, incidentally, we are shown; rather splendidly in fact, for as usual the filmed scenes have a life independent of the words.

This visually oriented perversity may explain the selection of Francesca Annis for the part of Lady Macbeth. She is beautiful and cannot speak verse. The sleepwalking scene is very perverse— a nude lady wandering about the freezing castle under the eye of her doctor, who, though he cannot minister to a mind diseased, can surely send the waiting woman for a cloak. Still, the break-up of Lady Macbeth is not wholly unconvincing. Jon Finch as Macbeth gets better and better as he grows more simply wicked, but is inadequate in the early stages, when violence on the screen is not a good enough substitute for the pressure in the poetry. John Stride, it must be said, makes a powerful impression as Ross, Mark II. But finally it should be repeated that this is nearly always a spectacularly good movie to look at, and one leaves it with a sort of discontented satisfaction. It's much better than it might have been. Some, though not the highest, possibilities of Shakespeare in the movies are realized, though at a rather high cost to whatever it is we might agree ought to be preserved.

Peter Brook's *Lear* had a bad press in England; it disappeared very quickly and is now hard to find. It wouldn't be difficult to say why it displeased people who think they know about movies, and why it displeased others who thought they knew about Shakespeare. Some of the reasons will emerge from what follows. In fact, the really difficult thing is to explain why it *is* very good, and so far beyond the more popular *Macbeth* that they aren't really comparable, and why the common judgment, that Brook is a genius in the theater but a bad movie director, is wrong. A genius, certainly; but he has also made the best of all Shakespeare movies. (We can rule out Kurosawa's *Throne of Blood*, which is an allusion to, rather than a version of, *Macbeth*.) How his *Lear* came to be so, despite all its apparent faults, is what has to be explained.

Manvell reports Brook as having said in 1965 (that is, some time after his classic Royal Shakespeare production of *Lear*, . . . that Shakespeare was impossible to film. What the verse does, he said, can't be done on film, though he thought there might be possibilities in a multiple screen using images in counterpoint, or projecting segments of a single image. Now this was the right way to begin: by despairing of the text in a film context. And when he decided after all to try to make the movie Brook continued, very fruitfully, to do so.

Manvell quotes a long and valuable statement by Michael Birkett, Brook's producer, concerning the origins of the movie. Briefly, Brook set about the task of de-creating the text. He did so by means that may appear extravagant, even absurd; for he invited Ted Hughes to translate the play "into a language which seemed to him to be expressive of the story as he saw it, in his own right as a poet." Kurosawa's solution was not available; and since it was the original text that was making the film impossible, this must have seemed an imaginative compromise. Hughes, we are told, did an excellent job (it would be very interesting to see it). But after comparing his text with Shakespeare's they decided that Shakespeare's was better. "Sooner or later it comes down to the fact that there are passages, obviously the greatest passages in the play, which have a force and emotional power that no translation, no paraphrase, can possibly match."

The important thing is not simply to have known this as "everybody" does, but to have seen the need to work for the knowledge. Thenceforth the director saw the whole play, and its verse, differently. His sense of its power, its unmatched force, was no longer *endoxal*, as the French critics say—no longer merely a function of what people conventionally say about it. So that whatever else he might do, he would always operate according to this luminous conviction. And when the great moments, on which all depends, arrive—say, the meeting of Lear and Gloucester on the beach at Dover—there will be in them nothing that simply reflects conventional opinion. It will not be a matter of being in a place which centuries of respect have made sacred, not a matter of whispering in church, but rather of being as near the source as we can, each in his own capacity, bear, of the greatest poetry that any of us can conceive of. To make such a scene is enough; and a production that made it would be a great human achievement if it seemed to botch nearly everything else.

Brook's version does make it. The closing stages of this film, in particular, have what Kent found and sought to serve in the face of Lear, namely, authority. Perhaps they could not have had it without some such purgative preliminary as Ted Hughes's paraphrase represented. It was a kind of ritual blasphemy, not unlike those of the play itself, when the young blind their fathers and deny them the right to be "in the basest things superfluous." The play needed, as it were, to be sent naked into the storm before it could know itself.

After rejecting the paraphrase, Brook wrote a narrative treatment without dialogue; then he cut the play to fit this treatment, and went on changing it in the course of shooting. This was done in Jutland, in a wintry setting of sand, snow, and mud which fitted the bleak and vague Dark Age idea Brook entertained of the setting—wooden compounds for castles, lumbering wooden wagons for transportation, of which there is rather a lot in *Lear*. The general misery of working in such conditions was no doubt a benefit in the end. This is a *Lear* that grows out of bitter soil.

Odd things happen as Brook engages his text, and so they ought; but it is still right to question detail. There are some shocking changes and omissions. To say so does not imply that one is a purist, as Lord Birkett, in the paper I mentioned, suggests. To be a purist in these matters is to be an idiot. But consider the great scene—which was the very heart of Brook's stage production—in which the blind Gloucester sits in silence while the battle rages off-stage; Edgar has left him with his new-found patience, but when he comes back with the news that the battle is lost the old man refuses to be dragged away: "a man may rot even here." Edgar, impatiently recommending patience yet again, hustles him away with the saying "Ripeness is all." Of all this we got only the last bit, not the great silence. As Lord Birkett remarks, silence is a tricky problem in the talkies.

Other apparent perversities: the libels invented by Edmund to blacken the character of his brother in the eyes of his father ("the father should be as ward to the son," etc.) are in the movie actually spoken by Edgar. Yet Edgar's truly horrible lines to the dying Edmund—"The gods are just . . . the dark and vicious place where thee he got/Cost him his eyes" —are transferred to the dying Cornwall; played with his usual splendid sadistic venom, by Patrick Magee.

For most people the opening of Act IV is fundamental to the play: Edgar, congratulating himself on his hopeless plight, says that nothing worse can happen to him, at which point his father enters, eyeless. Though much in the spirit of the Brook version, this passage is cut. So is much else: Gloucester's final happiness, Edmund's final repentance. The most famous line to disappear (though Scofield, at the appropriate moment, fumbles with his coat) is Lear's "Pray you, undo this button."

There are a great many other cuts not easily explicable on the sound principle that you have to have some, or as helping to strengthen the Brook version. Albany's "Humanity must prey upon itself/Like monsters of the deep" is shorn of its necessary prologue: "If that the heavens do not their visible spirits/Send quickly down to tame these vile offences/It will come. . . ." Lear himself, curiously, loses some of his sexual disgust ("But to the girdle do the gods inherit,/The rest is all the fiend's. There's hell, there's darkness, there the sulphurous pit . . ."). Kent, at the outset, says, in remonstrating against Lear's treatment of Cordelia, "Be Kent unmannerly when Lear is mad"; in the movie he simply shouts "Lear is mad," surely an unwise alteration. Cordelia loses too many of her very few lines; she is also shown for a second, and a second too long, with a rope around her neck.

I wonder whether Brook could explain in every case what he was up to; or how it is that after years with the play he still lets actors stress lines wrongly, even Scofield: "How *shall* your houseless heads. . . ." Or why he makes so much less of the Fool than he did on the stage, and reduces the role of Kent, and gives less scope to his Goneril. These may simply be faults, like some of the deliberately clumsy camera work and the muddles in the storm scene and the introduction of subtitles to explain scene changes, which was entirely avoidable.

330

Brook's decision to set the film in the Dark Ages has disadvantages as well as advantages: the jurisprudence of *Lear* and the talk of women at court whose finery "scarcely keeps them warm" and many other matters are medieval or Renaissance, and have nothing to do with the hovels and rudeness of the movie. No wonder Goneril and Regan found the king's knights an unruly mob and wanted them cut from a hundred to fifty, twenty-five, ten, five, one, and none. It wasn't, apparently, that the king had taught them in the opening scene to quantify love, just that the housing problem was insoluble.

One could go on talking about such details, but they don't really matter. The film has authority, promised at the outset, confirmed at the close. Much that troubles people very familiar with the original won't be noticed by most audiences, who will be making their first acquaintance with a fully realized and deeply imagined version of this great work. The playing is fine, especially, among the newer actors, Susan Engel's Regan, a performance of terrifying intelligence; Magee's Cornwall, Cyril Cusak's Albany, and Robert Lloyd's Edgar are as good as may be imagined. They are all, of course, servants of a masterly conception of the play. One noticed how Brook contrived to emphasize certain key words *(sight, nothing, know)* from the beginning, without encouraging the actors to lean on them; so that at the end, when Lear giggles about Gloucester's eyes, and when, in madness, he knows Kent, Gloucester, and Cordelia, the pressure is on, the effect as exactly close to unbearable as it ought to be.

Finally, the collaboration of Brook and Scofield is now such that it is impossible to conceive of anybody else matching this actor's performance. The strong, good-humored, ignorant, and willful old man of the opening still breathes power, is still wanton of fancy and judgment; arbitrary and self-assured, he has first to learn that his authority may be questioned, and then to discover the true nature of his old body, and then the true nature of justice, and then the true nature of love.

All this learning he must show in madness when he encounters Cordelia and Gloucester. In the second of these encounters, which I mentioned earlier as the great test of the whole, he must say what scarcely bears saying for terror and beauty. "I remember thine eyes well enough. Dost thou squiny at me? No, do thy worst, blind Cupid, I'll not love. . . . look with thine eyes. . . . When we are born we cry that we are come/To this great stage of fools. . . ." And Scofield is equal to this; especially in "I know thee well enough; thy name is Gloucester." All this is spoken on the shore, where Gloucester has just made his suicide attempt, and where (in the film) Lear will shortly bend over the body of his dead daughter. "Thou must be patient. . . ."

The point is simple: these texts, if we are to hold on to their greatness (and who says we can afford to lose it?), have to be reborn in the imagination of another. Hardly anybody is equal to this labor. It is not a task for the actor-manager, all self-regard is fatal to it. The true process is a violent one, and things will get distorted and torn. But the kind of truth this movie has in its last quarter of an hour can be got at in no other way. Here the right man was available, and he made a great film, which, unlike the relatively trivial *Macbeth* and the negligible *Antony*, cannot be seen in London, though New York honorably supports it, thus escaping a most serious censure. For Peter Brook should be honored in this. *C'est une belle âme, comme on ne fait plus à Londres.*

JAMES AGEE
HENRY V

It seems impertinent to discuss even briefly the excellence of Laurence Olivier's production of Shakespeare's *Henry V* without saying a few words, at least, about the author. If Shakespeare had been no more gifted with words than, say, I am, the depth and liveliness of his interest in people and predicaments, and his incredible hardness, practicality, and resource as a craftsman and maker of moods, rhythms, and points, could still have made him almost his actual equal as a playwright. I had never realized this so well until I saw this production, in which every nail in sight is so cleanly driven in with one blow; and I could watch the film for all that Shakespeare gave it in these terms alone, and for all that in these terms alone is done with what he gave, with great pleasure and gratitude. But then too, of course, there is the language of a brilliance, vigor, and absoluteness that make the craftsmanship and sometimes the people and their grandest emotions seem almost as negligibly pragmatic as a libretto beside an opera score. Some people, using I wonder what kind of dry ice for comfort, like to insist that *Henry V* is relatively uninteresting Shakespeare. This uninteresting poetry is such that after hearing it, in this production, I find it as hard to judge fairly even the best writing since Shakespeare as it is to see the objects in a room after looking into the sun.

The one great glory of the film is this language. The greatest credit I can assign to those who made the film is that they have loved and served the language so well. I don't feel that much of the delivery is inspired; it is merely so good, so right, that the words set loose in the graciously designed world of the screen, like so many uncaged birds, fully enjoy and take care of themselves. Neither of the grimmest Shakespearian vices, ancient or modern, is indulged: that is to say, none of the text is read in that human, down-to-earth, poetry-is-only-hopped-up-prose manner which is doubtless only proper when a character subscriber to *PM* reads the Lerner editorial to his shop-wise fellow traveler; nor is any of it intoned in the nobler manner, as if by a spoiled deacon celebrating the Black Mass down a section of sewer-pipe. Most of it is merely spoken by people who know and love poetry as poetry and have spent a lifetime learning how to speak it accordingly. Their voices, faces, and bodies are all in charge of a man who has selected them as shrewdly as a good orchestrator selects and blends his instruments; and he combines and directs them as a good conductor conducts an orchestral piece. It is, in fact, no surprise to learn that Mr. Olivier is fond of music; charming as it is to look at, the film is essentially less visual than musical.

I cannot compare it with many stage productions of Shakespeare; but so far as I can they were, by comparison, just so many slightly tired cultural summer-salads, now and then livened, thanks to an unkilled talent or an unkillable line, by an unexpected rose-petal or the sudden spasm of a rattlesnake: whereas this, down to the last fleeting bit of first-rate poetry in a minor character's mouth, was close to solid gold, almost every word given its own and its largest contextual value. Of course nothing prevents this kind of casting and playing on the stage, except talent and, more seriously, the money to buy enough talent and enough time to use it rightly in; and how often do you see anything to equal it on the Shakespearian stage? The specific advantages of the screen are obvious, but no less important for that. Microphones make possible a much more delicate and immediate use of the voice; reactions, in close-up, can color the lines more subtly and richly than on the stage. Thus it is possible, for instance, to get all the considerable excellence there is out of an aging player like Nicholas Hannen, who seemed weak in most scenes when, on the stage, he had to try to fill and dilate the whole Century Theater with unhappy majesty; and the exquisiteness of Renée Asherson's reactions to Olivier's spate of gallantry, in the wooing scene, did as much as he did toward making that scene, by no means the most inspired as writing, the crown of the film. When so much can be done, through proper understanding of these simple advantages, to open the beauties of poetry as relatively extroverted as this play, it is equally hard to imagine and to wait for the explorations that could be made of subtler, deeper poems like *Hamlet, Troilus and Cressida,* or *The Tempest.*

Speaking still of nothing except the skill with which the poetry is used in this film, I could go on far past the room I have. The sureness and seductive power of the pacing alone and its shifts and contrasts, in scene after scene, has seldom been equaled in a movie; the adjustments and relationships of tone are just as good. For just one example, the difference in tone between Olivier's almost schoolboyish "God-a-mercy" and his "Good old Knight," not long afterward, measures the King's growth in the time between with lovely strength, spaciousness, and cleanness; it earns, as craftsmanship, the triumph of bringing off the equivalent to an "impossibly" delayed false-rhyme; and psychologically or dramatically, it seems to me—though my guess may be far-fetched—it fully establishes the King's coming-of-age by raising honorable, brave, loyal, and dull old age (in Sir Thomas Erpingham) in the King's love and esteem to the level of any love he had ever felt for Falstaff.

Olivier does many other beautiful pieces of reading and playing. His blood-raising reply to the French Herald's ultimatum is not just that; it is a frank, bright exploitation of the moment for English ears, amusedly and desperately honored as such, in a still gallant and friendly way, by both Herald and King. His Crispin's Day oration is not just a brilliant bugle-blat; it is the calculated yet self-exceeding improvisation, at once self-enjoying and selfless, of a young and sleepless leader, rising to a situation wholly dangerous and glamorous, and wholly new to him. Only one of the many beauties of the speech as he gives it is the way in which the King seems now to exploit his sincerity, now to be possessed by it, riding like an unexpectedly mounting wave the astounding size of his sudden proud awareness of the country morning, of his moment in history, of his responsibility and competence, of being full-bloodedly alive, and of being about to die.

This kind of branching, nervous interpretive intelligence, so contemporary in quality except that it always keeps the main lines of its drive and meaning clear, never spiraling or strangling in awareness, is vivid in every way during all parts of the film.

335

It is tantalizing to be able to mention so few of the dozens of large and hundreds of small excellences which Mr. Olivier and his associates have developed to sustain Shakespeare's poem. They have done somewhere near all that talent, cultivation, taste, knowledgeability, love of one's work—every excellence, in fact, short of genius —can be expected to do; and that, the picture testifies, is a very great deal. Lacking space for anything further I would like to suggest that it be watched for all that it does in playing a hundred kinds of charming adventurousness against the incalculably responsive sounding-boards of tradition: for that is still, and will always be, a process essential in most, though not all, of the best kinds of art, and I have never before seen so much done with it in a moving picture. I am not a Tory, a monarchist, a Catholic, a medievalist, an Englishman, or, despite all the good that it engenders, a lover of war: but the beauty and power of this traditional exercise was such that, watching it, I wished I was, thought I was, and was proud of it. I was persuaded, and in part still am, that every time and place has since been in decline, save one, in which one Englishman used language better than anyone has before or since, or ever shall; and that nearly the best that our time can say for itself is that some of us are still capable of paying homage to the fact.

ANDRÉ BAZIN
OTHELLO

If one must be for or against *Othello*, I am for it. Doniol Valcroze and I were the only ones of this opinion upon emerging from the showing where Welles received both kudos and catcalls. Consequently, I feel free to say that I would not have awarded him the Grand Prix; it is appropriate neither to his failings nor to his strengths. The Special Award of the Jury would have been more appropriate. But I fear that Welles is forever destined to be misunderstood. After the insult in Venice the year *Macbeth* was shown, here we have a jury at Cannes, impressed beyond reason, awarding him the Grand Prix. One can see why they do so, and that this excess of honor is not occasioned by what is best in *Othello*. The same Jury would certainly not have so crowned *Macbeth*. The laurels seemed to be awarded for what was most academic in the audacities of *Othello*—for its Eisensteinian qualities, for instance. But I am putting myself in the place of the members of the Jury who may have liked the film for better reasons, had they been able to resist the enthusiasm shown by those who were discovering Orson Welles's genius *through* Shakespeare.

However that may be, Grand Prix or no, *Othello* seems to me an entrancing work. Before everything else, one must recognize a major achievement of Welles's adaptation: despite certain foolish liberties, it is profoundly faithful to Shakespeare's dramatic poetry. I can think of no other director in the world who could cut so much out of the original written text and replace it with visual spectacle without inviting ridicule. It is absurd to speculate about what

337

Shakespeare himself would have used in place of the written word if he had made films instead of writing tragedies; but one may wonder if Welles's solution is not at least one of the possible answers to this theoretical question. I am convinced that it is, and that it is no small achievement. From this point of view a comparison with *Hamlet* is very damaging to Laurence Olivier. His production was one possible framework for the Shakespeare text, but it could in no way replace that text (it is true that in this respect the production of *Henry V* was far superior).

Having acknowledged such a fundamental asset, one feels more free to mete out both praise and blame. Since I do not want to anticipate the review of Welles's film which I shall presently be writing, I shall limit my remarks here to *Othello's* greatest strength and its most obvious weakness, as I see them.

Here again I find confirmation of the idea that the problem of adapting theater to the cinema resides not in the choice of actors but in the conception of the decor. The theater stage is a closed centripetal universe spiraling toward its own center, like a seashell. The movie screen is a centrifugal surface, a photographer's mask set up before the limitless universe of nature. The language of the theater is designed to resound within a closed space; in a natural setting it dissolves and disperses irretrievably. In passing from the stage to the screen a play must find a new theatrical locale which will satisfy the two contradictory qualities inherent in cinematographic and theatrical space. In this Welles succeeds brilliantly by re-creating a completely dramatic architecture, but one which is almost solely composed of natural elements taken from Venice and the castle at Mogador. Through the use of montage and unusual camera angles (which effectively prevent the mind from reassembling in space the disparate elements of the set), Welles invents an imaginary architecture adorned with all the salient features, all of the predetermined as well as the unexpected beauties, that only real architecture—natural stone that has been worked by centuries of wind and sun—can possess. *Othello* unfolds, then, in the open sky, but not in nature. These walls, these vaults and corridors echo, reflect and multiply, like so many mirrors, the eloquence of the tragedy.

However, I cannot wholeheartedly praise Welles's editing, for it seems extremely fragmented, shattered like a mirror relentlessly struck with a hammer. Carried to such a degree, this stylistic idiosyncrasy becomes a tiresome device.

But my greatest disappointment is in Welles's own interpretation, which, I admit, sometimes lapses into exhibitionism of the sort which lacks that kind of enormous, cunning naïveté that made the closeups in *Macbeth* something quite different and remarkable.

Still, if there ever was a film that bears a second viewing, it is certainly this one. We shall be talking more about it at some future date.

J. BLUMENTHAL
MACBETH INTO
THRONE OF BLOOD

Akira Kurosawa's *Throne of Blood* (1957) is the only work, to my knowledge, that has ever completely succeeded in transforming a play of Shakespeare's into a film. What is important about this is that the film is a masterpiece in its own right, and the first of its kind. Up to now, Shakespeare adaptations for the screen have been perpetrated (this is the only word for it) mainly by those whose first love is the theatre. Maybe this is the way it has to be. Maybe *Throne of Blood* is an aberration, and truly gifted film-makers will always try to liberate themselves from the dreaded literary media so that they can concentrate on culling their own experience for film material. I guess it is even possible to argue that Shakespeare adaptations for the screen should be left to artists such as Olivier, so that they can bring the great soliloquies and reconstructions of the Globe Theatre to the provinces; for this, too, is an important function of the film. But then, who is to say where film-makers such as Kurosawa (as opposed to men of the theatre) should seek inspiration—especially when they succeed in turning out great films?

As easy as it may be to film a play, it is quite another thing to make a film out of one. Orson Welles, who has shown a genius for both media, is a good case in point. He has tried making films out of two of Shakespeare's plays and has failed—miserably with *Macbeth*, gracefully with *Othello*—both times. His *Othello*, beautiful as it is, fails because most of its cinematic flourishes are gratuitous. His toying with the medium remains toying for all its mastery. Welles is too often guilty of serving up chunks of pure Shakespeare that have been sugar-coated with an unusual camera angle or composition, or nicely sliced up by a bold cut. Although this is all very fascinating to look at, the experience of looking is empty at the centre. It is film as hobby, or ornament, but not as expression. No matter from what angle one photographs it, or the number of cute little pieces into which one cuts it, the material in its original form (the play, the individual scene with dialogue intact) remains essentially what it was. In such cases the filming is a more or less gratuitous decoration of the subject and not what it must be: an inevitable articulation of it.

THE FOREST

This Takes Us to Throne of Blood

At the same time, it takes us to Kurosawa's profound commitment to creating meaning by the manipulation of material reality. No doubt this is for him just as much an involuntary response to experience as it is a commitment; but whatever its sources, the form it takes in this film is revealing. To begin with, Kurosawa is doing much more here than simply letting us see the things that Shakespeare's characters describe, and the places where the action is set. This time-honoured but very limited device for filming plays is far from his only resource. The point is that Kurosawa actually thinks by manipulating material reality. Birnam Wood, for example, which has only a few lines of vague description devoted to it in the play, becomes in Kurosawa's hands a physical presence that is potent enough to embody the film's very complex network of themes. The forest in *Throne of Blood* was born with Kurosawa's conception of the film. It is not the result of a makeshift adaptation, nor is it even a fancy visualisation of the play. It is rather an offspring of the metamorphosis from play to film, and it is to a great degree responsible for charging *Throne of Blood* with an inner principle of motion, for making it an autonomous work of art.

It might help to look at the problem from Kurosawa's point of view. He feels deeply sympathetic to the theme of *Macbeth* and is moved to make a film out of it. The play is about a noble and highly ambitious warrior faced with the dire task of gaining control over his own vivid but treacherous imagination. He needs to prove himself to himself and can do so only by acting out his most horrible visions, wholly embracing whatever evil he encounters in his own soul. Self-control and self-destruction soon become identical, and this is the tragedy. As Kurosawa must have seen it, the crucial problem was to find a natural means of externalising, of objectifying, Macbeth's thoughts. By "natural" I mean that the object chosen had to appear to exist in the real world just as Macbeth did, living and growing there. For it is not enough that Macbeth's thoughts can be photographed; photographing them must bring them to life.

Birnam Wood, a marginal symbol from the original work, was perfect for the part. Even in the play, it is only when the forest defies the laws of nature (just as Macbeth subverts the moral order) that Macbeth's fate becomes explicit and he realises that the kind of self-control he sought was suicidal. In the film, however, the forest is more than a marginal objective correlative of the theme. It is both the battleground where the conflict rages and the very incitement to conflict. If this sounds like a fair description of what is called the "world" of a work of art, we are on the point. For this is precisely the role that the forest plays. It is the life at the centre of the film, what we always look for but seldom find in film versions of anyone's plays.

A sizable portion of *Throne of Blood* is devoted to the terrifying spectacle of Washizu (Macbeth) waging war on the forest. In an extended sequence near the beginning he and Miki (Banquo) thunder through a dense, murky forest on horses no less frightened than they. (The forest is referred to as "The Labyrinth" and much is made, here and later in the film, of the difficulty of finding one's way out of it.) Washizu is clearly the leader: *he* will find a way out, for he cannot bear the sense of dread and helplessness he feels before the blind paths, the unidentifiable shrieks and moans, the thunder, lightning, and fog. He starts at what he thinks an evil spirit, unsheathes his sword, and letting out a blood-curdling cry, half defiant and half hysterical, he plunges into the dark with Miki following him. The reality of this forest is overwhelming. It breathes, and sweats, and twitches, and speaks in the unknown tongue. It is easily as powerful a presence as Washizu himself; and this is exactly what it must be, since for Washizu this first encounter with the forest is nothing less than a headlong plunge into the self.

In this sequence Washizu and Miki are on their way to Forest

Castle, where their lord is waiting to reward them for leading the victorious battle against the rebel forces. Control of this castle soon becomes Washizu's obsession, and already he is struck by the thought that one would be truly invulnerable if he could control the forest, which is the only means of access to the castle. In a moment the crazed horses burst through the underbrush on to a small clearing that glows with an unholy light. Here, surrounded by heaps of carcases and bones, a chalk-white, sexless, ageless demon sits spinning a loom and chanting the prophecies that eventually drive Washizu on to the ultimate dare. "I must paint the forest with blood!" he will cry. The forest is Washizu's mind. As his ambitions reveal, it is no longer controlled by his lord. His lord is therefore vulnerable, but no more so than the doomed Washizu, whose position is ironically similar.

Kurosawa has at least this much in common with most other great film-makers: his ability to imbue a place with such deep moral meaning that the place often seems to take charge and structure the narrative on its own. I am not suggesting that the place equals the film. It is simply necessary that the place come alive and help shape the film. If it generates no conflict, if it does not partake of the reality of the characters' experiences, place remains meaningless. And if the place is meaningless, so is the film. A very painful example of this failing is the painted-backdrop universe of Olivier's *Henry V*. It is as if a novelist had tried to preserve *The Ring of the Niebelungen* by objectively reporting all the action, characters, dialogue, and scenery exactly as they appear on the stage. And then concluded his lark with a request that we actually read his work.

In *Throne of Blood*, however, place becomes an autonomous reality. The horses gallop through the forest and Kurosawa, always behind a maze of gnarled trunks and barren branches, gallops with them. The whole—the men and their horses, the composition of the frame, the narrative, and the theme itself—is galvanised by the hellish milieu. This applies equally to the interiors, whose simple theatricality constitutes a world within that of the all-encompassing forest. Behind the flimsy walls man makes to seal himself off from an amoral nature, there is a lucid, quiet geometry that is assaulted throughout the film and, in the end, shattered. Toward the end, before the forest moves, a futile war council between Washizu and his captains is thrown into confusion by a flock of squealing bats which suddenly comes flapping into the hall from the forest. Washizu understands only too well what this means. He screams for his horse (à la Richard III) and rides for the last time to that unholy clearing seeking the assurances he could not obtain from others. The forest, which is the objectification of Washizu's mind, both controls and contains the action of the film.

Finally, there are the tumultuous comings and goings of the men and their horses which function so importantly as the narrative link between castle and forest. They enable the director to tell his story with great economy and force and deserve a little section to themselves.

THE HORSES

I am reminded here of those two sleepy creatures who might conceivably have served as the drunken chamberlains but were forced instead to labour as mounts for Macbeth and Banquo at the beginning of Welles' film on the subject. Not that Welles should have made Kurosawa's film, but we do have some right to expect that a flair for phantasmagoria will show up in more than flashy editing and pretentiously symbolic sets—in the life surrounding the characters, for example.

ROSS
And Duncan's horses—a thing most strange and certain—
Beauteous, and swift, the minions of their race,
Turned wild in nature, broke their stalls, flung out,
Contending 'gainst obedience, as they would
Make war with mankind.

OLD MAN
'Tis said, they eat each other.
I grant that the old man's footnote would present problems. Ross's description, though, is the work of an excellent scenarist, and one whose talent Kurosawa did not fail to notice. From a lingering shot of Washizu and his wife retiring as the chaos loosed by the murder seems finally to have subsided, there is a jolting cut to the next morning, and we see the king's horses "contending 'gainst obedience," much as Duncan's did. The entire castle is aroused again as the horses, in their frantic rush to flee the thing they have sensed, stampede through a row of huge banners which flap resoundingly as they are dragged off towards the forest.

344

The sequence is typically Kurosawa in the calculated violence of its execution. All the action is shot from a worm's-eye view and up close; a few rapid-fire shots of the rebellious steeds and the stunned, helpless men and we move on immediately to the film's loose counterpart of Macduff, Noriashu, who is making off under cover of the excitement to warn Miki of his suspicions. The narrative takes an important step forward and nothing is left hanging. The brief turmoil here is anything but a decorative cinematic effect. We already know from the forest sequence at the beginning that Kurosawa is modelling his world on that of Shakespeare. The whole of nature is sensitive to moral traumas in this type of world, and the moral traumas themselves are often of such magnitude as to unhinge the whole of nature. Kurosawa's great gift is that he has the power as a film-maker to make us experience this world. If he had tried to abstract from the process the thing that Shakespeare, working as a dramatist, did—if he had given us a reaction to the event instead of the event itself—everything would have been lost. We would have neither play nor film.

Let me give another telling example, one for which Kurosawa did not have Shakespeare's potential genius as a scenarist to serve as inspiration. (Isn't this, by the way, at the heart of the matter? That Kurosawa relies on Shakespeare only as a scenarist whose vision is consonant with his own, and never as a maker of pentameters?) Miki decides, because of the prophecies, to throw in his lot with Washizu even though he is certain of Washizu's guilt. He is now a guest at Washizu's new residence, Forest Castle. The sequence opens in Washizu's chamber, with Lady Washizu playing the role of evil counsellor. She does not trust Miki and knows that Washizu doesn't either, so she gives voice to what he desires yet dreads even to think of: another murder. We cut immediately from Washizu's speechless, petrified face to the courtyard, where Miki's horse, normally gentle, seems to be going mad. It is charging around the courtyard and refuses to let the groom saddle it. Miki's son interprets this as a bad omen and pleads with his father not to ride forth that afternoon but to stay for the banquet and tend to his affairs the next morning. Miki laughs this off as childishness, but no sooner does he move to saddle the horse himself than we cut to a shot of the courtyard taken from the ramparts of the castle. It is night, and still, and the courtyard, far away and off in the lower left-hand corner of the frame, is deserted. Miki's men are seated up here in a circle discussing in hushed tones the strange turn of events during the last few days. Suddenly they fall silent. They hear something in the distance. It becomes louder and finally identifies itself as the sound of a galloping horse. The shot is held a moment longer, just long enough for Miki's beautiful white stallion to come racing into the courtyard, riderless. The cut is to Washizu at the banquet. Washizu, of course, is paying no attention to the entertainment or his guests; he cannot stop gaping at the one empty seat in the hall.

This passage, which lasts no more than three or four minutes, is film narrative at its most eloquent. Kurosawa edits with an unerring instinct for clipping each action at its climax so that it will reverberate throughout the whole, and movement and placement within the frame are always obliquely at the service of the story. But the sequence is also noteworthy because it allows us to catch Kurosawa in the act of narrating what Shakespeare dramatised, and in doing so it reveals how greatly film narrative depends on the material components of the world being depicted.

Kurosawa builds the entire sequence around the reactions of Miki's horse. The movements of this short-circuited creature are responsible for all the characteristic ellipses in the narrative; they say everything that has to be said until Washizu's own body and face take over again at the banquet. At the same time, they necessitate doing away with much of the play. The elaborate preparations with the murderers, and even the murder itself (presumably excellent cinematic material), are discarded. Kurosawa has no use for even the murder because the world he is creating already contains its own narrative potential. It is a world of morally sensitised objects (the forest, the horses, the bodies and faces of the characters) which throughout the film lead a life of their own. And in their autonomy they demand that the film-maker adhere to their logic. If the film-maker is really making a film, and not just filming a play, he is only too willing to accede.

All appearances to the contrary, I am not arguing for the horse-opera notion of film aesthetics. Silver, too, neighs when there is trouble in the air, but who hasn't had the urge to strike him mute? One does not need horses, or chases, or even the unleashing of stupendous natural forces whose mass can be hurtled across the screen, in order to make filmic films. One thing that is indispensable, though, is the ability to convince the spectator that the surfaces of body, face, and place, bristle with nerve-ends, and that the synapses between the three generate the meaning and control the structure of the film. Kurosawa does this again and again in *Throne of Blood.* I hope it is clear that what he does bears no relation to such things as Olivier's desperate attempt at the end of *Henry V* to add a dash of "cinema" to the recipe in the form of an equine extravaganza.

THE CHARACTERS

Probably the most radical result of this transformation from play to film is the total absence from the latter of Shakespeare's diction. That Kurosawa's characters in *Throne of Blood* speak Japanese is only half the point. The other and more important half is that they speak only when they can't communicate in any other way, and then in language that is terse, unadorned, brutally functional. As far as one can tell from the subtitles, Shakespeare's poetry is gone — not just translated and trimmed, but gone. In our discussion of the forest and the horses we saw some of the things that take its place. There it was best to concentrate on the fundamental similarity of the problems facing Macbeth and Washizu. But the film's scrupulous avoidance of Shakespeare's verse is closely related to some equally fundamental differences in plot and characterisation. These differences deserve attention because they take us deeper into the question of how character is developed in a film, and they may even provide some basis for a speculation on what types of character, if any, are most suitable to the medium.

LADY MACBETH

I have given suck, and know
How tender 'tis to love the babe that milks me —
I would while it was smiling in my face
Have plucked my nipple from his boneless gums,
And dashed the brains out, had I so sworn as you
Have done to this.

Such is the chilling eloquence that Shakespeare uses to build the character of Lady Macbeth. Lady Washizu, however, is denied this mode of self-expression. She is endowed instead with a purely physical power, one that reaches far beyond (although it includes) the immediately visible gesture. A short time before the action of the

347

film opens, she conceives Washizu's child. This pregnancy becomes the pitchfork with which she goads her husband into carrying out his evil intentions, and she needs few words to exploit her advantage. The child, who was to have been the ultimate beneficiary of the plot to kill the king and Miki, becomes with Lady Washizu's miscarriage one of its victims, and by the same token an incarnation of the plot itself. After Washizu gains control of Forest Castle, Lady Washizu acts out this perverse fertility rite by dancing, insane with joy, in the room where the king was murdered. But the pressures of approaching failure soon bring on the miscarriage, which in turn precipitates Lady Washizu's nervous breakdown. (The cause of Lady Washizu's madness is one of Kurosawa's most brilliant additions to the story.) In the mad scene she simply huddles in the middle of her empty chamber, scrubbing her hands and whimpering. We neither see nor hear of her again.

Earlier I mentioned the hero's vivid but treacherous imagination. Yet one would be hard pressed to find much evidence of a vivid imagination in what he says. What we are given is a barrage of gapes, grunts, shrieks, and snorts; and the taut motions of a trapped but still powerful animal. Washizu cannot articulate his nightmarish visions, but there is no doubt that he has them. Some of this we encountered in his reaction to the forest. There is more. When Miki's ghost appears to him at the banquet—that it does appear is also germane to the question at hand—he staggers all the way across the hall and back, the spasmodic thudding of his feet threatening at any moment to splinter the thin wooden floor. The delicate Japanese architecture is used throughout as a sounding board for the man's tremendous violence. He crashes into the wall, gasping for breath, his eyes half out of their sockets. The banquet soon ends and one of the murderers reports that Miki's son has escaped. The stricken Washizu kills him on the spot without saying a word; he screams, flings the sword away, and reels out of the room. We are meant to feel here that the powers of the forest are assaulting the fragile order of interiors that are not really interiors at all, but merely veneer, flimsy defences against the bestiality within. Although the faculty of speech eludes him, this is what Washizu feels (and expresses) with every bone in his body.

We are never allowed to forget the hero's primitive physicality. When Washizu finally glimpses the forest moving, he shudders and crouches in a corner of the ramparts unable to believe his eyes. With great effort he musters the courage to try to embolden his men. Pacing the rampart like a caged lion, he roars down into the terrified crowd. (The camera is placed well beneath him here and pans unsteadily back and forth, imitating his nervous motion.) But his men have had enough. The forest has moved and this creature's doom screams at them with his every gesture, no matter how brazen. They draw their bows and turn them on their master, denying him the honour of dying, as Macbeth did, with "harness on his back." The result is gruesome, for it is some time before Washizu, howling and writhing, with dozens of arrows stuck in him, is caught in the neck. He falls (in slow motion) into the courtyard and his body, which seems as if it will never stop bouncing, raises huge clouds of dust. The entire army backs off, fearing that the demon may not have been completely exorcised. It has, though, and when the body finally comes to rest, the film ends.

It seems to me that the main consequence of these various transformations is that the grotesque *rapprochement* between the human and animal kingdoms common to both works is more complete in *Throne of Blood* than in *Macbeth*. Essentially the same thing happens to both heroes, but this could not have been expressed filmically unless Macbeth were transformed into a more instinctive, more physical, creature; one for whom the moral dimension of behaviour exists but seldom crosses the threshold of conceptualisation into verbal poetry, or into philosophy. Washizu is no less sensitive than Macbeth, and no less moral. But because there is no place in the film (in any film, for that matter) for Shakespeare's poetry, he must of course be less of a poet, and less of a philosopher, and perhaps not quite the classical tragic hero that Macbeth is in the play.

Even at the news of the miscarriage and at the sight of his deranged wife, even in his attempt at the end to rally his men, meanings for him remain locked in their physiological symptoms. Given Macbeth's eloquence, Washizu might have succeeded in dying more nobly, with "harness on his back." But this is to confuse the two characters. For Washizu's character is controlled in this important respect by the requirements of the medium. His men turn on him because his body and face, awesome as they are in this final attempt to command, cannot conceal his awareness of his imminent destruction. Washizu is simply not articulate enough to mediate, in the lofty manner of the classical tragic hero, between his perceptions and his gestures. If he were, he would not present the powerful film image that he does. It is fitting that Kurosawa should exploit this by placing him on the ramparts in full view of everyone and at the mercy of those to whom he cannot help but reveal himself.

All this is not to say that Washizu cannot think. The point is that he thinks in another medium. When Macbeth hears of his wife's death he delivers the famous speech beginning "Tomorrow, and tomorrow, and tomorrow . . ." Washizu, looking into his wife's chamber, sees part of the result of his folly huddled in the centre of the room; his whole being sags and he moves off heavily to his own chamber. We follow him there. He enters the room and lets his limp body drop to the floor. "Fool!" he cries. "Fool!" These are the only words he speaks. Occupying the frame with his seated figure, however, are two other objects: his sword, and the throne. Kurosawa holds this eloquent shot for a long time. It is as good an indication as any that Washizu is not a brutish man incapable of reflection. He is rather the spirit of Macbeth distilled to almost pure materiality. Lady Washizu is the spirit of Lady Macbeth distilled in the same fashion. These distillations are the lifeblood of the film. Without them a meaningful and moving narrative would have been impossible.

As for the lesser characters, they receive much the same kind of treatment. Macduff (Noriashu) is an interesting example because in the process he loses not only his eloquence but also his glorious role as avenger. Although he is presumably among the forces attacking Forest Castle at the end, after he ineffectually warns Miki of his suspicions we never see him again. One result of this is that the effects of the central action on the body politic are not dwelt upon as they are in *Macbeth*. We may be thankful for the absence of all the tedious business between Macduff and the mealy-mouthed Malcolm, but we do demand that the social implications of the tragedy, which are integral, find some expression in the film. And this they find not in subtle political machinations, but in the monstrous betrayal that Washizu's men are forced to perform at the end. This is indeed a primal social situation. It can be seen (without stretching the point, I believe) as a re-enactment of the ritual replacement of the old king. In this the film seems even closer to the Dionysian roots of tragedy than the play; and seems also to descend, in its own way, just as deeply into the darker side of human nature and relationships. In his search for the surfaces he needed as a film-maker, Kurosawa had to chip some of the crust of civilisation off the drama. Macduff (and Malcolm) were part of that crust.

A final question arises. Are there certain types of character that are not really fit for film narrative? Let me venture into these deep waters with the speculation that no film-maker could help but grossly distort or over-simplify a character such as Hamlet's. I am not talking here about the problems that Olivier encountered in trying to preserve a theatrical performance of the role, but about those that would be involved in trying to create the character filmically. And the problem is not Hamlet's complexity, for Macbeth, too, is a very complex character and Kurosawa was able to recreate him filmically by means of a distillation that neither distorted nor simplified the fundamental meaning of his experience. Hamlet would be untranslatable because of the verbality of his experience. One can be verbal without one's experience being so. Macbeth, who is at bottom a man of action, is also a great poet, and therefore a good example of this. The verbal experience is typical of those who never wholly enter their experience, those who can only act at acting. It is typical of the theatrical, role-playing personality, which is *par excellence* Hamlet's. Macbeth, on the other hand, always lives his experiences, and thereby provides Kurosawa with the irreducible core of raw, unquestioned reality that is the first premise of most great films.

Polonius asks Hamlet what he is reading. "Words, words, words," Hamlet answers. A pun of this calibre should be able to withstand the strain of one more meaning. I submit it as a description of exactly the kind of self-conscious verbal construct that is the basic form of Hamlet's own character and experience. It is the theatre that has always nourished this sensibility and it seems therefore destined to remain outside the mainstream of film-making.

The Two Tendencies: Lumière's *Workers Leaving the Lumière Factory* (1895) and Méliès' *The Witch* (1900). "Lumière's lens did open on the world . . . Méliès' ignored the workings of nature out of the artist's delight in sheer fantasy" (KRACAUER, pages 11, 13).

Man Ray's *Étoile de Mer* (1928) and the slitting of the eyeball from Dali-Buñuel's *Un Chien Andalou* (1929). "In some of Man Ray's films, the bringing together of distant realities constructs a world closer to the hidden desires of the heart than the public reality could provide. . . ." Surrealism wishes to undermine the public reality, "hence the necessity for its jokes, outrages, scandals, manifestoes, demonstrations . . . and its love for gratuitous scandals . . ." (EARLE, pages 41, 39).

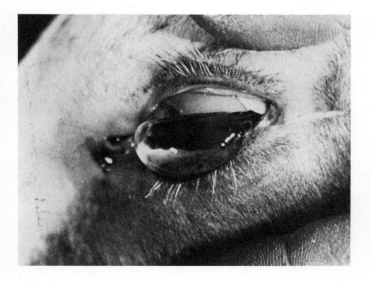

The concreteness of the husband who is not present in *Persona*
(1965) (Gunnar Björnstrand and Bibi Andersson), the photographer
(David Hemmings) searching for reality in the photograph in *Blow-
Up* (1966). "Bergman's film demonstrates the absurdity of the dream-
mode theory of film . . . Antonioni's . . . is a devastating sarcasm
indirectly commenting on the just as naïve physical-redemption theory
of film" (TYLER, page 55).

Ten shots from the montage sequence on the "Odessa Steps" from *Potemkin* (1925). "Step by step, by a process of comparing each new image with the common denotation, power is accumulated behind a process that can be formally identified with that of logical deduction" (EISENSTEIN, page 87). "The creation of a sense or meaning not proper to the images themselves but derived exclusively from their juxtaposition" (BAZIN, page 90).

From *Potemkin*. "An illustration of instantaneous action. Woman with pince-nez. Followed immediately—without transition—by the same woman with shattered pince-nez and bleeding eye: impression of a shot hitting the eye" (EISENSTEIN, page 81).

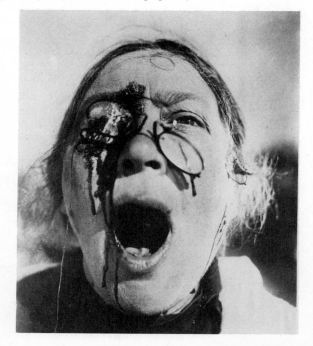

McTeague (Gibson Gowland) confronting Marcus Schouler (Jean Hersholt) in the wastes of Death Valley in *Greed* (1923); Nanook building his igloo in *Nanook of the North* (1922). Von Stroheim and Flaherty were two of "those who put their faith in reality" (BAZIN, page 89).

The shot-in-depth from *Citizen Kane* (1941). (Note the perfect focus of the image on all three planes—the three faces extremely close to the camera, the face in the middle distance, and the letters on the sign in the far distance.) "Thanks to the depth of field, whole scenes are covered in one take, the camera remaining motionless. . . . Director and cameraman have converted the screen into a dramatic checkerboard, planned down to the last detail" (BAZIN, pages 97, 98).

Laurence Olivier in *Henry V* (1944). The film "uses a device perhaps best designated as 'oblique close-up' (Mr. Oliviers' beautiful face inwardly listening to but not pronouncing the great soliloquy)." (PANOFSKY, page 159). "Microphones make possible a much more delicate and immediate use of the voice; reactions, in close-up, can color the lines more subtly and richly than on the stage" (AGEE, page 334).

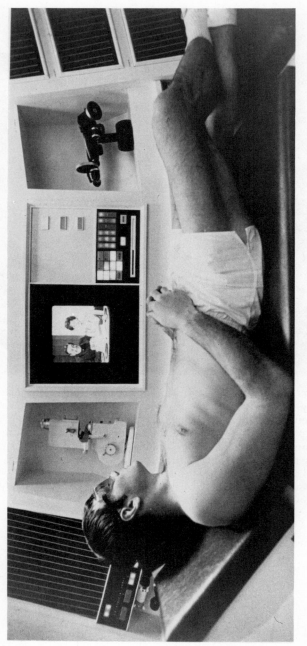

Composition in the wide screen. The astronaut (Gary Lockwood) receives birthday greetings from his parents in *2001: A Space Odyssey* (1968). "When the image is complex we *have* to be able to interpret it and the details within it . . . It is much easier to put together a complex scene synthetically out of separate details . . . but you sacrifice the possibility of real conviction, of real subtlety" (BARR, pages 138, 140).

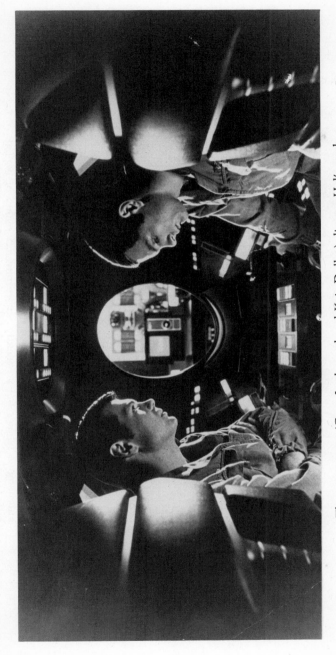

The astronauts (Gary Lockwood and Keir Dullea) discuss Hal's problems while Hal listens in the rearground in *2001: A Space Odyssey.* "The director . . . can have two faces in close shot together, instead of having to cut from one to the other, or to squeeze them in unnaturally close together" (BARR, page 144).

Caligari (Werner Krauss) feeding Cesare (Conrad Veidt) in *The Cabinet of Doctor Caligari* (1919). "The expressionist settings . . . could exert but little influence upon the general course of events. To prestylize reality prior to tackling it amounts to dodging the problem" (PANOFSKY, page 169). "Films of this type are not only intended as autonomous wholes but frequently ignore physical reality or exploit it for purposes alien to photographic veracity" (KRACAUER, page 20).

The accusers and Joan (Falconetti) in *The Passion of Joan of Arc* (1928). In "Dreyer's film . . . we move in the spiritual dimension of facial expression alone" (BALÁZS, page 194). "Carl Dreyer's basic problem as an artist is one that seems almost inevitably to confront the self-conscious creator of 'art' films: the conflict between a love for the purely visual and the tendencies of a medium that is not only visual but also dramatic" (WARSHOW, page 204). "It is a documentary of faces" (BAZIN, page 288).

Theater in Cinema. Jean Marais, Yvonne de Bray, Gabrielle Dorziat, Marcel André, and Josette Day in *Les Parents Terribles* (1948). It "deliberately deprives itself of the use of setting and of exterior nature" (BAZIN, page 282). Anna Magnani onstage in the *commedia dell'arte* of *The Golden Coach* (1952). Renoir incorporates the artifice of the theater into the cinema without destroying "that realism of space without which moving pictures do not constitute cinema" (BAZIN, page 290).

Toshiro Mifune in *Throne of Blood* (1957). The film reveals "Kurosawa's profound commitment to creating meaning by the manipulation of material reality. . . . In an extended sequence near the beginning [Washizu (Macbeth)] and Miki (Banquo) thunder through a dense, murky forest on horses no less frightened than they. (The forest is referred to as 'The Labyrinth' . . .). The forest in Washizu's mind . . ." (BLUMENTHAL, pages 341, 342, 343).

"In a moment the crazed horses burst through the underbrush on to a small clearing that glows with an unholy light" (BLUMENTHAL, page 343).

Above, Tex Avery's *Little Rural Riding Hood* (1949) and *below* Chuck Jones's *Robin Hood Daffy* (1958).

"Cartoon directors were always faced with . . . their own alternative to physical reality. The action in an animated cartoon is so completely under the director's control that it becomes a medium in which the film-maker's imagination not only *can* run absolutely riot, but *has* to . . ." (ADAMSON, page 395). "The one kind of movie which triumphantly asserts its non- or super-reality" (SELDES, page 379).

Easterners and Westerners. Paul Muni in *Scarface* (1932); John Car-
radine, Andy Devine, Chris Martin, George Bancroft, Louise Platt,
Donald Meek, Claire Trevor, and John Wayne in *Stagecoach* (1939).
"The two most successful creations of American movies are the
gangster and the Westerner: men with guns. . . . The land and the
horses have . . . a moral significance: the physical freedom they
represent belongs to the moral 'openness' of the West—corresponding to the fact that guns are carried where they can be seen. . . . The
gangster's world is less open . . ." (WARSHOW, pages 401, 404).

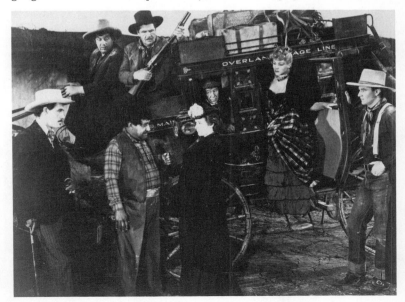

The aging Westerner—Gary Cooper (with Mary Brian) in *The Virginian* (1929) and (with Grace Kelly) in *High Noon* (1952). "As lines of age have come into Gary Cooper's face since *The Virginian*, so the outlines of the Western movie in general have become less smooth, its background more drab. . . . In *High Noon* we find Gary Cooper still the upholder of order that he was in *The Virginian*, but twenty-four years older, stooped, slower moving . . ." the flesh sagging . . ." (WARSHOW, pages 408, 411).

The lawyer from the East learns the law of the West: John Wayne
and James Stewart in John Ford's *The Man Who Shot Liberty
Valance* (1962). "Ford's . . . preoccupation with style" has the tendency "to destroy the outlines of the Western legend, assimilating it
to the more sentimental legend of rural America and making the
hero a more dangerous Mr. Deeds . . ." (WARSHOW, page 412).

Toshiro Mifune prepares for the "shoot-out" in *Yojimbo* (1961).
"Our Westerner, the freelance professional gunman, the fastest draw
in the West, has become the unemployed Samurai; the gun for hire
has become the sword for hire" (KAEL, page 417).

Attack of the Space Ship Invaders in *The War of the Worlds* (1953). "In *The War of the Worlds,* the ray which issues from the rocket ship disintegrates all persons and objects in its path, leaving no trace of them but a light ash" (SONTAG, page 433).

A shivering Tramp in *The Gold Rush* (1925). "Of all comedians he worked most deeply and most shrewdly within a realization of what a human being is, and is up against . . . The finest pantomime, the deepest emotion, the richest and most poignant poetry were in Chaplin's work" (AGEE, pages 445, 446). "The most outstanding film *picaro* . . . whose function is to bounce off the people and events around him, often, in the process, revealing the superiority of his comic bouncing to the social and human walls he hits" (MAST, page 461).

Harold Lloyd in trouble in *Safety Last* (1923). "Lloyd was outstanding . . . at setting up a gag clearly, culminating and getting out of it deftly, and linking it smoothly to the next" (AGEE, page 449).

A childish Harry Langdon (complete with bicycle) tips his hat to a gun moll in *Long Pants* (1927). "Langdon's magic was in his innocence . . . [he] looked like an elderly baby and, at times, a baby dope fiend . . ." (AGEE, pages 451, 445).

Buster Keaton surveying the situation in *The General* (1926). "He was by his whole style and nature so much the most deeply 'silent' of the silent comedians that even a smile was as deafeningly out of key as a yell" (AGEE, page 452). "*The General* is a heroic action performed by a comic character" (MAST, page 468).

Three films photographed by Gregg Toland—*Citizen Kane* (directed by Orson Welles), *Wuthering Heights* (directed by William Wyler), and *The Best Years of Our Lives* (also directed by Wyler). Note the triangular composition of all three and the use of screen depth. "Only those cameramen with the strongest personal styles were able to cross studio boundaries with impunity and imprint their own vision on everything" (KOSZARSKI, page 564).

Citizen Kane (1941): Joseph Cotton, Orson Welles, and Everett Sloan.

Wuthering Heights (1939): Geraldine Fitzgerald, Laurence Olivier, Leo G. Carroll, and Flora Robson.

The Best Years of Our Lives (1946): Dana Andrews, Teresa Wright, Myrna Loy, Fredric March, Harold Russell, and Cathy O'Donnell.

Greta Garbo in *Love* (1927) and *Anna Christie* (1930). "Garbo still belongs to that moment in cinema when capturing the human face still plunged audiences into the deepest ecstasy . . ." (BARTHES, page 567). "*Anna Christie*, where she could ensconce herself, most of the time, in mute or monosyllabic sullenness . . ." (PANOFSKY, page 164).

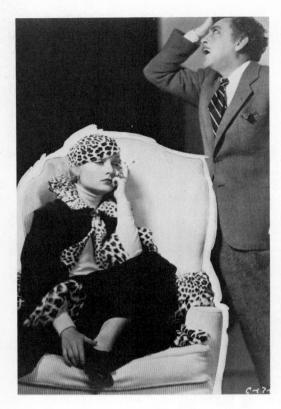

Howard Hawks's battle between the sexes. Carole Lombard and John Barrymore in *Twentieth Century* (1934), Cary Grant and Katharine Hepburn in *Bringing Up Baby* (1938). "Besides the covert pressure of the crowd outside, there is also an overt force which threatens: woman. Man is woman's 'prey' " (WOLLEN, page 536).

V

Kinds of Film

The study of artistic genres is as old as Aristotle, and at least one of his generic terms, "comedy," has been regularly applied to films. (Significantly, tragedy has not established itself as a film genre.) The generic approach to art has frequently been attacked, however, for its terms are often imprecise and its methods of categorization unclear. What, precisely, is a documentary film or a screwball comedy? Are films to be classified by their physical properties (silent, color), by their subject matter (gangster, western), or by their purpose or effect (comic, educational)? Further, are these categories legitimate? Of what interest is a category like the "educational" film? In any case, is it even proper to arrange works of art in classes, viewing them as instances of types? Benedetto Croce, the influential Italian philosopher and critic, argued that generic criticism was necessarily incompatible with an aesthetic point of view, which always treats works of art as individual and unique. Croce's views have not prevailed, however, and the concept of genre continues to be employed in film theory and criticism, as it is in all art theory and criticism, and with important results.

For Stanley Cavell, a contemporary American philosopher and aesthetician, the concept of genre is essential to an understanding of movies. Cavell wonders if one can discuss the medium of film except as the sum of its genres, in effect the film's "media." But he does not accept the traditional view that these genres are ways in which the possibilities of the medium can be "realized" or "exploited."

In Cavell's view speaking of a physical medium's possessing various artistic "possibilities" is a serious mistake. A medium is simply "something through which or by means of which something specific gets said or done in particular ways." It is a way of making sense. The first successful movies were not applications of a medium that possessed various possibilities, but the discovery of its various media, or genres—its ways of making sense.

Cavell argues that the classical Hollywood "world" was composed of three such media—stories or structures that revolve about the Military Man, the Dandy, and the Woman. The Military Man conquers evil for the sake of society (James Stewart in *The Man Who Shot Liberty Valance*, Gary Cooper in *Mr. Deeds Goes to Town*); the Dandy pursues his own interests, values, and self-respect (John Wayne in *Red River*, Cary Grant in anything); and The Woman attracts men as flames attract the moth (Garbo, Dietrich, Davis). With the loss of conviction in these genres, film reached (very belatedly in comparison to the other arts of the twentieth century) the period of modernism, in which the self-conscious artist seeks to produce a new genre, rather than simply producing more instances of a familiar genre.

In discussions of film, however, the concept of genre need not apply solely to forms of fictional narrative. The non-fictional film can be considered a genre in itself, in contrast to the fictional ones. If one argues (as Kracauer does) that film is photographic by nature and that it has a special affinity with the physical world, then the nonfiction film (Richard Barsam's more precise term for what is commonly called "documentary film") necessarily holds a special and privileged place among film genres.

On the other hand, Gilbert Seldes, an American student of popular culture, and Joe Adamson, a young American critic and animator, reject such thinking as dogmatic and untenable in view of the brilliant success of animated cartoons which, in Adamson's words, create "a new outpost of reality," a world "with its own set of physical laws and behavioral properties." Film, after all, is not essentially a photographic medium. A filmmaker can draw directly on celluloid, and even his photographs can be of drawings or of other photographs.

Robert Warshow's discussion of the gangster (the Easterner) and the Westerner is not far distant from Cavell's discussion of the Military Man and the Dandy. For Warshow, the power of the gangster film and the Western derives from their concern with the problem of violence. The hero of the Western asserts his honor and demonstrates the possibility of "style" in the face of inevitable defeat. He asserts that even in killing and being killed we are not freed from the necessity of establishing an admirable mode of behavior. Because the pattern of the classical Western is so firmly fixed, our pleasure is that of the connoisseur. We must appreciate minor variations in the characteristics of the actors who play the hero's role, and it is only in virtue of the film's ability to record such variations that these films can remain interesting to us. Any attempt to break the set pattern (to violate the "rules" of the genre), either by turning the Western into a "social drama" (as in *The Ox-Bow Incident*) or by aestheticizing it (as in *Shane*), destroys its power. According to Warshow, part of our pleasure in this kind of complete and self-contained art derives precisely from its contrast with the more complex, uncertain, and self-conscious creations of modernism. The art of the Western is not an art that precedes modernism (as it is for Cavell), but one that is contemporary with it and draws strength from the contrast.

Like Warshow, Pauline Kael dislikes the pretentious "mature" Western *(The Gunfighter, High Noon)* and the "static pictorial" Western (the later John Ford). But for her the genre is exhausted (she is, as she says elsewhere, "saddle sore"). Only a filmmaker like Kurosawa, who is willing to turn the conventions "inside out," debunking the concept of honor and turning the Westerner into a comic figure, can put this genre to further use.

Susan Sontag studies a later genre, the science fiction film that emerged in the 1950s. She shows how, because of the differences in the media, the science fiction film differs from the science fiction novel, and her account of the genre indicates the relationship, recognized by Kael and Warshow as well, between the rise and fall of genres and the social realities they reflect. Like the Western, the science fiction film has a typical hero and a recurrent structure. It too is concerned with the anxieties of contemporary life. But its fear of "depersonalization" is ambivalent and its attitude toward destruction is aesthetic; it fails to make the kind of authentic response to the contemporary situation that can be found in the best modernist works.

Warshow regards the gangster and the Westerner as significant figures and as Hollywood's finest successes. Others would reserve that honor for the comedies of the silent period, a genre to which Agee calls attention in his affectionate tribute. For Agee, however, sound comedy reveals a radical deterioration, which he is inclined to attribute to an incompatibility between comic style and speech. No doubt there is such an incompatibility between some comic styles (particularly the most physical ones) and speech, but the Hollywood dialogue comedies of the 1930s and early 1940s look as good in retrospect as many of the silent classics. Both Gilbert Seldes and Joe Adamson argue that the animated cartoon is a worthy successor to the achievement of silent comedy. And Gerald Mast does not believe that film comedy died with silence either. In his comprehensive study of film comedy, he defines the genre in terms of structure (the forms of comic plot), effect (its appeal to intellect), and spirit (its essential iconoclasm). Mast distinguishes eight types of comic structure, only one of which ("riffing") is peculiar to film. Comedy, in his view, is a genre that can manifest itself successfully in a variety of different media. For Mast, silent and sound film are really two different media.

Annette Michelson, a contemporary art critic and film aesthetician, does not believe modernism came to the film (as it did for Cavell) with the decline of Hollywood. Nor does she see modernism as a threat to the film, as Cavell does. On the contrary, Hollywood, and the triumph of the commercialism and mass culture which it represents, brought the first and classic phase of film modernism to an end. Never again would we see the combination of formal and political radicalism that reached its consummation in the Soviet film of the 1920s. But Michelson discerns a re-emergence of the radical spirit in a new kind of film, the film of radical aspiration. In Europe the post-Eisensteinian film accepts this "Fall from Grace," this "dissociation" of formal experimentation and radical political commitment, but attempts to exploit the divorce for valid aesthetic purposes. European filmmakers like Resnais and Godard have accepted the conventions of commercial Hollywood cinema and made it the basis for their radical formal advances. Godard's *Alphaville*, for instance, uses the genre of the Hitchcock suspense story to meditate on the agony and death of love, liberty, and language, on the fate of a society trapped in the self-perpetuating dialectic

356

of terrified progress. The American "independent" filmmakers, on the contrary, refuse to separate formal and political radicalism, attempting instead to re-establish their organic unity. The best recent work, such as Brakhage's and Snow's, is marked by its inquiry into this radical possibility, primarily by means of the filmmaker's questioning and exposing the ways that the cinema creates its illusions of reality. In both its European and American forms, the film of radical aspiration makes a kind of response to our situation that the Western as described by Warshow and the science fiction film as described by Sontag do not succeed in making.

STANLEY CAVELL
FROM THE WORLD VIEWED

TYPES; CYCLES AS GENRES

Our attention turns from the physical medium of cinema in general to the specific forms or genres the medium has taken in the course of its history.

Both Panofsky and Bazin begin at the beginning, noting and approving that early movies adapt popular or folk arts and themes and performers and characters: farce, melodrama, circus, music hall, romance, etc. And both are gratifyingly contemptuous of intellectuals who could not come to terms with those facts of life. (Such intellectuals are the alter egos of the film promoters they so heartily despise. Roxy once advertised a movie as "Art, in every sense of the word"; his better half declaims, "This is not art, in any sense of the word.") Our question is, why did such forms and themes and characters lend themselves to film? Bazin, in what I have read of him, is silent on the subject, except to express gratitude to film for revivifying these ancient forms, and to justify in general the legitimacy of adaptation from one art to another. Arnold Hauser, if I understand him, suggests wrong answers, in a passage that includes the remark "Only a young art can be popular," a remark that not only is in itself baffling (did Verdi and Dickens and Shakespeare and Chaplin and Frank Loesser work in young arts?) but suggests that it was only natural for the movies to pick up the forms they did. It *was* natural—anyway it happened fast enough—but not because movies were destined to popularity (they were at first no more popular than other forms of entertainment). In any case, popular arts are likely to pick up the forms and themes of high art for their material—popular theater naturally *burlesques*. And it means next to nothing to say that movies are young, because we do not know what the normal life span of an art is supposed to be, nor what would count as a unit of measure. Panofsky raises the question of the appropriateness of these original forms, but his answer is misleading.

> The legitimate paths of evolution [for the film] were opened, not by running away from the folk art character of the primitive film but by developing it within the limits of its own possibilities. Those primordial archetypes of film productions on the folk art level — success or retribution, sentiment, sensation, pornography, and crude humor — could blossom forth into genuine history, tragedy and romance, crime and adventure, and comedy, as soon as it was realized that they could be transfigured — not by an artificial injection of literary values but by the exploitation of the unique and specific possibilities of the new medium.

The instinct here is sound, but the region is full of traps. What are "the unique and specific possibilities of the new medium"? Panofsky defines them as dynamization of space and spatialization of time — that is, in a movie things move, and you can be moved instantaneously from anywhere to anywhere, and you can witness successively events happening at the same time. He speaks of these properties as "self-evident to the point of triviality" and, because of that, "easily forgotten or neglected." One hardly disputes this, or its importance. But we still do not understand what makes these properties "the possibilities of the medium." I am not now asking how one would know that these are *the* unique and specific possibilities (though I will soon get back to that); I am asking what it means to call them possibilities at all.

Why, for example, didn't the medium begin and remain in the condition of home movies, one shot just physically tacked on to another, cut and edited simply according to subject? (Newsreels essentially did, and they are nevertheless valuable, enough so to have justified the invention of moving pictures.) The answer seems obvious: narrative movies emerged because someone "saw the possibilities" of the medium — cutting and editing and taking shots at different distances from the subject. But again, these are mere actualities of film mechanics: every home movie and newsreel contains them. We could say: to make them "possibilities of the medium" is to realize what will give them *significance* — for example, the narrative and physical rhythms of melodrama, farce, American comedy of the 1930s. It is not as if film-makers saw these possibilities and then looked for something to apply them to. It is truer to say that someone with the wish to make a movie saw that certain established forms would give point to certain properties of film.

This perhaps sounds like quibbling, but what it means is that the aesthetic possibilities of a medium are not givens. You can no more tell what will give significance to the unique and specific aesthetic possibilities of projecting photographic images by thinking about them or seeing some, than you can tell what will give significance to the possibilities of paint by thinking about paint or by looking some over. You have to think about painting, and paintings; you have to think about motion pictures. What does this "thinking about them" consist in? Whatever the useful criticism of an art consists in. (Painters before Jackson Pollock had dripped paint, even deliberately. Pollock made dripping into a medium of painting.) I feel like saying: The first successful movies—i.e., the first moving pictures accepted as motion pictures—were not applications of a medium that was defined by given possibilities, but the *creation of a medium* by their giving significance to specific possibilities. Only the art itself can discover its possibilities, and the discovery of a new possibility is the discovery of a new medium. A medium is something through which or by means of which something specific gets done or said in particular ways. It provides, one might say, particular ways to get through to someone, to make sense; in art, they are forms, like forms of speech. To discover ways of making sense is always a matter of the relation of an artist to his art, each discovering the other.

Panofsky uncharacteristically skips a step when he describes the early silent films as an "unknown language . . . forced upon a public not yet capable of reading it." His notion is (with good reason, writing when he did) of a few industrialists forcing their productions upon an addicted multitude. But from the beginning the language was not "unknown"; it was known to its creators, those who found themselves speaking it; and in the beginning there was no "public" in question; there were just some curious people. There soon was a public, but that just proves how easy the thing was to know. If we are to say that there was an "unknown" something, it was less like a language than like a fact—in particular, the fact that something is intelligible. So while it may be true, as Panofsky says, that "for a Saxon peasant of around 800 it was not easy to understand the meaning of a picture showing a man as he pours water over the head of another man," this has nothing special to do with the problems of a moviegoer. The meaning of that act of pouring in certain communities is still not easy to understand; it was and is impossible to understand for anyone to whom the practice of baptism is unknown. Why did Panofsky suppose that comparable understanding is essential, or uniquely important, to the reading of movies? Apparently he needed an explanation for the persistence in movies of "fixed iconography"—"the well-remembered types of the Vamp and the Straight Girl . . . the Family Man, and the Villain," characters whose conduct was "predetermined accordingly"—an explanation for the persistence of an obviously primitive or folkloristic element in a rapidly developing medium. For he goes on, otherwise inexplicably, to say that "devices like these became gradually less necessary as the public grew accustomed to interpret the action by itself and were virtually abolished by the invention of the talking film." In fact such devices persist as long as there are still Westerns and gangster films and comedies and musicals and romances. *Which* specific iconography the Villain is given will alter with the times, but that his iconography remains specific (i.e., operates according to a "fixed attitude and attribute" principle) seems undeniable: if Jack Palance in *Shane* is not a Villain, no honest home was ever in danger. Films have changed, but that is not because we don't need such explanations any longer; it is because we can't *accept* them.

These facts are accounted for by the actualities of the film medium itself: types are exactly what carry the forms movies have relied upon. These media created new types, or combinations and ironic reversals of types; but there they were, and stayed. Does this mean that movies can never create individuals, only types? What it means is that this is the movies' way of creating individuals: they create *individualities*. For what makes someone a type is not his similarity with other members of that type but his striking separateness from other people.

Until recently, types of black human beings were not created in film: black people were stereotypes—mammies, shiftless servants, loyal retainers, entertainers. We were not given, and were not in a position to be given, individualities that projected particular *ways* of inhabiting a social role; we recognized only the role. Occasionally the humanity behind the role would manifest itself; and the result was a revelation not of a human individuality, but of an entire realm of humanity becoming visible. When in *Gone With the Wind* Vivien Leigh, having counted on Butterfly McQueen's professed knowledge of midwifery, and finding her as ignorant as herself, slaps her in rage and terror, the moment can stun us with a question: What was the white girl assuming about blackness when she believed the casual claim of a black girl, younger and duller and more ignorant than herself, to know all about the mysteries of childbirth? The assumption, though apparently complimentary, is dehumanizing—with such creatures knowledge of the body comes from nowhere, and in general they are to be trusted absolutely or not at all, like lions in a cage, with whom you either do or do not know how to deal. After the slap, we are left with two young girls equally frightened in a humanly desperate situation, one limited by a distraction which expects and forgets that it is to be bullied, the other by an energetic resourcefulness which knows only how to bully. At the end of Michael Curtiz' *Breaking Point*, as the wounded John Garfield is carried from his boat to the dock, awaited by his wife and children and, just outside the circle, by the other woman in his life (Patricia Neal), the camera pulls away, holding on the still waiting child of his black partner, who only the unconscious Garfield knows has been killed. The poignance of the silent and unnoticed black child overwhelms the yarn we had been shown. Is he supposed to symbolize the fact of general human isolation and abandonment? Or the fact that every action has consequences for innocent bystanders? Or that children are the real sufferers from the entangled efforts of adults to straighten out their lives? The effect here is to rebuke Garfield for attaching so much importance to the loss of his arm, and generally to blot out attention to individual suffering by invoking a massive social evil about which this film has nothing to say.

The general difference between a film type and a stage type is that the individuality captured on film naturally takes precedence over the social role in which that individuality gets expressed. Because on film social role appears arbitrary or incidental, movies have an inherent tendency toward the democratic, or anyway the idea of human equality. (But because of film's equally natural attraction to crowds, it has opposite tendencies toward the fascistic or populistic.) This depends upon recognizing film types as inhabited by figures we have met or may well meet in other circumstances. The recognized recurrence of film performers will become a central idea as we proceed. At the moment I am emphasizing only that in the case of black performers there was until recently no other place for them to recur in, except just the role within which we have already met them. For example, we would not have expected to see them as parents or siblings. I cannot at the moment remember a black person in a film making an ordinary purchase—say of a newspaper, or a ticket to a movie or for a train, let alone writing a check. (*Pinky* and *A Raisin in the Sun* prove the rule: in the former, the making of a purchase is a climactic scene in the film; in the latter, it provides the whole subject and structure.)

One recalls the list of stars of every magnitude who have provided the movie camera with human subjects—individuals capable of filling its need for individualities, whose individualities in turn, whose inflections of demeanor and disposition were given full play in its projection. They provided, and still provide, staples for impersonators: one gesture or syllable of mood, two strides, or a passing mannerism was enough to single them out from all other creatures. They realized the myth of singularity—that we can still be found, behind our disguises of bravado and cowardice, by someone, perhaps a god, capable of defeating our self-defeats. This was always more important than their distinction by beauty. Their singularity made them more like us—anyway, made their difference from us less a matter of metaphysics, to which we must accede, than a matter of responsibility, to which we must bend. But then that made them even more glamorous. That they should be able to stand upon their singularity! If one did that, one might be found, and called out, too soon, or at an inconvenient moment.

What was wrong with type-casting in films was not that it displaced some other, better principle of casting, but that factors irrelevant to film-making often influenced the particular figures chosen. Similarly, the familiar historical fact that there are movie cycles, taken by certain movie theorists as in itself a mark of unscrupulous commercialism, is a possibility internal to the medium; one could even say, it is the best emblem of the fact that a medium had been created. For a cycle is a genre (prison movies, Civil War movies, horror movies, etc.); and a genre is a medium.

As Hollywood developed, the original types ramified into individualities as various and subtle, as far-reaching in their capacities to inflect mood and release fantasy, as any set of characters who inhabited the great theaters of our world. We do not know them by such names as Pulcinella, Crispin, Harlequin, Pantaloon, the Doctor, the Captain, Columbine; we call them the Public Enemy, the Priest, James Cagney, Pat O'Brien, the Confederate Spy, the Army Scout, Randolph Scott, Gary Cooper, Gable, Paul Muni, the Reporter, the Sergeant, the Sheriff, the Deputy, the D.A., the Quack, the Shyster, the Other Woman, the Fallen Woman, the Moll, the Dance Hall Hostess. Hollywood was the theater in which they appeared, because the films of Hollywood constituted a world, with recurrent faces more familiar to me than the faces of the neighbors of all the places I have lived.

The great movie comedians—Chaplin, Keaton, W. C. Fields— form a set of types that could not have been adapted from any other medium. Its creation depended upon two conditions of the film medium mentioned earlier. These conditions seem to be necessities, not merely possibilities, so I will say that two necessities of the medium were discovered or expanded in the creation of these types. First, movie performers cannot project, but are projected. Second, photographs are of the world, in which human beings are not ontologically favored over the rest of nature, in which objects are not props but natural allies (or enemies) of the human character. The first necessity—projected visibility—permits the sublime comprehensibility of Chaplin's natural choreography; the second—ontological equality—permits his Proustian or Jamesian relationships with Murphy beds and flights of stairs and with vases on runners on tables on rollers: the heroism of momentary survival, Nietzsche's man as a tightrope across an abyss. These necessities permit not merely the locales of Keaton's extrications, but the philosophical mood of his countenance and the Olympic resourcefulness of his body; permit him to be perhaps the only constantly beautiful and continuously hilarious man ever seen, as though the ugliness in laughter should be redeemed. They permit Fields to mutter and suffer and curse obsessively, but heard and seen only by us; because his attributes are those of the gentleman (confident swagger and elegant manners, gloves, cane, outer heartiness), he can manifest continuously with the remorselessness of nature, the psychic brutalities of bourgeois civilization.

365

RICHARD MERAN BARSAM
FROM NONFICTION FILM :
A CRITICAL HISTORY

DEFINING NONFICTION FILM

The most familiar, but most abused and most misunderstood term in the film lexicon, *documentary*, has been applied to everything from newsreels to instructional films to travelogues and television specials. Its meaning has been extended by special film-making movements and special interest groups, by individual directors pursuing a specific goal, and by film historians and critics. Clearly it is time to reexamine the term, to reevaluate those films labeled by it, and to redefine it for purposes of clearer understanding. But, more important, it is necessary to see that *documentary* is a term which signifies only one approach to the making of nonfiction film. All documentaries are nonfiction films, but not all nonfiction films are documentaries.

In 1948, the World Union of Documentary defined documentary film as

> . . . all methods of recording on celluloid any aspect of reality interpreted either by factual shooting or by sincere and justifiable reconstruction, so as to appeal either to reason or emotion, for the purpose of stimulating the desire for, and the widening of human knowledge and understanding, and of truthfully posing problems and their solutions in the spheres of economics, culture, and human relations.

This material was adapted by Richard Meran Barsam from his *Nonfiction Film: A Critical History* (New York: E. P. Dutton and Co., Inc., 1973).

The word *documentary* was first used to describe Robert Flaherty's *Moana* (1926) by John Grierson, perhaps the single most important theorist and influence on the development of films which deserve that label. Grierson calls documentary film "a creative treatment of actuality," but he also thinks the word *documentary* is "clumsy." Other film makers and critics have added their own variations to this basic definition. Pare Lorentz, who did much to develop a wholly American approach to nonfiction film making, calls it "a factual film which is dramatic." British film maker Basil Wright insists that "documentary is not this or that type of film, but simply *a method of approach to public information.*" In his study of the American documentary film, Richard MacCann leans toward the belief that it is not "authenticity of the materials but the authenticity of the result" that matters in documentary film, while American film maker Willard Van Dyke says that the documentary is

> a film in which *the elements of dramatic conflict represent social or political forces rather than individual ones.* Therefore, it has an epic quality. Also, it cannot be a re-enactment. The social documentary deals with real people and real situations—with reality.

And another American film maker and producer, Philip Dunne, defines documentary this way:

> By its very nature the documentary is experimental and inventive. Contrary to the general impression it may even employ actors. It may deal in fantasy or fact. It may or may not possess a plot. But most documentaries have one thing in common: each springs from a definite need, each is conceived as an idea-weapon to strike a blow for whatever cause the originator has in mind. In the broadest sense, the documentary is almost always, therefore, an instrument of propaganda.

These are but a few of the many attempts to define the documentary film form, for a great deal has been said by film makers, historians, and critics. Recently, Andrew Sarris suggested that *all* films are documentary films in the sense that all films are *documents* of someone, something, some time, some place. Without further contributing to the complexity and confusion, it seems

367

desirable now to adopt a new term—*nonfiction film*—not to replace *documentary film* as a label, but to include it in a larger, more flexible concept, one that recognizes the many different approaches to this exciting form of film making.

To attempt the definition of any art form can often be a hazardous and meaningless task. For in his attempt to be precise in definition, the theorist or critic encounters the clarifying reality of each artist's vision and technique. Definitions are useful, of course, in the establishment of distinctions and categories, and certainly one can make these distinctions as precise as he wishes. However, in the approach to this study, it became increasingly clear that a concept such as "nonfiction film" should be broad enough to include *Nanook of the North* (1922) and *Woodstock* (1970). The former was made on a small budget in the frozen wastes with a crude hand-held camera, while the latter was made with every technical convenience available to the modern film maker, including helicopters and specially built editing equipment. It may be argued that there is a closer relation between these two films than a historical approach would suggest—that they both celebrate life, for instance—but it is apparent that the factors of time, technique, artistic vision, production budget, facilities, and audience are important factors in the defining of the cinematic art form to which they both belong.

It is not always possible, for example, to formulate a definition so workable as to include Eisenstein's *Old and New*, Flaherty's *Man of Aran*, Ivens' *The Spanish Earth*, Huston's *Let There Be Light*, Anderson's *Every Day Except Christmas*, and the Maysles brothers' *Salesman;* to try to define such a broad spectrum of film making with some comprehensive and all-inclusive terminology could be self-defeating. Broad lines can be drawn, of course, but even when drawn, they can be crossed without serious penalty.

NONFICTION FILM: SOME BASIC DISTINCTIONS

The nonfiction film dramatizes the factual rather than the fictional situation. The nonfiction film maker focuses his personal vision and his camera on actual situations—persons, processes, events—and attempts to render a creative interpretation of them.

A librarian once remarked to me that the difference between the two sections of the library was simple: the fiction section contains books that are "not true," while the nonfiction section contains the books that are "true." A perplexing distinction, to say the least, when one considers the problems of shelving *War and Peace*, *Ulysses*, or *Mein Kampf* under such a system. While there are some analogies between nonfiction and fiction books and films designated by the same labels, it is still necessary to distinguish the nonfiction film from its more familiar counterpart.

Generally, the nonfiction film originates in an immediate social situation: sometimes a problem, sometimes a crisis, sometimes an undramatic and seemingly unimportant person or event. It is usually filmed on the actual scene, with the actual people, without sets, costumes, written dialogue, or created sound effects. It tries to recreate the feeling of "being there," with as much fidelity to fact as the situation allows. The typical nonfiction film is structured in two or three parts, with an introduction and conclusion, and tends to follow a pattern from problem to solution. Even more typically, it is in black-and-white, with direct sound recording (or simulated sound), a musical score written expressly for the film and conceived as part of a cinematic whole, and, often as not, a spoken narration. Its typical running time is thirty minutes, but some films run less and some are ninety-minute feature-length films.

The nonfiction film maker can choose from many approaches in making his "creative treatment of actuality," but, from the beginning, two have been most apparent: the documentary approach and the factual approach. The direct cinema approach, a development of the 1960s, is an alternative approach.

DOCUMENTARY FILM

The documentary is distinguished from the factual film by its sociopolitical purpose, its "message." It attempts to fuse two concerns that often prove to be incompatible in art: medium and message. Great art is always powerful; in its most intimate way, it can create powerful personal reactions and emotions, while in its most public way, it can create powerful group actions and reactions. It can be an instrument for social influence and change, although it rarely sets out with this intention. However, the documentary film does have this purpose, and the film maker who works in this form wants to use cinema for purposes more important than entertainment or even an effective blend of entertainment and instruction. He wants to persuade, to influence, and to change his audience. His purpose can be an immediate one, such as the justification of his country's invasion of another in time of crisis *(Target for Tonight)*—or a general one, such as the romantic documentation of a primitive people for generations of viewers in the years to come *(Man of Aran)*. What becomes apparent, then, is that the content of the film is more important, at first, than the style by which that content is communicated. Here the distinctions between form and content are important ones, and while it is not the intention here to imply that the documentary film maker places politics above aesthetics, it should be emphasized that he has a job to do, a sponsor (usually) to whom he is responsible, and a specific goal to achieve. While these factors do not preclude great art, they do not always encourage it.

FACTUAL FILM

The second approach to nonfiction film making is that of the factual film maker. The difference between documentary and factual film is a basic one, but it is important and should not be overlooked. Essentially, the factual film lacks a specific message; however, if it happens to have one—and many factual films do—it does not necessarily take precedence over the other aspects of the film. Once again, the problem of formulating a definition for an artistic form occurs, but perhaps an analogy to another means of expression will help to clarify the matter. Nonfiction films share many characteristics of journalism, and the difference between documentary and factual film is roughly the difference between the editorial and the news pages of the daily newspaper. The editorial page is labeled as such, and the reader generally knows that he is reading opinions based, hopefully, on facts. The news pages, though, are a different thing. Sometimes they contain the homogenized press releases of the wire services, and at other times they contain the signed releases of reporters on the spot. No matter how "objective" they try to be, the reporters often filter the facts through the subjectivity of their own responses. Nonetheless, they are factual.

It should be apparent at this point, then, that to distinguish too precisely between the documentary and the factual approach would be to formulate inflexible concepts which would tend to defeat any fluent analysis. If we can remember that documentary films are concerned with facts *and* opinion, and that factual films are generally concerned with only the facts, then the problem is, if not solved, at least settled for the purposes of this study.

One final distinction should be made, and that is the difference between the fictional (theatrical) film and the nonfictional (nontheatrical) film. Theatrical films, or "story" films, as they are often called, are those generally made by independent producers or major studios for showing in public theaters; they feature actors or stars, real locations or constructed sets, and seek to make a profit. They are, of course, the major source of film entertainment, and one of the most important art forms of the twentieth century. *Theatrical* generally implies *commercial*, and the main purpose of most of these films is to make money, to turn a profit for the studio, at least until the producer or the studio can afford the losses frequently incurred by a film made by an unknown director. Because of the material, the costs, the political problems, and the distribution difficulties, the great nonfiction film makers of the past—Flaherty, Lorentz, Ivens, to name a few—made only a handful of films, in comparison to the great directors of fiction films. That pattern began to change in the 1960's as audiences and distributors developed a new interest in the nonfiction film, but it is too early to tell whether there will be prolific directors of nonfiction films to compare, in quality and quantity of output, with Renoir, Hitchcock, Ford, Bergman, Truffaut, and others.

Nonfiction films are not generally intended to be commercial, and are not distributed by commercial producers or shown in public theaters unless they are unusually broad in their appeal, or, as in the most recent cases, unless they appeal to a sufficiently large and specialized group, such as teen-agers, rock music enthusiasts, or those interested in wild animal conservation. "Nontheatrical" often means simply those films that are shown without admission charge in schools, colleges, churches, unions, industrial, social, and cultural organizations. While there are, of course, many exceptions, they are exceptions rather than the rule. Many great directors began their careers with nonfiction films, and many non-fiction films have been shown in large commercial theaters and have turned a profit, but the distinctions listed above will serve as a useful means by which to separate the two most obvious forms of film making: the theatrical and the nontheatrical. When there are films which successfully straddle the two fields—Sidney Meyers' *The Quiet One* (1949) for example—then one is only reminded of the infinite possibilities of the film art.

THE NEW NONFICTION FILM: DIRECT CINEMA

The "new" nonfiction film seems to pose as many problems in terminology as it presents approaches and techniques. Whatever one calls it, the new approach represents a decisive stage in the development of modern nonfiction film making. The French film maker Edgar Morin was influenced by Dziga Vertov's silent Kino-Pravda films, and used the term *cinéma vérité* ("film truth"), although others, Mario Ruspoli among them, insisted that *cinéma direct* was more appropriate. Whatever the term, the basic desire was the same: to use lightweight equipment in an informal attempt to break down the barriers between film maker and subject, to oversimplify procedure to get at the whole truth and nothing but the truth, and to catch events while they are happening, rather than to question events that have happened in the past. The technical characteristics of the new approach are simple: impromptu interviews, hand-held cameras, direct sound recording, and conscious informality.

But if there are problems with terminology, there are larger problems with the implications of these terms, implications which make the distinctions between *nonfiction* and *fiction* seem even simpler than they are. For instance, if direct cinema is "direct," can we assume that other films (fictional films, presumably) are "indirect"? If so, what does *indirect* mean? Does it mean that the films were produced with a script, with actors, with definite intentions? Does it mean that these considerations deflect the true nature of the film art into something that is indistinct and even indefensible? Does it suggest, on an even more important level, that *indi-*

rect is synonymous with *untrue*, while direct cinema is somehow "true"? A. William Bluem tries to clarify the matter when he suggests that direct cinema "assumes at the outset that the camera is the only real reporter and must not be subservient to script, to preconceived thematic statement, to plotted narrative, to someone's idea of a story—to anything, in fact, but the chronological unfolding of events. Such a comment seems the answer to some of the questions posed by the problem until we remember that film is an art, and that art presupposes an intrusion by the artist upon his subject matter. No artist merely records phenomena, as we know; as Andy Warhol has shown, even the simplest "home movie" reflects the attitude of the man behind the camera, and in that attitude is the foundation of the creative process. The film art is so highly complicated, so directly and indirectly affected by theories of time and space, by principles of editing, by types of film, by lenses, by weight of equipment, by finances, by dozens of factors, that anything like the kind of film making suggested by Bluem is more hypothetical than possible. And while it is possible to make a film based on the "chronological unfolding of events," it is in the presentation and interpretation of those events that the process of photography (an art in itself) becomes the art of film.

Both Jonas Mekas, the critic, and David Maysles, the film maker, agree that *nonfiction film* is a better term to apply to the new form. However, they use *nonfiction film* as a parallel to Truman Capote's paradoxical concept of the *nonfiction novel*, which, however successful it has proved to be in practice, is a term more notable for its contradictory quality than for its clarity as definition. Inherent in the art of film making is the process of selection: the selection of subject, of crew, of images (photography and editing), and of distribution. And what all these theories about direct cinema neglect to discuss is the importance of selecting the subject. It is easy enough to insist on objectivity once the subject has been chosen, but if the subject is inherently dull, devoid of the "spiritual energy" which D. A. Pennebaker insists is at the heart of these films, then the film will be dull. No amount of lighting, camera work, sound recording, editing, or music will erase that fact.

What, then, is the new nonfiction film? It is an attempt to capture a carefully selected aspect of reality as directly as possible, with a minimum of obstacles between the film maker and his subject; to this end, it is unscripted, unrehearsed (although internal evidence in many films indicates some preparation), and relatively unlimited as to where the persons in the film may move, what they may say, and where they may say it. The camera work is intimate, often giving the viewer the immediate sense that he is "there"; the sound recording is direct, and often clouded by pickup of background noise that lends even more reality; and the editing tends to be continuous, rather than discontinuous, striving for a chronological, rather than dramatic, presentation of events. Its pioneers include Lindsay Anderson, Karel Reisz, and Guy Brenton in England; Wolf Koenig, Roman Kroiter, Pierre Perrault, Allan King, and Michel Brault in Canada; and Jean Rouch, Edgar Morin, Mario Ruspoli, Chris Marker, and Georges Rouquier in France. However, the most important pioneers in developing and influencing the direction of the new nonfiction film have been American film makers (and, here *film makers* must be broad enough to include producers, directors, cameramen, sound-recording engineers, editors, and musicians, for many of the distinguished American films have been group efforts, rather than films signed by any single director); a list of these pioneers includes Richard Leacock, D. A. Pennebaker, Robert Drew, Gregory Shuker, Albert and David Maysles, Charlotte Zwerin, William C. Jersey, and Frederick Wiseman. They have influenced the course of nonfiction film making as significantly as John Grierson and his colleagues in the 1930's; they have encouraged others to join them, and they have attracted a large audience to their work.

BEGINNINGS OF THE NONFICTION FILM

Nonfiction film was pioneered and developed by the Americans, the Russians, and the British, in that order, but the most influential theories came from the British, notably from John Grierson and Paul Rotha.

John Grierson was truly the father of the documentary film. He was the first to apply the term *documentary*—when reviewing Flaherty's *Moana* in 1926—and he was the head of the first documentary film production unit, the Empire Marketing Board Film Unit, sponsored by the British government, and established in

1928. Grierson provided a sound, if not always systematic and consistent, philosophical foundation for the development of documentary film. From the beginning, he sought to develop a sense of community, and always placed his patriotism and his commitment to national goals over and above any personal achievement he might have made with his films. The British documentary movement began not so much in affection for film as art as in affection for national education. Its origins lay in sociological rather than in aesthetic aims.

Grierson was convinced that the documentary approach was basically propagandist rather than aesthetic, and, for him, the film medium happened to be the most convenient and the most dramatic means to implement his ideas of community and world peace. Grierson was deeply affected by the two world wars, although his major theories were formulated before World War II. To make films with a social message was all-important in the context of the world as he knew it. While other artists might have responded to war by analyzing the responses of others, Grierson was determined to prove that the world could be made a better place in which to live through mass education and communication. For him, art and aesthetics were only a means to an end: national education.

Grierson's principles of documentary are fundamental: he believed, first, that documentary was a new and vital art form which observed, selected, and opened up the real world; second, that the documentary film maker had a more imaginative degree of interpretation over his material than the maker of story films; and, third, that the materials and stories taken "from the raw" could be more real than the acted article. This so-called "minor manifesto of beliefs" is not without confusion and contradiction, but it does help to strengthen his essential convictions that documentary film should be a creative treatment of everyday actuality and that the film maker should be committed to crystallizing civic sentiments and to furthering national goals.

His position is not sufficiently consistent and systematic to be called a philosophy, but at its core is the simple belief that "somehow we had to make peace exciting, if we were to prevent wars. Simple notion that it is—that has been my propaganda ever since —to make peace exciting."

375

Paul Rotha has both produced and directed many documentary films and written a study of the genre. In the foreword to the first edition of his *Documentary Film* (1935), he speaks of a film with a message for the community of today as well as tomorrow. His concept of the documentary film is often idealistic, but his arguments reveals a sound and fundamental belief in the form. He suggests that documentary film makers take greater care in the production of their films, that they are more skillful craftsmen, and that there is "more profound reasoning" behind their choice of theme and approach than that of the theatrical film maker.

Rotha's emphasis has always been a humanistic one. He favors films which illuminate the past, explain the present, and enrich the future. He is concerned with issues that transcend time and place, and he is also concerned with finding immediate examples in the contemporary world that exemplify these issues. He asks that the documentary film maker be both a sociologist and a cameraman, and, when possible, a poet, too. Rotha stresses that the documentary film artist is a man of goodwill, a man who, in Grierson's words, can "make peace exciting." Indeed, he sees the role of the film maker much in the same way as Flaherty saw it long before and long after Rotha's influence was greatest — the role of the artist as educator, illuminator, and, finally, of conciliator. Like Shelley, Rotha would have his film makers be "legislators of mankind," but he would also have them be acknowledged, respected, and supported, and it is to this end that his writing and his films carry with them the unmistakable stamp of a man of faith and vision, and of a man whose art, however "political," was ultimately nonpolitical in its attempts to unite mankind. If the social consciousness of the 1930's characterizes Rotha's vision of art and society, it is founded on a belief that is, perhaps, naïve — that art and science can work together to solve the problems of this world. But we have been to the moon and back since then, and many of the same world problems exist still and with increasingly more deadly consequences. If Rotha's vision of the film maker as a true artist is a little tarnished today, that is not his fault, but ours. Grierson and Rotha assure us that nonfiction film, like its fictional counterpart, is an art, and that it can serve, as any art, to illuminate the human condition.

OTHER TYPES OF NONFICTION FILM

Nonfiction film includes documentary itself; factual films; travel films; educational, training, or classroom films; newsreels, and animated or cartoon films. We have seen above that documentary is as specifically different from factual film as form and technique can make it. But the following minor types are often grouped with the major types of the nonfiction film.

TRAVEL FILMS

Travel films, or travelogues, as they are more commonly called, are one of the oldest and most popular forms of nonfiction film. These films demonstrate the power of the camera to bring people together through a visual awareness of one another. Early travel films were so faithful in their visual depiction of other places and people that the French called them *documentaires*. But the meaning of the French term is different from the English term *documentary:* early travel films did create documents, or, to be more precise, factual visual records, but they did not function within the overall scope of documentary film as we have defined it.

EDUCATIONAL, TRAINING, OR CLASSROOM FILMS

The power of the nonfiction film to attract an audience, to engage its attention, and to influence its behavior is demonstrated with equal success in that large and generally undistinguished body of films that teach and train people. These training films are used everywhere, from kindergarten classrooms to battlefield information centers, and within their modest expectations, they are generally successful. Children can be introduced to safety procedures, teenagers to sex education, soldiers to the prevention of intelligence leaks, and farmers to the advantages of crop rotation. These training or information films are used extensively by such agencies as UNESCO in their efforts to inform and educate backward peoples to the benefits of such things as pest control and proper irrigation. They can be used to train salesmen how to sell more, to teach housewives how to spend less, to show Sunday golfers how to

377

drive the ball farther, and to instruct industrial workers in plant safety. In short, they can be used to teach almost anything to almost anyone, and their quality and success are limited only by the seriousness of the effort and the thoroughness of the approach used in making them.

NEWSREELS

A once-flourishing but now-vanishing species of nonfiction film is the biweekly or weekly newsreel. These newspapers of the screen were sometimes shown in special newsreel theaters in larger cities, or, more generally, on the same bill as a cartoon, a travel film, and one or two major feature films. Some of them, such as the "March of Time" or "This is America" series, reflected a particular editorial bias, while others—such as those of Paramount or Pathé—presented fairly objective reportage.

Except for rare instances, though, the newsreel is quickly becoming extinct. As with other nonfiction films, the newsreel relied on actual events for its raw material, and usually the more spectacular these events were, the better chance they had for inclusion. Newsreels presented this material in simple, descriptive terms, and within a minimum amount of time. Usually, they were without bias or viewpoint although they often took a humorous view of such topics as fashion. Frequently, there was a naïve and almost innocent approach to such items as transatlantic ship races or track meets, and, to be sure, the newsreel was part of the vanishing enthusiasm for day-to-day events that characterized America in the earlier decades of this century. The theatrical newsreel has been all-but-replaced by the broadcasting of news reports and editorial documentaries on television.

GILBERT SELDES
THE LOVELY ART: MAGIC

To little children and to aesthetes, the motion picture has always been sheer magic, and one of the complaints the aesthetes have consistently made against Hollywood is that its direction has steadily been toward reducing the magical content of the movies, making them more and more *real*. They are certainly justified in one respect: even the part of the movies which is most magical, the animated cartoon, has been pushed toward photographic realism. It has, however, resisted. Driven out of its natural habitat— sheer fantasy and illusion—by one practitioner, it has slipped out of his hands and returned with a flourish, as naïve-seeming, as saucy, as mystifying as ever, in the hands of another. So here, before we approach the newest technique by which the movies think they can make us forget that they are something more than photographic records of the actual, we can stop to consider the one kind of movie which triumphantly asserts its non- or super-reality.

If we were not so accustomed to it, if it were not on view day by day, we should celebrate, in reverence or by shouting in public places, the incredible wonder of the animated cartoon. Many years ago the aged Henri Matisse came to this country and it was said that, while he wished to see many men, he intended to pay his respects to two: Disney and Thurber. (An irony to which I am not partial: when Thurber came to be done in animations, Disney was off on other concerns and *The Unicorn in the Garden* was beautifully made by the supremely talented group of people who have the most forgettable trade name: UPA.)

379

The animated cartoon, the *Silly Symphonies*, the Mickey Mouse series, *Bambi* and *Snow White* and the other full-length features in animation, and the dreadful mistaken concept that let real people be surrounded by cartoon characters—the whole Disney enterprise and whatever went before it and came after can be taken as the typical, focal, symbolic creation in the popular arts. Whoever entirely dislikes this manifestation of money, machinery, and genius sets himself apart from humanity—as a saint perhaps, or a fool; I pass no judgments. Whoever takes them all, without making distinctions, is a happier man, but not the happiest man. For I take my stand on the principle that no harm is done by knowing—and that satisfaction increases with understanding. Or, in the specific instance, I would say that the animated cartoon is one of the three supreme examples of the multiple or diversified nature of these arts, in many respects more typical, purer, and consequently more of a test case than the two others, jazz and the feature picture. For in the animated drawing the use and abuse of the mechanism is perfectly displayed, the pressure of economic necessity, down and up, exists at high intensity, and the entire enterprise cannot come into being without pure genius of the simplest, most universal order.

And I should add that the curve of goodness (that essence which every professional recognizes) is in itself a case history of these dear and exasperating arts to which I am so devoted; should add that the pang of disappointment and the resurgence of delight are also characteristic of these arts, for they seem condemned by their own nature to destroy their sweetest qualities—and to recover. In the special case of the animated cartoon, the recovery has been made by Disney's successors while he has created at least three new careers for himself.

There were animations before Disney, and some of them were good. Even before the Keystone comedies were becoming fantastic, the animators were staking out their claims. To be sure, I can now recall only those bits I recorded at the time: the imp coming out of the inkpot and going back into it, protesting; the cow walking up the side of a barn; and the great, lovely, immortal Krazy Kat, who announced his arrival on the screen with the simple, often quoted words, "Envy me, Mice, I'm going into pictures." The mechanism of the animated cartoon had been known for generations and was used for a mild type of "feelthy pictures"—fifty drawings, packed rather like a paper-match book, when flicked presented the hootchy-kootchy dancer. To transfer the process to film was simple. Presently a disastrous discovery was made: the more single frames drawn for a step or a jump or any other action, the more lifelike it becomes. No one at that moment asked, "Who wants an animated cartoon to be life-like?"

Because the genius and the enchantment of the Disneys were so various, so overwhelming, for a long, long time the master of the business could do anything. Or let us say that at the heart of everything an animator does there is an animating principle—which here seems like a pun, but is the essence of the art. It is not the single situation created when Pluto is climbing a mountain, it is the fact that a drawn dog can move at all which captivates us first. After that we want these drawings to entertain us, to make us laugh. No one suggested in the early days that animations might make us do anything but laugh. (In 1923 I asked Picasso whether he would be interested in making some masterdrawings, and we also talked about using the *Goyescas* for a series. Picasso had, however, not seen any good animations, and unfortunately we never took the project up again. In 1953 UPA did *The Telltale Heart*, the first uncomic animation I have seen, outside of industrials and educational films, in the United States.)

To pile up the circumstances of good fortune surrounding Walt Disney is not to imply any lack of genius. Everything was in his favor—but genius was in his favor to begin with. The animated cartoon had followed the normal course of production—it had become routine. Disney arrived, a cartoonist dissatisfied with his own work; he had barely finished a few cartoons on his own when Vitaphone struck. Sound had come—and Disney took it in his stride, as if he had just been waiting for sound before starting his real work. Within a year he was using sound in counterpoint to his drawings; there was a scene in a cave, with icicles: the reverberations of sound were precisely adapted to the movements of the drops of water forming into ice—and the sense of unreality was superb.

And then, as if to challenge Disney's capacities once more, color came to Hollywood. Again there was no hesitation, no perplexity. Color, which was lacking in *Steamboat Willie* and the dance of the Egyptian characters around a frieze, was exactly what the *Silly*

Symphonies required. Let it be said at once that Disney made a few mistakes in the handling of color, slashing it about like a boy with a whitewash brush, but the major errors he never made; he never used color offensively. At worst, he used it without talent, and these occasions were few. He began by using a watercolor palette, a sort of wash in which his characters moved lightly; later he began to use the palette of an oil painter, which got thicker with every feature. I prefer the wash, because it seems to me to be within the tone of fantasy; oil is the medium of the real. But for a long time Disney had the instinctive feel for his work and seemed incapable of making a mistake. (I said this once a little more broadly; I wrote that he had never done a picture I did not like. That same week he released one about Midas, probably *The Golden Touch*, which was plodding and pretentious, and a year later he and I compared notes and I discovered that he disliked the picture almost as much as I did.) In those years he turned out masterpieces—not in comparison with the work of others, but absolutely, works that were perfect in detail as they were simple and, in a magnificent way, grand in their basic concepts. You can tick them off, this title and that, but you will run out of fingers because they came one after another, apparently without end, alternating the sheer magical loveliness of the *Silly Symphonies* and the intricate, ultralogical fantasies of Mickey Mouse and the great character who was to outshine him, Donald Duck, and the dear beasts who peopled the world in which these two lived.

There came a time, a few years after the shine and gaiety had become familiar, when people discovered a streak of cruelty in Disney; and it would be foolish to deny that it was there, as it was in Grimm and Hans Christian Andersen. But we have now the perspective of the years, and we can look at the Disney product as an entity, a single complete thing, and deliver ourselves of a nice judgment. And I think the first element in our judgment is the one no court would allow: it is sheer love. These fifteen-minute games played out in front of our eyes were—and to this day are—like candy and ice cream in our childhood, things about which we say, openly and freely, that we *love* them. They are like holidays about which we say "I can't wait . . ." because in a true sense we could hardly bear the long wait, in the early days, between Disney pictures.

I know that it is my business to say why and how these things occurred, since I am a professional critic, and if pushed, I think I can say why and how. But I think it also a good part of observation, if not of criticism, to utter the innocent childish cry of surprise and admiration with which we greet Roman candles in the summer night, or a moment in the circus when dexterity turns to loveliness. For Disney always had this moment when he was running true to his own form. It might be only the muted croak of a frog after the full chorus, it might be the sudden resemblance he showed us between a mammal and a machine, it might be the flow of one color into another or one sound into another sound, but always there was the special, sweetly knowing touch that skillful men before him had lacked. They had all his elements at their command, they seemed to do what he was doing, but the final ingredient was missing. It was not taste, not imagination, for these things Disney shared with others; and, while he developed a vast complexity in production, with machines as menacing as those that stamp out whole car-bodies in one operation, the difference between him and the others was never purely mechanical. I think that actually it was a moral difference, composed of two attitudes: a mischievous impertinence toward the public and a loving kindness toward his own creations.

I am still speaking of the short pictures, in which violence existed but was somehow held under control, as the fury of the hurricane was magisterially subdued to the beat of the music in *The Band Concert* or the tantrums of Donald Duck were justified and tamed. Since the animated cartoon, even more than the regular movie, can satisfy our wish to be omnipotent, defying the laws of gravitation, defying time and space, endowing animals with human attributes and making men and women into machines (and then giving the machines an apparent will and life of their own)—since these things are so, animations must have their own logic; we must rejoice when the Mouse or the Duck walks over the edge of a precipice and keeps on walking on air; we must rejoice because we would like also to be able to walk on air. And we must not let questions come into our minds, we must be under the spell of the picture. Then when the walker sees what has happened and panics and scrambles back to the cliff or falls and bounces back, we must recognize that also—the kind of morality of the cartoons, the laws by which they live; for it is their law that until we are afraid of what happens to us, we can do anything on earth or in the air or under the seas.

There was an additional quality in these early pictures: they missed completely the dreary quaintness of animal stories. They were partly Aesop with a touch of La Fontaine, perhaps, but they were never children's-book animals. They were carefully created characters with sustained motives, placed in situations which seemed plausible to them and in which they acted according to their lights. They were not Aesopian in any sense of delivering moral lessons, nor were their approaches to the society of human beings as satirical as those of La Fontaine; they were animals with lives of their own to lead.

The strangest thing about the early Disneys is that they did not make money—for Disney. The intricacies of the system of releasing movies can be of interest only to those in the business; they were defeating to Walt Disney, who saw his *Three Little Pigs* become an attraction capable of pulling in more money at the box office than the feature picture, yet was paid a lump sum, so much per week or per day, regardless of the take. This was the customary arrangement; everything except the feature was a filler and excluded from the percentage arrangements. There was a rough justice in this, but in the case of Disney it became intolerable and it compelled him to take the road to corporate enterprise, a big studio, big pictures, and eventually the virtual disappearance of the work that had made him famous.

The making of long pictures is in itself a natural outcome of making short ones. Chaplin had hardly arrived in the Keystone comedies when he was put into the support of Marie Dressler in *Tillie's Punctured Romance*, which some people professed to find pretentious on the silly ground that no comedy could last for seven reels. Actually, Disney waited ten years after the beginning of Mickey Mouse before doing his first feature cartoon: *Snow White and the Seven Dwarfs*. By that time his releasing arrangements were better and his studio was constantly enlarging and endless experiments were being made with color, with sound, and particularly with two qualities that Disney began to value more and more: depth and smoothness of motion, two qualities giving the effect of realness, as if he were in competition with regular movies. Some five years later he went back to a technique with which he had had a small success long before Mickey Mouse, a combination of cartoons and live actors. Eventually he made the picture that, one would have said, he was destined to make, as if the rest of his professional life was a preparation for it: *Alice in Wonderland.* Nothing so marked his fall as the tasteless, elaborate defeat he inflicted on the imagination and logic of the original—and I speak as a non-idolater.

Was it entirely the "curse of bigness" which had overtaken Disney? I am not sure. I know that midway in his work with one of his long features he wanted to call it off, but allowed his staff to go on, withdrawing only his supervision (it was either *Dumbo* or *The Reluctant Dragon,* both up to the Disney standard and, in parts, highly inventive). He had also made teaching films for one or more branches of the armed services which were miracles of inventiveness not only in his own field but in the field of education; the abstractions and fundamental principles and definitions that are so tedious and necessary were simplified, projected, and connected with happy devices, so that a mind positively allergic to ohms and amperes would remember the angle at which an animated and anguished arrow moved into a mass of bubbles, and even eyes not peculiarly observant learned to tell the nose and wing of a friendly plane from those of the enemy. And Disney made a feature in which he came to believe profoundly and passionately: *Victory Through Air Power.* The refusal of the high command to accept the thesis of this picture infuriated Disney. It was virtually that victory could be won by air power *alone,* that all other commitments of men and money and material were wasteful, and in the background was the implication that unless the Seversky principle were accepted, we could never hope for victory at all. Long after the picture was made and even when victory was beginning to be possible Disney spoke of it with a peculiar fanaticism, not with the genial enthusiasm he had for his entertainments. He was in rebellion against the government, and presently a less important event aggravated his feelings. A strike broke out at his studio.

It is hardly worth while to recall the passions of that time, but the effect on Disney was particularly strong because of the general assumption that all strikers were favored by the Administration. Disney was confused by the strike and kept saying to his friends, "I don't understand it. . . . Every one of them calls me Walt. I call them by their first names. . . ." He was back in the early days, the small studio, everybody sitting around the drawing tables, making a crack or a suggestion; he forgot the acres of buildings, the five or ten story boards simultaneously in use, the armory of sound effects, the huge machinery that photographed through several layers of gels to give perspective, the commitments to releasing organizations, the contracts, the income—he did remember the taxes. I have no position on the strike, having nothing to go on beyond Disney's own statements, which were not illuminating; I know that from that time on a certain sweetness left the studio and men of prodigious talent and pleasant natures found it difficult to work there. The last feature that seemed to me to capture anything of the quality of Disney's art was *Saludos Amigos*, which was really a grouping of unconnected shorts. In *Bambi*, which was made the same year, the naturalistic backgrounds and a mixture of the heavy and the arch brought the whole picture down to the level of illustration. The earlier elaborate *Fantasia* gave itself airs, but again, because it was made up of separate sections, seemed to have more brilliant episodes than the full-length single-story films. In addition to putting Carmen Miranda among cartoons, Disney also illustrated and hammed up *Casey at the Bat* as if its simple story needed to be helped to fame, and, laying a rough hand on whatever needed to be treated respectfully—not with reverence but with understanding—he finally came, as noted, to *Alice*.

And it must have been around this time that Stephen Bosustow and a few associates, some of whom had undergone the Disney treatment, began to make cartoons totally different in character—the first challengers to Disney sensible enough to know that they could not compete with him on his ground, the first to go back to basic principles in animations, perhaps the first since Disney to believe in their work and to enjoy it. They made a short, and suddenly everyone became aware of them and for several years they were constantly identified as "the people that made *Gerald McBoing Boing*." The surprise and elation brought by the first Disneys were again in the air, a kind of delight all the more pleasurable because it was remembered as well as new.

The men at UPA had the advantage of Disney's twenty years; they could begin with human figures—squat and round and unreal—where Disney had begun only with animals; they had all the experiments with comic sound to fall back on. The one thing they did not have was Disney's plant. They could not duplicate his backgrounds and perspectives, nor could they afford as many separate drawings per movement or gesture as Disney could give. They had to make flat backgrounds and spasmodic movements acceptable, and their particular stroke of genius was that they turned these two things into positive attractions, making them the essentials of their work. As I said, they reverted to first principles, which wouldn't have helped them if the pictures had not been supremely attractive; it is, however, agreeable to find that on occasion good theory results in practical success.

The theoretical approach is this: a caricature is not a photograph; an animation is exactly what the name implies—it makes a nonalive thing seem alive. The cartoon is not a series of photographs of reality, it is a series of photographs of drawings. A drawing has no real depth, only an appearance, and some drawings (notably cartoons) intentionally avoid even the appearance. So you have flat surfaces upon which a totally unreal movement appears to take place.

As a matter of pure speculation, I would say that without color these UPA pictures would not have succeeded; for color supplied what we might miss and accentuated the good things that we saw. In a wall of neutral color a rectangle of brightest blue was a door; colors distorted in a mirror showed us what the short-sighted Mr. Magoo imagined he saw. Sometimes a house is merely diagramed in white or brown, or with lines of different colors; sometimes all the rainbow is called on for a rich contrast. Color in the first years of UPA had the freshness and the innocence of the early Disneys; it came from a child's colorbox used with discretion and delight. (One thing Disney did which was beyond the UPA resources: when a hurricane or a whirlwind of passion started Donald in pursuit of an enemy, when a cyclone threatened Mickey and Minnie Mouse, these characters would take off, as characters always do in comic strips, in their equivalent of "a cloud of dust." Miraculously the Disney artists made this real, for as the characters moved faster, all the color in them changed and amalgamated until it became like a rubbing of crayons, the whole outline of the figures gone and the quality of the color changing as they gathered speed. The first time I saw this effect I felt that at last I understood the theory of relativity—for here the speed at which an object moved had altered its qualities; since Disney had shown it to me and it seemed perfectly logical, I need no longer worry at the thought of a yardstick being more or less than thirty-six inches long under certain circumstances. As usual, the "omnipotence effect" of the animated cartoon had brought a high degree of satisfaction.)

The satisfactions created by UPA are of two kinds. One is parallel to that of any other cartoon organization—a series in which a familiar figure appears. In UPA's case, it is Mr. Magoo, the myopic gentleman out of whose misfortunes you would have thought no comedy should be drawn. The comedy really lies in Mr. Magoo's sublime confidence and, of course, in his eventual success; it lies in his irascible scolding of other people for not looking where they are going, in his conviction that he has done the right thing when he takes off in the fire truck instead of the examiner's car to demonstrate his right to a driving license. The situations are ingenious, the drawings and the combinations of line and color are enchantments to the eye, and the tone of almost violent high spirits is exhilarating.

The other UPA cartoons are single shots with a wide range. In addition to the famous Gerald, who did things like sound effects with his voice, there was the child who demanded a jet plane under threat of turning himself into a rooster if refused. Another was about a child whose mother was going to have (or perhaps did have) a baby. A remarkably sound psychological lesson was conveyed in this cartoon with astounding virtuosity in its dream sequence, an intelligent use of symbolic images, and a wonderful scene at a circus in which the whole audience was like a painted curtain of faces, moving in unison as faces do at tennis matches at Forest Hills. And, among others, there has been *The Unicorn in the Garden*, a beginning perhaps of a whole series of Thurber. It moved intellectually out of the field of the usual cartoon, having a point, but it stayed well within the mode of comedy. *The Telltale Heart*, macabre in handling to match the material, was not entirely successful, but entire success was not to be looked for, and the question remaining is still whether a medium so "unreal" is suited to material as real in its significance as Poe's story or, to take another example, Orwell's *Animal Farm*. This was done by the British team of Halas and Batchelor, who have at times shown a light palette similar to UPA's, but in this satirical work chose to be somber, to work in semi-darkness much of the time, and to follow too literally a not-too-inspired original story. It was as if Disney's menagerie had suddenly turned pedantic, and I felt all the time that you cannot have animals in cartoons without letting us have at least a little fun out of them.

Outside of the field of entertainment, UPA has done the most entertaining TV commercials and also films for industry; some of these have been so good that they have been shown in regular movie houses. A film on cancer and when to be afraid of it, a film on the oil industry which was a brief history of the United States, and others have been as impressive in their way as the films made for fun.

The coda to the story of the cartoon is that Disney has for several years been making films of the actual lives of animals. At the beginning he insisted on making his animals behave the way his menagerie used to behave; by skillful cutting he could time the movements of a bear scratching his back or a beaver flapping his tail to the beat of a familiar piece of music, or the croaking of frogs, with the pulsation of their throats, would become a male chorus. This trick has been somewhat abated and Disney has gone forward to make serious reports on animal life in America, pictures of restrained power with just enough showmanship to make them popular. These reports grew gradually longer until a full-length feature, *The Living Desert*, was produced, and this held its own in the smaller houses at least. It was nice to know that Disney had found something interesting and important to do. Continuing these features, Disney also turned to television and won a dazzling and deserved success. He used his old materials and developed new ones; he made his television program an advertisement for a playground he had built in California; some of his material was not first-rate. But he was bold and enterprising. Even before he was established, he refused to conform to routine. Into his time period he put different kinds of programs—animation or movie, comedy or fact—until his Davy Crockett series (a straight filmed program) captured the imagination of the country. By that act he told a dreadful truth about the producers of those children's programs which were vile and violent and were presented "because children wouldn't look at anything else"—the truth being that their producers were not only liars but men of no talent whatever.

I said at the beginning of this brief history that the animated cartoon could be considered typical of the popular arts. It was typical of the best product in these arts because the trained and critical mind was totally in sympathy with the innocent spirit in admiring the cartoon and, in fact, the uninstructed turned away from the ill-conceived later features of the Disney studio, not as decisively as the critics did, but in a substantial way. All the stale equations in which good and bad and popular and highbrow figure were exploded by Disney first and by UPA later. At the same time the influence of technology on the arts was made visible in the various phases of Disney's work—from simple black-and-white through color to lavish and superfluous use of color. In the next phase the economics of the business affected the techniques of UPA by forcing them to use fewer masterframes and flat backgrounds, restoring some of the original freshness. The whole progression is a warning to us never to despair and equally a warning never to be satisfied with the second-rate, for the first-rate can be at least as popular.

JOE ADAMSON
SUSPENDED ANIMATION

I've just seen *Charlotte's Web*, and I want to say that any society which considers this a cute film and suitable to show to children is surely on the verge of collapse. This betrayal of the beautiful art form talented men labored decades to develop has generally been greeted as if it were a movie. "All the characters are delightful, as are the drawings, the colors, the songs, and, of course, the story itself," recommends *Good Housekeeping*. "The movie is beguiling. The children will love it," says *Time* Magazine. And *Newsweek* even goes so far as to gush, "This one leaves you with a warm afterglow."

Is there nowhere to turn? The kind of fraud Hanna and Barbera (the producers of *Charlotte's Web*) shamelessly palm off on innocent children every day (in TV series like *The Flintstones* and *The Jetsons*) is now brought to the neighborhood theater, and critics, charmed all to pieces by a film with no gratuitous violence in it, call it beguiling. It's like seeing "Hee Haw" gone filmic, and the newspapers applauding clean entertainment. Now Hanna-Barbera Productions has a new boom on, and *Charlotte* will spawn progeny, to outrage afresh every lover of real cartoons, and to leave *Newsweek* with a warm afterglow.

And the funny part of it is, there was a time when Hanna and Barbera made Tom & Jerry cartoons for MGM, and in all the beautiful animation that was turned out in the 40's and 50's, there was none to equal theirs. They have since discovered that it is easier to get rich by marketing quick-frozen imitations to somnambulist pre-teeners who were not alive to see the great stuff come alive before them on the screen.

Charlotte's Web, see, is about this pig named Wilbur and his horror at the thought of being butchered when September comes. Most of the film concerns the plight of Wilbur and the efforts of the barnyard mammals, geese, and insects to save his life. Now, it's no secret to you or me that hundreds of pigs are slaughtered every day, and if we're going to watch an hour and a half of one pig's attempts to preserve himself, there ought to be something *pretty special* about that pig, to provide a willing suspension of disinterest. But there's nothing special about Wilbur, not the way Hanna and Barbera have pictured him. He's a mummy to start with. The complimentary adjectives which Charlotte the Spider weaves into her web may spook out the countryside, but there's no reason why they should fool anybody who's been watching the movie. A really good cartoon would get me all absorbed in Wilbur's personality, so that I couldn't bear the thought of anybody killing him. If it was, let's say, *Porky Pig* they were going to butcher, I'd be perfectly horrified.

But the funny part of that is: Porky Pig doesn't exist. (Sorry, Virginia.) Where did I ever get the unreal idea that this character who never lived could ever die? It was all in my imagination. Or, better still, in the imaginations of the Warner Brothers Cartoon Wizards who endowed him with life.

The great cartoons of that era managed to put powerful characters into funny situations and spice them up with dynamic visuals as a matter of *course*. They would throw in things like individual style, cinematic experimentation, and, most amorphous, that innate artistic sense by which one perceives the world and transforms it into a vision of itself—just as marginal, unpaid-for fringe benefits. A reliable assaying of gems like *Bad Luck Blackie*, *Baton Bunny*, *Kitty Kornered*, and *Back Alley Oproar* will reveal that Agee's famous "Comedy's Greatest Era" did not end with *The Bank Dick*, but instead transferred its domain from the literal to the fantastic.

At that time, Warner Brothers Cartoons were directed by clever men like Friz Freleng, Bob Clampett, Bob McKimson, and Chuck Jones. And especially Chuck Jones. *My Little Duckaroo* (1954) opens with one shot rich in the kind of witty detail Jones was good at: Daffy Duck sits proud and erect on horseback, his noble beak arching forward in grim determination, to meet his noble hat, sloping downward in sultry languor; his left hand elegantly twisted into a lampoon of a horsemanship display; his kerchief floating gauzily like an aftermath behind him; his steel eyes steeling themselves for the trouble his steely gaze is sure to invite; his demure horse, an equine peacock, high-stepping like a ballerina, blushing at the preposterous grandeur he is all too clearly a part of. Behind him, stuttering, Porky Pig (as a character named Comedy Relief) sings, "The Flower of Gower Gulch."

There was a time when this sort of thing was taken for granted. Only now is it beginning to dawn on people that beautiful effects like this don't just *happen* in a magical place called Hollywood. Daffy was a fascinatingly neurotic character in Jones' hands, forever shouldering one absurd costume after another and going out to try and convince the world that he really was Protector of the Weak, or The Scarlet Pumpernickel, or Duck Dodgers of the 24½th Century. It soon becomes clear that he is none of these things, or he wouldn't spend so much time announcing that he is. Daffy becomes one of those people who isn't satisfied just to live his life, and so must establish for himself an ideal existence in the remotest outposts of his head, and, in the act of acting out Dragnet parodies and Wild West take-offs *(Robin Hood Daffy, Dripalong Daffy, Rocket Squad)*, he fails to live up to his own self-image. He is ironically accompanied in his exploits by a serene Porky Pig, whom he holds in little esteem, and who, less clever but far wiser, is fully aware of the mammoth unimportance of the escapades in which they engage together.

A pig *stood* for something in those days. Poor old Wilbur just stands there.

The ability to create characters out of moving drawings, the ability to set up cats and jackrabbits who assume prior existences and have life after the fadeout, is not a gift God grants to just anybody. The alternating expressions of fear, wonder, terror, dismay, malevolence, bewilderment, withdrawal, determination, defeat, smugness, futility, and wounded pride that register on the physiognomy of the Roadrunner's potential nemesis, The Coyote, are enough to illustrate the point. Chuck Jones' characters are out to prove themselves to an often unconcerned universe. You can see it

393

in their faces. Jones captures his characters in the act of reaching for something just beyond their grasp, of realizing that failure is inevitable, and of trying to tell themselves that it isn't so.

Look at the Coyote. Survival is not in question in his perpetual pursuit of that impossible bird. Most of us, having attempted to capture a roadrunner two or three times and failed, would give up and go chase a rabbit. But he is earnestly trying to prove to himself that such a thing is possible for him. And he has somehow gotten the idea that since simple schemes don't work, complicated ones must be the answer. Yet all he proves is that the more elaborate his preparations, the greater the chances of something going wrong, so that his obsession proves his undoing over and over. And secretly he knows it all the time: this we can tell from the heart-rending looks he gives us at the moment of failure, the haunted face of one who must live with the inevitability of disaster. There he is, staring at the dynamite, watching the impending onslaught of arrows, or, worst of all, sailing off one of those ubiquitous 5-mile cliffs, and nothing to do but submit to his fate—and then go on with the next scheme, momentarily restored by the fadeout, pretending none of this has happened.

The rest of Jones' menagerie display their hurts and fears just as graphically. There is a cat named Claude, who owns one half of a rivalry. Claude, the very picture of Mephistophelean cunning, never fails to get the best of himself by plotting remorseless torments for his chief rival in the household affection sweepstakes: a tiny terrier called Frisky who is too busy enjoying life to even realize there is a feud on, and is equally oblivious to the fact that the strongest, surest weapon is on his own side. All he has to do is bark, and the battle is won. He doesn't bark to be mean, he just barks because he's a dog, but it sends Claude straight to the ceiling every time, his claws stuck frantically into the plaster, his teeth clattering in panic. Two seconds later he is on the ground, mad as a hornet and scheming furiously, but Frisky is too good-natured even to fall for the schemes, and suddenly Claude is on the ceiling again, chattering like Morse Code. Justice, like the timing, is as swift, sure, and irrational as in the Roadrunner series. In cartoons like *No Barking* and *Two's a Crowd*, the action externalizes his internal tensions beautifully. His absolute, helpless fright at advances that so clearly bode no hostility make it painfully clear that his insecurities are hardly going to be solved by plots against a terrier, and that his fate is sealed so long as he goes on viewing the world upside down.

But there was more than character to contend with. Cartoon directors were always faced with the problem of coming up with their own alternative to physical reality. The action in an animated cartoon is so completely under the director's control that it becomes a medium in which the film-maker's imagination not only *can* run absolutely riot, but *has* to, if his films are going to rise to the expectations of the art. The cartoon director is granted a level of freedom that extends in all directions, in every dimension: all the way from deciding what kinds of conflicts will be set up to determining the way the trees will be drawn. But, like any freedom, the freedom of animation brings with it its own responsibility. The stylization, the exaggeration, the free-wheeling disregard for earthly reality are liberating enough for a scene or two, but it's a thrill that can wear out pretty quickly, unless it's given guidance beyond the momentary. The liberation is inherent in the medium; the control is up to the individual director.

Most of them, of course, settle for the comfortable rut of talking cats and mice, and the casual walking on air that comes to a halt when the character realizes the ground is gone. But the better directors don't let unreality get off so easy. Each one of them, when he puts his mind to the task, manages to come up with a separate set of physical laws and behavioral properties that constitutes his own world. Chuck Jones' Coyote can fall five miles from a precipice and still be alive when he gets to the bottom. Tex Avery's wolf could probably endure such a fall, but he is more likely to develop brakes on the way down.

Tex Avery was a mild-mannered madman who directed cartoons at MGM contemporaneously with Hanna and Barbera. He is not famous for any specific character like the Roadrunner, or Tom & Jerry (though he did forge Bugs Bunny's character in his short stay at Warners), but has an underground reputation for isolated masterworks such as *Bad Luck Blackie*, *King Size Canary*, and *Little Rural Riding Hood*. Avery tends to express himself less through his characters than through the outrageous gags that make up his individual world. In *Slap-Happy Lion*, a kangaroo hops into its own pocket and vanishes. In *Billy Boy*, a goat is rocketed to the moon and eats it. In *Northwest Hounded Police*, a fugitive wolf reaches his hideout in the wilderness, slams eight different doors into the same doorway, then turns around and, without uttering a gasp, drops his jaw to the floor with a thud.

Avery's world is the most Rabelaisian, the most fourth-dimensional in the cartoon universe, and his extra-terrestial lunacy is enormously funny and frighteningly vivid (the audience is "mesmerized with horror even as they laugh," says Raymond Durgnat). His comedy style consists of variations on Texas Tall Tales and on the kind of loose-knit panegyrics that used to pass for animation in the depressing days of the silent cartoon.

Once upon a time it was nothing for animated Mutt or Jeff to misplace his head and hardly notice. And Felix the Cat had a passion for detaching his tail and using it as a baseball bat matched only by his fondness for question marks and exclamation points as convenient props. But one is not surprised by such actions when they are carried on by spare little black and white drawings who speak in balloons and whose only audio impact is created by a convivial organist biding his time till the feature starts. One is simply not convinced of their presence. The animated cartoon never really caught on in the silent days, and Avery's cartoons are a good illustration of why: the creation of a specific universe was hardly even possible before the breaking of the soundtrack barrier. When Avery re-works in the 40's the rationale of the 20's we can see the degree to which sound and color (those twin Lucifers who earned the wrath of every God-fearing film aesthetician when they made their first appearance) were Heaven-sent for the particular needs of the cartoon. Avery can pull a gag that was meaningless on the silent screen, but is absolutely overwhelming with the full resources of the film medium behind it. The most unlikely events are suddenly so forceful and convincing that one daren't question them. In Avery's best cartoons, his animation has the power to make the most far-fetched event actually transpire before your very eyes, while his humor has the power to make the weightiest concern vanish in the light of its ridicule. Hallucinations assume the permanence of truths, and truth the shadowy form of hallucination.

One of Avery's favorite tricks is to hyperbolize out of all proportion some patent absurdity that is common to our mental makeup. *Bad Luck Blackie* (1949) ridicules the idea that a strolling black cat bodes trouble for some unwary pedestrian; this ancient superstition is one of those irrational notions we subconsciously accept, all the while knowing full well that it is perfectly senseless. Accompanied by a sprightly rendition of "Comin' Through the Rye," an angular, worldly-wise black cat dances methodically across the path of a treacherous bulldog, and forthwith the dog is beaned with a flowerpot. No source is even hinted at: it has come crashing down in perfect timing and that's that. As the film goes on, the villainous dog meets his various Dooms in the shape of a heavy trunk, a piano, a small bomb, a cash register, four horseshoes (and a horse, looking extremely puzzled), a fire hydrant, a safe, enough bricks to form a wall (which they do), an anvil, the kitchen sink, a bathtub, a steamroller, a passenger plane, a Greyhound bus, and, as a coup-de-grâce, the S.S. Arizona. We have been led in a logical progression from one common, well-accepted absurdity, on into the outward regions of an absurd universe. We can never look that superstition in the face again.

Another conjurer to conjure with is Walt Disney. When Disney set out to make a picture that was "beguiling," he generally succeeded. But it is important to realize that, especially in the 30's and early 40's, his art was not limited to the cuddlesome. At worst, his work was mere technical excellence in place of artistry, but often the artistry was undoubtedly there. In the carefully refined action you will find in a good Disney picture, the levels of subtlety and exaggeration, of exuberance and grace, of action and reaction, of reality and fantasy, merge so harmoniously into a Hymn to Movement that it bears repeated study in slow motion before it can all be absorbed. The "Plausible Impossible" was Disney's own articulation of what he was trying to accomplish by studying the physical principles of earthly movement (inertia, momentum, or the patterns of splashing raindrops) and inventing a stylized version for the cartoon world. The point was to make the fantasy come *alive* for an earth-bound audience, to connect the unreal actions with real human experience, so that the moving drawings up there on the screen had some meaning for the human people out there in their seats.

It was Disney who discovered, for all animators to follow, that establishing vivid characters was the surest means of effecting this

397

transposition. Cartoon characters in the silent days tended to be puppets. In 1933 Disney had the temerity to make a cartoon in which the three main characters looked exactly alike, but were readily distinguishable by their individual personalities, and *The Three Little Pigs* still stands as a milestone in animation. Where anybody else's version of *The Tortoise and the Hare* would have consisted of stale and convenient racing gags, Disney built the whole thing on a character contrast: the cocky hare, simultaneously impressive and annoying, and the pokey tortoise, both pathetic and sympathetic, are characterizations memorable enough to make the point of the story indelible. A mid-30s Disney cartoon like *The Band Concert* may make a clever comment on the self-absorption of musicians, but the great performances in the film belong to Mickey Mouse and Donald Duck, and their animators (Fred Moore and Dick Huemer, respectively) bring freshness and originality to the already-formulated principles of poetic movement and sharp characterization.

In the late 30's Disney began producing a succession of animated features, and sometimes was daring enough to have three in production at once. The whole concept of an animated feature is a touchy question. So long as film historians and critics restrict themselves to the feature film category it will be the only way an animator can attract any attention. But the incredible amount of patience, skill, and care that goes into every second of good animated motion renders the idea of dragging out the effort for a ninety-minute duration practically unthinkable. For this reason, many of Disney's features are more memorable in parts than as wholes, though, considering the peculiarities of the medium, this does not denigrate the level of achievement.

Bambi is probably the strongest and most consistently effective feature-length stretch of animation in existence, and deserves a place as one of the great films. Its naturalistic style of animation (a deer was kept on the studio lot for study throughout production, and stylization in the movement was subtly minimized) admirably suits its tone of devotion to the organic processes of Nature. *Bambi* is the story of innocence rising through adversity to an experienced maturity, and it alternates ingenuous humor with stark terror, its dramatic scenes (the death of Bambi's mother, the battle of the stags, the forest fire) presented with as much honesty and fervor as the "charming" scenes. The film also mixes naturalism with several powerful mythic elements: the human beings, who are treated as a mysterious, purposeless, unseen force, like a cancer on the face of the earth; and Bambi's father, a magnificent, god-like, superego personified, who materializes at moments of travail to summon the young deer's deepest resources and function as a Call to Destiny. In the same way, the rhapsodic texture of the film summons the deepest resources of the animation art, and in the carefully controlled visual exaltation (the opening track through the forest was done on the Multi-Plane camera and was reportedly a $40,000 single shot), every leaf of grass participates in the emotional effect.

Fantasia, another Disney hallmark, is one of those features more memorable in parts than as a whole. While "The Sorcerer's Apprentice" is a shining example of every one of the magical powers of this limitless art, "The Pastoral Symphony" is an encyclopedia of the mediocrities to which Hollywood often resigns itself.

But if *Fantasia* offers its delights piecemeal, no piece of the meal could be more enchanting than the "Night on Bald Mountain" segment, which (though hardly "delightful" in the *Good Housekeeping* sense), presents a phantasmagoria of grotesqueries that illuminates the dark side of human nature such as few demonic works have been able to do before or since. The images of evil in "Bald Mountain" are so uncompromised by any Mickey Mouse concept of cartooning (valkyries with bare breasts are even seen to populate the grimacing hillside) that you would think this sequence would have killed for Disney his cutey-pie stigma singlehanded. The awesome character of the Devil (designed by Albert Hurter and animated, with a respect for weight and power, by Bill Tytla), and the grisly visual distortions of the subsidiary demons (worked out by effects animators like Ub Iwerks and Joshua Meador) are demonstrative of the kind of visual magnificence Disney was able to achieve by organizing the work of many talented men in the direction of a single visual concept. When the subordinate ogres are coerced into hideous transmogrifications, and the Devil's eyes behind them burn *through* them, as if they were wisps of smoke, to glare directly at us, we are staring point blank at the awesome, barbarous underside of our own soul.

Fantasia points up, in its parallel of the twin art forms, the many ways in which animation, like music, strikes those chords that lie in the non-verbal realm, and deals with forces deeper within us than we sometimes care to admit. In the many dimensions of animation, the externalization of internal life proceeds in all directions. Ray Harryhausen's miracles with two-foot models in *The Seventh Voyage of Sinbad* and *Jason and the Argonauts* are filled with ingenious insights into such uncommon experiences as what it would be like to be a giant, one-eyed humanoid figure who has to walk on goat legs. Karel Zeman in *Baron Munchausen* and *The Fabulous World of Jules Verne* combines live action, pen and ink drawings, and model work with remorseless creativity that excites the eye and bends the mind. Norman McLaren animates human people in *Neighbors* and *A Chairy Tale* and combines abstraction with reality in unique and startling ways. Alexander Alexeieff moves pins on a pinboard to create the unearthly images in his own *Night on Bald Mountain*. And as far back as 1918, Winsor McCay, the first giant of animation, was turning a news item into a nightmare of Devastation and Despair in *The Sinking of the Lusitania*. In all these cases, flights of fantasy are emotionally charged, with whimsical character touches, whispers of true emotions, wisps of the world we know, to bridge the gulf to the world within, to excite in the mind of the spectator an atrophied spark, and transport him bodily into a new outpost of reality.

400

ROBERT WARSHOW
MOVIE CHRONICLE:
THE WESTERNER

They that have power to hurt and will do none,
That do not do the thing they most do show,
Who, moving others, are themselves as stone,
Unmoved, cold, and to temptation slow;
They rightly do inherit heaven's graces,
And husband nature's riches from expense;
They are the lords and owners of their faces,
Others but stewards of their excellence.

The two most successful creations of American movies are the gangster and the Westerner: men with guns. Guns as physical objects, and the postures associated with their use, form the visual and emotional center of both types of films. I suppose this reflects the importance of guns in the fantasy life of Americans; but that is a less illuminating point than it appears to be.

The gangster movie, which no longer exists in its "classical" form, is a story of enterprise and success ending in precipitate failure. Success is conceived as an increasing power to work injury, it belongs to the city, and it is of course a form of evil (though the gangster's death, presented usually as "punishment," is perceived simply as defeat). The peculiarity of the gangster is his unceasing, nervous activity. The exact nature of his enterprises may remain vague, but his commitment to enterprise is always clear, and all the more clear because he operates outside the field of utility. He is without culture, without manners, without leisure, or at any rate his leisure is likely to be spent in debauchery so compulsively aggressive as to seem only another aspect of his "work." But he is graceful, moving like a dancer among the crowded dangers of the city.

Like other tycoons, the gangster is crude in conceiving his ends but by no means inarticulate; on the contrary, he is usually expansive and noisy (the introspective gangster is a fairly recent development), and can state definitely what he wants: to take over the North Side, to own a hundred suits, to be Number One. But new "frontiers" will present themselves infinitely, and by a rigid convention it is understood that as soon as he wishes to rest on his gains, he is on the way to destruction.

The gangster is lonely and melancholy, and can give the impression of a profound worldly wisdom. He appeals most to adolescents with their impatience and their feeling of being outsiders, but more generally he appeals to that side of all of us which refuses to believe in the "normal" possibilities of happiness and achievement; the gangster is the "no" to that great American "yes" which is stamped so big over our official culture and yet has so little to do with the way we really feel about our lives. But the gangster's loneliness and melancholy are not "authentic"; like everything else that belongs to him, they are not honestly come by: he is lonely and melancholy not because life ultimately demands such feelings but because he has put himself in a position where everybody wants to kill him and eventually somebody will. He is wide open and defenseless, incomplete because unable to accept any limits or come to terms with his own nature, fearful, loveless. And the story of his career is a nightmare inversion of the values of ambition and opportunity. From the window of Scarface's bulletproof apartment can be seen an electric sign proclaiming: "The World Is Yours," and, if I remember, this sign is the last thing we see after Scarface lies dead in the street. In the end it is the gangster's weakness as much as his power and freedom that appeals to us; the world is not ours, but it is not his either, and in his death he "pays" for our fantasies, releasing us momentarily both from the concept of success, which he denies by caricaturing it, and from the need to succeed, which he shows to be dangerous.

The Western hero, by contrast, is a figure of repose. He resembles the gangster in being lonely and to some degree melancholy. But his melancholy comes from the "simple" recognition that life is unavoidably serious, not from the disproportions of his own temperament. And his loneliness is organic, not imposed on him by his situation but belonging to him intimately and testifying to his completeness. The gangster must reject others violently or draw them violently to him. The Westerner is not thus compelled to seek love; he is prepared to accept it, perhaps, but he never asks of it more than it can give, and we see him constantly in situations where love is at best an irrelevance. If there is a woman he loves, she is usually unable to understand his motives; she is against killing and being killed, and he finds it impossible to explain to her that there is no point in being "against" these things: they belong to his world.

Very often this woman is from the East and her failure to understand represents a clash of cultures. In the American mind, refinement, virtue, civilization, Christianity itself, are seen as feminine, and therefore women are often portrayed as possessing some kind of deeper wisdom, while the men, for all their apparent self-assurance, are fundamentally childish. But the West, lacking the graces of civilization, is the place "where men are men"; in Western movies, men have the deeper wisdom and the women are children. Those women in the Western movies who share the hero's understanding of life are prostitutes (or, as they are usually presented, barroom entertainers)—women, that is, who have come to understand in the most practical way how love can be an irrelevance, and therefore "fallen" women. The gangster, too, associates with prostitutes, but for him the important things about a prostitute are her passive availability and her costliness: she is part of his winnings. In Western movies, the important thing about a prostitute is her quasi-masculine independence: nobody owns her, nothing has to be explained to her, and she is not, like a virtuous woman, a "value" that demands to be protected. When the Westerner leaves the prostitute for a virtuous woman—for love—he is in fact forsaking a way of life, though the point of the choice is often obscured by having the prostitute killed by getting into the line of fire.

The Westerner is *par excellence* a man of leisure. Even when he wears the badge of a marshal or, more rarely, owns a ranch, he appears to be unemployed. We see him standing at a bar, or playing poker—a game which expresses perfectly his talent for remaining relaxed in the midst of tension—or perhaps camping out on the plains on some extraordinary errand. If he does own a ranch, it is in the background; we are not actually aware that he owns anything except his horse, his guns, and the one worn suit of clothing which is likely to remain unchanged all through the movie. It comes as a surprise to see him take money from his pocket or an extra shirt from his saddlebags. As a rule we do not even know where he sleeps at night and don't think of asking. Yet it never occurs to us that he is a poor man; there is no poverty in Western movies, and really no wealth either: those great cattle domains and shipments of gold which figure so largely in the plots are moral and not material quantities, not the objects of contention but only its occasion. Possessions too are irrelevant.

Employment of some kind—usually unproductive—is always open to the Westerner, but when he accepts it, it is not because he needs to make a living, much less from any idea of "getting ahead." Where could he want to "get ahead" to? By the time we see him, he is already "there": he can ride a horse faultlessly, keep his countenance in the face of death, and draw his gun a little faster and shoot it a little straighter than anyone he is likely to meet. These are sharply defined acquirements, giving to the figure of the Westerner an apparent moral clarity which corresponds to the clarity of his physical image against his bare landscape; initially, at any rate, the Western movie presents itself as being without mystery, its whole universe comprehended in what we see on the screen.

Much of this apparent simplicity arises directly from those "cinematic" elements which have long been understood to give the Western theme its special appropriateness for the movies: the wide expanses of land, the free movement of men on horses. As guns constitute the visible moral center of the Western movie, suggesting continually the possibility of violence, so land and horses represent the movie's material basis, its sphere of action. But the land and the horses have also a moral significance: the physical freedom they represent belongs to the moral "openness" of the West—corresponding to the fact that guns are carried where they can be seen. (And, as we shall see, the character of land and horses changes as the Western film becomes more complex.)

The gangster's world is less open, and his arts not so easily identifiable as the Westerner's. Perhaps he too can keep his countenance, but the mask he wears is really no mask: its purpose is precisely to make evident the fact that he desperately wants to "get ahead" and will stop at nothing. Where the Westerner imposes himself by the appearance of unshakable control, the gangster's pre-eminence lies in the suggestion that he may at any moment lose control; his strength is not in being able to shoot faster or straighter than others, but in being more willing to shoot. "Do it first," says Scarface expounding his mode of operation, "and keep on doing it!" With the Westerner, it is a crucial point of honor *not* to "do it first"; his gun remains in its holster until the moment of combat.

There is no suggestion, however, that he draws the gun reluctantly. The Westerner could not fulfill himself if the moment did not finally come when he can shoot his enemy down. But because that moment is so thoroughly the expression of his being, it must be kept pure. He will not violate the accepted forms of combat though by doing so he could save a city. And he can wait. "When you call me that—smile!"—the villain smiles weakly, soon he is laughing with horrible joviality, and the crisis is past. But it is allowed to pass because it must come again: sooner or later Trampas will "make his play," and the Virginian will be ready for him.

What does the Westerner fight for? We know he is on the side of justice and order, and of course it can be said he fights for these things. But such broad aims never correspond exactly to his real motives; they only offer him his opportunity. The Westerner himself, when an explanation is asked of him (usually by a woman), is likely to say that he does what he "has to do." If justice and order did not continually demand his protection, he would be without a calling. Indeed, we come upon him often in just that situation, as the reign of law settles over the West and he is forced to see that his day is over; those are the pictures which end with his death or with his departure for some more remote frontier. What he defends, at bottom, is the purity of his own image—in fact his honor. This is what makes him invulnerable. When the gangster is killed, his whole life is shown to have been a mistake, but the image the Westerner seeks to maintain can be presented as clearly in defeat as in victory: he fights not for advantage and not for the right, but to state what he is, and he must live in a world which permits that statement. The Westerner is the last gentleman, and the movies which over and over again tell his story are probably the last art form in which the concept of honor retains its strength.

Of course I do not mean to say that ideas of virtue and justice and courage have gone out of culture. Honor is more than these things: it is a style, concerned with harmonious appearances as much as with desirable consequences, and tending therefore toward the denial of life in favor of art. "Who hath it? he that died o' Wednesday." On the whole, a world that leans to Falstaff's view is a more civilized and even, finally, a more graceful world. It is just the march of civilization that forces the Westerner to move on; and if we actually had to confront the question it might turn out that the woman who refuses to understand him is right as often as she is wrong. But we do not confront the question. Where the Westerner lives it is always about 1870—not the real 1870, either, or the real West—and he is killed or goes away when his position becomes problematical. The fact that he continues to hold our attention is evidence enough that, in his proper frame, he presents an image of personal nobility that is still real for us.

Clearly, this image easily becomes ridiculous: we need only look at William S. Hart or Tom Mix, who in the wooden absoluteness of their virtue represented little that an adult could take seriously; and doubtless such figures as Gene Autry or Roy Rogers are no better, though I confess I have seen none of their movies. Some film enthusiasts claim to find in the early, unsophisticated Westerns a "cinematic purity" that has since been lost; this idea is as valid, and finally as misleading, as T. S. Eliot's statement that *Everyman* is the only play in English that stays within the limitations of art. The truth is that the Westerner comes into the field of serious art only when his moral code, without ceasing to be compelling, is seen also to be imperfect. The Westerner at his best exhibits a moral ambiguity which darkens his image and saves him from absurdity; this ambiguity arises from the fact that, whatever his justifications, he is a killer of men.

In *The Virginian*, which is an archetypal Western movie as *Scarface* or *Little Caesar* are archetypal gangster movies, there is a lynching in which the hero (Gary Cooper), as leader of a posse, must supervise the hanging of his best friend for stealing cattle. With the growth of American "social consciousness," it is no longer possible to present a lynching in the movies unless the point is the illegality and injustice of the lynching itself; *The Ox-Bow Incident*, made in 1943, explicitly puts forward the newer point of view and can be regarded as a kind of "anti-Western." But in 1929, when

The Virginian was made, the present inhibition about lynching was not yet in force; the justice, and therefore the necessity, of the hanging is never questioned—except by the school-teacher from the East, whose refusal to understand serves as usual to set forth more sharply the deeper seriousness of the West. The Virginian is thus in a tragic dilemma where one moral absolute conflicts with another and the choice of either must leave a moral stain. If he had chosen to save his friend, he would have violated the image of himself that he had made essential to his existence, and the movie would have had to end with his death, for only by his death could the image have been restored. Having chosen instead to sacrifice his friend to the higher demands of the "code"—the only choice worthy of him, as even the friend understands—he is none the less stained by the killing, but what is needed now to set accounts straight is not his death but the death of the villain Trampas, the leader of the cattle thieves, who had escaped the posse and abandoned the Virginian's friend to his fate. Again the woman intervenes: Why must there be *more* killing? If the hero really loved her, he would leave town, refusing Trampas's challenge. What good will it be if Trampas should kill him? But the Virginian does once more what he "has to do," and in avenging his friend's death wipes out the stain on his own honor. Yet his victory cannot be complete: no death can be paid for and no stain truly wiped out; the movie is still a tragedy, for though the hero escapes with his life, he has been forced to confront the ultimate limits of his moral ideas.

This mature sense of limitation and unavoidable guilt is what gives the Westerner a "right" to his melancholy. It is true that the gangster's story is also a tragedy—in certain formal ways more clearly a tragedy than the Westerner's—but it is a romantic tragedy, based on a hero whose defeat springs with almost mechanical inevitability from the outrageous presumption of his demands: the gangster is *bound* to go on until he is killed. The Westerner is a more classical figure, self-contained and limited to begin with, seeking not to extend his dominion but only to assert his personal value, and his tragedy lies in the fact that even this circumscribed demand cannot be fully realized. Since the Westerner is not a murderer but (most of the time) a man of virtue, and since he is always prepared for defeat, he retains his inner invulnerability and his story need not end with his death (and usually does not); but what we finally respond to is not his victory but his defeat.

Up to a point, it is plain that the deeper seriousness of the good Western films comes from the introduction of a realism, both physical and psychological, that was missing with Tom Mix and William S. Hart. As lines of age have come into Gary Cooper's face since *The Virginian*, so the outlines of the Western movie in general have become less smooth, its background more drab. The sun still beats upon the town, but the camera is likely now to take advantage of this illumination to seek out more closely the shabbiness of buildings and furniture, the loose, worn hang of clothing, the wrinkles and dirt of the faces. Once it has been discovered that the true theme of the Western movie is not the freedom and expansiveness of frontier life, but its limitations, its material bareness, the pressures of obligation, then even the landscape itself ceases to be quite the arena of free movement it once was, but becomes instead a great empty waste, cutting down more often than it exaggerates the stature of the horseman who rides across it. We are more likely now to see the Westerner struggling against the obstacles of the physical world (as in the wonderful scenes on the desert and among the rocks in *The Last Posse*) than carelessly surmounting them. Even the horses, no longer the "friends" of man or the inspired chargers of knight-errantry, have lost much of the moral significance that once seemed to belong to them in their careering across the screen. It seems to me the horses grow tired and stumble more often than they did, and that we see them less frequently at the gallop.

In *The Gunfighter*, a remarkable film of a couple of years ago, the landscape has virtually disappeared. Most of the action takes place indoors, in a cheerless saloon where a tired "bad man" (Gregory Peck) contemplates the waste of his life, to be senselessly killed at the end by a vicious youngster setting off on the same futile path. The movie is done in cold, quiet tones of gray, and every object in it—faces, clothing, a table, the hero's heavy mustache—is given an air of uncompromising authenticity, suggesting those dim photographs of the nineteenth-century West in which Wyatt Earp, say, turns out to be a blank untidy figure posing awkwardly before some uninteresting building. This "authenticity," to be sure, is only aesthetic; the chief fact about nineteenth-century photographs, to my eyes at any rate, is how stonily they refuse to yield up the truth. But that limitation is just what is needed: by preserving some hint of the rigidity of archaic photography (only in tone and décor, never in composition), *The Gunfighter* can permit us to feel that we are looking at a more "real" West than the one the movies have accustomed us to—harder, duller, less "romantic"—and yet without forcing us outside the boundaries which give the Western movie its validity.

We come upon the hero of *The Gunfighter* at the end of a career in which he has never upheld justice and order, and has been at times, apparently, an actual criminal; in this case, it is clear that the hero has been wrong and the woman who has rejected his way of life has been right. He is thus without any of the larger justifications, and knows himself a ruined man. There can be no question of his "redeeming" himself in any socially constructive way. He is too much the victim of his own reputation to turn marshal as one of his old friends has done, and he is not offered the sentimental solution of a chance to give up his life for some good end; the whole point is that he exists outside the field of social value. Indeed, if we were once allowed to see him in the days of his "success," he might become a figure like the gangster, for his career has been aggressively "anti-social" and the practical problem he faces is the gangster's problem: there will always be somebody trying to kill him. Yet it is obviously absurd to speak of him as "anti-social," not only because we do not see him acting as a criminal, but more fundamentally because we do not see his milieu as a society. Of course it has its "social problems" and a kind of static history: civilization is always just at the point of driving out the old freedom; there are women and children to represent the possibility of a settled life; and there is the marshal, a bad man turned good, determined to keep at least his area of jurisdiction at peace. But these elements are not, in fact, a part of the film's "realism," even though they come out of the real history of the West; they belong to the conventions of the form, to that accepted framework which makes the film possible in the first place, and they exist not to provide a standard by which the gunfighter can be judged, but only to set him off. The true "civilization" of the Western movie is always embodied in an individual, good or bad is more a matter of personal bearing than of social consequences, and the conflict of good and bad is a duel between two men. Deeply troubled and obviously doomed, the gunfighter is the Western hero still, perhaps all the more because his value must express itself entirely in his own being—in his presence, the way he holds our eyes—and in contradiction to the facts. No matter what he has done, he *looks* right, and he remains invulnerable because, without acknowledging anyone else's right to judge him, he has judged his own failure and has already assimilated it, understanding—as no one else understands except the marshal and the barroom girl—that he can do nothing but play out the drama of the gun fight again and again until the time comes when it will be he who gets killed. What "redeems" him is that he no longer believes in this drama and nevertheless will continue to play his role perfectly: the pattern is all.

The proper function of realism in the Western movie can only be to deepen the lines of that pattern. It is an art form for connoisseurs, where the spectator derives his pleasure from the appreciation of minor variations within the working out of a pre-established order. One does not want too much novelty: it comes as a shock, for instance, when the hero is made to operate without a gun, as has been done in several pictures (e.g., *Destry Rides Again*), and our uneasiness is allayed only when he is finally compelled to put his "pacifism" aside. If the hero can be shown to be troubled, complex, fallible, even eccentric, or the villain given some psychological taint or, better, some evocative physical mannerism, to shade the colors of his villainy, that is all to the good. Indeed, that kind of variation is absolutely necessary to keep the type from becoming sterile; we do not want to see the same movie over and over again, only the same form. But when the impulse toward realism is extended into a "reinterpretation" of the West as a developed society, drawing our eyes away from the hero if only to the extent of showing him as the one dominant figure in a complex social order, then the pattern is broken and the West itself begins to be uninteresting. If the "social problems" of the frontier are to be the movie's chief concern, there is no longer any point in reexamining these problems twenty times a year; they have been solved, and the people for whom they once were real are dead. Moreover, the hero himself, still the film's central figure, now tends to become its one unassimilable element, since he is the most "unreal."

The Ox-Bow Incident, by denying the convention of the lynching, presents us with a modern "social drama" and evokes a corresponding response, but in doing so it almost makes the Western setting irrelevant, a mere backdrop of beautiful scenery. (It is significant that *The Ox-Bow Incident* has no hero; a hero would have to stop the lynching or be killed in trying to stop it, and then the "problem" of lynching would no longer be central.) Even in *The Gunfighter* the women and children are a little too much in evidence, threatening constantly to become a real focus of concern instead of simply part of the given framework; and the young tough who kills the hero has too much the air of juvenile criminality: the hero himself could never have been like that, and the idea of a cycle being repeated therefore loses its sharpness. But the most striking example of the confusion created by a too conscientious "social" realism is in the celebrated *High Noon*.

In *High Noon* we find Gary Cooper still the upholder of order that he was in *The Virginian*, but twenty-four years older, stooped, slower moving, awkward, his face lined, the flesh sagging, a less beautiful and weaker figure, but with the suggestion of greater depth that belongs almost automatically to age. Like the hero of *The Gunfighter*, he no longer has to assert his character and is no longer interested in the drama of combat; it is hard to imagine that he might once have been so youthful as to say, "When you call me that—smile!" In fact, when we come upon him he is hanging up his guns and his marshal's badge in order to begin a new, peaceful life with his bride, who is a Quaker. But then the news comes that a man he had sent to prison has been pardoned and will get to town on the noon train; three friends of this man have come to wait for him at the station, and when the freed convict arrives the four of them will come to kill the marshal. He is thus trapped; the bride will object, the hero himself will waver much more than he would have done twenty-four years ago, but in the end he will play out the drama because it is what he "has to do." All this belongs to the established form (there is even the "fallen woman" who understands the marshal's position as his wife does not). Leaving aside the crudity of building up suspense by means of the clock, the actual Western drama of *High Noon* is well handled and forms a good companion piece to *The Virginian*, showing in both conception and technique the ways in which the Western movie has naturally developed.

But there is a second drama along with the first. As the marshal sets out to find deputies to help him deal with the four gunmen,

411

we are taken through the various social strata of the town, each group in turn refusing its assistance out of cowardice, malice, irresponsibility, or venality. With this we are in the field of "social drama"—of a very low order, incidentally, altogether unconvincing and displaying a vulgar anti-populism that has marred some other movies of Stanley Kramer's. But the falsity of the "social drama" is less important than the fact that it does not belong in the movie to begin with. The technical problem was to make it necessary for the marshal to face his enemies alone; to explain *why* the other townspeople are not at his side is to raise a question which does not exist in the proper frame of the Western movie, where the hero is "naturally" alone and it is only necessary to contrive the physical absence of those who might be his allies, if any contrivance is needed at all. In addition, though the hero of *High Noon* proves himself a better man than all around him, the actual effect of this contrast is to lessen his stature: he becomes only a rejected man of virtue. In our final glimpse of him, as he rides away through the town where he has spent most of his life without really imposing himself on it, he is a pathetic rather than a tragic figure. And his departure has another meaning as well; the "social drama" has no place for him.

But there is also a different way of violating the Western form. This is to yield entirely to its static quality as legend and to the "cinematic" temptations of its landscape, the horses, the quiet men. John Ford's famous *Stagecoach* (1938) had much of this unhappy preoccupation with style, and the same director's *My Darling Clementine* (1946), a soft and beautiful movie about Wyatt Earp, goes further along the same path, offering indeed a superficial accuracy of historical reconstruction, but so loving in execution as to destroy the outlines of the Western legend, assimilating it to the more sentimental legend of rural America and making the hero a more dangerous Mr. Deeds. (*Powder River*, a recent "routine" Western shamelessly copied from *My Darling Clementine*, is in most ways a better film; lacking the benefit of a serious director, it is necessarily more concerned with drama than with style.)

The highest expression of this aestheticizing tendency is in George Stevens' *Shane*, where the legend of the West is virtually reduced to its essentials and then fixed in the dreamy clarity of a fairly tale. There never was so broad and bare and lovely a landscape as Stevens puts before us, or so unimaginably comfortless a "town" as the little group of buildings on the prairie to which the settlers must come for their supplies and to buy a drink. The mere physical progress of the film, following the style of *A Place in the Sun,* is so deliberately graceful that everything seems to be happening at the bottom of a clear lake. The hero (Alan Ladd) is hardly a man at all, but something like the Spirit of the West, beautiful in fringed buckskins. He emerges mysteriously from the plains, breathing sweetness and a melancholy which is no longer simply the Westerner's natural response to experience but has taken on spirituality; and when he has accomplished his mission, meeting and destroying in the black figure of Jack Palance a Spirit of Evil just as metaphysical as his own embodiment of virtue, he fades away again into the more distant West, a man whose "day is over," leaving behind the wondering little boy who might have imagined the whole story. The choice of Alan Ladd to play the leading role is alone an indication of this film's tendency. Actors like Gary Cooper or Gregory Peck are in themselves, as material objects, "realistic," seeming to bear in their bodies and their faces mortality, limitation, the knowledge of good and evil. Ladd is a more "aesthetic" object, with some of the "universality" of a piece of sculpture; his special quality is in his physical smoothness and serenity, unworldly and yet not innocent, but suggesting that no experience can really touch him. Stevens has tried to freeze the Western myth once and for all in the immobility of Alan Ladd's countenance. If *Shane* were "right," and fully successful, it might be possible to say there was no point in making any more Western movies; once the hero is apotheosized, variation and development are closed off.

Shane is not "right," but it is still true that the possibilities of fruitful variation in the Western movie are limited. The form can keep its freshness through endless repetitions only because of the special character of the film medium, where the physical difference between one object and another—above all, between one actor and another—is of such enormous importance, serving the function that is served by the variety of language in the perpetuation of literary types. In this sense, the "vocabulary" of films is much larger than that of literature and falls more readily into pleasing and significant arrangements. (That may explain why the middle levels

413

of excellence are more easily reached in the movies than in literary forms, and perhaps also why the status of the movies as art is constantly being called into question.) But the advantage of this almost automatic particularity belongs to all films alike. Why does the Western movie especially have such a hold on our imagination?

Chiefly, I think, because it offers a serious orientation to the problem of violence such as can be found almost nowhere else in our culture. One of the well-known peculiarities of modern civilized opinion is its refusal to acknowledge the value of violence. This refusal is a virtue, but like many virtues it involves a certain willful blindness and it encourages hypocrisy. We train ourselves to be shocked or bored by cultural images of violence, and our very concept of heroism tends to be a passive one: we are less drawn to the brave young men who kill large numbers of our enemies than to the heroic prisoners who endure torture without capitulating. In art, though we may still be able to understand and participate in the values of the Iliad, a modern writer like Ernest Hemingway we find somewhat embarrassing: there is no doubt that he stirs us, but we cannot help recognizing also that he is a little childish. And in the criticism of popular culture, where the educated observer is usually under the illusion that he has nothing at stake, the presence of images of violence is often assumed to be in itself a sufficient ground for condemnation.

These attitudes, however, have not reduced the element of violence in our culture but, if anything, have helped to free it from moral control by letting it take on the aura of "emancipation." The celebration of acts of violence is left more and more to the irresponsible: on the higher cultural levels to writers like Céline, and lower down to Mickey Spillane or Horace McCoy, or to the comic books, television, and the movies. The gangster movie, with its numerous variations, belongs to this cultural "underground" which sets forth the attractions of violence in the face of all our higher social attitudes. It is a more "modern" genre than the Western, perhaps even more profound, because it confronts industrial society on its own ground—the city—and because, like much of our advanced art, it gains its effects by a gross insistence on its own narrow logic. But it is anti-social, resting on fantasies of irresponsible freedom. If we are brought finally to acquiesce in the denial of these fantasies, it is only because they have been shown to be dangerous, not because they have given way to a better vision of behavior.*

In war movies, to be sure, it is possible to present the uses of violence within a framework of responsibility. But there is the disadvantage that modern war is a co-operative enterprise; its violence is largely impersonal, and heroism belongs to the group more than to the individual. The hero of a war movie is most often simply a leader, and his superiority is likely to be expressed in a denial of the heroic: you are not supposed to be brave, you are supposed to get the job done and stay alive (this too, of course, is a kind of heroic posture, but a new—and "practical"—one). At its best, the war movie may represent a more civilized point of view than the Western, and if it were not continually marred by ideological sentimentality we might hope to find it developing into a higher form of drama. But it cannot supply the values we seek in the Western.

Those values are in the image of a single man who wears a gun on his thigh. The gun tells us that he lives in a world of violence, and even that he "believes in violence." But the drama is one of self-restraint: the moment of violence must come in its own time and according to its special laws, or else it is valueless. There is little cruelty in Western movies, and little sentimentality; our eyes are not focused on the sufferings of the defeated but on the deportment of the hero. Really, it is not violence at all which is the "point" of the Western movie, but a certain image of man, a style, which expresses itself most clearly in violence. Watch a child with his toy guns and you will see: what most interests him is not (as we so much fear) the fantasy of hurting others, but to work out how a man might look when he shoots or is shot. A hero is one who looks like a hero.

Whatever the limitations of such an idea in experience, it has always been valid in art, and has a special validity in an art where appearances are everything. The Western hero is necessarily an

---

* I am not concerned here with the actual social consequences of gangster movies, though I suspect they could not have been so pernicious as they were thought to be. Some of the compromises introduced to avoid the supposed bad effects of the old gangster movies may be, if anything, more dangerous, for the sadistic violence that once belonged only to the gangster is now commonly enlisted on the side of the law and thus goes undefeated, allowing us (if we wish) to find in the movies a sort of "confirmation" of our fantasies.

archaic figure; we do not really believe in him and would not have him step out of his rigidly conventionalized background. But his archaicism does not take away from his power; on the contrary, it adds to it by keeping him just a little beyond the reach both of common sense and of absolutized emotion, the two usual impulses of our art. And he has, after all, his own kind of relevance. He is there to remind us of the possibility of style in an age which has put on itself the burden of pretending that style has no meaning, and, in the midst of our anxieties over the problem of violence, to suggest that even in killing or being killed we are not freed from the necessity of establishing satisfactory modes of behavior. Above all, the movies in which the Westerner plays out his role preserve for us the pleasures of a complete and self-contained drama—and one which still effortlessly crosses the boundaries which divide our culture—in a time when other, more consciously serious art forms are increasingly complex, uncertain, and ill-defined.

PAULINE KAEL
YOJIMBO

Kurosawa has made the first great shaggy-man movie. *Yojimbo* (The Bodyguard) is a glorious comedy-satire of force: the story of the bodyguard who kills the bodies he is hired to guard. Our Westerner, the freelance professional gunman, the fastest draw in the West, has become the unemployed samurai; the gun for hire has become the sword for hire. But when our Westerner came into town, although his own past was often shady, he picked the *right* side, the farmers against the gamblers and cattle thieves, the side of advancing law and order and decency and schools and churches. Toshiro Mifune, the samurai without a master, the professional killer looking for employment, walks into a town divided by two rival merchants quarreling over a gambling concession, each supporting a gang of killers. The hero is the Westerner all right, the stranger in town, the disinterested outsider with his special skills and the remnants of a code of behavior, but to whom can he give his allegiance? Nobody represents any principle, the scattered weak are simply weak.

The Westerner has walked into the gangster movie: both sides are treacherous and ruthless (trigger-happy, they would be called in American pictures). He hires out to each and systematically eliminates both. He is the agent of their destruction because they offend his sense of how things should be: he destroys them because they disgust him. This black Robin Hood with his bemused contempt is more treacherous than the gangsters; he can defend his code only by a masterly use of the doublecross, and he enjoys him-

417

self with an occasional spree of demolition ("Destruction's our delight"). The excruciating humor of his last line, as he surveys the carnage—"Now there'll be a little quiet in this town"—is that we've heard it so many times before, but not amidst total devastation. His clean-up has been so thorough and so outrageously bloody that it has achieved a hilarious kind of style.

We would expect violence carried to extremity to be sickening; Kurosawa, in a triumph of bravura technique, makes it explosively comic and exhilarating. By taking the soft romantic focus off the Westerner as played by Gary Cooper or Alan Ladd or John Wayne, Kurosawa has made him a comic hero—just because of what he does, which was always incredible. Without his nimbus, he is unbelievably absurdly larger-than-life. In *Shane*, the rather ponderously "classic" version of the Western, good and evil were white and black. The settlers, morally strong but physically weak, naive and good but not very bright or glamorous, had to be represented in their fight against the rustling-gambling-murderous prince of darkness by a disinterested prince of light. Shane was Galahad. The Western dog, who howled at his master's grave in *Shane*, who crossed the road to frame the action at the beginning and end of *The Ox-Bow Incident*, has a new dimension in *Yojimbo*—he appears with a human hand for a bone. This dog signals us that in this movie the conventions of the form are going to be turned inside out, we'll have to shift expectations, abandon sentiments: in this terrain dog eats man. And if we think that man, having lost his best friend, can still count on his mother, Kurosawa has another shock for us. A boy from one gang, held prisoner by the other, is released; he rushes to his mother, crying "Oka" (ma or mother). She responds by slapping him. Mother isn't sentimental: first things first, and what she cares about is that gambling concession. This Eastern Western isn't merely a confusion in the points of the compass; Kurosawa's control and his sense of film rhythm are so sure that each new dislocation of values produces both surprise and delight, so that when the hero tries to free an old man who has been trussed-up and suspended in the air, and the old man protests that he's safer where he is, we giggle in agreement.

Other directors attempt to recreate the pastness of a story, to provide distance, perspective. For Kurosawa, the setting may be feudal or, as in this case, mid-nineteenth century, but we react (as we are supposed to react) as modern men. His time is now, his ac-

418

tion so immediate, sensuous, raging, that we are forced to disbe-
lieve, to react with incredulity, to admire. (This is partly the result
of using telephoto lenses that put us right into the fighting, into
the confusion of bared teeth and gasps and howls.) He shakes spears
in our faces. This is more alive than any living we know; this, all
our senses tell us, is art, not life. Ironic detachment is our saving
grace.

Of all art forms, movies are most in need of having their concepts of heroism undermined. The greatest action pictures have
often been satirical: even before Douglas Fairbanks, Sr., mocked
the American dreams, our two-reelers used the new techniques of
the screen to parody the vacuous heroics of stage melodrama.
George Stevens' *Gunga Din*, a model of the action genre, was so
exuberant and high-spirited that it both exalted and mocked a
schoolboy's version of heroism. But in recent years John Ford,
particularly, has turned the Western into an almost static pictorial
genre, a devitalized, dehydrated form which is "enriched" with
pastoral beauty and evocative nostalgia for a simple, heroic way
of life. The clichés we retained from childhood pirate, buccaneer,
gangster, and Western movies have been awarded the status of
myths, and writers and directors have been making infatuated
tributes to the myths of our old movies. If, by now, we dread going
to see a "great" Western, it's because "great" has come to mean
slow and pictorially composed. We'll be lulled to sleep in the "affectionate," "pure," "authentic" scenery of the West (in "epics" like
My Darling Clementine, She Wore a Yellow Ribbon, Fort Apache)
or, for a change, we'll be clobbered by messages in "mature" Westerns like *The Gunfighter* and *High Noon* (the message is that the
myths we never believed in anyway were false). Kurosawa slashes
the screen with action, and liberates us from the pretensions of our
"serious" Westerns. After all those long, lean-hipped walks across
the screen with Cooper or Fonda (the man who knows how to use
a gun is, by movie convention, the man without an ass), we are restored to sanity by Mifune's heroic personal characteristic—a
titanic shoulder twitch.

The Western has always been a rather hypocritical form. The
hero represents a way of life that is becoming antiquated. The
solitary defender of justice is the last of the line; the era of law-
lessness is over, courts are coming in. But the climax is the demonstration that the old way is the only way that works—though we

are told that it is the last triumph of violence. The Westerner, the loner, must take the law into his hands for one last time in order to wipe out the enemies of the new system of justice. *Yojimbo* employs an extraordinary number of the conventions of the form, but takes the hypocrisy for a ride. The samurai is a killer with a code of honor and all that, but no system of justice is supplanting him. He's the last of the line not because law and order will prevail, but because his sword for hire is already anachronistic. Guns are coming in. One of his enemies is a gun-slinger, who looks and acts a parody of American Method actors. That ridiculous little gun means the end of the warrior caste: killing is going to become so easy that it will be democratically available to all. In *Yojimbo* goodness triumphs satirically: the foil at the point of the sword is a huge joke. The samurai is not a man with a poker face, and he's not an executioner who hates his job. He's a man of passion who takes savage satisfaction in his special talents. Violence triumphs whoever wins, and our ideas of courage, chivalry, strength, and honor bite the dust along with the "bad" men. The dogs will have their human fodder.

Yojimbo is not a film that needs much critical analysis; its boisterous power and good spirits are right there on the surface. Lechery, avarice, cowardice, coarseness, animality, are rendered by fire; they become joy in life, in even the lowest forms of human life. (Kurosawa's grotesque variants of the John Ford stock company include a giant—a bit mentally retarded, perhaps.) The whimpering, maimed and cringing are so vivid they seem joyful; what in life might be pathetic, loathsome, offensive is made comic and beautiful. Kurosawa makes us accept even the most brutish of his creatures as more alive than the man who doesn't yield to temptation. There is so much displacement that we don't have time or inclination to ask why we are enjoying the action; we respond kinesthetically. It's hard to believe that others don't share this response. Still, I should remember Bosley Crowther with his "the dramatic penetration is not deep, and the plot complications are many and hard to follow in Japanese." And Dwight Macdonald, who writes, "It is a dark, neurotic, claustrophobic film . . ." and, "The Japanese have long been noted for their clever mimicry of the West. *Yojimbo* is the cinematic equivalent of their ten-cent ballpoint pens and their ninety-eight-cent mini-cameras. But one expects more of Kurosawa."

420

More? Kurosawa, one of the few great new masters of the medium, has had one weakness: he has often failed to find themes that were commensurate with the surge and energy of his images. At times he has seemed to be merely a virtuoso stylist, a painter turned director whose visual imagination had outstripped his content. But in at least three films, eye and mind have worked together at the highest levels. His first major international success, *Rashomon* (1950)—despite the longeurs of the opening and closing sequences —is still the classic film statement of the relativism, the unknowability of truth. *The Seven Samurai* (1954) is incomparable as a modern poem of force. It is the Western form carried to apotheosis —a vast celebration of the joys and torments of fighting, seen in new depth and scale, a brutal imaginative ballet on the nature of strength and weakness. Now, in *Yojimbo*, Kurosawa has made a farce of force. And now that he has done it, we can remember how good his comic scenes always were and that he frequently tended toward parody.

Ikiru is often called Kurosawa's masterpiece. (It *does* have one great moment—the old man's song in the swing. *Throne of Blood*, which I much prefer, has at least two great moments—Isuzu Yamada's handwashing scene, and that dazzling filmic achievement of Shakespeare's vision when Birnam Wood does come to Dunsinane.) Movies are, happily, a popular medium (which makes it difficult to understand why Dwight Macdonald with his dedication to high art sacrifices his time to them), but does that mean that people must look to them for confirmation of their soggiest humanitarian sentiments? The prissy liberals who wouldn't give a man with the D.T.'s a quarter for a shot ("He'll waste it on drink") are just the ones who love the message they take out of *Ikiru*, not that one man did manage to triumph over bureaucracy but that the meaning of life is in doing a bit of goody good good for others. I have talked to a number of these people about why they hated *The Manchurian Candidate* and I swear not one of them can remember that when the liberal senator is killed, milk pours out. *Yojimbo* seems so simple, so marvelously obvious, but those who are sentimental don't get it: they think it's a mistake, that it couldn't have been intended as a killing comedy. It's true that even Shakespeare didn't dare give his clowns hot blood to drink. But Kurosawa dares.

421

SUSAN SONTAG
THE IMAGINATION
OF
DISASTER

The typical science fiction film has a form as predictable as a Western, and is made up of elements which, to a practiced eye, are as classic as the saloon brawl, the blonde schoolteacher from the East, and the gun duel on the deserted main street.

One model scenario proceeds through five phases.

(1) The arrival of the thing. (Emergence of the monsters, landing of the alien spaceship, etc.) This is usually witnessed or suspected by just one person, a young scientist on a field trip. Nobody, neither his neighbors nor his colleagues, will believe him for some time. The hero is not married, but has a sympathetic though also incredulous girl friend.

(2) Confirmation of the hero's report by a host of witnesses to a great act of destruction. (If the invaders are beings from another planet, a fruitless attempt to parley with them and get them to leave peacefully.) The local police are summoned to deal with the situation and massacred.

(3) In the capital of the country, conferences between scientists and the military take place, with the hero lecturing before a chart, map, or blackboard. A national emergency is declared. Reports of further destruction. Authorities from other countries arrive in black limousines. All international tensions are suspended in view of the planetary emergency. This stage often includes a rapid montage of news broadcasts in various languages, a meeting at the UN, and more conferences between the military and the scientists. Plans are made for destroying the enemy.

(4) Further atrocities. At some point the hero's girl friend is in

422

grave danger. Massive counter-attacks by international forces, with brilliant displays of rocketry, rays, and other advanced weapons, are all unsuccessful. Enormous military casualties, usually by incineration. Cities are destroyed and/or evacuated. There is an obligatory scene here of panicked crowds stampeding along a highway or a big bridge, being waved on by numerous policemen who, if the film is Japanese, are immaculately white-gloved, preternaturally calm, and call out in dubbed English, "Keep moving. There is no need to be alarmed."

(5) More conferences, whose motif is: "They must be vulnerable to something." Throughout the hero has been working in his lab to this end. The final strategy, upon which all hopes depend, is drawn up; the ultimate weapon—often a super-powerful, as yet untested, nuclear device—is mounted. Countdown. Final repulse of the monster or invaders. Mutual congratulations, while the hero and girl friend embrace cheek to cheek and scan the skies sturdily. "But have we seen the last of them?"

The film I have just described should be in color and on a wide screen. Another typical scenario, which follows, is simpler and suited to black-and-white films with a lower budget. It has four phases.

(1) The hero (usually, but not always, a scientist) and his girl friend, or his wife and two children, are disporting themselves in some innocent ultra-normal middle-class surroundings—their house in a small town, or on vacation (camping, boating). Suddenly, someone starts behaving strangely; or some innocent form of vegetation becomes monstrously enlarged and ambulatory. If a character is pictured driving an automobile, something gruesome looms up in the middle of the road. If it is night, strange lights hurtle across the sky.

(2) After following the thing's tracks, or determining that It is radioactive, or poking around a huge crater—in short, conducting some sort of crude investigation—the hero tries to warn the local authorities, without effect; nobody believes anything is amiss. The hero knows better. If the thing is tangible, the house is elaborately barricaded. If the invading alien is an invisible parasite, a doctor or friend is called in, who is himself rather quickly killed or "taken possession of" by the thing.

(3) The advice of whoever further is consulted proves useless. Meanwhile, It continues to claim other victims in the town, which remains implausibly isolated from the rest of the world. General helplessness.

(4) One of two possibilities. Either the hero prepares to do battle alone, accidentally discovers the thing's one vulnerable point, and destroys it. Or, he somehow manages to get out of town and succeeds in laying his case before competent authorities. They, along the lines of the first script but abridged, deploy a complex technology which (after initial setbacks) finally prevails against the invaders.

Another version of the second script opens with the scientist-hero in his laboratory, which is located in the basement or on the grounds of his tasteful, prosperous house. Through his experiments, he unwittingly causes a frightful metamorphosis in some class of plants or animals which turn carnivorous and go on a rampage. Or else, his experiments have caused him to be injured (sometimes irrevocably) or "invaded" himself. Perhaps he has been experimenting with radiation, or has built a machine to communicate with beings from other planets or transport him to other places or times.

Another version of the first script involves the discovery of some fundamental alteration in the conditions of existence of our planet, brought about by nuclear testing, which will lead to the extinction in a few months of all human life. For example: the temperature of the earth is becoming too high or too low to support life, or the earth is cracking in two, or it is gradually being blanketed by lethal fallout.

A third script, somewhat but not altogether different from the first two, concerns a journey through space—to the moon, or some other planet. What the space-voyagers discover commonly is that the alien terrain is in a state of dire emergency, itself threatened by extra-planetary invaders or nearing extinction through the practice of nuclear warfare. The terminal dramas of the first and second scripts are played out there, to which is added the problem of getting away from the doomed and/or hostile planet and back to Earth.

I am aware, of course, that there are thousands of science fiction novels (their heyday was the late 1940s), not to mention the transcriptions of science fiction themes which, more and more, provide the principal subject-matter of comic books. But I propose to discuss science fiction films (the present period began in 1950 and continues, considerably abated, to this day) as an independent subgenre, without reference to other media—and, most particularly, without reference to the novels from which, in many cases, they were adapted. For, while novel and film may share the same plot, the fundamental difference between the resources of the novel and the film makes them quite dissimilar.

Certainly, compared with the science fiction novels, their film counterparts have unique strengths, one of which is the immediate representation of the extraordinary: physical deformity and mutation, missile and rocket combat, toppling skyscrapers. The movies are, naturally, weak just where the science fiction novels (some of them) are strong—on science. But in place of an intellectual workout, they can supply something the novels can never provide—sensuous elaboration. In the films it is by means of images and sounds, not words that have to be translated by the imagination, that one can participate in the fantasy of living through one's own death and more, the death of cities, the destruction of humanity itself.

Science fiction films are not about science. They are about disaster, which is one of the oldest subjects of art. In science fiction films disaster is rarely viewed intensively; it is always extensive. It is a matter of quantity and ingenuity. If you will, it is a question of scale. But the scale, particularly in the wide-screen color films (of which the ones by the Japanese director Inoshiro Honda and the American director George Pal are technically the most convincing and visually the most exciting), does raise the matter to another level.

Thus, the science fiction film (like that of a very different contemporary genre, the Happening) is concerned with the aesthetics of destruction, with the peculiar beauties to be found in wreaking havoc, making a mess. And it is in the imagery of destruction that the core of a good science fiction film lies. Hence, the disadvantage of the cheap film—in which the monster appears or the rocket lands in a small dull-looking town. (Hollywood budget needs usually dictate that the town be in the Arizona or California desert. In *The Thing From Another World* [1951] the rather sleazy and confined set is supposed to be an encampment near the North Pole.)

Still, good black-and-white science fiction films have been made. But a bigger budget, which usually means color, allows a much greater play back and forth among several model environments. There is the populous city. There is the lavish but ascetic interior of the spaceship—either the invaders' or ours—replete with stream-lined chromium fixtures and dials and machines whose complexity is indicated by the number of colored lights they flash and strange noises they emit. There is the laboratory crowded with formidable boxes and scientific apparatus. There is a comparatively old-fashioned-looking conference room, where the scientists unfurl charts to explain the desperate state of things to the military. And each of these standard locales or backgrounds is subject to two modalities—intact and destroyed. We may, if we are lucky, be treated to a panorama of melting tanks, flying bodies, crashing walls, awesome craters and fissures in the earth, plummeting spacecraft, colorful deadly rays; and to a symphony of screams, weird electronic signals, the noisiest military hardware going, and the leaden tones of the laconic denizens of alien planets and their subjugated earthlings.

Certain of the primitive gratifications of science fiction films—for instance, the depiction of urban disaster on a colossally magnified scale—are shared with other types of films. Visually there is little difference between mass havoc as represented in the old horror and monster films and what we find in science fiction films, except (again) scale. In the old monster films, the monster always headed for the great city, where he had to do a fair bit of rampaging, hurling busses off bridges, crumpling trains in his bare hands, toppling buildings, and so forth. The archetype is King Kong, in Schoedsack and Cooper's great film of 1933, running amok, first in the native village (trampling babies, a bit of footage excised from most prints), then in New York. This is really no different in spirit from the scene in Inoshiro Honda's *Rodan* (1957) in which two giant reptiles—with a wingspan of 500 feet and supersonic speeds—by flapping their wings whip up a cyclone that blows most of Tokyo to smithereens. Or the destruction of half of Japan by the gigantic robot with the great incinerating ray that shoots forth from his eyes, at the beginning of Honda's *The Mysterians* (1959). Or, the devastation by the rays from a fleet of flying saucers of New York, Paris, and Tokyo, in *Battle in Outer Space* (1960). Or, the inundation of New York in *When Worlds Collide* (1951). Or, the end of London in 1966 depicted in George Pal's *The Time Machine* (1960). Neither do these sequences differ in aesthetic intention from the destruction scenes in the big sword, sandal, and orgy color spectaculars set in Biblical and Roman times—the end of Sodom in Aldrich's *Sodom and Gomorrah*, of Gaza in De Mille's *Samson and Delilah*, of Rhodes in *The Colossus of Rhodes*, and of Rome in a dozen Nero movies. Griffith began it with the Babylon sequence in *Intolerance*, and to this day there is nothing like the thrill of watching all those expensive sets come tumbling down.

In other respects as well, the science fiction films of the 1950s take up familiar themes. The famous 1930s movie serials and comics of the adventures of Flash Gordon and Buck Rogers, as well as the more recent spate of comic book super-heroes with extraterrestrial origins (the most famous is Superman, a foundling from the planet Krypton, currently described as having been exploded by a nuclear blast), share motifs with more recent science fiction movies. But there is an important difference. The old science fiction films, and most of the comics, still have an essentially innocent relation to disaster. Mainly they offer new versions of the oldest romance of all—of the strong invulnerable hero with a mysterious lineage come to do battle on behalf of good and against evil. Recent science fiction films have a decided grimness, bolstered by their much greater degree of visual credibility, which contrasts strongly with the older films. Modern historical reality has greatly enlarged the imagination of disaster, and the protagonists—perhaps by the very nature of what is visited upon them—no longer seem wholly innocent.

The lure of such generalized disaster as a fantasy is that it releases one from normal obligations. The trump card of the end-of-the-world movies—like *The Day the Earth Caught Fire* (1962)—is that great scene with New York or London or Tokyo discovered empty, its entire population annihilated. Or, as in *The World, The Flesh, and The Devil* (1957), the whole movie can be devoted to the fantasy of occupying the deserted metropolis and starting all over again, a world Robinson Crusoe.

Another kind of satisfaction these films supply is extreme moral simplification—that is to say, a morally acceptable fantasy where one can give outlet to cruel or at least amoral feelings. In this respect, science fiction films partly overlap with horror films. This is the undeniable pleasure we derive from looking at freaks, beings excluded from the category of the human. The sense of superiority over the freak conjoined in varying proportions with the titillation of fear and aversion makes it possible for moral scruples to be lifted, for cruelty to be enjoyed. The same thing happens in science fiction films. In the figure of the monster from outer space, the freakish, the ugly, and the predatory all converge—and provide a fantasy target for righteous bellicosity to discharge itself, and for the aesthetic enjoyment of suffering and disaster. Science fiction films are one of the purest forms of spectacle; that is, we are rarely inside anyone's feelings. (An exception is Jack Arnold's *The Incredible Shrinking Man* [1957].) We are merely spectators; we watch.

But in science fiction films, unlike horror films, there is not much horror. Suspense, shocks, surprises are mostly abjured in favor of a steady, inexorable plot. Science fiction films invite a dispassionate, aesthetic view of destruction and violence—a *technological* view. Things, objects, machinery play a major role in these films. A greater range of ethical values is embodied in the décor of these films than in the people. Things, rather than the helpless humans, are the locus of values because we experience them, rather than people, as the sources of power. According to science fiction films, man is naked without his artifacts. *They* stand for different values, they are potent, they are what get destroyed, and they are the indispensable tools for the repulse of the alien invaders or the repair of the damaged environment.

The science fiction films are strongly moralistic. The standard message is the one about the proper, or humane, use of science, versus the mad, obsessional use of science. This message the science fiction films share in common with the classic horror films of the 1930s, like *Frankenstein*, *The Mummy*, *Island of Lost Souls*, *Dr. Jekyll and Mr. Hyde*. (George Franju's brilliant *Les Yeux Sans Visage* [1959], called here *The Horror Chamber of Doctor Faustus*, is a more recent example.) In the horror films, we have the mad or obsessed or misguided scientist who pursues his experiments against good advice to the contrary, creates a monster or monsters, and is himself destroyed—often recognizing his folly himself, and dying

428

in the successful effort to destroy his own creation. One science fiction equivalent of this is the scientist, usually a member of a team, who defects to the planetary invaders because "their" science is more advanced than "ours."

This is the case in *The Mysterians*, and, true to form, the renegade sees his error in the end, and from within the Mysterian spaceship destroys it and himself. In *This Island Earth* (1955), the inhabitants of the beleaguered planet Metaluna propose to conquer earth, but their project is foiled by a Metalunan scientist named Exeter who, having lived on earth a while and learned to love Mozart, cannot abide such viciousness. Exeter plunges his spaceship into the ocean after returning a glamorous pair (male and female) of American physicists to earth. Metaluna dies. In *The Fly* (1958), the hero, engrossed in his basement-laboratory experiments on a matter-transmitting machine, uses himself as a subject, exchanges head and one arm with a housefly which had accidentally gotten into the machine, becomes a monster, and with his last shred of human will destroys his laboratory and orders his wife to kill him. His discovery, for the good of mankind, is lost.

Being a clearly labeled species of intellectual, scientists in science fiction films are always liable to crack up or go off the deep end. In *Conquest of Space* (1955), the scientist-commander of an international expedition to Mars suddenly acquires scruples about the blasphemy involved in the undertaking, and begins reading the Bible mid-journey instead of attending to his duties. The commander's son, who is his junior officer and always addresses his father as "General," is forced to kill the old man when he tries to prevent the ship from landing on Mars. In this film, both sides of the ambivalence toward scientists are given voice. Generally, for a scientific enterprise to be treated entirely sympathetically in these films, it needs the certificate of utility. Science, viewed without ambivalence, means an efficacious response to danger. Disinterested intellectual curiosity rarely appears in any form other than caricature, as a maniacal dementia that cuts one off from normal human relations. But this suspicion is usually directed at the scientist rather than his work. The creative scientist may become a martyr to his own discovery, through an accident or by pushing things too far. But the implication remains that other men, less imaginative—in short, technicians—could have administered the same discovery better and more safely. The most ingrained contemporary mistrust of the intellect is visited, in these movies, upon the scientist-as-intellectual.

The message that the scientist is one who releases forces which, if not controlled for good, could destroy man himself seems innocuous enough. One of the oldest images of the scientist is Shakespeare's Prospero, the overdetached scholar forcibly retired from society to a desert island, only partly in control of the magic forces in which he dabbles. Equally classic is the figure of the scientist as satanist (*Doctor Faustus*, and stories of Poe and Hawthorne). Science is magic, and man has always known that there is black magic as well as white. But it is not enough to remark that contemporary attitudes—as reflected in science fiction films—remain ambivalent, that the scientist is treated as both satanist and savior. The proportions have changed, because of the new context in which the old admiration and fear of the scientist are located. For his sphere of influence is no longer local, himself or his immediate community. It is planetary, cosmic.

One gets the feeling, particularly in the Japanese films but not only there, that a mass trauma exists over the use of nuclear weapons and the possibility of future nuclear wars. Most of the science fiction films bear witness to this trauma, and, in a way, attempt to exorcise it.

The accidental awakening of the super-destructive monster who has slept in the earth since prehistory is, often, an obvious metaphor for the Bomb. But there are many explicit references as well. In *The Mysterians*, a probe ship from the planet Mysteroid has landed on earth, near Tokyo. Nuclear warfare having been practiced on Mysteroid for centuries (their civilization is "more advanced than ours"), ninety percent of those now born on the planet have to be destroyed at birth, because of defects caused by the huge amounts of Strontium 90 in their diet. The Mysterians have come to earth to marry earth women, and possibly to take over our relatively uncontaminated planet. . . . In *The Incredible Shrinking Man*, the John Doe hero is the victim of a gust of radiation which blows over the water, while he is out boating with his wife; the radiation causes him to grow smaller and smaller, until at the end of the movie he steps through the fine mesh of a window screen to become "the infinitely small." . . . In *Rodan*, a horde of monstrous carnivorous prehistoric insects, and finally a pair of giant flying reptiles (the prehistoric Archeopteryx), are hatched from dormant eggs in the depths of a mine shaft by the impact of nuclear test explosions, and go on to destroy a good part of the world before they are felled by the molten lava of a volcanic eruption. . . . In the English film, *The Day the Earth Caught Fire*, two simultaneous hydrogen bomb tests by the United States and Russia change by 11 degrees the tilt of the earth on its axis and alter the earth's orbit so that it begins to approach the sun.

Radiation casualties—ultimately, the conception of the whole world as a casualty of nuclear testing and nuclear warfare—is the most ominous of all the notions with which science fiction films deal. Universes become expendable. Worlds become contaminated, burnt out, exhausted, obsolete. In *Rocketship X-M* (1950) explorers from the earth land on Mars, where they learn that atomic warfare has destroyed Martian civilization. In George Pal's *The War of the Worlds* (1953), reddish spindly alligator-skinned creatures from Mars invade the earth because their planet is becoming too cold to be inhabitable. In *This Island Earth*, also American, the planet Metaluna, whose population has long ago been driven underground by warfare, is dying under the missile attacks of an enemy planet. Stocks of uranium, which power the force field shielding Metaluna, have been used up; and an unsuccessful expedition is sent to earth to enlist earth scientists to devise new sources for nuclear power. In Joseph Losey's *The Damned* (1961), nine icy-cold radioactive children are being reared by a fanatical scientist in a dark cave on the English coast to be the only survivors of the inevitable nuclear Armageddon.

There is a vast amount of wishful thinking in science fiction films, some of it touching, some of it depressing. Again and again, one detects the hunger for a "good war," which poses no moral problems, admits of no moral qualifications. The imagery of science fiction films will satisfy the most bellicose addict of war films, for a lot of the satisfactions of war films pass, untransformed, into science fiction films. Examples: the dogfights between earth "fighter rockets" and alien spacecraft in the *Battle in Outer Space* (1960); the escalating firepower in the successive assaults upon the invaders in *The Mysterians*, which Dan Talbot correctly described as a non-stop holocaust; the spectacular bombardment of the underground fortress of Metaluna in *This Island Earth*.

Yet at the same time the bellicosity of science fiction films is neatly channeled into the yearning for peace, or for at least peaceful coexistence. Some scientist generally takes sententious note of the fact that it took the planetary invasion to make the warring nations of the earth come to their senses and suspend their own conflicts. One of the main themes of many science fiction films—the color ones usually, because they have the budget and resources to develop the military spectacle—is this UN fantasy, a fantasy of united warfare. (The same wishful UN theme cropped up in a recent spectacular which is not science fiction, *Fifty-Five Days in Peking* [1963]. There, topically enough, the Chinese, the Boxers, play the role of Martian invaders who unite the earthmen, in this case the United States, England, Russia, France, Germany, Italy, and Japan.) A great enough disaster cancels all enmities and calls upon the utmost concentration of earth resources.

Science—technology—is conceived of as the great unifier. Thus the science fiction films also project a Utopian fantasy. In the classic models of Utopian thinking—Plato's Republic, Campanella's City of the Sun, More's Utopia, Swift's land of the Houyhnhnms, Voltaire's Eldorado—society had worked out a perfect consensus. In these societies reasonableness had achieved an unbreakable supremacy over the emotions. Since no disagreement or social conflict was intellectually plausible, none was possible. As in Melville's *Typee*, "they all think the same." The universal rule of reason meant universal agreement. It is interesting, too, that societies in which reason was pictured as totally ascendant were also traditionally pictured as having an ascetic or materially frugal and economically simple mode of life. But in the Utopian world community projected by science fiction films, totally pacified and ruled by scientific consensus, the demand for simplicity of material existence would be absurd.

Yet alongside the hopeful fantasy of moral simplification and international unity embodied in the science fiction films lurk the deepest anxieties about contemporary existence. I don't mean only the very real trauma of the Bomb—that it has been used, that there

432

are enough now to kill everyone on earth many times over, that those new bombs may very well be used. Besides these new anxieties about physical disaster, the prospect of universal mutilation and even annihilation, the science fiction films reflect powerful anxieties about the condition of the individual psyche.

For science fiction films may also be described as a popular mythology for the contemporary *negative* imagination about the impersonal. The other-world creatures that seek to take "us" over are an "it," not a "they." The planetary invaders are usually zombie-like. Their movements are either cool, mechanical, or lumbering, blobby. But it amounts to the same thing. If they are non-human in form, they proceed with an absolutely regular, unalterable movement (unalterable save by destruction). If they are human in form—dressed in space suits, etc.—then they obey the most rigid military discipline, and display no personal characteristics whatsoever. And it is this regime of emotionlessness, of impersonality, of regimentation, which they will impose on the earth if they are successful. "No more love, no more beauty, no more pain," boasts a converted earthling in *The Invasion of the Body Snatchers* (1956). The half-earthling, half-alien children in *The Children of the Damned* (1960) are absolutely emotionless, move as a group and understand each others' thoughts, and are all prodigious intellects. They are the wave of the future, man in his next stage of development.

These alien invaders practice a crime which is worse than murder. They do not simply kill the person. They obliterate him. In *The War of the Worlds*, the ray which issues from the rocket ship disintegrates all persons and objects in its path, leaving no trace of them but a light ash. In Honda's *The H-Man* (1959), the creeping blob melts all flesh with which it comes in contact. If the blob, which looks like a huge hunk of red Jello and can crawl across floors and up and down walls, so much as touches your bare foot, all that is left of you is a heap of clothes on the floor. (A more articulated, size-multiplying blob is the villain in the English film *The Creeping Unknown* [1956].) In another version of this fantasy, the body is preserved but the person is entirely reconstituted as the automatized servant or agent of the alien powers. This is, of course, the vampire fantasy in new dress. The person is really dead, but he doesn't know it. He is "undead," he has become an "unperson." It

433

happens to a whole California town in *The Invasion of the Body Snatchers*, to several earth scientists in *This Island Earth*, and to assorted innocents in *It Came From Outer Space*, *Attack of the Puppet People* (1958), and *The Brain Eaters* (1958). As the victim always backs away from the vampire's horrifying embrace, so in science fiction films the person always fights being "taken over"; he wants to retain his humanity. But once the deed has been done, the victim is eminently satisfied with his condition. He has not been converted from human amiability to monstrous "animal" bloodlust (a metaphoric exaggeration of sexual desire), as in the old vampire fantasy. No, he has simply become far more efficient—the very model of technocratic man, purged of emotions, volitionless, tranquil, obedient to all orders. (The dark secret behind human nature used to be the upsurge of the animal—as in *King Kong*. The threat to man, his availability to dehumanization, lay in his own animality. Now the danger is understood as residing in man's ability to be turned into a machine.)

The rule, of course, is that this horrible and irremediable form of murder can strike anyone in the film except the hero. The hero and his family, while greatly threatened, always escape this fate and by the end of the film the invaders have been repulsed or destroyed. I know of only one exception, *The Day That Mars Invaded Earth* (1963), in which after all the standard struggles the scientist-hero, his wife, and their two children are "taken over" by the alien invaders—and that's that. (The last minutes of the film show them being incinerated by the Martians' rays and their ash silhouettes flushed down their empty swimming pool, while their simulacra drive off in the family car.) Another variant but upbeat switch on the rule occurs in *The Creation of the Humanoids* (1964), where the hero discovers at the end of the film that he, too, has been turned into a metal robot, complete with highly efficient and virtually indestructible mechanical insides, although he didn't know it and detected no difference in himself. He learns, however, that he will shortly be upgraded into a "humanoid" having all the properties of a real man.

Of all the standard motifs of science fiction films, this theme of dehumanization is perhaps the most fascinating. For, as I have indicated, it is scarcely a black-and-white situation, as in the old vampire films. The attitude of the science fiction films toward depersonalization is mixed. On the one hand, they deplore it as the ultimate horror. On the other hand, certain characteristics of the dehumanized invaders, modulated and disguised—such as the ascendancy of reason over feelings, the idealization of teamwork and the consensus-creating activities of science, a marked degree of moral simplification—are precisely traits of the savior-scientist. It is interesting that when the scientist in these films is treated negatively, it is usually done through the portrayal of an individual scientist who holes up in his laboratory and neglects his fiancée or his loving wife and children, obsessed by his daring and dangerous experiments. The scientist as a loyal member of a team, and therefore considerably less individualized, is treated quite respectfully.

There is absolutely no social criticism, of even the most implicit kind, in science fiction films. No criticism, for example, of the conditions of our society which create the impersonality and dehumanization which science fiction fantasies displace onto the influence of an alien It. Also, the notion of science as a social activity, interlocking with social and political interests, is unacknowledged. Science is simply either adventure (for good or evil) or a technical response to danger. And, typically, when the fear of science is paramount—when science is conceived of as black magic rather than white—the evil has no attribution beyond that of the perverse will of an individual scientist. In science fiction films the antithesis of black magic and white is drawn as a split between technology, which is beneficent, and the errant individual will of a lone intellectual.

Thus, science fiction films can be looked at as thematically central allegory, replete with standard modern attitudes. The theme of depersonalization (being "taken over") which I have been talking about is a new allegory reflecting the age-old awareness of man that, sane, he is always perilously close to insanity and unreason. But there is something more here than just a recent, popular image which expresses man's perennial, but largely unconscious, anxiety about his sanity. The image derives most of its power from a supplementary and historical anxiety, also not experienced *consciously* by most people, about the depersonalizing conditions of modern urban life. Similarly, it is not enough to note that science fiction allegories are one of the new myths about—that is, one of the ways of accommodating to and negating—the perennial human anxiety

435

about death. (Myths of heaven and hell, and of ghosts, had the same function.) For, again, there is a historically specifiable twist which intensifies the anxiety. I mean, the trauma suffered by everyone in the middle of the 20th century when it became clear that, from now on to the end of human history, every person would spend his individual life under the threat not only of individual death, which is certain, but of something almost insupportable psychologically—collective incineration and extinction which could come at any time, virtually without warning.

From a psychological point of view, the imagination of disaster does not greatly differ from one period in history to another. But from a political and moral point of view, it does. The expectation of the apocalypse may be the occasion for a radical disaffiliation from society, as when thousands of Eastern European Jews in the 17th century, hearing that Sabbatai Zevi had been proclaimed the Messiah and that the end of the world was imminent, gave up their homes and businesses and began the trek to Palestine. But people take the news of their doom in diverse ways. It is reported that in 1945 the populace of Berlin received without great agitation the news that Hitler had decided to kill them all, before the Allies arrived, because they had not been worthy enough to win the war. We are, alas, more in the position of the Berliners of 1945 than of the Jews of 17th century Eastern Europe; and our response is closer to theirs, too. What I am suggesting is that the imagery of disaster in science fiction is above all the emblem of an *inadequate response*. I don't mean to bear down on the films for this. They themselves are only a sampling, stripped of sophistication, of the inadequacy of most people's response to the unassimilable terrors that infect their consciousness. The interest of the films, aside from their considerable amount of cinematic charm, consists in this intersection between a naïve and largely debased commercial art product and the most profound dilemmas of the contemporary situation.

Ours is indeed an age of extremity. For we live under continual threat of two equally fearful, but seemingly opposed, destinies: unremitting banality and inconceivable terror. It is fantasy, served out in large rations by the popular arts, which allows most people to cope with these twin specters. For one job that fantasy can do is to lift us out of the unbearably humdrum and to distract us from terrors—real or anticipated—by an escape into exotic, dangerous situations which have last-minute happy endings. But another of the things that fantasy can do is to normalize what is psychologically unbearable, thereby inuring us to it. In one case, fantasy beautifies the world. In the other, it neutralizes it.

The fantasy in science fiction films does both jobs. The films reflect world-wide anxieties, and they serve to allay them. They inculcate a strange apathy concerning the processes of radiation, contamination, and destruction which I for one find haunting and depressing. The naïve level of the films neatly tempers the sense of otherness, of alien-ness, with the grossly familiar. In particular, the dialogue of most science fiction films, which is of a monumental but often touching banality, makes them wonderfully, unintentionally funny. Lines like "Come quickly, there's a monster in my bathtub," "We must do something about this," "Wait, Professor. There's someone on the telephone," "But that's incredible," and the old American stand-by, "I hope it works!" are hilarious in the context of picturesque and deafening holocaust. Yet the films also contain something that is painful and in deadly earnest.

There is a sense in which all these movies are in complicity with the abhorrent. They neutralize it, as I have said. It is no more, perhaps, than the way all art draws its audience into a circle of complicity with the thing represented. But in these films we have to do with things which are (quite literally) unthinkable. Here, "thinking about the unthinkable"—not in the way of Herman Kahn, as a subject for calculation, but as a subject for fantasy—becomes, however inadvertently, itself a somewhat questionable act from a moral point of view. The films perpetuate clichés about identity, volition, power, knowledge, happiness, social consensus, guilt, responsibility which are, to say the least, not serviceable in our present extremity. But collective nightmares cannot be banished by demonstrating that they are, intellectually and morally, fallacious. This nightmare—the one reflected, in various registers, in the science fiction films—is too close to our reality.

JAMES AGEE
COMEDY'S GREATEST ERA

In the language of screen comedians four of the main grades of laugh are the titter, the yowl, the belly laugh and the boffo. The titter is just a titter. The yowl is a runaway titter. Anyone who has ever had the pleasure knows all about a belly laugh. The boffo is the laugh that kills. An ideally good gag, perfectly constructed and played, would bring the victim up this ladder of laughs by cruelly controlled degrees to the top rung, and would then proceed to wobble, shake, wave and brandish the ladder until he groaned for mercy. Then, after the shortest possible time out for recuperation, he would feel the first wicked tickling of the comedian's whip once more and start up *a new ladder*.

The reader can get a fair enough idea of the current state of screen comedy by asking himself how long it has been since he has had that treatment. The best of comedies these days hand out plenty of titters and once in a while it is possible to achieve a yowl without overstraining. Even those who have never seen anything better must occasionally have the feeling, as they watch the current run or, rather, trickle of screen comedy, that they are having to make a little cause for laughter go an awfully long way. And anyone who has watched screen comedy over the past ten or fifteen years is bound to realize that it has quietly but steadily deteriorated. As for those happy atavists who remember silent comedy in its heyday and the belly laughs and boffos that went with it, they have something close to an absolute standard by which to measure the deterioration.

When a modern comedian gets hit on the head, for example, the most he is apt to do is look sleepy. When a silent comedian got hit on the head he seldom let it go so flatly. He realized a broad license, and a ruthless discipline within that license. It was his business to be as funny as possible physically, without the help or hindrance of words. So he gave us a figure of speech, or rather of vision, for loss of consciousness. In other words he gave us a poem, a kind of poem, moreover, that everybody understands. The least he might do was to straighten up stiff as a plank and fall over backward with such skill that his whole length seemed to slap the floor at the same instant. Or he might make a cadenza of it — look vague, smile like an angel, roll up his eyes, lace his fingers, thrust his hands palms downward as far as they would go, hunch his shoulders, rise on tiptoe, prance ecstatically in narrowing circles until, with tallow knees, he sank down the vortex of his dizziness to the floor and there signified nirvana by kicking his heels twice, like a swimming frog.

Startled by a cop, this same comedian might grab his hatbrim with both hands and yank it down over his ears, jump high in the air, come to earth in a split violent enough to telescope his spine, spring thence into a coattail-flattening sprint and dwindle at rocket speed to the size of a gnat along the grand, forlorn perspective of some lazy back boulevard.

Those are fine clichés from the language of silent comedy in its infancy. The man who could handle them properly combined several of the more difficult accomplishments of the *acrobat*, the *dancer*, the *clown* and the *mime*. Some very gifted comedians, unforgettably Ben Turpin, had an immense vocabulary of these clichés and were in part so lovable because they were deep conservative classicists and never tried to break away from them. The still more gifted men, of course, simplified and invented, finding out new and much deeper uses for the idiom. They learned to show emotion through it, and comic psychology, more eloquently than most language has ever managed to, and they discovered beauties of comic motion which are hopelessly beyond reach of words.

It is hard to find a theater these days where a comedy is playing; in the days of the silents it was equally hard to find a theater which was not showing one. The laughs today are pitifully few, far between, shallow, quiet and short. They almost never build, as they

439

used to, into something combining the jabbering frequency of a machine gun with the delirious momentum of a roller coaster. Saddest of all, there are few comedians now below middle age and there are none who seem to learn much from picture to picture, or to try anything new.

To put it unkindly, the only thing wrong with screen comedy today is that it takes place on a screen which talks. Because it talks, the only comedians who ever mastered the screen cannot work, for they cannot combine their comic style with talk. Because there is a screen, talking comedians are trapped into a continual exhibition of their inadequacy as screen comedians on a surface as big as the side of a barn.

At the moment, as for many years, the chances to see silent comedy are rare. There is a smattering of it on television—too often treated as something quaintly archaic, to be laughed at, not with. Some two hundred comedies—long and short—can be rented for home projection. And a lucky minority has access to the comedies in the collection of New York's Museum of Modern Art, which is still incomplete but which is probably the best in the world. In the near future, however, something of this lost art will return to regular theaters. A thick straw in the wind is the big business now being done by a series of revivals of W. C. Field's memorable movies, a kind of comedy more akin to the old silent variety than anything which is being made today. Mack Sennett now is preparing a sort of potpourri variety show called *Down Memory Lane* made up out of his old movies, featuring people like Fields and Bing Crosby when they were movie beginners, but including also interludes from silents. Harold Lloyd has re-released *Movie Crazy*, a talkie, and plans to revive four of his best silent comedies, *Grandma's Boy*, *Safety Last*, *Speedy* and *The Freshman*. Buster Keaton hopes to remake at feature length, with a minimum of dialogue, two of the funniest short comedies ever made, one about a porous homemade boat and one about a prefabricated house.

Awaiting these happy events, we will discuss here what has gone wrong with screen comedy and what, if anything, can be done about it. But mainly we will try to suggest what it was like in its glory in the years from 1912 to 1930, as practiced by the employees of Mack Sennett, the father of American screen comedy, and by the four most eminent masters: Charlie Chaplin, Harold Lloyd, the late Harry Langdon and Buster Keaton.

440

Mack Sennett made two kinds of comedy: parody laced with slapstick, and plain slapstick. The parodies were the unceremonious burial of a century of hamming, including the new hamming in serious movies, and nobody who has missed Ben Turpin in *A Small Town Idol*, or kidding Erich von Stroheim in *Three Foolish Weeks* or as *The Shriek of Araby*, can imagine how rough parody can get and still remain subtle and roaringly funny. The plain slapstick, at its best, was even better: a profusion of hearty young women in disconcerting bathing suits, frisking around with a gaggle of insanely incompetent policemen and of equally certifiable male civilians sporting museum-piece mustaches. All these people zipped and caromed about the pristine world of the screen as jazzily as a convention of water bugs. Words can hardly suggest how energetically they collided and bounced apart, meeting in full gallop around the corner of a house; how hard and how often they fell on their backsides; or with what fantastically adroit clumsiness they got themselves fouled up in folding ladders, garden hoses, tethered animals and each other's headlong cross-purposes. The gestures were ferociously emphatic; not a line or motion of the body was wasted or inarticulate. The reader may remember how splendidly upright wandlike old Ben Turpin could stand for a Renunciation Scene, with his lampshade mustache twittering and his sparrowy chest stuck out and his head flung back like Paderewski assaulting a climax and the long babyish back hair trying to look lionlike, while his Adam's apple, an orange in a Christmas stocking, pumped with noble emotion. Or huge Mack Swain, who looked like a hairy mushroom, rolling his eyes in a manner patented by French romantics and gasping in some dubious ectasy. Or Louise Fazenda, the perennial farmer's daughter and the perfect low-comedy housemaid, primping her spit curl; and how her hair tightened a good-looking face into the incarnation of rampant gullibility. Or snouty James Finlayson, gleefully foreclosing a mortgage, with his look of eternally tasting a spoiled pickle. Or Chester Conklin, a myopic and inebriated little walrus stumbling around in outsize pants. Or Fatty Arbuckle, with his cold eye and his loose, serene smile, his silky manipulation of his bulk and his satanic marksmanship with pies (he was ambidextrous and could simultaneously blind two people in opposite directions).

The intimate tastes and secret hopes of these poor ineligible dunces were ruthlessly exposed whenever a hot stove, an electric fan or a bulldog took a dislike to their outer garments: agonizingly elaborate drawers, worked up on some lonely evening out of some Godforsaken lace curtain; or men's underpants with big round black spots on them. The Sennett sets—delirious wallpaper, megalomaniacally scrolled iron beds, Grand Rapids *in extremis*—outdid even the underwear. It was their business, after all, to kid the squalid braggadocio which infested the domestic interiors of the period, and that was almost beyond parody. These comedies told their stores to the unaided eye, and by every means possible they screamed to it. That is one reason for the India ink silhouettes of the cops, and for convicts and prison bars and their shadows in hard sunlight, and for bare-footed husbands, in tigerish pajamas, reacting like dervishes to stepped-on tacks.

The early silent comedians never strove for or consciously thought of anything which could be called artistic "form," but they achieved it. For Sennett's rival, Hal Roach, Leo McCarey once devoted almost the whole of a Laurel and Hardy two-reeler to pie throwing. The first pies were thrown thoughtfully, almost philosophically. Then innocent bystanders began to get caught into the vortex. At full pitch it was Armageddon. But everything was calculated so nicely that until late in the picture, when havoc took over, every pie made its special kind of point and piled on its special kind of laugh.

Sennett's comedies were just a shade faster and fizzier than life. According to legend (and according to Sennett) he discovered the tempo proper to screen comedy when a green cameraman, trying to save money, cranked too slow. Realizing the tremendous drumlike power of mere motion to exhilarate, he gave inanimate objects a mischievous life of their own, broke every law of nature the tricked camera would serve him for and made the screen dance like a witches' Sabbath. The thing one is surest of all to remember is how toward the end of nearly every Sennett comedy, a chase (usually called the "rally") built up such a majestic trajectory of pure anarchic motion that bathing girls, cops, comics, dogs, cats, babies, automobiles, locomotives, innocent bystanders, sometimes what seemed like a whole city, an entire civilization, were hauled along head over heels in the wake of that energy like dry leaves following an express train.

"Nice" people, who shunned all movies in the early days, con-

demned the Sennett comedies as vulgar and naïve. But millions
of less pretentious people loved their sincerity and sweetness, their
wild-animal innocence and glorious vitality. They could not put
these feelings into words, but they flocked to the silents. The reader
who gets back deep enough into that world will probably even
remember the theater: the barefaced honky-tonk and the waltzes
by Waldteufel, slammed out on a mechanical piano; the searing
redolence of peanuts and demirep perfumery, tobacco and feet
and sweat; the laughter of unrespectable people having a hell of
a fine time, laughter as violent and steady and deafening as standing
under a waterfall.

Sennett wheedled his first financing out of a couple of ex-bookies
to whom he was already in debt. He took his comics out of music
halls, burlesque, vaudeville, circuses and limbo, and through them
he tapped in on that great pipeline of horsing and miming which
runs back unbroken through the fairs of the Middle Ages at least
to ancient Greece. He added all that he himself had learned about
the large and spurious gesture, the late decadence of the Grand
Manner, as a stage-struck boy in East Berlin, Connecticut, and
as a frustrated opera singer and actor. The only thing he claims
to have invented is the pie in the face, and he insists, "Anyone
who tells you he has discovered something new is a fool or a liar
or both."

The silent-comedy studio was about the best training school
the movies have ever known, and the Sennett studio was about
as free and easy and as fecund of talent as they came. All the major
comedians we will mention worked there, at least briefly. So did
some of the major stars of the '20s and since—notably Gloria Swan-
son, Phyllis Haver, Wallace Beery, Marie Dressler and Carole
Lombard. Directors Frank Capra, Leo McCarey and George Stevens also got their start in silent comedy; much that remains most
flexible, spontaneous and visually alive in sound movies can be
traced, through them and others, to this silent apprenticeship.
Everybody did pretty much as he pleased on the Sennett lot, and
everybody's ideas were welcome. Sennett posted no rules, and
the only thing he strictly forbade was liquor. A Sennett story conference was a most informal affair. During the early years, at least,
only the most important scenario might be jotted on the back of
an envelope. Mainly Sennett's men thrashed out a few primary

443

ideas and carried them in their heads, sure that better stuff would turn up while they were shooting, in the heat of physical action. This put quite a load on the prop man; he had to have the most improbable apparatus on hand—bombs, trick telephones, what not—to implement whatever idea might suddenly turn up. All kinds of things did—and were recklessly used. Once a low-comedy auto got out of control and killed the cameraman, but he was not visible in the shot, which was thrilling and undamaged; the audience never knew the difference.

Sennett used to hire a "wild man" to sit in on his gag conferences, whose whole job was to think up "wildies." Usually he was an all but brainless, speechless man, scarcely able to communicate his idea; but he had a totally uninhibited imagination. He might say nothing for an hour; then he'd mutter, "You take . . ." and all the relatively rational others would shut up and wait. "You take this cloud . . ." he would get out, sketching vague shapes in the air. Often he could get no further; but thanks to some kind of thought transference, saner men would take this cloud and make something of it. The wild man seems in fact to have functioned as the group's subconscious mind, the source of all creative energy. His ideas were so weird and amorphous that Sennett can no longer remember a one of them, or even how it turned out after rational processing. But a fair equivalent might be one of the best comic sequences in a Laurel and Hardy picture. It is simple enough—simple and real, in fact, as a nightmare. Laurel and Hardy are trying to move a piano across a narrow suspension bridge. The bridge is slung over a sickening chasm, between a couple of Alps. Midway they meet a gorilla.

Had he done nothing else, Sennett would be remembered for giving a start to three of the four comedians who now began to apply their sharp individual talents to this newborn language. The one whom he did not train (he was on the lot briefly but Sennett barely remembers seeing him around) wore glasses, smiled a great deal and looked like the sort of eager young man who might have quit divinity school to hustle brushes. That was Harold Lloyd. The others were grotesque and poetic in their screen characters in degrees which appear to be impossible when the magic of silence is broken. One, who never smiled, carried a face as still and sad as a daguerreotype through some of the most preposterously ingenious and visually satisfying physical comedy ever invented. That was Buster Keaton. One looked like an elderly baby and, at times, a baby dope fiend; he could do more with less than any other comedian. That was Harry Langdon. One looked like Charlie Chaplin, and he was the first man to give the silent language a soul.

When Charlie Chaplin started to work for Sennett he had chiefly to reckon with Ford Sterling, the reigning comedian. Their first picture together amounted to a duel before the assembled professionals. Sterling, by no means untalented, was a big man with a florid Teutonic style which, under this special pressure, he turned on full blast. Chaplin defeated him within a few minutes with a wink of the mustache, a hitch of the trousers, a quirk of the little finger.

With *Tillie's Punctured Romance*, in 1914, he became a major star. Soon after, he left Sennett when Sennett refused to start a landslide among the other comedians by meeting the raise Chaplin demanded. Sennett is understandably wry about it in retrospect, but he still says, "I was right at the time." Of Chaplin he says simply, "Oh well, he's just the greatest artist that ever lived." None of Chaplin's former rivals rates him much lower than that; they speak of him no more jealously than they might of God. We will try here only to suggest the essence of his supremacy. Of all comedians he worked most deeply and most shrewdly within a realization of what a human being is, and is up against. The Tramp is as centrally representative of humanity, as many-sided and as mysterious, as Hamlet, and it seems unlikely that any dancer or actor can ever have excelled him in eloquence, variety or poignancy of motion. As for pure motion, even if he had never gone on to make his magnificent feature-length comedies, Chaplin would have made his period in movies a great one singlehanded even if he had made nothing except *The Cure*, or *One A.M.* In the latter, barring one immobile taxi driver, Chaplin plays alone, as a drunk trying to get upstairs and into bed. It is a sort of inspired elaboration on a soft-shoe dance, involving an angry stuffed wildcat, small rugs on slippery floors, a Lazy Susan table, exquisite footwork on a flight of stairs, a contretemps with a huge, ferocious pendulum and the funniest and most perverse Murphy bed in movie history—

445

and, always made physically lucid, the delicately weird mental processes of a man ethereally sozzled.

Before Chaplin came to pictures people were content with a couple of gags per comedy; he got some kind of laugh every second. The minute he began to work he set standards—and continually forced them higher. Anyone who saw Chaplin eating a boiled shoe like brook trout in *The Gold Rush*, or embarrassed by a swallowed whistle in *City Lights*, has seen perfection. Most of the time, however, Chaplin got his laughter less from the gags, or from milking them in any ordinary sense, than through his genius for what may be called *inflection*—the perfect, changeful shading of his physical and emotional attitudes toward the gag. Funny as his bout with the Murphy bed is, the glances of awe, expostulation and helpless, almost whimpering desire for vengeance which he darts at this infernal machine are even better.

A painful and frequent error among tyros is breaking the comic line with a too-big laugh, then a letdown; or with a laugh which is out of key or irrelevant. The masters could ornament the main line beautifully; they never addled it. In *A Night Out* Chaplin, passed out, is hauled along the sidewalk by the scruff of his coat by staggering Ben Turpin. His toes trail; he is as supine as a sled. Turpin himself is so drunk he can hardly drag him. Chaplin comes quietly to, realizes how well he is being served by his struggling pal, and with a royally delicate gesture plucks and savors a flower.

The finest pantomime, the deepest emotion, the richest and most poignant poetry were in Chaplin's work. He could probably pantomime Bryce's *The American Commonwealth* without ever blurring a syllable and make it paralyzingly funny into the bargain. At the end of *City Lights* the blind girl who has regained her sight, thanks to the Tramp, sees him for the first time. She has imagined and anticipated him as princely, to say the least; and it has never seriously occurred to him that he is inadequate. She recognizes who he must be by his shy, confident, shining joy as he comes silently toward her. And he recognizes himself, for the first time, through the terrible changes in her face. The camera just exchanges a few quiet close-ups of the emotions which shift and intensify in each face. It is enough to shrivel the heart to see, and it is the greatest piece of acting and the highest moment in movies.

446

Harold Lloyd worked only a little while with Sennett. During most of his career he acted for another major comedy producer, Hal Roach. He tried at first to offset Chaplin's influence and establish his own individuality by playing Chaplin's exact opposite, a character named Lonesome Luke who wore clothes much too small for him and whose gestures were likewise as un-Chaplinesque as possible. But he soon realized that an opposite in itself was a kind of slavishness. He discovered his own comic identify when he saw a movie about a fighting parson: a hero who wore glasses. He began to think about those glasses day and night. He decided on horn rims because they were youthful, ultravisible on the screen and on the verge of becoming fashionable (he was to make them so). Around these large lensless horn rims he began to develop a new character, nothing grotesque or eccentric, but a fresh, believable young man who could fit into a wide variety of stories.

Lloyd depended more on story and situation than any of the other major comedians (he kept the best stable of gagmen in Hollywood, at one time hiring six); but unlike most "story" comedians he was also a very funny man from inside. He had, as he has written, "an unusually large comic vocabulary." More particularly he had an expertly expressive body and even more expressive teeth, and out of this thesaurus of smiles he could at a moment's notice blend prissiness, breeziness and asininity, and still remain tremendously likable. His movies were more extroverted and closer to ordinary life than any others of the best comedies: the vicissitudes of a New York taxi driver; the unaccepted college boy who, by desperate courage and inspired ineptitude, wins the Big Game. He was especially good at putting a very timid, spoiled or brassy young fellow through devastating embarrassments. He went through one of his most uproarious Gethsemanes as a shy country youth courting the nicest girl in town in *Grandma's Boy*. He arrived dressed "strictly up to date for the Spring of 1862," as a subtitle observed, and found that the ancient colored butler wore a similar flowered waistcoat and moldering cut-away. He got one wandering, nervous forefinger dreadfully stuck in a fancy little vase. The girl began cheerfully to try to identify that queer smell which dilated from him; Grandpa's best suit was rife with mothballs. A tenacious litter of kittens feasted off the goose grease on his home-shined shoes.

447

Lloyd was even better at the comedy of thrills. In *Safety Last*, as a rank amateur, he is forced to substitute for a human fly and to climb a medium-sized skyscraper. Dozens of awful things happen to him. He gets fouled up in a tennis net. Popcorn falls on him from a window above, and the local pigeons treat him like a cross between a lunch wagon and St. Francis of Assisi. A mouse runs up his britches leg, and the crowd below salutes his desperate dance on the window ledge with wild applause of the daredevil. A good deal of this full-length picture hangs thus by its eyelashes along the face of a building. Each new floor is like a new stanza in a poem; and the higher and more horrifying it gets, the funnier it gets.

In this movie Lloyd demonstrates beautifully his ability to do more than merely milk a gag, but to top it. (In an old, simple example of topping, an incredible number of tall men get, one by one, out of a small closed auto. After as many have clambered out as the joke will bear, one more steps out: a midget. That tops the gag. Then the auto collapses. That tops the topper.) In *Safety Last* Lloyd is driven out to the dirty end of a flagpole by a furious dog; the pole breaks and he falls, just managing to grab the minute hand of a huge clock. His weight promptly pulls the hand down from IX to VI. That would be more than enough for any ordinary comedian, but there is further logic in the situation. Now, hideously, the whole clockface pulls loose and slants from its trembling springs above the street. Getting out of difficulty with the clock, he makes still further use of the instrument by getting one foot caught in one of these obstinate springs.

A proper delaying of the ultrapredictable can of course be just as funny as a properly timed explosion of the unexpected. As Lloyd approaches the end of his horrible hegira up the side of the building in *Safety Last*, it becomes clear to the audience, but not to him, that if he raises his head another couple of inches he is going to get murderously conked by one of the four arms of a revolving wind gauge. He delays the evil moment almost interminably, with one distraction and another, and every delay is a suspense-tightening laugh; he also gets his foot nicely entangled in a rope, so that when he does get hit, the payoff of one gag sends him careening head downward through the abyss into another. Lloyd was outstanding even among the master craftsmen at setting up a gag clearly, culminating and getting out of it deftly, and linking it smoothly to the next. Harsh experience also taught him a deep and fundamental rule: Never try to get "above" the audience.

Lloyd tried it in *The Freshman*. He was to wear an unfinished, basted-together tuxedo to a college party, which would gradually fall apart as he danced. Lloyd decided to skip the pants, a low-comedy cliché, and lose just the coat. His gag men warned him. A preview proved how right they were. Lloyd had to reshoot the whole expensive sequence, build it around defective pants and climax it with the inevitable. It was one of the funniest things he ever did.

When Lloyd was still a very young man he lost about half his right hand (and nearly lost his sight) when a comedy bomb exploded prematurely. But in spite of his artificially built-out hand he continued to do his own dirty work, like all of the best comedians. The side of the building he climbed in *Safety Last* did not overhang the street, as it appears to. But the nearest landing place was a roof three floors below him, as he approached the top, and he did everything, of course, the hard way, i.e., the comic way, keeping his bottom stuck well out, his shoulders hunched, his hands and feet skidding over perdition.

If great comedy must involve something beyond laughter, Lloyd was not a great comedian. If plain laughter is any criterion—and it is a healthy counterbalance to the other—few people have equaled him, and nobody has ever beaten him.

Chaplin and Keaton and Lloyd were all more like each other, in one important way, than Harry Langdon was like any of them. Whatever else the others might be doing, they all used more or less elaborate physical comedy; Langdon showed how little of that one might use and still be a great silent-screen comedian. In his screen character he symbolized something as deeply and centrally human, though by no means as rangily so, as the Tramp. There was, of course, an immense difference in inventiveness and range of virtuosity. It seemed as if Chaplin could do literally anything, on any instrument in the orchestra. Langdon had one queerly toned, unique little reed. But out of it he could get incredible melodies.

Like Chaplin, Langdon wore a coat which buttoned on his wishbone and swung out wide below, but the effect was very different:

he seemed like an outsized baby who had begun to outgrow his clothes. The crown of his hat was rounded and the brim was turned up all around, like a little boy's hat, and he looked as if he wore diapers under his pants. His walk was that of a child which has just got sure on its feet, and his body and hands fitted that age. His face was kept pale to show off, with the simplicity of a nursery school drawing, the bright, ignorant, gentle eyes and the little twirling mouth. He had big moon cheeks, with dimples, and a Napoleonic forelock of mousy hair; the round, docile head seemed large in ratio to the cream-puff body. Twitchings of his face were signals of tiny discomforts too slowly registered by a tinier brain; quick, squirty little smiles showed his almost prehuman pleasures, his incurably premature trustfulness. He was a virtuoso of hesitations and of delicately indecisive motions, and he was particularly fine in a high wind, rounding a corner with a kind of skittering toddle, both hands nursing his hatbrim.

He was as remarkable a master as Chaplin of subtle emotional and mental process and operated much more at leisure. He once got a good three hundred feet of continuously bigger laughs out of rubbing his chest, in a crowded vehicle, with Limburger cheese, under the misapprehension that it was a cold salve. In another long scene, watching a brazen show girl change her clothes, he sat motionless, back to the camera, and registered the whole lexicon of lost innocence, shock, disapproval and disgust, with the back of his neck. His scenes with women were nearly always something special. Once a lady spy did everything in her power (under the Hays Office) to seduce him. Harry was polite, willing, even flirtatious in his little way. The only trouble was that he couldn't imagine what in the world she was leering and pawing at him for, and that he was terribly ticklish. The Mata Hari wound up foaming at the mouth.

There was also a sinister flicker of depravity about the Langdon character, all the more disturbing because babies are premoral. He had an instinct for bringing his actual adulthood and figurative babyishness into frictions as crawly as a fingernail on a slate blackboard, and he wandered into areas of strangeness which were beyond the other comedians. In a nightmare in one movie he was forced to fight a large, muscular young man; the girl Harry loved was the prize. The young man was a good boxer; Harry could scarcely lift his gloves. The contest took place in a fiercely lighted prize ring, in a prodigious pitch-dark arena. The only spectator was the girl, and she was rooting against Harry. As the fight went on, her eyes glittered ever more brightly with blood lust and, with glittering teeth, she tore her big straw hat to shreds.

Langdon came to Sennett from a vaudeville act in which he had fought a losing battle with a recalcitrant automobile. The minute Frank Capra saw him he begged Sennett to let him work with him. Langdon was almost as childlike as the character he played. He had only a vague idea of his story or even of each scene as he played it; each time he went before the camera Capra would brief him on the general situation and then, as this finest of intuitive improvisers once tried to explain his work, "I'd go into my routine." The whole tragedy of the coming of dialogue as far as these comedians were concerned—and one reason for the increasing rigidity of comedy ever since—can be epitomized in the mere thought of Harry Langdon confronted with a script.

Langdon's magic was in his innocence, and Capra took beautiful care not to meddle with it. The key to the proper use of Langdon, Capra always knew, was "the principle of the brick." "If there was a rule for writing Langdon material," he explains, "it was this: His only ally was God. Langdon might be saved by the brick falling on the cop, but it was *verboten* that he in any way motivate the brick's fall." Langdon became quickly and fantastically popular with three pictures, *Tramp, Tramp, Tramp, The Strong Man* and *Long Pants;* from then on he went downhill even faster. "The trouble was," Capra says, "that high-brow critics came around to explain his art to him. Also he developed an interest in dames. It was a pretty high life for such a little fellow." Langdon made two more pictures with highbrow writers, one of which *(Three's a Crowd)* had some wonderful passages in it, including the prize-ring nightmare; then First National canceled his contract. He was reduced to mediocre roles and two-reelers which were more rehashes of his old gags; this time around they no longer seemed funny. "He never did really understand what hit him," says Capra. "He died broke [in 1944]. And he died of a broken heart. He was the most tragic figure I ever came across in show business."

Buster Keaton started work at the age of three and a half with his parents in one of the roughest acts in vaudeville ("The Three Keatons"); Harry Houdini gave the child the name Buster in admiration for a fall he took down a flight of stairs. In his first movies Keaton teamed with Fatty Arbuckle under Sennett. He went on to become one of Metro's biggest stars and earners; a Keaton feature cost about $200,000 to make and reliably grossed $2 million. Very early in his movie career friends asked him why he never smiled on the screen. He didn't realize he didn't. He had got the deadpan habit in variety; on the screen he had merely been so hard at work it had never occurred to him there was anything to smile about. Now he tried it just once and never again. He was by his whole style and nature so much the most deeply "silent" of the silent comedians that even a smile was as deafeningly out of key as a yell. In a way his pictures are like a transcendent juggling act in which it seems that the whole universe is in exquisite flying motion and the one point of repose is the juggler's effortless, uninterested face.

Keaton's face ranked almost with Lincoln's as an early American archetype; it was haunting, handsome, almost beautiful, yet it was irreducibly funny; he improved matters by topping it off with a deadly horizontal hat, as flat and thin as a phonograph record. One can never forget Keaton wearing it, standing erect at the prow as his little boat is being launched. The boat goes grandly down the skids and, just as grandly, straight on to the bottom. Keaton never budges. The last you see of him, the water lifts the hat off the stoic head and it floats away.

No other comedian could do as much with the deadpan. He used this great, sad, motionless face to suggest various related things: a one-track mind near the track's end of pure insanity; mulish imperturbability under the wildest of circumstances; how dead a human being can get and still be alive; an awe-inspiring sort of patience and power to endure, proper to granite but uncanny in flesh and blood. Everything that he was and did bore out this rigid face and played laughs against it. When he moved his eyes, it was like seeing them move in a statue. His short-legged body was all sudden, machinelike angles, governed by a daft aplomb. When he swept a semaphorelike arm to point, you could almost hear the electrical impulse in the signal block. When he ran from a cop his transitions from accelerating walk to easy jog trot to brisk canter to headlong gallop to flogged-piston sprint— always floating, above this frenzy, the untroubled, untouchable face—were as distinct and as soberly in order as an automatic gearshift.

Keaton was a wonderfully resourceful inventor of mechanistic gags (he still spends much of his time fooling with Erector sets); as he ran afoul of locomotives, steamships, prefabricated and over-electrified houses, he put himself through some of the hardest and cleverest punishment ever designed for laughs. In *Sherlock Jr.*, boiling along on the handlebars of a motorcycle quite unaware that he has lost his driver, Keaton whips through city traffic, breaks up a tug-of-war, gets a shovelful of dirt in the face from each of a long line of Rockette-timed ditchdiggers, approaches at high speed a log which is hinged open by dynamite precisely soon enough to let him through and, hitting an obstruction, leaves the handlebars like an arrow leaving a bow, whams through the window of a shack in which the heroine is about to be violated, and hits the heavy feet first, knocking him through the opposite wall. The whole sequence is as clean in motion as the trajectory of a bullet.

Much of the charm and edge of Keaton's comedy, however, lay in the subtle leverages of expression he could work against his nominal deadpan. Trapped in the side wheel of a ferryboat, saving himself from drowning only by walking, then desperately running, inside the accelerating wheel like a squirrel in a cage, his only real concern was, obviously, to keep his hat on. Confronted by Love, he was not as deadpan as he was cracked up to be, either; there was an odd, abrupt motion of his head which suggested a horse nipping after a sugar lump.

Keaton worked strictly for laughs, but his work came from so far inside a curious and original spirit that he achieved a great deal besides, especially in his feature-length comedies. (For plain hard laughter his nineteen short comedies—the negatives of which have been lost—were even better.) He was the only major comedian who kept sentiment almost entirely out of his work, and he brought pure physical comedy to its greatest heights. Beneath his lack of emotion he was also uninsistently sardonic; deep below that, giving a disturbing tension and grandeur to the foolishness, for those who sensed it, there was in his comedy a freezing whisper not of pathos but of melancholia. With the humor, the craftsmanship and the action there was often, besides, a fine, still and sometimes dreamlike beauty. Much of his Civil War picture *The General* is within hailing distance of Mathew Brady. And there is a ghostly, unforgettable moment in *The Navigator* when, on a deserted, softly, rolling ship, all the pale doors along a deck swing open as one behind Keaton and, as one, slam shut, in a hair-raising illusion of noise.

Perhaps because "dry" comedy is so much more rare and odd than "dry" wit, there are people who never much cared for Keaton. Those who do cannot care mildly.

As soon as the screen began to talk, silent comedy was pretty well finished. The hardy and prolific Mack Sennett made the transfer; he was the first man to put Bing Crosby and W. C. Fields on the screen. But he was essentially a silent-picture man, and by the time the Academy awarded him a special Oscar for his "lasting contribution to the comedy technique of the screen" (in 1938), he was no longer active. As for the comedians we have spoken of in particular, they were as badly off as fine dancers suddenly required to appear in plays.

Harold Lloyd, whose work was most nearly realistic, naturally coped least unhappily with the added realism of speech; he made several talking comedies. But good as the best were, they were not so good as his silent work, and by the late '30s he quit acting. A few years ago he returned to play the lead (and play it beautifully) in Preston Sturges' *The Sin of Harold Diddlebock*, but this exceptional picture—which opened, brilliantly, with the closing reel of Lloyd's *The Freshman*—has not yet been generally released.

Like Chaplin, Lloyd was careful of his money; he is still rich and active. Last June, in the presence of President Truman, he became Imperial Potentate of the A.A.O.N.M.S. (Shriners). Harry Langdon, as we have said, was a broken man when sound came in.

Up to the middle '30s Buster Keaton made several feature-length pictures (with such players as Jimmy Durante, Wallace Beery and Robert Montgomery); he also made a couple of dozen talking shorts. Now and again he managed to get loose into motion, without having to talk, and for a moment or so the screen would start singing again. But his dark, dead voice, though it was in keeping with the visual character, tore his intensely silent style to bits and destroyed the illusion within which he worked. He gallantly and correctly refuses to regard himself as "retired." Besides occasional bits, spots and minor roles in Hollywood pictures, he has worked on summer stages, made talking comedies in France and Mexico and clowned in a French circus. This summer he has played the straw hats in *Three Men on a Horse*. He is planning a television program. He also has a working agreement with Metro. One of his jobs there is to construct comedy sequences for Red Skelton.

The only man who really survived the flood was Chaplin, the only one who was rich, proud and popular enough to afford to stay silent. He brought out two of his greatest nontalking comedies, *City Lights* and *Modern Times*, in the middle of an avalanche of talk, spoke gibberish and, in the closing moments, plain English in *The Great Dictator*, and at last made an all-talking picture, *Monsieur Verdoux*, creating for that purpose an entirely new character who might properly talk a blue streak. *Verdoux* is the greatest of talking comedies though so cold and savage that it had to find its public in grimly experienced Europe.

Good comedy, and some that was better than good, outlived silence, but there has been less and less of it. The talkies brought one great comedian, the late, majestically lethargic W. C. Fields, who could not possibly have worked as well in silence; he was the toughest and the most warmly human of all screen comedians, and *It's a Gift* and *The Bank Dick*, fiendishly funny and incisive white-collar comedies, rank high among the best comedies (and best movies) ever made. Laurel and Hardy, the only comedians who managed to preserve much of the large, low style of silence and who began to explore the comedy of sound, have made nothing since 1945. Walt Disney, at his best an inspired comic inventor and teller of fairy stories, lost his stride during the war and has since regained it only at moments. Preston Sturges has made brilliant, satirical comedies, but his pictures are smart, nervous comedy-dramas merely italicized with slapstick. The Marx Brothers were sidesplitters but they made their best comedies years ago. Jimmy Durante is mainly a night-club genius; Abbott and Costello are semiskilled laborers, at best; Bob Hope is a good radio comedian with a pleasing presence, but not much more, on the screen.

There is no hope that screen comedy will get much better than it is without new, gifted young comedians who really belong in movies, and without freedom for their experiments. For everyone who may appear we have one last, invidious comparison to offer as a guidepost.

One of the most popular recent comedies is Bob Hope's *The Paleface*. We take no pleasure in blackening *The Paleface*; we single it out, rather, because it is as good as we've got. Anything that is said of it here could be said, with interest, of other comedies of our time. Most of the laughs in *The Paleface* are verbal. Bob Hope is very adroit with his lines and now and then, when the words don't get in the way, he makes a good beginning as a visual comedian. But only the beginning, never the middle or the end. He is funny, for instance, reacting to a shot of violent whisky. But he does not know how to get still funnier (i.e., how to build and milk) or how to be funniest last (i.e., how to top or cap his gag). The camera has to fade out on the same old face he started with.

One sequence is promisingly set up for visual comedy. In it, Hope and a lethal local boy stalk each other all over a cow town through streets which have been emptied in fear of their duel. The gag here is that through accident and stupidity they keep just failing to find each other. Some of it is quite funny. But the fun slackens between laughs like a weak clothesline, and by all the logic of humor (which is ruthlessly logical) the biggest laugh should come at the moment, and through the way, they finally spot each other. The sequence is so weakly thought out that at that crucial moment the camera can't afford to watch them; it switches to Jane Russell.

Now we turn to a masterpiece. In *The Navigator* Buster Keaton works with practically the same gag as Hope's duel. Adrift on a ship which he believes is otherwise empty, he drops a lighted cigarette. A girl finds it. She calls out and he hears her; each then tries to find the other. First each walks purposefully down the long, vacant starboard deck, the girl, then Keaton, turning the corner just in time not to see each other. Next time around each of them is trotting briskly, very much in earnest; going at the same pace, they miss each other just the same. Next time around each of them is going like a bat out of hell. Again they miss. Then the camera withdraws to a point of vantage at the stern, leans its chin in its hand and just watches the whole intricate superstructure of the ship as the protagonists stroll, steal and scuttle from level to level, up, down and sidewise, always managing to miss each other by hairbreadths, in an enchantingly neat and elaborate piece of timing. There are no subsidiary gags to get laughs in this sequence and there is little loud laughter; merely a quiet and steadily increasing kind of delight. When Keaton has got all he can out of this fine modification of the movie chase he invents a fine device to bring the two together: the girl, thoroughly winded, sits down for a breather, indoors, on a plank which workmen have left across sawhorses. Keaton pauses on an upper deck, equally winded and puzzled. What follows happens in a couple of seconds at most: Air suction whips his silk topper backward down a ventilator; grabbing frantically for it, he backs against the lip of the ventilator, jackknifes and falls in backward. Instantly the camera cuts back to the girl. A topper falls through the ceiling and lands tidily, right side up, on the plank beside her. Before she can look more than startled, its owner follows, head between his knees, crushes the topper, breaks the plank with the point of his spine and proceeds to the floor. The breaking of the plank smacks Boy and Girl together.

It is only fair to remember that the silent comedians would have as hard a time playing a talking scene as Hope has playing his visual ones, and that writing and directing are as accountable for the failure as Hope himself. But not even the humblest journeyman of the silent years would have let themselves off so easily. Like the masters, they knew, and sweated to obey, the laws of their craft.

GERALD MAST
FROM THE COMIC MIND: COMEDY AND THE MOVIES

COMIC STRUCTURES

COMIC PLOTS

There are eight comic film plots, eight basic structures by which film comedies have organized their human material. The film shares six of the eight with both the drama and the novel, one of the eight with only the novel, and one seems completely indigenous to the cinema.

1. The first is the familiar plot of New Comedy—the young lovers finally wed despite the obstacles (either within themselves or external) to their union. Boy meets girl; boy loses girl; boy gets girl. Many twists and surprises have been injected into this structure— in fact, it was full of twists and surprises in its infancy with Plautus and Terence. Shakespeare used trans-sexual twists in *Twelfth Night* and *As You Like It;* in *A Midsummer Night's Dream* he twists the romantic platitude that beauty is in the eye of the beholder; in *Much Ado About Nothing* the twist is the irony that the boy and girl do not know they are the boy and girl. Shaw reversed the active and passive sexes of New Comedy in *Man and Superman.* Ionesco burlesqued boy-gets-girl in *Jack, or The Submission.* This plot, with or without unexpected wrinkles, serves as the structural model for such films as *Bringing Up Baby* (the girl is the aggressive kook), *The Marriage Circle, Adam's Rib,* and *The Awful Truth* (boy and girl happen to be husband and wife), *It Happened One Night, Trouble in Paradise, Seven Chances, The Graduate* ("the other woman" is the girl's mother), and many, many more.

Merely concluding the action with a marriage (or an implied union of the romantic couple) is not sufficient for creating a comic plot. Many non-comic films end that way—*The Birth of a Nation, Stagecoach, The 39 Steps, Way Down East, Spellbound.* But in such films the final romantic union is parenthetic to the central action—the overcoming of a series of dangerous, murderous problems. After successfully combating terrible foes, the protagonist earns both life and love as his rewards. This is the typical plot of melodrama (in more dignified terms, "action" or "adventure" films). The adventure plot is a contemporary, totally secularized descendant of the medieval romance, and such films might be truly labeled "romances." In the comic plot, however, the amorous conclusion grows directly and exclusively from amorous complications.

The next three comic plots are all distillations of elements that were combined in Aristophanic Old Comedy.

2. The film's structure can be an intentional parody or burlesque of some other film or genre of films. Aristophanes parodied Euripides; Shakespeare parodied both classical heroism and courtly romance in *Troilus and Cressida;* Fielding began by parodying Richardson in *Joseph Andrews* and heroic tragedy in *The Tragedy of Tragedies* and *The Covent Garden Tragedy;* Ionesco parodies the well-made *boulevard* play in *The Bald Soprano.* In films there were specific parodies of silent hits—*The Iron Nag, The Halfback of Notre Dame.* Mack Sennett parodied melodrama and Griffith's last-minute rescues in *Barney Oldfield's Race for Life* and *Teddy at the Throttle.*

Parody plots flourished in the days of the one- and two-reelers. Feature-length parodies have been rarer. Keaton's *The Three Ages* is a parody of *Intolerance,* and his *Our Hospitality* parodies both the stories of the Hatfield-McCoy feuds and Griffith's last-minute rescue from the murderous falls in *Way Down East.* Many Abbott and Costello films parodied serious horror films. Woody Allen's *Take the Money and Run* is a series of parodies of film genres and styles; his *Bananas,* a series of parodies of specific films. The parodic plot is deliberately contrived and artificial; it is not an "imitation of a human action" but an imitation of an imitation. Perhaps, for this reason, it is best suited to the short form.

3. The *reductio ad absurdum* is a third kind of comic plot. A simple human mistake or social question is magnified, reducing the

action to chaos and the social question to absurdity. The typical progression of such a plot—rhythmically—is from one to infinity. Perfect for revealing the ridiculousness of social or human attitudes, such a plot frequently serves a didactic function. After all, reduction to the absurd is a form of argument. Aristophanes used it by taking a proposition (if you want peace, if you want a utopian community, if you want to speculate abstractly) and then reducing the proposition to nonsense—thereby implying some more sensible alternative.

But the *reductio ad absurdum* need not serve didactic purposes exclusively. Feydeau typically takes a small human trait—jealousy, extreme moral fastidiousness—and multiplies it to infinity. Ionesco combines the farcical and intellectual potential of the *reductio ad absurdum* in plays such as *The Lesson*—which reduces the process of education to the absurd—and *The New Tenant*—which reduces man's dependence on material objects to the absurd.

In films, too, the *reductio ad absurdum* has served as the basis for both pure farce and bitter intellectual argument. The Laurel and Hardy two-reelers are the perfect example of the *reductio ad absurdum* as pure fun—a single mistake in the opening minutes leads inexorably to final chaos. However, some of the most haunting and bitter film comedies are those which take some intellectual position and reduce it to horrifying nonsense. The reason both *Monsieur Verdoux* and *Doctor Strangelove* are comedies *structurally* (they are comedies for other reasons, too), despite their emphasis on deaths and horrors, is that they share this common comic shape. *Verdoux* reduces to the absurd the proposition that murder serves socially useful and emotionally necessary purposes; *Strangelove* deflates the proposition that man needs atomic weapons and military minds to preserve the human race. There is also an implied reduction to the absurd in Renoir's *The Rules of the Game*, although that is not its primary structural principle. Renoir's film is built on the proposition that good form is more important than sincere expressions of feeling. He reduces the proposition to death.

4. The structural principle of this Renoir film is more leisurely, analytical, and discursive than the taut, unidirectional, rhythmically accelerating *reductio ad absurdum*. This structure might be described as an investigation of the workings of a particular so-

ciety, comparing the responses of one social group or class with those of another, contrasting people's different responses to the same stimuli and similar responses to different stimuli. Such plots are usually multileveled, containing two, three, or even more parallel lines of action. The most obvious examples of such plots are Shakespeare's comedies in which love *(A Midsummer Night's Dream)*, deceptive appearances *(Much Ado About Nothing)*, or the interrelation of human conduct and social environment *(As You Like It)* is examined from several social and human perspectives. Many Restoration comedies (Congreve's *Love for Love*, Wycherley's *The Country Wife*) and their descendants (Sheridan's *The Rivals*) are constructed on similar principles. In films, this multilevel social analysis serves as the basis of many Renoir films *(Boudu sauvé des eaux, The Rules of the Game, The Golden Coach)*, of Clair's *À Nous la liberté*, Carné's *Bizarre, Bizarre*, and Chaplin's *The Great Dictator*. In films there is something very French about this structure.

5. The fifth comic-film structure is familiar in narrative fiction but very uncommon on the stage. It is unified by the central figure of the film's action. The film follows him around, examining his responses and reactions to various situations. This is the familiar journey of the picaresque hero—Don Quixote, Huck Finn, Augie March—whose function is to bounce off the people and events around him, often, in the process, revealing the superiority of his comic bouncing to the social and human walls he hits.

This form is probably less suited to the stage simply because its sprawling structure requires a series of imaginative encounters for the *picaro* that could not be effectively depicted on a stage, given the theater's boundaries of time and space. But the film, completely free from such tyrannies (one of the points at which the film is closer to narrative fiction than to the drama), can give the *picaro* as interesting and believable a series of opponents as any novelist. The most outstanding film *picaro* is, of course, Chaplin. Significantly, he begins to use the picaresque structure as he begins to mature with the Essanay films of 1915 (very few of his Keystones use it) and keeps it until *Modern Times* (1936), after which he drops it. The other major film *picaro* is Jacques Tati. But few of Chaplin's silent rivals ever used the loose, personality-centered structure: Langdon (traces of the picaresque only in *Tramp, Tramp, Tramp* and *The Strong Man*), Keaton (perhaps in a few two-reelers but not in the features), Lloyd (never the *picaro;* always up to his neck in a very clear, goal-oriented plot). The picaresque structure also shapes such bitter comedies as *Nights of Cabiria* and *A Clockwork Orange.*

6. The next comic-film plot is one that would seem to have no analogue in any other fictional form. The structure might best be described with a musical term—"riffing." But it could as easily be called "goofing," or "miscellaneous bits," or "improvised and anomalous gaggery." This was the structure of most of Chaplin's Keystones, simply because it was one of the two major Sennett structures (parody was the other). The Sennett riffing films take some initial situation—perhaps a place (a beach, a lake, a field), an event (auto races, a dance contest, a circus), an object (Tin Lizzies), an animal (lion), and then run off a series of gags that revolve around this central situation. The only sources of such a film's unity (other than the place, event, thing, or animal) are the performers' tendency to reappear from gag to gag and the film's unceasing rhythmic motion. Pace and motion become unifying principles in themselves. Perhaps the riffing film has no literary analogue because no other form (dance and music would be the closest) is so dependent on pace, motion, and physical energy. The outstanding examples of more recent riffing films are the two Richard Lester-Beatles pictures, *A Hard Day's Night* and *Help,* Louis Malle's *Zazie dans le métro,* and the Woody Allen comedies, which riff with a fairly anomalous collection of parodies and jokes.

Each of these six plots usually produces a comedy, though there are obvious exceptions. *King Lear* uses the multi-plot structure (4) for tragic ends, and many Elizabethan and Jacobean plays (*Doctor Faustus, The Changeling,* Beaumont and Fletcher's) interweave multiple lines of action for non-comic effects. In films, *Children of Paradise, Ship of Fools,* and *The Magnificent Ambersons* might be described as non-comic films with multilevel structures. And the amorous plot of boy-eventually-gets-girl (1) can serve as the basis of weepy melodramas as well as comedies. The difference between Lubitsch's *The Merry Widow* (1934) and von Stroheim's (1925) is the difference between a comic and non-comic use of the same structural pattern.

Finally, there are two other plots that have been used as frequently for non-comic ends as comic ones.

7. One is the kind that is also typical of melodramatic (or adventure or "romance") films. The central character either chooses to perform or is forced to accept a difficult task, often risking his life in the process. The plot then traces his successful accomplishment of the task, often with his winning the battle, the girl, and the pot of gold at the end of the rainbow. Non-comic versions of this plot include *My Darling Clementine, North by Northwest, Rio Bravo, Tol'able David, The Maltese Falcon, The Thief of Bagdad* (1924), and thousands of other films—many of which contain comic elements and touches. Comic versions of the plot include *The General, The Navigator* (indeed, most of Keaton), *The Kid Brother, The Mollycoddle, The Lavender Hill Mob,* and many others. The difference between a comic and non-comic use of the plot depends entirely on whether the film creates a comic "climate" in the interest of arousing laughter or a non-comic one in the interest of arousing suspense, excitement, and expectation.

8. The same distinction holds true for the final plot form of comic films—the story of the central figure who eventually discovers an error he has been committing in the course of his life. This is, of course, the plot of *Oedipus Rex, Macbeth, Othello,* and any prototypic Aristotelian-Sophoclean tragedy. But it is also the plot of *Tartuffe, The Plain Dealer,* and *Major Barbara.* In films, the plot serves comically in *Mr. Smith Goes to Washington, The Freshman, Sullivan's Travels, Hail the Conquering Hero* (indeed, much of Sturges), *The Apartment* (and much of Wilder), and many others. The comic versions of the plot take place in a comic climate, which is a function of who makes the discovery, what the discovery is, and what the consequences of the discovery are.

COMIC CLIMATE

This term condenses the notion that an artist builds signs into a work to let us know that he considers it a comedy and wishes us to take it as such. It is functional to sidestep theory on the premise that we pretty much know what *a* comedy is even if we do not know what Comedy is. What are the signs by which we recognize that we are in the presence of a comic work?

Here Elder Olson's concept of "worthlessness" is useful. A worthless action is one that we do not take seriously, that we consider

trivial and unimportant rather than a matter of extreme importance, of life and death.* Now, if comedy does indeed depict matters of life and death, then the reason such a depiction remains
comic is because it *has not been handled as if it were* a matter of life
and death. This device will, at some point, lead the audience to reflect that it has been lulled into taking the supremely serious as
trivial—a reflection that is precisely the aim of much contemporary
comedy. But whether a comedy asks for such reflection or not, the
comic craftsman plants a series of signs that lets us know the action
is taking place in a comic world, that it will be "fun" (even if at
some moments it will not be), that we are to enjoy and not to
worry.

1. When the film begins, perhaps even before it, the filmmaker
transmits cues to our responses. The first might be the title. It is
not worth making too much of titles, and obviously titles such as
The General, Modern Times, and *The Marriage Circle* do not tell
us a lot—although Bergson notes that most comedies bear generic
titles *(The Alchemist)* rather than specific names *(Macbeth)*. But
titles such as *Much Ado About Nothing, Super-Hooper-Dyne
Lizzies, Three's a Crowd, Sullivan's Travels,* and *Doctor Strangelove: or How I Learned to Stop Worrying and Love the Bomb*
tell us a good deal about what to expect from what follows.

2. The characters of the film rather quickly tell us if the climate
is comic. If a familiar comedian plays the central role, we can be
almost certain that the climate is comic (unless the filmmaker deliberately plays on our assumptions). Keaton's presence makes *The
General* take place in a comic world—despite the fact that the film
is full of adventure, suspense, war, and death. When Chaplin
dropped the picaresque journey for other plot structures, he still
used our expectations about Charlie to tell us in what light to view
the action. He first appears in *Monsieur Verdoux* trimming flowers,
showing great concern for a tiny caterpillar, his familiar mustache
turned up in an insane, amputated version of Dali's. Meanwhile the
remains of his last wife are going up in smoke (literally) in an
incinerator in the rearground of the frame. Chaplin's comically
finicky character informs us how to view the grisly activities in his

---

*Olson defines comedy as "the imitation of a worthless action . . . effecting a
katastasis of concern through the absurd."

incinerator. His familiar comic *persona* influences every reaction we have to the film, much as the sight of Will Kemp or Robert Armin must have done for audiences in the Theater or the Globe.

One-dimensional characters who represent comic types, either physically or psychologically, also line up our responses in the intended direction. Because of the pervasiveness of these types, critics have consistently identified comic character with "the base," the lowly," "the mechanical," or "the ridiculous." But such identifications are not necessarily valid. Such terms fail to fit any of the great comic film *personae*. Many comic films deliberately use inelastic, mechanical types in the minor roles and perfectly supple, non-stereotypic human beings in the major ones—just as Shakespeare did in his comedies.

3. The subject matter of the film's story might also inform us of a comic climate. Subjects such as trying to invent doughnuts without holes or participating in a cross-country walking race are necessarily comic. But if the subject matter is not intrinsically trivial, a comedy reduces important subject matter to trivia. In *Doctor Strangelove* a serious subject, the destruction of the human race, is treated as if it were no more important than inventing hole-free doughnuts. And in *Bananas*, a political assassination (a topic horrifyingly fresh in the American memory) is staged as if it were a televised sporting contest.

4. The dialogue can let us know the climate is comic—because it either is funny or is delivered in a funny, incongruous, mechanical, or some other unnatural way. The opening sequence of Preston Sturges' *Sullivan's Travels* is a breathless series of one-line jokes in which a studio chief and a young, idealistic director debate the validity of making films with a social message. The comic dialogue of this opening scene is essential to the effect of the rest of the film, which gets precariously close to the edge of bathos in its later sequences (indeed it may fall over that edge despite the opening jokes). The suave dialogue between Herbert Marshall and the waiter taking his order for supper in *Trouble in Paradise* informs us that the action and world to follow are comic, as do the subjects and manner of Cary Grant's breathlessly rapid discussion with his former wife in the opening scene of *His Girl Friday*.

5. Any hint of artistic self-consciousness—that the filmmaker knows he is making a film—can wrench us out of the illusion of the

film and let us know that the action is not to be taken seriously. Such self-consciousness can assert itself in moments of burlesque or parody of topical issues or figures, parodies of other films or film styles, in gimmicky cinematic tricks, or in any other device that reminds the audience it is watching something artificial, "worthless." *Singin' in the Rain* self-consciously parodies the story of a star's meteoric rise from obscurity to fame and fortune; *Trouble in Paradise* parodies picture-postcard romance by juxtaposing a garbage collector and a shot of romantic Venice; *Doctor Strangelove* begins with a parody of a love scene as two planes enjoy sexual intercourse to the violinic strains of "Try a Little Tenderness." One trend in recent films is to add self-conscious, intrusive manipulation of cinematic elements to non-comic films as well. Such films, while proclaiming the film event as "not real," attempt to create an intense kinetic metaphor for the feeling of an event rather than comic detachment.

6. The examples above reveal that the motion picture can use distinctly cinematic tools to create its comic or non-comic climate. What the director shoots, how he shoots and edits it, and how he underscores the pictures for the ear establish the way an audience responds. A piece of comic business at the beginning of a film can color our responses for the next two hours—or until the film informs us to alter them.* Chaplin and Lubitsch are two masters at creating hilariously informative business for the beginnings of their films. In *The Gold Rush* Charlie enters the screen world unknowingly pursued by a bear; in *City Lights* he is grandiosely unveiled as he sleeps on the statue of Civic Virtue and Justice. Whatever else such shots mean in the films—and they mean plenty—they are hilariously funny surprises. Lubitsch's *So This Is Paris* begins as an apparent parody of a Valentino sheik-type movie, only to surprise us by revealing an ordinary domestic couple practicing a dance routine. *The Merry Widow* captures a gaudy military parade as Maurice Chevalier sings "Girls, Girls, Girls." Then two oxen walk ploddingly down the street in the opposite direction, disrupting the order and precision of the singer and the marching band. The ap-

---

* Although the comic climate persists throughout a comic film, I have been concentrating on how we feel that climate at a film's beginning. Establishing the comic climate is, in effect, an element of exposition.

parent "seriousness" of this display of European pageantry has been permanently and effectively ruptured. The manipulation of physical business, so important to an art that depends on the visual and, hence, physical, provides one of the important clues about a film's emotional climate.

So does the director's handling of camera angle, editing, lighting, and sound. Are the shots close or distant? Does he shoot from below, from above, or at eye level? Is the lighting bright and even, or somberly tonal? Is the editing invisible or obtrusive, rapid or languid with dissolves? Is the sound track cheery, tense, contrapuntal, silent? There are no formulas as to what techniques and methods will or won't inevitably produce comic effects, but that the union and combination of lighting, camera angle, decor, editing rhythm, music, etc. do shape the way we respond is undeniable.

In the film medium the handling of physical action, the photographing of images, the styles of camera, editing, and sound have far more importance than Aristotle accorded "melody" and "spectacle" in the drama. Whereas Aristotle relegated these two concrete physical assaults of the drama to the two least important aesthetic places, the motion picture, given its greater physical freedom, is far more dependent on them. The handling of image and sound becomes literally, a part of a film's "diction"—its method of "saying" what it has to "say." The common view that there is a grammar and rhetoric of film underscores the fact that cinematic technique is a kind of language. Whereas imagery in a literary form transmits itself verbally, imagery in the films is explicitly visual. Just as jokes, puns, wit, or comic imagery shape our reaction to a comic novel or play, a film's cinematic "diction" shapes our awareness that the action takes place in a comic or non-comic world.

A comic film, then, is either *(a)* one with a comic plot and comic climate or *(b)* one with a not necessarily comic plot but a pervasive enough comic climate so that the overall effect is comic. For example, the reason von Stroheim's *Merry Widow* is melodrama while Lubitsch's *Merry Widow* is comedy is that Lubitsch has created a comic climate for his film by almost all available means. Von Stroheim's subject matter is gloomy and brutal (duels, deaths, and semi-rapes); his characters are often vicious and perverted; and his manipulation of cinematic devices—camera angle, rhythms of cutting, lighting—is quiet and gloomily tonal. Lubitsch, using the same basic story and characters with the same names, fleshes out the structure with frivolous incidents; and he uses song, farcical minor characters, clever physical business, and self-conscious games with the camera and sound track.

An even more revealing (and more complicated) contrast is that between a comic film such as *The General* and a non-comic one such as *The 39 Steps*. Both use the same plot (the series of dangerous obstacles), the same motivation (both protagonists must overcome obstacles to survive), the same conclusion (both men succeed and win the lady fair). Both films are journeys. Both turn upon accidents and ironies.

But *The 39 Steps* is a heroic action performed by a non-heroic character; *The General* is a heroic action performed by a comic character. *The General* establishes a comic climate early and maintains it throughout the film. Gags define Buster Keaton's character as comic before he ever begins his adventure in search of a locomotive; *The General* introduces slapstick gags even at the most perilous moments. While *The 39 Steps* has wonderful comic moments—the feuding man and woman handcuffed together in a double bed; the man delivering a rousing impromptu political speech although ignorant of the views of the expected speaker—these moments of themselves do not, and are not intended to, create a comic climate.

ANNETTE MICHELSON
FILM
AND THE RADICAL ASPIRATION

The history of Cinema is, like that of Revolution in our time, a chronicle of hopes and expectations, aroused and suspended, tested and deceived. I came to know and care for film in a city which has traditionally sheltered and animated these hopes and expectations. It is not only the political and intellectual capital of its country, but that of filmmaking, as well. Quite simply, the distance between the Place de l'Opéra and the studios at Joinville is a matter of a subway ride, not of a transcontinental jet flight. I shall ask you to bear this elementary fact in mind because it has determined much of what I would ever have to say about most things. More than that it provides the terms of a general, if somewhat crude, metaphor for my concern today. To speak of Film and the Radical Aspiration is necessarily to evoke instances of convergence and dissociation.

Two statements, first, however: not mine, but drawn from the writings of men of quite dissimilar sensibilities and vocations, living and working at a distance of almost two generations. The first, Benjamin Fondane, a writer and critic, and man of the left, died, when still young, in a German concentration camp. Writing in 1933, he said,

> We are committed with all our strength to the denunciation of a world whose catastrophic end seems more than ever before inevi-

This essay, originally delivered as a talk at the New York Film Festival in 1966 and published in another version, has been rewritten specifically for this volume.

469

table. We demand its rightful liquidation, whether that liquidation produces an irremediable vacuum of nothingness or a sovereign renewal through revolutionary means. Such should be—and this regardless of the deep inner wounds inevitably involved in such an aspiration—the aims of will and consciousness today. . . . As for film, the curve of its development has rapidly ascended, only to sink into an immediate decline. Stuffed to bursting, tricked out with an absurd and meretricious pomp, with every kind of frill imaginable, it has hypertrophied into a monstrous industry. The attraction was merely potential, the magic contained . . . the seeds of an unpardonable decay until, with the abruptness of a volcanic eruption, the huge shambles collapsed beneath the weight of its own emptiness. And yet, the cinema continues to interest us for that which it is not, for that which it failed to become, for its ultimate possibilities. . . . It may be that film is the expression of a society unable to sustain a world . . . of the mind. It may be that this tardily conceived art, child of an aged continent, will perish in its infancy. It may be, too, that the Revolution is not utterly to be despaired of.

The second statement—just one sentence—was written by a Movie Star and published in *Film Culture* a year or two ago. The Movie Star in question, a performer of quite extraordinary charm and originality, is Taylor Mead, and I presume that some of you have seen him in independently produced films. Taylor Mead has said, "The movies are a Revolution."

Film, our most vivacious art, is young enough to remember its first dreams, its limitless promise, and it is haunted, scarred, by a central, ineradicable trauma of dissociation. The attendant guilt and ambivalence, their repressive effects, the manner above all, in which a dissociative principle has been alternately resisted or assumed, converted into an aesthetic principle, the manner in which this resistance or conversion modifies or re-defines cinematic aspirations are, like everything concerning film, unique in the history of western culture.

A dream, a presentiment of the medium, inhabits and traverses the 19th century. Almost every form of popular diversion characteristic of the era—the family album, the wax museum, the novel itself, the panopticon in all its forms—can be read as an obscure, wistful prefiguration of cinema. My own revelation of the wax museum as prefiguration came a year or so ago when I chose, as a

Christmas treat, to accompany a bright little American, French-educated boy to the Musée Grevin. It struck me, as we went slowly through the long, dark, labyrinthine corridors, punctuated by the rather grand and spectacular tableaux which chronicle the whole of French history, from early Gauls until the Gaullist regime, that the wax museum, in its very special, hallucinatory darkness, its spatial ambiguity, its forcing of movement upon the spectator, its mixture of diversion and didacticism, is a kind of proto-cinema. And of course the historical mode of discourse is, above all, that of the earliest films which celebrated state occasions, public festivities, followed monarchs to christenings and assassinations. The extraordinary rapidity of the cinema's growth seemed to confirm this vision of a century's wistful fantasy (only seventy years have passed since Méliès witnessed the Lumières' demonstration and produced his own first reel). So, too, did the general climate of anticipatory enthusiasm and accord which animated filmmaking and criticism in their early, heroic period. That climate seems, in retrospect, Edenic.

Consider the atmosphere surrounding the early theoretical discussions: the Eisenstein-Pudovkin debate on the nature of montage, involving the conception of images as "cells, not elements" engaged in dialectical conflicts, as opposed to the "linkage of chains." Or the discussion, somewhat less familiar to historians, of the function of the subtitle as it crystallized during the 1920's in France: Kirsanov's elimination of the title in the interest of visual explicitness, René Clair's reduction of the title's role to the strictest minimum, the stress placed by Desnos and Surrealists on its exclusively poetic use, on the subversion of "sense in the interests of poetry." While the controversy developed—and with the unique intensity and inventiveness which characterise critical discourse in France—technology was preparing to transcend the problem. The claim that the "shriek" or "grinding of brakes" was no less real or "present" for being understood rather than heard was rendered comically irrelevant; the problem was simply cancelled by the arrival of sound.

Generally speaking, however, discussion, fruitful or academic, took place within a context of broad agreement as to the probable or desirable directions of the medium. Styles, forms, inventions and theoretical preoccupations were largely complementary, not

471

contradictory. A spectrum, rather than a polarity of possibilities was involved. The Surrealist's admiration of American silent comedy, reflected in the work of Artaud and Epstein among others, the universal excitement over the achievements of Russian film, Eisenstein's openly acknowledged debt to Griffith, testify to a certain community of aspiration. Eisenstein, in the very beautiful essay on "Griffith, Dickens and the Film Today" said that "what enthralled us was not only these films, it was also their possibilities." And speaking of montage: "Its foundation had been laid by American film-culture, but its full, completed, conscious use and world recognition was established by our films."

The excitement, the exhilaration of artists and intellectuals not directly involved in the medium was enormous. Indeed, a certain euphoria enveloped the early filmmaking and theory. For there was, ultimately, a very real sense in which the revolutionary aspirations of the modernist movement in literature and the arts, on the one hand, and of a Marxist or Utopian tradition, on the other, could converge in the hopes and promises, as yet undefined, of the new medium.

There was, among the intellectuals concerned with cinema's revolutionary potential, both social and formal, a general and touching reverence for an idea of its specificity. There was, above all, an immediate apprehension, cutting quite across theoretical differences, of its privileged status, its unique destiny.

In the celebrated essay on "The Work of Art in the Era of Reproduction Techniques,"* Walter Benjamin attacked as reactionaries, men such as Werfel, who, by relegating the movie to the articulation of fantasy and faery, were engaged in a reduction of its scope, a tactics of repression. The most intensely euphoric expression of the new passion, of the convergence of modernist aesthetics and an Utopian ideology is Elie Faure's "Art of Cineplastics," really an essay in aesthetics-as-science-fiction which predicts the cinema's radical transformation of the very nature of spatio-temporal perception, of historical consciousness and process.

Anticipations and speculations and, more significantly still, the inventions and achievements of the Americans, Russians, French,

---

* This essay appears as the final piece in the present collection under the title, "The Work of Art in the Age of Mechanical Reproduction" [eds.].

Germans and Scandinavians were predicated, then, upon complementary apprehensions of the morphological and syntactical possibilities of the medium evolving within a framework of concord and mutual recognition, shattered, ultimately, by the growing awareness of a principle of dissociation inherent in the art and its situation.

The point of shock is easily located in history: that moment, at the end of the 1920's in which the "hermaphroditic" nature of a craft which had already expanded and hardened into an industry, could no longer be ignored. The classical instrument of industrial revolution being division of labor, a generation of hardy adventurers, artist-entrepreneurs, director-producers, such as Griffith, were replaced by paid employees. The ultimate consequences involved something analogous to a dissociation of sensibility, which, in turn, rapidly engendered a register of limits and conventions that have acted to inhibit, displace, and reshape cinematic effort.

We are dealing with a Fall from Grace. For men like Griffith, Eisenstein, von Stroheim, Welles and many more of the most brilliant and radical talents, it created, as we know, in the gardens of California, an irrespirable atmosphere, a corruption which was to impair much of the best work done anywhere.

Intellectuals and filmmakers alike, here and abroad, reacted with an immediate tension of distrust and, in many instances, withdrawal. The widespread resistance to the introduction of the sound track, for example, could certainly be shown to mask or reflect an hostility to the prospect of the medium's accelerated development into an instrument of mass culture. A French philosopher of my acquaintance claims to have stopped going to the movies in 1929. For Fondane, "the sound film is good only in so far as it is dumb." And for Artaud, "cinematic truth lies within the image, not beyond it." The resistance to sound—and it was a resistance to the Word, not ever to music which had, from the beginning, found a place in cinematic convention—expressed a nostalgia for an era of mute innocence and untested hope. It was, in short, a pastoral attitude.

The disenchantment, the sense of moral and esthetic frustration expressed by Fondane, was general. The history of modern cinema is, nevertheless, to a large degree, that of its accommodation to those very repressive and corrupting forces of the post-1929

473

situation. A complex register of limits and conventions engendered by that situation has been *productively* used. Historical precedents abound, but few or none have attained a comparable degree of dialectical paradox, intricacy, and scandalousness.

It is the acceptance of the dissociative principle, its sublimation or conversion to aesthetic purposes, which characterise recent, advanced filmmaking in France and elsewhere in Europe. It is the almost categorical rejection of that principle and the aspiration to a radical organicity which animates the efforts of the "independent" filmmakers who compose something of an American *avant-garde*. All discussion of the nature and possibilities of advanced filmmaking today, of film aesthetics and of future possibilities must, I believe, take this divergence into account. It must also take into account the fact that the question is, as Walter Benjamin remarked, "not whether we are dealing with an art" (and some, apparently, still ask that question), "but whether or not the emergence of this medium has not transformed the nature of all art."

The general resistance in this country to the notion of this transformation assumes its most crucial aspect, not in circles unconcerned with film, but rather in those presumably animated by a commitment to its development. The discomfort and hostility of many, indeed most, film critics to those aspects of contemporary cinema which bypass, contradict or transcend the modes and values of psycho-social observation is familiar. The generally *rétardataire* character of our film criticism reflects a regressive anxiety about the manner in which postwar cinema, in Europe and America alike, has, at its best, transcended the conventions of a sensibility formed by the pre-modernist canon of a primarily literary 19th-century. One simply has to face the fact that a great part of a generation who came to maturity in the twenties, who were nourished by and committed to the formal radicalism of a Pound, a Stein or a Joyce, are these days concerned with, let us say, the novels of Saul Bellow and Norman Mailer! If the crux of cinematic development lies—as I think it largely does—in the evaluation and re-definition of the nature and role of narrative structure, we may say that the history of academicism in filmmaking and film criticism has been that of the substitution of novelistic forms and values for theatrical ones— and this in a century which saw a flowering of American poetry.

Critical malaise and contradictions, therefore, quite logically focussed last season on two films of Jean-Luc Godard: *Le Petit Soldat* and *Alphaville*, first presented in New York within the context of the Lincoln Center Festival. I say "logically" because it is precisely in so far as *Alphaville* constitutes a really remarkable instance of a reconsideration of the nature and possibilities of certain narrative conventions that I wish to consider it ever so briefly at this point.

Alphaville is an anxious meditation, in the form of a suspense story, on the agony and death of love, liberty and language in a society which is trapped in the self-perpetuating dialectic of technical progress. It is about feeling in deep freeze. The violent rehearsal of the content-versus-style liturgies which greeted *Alphaville* testified, in negative fashion, to Godard's central importance. Together with a few of his European contemporaries he does dominate cinema now and much of what is done anywhere has to be situated in relation to the work of these men. Above all, however, the complex *statement* of the film in regard to the possibilities of narrative convention transcends, in interest and importance, the nature of its *discourse*, and the hostility displayed towards that *discourse*, I take to represent simply a displacement (or dislocation) of hostility to its formal, cinematic *statement*.

François Truffaut, reflecting somewhat casually on the history of film, once divided its protagonists into two sorts: the creators of *"spectacle"* or entertainment, such as Méliès, and the experimenters or inventors, such as Lumière. To this Godard replied that he had always tried to make "experimental" films in the guise of entertainments. *Alphaville* is such a film. Its conceptual and formal complexities fuse into an elaborate and precisely articulated metaphor of Immanence, of the ambiguity of location and dis-location, in both their spatial and temporal modes.

Paris now, her public buildings, offices, hotels, garages, corridors, staircases and escalators are revealed as invaded by the Future. Frontiers between past, present and future are—like the distinctions between invention and entertainment—abolished through a series of formal strategies: a *prise de conscience* secured through a *prise de vues*. This film, shot entirely on location, is the film of dis-location. And as narrative structure, lighting, cutting, produce a visual, temporal or situational transformation, so a continual play with language transforms things known and seen.

Thus, the low-income housing developments of post-1945 Paris, known as *Habitations à Loyers Modiques* are the clinics and insane asylums of the future: *les Hôpitaux des Longues Maladies*. The city's peripheral avenues, *les boulevards extérieurs*, shift and expand into an irrevocably disquieting suggestion of the routes of interplanetary space. Function and scale of object and place are continuously altered, as image and sound converge upon site and situation in the exploration of the cinematic figuration of dislocation, of the ambiguities of time and history. One thinks of Gertrude Stein: "Composition is not there, it is going to be there and we are here. *This is some time ago for us naturally.*" The shifting—within—simultaneity of sameness and difference, of being and going-to-be, while we *are*, "some time ago, naturally," structures the time-space within which the mind (and *Alphaville* is *"about"* the birth of mind and sensibility, the rebirth of language as a rebirth of love) is constrained to function: that of a dislocation with respect to time. The "past-future" tense of which Godard speaks is our *present situation*.

The progress or plot of *Alphaville*, is, therefore, the passage from one revelation to another; its peripeties are perceptions, structured by the pace and tension of a detective story, of "finding truth." In the face of this, the accusations of "triviality" or "pretentiousness" became embarrassingly irrelevant. The film "states" its concern with the creation of a morphology; the concentration is on pace, tension, weight and syntactic coherence through narration—narration being in this instance a form of "relating" in the fullest possible sense of the word: a manner of creating *relational* strategies through *telling*.

Alphaville constitutes a remarkable instance of a critical allegiance, shared by the major European filmmakers, to the conventions of Hollywood's commercial cinema, and of the conversion of those conventions to the uses of advanced cinema. For the allegiance has acted as context and pre-condition of formal radicalism. (And it is interesting to consider that Godard's attachment to the Monogram film, the "B series" production, is paralleled, or anticipated, by Eisenstein's life-long affection for the early films that began to come to Russia when he was a boy. He speaks with tenderness of films like *The House Of Hate* and *The Mark of Zorro*.) The importance of the suspense story, as refined by Hitchcock for the further use of men such as Resnais and Godard, lies in its paradigmatic character as narrative form, as a "vehicle" of dramatic and formal invention. Perfected in the Hollywood of an era following upon the Fall, it was adopted and refined, sublimated in the interests of a formal radicalism.

The earliest, and certainly the most sumptuous, anticipation of this strategy is Feuillade's *Vampires*, shown in its entirety here for the first time during last year's New York Film Festival. Together with *Alphaville*, it dominated the occasion. Made by a man of utterly intrepid imagination, its formal inventiveness is supported by a firm commitment to a notion of film as a technique of narrative for a mass public. I have discussed elsewhere the manner in which *Vampires* not only sets forth the themes developed in *Alphaville*, and the way in which the cinema of Méliès and Feuillade adumbrated, within the context of the medium's earliest stages, the principles and strategies of which Surrealist art and film provided a subsequent development.

"Please believe me," said Feuillade, "when I tell you that it is not the experimenters who will eventually obtain film's rightful recognition, but rather the makers of melodrama—and I count myself among the most devoted of their number. . . . I won't in the least attempt to excuse (this view). . . . I believe I come closer to the truth." It was strict adherence to the logic of this view which guaranteed, for Feuillade, a margin of improbability, of open-ness, of that oneiric intensity which gives *Vampires* its place among the masterworks of cinema.

Predicated on the development of a narrative convention both strict and elastic enough to accomodate a tension between dramatic probability and fantasy—between discourse and poetry—Feuillade's work opens out upon the future of film rather than upon its past. Which is to say, as Robbe-Grillet has said, that "Imagination, when really alive, is always of the present." And we might find a partial confirmation of this in Alain Resnais' fascination with Feuillade. Resnais' work, like that of his European contemporaries, perpetuates the commitment to the constraints and stimuli of a given form; above all, in its straining of the limits of that form, it exemplifies a commitment to the value of Form as such which animates the best of advanced European cinema today.

Now, if we assume, as I shall, that the revolutionary aspiration,

477

aesthetic and political, achieved a moment of consummation in the Russian film of the twenties and early thirties, we know, too, that the paradigmatic fusion was dissolved by the counter-revolution of Stalinism. As this happened (and the installation of Stalinism in its more or less definitive form is contemporary with the introduction of sound into film), European cinema and European art as a whole abandoned a certain totality of aspiration. The process of dissociation, the split between formal and political aspects of radical or revolutionary efforts, was created, irremediably so — at least through our time. The result was either reaction, or a sublimation of the revolutionary aspiration into a purely formal radicalism. The vestiges of the politically revolutionary experience and tradition are henceforth expressed in the form of nostalgia and frustration. Politically oriented art at its best became a chronicle of absence, of negation, an analysis of dissociation, and, in the best modernist tradition, a *formal statement of the impossibility of discourse.*

The nostalgia and frustration are explicitly stated in Godard's *Le Petit Soldat*, by Michel, the hero: "In the early thirties, young people had the revolution. Malraux, for example, Drieu la Rochelle and Aragon. We don't have anything any more. They had the Spanish Civil War. We don't even have a war of our own." The formal articulation of this nostalgia for a revolutionary impulse and hope involves a succession of fascinating paradoxes and failures. The case of Resnais, who almost alone of his particular generation has attempted to articulate a strong personal political commitment, is particularly fascinating. I have in mind not only *Hiroshima* but *Muriel*. In both films he has visible difficulty in situating the commitment within the total structure of his work, in finding a visual trope that will not inflect the style, or distend the structure. The result is a rhythmical, dramatic, and visual caesura, the stylistic articulation of aphony.

The two explicitly political passages in these films are both distanced, bracketed as spectacles or diversions. In *Hiroshima* the anti-war demonstration is inserted as a film sequence enacted within the film, while in *Muriel*, the Algerian war is evoked, not shown, in an amateur movie, by an agonised verbal commentary (the account of a young girl's torture by French soldiers) in counterpoint to the series of innocuous amateur shots which parody the myth of barracks'-life hilarity.

478

This sequence constitutes the most brilliant, the definitive articulation of the disintegration of a cinematic arena for political discourse. The despair over that disintegration is the film's central political "statement." The "statement's" intensity, however, is further amplified through the further distancing of the bracketed statement from *itself* (the distance between image and commentary). Its isolation within the texture of the total work, its particular, stylistic disjunctiveness, its own colourless colour, are slightly at odds with the disjunctiveness and invented colour of the whole. Through a speculative and stylistic refraction Resnais proposes an image of the shameful scandal which generated the Fifth Republic. His trope is that of the caesura. The crack, the flaw, the rhythmic, visual gap or caesura created by this interlude or "diversion" is the *form* of Resnais' declaration of aphony. It declares his nostalgia for the film which could *not* be made; it renders the artist's struggle with the dissociative principle and its politics.

And it is fascinating, but distressing beyond telling, to see, in *La Guerre Est Finie*, Resnais' ultimate attempt to assume what he obviously regards as the discursive responsibility of his position, the diabolical logic of that principle in operation. Like *Alexander Nevsky*, *La Guerre Est Finie* is the chronicle of an artist's defeat; it represents a total inversion, the most concrete negation of a form and style. In this film, it is the erotic sequences which assume the aspect of interludes or diversions within the total structure, and the bracketing or distancing is achieved through a reversion to a hieraticism of style we have, of course, known and loved: that of *Hiroshima* and, above all, of *Marienbad*. These passages now produce the caesuras which arouse our nostalgia. Far more painfully, however, they declare Resnais' *own* nostalgia for his past achievements. *Vivement Harry Dickson!*

Lucien Goldmann, writing a few years ago in *Les Temps Modernes* of the supposed atrophy of historical and social consciousness in the New Wave directors, remarked with a sigh that political energy and vitality seemed concentrated in the Left, while cinematic talent was reserved for the Right. Goldmann's characteristically Lukacsian conservative taste and aesthetics aside, the problem needs to be restated—and far more explicitly than one can do here and now. Most briefly put, however, one might formulate it in the following manner: if, for the young Russians of the immediately post-Revolutionary period the problem was, as Eisenstein said, "to advance towards new and as yet unrealized qualities and means of expression, to raise form once more to the level of ideological content," the problem for Resnais and his peers is to accommodate ideological content to the formal exigencies of a modernist sensibility. Ultimately, ideology of any kind—whether that of Surrealism, Marxism, or the anti-humanism of the New Novel—provides, at best, a fruitful working hypothesis for the artist. Eisenstein's conception of montage as the triadic rehearsal of the Dialectic was aesthetically regenerative. The energy, courage and intellectual passion which sustained both theory and work were, of course, among the noblest of our century. Eisenstein is a model of the culture of our era—in his defeat as in his achievement, and down to the very fragmentary quality of his work!

There is a passage in his writings and it is the most tantalizing page he has bequeathed us—in which he describes a cinema of the mind, a film "capable of reconstructing all phases and all specifics of the course of thought."* He is shifting, at this point, from a pristine conception of "intellectual cinema" which had culminated in a projected film version of *Capital*, a rendering of analytic method, to another aspiration, more complex, even more problematic: the rendering of the movement of consciousness itself. He envisages the filmic "interior monologue" as the agent of the dissolution of "the distinction between subject and object," first undertaken in the novels of Eduard Dujardin, that "pioneer on the stream of consciousness," a dissolution completed in the work of Joyce. *Ulysses*, then, becomes the other prime Utopian project of the 1930's out of which Eisenstein's notion of "intellectual cinema" continues to be refined. He informs us, in his excitement, of a period of preliminary work upon his script for *An American Tragedy*, another project of that period which stimulated this sort of speculation, and of the "wonderful sketches" produced in the process.

Like thought, they would sometimes proceed with visual images. With sound. Synchronized or non-synchronized. Then as sounds. Formless. Or with sound-images: with objectively representational sounds . . .

Then suddenly, definite intellectually formulated words—as "in-

---

*Sergei Eisenstein, *Film Form, Essays in Film Theory*, ed. and trans. by Jay Leyda, New York: Harcourt, Brace and World, p. 105.

tellectual" and dispassionate as pronounced words. With a black screen, a rushing imageless visuality.

Then in passionate disconnected speech. Nothing but nouns. Or nothing but verbs. Then interjections. With zigzags of aimless shapes, whirling along with these in synchronization.

Then racing visual images over complete silence.

Then linked with polyphonic sounds. Then polyphonic images. Then both at once.

Then interpolated into the outer course of action, then interpolating elements of the outer action into the inner monologue.

As if presenting inside the characters the inner play, the conflict of doubts, the explosions of passion, the voice of reason, rapidly or in slow-motion, marking the differing rhythms of one and the other and, at the same time, contrasting with the almost complete absence of outer action: a feverish inner debate behind the stony mask of the face.

. . . The syntax of inner speech as distinct from outer speech. The quivering inner words that correspond with the visual images. Contrasts with outer circumstances. How they work reciprocally . . .

And Eisenstein ends by noting that "These notes for this 180° advance in sound film culture languished in a suitcase—and were eventually buried, Pompeii-like, beneath a mass of books. . . ." There they remained. Sound was to take Eisenstein in quite another direction, to the splendidly hieratic exacerbation of *Ivan the Terrible*.

This buried page, however, might figure as a blueprint for a cinema that was still to come. Its affirmation of disjunction, of abstraction, of the shifting relations of image and sound, its stress on polyphony, upon the use of silence and of the black screen as dynamic formal elements are familiar to us: Eisenstein, in a dazzling leap of the imagination, had invented on paper the essential tenor, the formal strategies of American Independent Cinema of our own last two decades.

It is exactly nineteen years—about the time we say we take to come of age—since "Cinema 16," a pioneer film society presenting work by artists of the independent persuasion to a New York audience, held a symposium on "Poetry and the Film." The proceedings, published in somewhat abridged form,* constitute a

---

The Film Culture Reader, P. Adams Sitney, ed., Praeger Publishers, New York, 1970.

document of enormous and multiple interest. Re-reading it now one is startled by an intensity and level of exchange to which we have grown unaccustomed in the present proliferation of such occasions; the text now stands as a major document of the period, a chapter in a polemical mode of the intellectual history of its time, its scene.

That time, that scene are the early '50's, and here are its players: Parker Tyler, a film critic already distinguished and actively involved, from the time of its wartime exile in New York, in the Surrealist tradition; Willard Maas, filmmaker; Arthur Miller, then the white hope of a certain native theatrical realism and Dylan Thomas, the visiting star performer of that period are there as "prose" and "poetry." With Maas acting as chairman or "moderator," as we've come to say, film and film-as-poetry are most strongly represented by Maya Deren, unquestionably one of the most gifted filmmakers and theoreticians of her generation.

The occasion fuses and opposes forces, notions about what such an occasion might be, its use, pre-suppositions about the conventions of a possible discourse on film. Inscribed within it, by the way, is the plain evidence of what it was to be both a woman and an independent filmmaker at that time—someone exposed to the lordly contempt affected by intellectuals for seriousness in film and seriousness in women. Thomas' wit and grandstanding joviality are thus directed against Deren's passionate attempt to define a subject about which they might profitably converse.

Miller, less narcissistic and more interesting, has obviously given more thought to the general matter at hand and there is, near the end, a remarkable moment, when he suddenly says, "I think that it would be profitable to speak about the special nature of any film, of the fact of images unwinding off a machine. Until that's understood, and I don't know that it's understood (I have some theories about it myself), we can't begin to create on a methodical basis, an aesthetic for that film. We don't understand the psychological meaning of images—any image—coming off a machine. There are basic problems, it seems to me, that could be discussed here." The remarks are offered, most likely, as antidote to what Miller obviously considers to be the questionable rhetoric of Deren's poetics, but the trajectory towards the assumption of that challenge is, of course, the history of our American filmic avant-garde and the re-examination of the materiality, the conditions and practical contingencies of filmmaking and projection have inflected an avant-garde which moves from the psychological to the epistemological mode of discourse.

Deren had proposed the poetic film as representing "an approach to experience in the sense that a poet is looking at the same experience that a dramatist may be looking at." Distinguishing it somewhat more specifically, she describes it as "vertical" in structure, "an investigation of a situation, in that it probes the ramifications of the moment, and is concerned with its qualities and its depth, so that you have poetry concerned, in a sense not with what is occurring but with what it feels like or what it means. A poem to my mind, creates visible or auditory form for something that is invisible, which is the feeling, or the emotion or the metaphysical content of the statement. Now it also may include action, but its attack is what I would call the vertical attack, and this may be a little bit clearer if you will contrast it to what I would call the horizontal attack to drama which is concerned with the development, let's say, within a very small situation from feeling to feeling. Perhaps it would be made most clear if you take a Shakespearean work that combines the two movements. In Shakespeare, you have the drama moving forward on a 'horizontal' plane of development of one circumstance — one action leading to another and this delineates the character. Every once in a while, however, he arrives at a point of action where he wants to illuminate the meaning to 'this' moment of drama and, at that moment, he builds a pyramid or investigates it 'vertically' if you will, so that you have a 'horizontal' development with periodic 'vertical' investigations which are the poems, which are the monologues. Now if you consider it this way, then you can think of any kind of combination being possible. You can have operas where the 'horizontal' development is virtually unimportant — the plots are very silly, but they serve as an excuse for stringing together a number of arias that are essentially lyric statements. Lieder are, in singing, comparable to the lyric poem, and you can see that all sorts of combinations would be possible."

One thing we note immediately: Deren is defining poetry in a manner quite natural, indeed endemic in her time, as being exclusively of the lyric mode. And referring to the tradition of the "lied," she assumes this as well to be quite unrelated to or disengaged from, the narrative. Though one might argue that view of "Gretchen am Spinnrade," one might dispute it for "Der Erlkonig." She is arguing, in any case, passionately and well for something one does sense as fundamental for her and her time. In positing her horizontal and vertical structures, she is positing disjunctiveness against linearity, claiming for film the strategic polarity of discourse which Jakobson, examining the structure of speech through its disorders in aphasia, proposed in the metonymic and metaphoric modes. Some questions, then: are such polarities valid, do they hold, do they concern us here and now?

We may now say, I think, "No, they are not and do not," but the last of these three questions is the one of major interest to us and demands our assent.

These polarisations serve to crystallize for their own time the thinking, feeling and, above all, the working impulse of a major film-maker initiating a tradition of criticism. Deren's concern with the lyric was essentially a step towards a radical revision of filmic temporality as a source of formal innovation. Reflecting 19 years later upon the best and most innovative of recent work in this country, one realizes that its common critical context is to be found not through definition of aspects of style or texture—not even that style and texture which have been called "structural"—but rather through the recognition that the best of recent work takes its place as an extended moment in a continuum of inquiry, constituting the most recent and most complete interplay of "verticality" and "horizontality" within that continuum.

Deren's own preoccupation with the "vertical" begins as an extension of that extraordinary intuition of film's temporal vistas which inserts within the literally split (spliced) second of a tower's crash, that odyssey of a "poet" whose "blood" had congealed, somehow, into a film. And that "Poet" had, indeed, spattered himself over that film's entire surface. Here is the model of his appearance: the narrator's voice, the signature, the plaster masks of hand and of face, the wire mask revolving in space, the autobiographical tableaux, the autobiographical incidents climaxing in a snowball fight which intensifies the referential dimension, recapitulating as it does the opening scene of an already celebrated work, *Les Enfants Terribles*. And then there is the opening dedication, the injunction to read, to decipher, the work as a coat of arms, the homage paid in the "Poet's" name, to the masters of Renaissance perspective from one who confesses his reluctance to "deform" space. Fearing no doubt the "Caligarism" which was the French film world's name for an expressionism more generally feared and detested, the Poet confines himself to a play, an assault upon the time of action while respecting its spatial integrity.

Deren, then, arguing for "her" "personal," "vertical," "poetic" film was to work in a direction which reversed Cocteau's. Rather than splice a moment through a moment of time in which she could insert the integrality of a film, she attempted to work with the moment, distending it into a structure of exquisite ambiguity, underwritten by the braver spatial strategies that came perhaps more easily to the developed kinetic sense of a dancer.

It then came to Stan Brakhage to radicalize the revision of filmic temporality in positing the sense of a continuous present, of a filmic time which devours memory and expectation in the presentation of presentness. To do this one had, of course, to destroy the spatio-temporal coordinates by which past and present events define themselves as against each other. The assault of Brakhage upon the space of representation, then, is the final and most radical break with that spatial integrity which Cocteau had been at pains, neo-classicist that he was, to preserve. It consummates the break with narrative structure, and Brakhage now moves into the climate of expressionism, pushing the abstractive process, contracting the depth of the visual field to the point where he destroys the spatiality of narrative, redefining time as purely that of vision, the time of appearance. In doing so he replaces the scene of action by the screen of eidetic imagery, projecting, as it were, the nature of vision itself as the subject of a new temporal mode. His editing style, at once assertive and uniquely fluid, creates that "convergence of a hundred spaces" which Klee had called for and which only a radically redefined cinematic temporality could provide. It is Utopian.

Doing this, Brakhage was to do more still—re-examining the photographic and projective processes themselves, opening them up as it were, reclaiming them for inclusion in the total work. Thus, in an unmailed proposal written for the Guggenheim Foundation:

> These films would be created not only with a sense of the projected experience but also (as in all my work recently) with an eye to their

speaking just as strips of celluloid held in the hand and to the light which can illuminate their multi-colored forms. They will be created out of the deepest possible conviction that such a viewing (or any other, such as a frame at a time through a slide projector) can and should be so integral with the projected experience as to add another dimension to that projected experience. Please understand that I arrive at such a conclusion from a working relationship with film and a realization that all my significant splices (adding moving image to moving image) are the result of viewing the film to be edited both through the editor at an approximate 24 frames a second and also as stilled strips of film. Similarly, out of an aesthetic understanding of time relativity, I have the sense that my finished films should be viewable either 16 frames a second or 24 frames a second. Very recently I have begun working toward a filmic realisation which will retain its integral form (considering the structure of the work of art as integral with all its emotional and intellectual statements) even when run backwards.*

The assault, then, upon the space of representation is accompanied by a reclamation of the elements and materials of the filmmaking and film-viewing experience, an extension of the ways in which light may be projected through the film, the creation of another surface through which the image is perceived, the painting, scratching or application of "foreign matter" to the surface of the film so that our heightened sense of a surface through which the image is viewed brings with it the heightened sense of the illusionism in which that apperception is grounded. All this, then, meant proposing—as Stein had done—that everything, including the materiality and contingencies of the making process, was food for poetry.

It is this proposal—and, though a curious prank of history—Arthur Miller's, that is accepted and developed in the best of recent work. The assertion of the still photographic frame composing the strip, the assertion, through the flicker, of the medium as projection of light, the assertion of the nature of projection through the use of sound, the assertion of the persistence of vision in the work of Jacobs, Sharits, Frampton, Gehr, Landow, Wieland and Snow, propose the terms of an epistemological concern with the nature of filmic process and experience which will require another space, another time, those of a new cinematic discourse.

---

*Stan Brakhage, "Metaphors on Vision," *Film Culture*, No. 30, Fall 1963.

For that discourse, then, spatio-temporal co-ordinates had to be re-invented and they quite naturally have been. In *Wavelength*, in the empty loft traversed by the zoom, Snow, voiding the film of the metaphoric proclivity of montage, re-creates a grand metaphor for narrative form. In the re-definition of "action" as the investigation of space through camera movement, Snow redefined the filmic form as the narrative of "one thing leading to another." *La Région Centrale* explores a landscape, pushes one's sense of space inward, obliterating the coordinates once again in the interests of an increasingly kinetic sense of seeing. Frampton plays in *Nostalgia* on the tension of past and present, of memory and expectation. Jacobs, distending the time and space of *Tom, Tom, the Piper's Son*, inscribes within a single work a history of film. Gehr, positing, in *Still* a space which we must interrogate, saying to ourselves, "Where is the surface in relation to which I am seeing what I see?" thereby poses the question of the time and space which might contain the multiple duration of superimposition. Landow, playing viewing against reading and reading against mis-reading, multiplies the modes of perception in time. Sharits substitutes or exchanges, as in *N.O.T.H.I.N.G.*, cause for effect. And Wieland prints and holds 1933, a static sign of time whose existence is made problematic by the continuous action in her loop film.

The cinema of *this* time, then, articulates an investigation of the terms of cinematic illusionism. It turns, from the fascinated consciousness of the eidetic, lyric mode, to precisely that "course of genuine investigation" which so preoccupied Eisenstein in his speculations upon the nature of "intellectual cinema" as instantiating the dynamics of analytic consciousness, recalling to us the view of Marx: "Not only the result, but the road to it also, is a part of the truth. The investigation of truth must itself be true; true investigation is unfolded truth, the disjunct members of which unite in the result."*

1966–73

---

*Sergei Eisenstein, *The Film Sense*, ed. and trans. by Jay Leyda, New York: Harcourt Brace and World, p. 82.

VI

The Film Artist

Otis Ferguson's essay, "Before the Cameras Roll," vividly demonstrates the overwhelming variety of considerations, both commercial and personal, that influence the making of a Hollywood movie. When this *New Republic* critic of the late 1930s and early 40s traveled west to Hollywood, he was amazed by the number of workers who contributed to the final product—the producer, the writers, the director, the researchers, the costume designers, the musicians, the cinematographer, the cutters, and the special effects men. The question necessarily arises: How can a work of art result from such varied intentions and collective labor? Many argue that it could not possibly issue from such collective chaos, and they regard the products of Hollywood as mere commercial entertainments that cannot be compared to the "art films" of Europe or the "underground" works of the personal, experimental filmmaker.

One reply to this argument is to deny that a purely aesthetic intention or the vision of a single artist is necessary to create a work of art. Panofsky specifically compares the making of a film to the building of a cathedral, for the cathedral was built for the greater glory of God and was the result of the collective labor of as many specialists as a Hollywood film. François Truffaut, in his essay, "Certain Tendencies in the French Cinema," developed his *"politique des auteurs,"* which defended the Hollywood film in a different manner. Truffaut maintained that, although unappreciated or even unnoticed, the work of an author, an *auteur*, could be seen in many Hollywood films. This *auteur* was, typically, the film's director, and his "signature" could be discerned by the sensitive critic.

Truffaut's·aim in this article was not to posit a general theory; the piece was a polemic, a specific response to the French critics in the period just after World War II who falsely assumed that the scenarist was a film's author—if there was an author at all.

According to what has become known as the *"auteur* theory," the director's "style" or his "basic motifs," as the British critic Peter Wollen calls them, can be discerned by viewing his work as a whole—for these marks of directorial authorship will manifest themselves in all of a true *auteur*'s films, even as he works with different writers, cinematographers, and stars. Andrew Sarris, the primary American spokesman for the *auteur* theory, suggests that not only is the distinguishable personality of the director a criterion of value, but that the "meaning" which he is able to impose on the material with which he must work is the "ultimate" glory of the cinema. This observation raises a problem, however, concerning Wollen's two key terms—"style" and "basic motifs." Does Sarris mean that the "ultimate" glory is a director's imposition of "style" (e.g., the use of deep-focus photography) on a film's given "basic motifs" (e.g., domestic melodrama) or does he mean that the glory is the director's imposition of a "style" that elicits new "basic motifs" (i.e., the meaning of love) from that melodrama? If the latter, does Sarris realize that the same can be said of any artist (say, Shakespeare in *King Lear* or *Othello*)? If the former, does Sarris mean that a director whose films deal with trash stylishly is an artist worthy of our attention?

Pauline Kael's reply to Sarris's "Notes on the Auteur Theory in 1962," is fiercely critical of Sarris's version of the *auteur* theory—precisely because of the fuzziness about content and style. First, she finds it platitudinous to observe that one can find an artistic "signature" or "basic motifs" in the work of an artist. Critics in all the arts assume that the artist has such a "signature," otherwise they would not bother to study him at all. Besides, as she observes, the sheer distinguishability of an artistic personality has no bearing on the value of that personality or his work. What an artist's works have in common may simply be signs of his ineptitude or his limitations. Finally, she thinks, there is something perverse about admiring an artist for managing to make an artistic silk purse out of the sow's ear of Hollywood trash. Isn't the true artist responsible for the choice of his materials and for finding an appropriate form for his chosen subject?

490

Although Kael's refutation of Sarris is largely correct, it is worth remarking that those who proposed the *auteur* theory were not simply arguing that an artist's personality will manifest itself in his works. They were seeking to establish that there was, indeed, an artist at work where many had never seen one. In doing so, they unquestionably helped to establish or re-establish the reputations of certain directors who worked within the Hollywood system, directors who did not exert much more control over the total project than many studio hacks, but who managed to make the kind of personal, significant statement that John Ford or (as Peter Wollen shows) Howard Hawks did. But Sarris's insistence on the sheer value of an artist's triumphing over his material seems a mistake, even from Sarris's own point of view. This is a useful strategy for rescuing some Hollywood reputations, but it lays the wrong groundwork for demonstrating the merits of the directors that Sarris (and almost everyone else) most admires. Directors such as Lubitsch, Renoir, Chaplin, Welles, and Keaton in fact enjoyed a large measure of individual control over scripts, shooting, and cutting. One does not, as Kael puts it, admire these directors for "shoving bits of style up the crevasses of the plots." In extending Truffaut's defense of the effective Hollywood studio director to cinema in general, Sarris has betrayed its limitations.

There are other problems with such a director-centered theory. If a director's signature can be discovered by a careful examination of all his works, this is equally true of certain screen writers, cinematographers, and stars. Often the mark they leave on a film will be far greater than that of its director. Both Gerald Mast and Richard Corliss point out, for instance, that a film whose script is written by a Preston Sturges or a Norman Krasna will more likely display their personality than that of its director, say a Mitchell Leisen. Similarly, Richard Koszarski argues that various studio styles and even the Hollywood style itself is better explained by the dominance of certain cinematographers than it is by reference to any directors or group of directors. In this same spirit, Pauline Kael's now famous essay, "Raising Kane," consciously attacks the *auteurist*'s *auteur* and the *auteurist*'s *auteur*-film by developing in detail the crucial contributions of *Citizen Kane*'s writer (Herman J. Mankiewicz), its cinematographer (Gregg Toland), and its leading actor (Welles the actor not the *auteur*).

Indeed, the most serious difficulty for any theory of the film *maker* as artist is the fact that many stars have made the most decisive contributions to the Hollywood films in which they have appeared, and that their unique "presence" can also be determined by viewing the totality of their works. In *The World Viewed* Stanley Cavell remarks how surprising he found the *auteur* theory, for it never previously occurred to him that anyone *made* a Hollywood film. For Cavell, the world of film revolved about, and was determined by, the star. When the European semiologist, Roland Barthes, writes of Garbo's "face," he implies that it is the main object of interest and the main conveyer of meaning in most of the films in which she appears. And Kenneth Tynan, the British film and theater critic, observes that "often during the decade in which [Garbo] talked to us, she gave signs that she was on the side of life against darkness: they seeped through a series of banal, barrel-scraping scripts like code-messages borne through enemy lines."

It may be, as Sarris observes in *The American Cinema*, his later attempt to repair the excesses of his original theory, that the film will most likely fulfill the criterion of being a unified work of art when the director dominates. But even this claim, however plausible and pragmatic, has not been established either by the arguments of the *auteur* theorists or by the complex facts of the history of the American film. For every *Modern Times*, which is obviously the work of a single artistic vision, there is a *Casablanca*, whose success may be the result of its director, of the men who conceived the original script, of the writer who amended that original script and wrote much of the dialogue, of its male star, of the particular chemistry between its male and female stars, or of some mysterious compound of all those elements.

OTIS FERGUSON
BEFORE THE CAMERAS ROLL

The worst things that happen in pictures happen previous to the first day of actual shooting, usually. In many cases they happen before the story is considered and bought. Yet these things are vital in the art of making pictures, and though they may be improved, I know of no happy state where they may be eliminated, just in the nature of things.

In the book of How to Make a Picture, item one is, first get an audience. To get and hold a body of followers large enough to support this fabulous expense in production is the prime moving force of the whole industry, however clumsy its lunges and however many times it cuts its own throat out of jealousy and meanness. Audience support is the one reason for the emergence of men with talent and push enough to go against the current (you'd never have heard of them in a closed subsidy); it is responsible for both the best and the worst, and I do not know how many thousands of times someone has said, as I have heard them: I made that one so I could make them give me this one. At the same time it has been a powerful brake on the tendency of all art toward obscure faddism; American writers and directors have had to learn to do it the hard way, and it is the way they have learned to tell stories with a camera and a pair of cutting scissors which has come to lead the world, to influence the technique of even the best filmmaking everywhere.

But that is all in the what-I-think-about-the-moon realm of picturemaking. The audience is there. It is always there. It is there now in such a steady multiple vigor that anybody with a brass voice and craft enough to promote one or two thousand can make the world's worst picture and get away with it (the world's worst picture either will never be made or is made every second Monday after the first Tuesday). But to understand the relationship between those who pay their money to see, and those who make, buy, sell, distribute, and exhibit, you will have to be familiar with the subject or read some of the books in its endless library: this is not the class for beginners, and there is not space here for a subject so wide and intricate. The point is that any understanding of the making of any single picture demands this background of for-whom and to-what-end—as who in civilization would listen to his mouth clapping up and down on the subject of Shakespeare and think himself a critic if he had never so much as heard of the terms Elizabethan, Renaissance, Globe, Holinshed, buskin, blank verse? We must simply remember that when the act of creation involves a thousand people and a million dollars, and wonders of science too deep to see, there must be some kind of monumental and sometimes monstrous plant set up to manufacture and purvey this entertainment for millions.

The plant is Hollywood as a center with lines running out over the world, and the second chapter in the book is: To make a picture you have to have the backing *and* equipment. Now in most cases, the backing comes from one of the major or minor established companies. Not because it comes more readily, and certainly not because it will give you any scope to work in, but because these companies control the channels of distribution—you want to make a picture but you want it to be seen too, don't you? There is a long history of seesaw and confusion in this struggle for the upper hand as between the man who shows and the man who makes the shows. Great companies have swallowed up minor companies by buying up theater chains, *i.e.*, the means of their expansion and their competitors' dwindling revenue; great companies have then staggered under the load and gone down. Great chain owners have tried to dominate the companies, bought them or starved them out, and then failed because they had dried up the very thing they were selling at its source. Men like William Fox, not essentially a picture man, have grown to giant size in the field of build-and-buy-and-produce-for-it, and then been chivvied out by the bankers. The bankers have seen those billions lying around and got in to pick them up, only to discover that their brusque pirate's idea of how to run a picture studio left out the ingredient of how pictures could be made. In the long and varied contest, it is always the working producers who win out in the end. Individuals among them are constantly losing their shirts, but those who make pictures and know pictures must have the final say, as a whole. They are the geese who lay those golden eggs; bankers, exhibitors, distributors, operators, and the like can lay eggs only in the figurative sense. So helpless are they, one after the other, that you take as accepted such facts as that little Shirley Temple alone saved the farflung glory of Twentieth Century-Fox; that Deanna Durbin, also alone, kept Universal off the bread line.

The golden egg itself, of course, is the patents racket. So much costly and marvelous equipment is necessary in the processes of building cameras, making sound and color, that it was impossible the original small inventors or owners should not be bought or buried, until some powerful and unscrupulous monopoly like the American Telephone and Telegraph Company controlled or tied up all the patents being used in some important process or other, and naturally will never sell anything outright because the lease is so rich, beyond fable. Or that an outfit like Electrical Research Products Incorporated should not only control patents but own studios and lend money and generally be the people you have to see, always at your cost. There is du Pont too. There is Eastman. Names fill the sky like buzzards.

The best analysis of these financial, and all-powerful, ends of the business will probably be Leo Rosten's forthcoming book, though from what very little I know of it, it will not have understanding of the philosophy of showmanship, which has no philosopher. The best book on the movie man as operator is still *Upton Sinclair Presents William Fox*—an amazing book but again deficient in knowledge of movies, their cause and effect. For the strange rank growth of the industry in general through the early days, the book is Terry Ramsaye's *Million and One Nights*, if you can read it and remember that Ramsaye is on the whole a journalist whose feet hurt and that he works today as the right hand of the practically unspeakable Martin Quigley. Thousands have fussed and fumed, but I doubt anything else has been written with much pertinence to the forbidding factual mountain of make and sell, buy and beat the drum.

495

To go back to where we came from, you *can* go to one of the pic-ture-loan promoters and prove to his satisfaction that you have an idea for a picture which will sell, and get financing. In that case you rent a studio and equipment at exorbitant cost, and make the picture, hiring your writers, directors, actors, and so forth. And then you get into the problem of what a picture is, what it takes.

The picture always starts at the beginning, which is (1) a writer's idea, (2) a successful book or play if you can buy it, (3) in some other studio. The toughest on the writer, and often on the public, is when the idea comes from a producer and is therefore not an idea —such not being his business—but an impulse. Budd Schulberg has written in these very pages how he and Scott Fitzgerald were sent by Walter Wanger to Hanover to cook up a story "around" Dartmouth simply because Walter Wanger went to Dartmouth and hasn't got out from under it yet. You didn't think that was an exception? Or the story I told last time about the producer who had an idea which boiled down to the title *Tomorrow's Generals*. Or the big-company executive who says, There's a lot of interest in the Lindbergh kidnaping, and it's safe by now, only it can't be Lind-bergh and it can't be a kidnaping. Or the company which says, We are due for an ice-carnival picture, or a Colbert picture, or a non-gangster picture, or something like an Abbot and Costello, or some-thing like what the hell is the name of that musical Fox is cleaning up on, or a period picture—everybody's still hot for the Civil War after *Gone with the Wind*.

On the whole it is the writer who takes the big rap. Stuff is shoved at him which should never even be considered for pictures, yet he must make a screenplay out of it because the company has money tied up in it and he is tied up with the company, just for the living. It will be done and will go out under his name, and I think it was Sidney Skolsky who broke the story about two writers com-ing home from work at Republic, one saying: "*You* take the credit title on this one; I had to take it last time." Or the writer shapes up a good screenplay and then has one to five expensive names called in to jigger it all out of true. Or he does some good work and everybody says that is really good work, and the picture is never made, and two months later the same everybodies are saying, Yes, I know, but I don't seem to remember the name.

Whatever the actual genesis, the picture has to start with a writer. If he has an idea of his own, fine, he will sell it as an original and maybe clean up by doing what is called the treatment on salary. But most of the time he has no time for ideas of his own. The company wants a Western, a South Sea Islands, a Hedy Lamarr, or some damn thing. It's a book or a play or a magazine series the company has on the shelf; it has to be done to write off a book loss that would worry the bankers; and it may have to be stretched to include a big deathbed sequence in the gutter at Tia Juana because Paramount has just finished with a whole Mexican street and square they built, and have it uneasy on their hands; or it may have to have a sea episode, to make use of the white-elephant tank and enormous ship models Korda has on his hands over at General Service.

You have a picture cooking, and you have a producer. You have to have a producer because that is the movies' middleman. He takes care of promoting the money, hiring the sound stages, the director, the actors; figuring costs and time elements, getting the thing cut and sound-tracked, ready and distributed. The producer may work in one of three ways. He may be a free-lance, completely free-lance, trusting in his own judgment to make a picture in the expectation that it will be good enough to force the big chains to buy and show it. He may be a semi-free-lance, a man who has got his own unit, and his own say in everything (the everything is a pipe dream) on a major lot. He may be just a yes-man to the executive in charge of production—and that is what he usually is. But in the present setup he is there, taking the responsibility for smash or flop; and the present setup is not considered all to the good by the men who make pictures, more and more of whom are taking over the producer's job themselves, demanding: Give the movies back to us, the moviemakers.

The independent producer is up against long odds. He may move in on, say, RKO. He has his own writers, director. But wait. It is very hard to tell where the equipment you are renting stops: you rent the carpenters, grips, gaffers, cameramen, sound men; why aren't you renting the chiefs of these departments? The director-producer either spends valuable days fighting it out with the front office or uses the company men. He may be somebody like Sam Goldwyn, who has a name that will strike anybody to silence, but even after his picture has been made, he has to fight United Artists on the way it is released, delayed, and generally hamstrung.

Or he may be a producer who is making a picture for one of the majors, and finds that although he has signed his director and stars, as of now, as of high salaries starting today, he has a rather weird time getting the stages and the general go-ahead from the company anxious to produce his production. What goes? After a while of negotiations he finds out. The producer has his own female lead signed up; the company does not mention her. After a few days of objecting to the story or the Toronto sequence, the company calls him up, surprise! With envy and with wonder it says, Why you lucky dog, you, we've *got* it. Are you lucky? Listen, get this: we just found we haven't a lead spot for May Bonnet, and, get this, you can have her! Jesus what a lucky guy. May Bonnet!

So he guessed it all along. May Bonnet is the cow this company signed a contract of $60,000 for two pictures and wants to pull out of making the second with, the first was so sad. They were stuck with her and they were doing the holdup on the producer who wanted to make a picture for them. And the final arrangement, the producer knowing necessity when he saw it, was that he bought the remainder of May Bonnet's contract for $30,000, tore it up, and told her to go back to her telephone and stay there, all alone, and found stages available for his picture with his own lead, and enough red ink to write the three-o into the budget.

But when a picture is started, many departments get to work, outside of the producer with his balances and arrangements, the writer and director dreaming up the story they are to tell (if the director is a fair name and not on the Metro or Warners' payroll — which is to say, lucky). The research department gets the script, and looks up the likeness with wonderful pertinacity and skill. The art department gets the green light and the art director delegates his draftsmen, painters, model builders, and curators to work up a rough draft, scene by scene, and then practically the whole picture in drawings, in miniatures, in paintings and models. These men build the thing you see, and change it as the camera requires; but it is always the art director himself who has laid it out, it is his department that has sketched out and painted in the things you see, from beautiful to bum. You have to have an art director, if only because he is the man who sees it in advance and starts the wheels moving for its realization.

Then there is sound, and with sound comes the musical director, who works after the picture has been made. He is a vital man in a picture's effect—at least he is when he is good enough and given any freedom; but like the cutters and special-effects men, he is not at work until after the cameras start rolling. You have to catch him later.

ANDREW SARRIS
NOTES ON
THE AUTEUR THEORY IN 1962

I call these sketches Shadowgraphs, partly by the designation to remind you at once that they derive from the darker side of life, partly because, like other shadowgraphs, they are not directly visible. When I take a shadowgraph in my hand, it makes no impression on me, and gives me no clear conception of it. Only when I hold it up opposite the wall, and now look not directly at it, but at that which appears on the wall, am I able to see it. So also with the picture I wish to show here, an inward picture that does not become perceptible until I see it through the external. This external is perhaps not quite unobtrusive, but, not until I look through it, do I discover that inner picture that I desire to show you, an inner picture too delicately drawn to be outwardly visible, woven as it is of the tenderest moods of the soul.

SØREN KIERKEGAARD, in *Either/Or*

An exhibitor once asked me if an old film I had recommended was *really* good or good only according to the *auteur* theory. I appreciate the distinction. Like the alchemists of old, *auteur* critics are notorious for rationalizing leaden clinkers into golden nuggets. Their judgments are seldom vindicated, because few spectators are conditioned to perceive in individual works the organic unity of a director's career. On a given evening, a film by John Ford must take its chances as if it were a film by Henry King. Am I implying that the weakest Ford is superior to the strongest King? Yes! This kind of unqualified affirmation seems to reduce the *auteur* theory to a game of aesthetic solitaire with all the cards turned face up. By *auteur* rules, the Fords will come up aces as invariably as the Kings will come up deuces. Presumably, we can all go home as soon as the directorial signature is flashed on the screen. To those who linger, *The Gunfighter* (King 1950) may appear worthier than *Flesh* (Ford 1932). (And how deeply one must burrow to undermine Ford!) No matter. The *auteur* theory is unyielding. If, by definition, Ford is invariably superior to King, any evidence to the contrary is merely an optical illusion. Now what could be sillier than this inflexible attitude? Let us abandon the absurdities of the *auteur* theory so that we may return to the chaos of common sense.

My labored performance as devil's advocate notwithstanding, I intend to praise the *auteur* theory, not to bury it. At the very least, I would like to grant the condemned system a hearing before its execution. The trial has dragged on for years, I know, and everyone is now bored by the abstract reasoning involved. I have little in the way of new evidence or new arguments, but I would like to change some of my previous testimony. What follows is, consequently, less a manifesto than a credo, a somewhat disorganized credo, to be sure, expressed in formless notes rather than in formal brief.

I. AIMEZ-VOUS BRAHMS?

Goethe? Shakespeare? Everything signed with their names is considered good, and one wracks one's brains to find beauty in their stupidities and failures, thus distorting the general taste. All these great talents, the Goethes, the Shakespeares, the Beethovens, the Michelangelos, created, side by side with their masterpieces, works not merely mediocre, but quite simply frightful.

—Leo Tolstoy, *Journal*, 1895–99

The preceding quotation prefaces the late André Bazin's famous critique of *"la politique des auteurs,"* which appeared in the *Cahiers du Cinéma* of April, 1957. Because no comparably lucid statement opposing the *politique* has appeared since that time, I would like to discuss some of Bazin's arguments with reference to the current situation. (I except, of course, Richard Roud's penetrating article "The French Line," which dealt mainly with the post-*Nou-*

velle Vague situation when the *politique* had degenerated into McMahonism.)

As Tolstoy's observation indicates, *la politique des auteurs* ante-dates the cinema. For centuries, the Elizabethan *politique* has decreed the reading of every Shakespearean play before any encounter with the Jonsonian repertory. At some point between *Timon of Athens* and *Volpone*, this procedure is patently unfair to Jonson's reputation. But not really. On the most superficial level of artistic reputations, the *auteur* theory is merely a figure of speech. If the man in the street could not invoke Shakespeare's name as an identifiable cultural reference, he would probably have less contact with all things artistic. The Shakespearean scholar, by contrast, will always be driven to explore the surrounding terrain, with the result that all the Elizabethan dramatists gain more rather than less recognition through the pre-eminence of one of their number. Therefore, on balance, the *politique*, as a figure of speech, does more good than harm.

Occasionally, some iconoclast will attempt to demonstrate the fallacy of this figure of speech. We will be solemnly informed that *The Gambler* was a potboiler for Dostoyevsky in the most literal sense of the word. In Jacques Rivette's *Paris Nous Appartient*, Jean-Claude Brialy asks Betty Schneider if she would still admire *Pericles* if it were not signed by Shakespeare. Zealous musicologists have played *Wellington's Victory* so often as an example of inferior Beethoven that I have grown fond of the piece, atrocious as it is. The trouble with such iconoclasm is that it presupposes an encyclopedic awareness of the *auteur* in question. If one is familiar with every Beethoven composition, *Wellington's Victory*, in itself, will hardly tip the scale toward Mozart, Bach, or Schubert. Yet that is the issue raised by the *auteur* theory. If not Beethoven, who? And why? Let us say that the *politique* for composers went Mozart, Beethoven, Bach, and Schubert. Each composer would represent a task force of compositions, arrayed by type and quality with the mighty battleships and aircraft carriers flanked by flotillas of cruisers, destroyers, and mine sweepers. When the Mozart task force collides with the Beethoven task force, symphonies roar against symphonies, quartets maneuver against quartets, and it is simply no contest with the operas. As a single force, Beethoven's nine symphonies, outgun any nine of Mozart's forty-one symphonies, both sets of quartets are almost on a par with Schubert's, but *The Magic Flute*, *The Marriage of Figaro*, and *Don Giovanni* will blow poor *Fidelio* out of the water. Then, of course, there is Bach with an entirely different deployment of composition and instrumentation. The Haydn and Handel cultists are moored in their inlets ready to join the fray, and the moderns with their nuclear noises are still mobilizing their forces.

It can be argued that any exact ranking of artists is arbitrary and pointless. Arbitrary up to a point, perhaps, but pointless, no. Even Bazin concedes the polemical value of the *politique*. Many film critics would rather not commit themselves to specific rankings ostensibly because every film should be judged on its own merits. In many instances, this reticence masks the critic's condescension to the medium. Because it has not been firmly established that the cinema is an art at all, it requires cultural audacity to establish a pantheon for film directors. Without such audacity, I see little point in being a film critic. Anyway, is it possible to honor a work of art without honoring the artist involved? I think not. Of course, any idiot can erect a pantheon out of hearsay and gossip. Without specifying any work, the Saganesque seducer will ask quite cynically, "Aimez-vous Brahms?" The fact that Brahms is included in the pantheon of high-brow pickups does not invalidate the industrious criticism that justifies the composer as a figure of speech.

Unfortunately, some critics have embraced the *auteur* theory as a short-cut to film scholarship. With a "you-see-it-or-you-don't" attitude toward the reader, the particularly lazy *auteur* critic can save himself the drudgery of communication and explanation. Indeed, at their worst, *auteur* critiques are less meaningful than the straight-forward plot reviews that pass for criticism in America. Without the necessary research and analysis, the *auteur* theory can degenerate into the kind of snobbish racket that is associated with the merchandising of paintings.

It was largely against the inadequate theoretical formulation of *la politique des auteurs* that Bazin was reacting in his friendly critique. (Henceforth, I will abbreviate *la politique des auteurs* as the *auteur* theory to avoid confusion.) Bazin introduces his arguments within the context of a family quarrel over the editorial policies of *Cahiers*. He fears that, by assigning reviews to admirers of given directors, notably Alfred Hitchcock, Jean Renoir, Roberto

Rossellini, Fritz Lang, Howard Hawks, and Nicholas Ray, every work, major and minor, of these exalted figures is made to radiate the same beauties of style and meaning. Specifically, Bazin notes a distortion when the kindly indulgence accorded the imperfect work of a Minnelli is coldly withheld from the imperfect work of Huston. The inherent bias of the *auteur* theory magnifies the gap between the two films.

I would make two points here. First, Bazin's greatness as a critic, (and I believe strongly that he was the greatest film critic who ever lived) rested in his disinterested conception of the cinema as a universal entity. It follows that he would react against a theory that cultivated what he felt were inaccurate judgments for the sake of dramatic paradoxes. He was, if anything, generous to a fault, seeking in every film some vestige of the cinematic art. That he would seek justice for Huston vis-à-vis Minnelli on even the secondary levels of creation indicates the scrupulousness of his critical personality.

However, my second point would seem to contradict my first. Bazin was wrong in this instance, insofar as any critic can be said to be wrong in retrospect. We are dealing here with Minnelli in his *Lust for Life* period and Huston in his *Moby Dick* period. Both films can be considered failures on almost any level. The miscasting alone is disastrous. The snarling force of Kirk Douglas as the tormented Van Gogh, the brutish insensibility of Anthony Quinn as Gauguin, and the nervously scraping tension between these two absurdly limited actors, deface Minnelli's meticulously objective decor, itself inappropriate for the mood of its subject. The director's presentation of the paintings themselves is singularly unperceptive in the repeated failure to maintain the proper optical distance from canvases that arouse the spectator less by their detailed draughtsmanship than by the shock of a *gestalt* wholeness. As for *Moby Dick*, Gregory Peck's Ahab deliberates long enough to let all the demons flee the Pequod, taking Melville's Lear-like fantasies with them. Huston's epic technique with its casually shifting camera viewpoint then drifts on an intellectually becalmed sea toward a fitting rendezvous with a rubber whale. These two films are neither the best nor the worst of their time. The question is: Which deserves the harder review? And there's the rub. At the time, Huston's stock in America was higher than Minnelli's. Most critics expected Huston to do "big" things, and, if they thought about it at all, expected

Minnelli to stick to "small" things like musicals. Although neither film was a critical failure, audiences stayed away in large enough numbers to make the cultural respectability of the projects suspect. On the whole, *Lust for Life* was more successful with the audiences it did reach than was *Moby Dick*.

In retrospect, *Moby Dick* represents the turning downward of Huston as a director to be taken seriously. By contrast, *Lust for Life* is simply an isolated episode in the erratic career of an interesting stylist. The exact size of Minnelli's talent may inspire controversy, but he does represent something in the cinema today. Huston is virtually a forgotten man with a few actors' classics behind him surviving as the ruins of a once-promising career. Both Eric Rohmer, who denigrated Huston in 1957, and Jean Domarchi, who was kind to Minnelli that same year, somehow saw the future more clearly on an *auteur* level than did Bazin. As Santayana has remarked: "It is a great advantage for a system of philosophy to be substantially true." If the *auteur* critics of the 1950's had not scored so many coups of clairvoyance, the *auteur* theory would not be worth discussing in the 1960's. I must add that, at the time, I would have agreed with Bazin on this and every other objection to the *auteur* theory, but subsequent history, that history about which Bazin was always so mystical, has substantially confirmed most of the principles of the *auteur* theory. Ironically, most of the original supporters of the *auteur* theory have now abandoned it. Some have discovered more useful *politiques* as directors and would-be directors. Others have succumbed to a European-oriented pragmatism where intention is now more nearly equal to talent in critical relevance. Luc Moullet's belated discovery that Samuel Fuller was, in fact, fifty years old, signaled a reorientation of *Cahiers* away from the American cinema. (The handwriting was already on the wall when Truffaut remarked recently that, whereas he and his colleagues had "discovered" *auteurs*, his successors have "invented" them.)

Bazin then explores the implications of Giraudoux's epigram: "There are no works; there are only authors." Truffaut has seized upon this paradox as the battle cry of *la politique des auteurs*. Bazin casually demonstrates how the contrary can be argued with equal probability of truth or error. He subsequently dredges up the equivalents of *Wellington's Victory* for Voltaire, Beaumarchais, Flaubert, and Gide to document his point. Bazin then yields some ground to Rohmer's argument that the history of art does not confirm the decline with age of authentic geniuses like Titian, Rembrandt, Beethoven, or nearer to us, Bonnard, Matisse, and Stravinsky. Bazin agrees with Rohmer that it is inconsistent to attribute senility only to aging film directors while, at the same time, honoring the gnarled austerity of Rembrandt's later style. This is one of the crucial propositions of the *auteur* theory, because it refutes the popular theory of decline for aging giants like Renoir and Chaplin and asserts, instead, that, as a director grows older, he is likely to become more profoundly personal than most audiences and critics can appreciate. However, Bazin immediately retrieves his lost ground by arguing that, whereas the senility of directors is no longer at issue, the evolution of an art form is. Where directors fail and fall is in the realm not of psychology but of history. If a director fails to keep pace with the development of his medium, his work will become obsolescent. What seems like senility is, in reality, a disharmony between the subjective inspiration of the director and the objective evolution of the medium. By making this distinction between the subjective capability of an *auteur* and the objective value of a work in film history, Bazin reinforces the popular impression that the Griffith of *Birth of a Nation* is superior to the Griffith of *Abraham Lincoln* in the perspective of timing, which similarly distinguishes the Eisenstein of *Potemkin* from the Eisenstein of *Ivan the Terrible*, the Renoir of *La Grande Illusion* from the Renoir of *Picnic in the Grass*, and the Welles of *Citizen Kane* from the Welles of *Mr. Arkadin*.

I have embroidered Bazin's actual examples for the sake of greater contact with the American scene. In fact, Bazin implicitly denies a decline in the later works of Chaplin and Renoir and never mentions Griffith. He suggests circuitously that Hawks's *Scarface* is clearly superior to Hawks's *Gentlemen Prefer Blondes*, although the *auteur* critics would argue the contrary. Bazin is particularly critical of Rivette's circular reasoning on *Monkey Business* as the proof of Hawks's genius. "One sees the danger," Bazin warns, "which is an aesthetic cult of personality."

Bazin's taste, it should be noted, was far more discriminating than that of American film historians. Films Bazin cites as unquestionable classics are still quite debatable here in America. After all, *Citizen Kane* was originally panned by James Agee, Richard Griffith, and Bosley Crowther, and *Scarface* has never been regarded as one of the landmarks of the American cinema by native critics. I would say that the American public has been ahead of its critics on both *Kane* and *Scarface*. Thus, to argue against the *auteur* theory in America is to assume that we have anyone of Bazin's sensibility and dedication to provide an alternative, and we simply don't.

Bazin, finally, concentrates on the American cinema, which invariably serves as the decisive battleground of the *auteur* theory, whether over *Monkey Business* or *Party Girl*. Unlike most "serious" American critics, Bazin likes Hollywood films, but not solely because of the talent of this or that director. For Bazin, the distinctively American comedy, western, and gangster genres have their own mystiques apart from the personalities of the directors concerned. How can one review an Anthony Mann western, Bazin asks, as if it were not an expression of the genre's conventions. Not that Bazin dislikes Anthony Mann's westerns. He is more concerned with otherwise admirable westerns that the *auteur* theory rejects because their directors happen to be unfashionable. Again, Bazin's critical generosity comes to the fore against the negative aspects of the *auteur* theory.

Some of Bazin's arguments tend to overlap each other as if to counter rebuttals from any direction. He argues, in turn, that the cinema is less individualistic an art than painting or literature, that Hollywood is less individualistic than other cinemas, and that, even so, the *auteur* theory never really applies anywhere. In upholding historical determinism, Bazin goes so far as to speculate that, if Racine had lived in Voltaire's century, it is unlikely that Racine's tragedies would have been any more inspired than Voltaire's. Presumably, the Age of Reason would have stifled Racine's neoclassical impulses. Perhaps. Perhaps not. Bazin's hypothesis can hardly be argued to a verifiable conclusion, but I suspect somewhat greater reciprocity between an artist and his *zeitgeist* than Bazin would allow. He mentions, more than once and in other contexts, capitalism's influence on the cinema. Without denying this influence, I still find it impossible to attribute X directors and Y films to any particular system or culture. Why should the Italian cinema be superior to the German cinema after one war, when the reverse was true after the previous one? As for artists conforming to the spirit of their age, that spirit is often expressed in contradictions, whether between Stravinsky and Sibelius, Fielding and Richardson, Picasso and Matisse, Chateaubriand and Stendhal. Even if the artist does not spring from the idealized head of Zeus, free of the embryonic stains of history, history itself is profoundly affected by his arrival. If we cannot imagine Griffith's *October* or Eisenstein's *Birth of a Nation* because we find it difficult to transpose one artist's unifying conceptions of Lee and Lincoln to the other's dialectical conceptions of Lenin and Kerensky, we are, nevertheless, compelled to recognize other differences in the personalities of these two pioneers beyond their respective cultural complexes. It is with these latter differences that the *auteur* theory is most deeply concerned. If directors and other artists cannot be wrenched from their historical environments, aesthetics is reduced to a subordinate branch of ethnography.

I have not done full justice to the subtlety of Bazin's reasoning and to the civilized skepticism with which he propounds his own arguments as slight probabilities rather than absolute certainties. Contemporary opponents of the *auteur* theory may feel that Bazin himself is suspect as a member of the *Cahiers* family. After all, Bazin does express qualified approval of the *auteur* theory as a relatively objective method of evaluating films apart from the subjective perils of impressionistic and ideological criticism. Better to analyze the director's personality than the critic's nerve centers or politics. Nevertheless, Bazin makes his stand clear by concluding: "This is not to deny the role of the author, but to restore to him the preposition without which the noun is only a limp concept. 'Author,' undoubtedly, but of what?"

Bazin's syntactical flourish raises an interesting problem in English usage. The French preposition "de" serves many functions, but among others, those of possession and authorship. In English, the preposition "by" once created a scandal in the American film industry when Otto Preminger had the temerity to advertise *The Man With the Golden Arm* as a film "by Otto Preminger." Novelist Nelson Algren and the Screenwriters' Guild raised such an outcry that the offending preposition was deleted. Even the noun "author" (which I cunningly mask as *"auteur"*) has a literary connotation in English. In general conversation, an "author" is invariably taken to be a writer. Since "by" is a preposition of authorship and not of ownership like the ambiguous "de," the fact that Preminger both

produced and directed *The Man with the Golden Arm* did not en-
title him in America to the preposition "by." No one would have
objected to the possessive form: "Otto Preminger's *The Man with
the Golden Arm.*" But, even in this case, a novelist of sufficient
reputation is usually honored with the possessive designation.
Now, this is hardly the case in France, where *The Red and the Black*
is advertised as "un film de Claude Autant-Lara." In America,
"directed by" is all the director can claim, when he is not also a well-
known producer like Alfred Hitchcock or Cecil B. de Mille.

Since most American film critics are oriented toward literature
or journalism, rather than toward future film-making, most American film criticism is directed toward the script instead of toward
the screen. The writer-hero in *Sunset Boulevard* complains that
people don't realize that someone "writes a picture; they think the
actors make it up as they go along." It would never occur to this
writer or most of his colleagues that people are even less aware
of the director's function.

Of course, the much-abused man in the street has a good excuse
not to be aware of the *auteur* theory even as a figure of speech.
Even on the so-called classic level, he is not encouraged to ask
"Aimez-vous Griffith?" or "Aimez-vous Eisenstein?" Instead, it is
which Griffith or which Eisenstein? As for less acclaimed directors,
he is lucky to find their names in the fourth paragraph of the typical review. I doubt that most American film critics really believe
that an indifferently directed film is comparable to an indifferently
written book. However, there is little point in wailing at the Philis-
tines on this issue, particularly when some progress is being made
in telling one director from another, at least when the film comes
from abroad. The Fellini, Bergman, Kurosawa, and Antonioni
promotions have helped push more directors up to the first paragraph of a review, even ahead of the plot synopsis. So, we mustn't
complain.

Where I wish to redirect the argument is toward the relative
position of the American cinema as opposed to the foreign cinema.
Some critics have advised me that the *auteur* theory only applies
to a small number of artists who make personal films, not to the
run-of-the-mill Hollywood director who takes whatever assignment is available. Like most Americans who take films seriously,
I have always felt a cultural inferiority complex about Hollywood.

509

Just a few years ago, I would have thought it unthinkable to speak in the same breath of a "commercial" director like Hitchcock and a "pure" director like Bresson. Even today, *Sight and Sound* uses different type sizes for Bresson and Hitchcock films. After years of tortured revaluation, I am now prepared to stake my critical reputation, such as it is, on the proposition that Alfred Hitchcock is artistically superior to Robert Bresson by every criterion of excellence and, further, that, film for film, director for director, the American cinema has been consistently superior to that of the rest of the world from 1915 through 1962. Consequently, I now regard the *auteur* theory primarily as a critical device for recording the history of the American cinema, the only cinema in the world worth exploring in depth beneath the frosting of a few great directors at the top.

These propositions remain to be proven and, I hope, debated. The proof will be difficult because direction in the cinema is a nebulous force in literary terms. In addition to its own jargon, the director's craft often pulls in the related jargon of music, painting, sculpture, dance, literature, theatre, architecture, all in a generally futile attempt to describe the indescribable. What is it the old jazz man says of his art? If you gotta ask what it is, it ain't? Well, the cinema is like that. Criticism can only attempt an approximation, a reasonable preponderance of accuracy over inaccuracy. I know the exceptions to the *auteur* theory as well as anyone. I can feel the human attraction of an audience going one way when I am going the other. The temptations of cynicism, common sense, and facile culture-mongering are always very strong, but, somehow, I feel that the *auteur* theory is the only hope for extending the appreciation of personal qualities in the cinema. By grouping and evaluating films according to directors, the critic can rescue individual achievements from an unjustifiable anonymity. If medieval architects and African sculptors are anonymous today, it is not because they deserved to be. When Ingmar Bergman bemoans the alienation of the modern artist from the collective spirit that rebuilt the cathedral at Chartres, he is only dramatizing his own individuality for an age that has rewarded him handsomely for the travail of his alienation. There is no justification for penalizing Hollywood directors for the sake of collective mythology. So, invective aside, "Aimez-vous Cukor?"

510

II. WHAT IS THE *AUTEUR* THEORY?

As far as I know, there is no definition of the *auteur* theory in the English language, that is, by any American or British critic. Truffaut has recently gone to great pains to emphasize that the *auteur* theory was merely a polemical weapon for a given time and a given place, and I am willing to take him at his word. But, lest I be accused of misappropriating a theory no one wants anymore, I will give the *Cahiers* critics full credit for the original formulation of an idea that reshaped my thinking on the cinema. First of all, how does the *auteur* theory differ from a straightforward theory of directors. Ian Cameron's article "Films, Directors, and Critics," in *Movie* of September, 1962, makes an interesting comment on this issue: "The assumption that underlies all the writing in *Movie* is that the director is the author of a film, the person who gives it any distinctive quality. There are quite large exceptions, with which I shall deal later." So far, so good, at least for the *auteur* theory, which even allows for exceptions. However, Cameron continues: "On the whole, we accept the cinema of directors, although without going to the farthest-out extremes of the *la politique des auteurs*, which makes it difficult to think of a bad director making a good film and almost impossible to think of a good director making a bad one." We are back to Bazin again, although Cameron naturally uses different examples. That three otherwise divergent critics like Bazin, Roud, and Cameron make essentially the same point about the *auteur* theory suggests a common fear of its abuses. I believe there is a misunderstanding here about what the *auteur* theory actually claims, particularly since the theory itself is so vague at the present time.

First of all, the *auteur* theory, at least as I understand it and now intend to express it, claims neither the gift of prophecy nor the option of extracinematic perception. Directors, even *auteurs*, do not always run true to form, and the critic can never assume that a bad director will always make a bad film. No, not always, but almost always, and that is the point. What is a bad director, but a director who has made many bad films? What is the problem then? Simply this: The badness of a director is not necessarily considered the badness of a film. If Joseph Pevney directed Garbo, Cherkassov, Olivier, Belmondo, and Harriet Andersson in *The Cherry Orchard*, the resulting spectacle might not be entirely devoid of merit with so many subsidiary *auteurs* to cover up for Joe. In fact, with this cast and this literary property, a Lumet might be safer than a Welles. The realities of casting apply to directors as well as to actors, but the *auteur* theory would demand the gamble with Welles, if he were willing.

Marlon Brando has shown us that a film can be made without a director. Indeed, *One-Eyed Jacks* is more entertaining than many films with directors. A director-conscious critic would find it difficult to say anything good or bad about direction that is nonexistent. One can talk here about photography, editing, acting, but not direction. The film even has personality, but, like *The Longest Day* and *Mutiny on the Bounty*, it is a cipher directorially. Obviously, the *auteur* theory cannot possibly cover every vagrant charm of the cinema. Nevertheless, the first premise of the *auteur* theory is the technical competence of a director as a criterion of value. A badly directed or an undirected film has no importance in a critical scale of values, but one can make interesting conversation about the subject, the script, the acting, the color, the photography, the editing, the music, the costumes, the decor, and so forth. That is the nature of the medium. You always get more for your money than mere art. Now, by the *auteur* theory, if a director has no technical competence, no elementary flair for the cinema, he is automatically cast out from the pantheon of directors. A great director has to be at least a good director. This is true in any art. What constitutes directorial talent is more difficult to define abstractly. There is less disagreement, however, on this first level of the *auteur* theory than there will be later.

The second premise of the *auteur* theory is the distinguishable personality of the director as a criterion of value. Over a group of films, a director must exhibit certain recurring characteristics of style, which serve as his signature. The way a film looks and moves should have some relationship to the way a director thinks and feels. This is an area where American directors are generally superior to foreign directors. Because so much of the American cinema is commissioned, a director is forced to express his personality through the visual treatment of material rather than through the literary content of the material. A Cukor, who works with all sorts of projects, has a more developed abstract style than a Bergman, who is free to develop his own scripts. Not that Bergman lacks personality, but his work has declined with the depletion of his ideas largely because his technique never equaled his sensibility. Joseph L. Mankiewicz and Billy Wilder are other examples of writer-directors without adequate technical mastery. By contrast, Douglas Sirk and Otto Preminger have moved up the scale because their miscellaneous projects reveal a stylistic consistency.

The third and ultimate premise of the *auteur* theory is concerned with interior meaning, the ultimate glory of the cinema as an art. Interior meaning is extrapolated from the tension between a director's personality and his material. This conception of interior meaning comes close to what Astruc defines as *mise en scène*, but not quite. It is not quite the vision of the world a director projects nor quite his attitude toward life. It is ambiguous, in any literary sense, because part of it is imbedded in the stuff of the cinema and cannot be rendered in noncinematic terms. Truffaut has called it the temperature of the director on the set, and that is a close approximation of its professional aspect. Dare I come out and say what I think it to be is an *élan* of the soul?

Lest I seem unduly mystical, let me hasten to add that all I mean by "soul" is that intangible difference between one personality and another, all other things being equal. Sometimes, this difference is expressed by no more than a beat's hesitation in the rhythm of a film. In one sequence of *La Règle du Jeu*, Renoir gallops up the stairs, turns to his right with a lurching movement, stops in hoplike uncertainty when his name is called by a coquettish maid, and, then, with marvelous postreflex continuity, resumes his bearishly shambling journey to the heroine's boudoir. If I could describe the musical grace note of that momentary suspension, and I can't, I might be able to provide a more precise definition of the *auteur* theory. As it is, all I can do is point at the specific beauties of interior meaning on the screen and, later, catalogue the moments of recognition.

The three premises of the *auteur* theory may be visualized as three concentric circles: the outer circle as technique; the middle circle, personal style; and the inner circle, interior meaning. The corresponding roles of the director may be designated as those of a technician, a stylist, and an *auteur*. There is no prescribed course by which a director passes through the three circles. Godard once remarked that Visconti had evolved from a *metteur en scène* to an *auteur*, whereas Rossellini had evolved from an *auteur* to a *metteur en scène*. From opposite directions, they emerged with comparable status. Minnelli began and remained in the second circle as a stylist; Buñuel was an *auteur* even before he had assembled the technique of the first circle. Technique is simply the ability to put a film together with some clarity and coherence. Nowadays, it is possible to become a director without knowing too much about the technical side, even the crucial functions of photography and editing. An expert production crew could probably cover up for a chimpanzee in the director's chair. How do you tell the genuine director from the quasichimpanzee? After a given number of films, a pattern is established.

In fact, the *auteur* theory itself is a pattern theory in constant flux. I would never endorse a Ptolemaic constellation of directors in a fixed orbit. At the moment, my list of *auteurs* runs something like this through the first twenty: Ophuls, Renoir, Mizoguchi, Hitchcock, Chaplin, Ford, Welles, Dreyer, Rossellini, Murnau, Griffith, Sternberg, Eisenstein, von Stroheim, Buñuel, Bresson, Hawks, Lang, Flaherty, Vigo. This list is somewhat weighted toward seniority and established reputations. In time, some of these *auteurs* will rise, some will fall, and some will be displaced either by new directors or rediscovered ancients. Again, the exact order is less important than the specific definitions of these and as many as two hundred other potential *auteurs*. I would hardly expect any other critic in the world fully to endorse this list, especially on faith. Only after thousands of films have been revaluated, will any personal pantheon have a reasonably objective validity. The task of validating the *auteur* theory is an enormous one, and the end will never be in sight. Meanwhile, the *auteur* habit of collecting random films in directorial bundles will serve posterity with at least a tentative classification.

Although the *auteur* theory emphasizes the body of a director's work rather than isolated masterpieces, it is expected of great directors that they make great films every so often. The only possible exception to his rule I can think of is Abel Gance, whose greatness is largely a function of his aspiration. Even with Gance, *La Roue* is as close to being a great film as any single work of Flaherty's. Not that single works matter that much. As Renoir has observed, a director spends his life on variations of the same film.

Two recent films—*Boccaccio '70* and *The Seven Capital Sins*—unwittingly reinforced the *auteur* theory by confirming the relative standing of the many directors involved. If I had not seen either film, I would have anticipated that the order of merit in *Boccaccio '70* would be Visconti, Fellini, and De Sica, and in *The Seven Capital Sins* Godard, Chabrol, Demy, Vadim, De Broca, Molinaro. (Dhomme, Ionesco's stage director and an unknown quantity in advance, turned out to be the worst of the lot.) There might be some argument about the relative badness of De Broca and Molinaro, but, otherwise, the directors ran true to form by almost any objective criterion of value. However, the main point here is that even in these frothy, ultracommercial servings of entertainment, the contribution of each director had less in common stylistically with the work of other directors on the project than with his own previous work.

Sometimes, a great deal of corn must be husked to yield a few kernels of internal meaning. I recently saw *Every Night at Eight*, one of the many maddeningly routine films Raoul Walsh has directed in his long career. This 1935 effort featured George Raft, Alice Faye, Frances Langford, and Patsy Kelly in one of those familiar plots about radio shows of the period. The film keeps moving along in the pleasantly unpretentious manner one would expect of Walsh until one incongruously intense scene with George Raft thrashing about in his sleep, revealing his inner fears in mumbling dream-talk. The girl he loves comes into the room in the midst of his unconscious avowals of feeling and listens sympathetically. This unusual scene was later amplified in *High Sierra* with Humphrey Bogart and Ida Lupino. The point is that one of the screen's most virile directors employed an essentially feminine narrative device to dramatize the emotional vulnerability of his heroes. If I had not been aware of Walsh in *Every Night at Eight*, the crucial link to *High Sierra* would have passed unnoticed. Such are the joys of the *auteur* theory.

PAULINE KAEL
CIRCLES AND SQUARES

. . . the first premise of the auteur *theory is the technical competence of a director as a criterion of value . . . The second premise
of the* auteur *theory is the distinguishable personality of the director as a criterion of value. . . . The third and ultimate premise of
the* auteur *theory is concerned with interior meaning, the ultimate
glory of the cinema as an art. Interior meaning is extrapolated from
the tension between a director's personality and his material. . . .*

*Sometimes a great deal of corn must be husked to yield a few ker-
nels of internal meaning. I recently saw* Every Night at Eight, *one of
the many maddeningly routine films Raoul Walsh has directed in
his long career. This 1935 effort featured George Raft, Alice Faye,
Frances Langford and Patsy Kelly in one of those familiar plots
about radio shows of the period. The film keeps moving along in
the pleasantly unpretentious manner one would expect of Walsh
until one incongruously intense scene with George Raft thrashing
about in his sleep, revealing his inner fears in mumbling dream
talk. The girl he loves comes into the room in the midst of his unconscious avowals of feeling, and listens sympathetically. This
unusual scene was later amplified in* High Sierra *with Humphrey
Bogart and Ida Lupino. The point is that one of the screen's most
virile directors employed an essentially feminine narrative device
to dramatize the emotional vulnerability of his heroes. If I had not
been aware of Walsh in* Every Night at Eight, *the crucial link to*

516

High Sierra *would have passed unnoticed. Such are the joys of the* auteur *theory.*

—Andrew Sarris, "Notes on the Auteur Theory in 1962," *Film Culture*, Winter 1962–1963.

Perhaps a little more corn should be husked; perhaps, for example, we can husk away the word "internal" (is "internal meaning" any different from "meaning"?). We might ask why the link is "crucial"? Is it because the device was "incongruously intense" in *Every Night at Eight* and so demonstrated a try for something *deeper* on Walsh's part? But if his merit is his "pleasantly unpretentious manner" (which is to say, I suppose, that, recognizing the limitations of the script, he wasn't trying to do much) then the incongruous device was probably a misconceived attempt that disturbed the manner—like a bad playwright interrupting a comedy scene because he cannot resist the opportunity to tug at your heartstrings. We might also ask why this narrative device is "essentially feminine": is it more feminine than masculine to be asleep, or to talk in one's sleep, or to reveal feelings? Or, possibly, does Sarris regard the device as feminine because the listening woman becomes a sympathetic figure and emotional understanding is, in this "virile" context, assumed to be essentially feminine? Perhaps only if one accepts the narrow notions of virility so common in our action films can this sequence be seen as "essentially feminine," and it is amusing that a critic can both support these clichés of the male world and be so happy when they are violated.

This is how we might quibble with a different *kind* of critic but we would never get anywhere with Sarris if we tried to examine what he is saying sentence by sentence.

So let us ask, what is the meaning of the passage? Sarris has noticed that in *High Sierra* (not a very good movie) Raoul Walsh repeated an uninteresting and obvious device that he had earlier used in a worse movie. And for some inexplicable reason, Sarris concludes that he would not have had this joy of discovery without the *auteur* theory.

But in every art form, critics traditionally notice and point out the way the artists borrow from themselves (as well as from others) and how the same devices, techniques, and themes reappear in their work. This is obvious in listening to music, seeing plays, reading

517

novels, watching actors; we take it for granted that this is how we perceive the development or the decline of an artist (and it may be necessary to point out to *auteur* critics that repetition without development is decline). When you see Hitchcock's *Saboteur* there is no doubt that he drew heavily and clumsily from *The 39 Steps*, and when you see *North by Northwest* you can see that he is once again toying with the ingredients of *The 39 Steps* — and apparently having a good time with them. Would Sarris not notice the repetition in the Walsh films without the *auteur* theory? Or shall we take the more cynical view that without some commitment to Walsh as an *auteur*, he probably wouldn't be spending his time looking at these movies?

If we may be permitted a literary analogy, we can visualize Sarris researching in the archives of the *Saturday Evening Post*, tracing the development of Clarence Budington Kelland, who, by the application of something like the *auteur* theory, would emerge as a much more important writer than Dostoyevsky; for in Kelland's case Sarris's three circles, the three premises of the *auteur* theory, have been consistently congruent. Kelland is technically competent (even "pleasantly unpretentious"), no writer has a more "distinguishable personality," and if "interior meaning" is what can be extrapolated from, say, *Hatari!* or *Advise and Consent* or *What Ever Happened to Baby Jane?* then surely Kelland's stories with their attempts to force a bit of character and humor into the familiar plot outlines are loaded with it. Poor misguided Dostoyevsky, too full of what he has to say to bother with "technical competence," tackling important themes in each work (surely the worst crime in the *auteur* book) and with his almost incredible unity of personality and material leaving you nothing to extrapolate from, he'll never make it. If the editors of *Movie* ranked authors the way they do directors, Dostoyevsky would probably be in that almost untouchable category of the "ambitious."

It should be pointed out that Sarris's defense of the *auteur* theory is based not only on aesthetics but on a rather odd pragmatic statement: "Thus to argue against the *auteur* theory in America is to assume that we have anyone of Bazin's sensibility and dedication to provide an alternative, and we simply don't." Which I take to mean that the *auteur* theory is necessary in the absence of a critic who wouldn't need it. This is a new approach to aesthetics, and I hope

Sarris's humility does not camouflage his double-edged argument. If his aesthetics is based on expediency, then it may be expedient to point out that it takes extraordinary intelligence and discrimination and taste to *use* any theory in the arts, and that without those qualities, a theory becomes a rigid formula (which is indeed what is happening among *auteur* critics). The greatness of critics like Bazin in France and Agee in America may have something to do with their using their full range of intelligence and intuition, rather than relying on formulas. Criticism is an art, not a science, and a critic who follows rules will fail in one of his most important functions: perceiving what is original and important in *new* work and helping others to see.

THE OUTER CIRCLE

. . . the first premise of the auteur *theory is the technical competence of a director as a criterion of value.*

This seems less the premise of a theory than a commonplace of judgment, as Sarris himself indicates when he paraphrases it as, "A great director has to be at least a good director." But this commonplace, though it *sounds* reasonable and basic, is a shaky premise: sometimes the greatest artists in a medium bypass or violate the simple technical competence that is so necessary for hacks. For example, it is doubtful if Antonioni could handle a routine directorial assignment of the type at which John Struges is so proficient *(Escape from Fort Bravo* or *Bad Day at Black Rock*), but surely Antonioni's *L'Avventura* is the work of a great director. And the greatness of a director like Cocteau has nothing to do with mere technical competence: his greatness is in being able to achieve his own personal expression and style. And just as there were writers like Melville or Dreiser who triumphed over various kinds of technical incompetence, and who were, as artists, incomparably greater than the facile technicians of their day, a new great film director may appear whose very greatness is in his struggling toward grandeur or in massive accumulation of detail. An artist who is not a good technician can indeed create new standards, because standards of technical competence are based on comparisons with work already done.

Just as new work in other arts is often attacked because it violates the accepted standards and thus seems crude and ugly and incoherent, great new directors are very likely to be condemned precisely on the grounds that they're not even good directors, that they don't know their "business." Which, in some cases, is true, but does it matter when that "business" has little to do with what they want to express in films? It may even be a hindrance, leading them to banal slickness, instead of discovery of their own methods. For some, at least, Cocteau may be right: "The only technique worth having is the technique you invent for yourself." The director must be judged on the basis of what he produces—his films—and if he can make great films without knowing the standard methods, without the usual craftsmanship of the "good director," then that is the way he works. I would amend Sarris's premise to, "In works of a lesser rank, technical competence can help to redeem the weaknesses of the material." In fact it seems to be precisely this category that the *auteur* critics are most interested in—the routine material that a good craftsman can make into a fast and enjoyable movie. What, however, makes the *auteur* critics so incomprehensible, is not their *preference* for works of this category (in this they merely follow the lead of children who also prefer simple action films and westerns and horror films to works that make demands on their understanding) but their truly astonishing inability to exercise taste and judgment *within* their area of preference. Moviegoing kids are, I think, much more reliable guides to this kind of movie than the *auteur* critics: every kid I've talked to knows that Henry Hathaway's *North to Alaska* was a surprisingly funny, entertaining movie and *Hatari!* (classified as a "masterpiece" by half the *Cahiers* Conseil des Dix, Peter Bogdanovich, and others) was a terrible bore.

THE MIDDLE CIRCLE

. . . the second premise of the auteur *theory is the distinguishable personality of the director as a criterion of value.*

Up to this point there has really been no theory, and now, when Sarris begins to work on his foundation, the entire edifice of civilized standards of taste collapses while he's tacking down his floorboards. Traditionally, in any art, the personalities of all those involved in a production have been a factor in judgment, but that the *distinguishability* of personality should in itself be a criterion of value completely confuses *normal* judgment. The smell of a skunk is more distinguishable than the perfume of a rose; does that make it better? Hitchcock's personality is certainly more distinguishable in *Dial M for Murder, Rear Window, Vertigo*, than Carol Reed's in *The Stars Look Down, Odd Man Out, The Fallen Idol, The Third Man, An Outcast of the Islands,* if for no other reason than because Hitchcock repeats while Reed tackles new subject matter. But how does this distinguishable personality function as a criterion for judging the works? We recognize the hands of Carné and Prévert in *Le Jour se Lève,* but that is not what makes it a beautiful film; we can just as easily recognize their hands in *Quai des Brumes* —which is not such a good film. We can recognize that *Le Plaisir* and *The Earrings of Madame de . . .* are both the work of Ophuls, but *Le Plaisir* is not a great film, and *Madame de . . .* is.

Often the works in which we are most aware of the personality of the director are his worst films—when he falls back on the devices he has already done to death. When a famous director makes a good movie, we look at the movie, we don't think about the director's personality; when he makes a stinker we notice his familiar touches because there's not much else to watch. When Preminger makes an expert, entertaining whodunit like *Laura,* we don't look for his personality (it has become part of the texture of the film); when he makes an atrocity like *Whirlpool,* there's plenty of time to look for his "personality"—if that's your idea of a good time.

It could even be argued, I think, that Hitchcock's uniformity, his mastery of tricks, and his cleverness at getting audiences to respond according to his calculations—the feedback he wants and gets from them—reveal not so much a personal style as a personal theory of audience psychology, that his methods and approach are not those of an artist but a prestidigitator. The *auteur* critics respond just as Hitchcock expects the gullible to respond. This is not so surprising —often the works *auteur* critics call masterpieces are ones that seem to reveal the contempt of the director for the audience.

It's hard to believe that Sarris seriously attempts to apply "the distinguishable personality of the director as a criterion of value" because when this premise becomes troublesome, he just tries to brazen his way out of difficulties. For example, now that John

Huston's work has gone flat* Sarris casually dismisses him with: "Huston is virtually a forgotten man with a few actors' classics behind him . . ." If *The Maltese Falcon*, perhaps the most high-style thriller ever made in America, a film Huston both wrote and directed, is not a director's film, what is? And if the distinguishable personality of the director is a criterion of value, then how can Sarris dismiss the Huston who comes through so unmistakably in *The Treasure of Sierra Madre*, *The African Queen*, or *Beat the Devil*, or even in a muddled Huston film like *Key Largo*? If these are actors' movies, then what on earth is a director's movie?

Isn't the *auteur* theory a hindrance to clear judgment of Huston's movies and of his career? Disregarding the theory, we see some fine film achievements and we perceive a remarkably distinctive directorial talent; we also see intervals of weak, half-hearted assignments like *Across the Pacific* and *In This Our Life*. Then, after *Moulin Rouge*, except for the blessing of *Beat the Devil*, we see a career that splutters out in ambitious failures like *Moby Dick* and confused projects like *The Roots of Heaven* and *The Misfits*, and strictly commercial projects like *Heaven Knows, Mr. Allison*. And this kind of career seems more characteristic of film history, especially in the United States, than the ripening development and final mastery envisaged by the *auteur* theory—a theory that makes it almost de rigeur to regard Hitchcock's American films as superior to his early English films. Is Huston's career so different, say, from Fritz Lang's? How is it that Huston's early good—almost great—work, must be rejected along with his mediocre recent work, but Fritz Lang, being sanctified as an *auteur*, has his bad recent work praised along with his good? Employing more usual norms, if you respect the Fritz Lang who made *M* and *You Only Live Once*, if you enjoy the excesses of style and the magnificent absurbities of a film like *Metropolis*, then it is only good sense to reject the ugly stupidity of *Journey to the Lost City*. It is an insult to an artist to praise

---

* And, by the way, the turning point came, I think, not with *Moby Dick*, as Sarris indicates, but much earlier, with *Moulin Rouge*. This may not be so apparent to *auteur* critics concerned primarily with style and individual touches, because what was shocking about *Moulin Rouge* was that the content was sentimental mush. But critics who accept even the worst of Minnelli probably wouldn't have been bothered by the fact that *Moulin Rouge* was soft in the center, it had so many fancy touches at the edges.

his bad work along with his good; it indicates that you are incapable of judging either.

A few years ago, a friend who reviewed Jean Renoir's University of California production of his play *Carola*, hailed it as "a work of genius." When I asked my friend how he could so describe this very unfortunate play, he said, "Why, of course, it's a work of genius. Renoir's a genius, so anything he does is a work of genius." This could almost be a capsule version of the *auteur* theory (just substitute *Hatari!* for *Carola*) and in this reductio ad absurdum, viewing a work is superfluous, as the judgment is a priori. It's like buying clothes by the label: this is Dior, so it's good. (This is not so far from the way the *auteur* critics work, either.)

Sarris doesn't even play his own game with any decent attention to the rules: it is as absurd to praise Lang's recent bad work as to dismiss Huston's early good work; surely it would be more consistent if he also tried to make a case for Huston's bad pictures? That would be more consistent than devising a category called "actors' classics" to explain his good pictures away. If *The Maltese Falcon* and *The Treasure of Sierra Madre* are actors' classics, then what makes Hawks's *To Have and Have Not* and *The Big Sleep* (which were obviously tailored to the personalities of Bogart and Bacall) the work of an *auteur*?

Sarris believes that what makes an *auteur* is "an élan of the soul." (This critical language is barbarous. Where else should élan come from? It's like saying "a digestion of the stomach." A film critic need not be a theoretician, but it is necessary that he know how to use words. This might, indeed, be a first premise for a theory.) Those who have this élan presumably have it forever and their films reveal the "organic unity" of the directors' careers; and those who don't have it—well, they can only make "actors' classics." It's ironic that a critic trying to establish simple "objective" rules as a guide for critics who he thinks aren't gifted enough to use taste and intelligence, ends up—where, actually, he began—with a theory based on mystical insight. This might really make demands on the *auteur* critics if they did not simply take the easy way out by arbitrary decisions of who's got "it" and who hasn't. Their decisions are not merely not based on their theory; their decisions are *beyond* criticism. It's like a woman's telling us that she feels a certain dress *does* something for her: her feeling has about as much to do with

523

critical judgment as the *auteur* critics' feeling that Minnelli *has* "it," but Huston never had "it."

Even if a girl had plenty of "it," she wasn't expected to keep it forever. But this "élan" is not supposed to be affected by the vicissitudes of fortune, the industrial conditions of moviemaking, the turmoil of a country, or the health of a director. Indeed, Sarris says, "If directors and other artists cannot be wrenched from their historical environments, aesthetics is reduced to a subordinate branch of ethnography." May I suggest that if, in order to judge movies, the *auteur* critics must wrench the directors from their historical environments (which is, to put it mildly, impossible) so that they can concentrate on the detection of that "élan," they are reducing aesthetics to a form of idiocy. Élan as the permanent attribute Sarris posits can only be explained in terms of a cult of personality. May I suggest that a more meaningful description of élan is what a man feels when he is working at the height of his powers—and what we respond to in works of art with the excited cry of "This time, he's really done it" or "This shows what he could do when he got the chance" or "He's found his style" or "I never realized he had it in him to do anything so good," a response to his joy in creativity.

Sarris experiences "joy" when he recognizes a pathetic little link between two Raoul Walsh pictures (he never does explain whether the discovery makes him think the pictures are any better) but he wants to see artists in a pristine state—their essences, perhaps? —separated from all the life that has formed them and to which they try to give expression.

THE INNER CIRCLE

The third and ultimate premise of the auteur *theory is concerned with interior meaning, the ultimate glory of the cinema as an art. Interior meaning is extrapolated from the tension between a director's personality and his material.*

This is a remarkable formulation: it is the opposite of what we have always taken for granted in the arts, that the artist expresses himself in the unity of form and content. What Sarris believes to be "the ultimate glory of the cinema as an art" is what has generally been considered the frustrations of a man working against the given material. Fantastic as this formulation is, it does something that the first two premises didn't do: it clarifies the interests of the *auteur* critics. If we have been puzzled because the *auteur* critics seemed so deeply involved, even dedicated, in becoming connoisseurs of trash, now we can see by this theoretical formulation that trash is indeed their chosen province of film.

Their ideal *auteur* is the man who signs a long-term contract, directs any script that's handed to him, and expresses himself by shoving bits of style up the crevasses of the plots. If his "style" is in conflict with the story line or subject matter, so much the better —more chance for tension. Now we can see why there has been so much use of the term "personality" in this aesthetics (the term which seems so inadequate when discussing the art of Griffith or Renoir or Murnau or Dreyer)—a routine, commercial movie can sure use a little "personality."

Now that we have reached the inner circle (the bull's eye turns out to be an empty socket) we can see why the shoddiest films are often praised the most. Subject matter is irrelevant (so long as it isn't treated sensitively—which is bad) and will quickly be disposed of by *auteur* critics who know that the smart director isn't responsible for that anyway; they'll get on to the important subject—his *mise-en-scène:* The director who fights to do something he cares about is a square. Now we can at least begin to understand why there was such contempt toward Huston for what was, in its way, a rather extraordinary effort—the *Moby Dick* that failed; why *Movie* considers Roger Corman a better director than Fred Zinnemann and ranks Joseph Losey next to God, why Bogdanovich, Mekas, and Sarris give their highest critical ratings to *What Ever Happened to Baby Jane?* (mighty big crevasses there). If Carol Reed had made only movies like *The Man Between*—in which he obviously worked to try to make something out of a ragbag of worn-out bits of material—he might be considered "brilliant" too. (But this is doubtful: although even the worst Reed is superior to Aldrich's *Baby Jane*, Reed would probably be detected, and rejected, as a man interested in substance rather than sensationalism.)

I am angry, but am I unjust? Here's Sarris:

> A Cukor who works with all sorts of projects has a more developed abstract style than a Bergman who is free to develop his own scripts. Not that Bergman lacks personality, but his work has declined with

the depletion of his ideas largely because his technique never equaled his sensibility. Joseph L. Mankiewicz and Billy Wilder are other examples of writer-directors without adequate technical mastery. By contrast, Douglas Sirk and Otto Preminger have moved up the scale because their miscellaneous projects reveal a stylistic consistency.

How neat it all is — Bergman's "work has declined with the depletion of his ideas largely because his technique never equaled his sensibility." But what on earth does that mean? How did Sarris perceive Bergman's sensibility except through his technique? Is Sarris saying what he seems to be saying, that if Bergman had developed more "technique," his work wouldn't be dependent on his ideas? I'm afraid this *is* what he means, and that when he refers to Cukor's "more developed abstract style" he means by "abstract" something unrelated to ideas, a technique not dependent on the content of the films. This is curiously reminiscent of a view common enough in the business world, that it's better not to get too involved, too personally interested in business problems, or they take over your life; and besides, you don't function as well when you've lost your objectivity. But this is the *opposite* of how an artist works. His technique, his *style*, is determined by his range of involvements, and his preference for certain themes. Cukor's style is no more *abstract*(!) than Bergman's: Cukor has a range of subject matter that he can handle and when he gets a good script within his range (like *The Philadelphia Story* or *Pat and Mike*) he does a good job; but he is at an immense *artistic* disadvantage, compared with Bergman, because he is dependent on the ideas of so many (and often bad) scriptwriters and on material which is often alien to his talents. It's amusing (and/or depressing) to see the way *auteur* critics tend to downgrade writer-directors — who are in the *best* position to use the film medium for personal expression.

Sarris does some pretty fast shuffling with Huston and Bergman; why doesn't he just come out and admit that writer-directors are disqualified by his third premise? They can't arrive at that "interior meaning, the ultimate glory of the cinema" because a writer-director has no tension between his personality and his material, so there's nothing for the *auteur* critic to extrapolate from.

What is all this nonsense about extrapolating "interior" meaning from the tension between a director's personality and his material?

A competent commercial director generally does the best he can with what he's got to work with. Where is the "tension"? And if you can locate some, what kind of meaning could you draw out of it except that the director's having a bad time with lousy material or material he doesn't like? Or maybe he's trying to speed up the damned production so he can do something else that he has some *hopes* for? Are these critics honestly (and futilely) looking for "interior meanings" or is this just some form of intellectual diddling that helps to sustain their pride while they're viewing silly movies? Where is the tension in Howard Hawks's films? When he has good material, he's capable of better than good direction, as he demonstrates in films like *Twentieth Century, Bringing Up Baby, His Girl Friday*; and in *To Have and Have Not* and *The Big Sleep* he demonstrates that with help from the actors, he can jazz up ridiculous scripts. But what "interior meaning" can be extrapolated from an enjoyable, harmless, piece of kitsch like *Only Angels Have Wings;* what can the *auteur* critics see in it beyond the sex and glamor and fantasies of the high-school boys' universe—exactly what the mass audience liked it for? And when Hawks's material and/or cast is dull and when his heart isn't in the production—when by the *auteur* theory he should show his "personality," the result is something soggy like *The Big Sky.*

George Cukor's modest statement, "Give me a good script and I'll be a hundred times better as a director"* provides some notion of how a director may experience the problem of the given material. What can Cukor do with a script like *The Chapman Report* but try to kid it, to dress it up a bit, to show off the talents of Jane Fonda and Claire Bloom and Glynis Johns, and to give the total production a little flair and craftsmanship. At best, he can make an entertaining bad movie. A director with something like magical gifts *can* make a silk purse out of a sow's ear. But if he has it in him to do

---

* In another sense, it is perhaps immodest. I would say, give Cukor a clever script with light, witty dialogue, and he will know what to do with it. But I wouldn't expect more than glossy entertainment. (It seems almost too obvious to mention it, but can Sarris really discern the "distinguishable personality" of George Cukor and his "abstract" style in films like *Bhowani Junction, Les Girls, The Actress, A Life of Her Own, The Model and the Marriage Broker, Edward, My Son, A Woman's Face, Romeo and Juliet, A Double Life?* I wish I could put him to the test. I can only *suspect* that many *auteur* critics would have a hard time seeing those telltale traces of the beloved in their works.)

527

more in life than make silk purses, the triumph is minor—even if the purse is lined with gold. Only by the use of the *auteur* theory does this little victory become "ultimate glory." For some unexplained reason those traveling in *auteur* circles believe that making that purse out of a sow's ear is an infinitely greater accomplishment than making a solid carrying case out of a good piece of leather (as, for example, a Zinnemann does with *From Here to Eternity* or *The Nun's Story*).

I suppose we should be happy for Sirk and Preminger elevated up the glory "scale," but I suspect that the "stylistic consistency" of say, Preminger, could be a matter of his *limitations*, and that the only way you could tell he made some of his movies was that he used the same players so often (Linda Darnell, Jeanne Crain, Gene Tierney, Dana Andrews, et al., gave his movies the Preminger look). But the argument is ludicrous anyway, because if Preminger shows stylistic consistency with subject matter as varied as *Carmen Jones*, *Anatomy of a Murder*, and *Advise and Consent*, then by any rational standards he should be attacked rather than elevated. I don't think these films are stylistically consistent, nor do I think Preminger is a great director—for the very simple reason that his films are consistently superficial and facile. (*Advise and Consent*, an *auteur* "masterpiece"—Ian Cameron, Paul Mayersberg, and Mark Shivas of *Movie* and Jean Douchet of *Cahiers du Cinéma* rate it first on their ten best lists of 1962 and Sarris gives it his top rating—seems not so much Preminger-directed as other-directed. That is to say, it seems calculated to provide what as many different groups as possible want to see: there's something for the liberals, something for the conservatives, something for the homosexuals, something for the family.) An editorial in *Movie* states: "In order to enjoy Preminger's films the spectator must apply an unprejudiced intelligence; he is constantly required to examine the quality not only of the characters' decisions but also of his own reactions," and "He presupposes an intelligence active enough to allow the spectator to make connections, comparisons and judgments." May I suggest that this spectator would have better things to do than the editors of *Movie* who put out Preminger issues? They may have, of course, the joys of discovering links between *Centennial Summer*, *Forever Amber*, *That Lady in Ermine*, and *The Thirteenth Letter*, but I refuse to believe in these ever-so-intellectual protestations. The *auteur* critics aren't a very *convincing* group.

I assume that Sarris's theory is not based on his premises (the necessary causal relationships are absent), but rather that the premises were devised in a clumsy attempt to prop up the "theory." (It's a good thing he stopped at three: a few more circles and we'd really be in hell, which might turn out to be the last refinement of film tastes — Abbott and Costello comedies, perhaps?) These critics work embarrassingly hard trying to give some semblance of intellectual respectability to a preoccupation with mindless, repetitious commercial products — the kind of action movies that the restless, rootless men who wander on Forty-Second Street and in the Tenderloin of all our big cities have always preferred just because they could respond to them without thought. These movies soak up your time. I would suggest that they don't serve a very different function for Sarris or Bogdanovich or the young men of *Movie* — even though they devise elaborate theories to justify soaking up their time. An educated man must have to work pretty hard to set his intellectual horizons at the level of *I Was a Male War Bride* (which, incidentally, wasn't even a good *commercial* movie).

"Interior meaning" seems to be what those in the know know. It's a mystique — and a mistake. The *auteur* critics never tell us by what divining rods they have discovered the élan of a Minnelli or a Nicholas Ray or a Leo McCarey. They're not critics; they're inside dopesters. There must be another circle that Sarris forgot to get to — the one where the secrets are kept. . . .

PETER WOLLEN
FROM SIGNS AND MEANING IN THE CINEMA

THE AUTEUR THEORY

The *politique des auteurs* —the *auteur* theory, as Andrew Sarris calls it —was developed by the loosely knit group of critics who wrote for *Cahiers du Cinéma* and made it the leading film magazine in the world. It sprang from the conviction that the American cinema was worth studying in depth, that masterpieces were made not only by a small upper crust of directors, the cultured gilt on the commercial gingerbread, but by a whole range of authors, whose work had previously been dismissed and consigned to oblivion. There were special conditions in Paris which made this conviction possible. Firstly, there was the fact that American films were banned from France under the Vichy government and the German Occupation. Consequently, when they reappeared after the Liberation they came with a force—and an emotional impact—which was necessarily missing in the Anglo-Saxon countries themselves. And, secondly, there was a thriving ciné-club movement, due in part to the close connections there had always been in France between the cinema and the intelligentsia: witness the example of Jean Cocteau or André Malraux. Connected with this ciné-club movement was the magnificent Paris *Cinémathèque*, the work of Henri Langlois, a great *auteur*, as Jean-Luc Godard described him. The policy of the *Cinémathèque* was to show the maximum number of films, to plough back the production of the past in order to produce the culture in which the cinema of the future could thrive. It gave French *cinéphiles* an unmatched perception of the historical dimensions of Hollywood and the careers of individual directors.

The *auteur* theory grew up rather haphazardly; it was never elaborated in programmatic terms, in a manifesto or collective statement. As a result, it could be interpreted and applied on rather broad lines; different critics developed somewhat different methods within a loose framework of common attitudes. This looseness and diffuseness of the theory has allowed flagrant misunderstandings to take root, particularly among critics in Britain and the United States. Ignorance has been compounded by a vein of hostility to foreign ideas and a taste for travesty and caricature. However, the fruitfulness of the *auteur* approach has been such that it has made headway even on the most unfavorable terrain. For instance, a recent straw poll of British critics, conducted in conjunction with a Don Siegel Retrospective at the National Film Theatre, revealed that, among American directors most admired, a group consisting of Budd Boetticher, Samuel Fuller and Howard Hawks ran immediately behind Ford, Hitchcock and Welles, who topped the poll, but ahead of Billy Wilder, Josef Von Sternberg and Preston Sturges.

Of course, some individual directors have always been recognised as outstanding: Charles Chaplin, John Ford, Orson Welles. The *auteur* theory does not limit itself to acclaiming the director as the main author of a film. It implies an operation of decipherment; it reveals authors where none had been seen before. For years, the model of an author in the cinema was that of the European director, with open artistic aspirations and full control over his films. This model still lingers on; it lies behind the existential distinction between art films and popular films. Directors who built their reputations in Europe were dismissed after they crossed the Atlantic, reduced to anonymity. American Hitchcock was contrasted unfavourably with English Hitchcock, American Renoir with French Renoir, American Fritz Lang with German Fritz Lang. The *auteur* theory has led to the revaluation of the second, Hollywood careers of these and other European directors; without it, masterpieces such as *Scarlet Street* or *Vertigo* would never have been perceived. Conversely, the *auteur* theory has been sceptical when offered an American director whose salvation has been exile to Europe. It is difficult now to argue that *Brute Force* has ever been excelled by Jules Dassin or that Joseph Losey's recent work is markedly superior to, say, *The Prowler*.

531

In time, owing to the diffuseness of the original theory, two main schools of *auteur* critics grew up: those who insisted on revealing a core of meanings, of thematic motifs, and those who stressed style and *mise en scène*. There is an important distinction here, which I shall return to later. The work of the *auteur* has a semantic dimension, it is not purely formal; the work of the *metteur en scène*, on the other hand, does not go beyond the realm of performance, of transposing into the special complex of cinematic codes and channels a pre-existing text: a scenario, a book or a play. As we shall see, the meaning of the films of an *auteur* is constructed *a posteriori*; the meaning — semantic, rather than stylistic or expressive — of the films of a *metteur en scène* exists *a priori*. In concrete cases, of course, this distinction is not always clear-cut. There is controversy over whether some directors should be seen as *auteurs* or *metteurs en scène*. For example, though it is possible to make intuitive ascriptions, there have been no really persuasive accounts as yet of Raoul Walsh or William Wyler as *auteurs*, to take two very different directors. Opinions might differ about Don Siegel or George Cukor. Because of the difficulty of fixing the distinction in these concrete cases, it has often become blurred; indeed, some French critics have tended to value the *metteur en scène* above the *auteur*. MacMahonism sprang up, with its cult of Walsh, Lang, Losey and Preminger, its fascination with violence and its notorious text: "Charlton Heston is an axiom of the cinema." What André Bazin called "aesthetic cults of personality" began to be formed. Minor directors were acclaimed before they had, in any real sense, been identified and defined.

Yet the *auteur* theory has survived despite all the hallucinating critical extravaganzas which it has fathered. It has survived because it is indispensable. Geoffrey Nowell-Smith has summed up the *auteur* theory as it is normally presented today:

> One essential corollary of the theory as it has been developed is the discovery that the defining characteristics of an author's work are not necessarily those which are most readily apparent. The purpose of criticism thus becomes to uncover behind the superficial contrasts of subject and treatment a hard core of basic and often recondite motifs. The pattern formed by these motifs . . . is what gives an author's work its particular structure, both defining it internally and distinguishing one body of work from another.

It is this "structural approach," as Nowell-Smith calls it, which is indispensable for the critic.

The test case for the *auteur* theory is provided by the work of Howard Hawks. Why Hawks, rather than, say, Frank Borzage or King Vidor? Firstly, Hawks is a director who has worked for years within the Hollywood system. His first film, *Road to Glory*, was made in 1926. Yet throughout his long career he has only once received general critical acclaim, for his wartime film, *Sergeant York*, which closer inspection reveals to be eccentric and atypical of the main *corpus* of Hawks's films. Secondly, Hawks has worked in almost every genre. He has made westerns *(Rio Bravo)*, gangsters *(Scarface)*, war films *(Air Force)*, thrillers *(The Big Sleep)*, science fiction *(The Thing from Another World)*, musicals *(Gentlemen Prefer Blondes)*, comedies *(Bringing up Baby)*, even a Biblical epic *(Land of the Pharaohs)*. Yet all of these films (except perhaps *Land of the Pharaohs*, which he himself was not happy about) exhibit the same thematic preoccupations, the same recurring motifs and incidents, the same visual style and tempo. In the same way that Roland Barthes constructed a species of *homo racinianus*, the critic can construct a *homo hawksianus*, the protagonist of Hawksian values in the problematic Hawksian world.

Hawks achieved this by reducing the genres to two basic types: the adventure drama and the crazy comedy. These two types express inverse views of the world, the positive and negative poles of the Hawksian vision. Hawks stands opposed, on the one hand, to John Ford and, on the other hand, to Budd Boetticher. All these directors are concerned with the problem of heroism. For the hero, as an individual, death is an absolute limit which cannot be transcended: it renders the life which preceded it meaningless, absurd. How then can there be any meaningful individual action during life? How can individual action have any value—be heroic— if it cannot have transcendent value, because of the absolutely devaluing limit of death? John Ford finds the answer to this question by placing and situating the individual within society and within history, specifically within American history. Ford finds transcendent values in the historic vocation of America as a nation, to bring civilisation to a savage land, the garden to the wilderness. At the same time, Ford also sees these values themselves as problematic; he begins to question the movement of American history itself. Boetticher, on the contrary, insists on a radical individualism.

"I am not interested in making films about mass feelings. I am for the individual." He looks for values in the encounter with death itself: the underlying metaphor is always that of the bull-fighter in the arena. The hero enters a group of companions, but there is no possibility of group solidarity. Boetticher's hero acts by dissolving groups and collectives of any kind into their constituent individuals, so that he confronts each person face-to-face; the films develop, in Andrew Sarris's words, into "floating poker games, where every character takes turns at bluffing about his hand until the final showdown." Hawks, unlike Boetticher, seeks transcendent values beyond the individual, in solidarity with others. But, unlike Ford, he does not give his heroes any historical dimension, any destiny in time.

For Hawks the highest human emotion is the camaraderie of the exclusive, self-sufficient, all-male group. Hawk's heroes are cattlemen, marlin-fishermen, racing-drivers, pilots, big-game hunters, habituated to danger and living apart from society, actually cut off from it physically by dense forest, sea, snow or desert. Their aerodromes are fog-bound; the radio has cracked up; the next mail-coach or packet-boat does not leave for a week. The *élite* group strictly preserves its exclusivity. It is necessary to pass a test of ability and courage to win admittance. The group's only internal tensions come when one member lets the other down (the drunk deputy in *Rio Bravo*, the panicky pilot in *Only Angels Have Wings)* and must redeem himself by some act of exceptional bravery, or occasionally when too much 'individualism' threatens to disrupt the close-knit circle (the rivalry between drivers in *Red Line 7000*, the fighter pilot among the bomber crew in *Air Force).* The group's security is the first commandment: "You get a stunt team in acrobatics in the air—if one of them is no good, then they're all in trouble. If someone loses his nerve catching animals, then the whole bunch can be in trouble." The group members are bound together by rituals (in *Hatari!* blood is exchanged by transfusion) and express themselves univocally in communal sing-songs. There is a famous example of this in *Rio Bravo*. In *Dawn Patrol* the camaraderie of the pilots stretches even across the enemy lines: a captured German ace is immediately drafted into the group and joins in the sing-song; in *Hatari!* hunters of different nationality and in different places join together in a song over an intercom radio system.

Hawks's heroes pride themselves on their professionalism. They ask: "How good is he? He'd better be good." They expect no praise for doing their job well. Indeed, none is given except: 'The boys did all right.' When they die, they leave behind them only the most meagre personal belongings, perhaps a handful of medals. Hawks himself has summed up this desolate and barren view of life:

> It's just a calm acceptance of a fact. In *Only Angels Have Wings*, after Joe dies, Cary Grant says: "He just wasn't good enough." Well, that's the only thing that keeps people going. They just have to say: "Joe wasn't good enough, and I'm better than Joe, so I go ahead and do it." And they find out they're not any better than Joe, but then it's too late, you see.

In Ford films, death is celebrated by funeral services, an impromptu prayer, a few staves of "Shall we gather at the river?"—it is inserted into an ongoing system of ritual institutions, along with the wedding, the dance, the parade. But for Hawks it is enough that the routine of the group's life goes on, a routine whose only relieving features are "danger" *(Hatari!)* and "fun." Danger gives existence pungency: "Every time you get real action, then you have danger. And the question, 'Are you living or not living?' is probably the biggest drama we have." This nihilism, in which 'living' means no more than being in danger of losing your life—a danger entered into quite gratuitously—is augmented by the Hawksian concept of having "fun." The word "fun" crops up constantly in Hawks's interviews and scripts. It masks his despair.

When one of Hawks's *élite* is asked, usually by a woman, why he risks his life, he replies: "No reason I can think of makes any sense. I guess we're just crazy." Or Feathers, sardonically, to Colorado in *Rio Bravo:* "You haven't even the excuse I have. We're all fools." By "crazy" Hawks does not mean psychopathic: none of his characters are like Turkey in Peckinpah's *The Deadly Companions* or Billy the Kid in Penn's *The Left-Handed Gun.* Nor is there the sense of the absurdity of life which we sometimes find in Boetticher's films: death, as we have seen, is for Hawks simply a routine occurrence, not a *grotesquerie*, as in *The Tall T* ('Pretty soon that well's going to be chock-a-block') or *The Rise and Fall of Legs Diamond.* For Hawks "craziness" implies difference, a sense

535

of apartness from the ordinary, everyday, social world. At the same time, Hawks sees the ordinary world as being "crazy" in a much more fundamental sense, because devoid of any meaning or values. "I mean crazy reactions—I don't think they're crazy, I think they're normal—but according to bad habits we've fallen into they seemed crazy." Which is the normal, which the abnormal? Hawks recognises, inchoately, that to most people his heroes, far from embodying rational values, are only a dwindling band of eccentrics. Hawks's 'kind of men' have no place in the world.

The Hawksian heroes, who exclude others from their own *élite* group, are themselves excluded from society, exiled to the African bush or to the Arctic. Outsiders, other people in general, are perceived by the group as an undifferentiated crowd. Their role is to gape at the deeds of the heroes whom, at the same time, they hate. The crowd assembles to watch the showdown in *Rio Bravo*, to see the cars spin off the track in *The Crowd Roars*. The gulf between the outsider and the heroes transcends enmities among the *élite*: witness *Dawn Patrol* or Nelse in *El Dorado*. Most dehumanised of all is the crowd in *Land of the Pharaohs*, employed in building the Pyramids. Originally the film was to have been about Chinese labourers building a "magnificent airfield" for the American army, but the victory of the Chinese Revolution forced Hawks to change his plans. ("Then I thought of the building of the Pyramids; I thought it was the same kind of story.") But the presence of the crowd, of external society, is a constant covert threat to the Hawksian *élite*, who retaliate by having "fun." In the crazy comedies ordinary citizens are turned into comic butts, lampooned and tormented: the most obvious target is the insurance salesman in *His Girl Friday*. Often Hawks's revenge becomes grim and macabre. In *Sergeant York* it is "fun" to shoot Germans "like turkeys"; in *Air Force* it is "fun" to blow up the Japanese fleet. In *Rio Bravo* the geligniting of the badmen "was very funny." It is at these moments that the *élite* turns against the world outside and takes the opportunity to be brutal and destructive.

Besides the covert pressure of the crowd outside, there is also an overt force which threatens: woman. Man is woman's "prey." Women are admitted to the male group only after much disquiet and a long ritual courtship, phased round the offering, lighting and exchange of cigarettes, during which they prove themselves worthy of entry. Often they perform minor feats of valour. Even then though they are never really full members. A typical dialogue sums up their position:

Woman: You love him, don't you?

Man (embarrassed): Yes . . . I guess so. . . .

Woman: How can I love him like you?

Man: Just stick around.

The undercurrent of homosexuality in Hawks's films is never crystallised, though in *The Big Sky*, for example, it runs very close to the surface. And he himself described *A Girl in Every Port* as "really a love story between two men." For Hawks men are equals, within the group at least, whereas there is a clear identification between women and the animal world, most explicit in *Bringing Up Baby*, *Gentlemen Prefer Blondes* and *Hatari!* Man must strive to maintain his mastery. It is also worth noting that, in Hawks's adventure dramas and even in many of his comedies, there is no married life. Often the heroes were married or at least intimately committed, to a woman at some time in the distant past but have suffered an unspecified trauma, with the result that they have been suspicious of women ever since. Their attitude is "Once bitten, twice shy." This is in contrast to the films of Ford, which almost always include domestic scenes. Woman is not a threat to Ford's heroes; she falls into her allotted social place as wife and mother, bringing up the children, cooking, sewing, a life of service, drudgery and subordination. She is repaid for this by being sentimentalised. Boetticher, on the other hand, has no obvious place for women at all; they are phantoms, who provoke action, are pretexts for male modes of conduct, but have no authentic significance in themselves. "In herself, the woman has not the slightest importance."

Hawks sees the all-male community as an ultimate; obviously it is very retrograde. His Spartan heroes are, in fact, cruelly stunted. Hawks would be a lesser director if he was unaffected by this, if his adventure dramas were the sum total of his work. His real claim as an author lies in the presence, together with the dramas, of their inverse, the crazy comedies. They are the agonised exposure of the underlying tensions of the heroic dramas. There are two principal themes, zones of tension. The first is the theme of regression: of regression to childhood, infantilism, as in *Monkey Business*, or regression to savagery: witness the repeated scene of the adult about to be scalped by painted children, in *Monkey Business* and in *The Ransom of Red Chief*. With brilliant insight, Robin Wood has shown how *Scarface* should be categorised among the comedies rather than the dramas: Camonte is perceived as savage, child-like, subhuman. The second principal comedy theme is that of sex-reversal and role-reversal. *I Was A Male War Bride* is the most extreme example. Many of Hawks's comedies are centred round domineering women and timid, pliable men: *Bringing Up Baby* and *Man's Favourite Sport*, for example. There are often scenes of male sexual humiliation, such as the trousers being pulled off the hapless private eye in *Gentlemen Prefer Blondes*. In the same film, the Olympic Team of athletes are reduced to passive objects in an extraordinary Jane Russell song number; big-game hunting is lampooned, like fishing in *Man's Favourite Sport*; the theme of infantilism crops up again: "The child was the most mature one on board the ship, and I think he was a lot of fun."

Whereas the dramas show the mastery of man over nature, over woman, over the animal and childish; the comedies show his humiliation, his regression. The heroes become victims; society, instead of being excluded and despised, breaks in with irruptions of monstrous farce. It could well be argued that Hawks's outlook, the alternative world which he constructs in the cinema, the Hawksian heterocosm, is not one imbued with particular intellectual subtlety or sophistication. This does not detract from its force. Hawks first attracted attention because he was regarded naïvely as an action director. Later, the thematic content which I have outlined was detected and revealed. Beyond the stylemes, semantemes were found to exist; the films were anchored in an objective stratum of meaning, a plerematic stratum, as the Danish linguist Hjelmslev would put it. Thus the stylistic expressiveness of Hawks's films was shown to be not purely contingent, but grounded in significance.

Something further needs to be said about the theoretical basis of the kind of schematic exposition of Hawks's work which I have outlined. The 'structural approach' which underlies it, the definition of a core of repeated motifs, has evident affinities with methods which have been developed for the study of folklore and mythology. In the work of Olrik and others, it was noted that in different folk-tales the same motifs reappeared time and time again. It became possible to build up a lexicon of these motifs. Eventually Propp showed how a whole cycle of Russian fairy-tales could be analysed into variations of a very limited set of basic motifs (or moves, as he called them). Underlying the different, individual tales was an archi-tale, of which they were all variants. One important point needs to be made about this type of structural analysis. There is a danger, as Lévi-Strauss has pointed out, that by simply noting and mapping resemblances, all the texts which are studied (whether Russian fairy-tales or American movies) will be reduced to one, abstract and impoverished. There must be a moment of synthesis as well as a moment of analysis: otherwise, the method is formalist, rather than truly structuralist. Structuralist criticism cannot rest at the perception of resemblances or repetitions (redundancies, in fact), but must also comprehend a system of differences and oppositions. In this way, texts can be studied not only in their universality (what they all have in common) but also in their singularity (what differentiates them from each other). This means of course that the test of a structural analysis lies not in the orthodox canon of a director's work, where resemblances are clustered, but in films which at first sight may seem eccentricities.

In the films of Howard Hawks a systematic series of oppositions can be seen very near the surface, in the contrast between the adventure dramas and the crazy comedies. If we take the adventure dramas alone it would seem that Hawks's work is flaccid, lacking in dynamism; it is only when we consider the crazy comedies that it becomes rich, begins to ferment: alongside every dramatic hero we are aware of a phantom, stripped of mastery, humiliated, inverted. With other directors, the system of oppositions is much more complex: instead of there being two broad strata of films there are a whole series of shifting variations. In these cases, we need to analyse the roles of the protagonists themselves, rather than simply the worlds in which they operate. The protagonists of fairy-tales or myths, as Lévi-Strauss has pointed out, can be dissolved into bundles of differential elements, pairs of opposites. Thus the difference between the prince and the goose-girl can be reduced to two antinomic pairs: one natural, male versus female, and the other cultural, high versus low. We can proceed with the same kind of operation in the study of films, though, as we shall see, we shall find them more complex than fairy-tales. . . .

RICHARD CORLISS
THE
HOLLYWOOD SCREENWRITER

Eight years ago, when popular movie criticism consisted mainly
of plot summaries and star-gazing, and Bosley Crowther of *The
New York Times* was scorning Godard and ignoring Ford and
Hawks, *Film Culture* magazine published two articles by Andrew
Sarris that were to revolutionize film criticism in the United
States. In the first article, "Notes on the Auteur Theory in 1962,"
Sarris proposed an Americanization of the *politique des auteurs*,
which held that the director is the author of a film and that visual
style is the key to assessing a director's standing as an *auteur*. In
The American Cinema, he evaluated—indeed, he rated—106 Amer-
ican directors (and seven foreigners) in categories ranging from the
"Pantheon" to "Oddities and One Shots."

It took some time for the importance of Sarris' work to become
evident to the community of film scholars. Hadn't Pauline Kael
demolished his stratified silliness for good in a *Film Quarterly*
polemic read by far more people than Sarris' original articles?
Hadn't Dwight Macdonald resigned his regular column in *Film
Quarterly* because Sarris was invited to contribute, and hadn't
he done so with a venom that suggested an angry redneck burning
a cross on the lawn of his new Negro neighbor's house? Hadn't
Richard Dyer MacCann conspicuously omitted Sarris' writing
(or any *auteur* criticism) from his anthology, *Film: A Montage of
Theories*, which did include a piece by Kael the theory-baiter?

It's a pity that Academia didn't notice what Sarris had going for
him: an engaging prose style that ranged from entertainingly analytical to deliriously lyrical; a popular, hip publication *(The Village*

Voice) just right for reaching the young intellectuals for whom film was the most exciting art; a subject matter (the Hollywood sound film) that he knew almost viscerally, and whose product was bound to interest his readers more than the "serious" European films praised by his detractors; and a burgeoning group of articulate acolytes (like Roger Greenspun and James Stoller) who could spread the faith without his losing face.

Came the Revolution, which coincided with the growing number of film courses and monographs. Sarris' thoughtful and well-timed challenge to the near-monopoly of social-realist criticism was adopted by most of the younger critics, and even adapted by some of the less secure older ones. It was refreshing to examine films as the creations of artists rather than of social forces, and to be able to do so in a manner that was serious without being solemn. Americans could finally admit that their movies weren't sinful just because they were entertaining, and that the films deserved to be judged by the same artistic standards applicable to any film.

By 1969, when Sarris expanded *The American Cinema* to book length, the critical attitude that had begun as a reaction to the party line was in serious danger of hardening into the Gospel According to St. Andrew. *The New York Times* had been converted into a veritable *auteur* shrine; its first- and second-string critics adhered closely to Sarris' tastes and standards, and its Almanac welcomed the word *auteur* into the English language, along with *acid, activist* and *Afro.* Film societies mounted ambitious retrospectives of directors, from John Ford and Jean Renoir to Sam Fuller and Russ Meyer. Publishers commissioned extended studies of Fritz Lang (who has made forty-three films) and Roman Polanski (who has made five). The Revolution was victorious.

In some respects, however, the anarchists show tendencies of close-minded classicism. They put the spotlight on the once-despised Hollywood movie system and sprinkled a little cultural respectability on the industry's "hack" directors—fine. But in doing so they retarded investigation of other, equally vital film crafts, especially that of the screenwriter, who creates (or creatively adapts) a film's plot, characters, dialogue and theme.

The director *is* right in the middle of things. At the very least, he's on the sound stage while the director of photography is lighting the set that the art director has designed and, later, while the actors are speaking the lines that the screenwriter wrote. Quite often, he steers all these factors—story, actors, camera—in the right *direction*. So why not just say it's his film, that he is the author? Simply because the director is almost always an interpretive artist, not a creative one, and because the Hollywood film is a corporate art, not an individual one. This doesn't diminish the importance of the director, or the validity of the Hollywood film as an art. Both Chartres and *Charade* were the work of a number of individuals who contributed their unique talents to a corporate enterprise, but this fact doesn't necessarily make either work less appropriate for serious study than, say, the Mona Lisa or *Mothlight*. It just makes it more difficult for the critic to assign sole authorship to the work—and why should he waste time on a Name Game like this?

In the same way, both Stanley Donen and Stan Brakhage may be called film artists, but Donen is an interpretive artist while Brakhage is a creative one; Donen is a conductor and Brakhage is a composer. Donen is a film *director* who collaborates with his writers, actors and technicians in a completely different way than Brakhage, the film*maker*, collaborates with his film strips and viewer. The case can be made that Donen is a better film director than Brakhage is a filmmaker; they work in separate but equal film traditions, and it is possible that Donen succeeds in his genre, whereas Brakhage may fail in his. The theory used to be that the solitary, creative artist produced Art, and the corporate, interpretive craftsman produced Entertainment—a prejudice that kept people from examining the Hollywood movie. The *auteur* theory says, in effect, "What you thought was just Entertainment is really Art, because it is the work of an individual creator—an *auteur*. Therefore the Hollywood movie is worthy to be examined."

Many films are indeed dominated by the personality of the director, although not, perhaps, in the way the auteurists mean. The phrase "directorial personality" makes more sense if taken quite literally. The good director is usually a man with a strong, persuasive personality. He has to be a combination of tough guy, to make the technicians respond to his commands, and best friend, to coax a good performance out of a sensitive actress. Whether he directs with a riding crop (Stroheim), an icy stare (Sternberg), or a few soft-spoken words (Cukor), his personality is often crucial to the success of a film. The importance of a director's personal—or even visual—style is not questioned here, only the assumption that he creates a style out of thin air (with his collaborating craftsmen acting merely as paint, canvas, bowl of fruit, and patron), instead of adapting it to the equally important styles of the story and performers. The same literal meaning can apply to a director's "authority," which accurately describes his function on the set.

But the director need not be the only dominant force in a successful film. Often the actor is the *auteur*. Keaton and Chaplin may be fine directors, but it is their screen personalities that we especially cherish. Who would trade Keaton the actor for Keaton the director? And who would prefer analyzing the directorial styles of James W. Horne, Donald Crisp, Edward Sedgwick or Charles F. Reisner to savoring that sublime bodily mechanism that Buster controls so beautifully? The unique cinema personae of W. C. Fields, Mae West and Laurel and Hardy also flourished with little regard to the director of record, and can be defined without much reference to him — although, quite naturally, the combination of the comedians with different scripts and directors produced varying results. The same can be said of such incandescent performers as Greta Garbo, Katharine Hepburn and Cary Grant. Just as one can be drawn to an exercise in visual style like Blake Edwards' *Darling Lili* without finding it a completely successful film, so can one delight in the way Garbo dignifies and illuminates a rickety melodrama like *Mata Hari* with her beauty, her passion, and her ironic acceptance of an innate and tragic superiority.

It's instructive — indeed, it's often fun — to see a great actor transcend a ridiculous script and unfeeling direction; it's interesting to watch a fine director play around with an incredible story and poor performers. But the real joy in movies comes from seeing the fortuitous communion of forces (story, script, direction, acting, lighting, editing, design, scoring) that results in a great Hollywood film. *Frankenstein, Scarface, Love Me Tonight, Camille, Holiday, Mr. Smith Goes to Washington, His Girl Friday, Citizen Kane, Penny Serenade, Casablanca, Double Indemnity, Body and Soul, Rachel and the Stranger, Born Yesterday, Seven Brides for Seven Brothers, The Searchers, Invasion of the Body Snatchers, Psycho, The Manchurian Candidate, Charade* and *Planet of the Apes* are just a few examples of collaborative movie-making at its best. Intelligent appreciation of films like these, and not scholastic disputes over the validity of individual signatures, should be our first critical concern.

The cry *"cherchez l' auteur"* can lead unwary film scholars astray when the *auteur* happens to be the author—or rather, when the script is the basis for a film's success. More often than not, when a fine film is signed by a mediocre director, the film's distinctive qualities can be traced to the screenwriter. There's no need to rescue Mitchell Leisen, Garson Kanin, Sam Wood and William D. Russell from the underworld of neglected directors simply because they were each fortunate enough to direct a comedy written by Norman Krasna (*Hands Across the Table, Bachelor Mother, The Devil and Miss Jones,* and *Dear Ruth,* respectively). The direction of these films is usually adroit and sensitive, and the presence of charming comediennes enhances them even further; but the delightfully dominant personality behind the screen is undoubtedly Krasna's. Similarly, the team of Sydney Gilliatt and Frank Launder constructed the frame—and contributed most of the furnishings— for two witty thrillers of the Thirties, Alfred Hitchcock's *The Lady Vanishes* and Carol Reed's *Night Train.* With the credits and Hitchcock's cameo cut from the films (but with the Gilliatt and Launder figures, in the puckish persons of Naunton Wayne and Basil Radford, left in), even an auteurist might have trouble determining which director was responsible for which film. That is because the authorship, and thus the responsibility, belonged to the two writers.

Body and Soul, written by Abraham Polonsky and directed by Robert Rossen, fits securely into Polonsky's very personal urban Hellmouth, with its Breughelesque, subway-at-rush-hour density, its stylized but fiercely realistic dialogue, and its cheeky characters who seem to carry both a chip and an albatross on their shoulders. His authorship of *Body and Soul* can be certified, if need be, by a look at his next film, the malignant *Force of Evil,* which he also directed, and which extends and enriches the penny-ante pessimism of *Body and Soul.* Waldo Salt's adaptations of *Rachel and the Stranger* (1948) and *Midnight Cowboy* (1969) are both graced by intelligent empathy for some very unusual characters, and by the gentle humor he evokes from the most improbable situations. Ring Lardner Jr.'s penchant for bantering, overlapping dialogue distinguishes *Woman of the Year* (1942) and *M*a*s*h* (1970), although most of his other assignments during those three decades offered him little chance to display his talent. Paul Mazursky and Larry Tucker, not director Hy Averback, are surely the authors of *I Love You, Alice B. Toklas;* its successor, *Bob & Carol & Ted & Alice,* evinced the same social concerns and behavioral absurdities, while Averback has loped further into obscurity with each new film. (Significantly, now that Mazursky is a director, he tends to ignore the contribution of his writing partner.)

It's clear that some method of classification and evaluation is necessary, both to identify and to assess the contributions of the over-paid but underrated *genus* known as the screenwriter. But that is a game that conceals even more perils than Sarris' Hit Parade of Directors. Once the *auteur* scholar accepts the myth of the omnipotent director, his game is won: he can Pass Kael and Collect $200. Indeed, even an adherent of the *politique des collaborateurs* can be fairly sure that the director of record is the man who hollered "Action!" and "Cut!"—though his importance in controlling what went on between those two commands may be disputed. But the size of a screenwriter's contribution to any given film is often far more difficult to ascertain. A writer may have received screen credit for work he didn't do (such as Sidney Buchman on *Holiday*) or for a few minor suggestions (Orson Welles on *Citizen Kane*). More likely, his name may not appear on the screen even if he has written virtually the entire script. Ben Hecht was responsible for far more of *Gone with the Wind*'s dialogue than Sidney Howard, who had merely written a treatment of the Margaret Mitchell novel for producer David O. Selznick. But it was Howard who received sole screen credit, as well as a posthumous Oscar— for Hecht's work. Michael Wilson wrote the screenplay for *Friendly Persuasion* and co-scripted *The Bridge on the River Kwai.* But the Hollywood Blacklist kept his name off both films, and the writing Oscar for *Kwai* was awarded to Pierre Boulle, who had nothing to do with the film adapted from his novel.

A more subtle problem is appraising the work of a screenwriter who specializes in adaptations. Few screenwriters can boast a more impressive list of credits than Donald Ogden Stewart. As with George Cukor, the director for whom he produced his finest scripts, Stewart's "filmography is his most eloquent defense." Both Stewart and Cukor, however, had the good luck to be assigned adaptations of some of the wittiest and most actable theatre pieces of their time —*Holiday, The Women* (for which Stewart received no screen credit), *The Philadelphia Story,* and *Edward, My Son,* among others—and Stewart adhered closely to both in spirit and letter. Stewart's achievement should not be degraded; many screenwriters failed at the delicate craft he mastered. But, as with directors, one can distinguish several levels of screenwriting: the indifferent work of a mediocre writer, whether an original script or an adaptation (which we may call procrustean); the gem polishing of a gifted adaptor like Stewart (protean); and the creation of a superior original script, like Herman J. Mankiewicz's *Citizen Kane* or Polonsky's *Body and Soul* (promethean). When faced with the career of a Stewart, the critic who has discarded the convenience of the *auteur* theory must compare Stewart's adaptation with the source work, in hopes of detecting such changes as plot compression or expansion, bowdlerization, addition or deletion of dialogue, and differences in theme and tone. At worst, this research will exhaust and discourage the critic; at best, it will convince him that the creation of a Hollywood movie involves a complex weave of talents, properties, and personalities.

When a screenwriter, like Preston Sturges or George Axelrod, has a distinctive style, his contributions to films with multiple script credits can usually be discerned. But the hallmark of many of the best screenwriters is versatility, not consistency. Subject matter dictates style. Given the chameleon-like quality of these writers, how are we to know which part of the *Casablanca* script is the work of the sophisticated but self-effacing Howard Koch, and which part was written by Warners' prolific Epstein brothers? Luckily, Koch himself has told the *Casablanca* production story, and revealed that the Epsteins fabricated a plot around the name of a saloon—Rick's—they had found in an unproduced play, and that, when the brothers moved on to another assignment, Koch developed the strands of their story into a full-blooded screenplay that reads as well as it plays. We don't have many of these memoirs, though, and since most Hollywood egos are about as large as the Graf Zeppelin, the accounts of screenwriters may be taken with the same pillar of salt we keep handy for directors' interviews and actors' autobiographies.

Nevertheless, a screenwriter's work should, and can, be judged by considering his entire career, as is done with a director. If a writer has been associated with a number of favorite films, if we can distinguish a common style in films with different directors and actors, and if he has received sole writing credit on several films, an authorial personality begins to appear. The high polish and excitement of Koch's other work, for example (he wrote *Invasion from Mars*, better known as *War of the Worlds*, for the Orson Welles Mercury Theatre, and his film scripts include *The Letter*, *Sergeant York*, *Three Strangers*, *Letter from an Unknown Woman*, and *The Thirteenth Letter*), and his fulfillment of the three conditions mentioned above, give credence to his account of the writing of *Casablanca*. In fact, most of the best screenwriters were the sole authors of a substantial number of scripts.

The paucity of critical and historical literature makes all screenwriters "Subjects for Further Research." The cavalier group-headings on the following lists are meant only to emphasize the tentative nature of the classifications. As more films are seen from a screenwriter's point of view, names will be shuffled from one list to another. Ultimately, each of these fine screenwriters, and a hundred more, should have an artistic identity clear enough so that such capricious classifications will be unnecessary. Until that enlightened time comes to pass, we must make do with an Acropolis of Screenwriters something like the one which follows. (To make matters even more delphic, the screenwriter's work is defined simply by three of his finest films.)

The men and women so honored, by adapting their conspicuous talents to the byzantine demands of the trade, developed the most successful screenwriting techniques. Success usually begat power, and power begat authority. By authority is meant the right to complete your own script without being forced to surrender it to the next fellow on the assembly line, the right to consult with any actor or director who wants changes, and the right to fight for your film through the taffy pull of front-office politics, pressure groups, and publicists. The power of the most important screenwriters often resulted in superior films, in which the distinctive contributions of writer and director can be analyzed with greater assurance. Inevitably, some writers had literary pretensions, not only for themselves but for the cinemah, and when these men achieved some measure of autonomy, the cheerful cynicism of their earlier, more successful scripts was replaced by sesquipedalian platitudes on The Brotherhood of Man Through World Government. Thus, the most famous screenwriters, such as Dudley Nichols, Dalton Trumbo and, of late, Buck Henry, are not necessarily the best. Nichols' thoughtful articles on the need for sparse, realistic dialogue were not often matched by his actual scripts, which tend to talk the characters into the ground with palaver and pontification. Dalton Trumbo's private letters (now published in book form) reveal an easy-going but pungent wit that was concealed by his attempts to radicalize bourgeois movie melodrama. The pomp currently surrounding Buck Henry derives largely from the fortuitous circumstance of his visible connection with Mike Nichols and *The Graduate*, a film whose dialogue was lifted, almost word for word, from Charles Webb's novel. When on his own (in *The Troublemaker* and *Candy*), Henry's humor is decidedly undergraduate, even sophomoric.

Unfortunately, the best screenwriters are likely to be ignored by film critics and historians. It's a minor scandal that film students are aware of Don Siegel's montages for *Casablanca* but not of Howard Koch's script; that Jules Furthman is trampled under foot in the mad rush to canonize Hawks and Sternberg; that film buffs, who can trace Gregg Toland's deep-focus work from *Wuthering Heights* through *Citizen Kane*, don't know, and probably don't care, that Herman Mankiewicz wrote *Citizen Kane* with only nominal assistance from Orson Welles. "In my opinion," Welles said twenty years ago, "the writer should have the first and last word in filmmaking, the only better alternative being the writer-director, but with the stress on the first word."

Perhaps the day of the hyphenate, the writer-director, has already dawned, and the screenwriter will become just another high-priced artifact in that great Hollywood auction in the sky. Perhaps not. Some of the most successful and popular films of the Right-Now Generation have been close adaptations of novels, with tight, efficient scripts (such as *The Graduate*, *Rosemary's Baby* and *Midnight Cowboy*). It's also encouraging to note the return to prominence of veteran screenwriters who have learned to meet the demands of a youth market while doing work that an adult can be proud of: Waldo Salt with *Midnight Cowboy*, Ring Lardner Jr. with *M*a*s*h*, Abraham Polonsky with *Tell Them Willie Boy is Here*, and Albert Maltz with *Two Mules for Sister Sara*. But whether these trends are heralding the screenwriter's second wind or portending his last gasp, the first forty years of the American commercial sound film cannot be evaluated without considering the crucial role he has played. The best screenwriters were talented and tenacious enough to assure that their visions and countless revisions would be realized on the screen. Now it is time for them to be remembered in film history.

PARTHENON

Sidney Buchman
Mr. Smith Goes
  to Washington
Theodora Goes Wild
Here Comes Mr. Jordan
Jules Furthman
Rio Bravo
The Big Sleep
Shanghai Express
Ben Hecht
Scarface
Gone With the Wind
The Scoundrel
Howard Koch
Casablanca
Letter from
  an Unknown Woman
The Letter
Norman Krasna
Bachelor Mother
Hands Across the Table
The Devil and Miss Jones
Frances Marion
Camille [1936]
Stella Maris
The Scarlet Letter
Frank S. Nugent
The Searchers
Wagonmaster
Two Rode Together
Samson Raphaelson
Trouble in Paradise
Suspicion
The Shop Around
  the Corner
Preston Sturges
The Lady Eve
Sullivan's Travels
Easy Living
Billy Wilder
Ninotchka
Sunset Boulevard
Some Like It Hot

ERECHTHEION

George Axelrod
The Manchurian Candidate
How to Murder Your Wife
Lord Love a Duck
Borden Chase
Red River
Winchester 73
The Far Country
Garson Kanin
Born Yesterday
Pat and Mike
Adam's Rib
Charles Lederer
His Girl Friday
The Thing
The Front Page
Anita Loos
Reaching for the Moon
Hold Your Man
Down to Earth
Daniel Mainwearing
Invasion of the
  Body Snatchers
Out of the Past
The Tall Target
Herman J. Mankiewicz
Citizen Kane
Citizen Kane
Citizen Kane
Robert Riskin
It Happened One Night
Platinum Blonde
The Whole Town's Talking
Donald Ogden Stewart
Holiday
Love Affair
Edward My Son
Michael Wilson
Five Fingers
Lawrence of Arabia
A Place in the Sun

BRAURONION

W. R. Burnett
High Sierra
The Asphalt Jungle
The Great Escape
John Huston
The African Queen
Jezebel
The Maltese Falcon
Nunnally Johnson
Jesse James
Prisoner of Shark Island
The Dirty Dozen
John Lee Mahin
North to Alaska
Red Dust
The Horse Soldiers
Joseph L. Mankiewicz
All About Eve
A Letter to Three Wives
Million Dollar Legs
Seton I. Miller
The Criminal Code
Ministry of Fear
The Dawn Patrol [1930]
Dudley Nichols
Judge Priest
Sister Kenny
Swamp Water
Abraham Polonsky
Force of Evil
Body and Soul
Madigan
Morrie Ryskind
Penny Serenade
A Night at the Opera
Stage Door
Jo Swerling
Leave Her to Heaven
Lifeboat
Man's Castle

PANDROSEION

Charles Brackett
Midnight
To Each His Own
The Model and the Marriage
  Broker
Delmer Daves
An Affair to Remember
Dark Passage
Professor Beware
Philip Dunne
How Green Was My Valley
The Ghost and Mrs. Muir
Hilda Crane
**Frances Goodrich and
Albert Hackett**
The Thin Man
Seven Brides
  for Seven Brothers
It's a Wonderful Life
Casey Robinson
Now Voyager
Dark Victory
Captain Blood
Charles Schnee
The Bad and The Beautiful
They Live By Night
I Walk Alone
R. C. Sheriff
The Invisible Man
Odd Man Out
The Old Dark House
Frank Tashlin
Will Success Spoil
  Rock Hunter?
The Paleface
Bachelor Flat
Anthony Veiller
The Killers
The List of
  Adrian Messenger
The Stranger
Phillip Yordan
The Man From Laramie
The Fall of the
  Roman Empire
Johnny Guitar [disputed by
  the authors of *Trente Ans
  du Cinéma Americain* who
  contend that Ben Maddow
  is the film's
  sole screenwriter.]

GERALD MAST
FROM THE COMIC MIND :
COMEDY AND THE MOVIES

PRESTON STURGES AND
THE DIALOGUE TRADITION

One of the major traditions of sound comedy is the American film that generates its comedy through talk. Creating within the confines of the Hollywood studio system, several directors made distinctive, clever, and intelligent comedies that, like most American films of the 1930s and 1940s, were dialogue films in which pictures primarily supported the talk. But if the talk was good, the pictures pleasant and functional, the performances energetic and compelling, and the structural conception careful and clever, the comedy could be very entertaining indeed.

Because the dialogue comedy was so dependent on talk and structure, it was equally dependent on the scriptwriter who devised the talk and structure. The dialogue comedies were *written* comedies, and the writer played almost as great a role in shaping the film as its director. The scripts of Ben Hecht, Preston Sturges, Robert Riskin, Dudley Nichols, Herman J. Mankiewicz, Charles Lederer, Garson Kanin, and Ruth Gordon frequently overwhelmed the weak director, exerting far more influence over the film than the director's "auteurial" style. If that fact seems to contradict the assumption that the director is a film's prime mover, it is equally true that in the best dialogue comedies the insight of the writers fused perfectly with the style and attitudes of the director, who expanded the sharp script into the full and final comic conception.

Underlying the best of the dialogue comedies was usually a subtle and silent rebellion against the very studio system and values that produced them. Most of these films slyly bit the hand that fed them, but the bite was very coy and the teeth were often capped with the same tinsel and rhinestones that Hollywood so adored. The comedies developed a unique aesthetic for destroying Hollywood assumptions and conventions while appearing to subscribe to them. Their primary targets were the familiar movie definitions of love, sex, success, and propriety. And by shredding the Hollywood clichés, the comedies frequently implied a more human, sensible, and sensitive system of emotional relationships and moral values. As in the earliest American comedies, the sting of raucous, vulgar sincerity popped the balloon of pretentious gentility. . . .

No one made better dialogue comedies than Preston Sturges, primarily because no one wrote better dialogue. Sturges is one of those filmmakers whose one-liners are often as memorable as his whole films. In *Easy Living* (a Sturges screenplay that completely dominates its director, Mitchell Leisen), Jean Arthur is sitting on a Fifth Avenue bus when a sable coat descends from the skies to land on her head. She angrily turns to the man behind her, a Hindu wearing a turban, and snaps, "What's the big idea, anyway?" His answer, "Kismet." Ironically, the joke also functions in the film, for Kismet, fate, is the driving force in the film's plot.

In *The Great McGinty*, a crooked politician remarks, "If it wasn't for graft, you'd get a very low type of people in politics." When McGinty subsequently runs out on his wife, he tells her about the money he stashed away "to send the kids through college—without selling magazines." And the most brilliant collection of Sturgesisms opens *Sullivan's Travels*, as an idealistic director discusses a socially conscious film with his money-minded producers:

"You see the symbolism of it? Capital and Labor destroying each other."
"It gives me the creeps."

"It was held over a fifth week at the Music Hall."
"Who goes to the Music Hall? Communists."

"It died in Pittsburgh."
"What do they know in Pittsburgh?"
"They know what they like."
"Then why do they live in Pittsburgh?"

The Sturges emphasis on dialogue determines his film technique, which relies on the conventional American two-shot to capture the faces and features while the characters talk, talk, talk. But it is such good talk—incredibly rapid, crackling, brittle—that the film has plenty of life. Like Hawks, Sturges was a master of the lightning pace. When Sturges uses special, cinematic devices, he inevitably turns them into self-conscious bits of trickery and gimmickry that harmonize well with the parodic spirit of the film. His favorite game with the sound track is to use musical backgrounds that comment parodically on the action in the scene. The opening of *Sullivan's Travels* uses melodramatic "movie music" that underscores a stagey, predictable gunfight on top of a speeding train. We later discover the scene was indeed part of a melodramatic movie within the movie. *The Palm Beach Story* opens with the William Tell Overture to underscore a breathtakingly funny pseudo-melodramatic montage sequence that finally brings a future husband and wife to the altar. The film's final use of music is just as clever. While Rudy Vallee serenades Claudette Colbert with "Goodnight, Sweetheart" (complete with full orchestra) outside her window, the sweetheart takes refuge in the arms (and, by implication, bed) of her husband inside the room. Rudy's romantic singing drives her into the arms of his rival. And perhaps Sturges uses music most effectively and wittily in *Unfaithfully Yours* (1948) when an orchestra conductor imagines three separate strategies for handling his adulterous wife, each perfectly correlated with the musical feeling of the piece he is conducting.

Sturges also reserves his manipulation of editing and the camera for the occasional tricky effect. *Christmas in July* uses a comically obtrusive zoom shot accompanied by a whistling kazoo to achieve its final miraculous solution. *The Lady Eve* combines jarring shock-cuts and screaming train whistles as comic punctuation for each of Eve's "revelations" of her previous affairs to her innocent husband. The opening sequence of *The Palm Beach Story* is a dizzying, almost illogical montage that parallels a melodramatic murder in a closet with a wedding (breaking out of the closet?). Sturges similarly punctuates his scenes of talk with an occasional bit of physical, slapstick comedy (the automat scene in *Easy Living*, the racing land yacht in *Sullivan's Travels*, the escape from prison in *McGinty*, the rifle-shooting sequence aboard the train in *Palm*

Beach) that cunningly—sometimes too cunningly—injects motion into his motion pictures.

Sturges' cleverness also shows itself in the unconventional, unexpected people and situations with which he filled his films. His crazy foreigners—Louis Louis in *Easy Living*, the Boss in *McGinty*, Toto in *Palm Beach*—are burlesques of the Hollywood cliché. Where most of Sturges' contemporaries contrasted the pure, natural American with the corrupt, suave European (Henry James in Hollywood terms), Sturges' foreigners parody American ideals by trying to imitate them. Louis tries to open a huge, grotesque hotel rather than remain a brilliant French chef. His aspirations to gentility and class are undercut by his vulgarity and pronunciation—the Imperial "Suit" (suite), "phenonemom," "inwisibles." The Boss explains his American success by referring to the romantic tradition of the robber baron and by pointing out that, if it weren't for him, "everyone would be at the mercy" (but he never says at the mercy of what). Toto is the looniest foreigner of all, a slimy gigolo, ugly and wormlike, whose sole functions seem to be to parade around in a series of different costumes, to intrude into conversations with his single coherent word, "Greetings" ("His English is a little elementary"), and to chatter in some stew of languages that makes it impossible to tell to which tongue he owes his original allegiance.

Among the other wonderful Sturges caprices is "the Wienie King" in *Palm Beach*, a gruff, testy, deaf old gentleman who still loves the ladies and who can carry on whole conversations without understanding a single word. To Sturges we owe the comic and rare opportunity to hear Eugene Pallette, the human bullfrog, sing "For Tonight We'll Merry Merry Be" in *The Lady Eve*. *Easy Living* features a youth magazine called *The Boys' Constant Companion*. Ironically, this magazine is staffed entirely by prune-faced, moralistic old maids and misters. And about this magazine Sturges sneaks in a wonderfully sly bit of obscenity (Sturges, like Lubitsch, was a master at ducking the censor) when the rich businessman mistakenly refers to the publication as *The Boys' Constant Reminder*.

Sturges also delighted in showing apparently conventional Hollywood characters and scenes in a very unconventional light. The conventional boy and girl in *Christmas in July* engage in verbal battles that no Hollywood juvenile and ingenue ought to have.

(He even tells her to shut up.) *The Lady Eve* contains two seduction scenes in which the lady throws herself at the recalcitrant gentleman, who insists on protecting both her and his virtue. The idyllic, conventional life of the rich receives rough treatment in the opening scene of *Easy Living*, when the wealthy husband and wife fight (almost to the death) over her newest sable coat. The Hollywood clichés of loving father and daughter get a tough beating from the continual violent arguments between Diana Lynn and William Demarest in *The Miracle of Morgan's Creek*. *Sullivan's Travels* reverses the clichés of city sensuality and country purity as a fat, lecherous farm widow does her utmost to enjoy the physical pleasures of Sullivan's young, firm body. The best things in the Sturges films are these surprising pieces of reversal and burlesque.

As for their wholes, each of the Sturges films begins with a parodic premise. *The Great McGinty* (1940) parodies both Hollywood "flashback" stories and the American ideal that anyone can rise to greatness; *Sullivan's Travels* (1941), Hollywood production values and the Hollywood iconoclast's urge to say something significant; *The Lady Eve* (1941), shipboard romance and virginal innocence; *The Miracle of Morgan's Creek* (1943), small-town Americana, the sanctity of motherhood, and patriotism; *The Palm Beach Story* (1942), marital tensions; *Unfaithfully Yours* (1948), marital infidelity; and so forth. The best Sturges films never desert delicate, fast-paced parody for moralistic, sentimental conclusions.

The Great McGinty is unrelentingly ironic. It begins with a delicious red herring, a framework story that seems to promise the tale of an erring bank clerk in a South American "banana republic." But the film couldn't care less about this bank clerk. The real story turns out to be about the bartender (Brian Donlevy), the man who stops the clerk from shooting himself. The bartender (only several reels later do we discover his name is McGinty) tells of his rise from hobo to governor. He begins his political career as a two-dollar voter for the political machine of some big city, substituting for those registered voters who are no longer alive to vote for the machine candidates. In his zeal, an ironic burlesque of "get out and vote," the hobo votes 37 times, earning himself $74. That is American ingenuity and gumption doubled and redoubled.

From this auspicious beginning the hobo rises through the machine's ranks. He first shakes down the shady businessmen (and women) who don't want to pay protection; for example, Madame

LaJolla (pronounced "Hoya"), a "fortune-teller," must come up with $250 or "Madame LaJolla doesn't jolla any more." Then Dan McGinty wins his first office—alderman. He develops more refined methods for plucking higher sums. Finally, after acquiring a wife and kids, McGinty becomes "reform" mayor. (The Boss ironically runs the "Reform Party" as well as the machine.) In each of McGinty's steps up the political ladder, his style gets smoother (he even grows a mustache), his clothes get slicker (from hobo rags to a ridiculous plaid suit referred to as a "horse blanket" to a dapper three-piece business suit to a top hat and tails).

But McGinty gets into trouble when he falls in love with the woman he married for political convenience. She suddenly feels qualms about McGinty's "municipal improvements" (euphemism for graft) and the grafters who support him—slum landlords, owners of sweatshops. She urges McGinty to institute genuine reform, to buck the party, to make the world safe for the children. McGinty has his doubts. To his wife's sentimentalities about the "dark, airless factories," McGinty retorts with his own sentimentalities: the factory where he worked as a kid was clean and neat, a place where he labored profitably "instead of playing on the streets learning a lot of dirty words." But the wife's sentimentalities triumph—and Sturges clearly parodies yet another political cliché, the woman behind the man. (These were, after all, the years of Franklin D. and Eleanor.) Ironically, McGinty's one honest moment costs him his family, his power, his wife, and his fortune. When he bucks the Boss, the Boss bucks back, and the two of them end up in the "banana republic," continuing their long feud over who exactly is boss.

The unadulterated cynicism of *The Great McGinty*, its burlesque of the democratic political process and its reduction of an ideal—America as "the land of opportunity"—to the absurd would never have been accepted by audiences one year later. During the war years Sturges had to worry not only about the censor but also about stepping on the sensitive moral toes of a country sacrificing its young men to preserve the very ideals that *McGinty* burlesques. Sturges' greater consciousness of audience values is clear in *Sullivan's Travels*, in which the cynicism is tempered by an uplifting moral affirmation. The plot of this film springs from the tension between an intellectual film director who wants to make a "significant," socially conscious film, *Oh Brother, Where Art Thou?* and the producers who want him to keep making the escapist fluff at which he excels, *Ants in Your Pants of 1941.* The first part of the film convincingly demonstrates that a man with a college education, swimming pool, alimony payments, butler, and a troop of publicity men on his tail is incapable of capturing the desperation and misery of the poor and suffering. (There is perhaps a conscious reference to Ford's *The Grapes of Wrath* and the Pare Lorenz documentaries in the film's depiction of starving tramps and government camps.)

But the second half of the film takes Sullivan and the audience in a very different direction and toward a very different conclusion. Through a series of bizarre accidents, Sullivan winds up truly wretched and helpless, an inmate of a brutal Southern prison (evoking the Hollywood chain-gang genre). In the midst of his misery, Sullivan goes to the movies; the prisoners are guests of a black congregation on its movie night. Sturges shows the parallel misery of both blacks and prisoners; as the convicts shuffle into the humble chapel wearing chains, the blacks sing, "Let My People Go." After this rather idealized display of social misery, the movie flashes on the screen (the third film within this film about films), a Walt Disney cartoon with Mickey Mouse and Pluto. And all the downtrodden members of the audience respond in unison to the funny film—with laughter. From this demonstration, Sullivan concludes (after he gets out of prison as bizarrely as he got in) that *Oh Brother, Where Art Thou?* is not worth making. He directly proclaims, "There's a lot to be said for making people laugh. That's all some people have. It isn't much, but it's better than nothing in this cockeyed caravan." After the explicit proclamation, only slightly softened by the fancy metaphor, Sturges ends the film with an equally explicit montage of laughing faces.

Christmas in July also insists on a moralistic ending, for the young man learns that his own ability is a stronger asset than any windfall (after which Sturges gives him the windfall). *Hail the Conquering Hero* ends with the young man's confession of his dishonesty to the whole town, a greater act of personal heroism than the very clichés that forced the man into his initial lie (after which the town elects him mayor). *Mad Wednesday* ends with the implication that it is better to be "mad," spontaneous, and free than to be chained to a stifling, deadening routine (and after Harold Diddle-bock's lesson in spontaneity, he discovers he has miraculously won both riches and the hand of the woman he loves).

So many of the Sturges films end with these "miracles"—like those sextuplets which are the miracle of Morgan's Creek. Such miracles are cop-outs. Despite their obvious parodies of Hollywood success stories and the Hollywood homily that the rewards go to the virtuous, Sturges' endings, like René Clair's, are incapable of tracing the implications of the issues that he himself has introduced. Either Sturges sells out to Hollywood's commercial necessities, or he is a lazy, sloppy thinker who cannot refuse the easy road (as James Agee suggests), or, like René Clair, he simply "likes happy endings"—whether they make intellectual sense or not.

The absence of these moralizing and miraculous solutions in Sturges' domestic films perhaps accounts for their greater unity and consistency. *Easy Living*, *The Lady Eve*, and *The Palm Beach Story* do not desert irony and satire to give the audience an obligatory piece of optimistic inspiration. In its own way *Easy Living* is a much better film about the Depression than *Sullivan's Travels*, simply because it plays on the irony that for some people a $58,000 sable coat is so valueless that it can be thrown away like a piece of trash, and for others a $58,000 sable coat is so valueless that it can't provide a nourishing meal or a necessary job.

Despite the Sturges toughness, his scorn for fakery and poses, his ridiculing of false ideals, it is more difficult to see what he accepts than what he rejects. If there is a positive Sturges ideal, it can be seen more easily in his people than in the moral summaries that conclude so many of his films. The members of the Sturges troupe —the character actors he uses over and over again—say much about Sturges' values. William Demarest is Sturges' alter ego; tough, cynical, anti-sentimental, he owes no allegiance to abstractions, but is always loyal to his friends. Jimmy Conlin—the owlish flea, nervous, squeaky-voiced—usually comforts those in trouble. Eric Blore, a man of words and poses, knows how to twist appearances to make people accept the fake as real. Robert Greig, the inevitable butler, enjoys the luxury of being a butler and is a loyal cynic who refuses to romanticize the class question. Edgar Kennedy —bartender, private detective—never lets his gruff voice and appearance interfere with his human compassion. And so forth. Most of the Sturges players are mixtures of toughness and softness (even the mincing Franklin Pangborn), scornful of idealistic clichés, usually responsive to each other as people.

In his attack on sentimental and pretentious clichés, Sturges is clearly part of the great American comic tradition that stretches back to the earliest comic jests. Like Lubitsch, Hawks, and Ben Hecht, Sturges disguised his contempt for the Hollywood beatitudes with cinematic conventions that looked very much like the usual Hollywood product. For most members of the audience, *Easy Living* was a wonderful chance to indulge fantasies about incredible luxuries dropping from the skies. The ornate, lavish sets—particularly the Imperial "Suit"—looked exactly like the gaudy settings of their favorite M-G-M films. But for a few members of the audience, the film was a chance to see the grotesque excesses of wealth, the immense gap between rich and poor, and the instability of a stock market that could rise and fall crazily on the whims of a dizzy lady. Further, the film coyly exposes the importance of sex in our supposedly puritanical society; Mary Smith derives all her power from everyone else's assumption that she is sleeping with the powerful financier. In his delightful games with Hollywood expectations, Sturges' cleverness and iconoclasm are more impressive than the depth and complexity of his vision. Sturges very quickly ran out of that iconoclastic energy in the years following the war.

RICHARD KOSZARSKI
THE MEN WITH
THE MOVIE CAMERAS

When applying the spotlight theory of film history, attention is directed from one "golden age" to another, flitting back and forth across Europe, back and forth across the Atlantic, following the cinematic muse as it settles first with one national cinema and then another. This theory is quite serviceable in the writing of cursory film histories, but always raises the problem of specifically delineating each national cinema to which the author seeks to attribute greatness. Those who apply this technique most strictly tend to choose movements that are easy to talk about in terms commonly employed in literary analysis. It is a strong thematic quality which unites the Soviet, German, or post-war Italian schools for these writers, and any utilization of editing, design or camerawork is shuffled uncomfortably to a far corner and discussed as ancillary technique. This is only to be expected, given the state of film historical study and the predilections of many film historians. Occasionally the more daring among them will try to relate the "style" of a particular movement to the "content" of that movement, but seldom will you find any admission that the style *is* the movement, and the way a story is told *is* the story. Our conditioned vocabularies resist defining a movement in terms of juxtaposition or spacial relationships, and consequently, the only film movements that get generally discussed *as* movements are those who have a strong and unifying thematic core susceptible to analysis in literary fashion.

When film criticism grew into a more artist-centered format, it was still these thematic values that dominated the conversation.

Directors, even such obvious visual stylists as Ophuls or Dreyer, were discussed primarily in terms of the story content of their work, certainly a strange approach for criticism of this most modern of art forms. Recently the grip of director-as-auteur criticism has loosened, and fleeting spotlights of attention have been directed to other participants in the filmmaking process. Last year *Film Comment* devoted a whole issue to the work of the screenwriter, certainly a fresh approach in the welter of director-centered criticism that has appeared in the past decade, but predictably devoted to a type of filmmaker intimately bound up with story and narrative elements, and thus susceptible to the standard forms of literary/thematic analysis employed previously.

Written criticism necessarily tends towards what can be verbalized most satisfactorily, and so film criticism has always centered on those elements of this variegated art form which are most manageable in literary terms. But the form demands critics equipped to discuss it not only in the terms of written literature, but with a critical vocabulary conscious of developments in post-war music and art as well, prepared to discuss the *moving picture* in terms of the questions raised by these related disciplines. Only then can we successfully appreciate the work of those whose creative contribution is involved most directly with the more plastic and rhythmic elements of the medium, those who lend form and movement to the structure of the moving image. At this state in film history a monograph on Margaret Booth would be most welcome. Or on the other hand, a study of those who put the images on the film in the first place. It is simply preposterous that there is not a *sentence* on the art of Lee Garmes or Gregg Toland, not any proper critical evaluation. What were these men doing? It is a very hopeful sign that the American Film Institute has been spending more attention lately in compiling oral histories of cinematographers, and that several books have appeared recently with similar information. But these are only tools for scholars and critics, with little value as ends in themselves.

They are only starting points in analysis. They do, however, represent new material not previously collected and absolutely crucial to any understanding of the work of the film artists involved. Even more importantly, they illuminate still another "golden age," which unlike that of Germany or Italy or Great Brit-

561

ain was not one defined so easily by its content as by its style—the Hollywood golden age, the classic period of the American studios, from 1915 up to the Fifties. It becomes clear that here was the key unifying element of the Hollywood style, a visual hallmark which effectively evaded the attentions of most previous historians.

The process of absorption, synthesis and change is what marks Hollywood photography throughout, the idea of building on earlier models, foreign models, contemporary models, taking everything of quality in sight and putting it to use for their own particular ends. This eclecticism was developed into an unmistakeably fluid and dynamic style by Hollywood cameramen over the four or five decades of Hollywood's ascendance, and its roots may be traced back to the very beginnings of American production. When G. W. Bitzer began work at Biograph in 1898 the motion picture had just left the laboratories of its inventors. Lumière, Dickson—Friese-Greene if you insist—had demonstrated just before the turn of the century the success of their mechanical contrivances in catching and reduplicating action in movement. But after perfecting the device they left its development to other hands, and the motion picture passed from inventors and mechanics fascinated by the problem of movement to businessmen and artists enthralled by the fact of movement itself. To Méliès and Porter, to Smith and Selig and Lubin and dozens of other vague figures of this transitional period, the fate of this latest Victorian marvel was entrusted. The manner of their success is still something that awaits the proper Gordon Hendricks treatment, but one factor which unified all of their work was an intense personal contact with all the elements of the film-making process.

This was the scene into which Bitzer wandered in 1898. A film was generally conceived, shot, developed and printed by one man —a not infelicitous situation for 50- or 100-foot productions. This is the way Bitzer himself learned filmmaking, and his early work preserved on Library of Congress paper prints casts an interesting light on the nature of his collaboration with Griffith years later. But of all these functions, by far the chief was photography. "Making a moving picture" meant turning the crank; thinking up a story, handling the actors and cutting the material together was just icing on the cake. Soon a primitive division of labor was introduced for the more complicated productions, and specialized film "directors" like Wallace McCutcheon began to restrict themselves to working solely with the stories and actors of the increasingly complicated narrative films. But the mechanical portion of the machine art was left to the cameramen, and when the time came this is what Bitzer and many others chose to specialize in. The responsibility of this position was such that when Griffith arrived in 1908 he found his cameramen were often slow to implement the suggestions and improvements he thought of for his films. They reasoned that if anything went wrong with the film, if an image failed to register, it was the cameraman and not the director who was in trouble. The camera was still the whole show.

But the growth of the modern cinema restructured all of this again. The Hollywood studio tradition grew up around the idea of division of labor, of departmentalization, of a specialist for every aspect of the production—literary, scenic, photographic, or whatever. Screenwriters decided what Hollywood films had to say, and directors how it would be said. But putting the image on film—"making the moving picture"—was still the responsibility of the cameraman. And in the pre-war years this was no mean accomplishment. Lethargic emulsions, sputtering or non-existent lighting, crotchety camera mechanisms and super-slow lenses made great cameramen out of anyone who could succeed in getting a clearly focussed image on the film—yet those troublesome days were certainly a fruitful training ground. By 1915 mechanical difficulties had been swept away and expression in terms of light was made possible on a major scale.

Three films of that year, fortunately all extant in fine quality prints, offer good examples: De Mille's *The Cheat*, shot by Alvin Wyckoff; Dwan's *David Harum*, shot by Hal Rosson; and Griffith's *The Birth of a Nation*, shot by Billy Bitzer. In these three films one can see already formed the basis of the whole tradition of American cinematography. Wyckoff's use of shadows for psychological effect, of superb figure molding, of intricately accomplished trick work, points to the whole romantic-expressionist tradition of Lee Garmes, John Seitz and Bert Glennon. Rosson's warm and documentary-like examination of the countryside (complete with precocious deep focus and tracking movements) prefigures the deceptively uncomplicated styles of George Schneiderman or William

Clothier. And Bitzer's bravura camerawork, which can encompass intimate human drama and grandscale panorama in the same shot (as in Sherman's march to the sea), has been carried on by such men as Leon Shamroy and Robert Surtees.

Over the intervening years the continuity of this visual style was fostered by a number of methods which enabled younger cameramen to work under more experienced veterans in a direct way, either as operators, second cameramen, or assistants. Thus, an informal "school" of one particular visual style can be traced in a reasonably clear manner (something which can't be done with directors, for example, whose assistants were usually busy rounding up extras). Many cameramen were under contract to studios for years, and such cross-pollination no doubt resulted in one particular style heavily influencing a wide variety of younger assistants who were also under contract at the time. One can discuss an Ernest Palmer or Arthur Miller or Leon Shamroy style at Fox, for example, which would exist outside of any particular trend in studio production. Of course, when such a studio style was definitely promoted, it was the cameraman who carried it along. Warner Brothers films of the Thirties are probably visualized more clearly in terms of Sol Polito, Tony Gaudio and Barney McGill, than through Wellman, LeRoy or even Curtiz. Paramount's glossiest period was the result of Victor Milner and Lee Garmes as much as Lubitsch, Sternberg or Mamoulian. William Daniels, Oliver Marsh and Harry Stradling Sr. went a long way toward producing the MGM look. And Joe Walker was Columbia all by himself.

Once such a studio style had been fixed it seemed to pervade the rafters of the studio itself. George Folsey moved from Paramount *(Applause, The Smiling Lieutenant)* to Metro *(Meet Me in St. Louis, The White Cliffs of Dover)* but his style didn't move with him. Only those cameramen with the strongest personal styles were able to cross studio boundaries with impunity and imprint their own vision on everything. Hal Rosson could make a Metro Fleming *(Red Dust)* look like a Paramount Sternberg *(The Docks of New York)*, and Bert Glennon, Joe August or Gregg Toland could do the same thing.

Just as many of the great cameramen were associated most strongly with individual studios, another group was so linked to individual directors that their work together created a fusion of personal styles similar to some of the studio/cameraman associations. Bitzer and Griffith are the chief examples, but John Seitz and Rex Ingram (and later Billy Wilder), Karl Brown and James Cruze, and Robert Burks and Alfred Hitchcock are also notable pairings and, when these associations broke up, the effect on the visual style of both partners was often quite noticeable (Hitchcock's work after Burks' death, for example).

But Hollywood's visual style was not a purely inbred tradition. As with everything else, the studios could appropriate a pictorial style from overseas and make it their own. In the late Twenties and early Thirties a "German look" was highly cultivated, but there was no mistaking *Flesh and The Devil* or *Svengali* as anything but pure Hollywood, no matter how hard they tried. The finest Hollywood cameramen always added to the techniques they adopted from overseas, and to see this most clearly look at *Sunrise* against the context of Murnau's earlier films. The German cameramen had retained their primary interest in engineering; creative photography was concerned with the designing of tracking and dollying equipment. But Struss and Rosher quickly adapted to the moving style called for by Murnau and combined with this their own backgrounds in portrait photography. The visual difference between *Sunrise* and *The Last Laugh* can be seen in the figure molding on the faces of George O'Brien and Janet Gaynor, a lighting sophistication undreamed of in Germany at the time, but well grounded in American camerawork throughout the Twenties. Karl Freund and the other German cameramen who successfully worked in America quickly adapted themselves to these new complexities of shading, and we can trace this change by watching their earliest American work.

The post-World War II period brought the influence of the documentarists and Italian neo-realists, but here again it was digested and made part of the evolving tradition. Look at James Wong Howe's *The Rose Tattoo*, which echoes the grim texture of Magnani's Italian films—an amazing hybrid, but still a most polished piece of Hollywood craftsmanship underneath. And when the studios weren't borrowing stylistic touches from overseas they were often borrowing the cameramen themselves: Freund, Maté, Planer and others came over and brought part of the European tradition with them. Karl Freund made *Murders in the Rue Morgue* a sequel to *Caligari* and *The Golem*. One can see Dreyer's wall-eyed lighting effects behind Rita Hayworth in Rudolph Maté's photography of *Gilda*. As for Franz Planer, his work with Ophuls on both sides of the Atlantic is reflected in the elegance of such diverse work as *Holiday* and *Breakfast at Tiffany's*. The list could go on and on.

In the flow of these influences, as well as their absorption into the general fabric of Hollywood style, . . . one not only sees the growth of the individual artist, but the historical context that prompted certain developments and his reactions and contributions to them. . . . Taken together these form the fabric of Hollywood's visual style with all the individual strands showing through. Combined with the work of directors, writers, designers and others, they form a picture of classic Hollywood as the Florence of the West, bringing together creative ideas and creative talents from all over the world, then blending them into a new and dynamic synthesis.

This fabled mixture held so long as there was a framework to support it all. When that dropped out it meant more than the collapse of the studio method of filmmaking. Without this structure to support growth and change, American cinematography turned from inspired eclecticism to fragmented inspiration. It came full circle again to the days of Billy Bitzer, as today's pioneers roam the streets with portable equipment and Angenieux lenses, starting their own traditions.

ROLAND BARTHES
THE FACE OF GARBO

Garbo still belongs to that moment in cinema when capturing the human face still plunged audiences into the deepest ecstasy, when one literally lost oneself in a human image as one would in a philtre, when the face represented a kind of absolute state of the flesh, which could be neither reached nor renounced. A few years earlier the face of Valentino was causing suicides; that of Garbo still partakes of the same rule of Courtly Love, where the flesh gives rise to mystical feelings of perdition.

It is indeed an admirable face-object. In *Queen Christina*, a film which has again been shown in Paris in the last few years, the make-up has the snowy thickness of a mask: it is not a painted face, but one set in plaster, protected by the surface of the colour, not by its lineaments. Amid all this snow at once fragile and compact, the eyes alone, black like strange soft flesh, but not in the least expressive, are two faintly tremulous wounds. In spite of its extreme beauty, this face, not drawn but sculpted in something smooth and friable, that is, at once perfect and ephemeral, comes to resemble the flour-white complexion of Charlie Chaplin, the dark vegetation of his eyes, his totem-like countenance.

Now the temptation of the absolute mask (the mask of antiquity, for instance) perhaps implies less the theme of the secret (as is the case with Italian half mask) than that of an archetype of the human face. Garbo offered to one's gaze a sort of Platonic Idea of the human creature, which explains why her face is almost sexually undefined, without however leaving one in doubt. It is true that this film (in which Queen Christina is by turns a woman and a young cavalier) lends itself to this lack of differentiation; but Garbo does not perform in it any feat of transvestism; she is always herself, and carries without pretence, under her crown or her wide-brimmed hats, the same snowy solitary face. The name given to her, *the Divine*, probably aimed to convey less a superlative state of beauty than the essence of her corporeal person, descended from a heaven where all things are formed and perfected in the clearest light. She herself knew this: how many actresses have consented to let the crowd see the ominous maturing of their beauty. Not she, however; the essence was not to be degraded, her face was not to have any reality except that of its perfection, which was intellectual even more than formal. The Essence became gradually obscured, progressively veiled with dark glasses, broad hats and exiles: but it never deteriorated.

And yet, in this deified face, something sharper than a mask is looming: a kind of voluntary and therefore human relation between the curve of the nostrils and the arch of the eyebrows; a rare, individual function relating two regions of the face. A mask is but a sum of lines; a face, on the contrary, is above all their thematic harmony. Garbo's face represents this fragile moment when the cinema is about to draw an existential from an essential beauty, when the archetype leans towards the fascination of mortal faces, when the clarity of the flesh as essence yields its place to a lyricism of Woman.

Viewed as a transition the face of Garbo reconciles two iconographic ages, it assures the passage from awe to charm. As is well known, we are today at the other pole of this evolution: the face of Audrey Hepburn, for instance, is individualized, not only because of its peculiar thematics (woman as child, woman as kitten) but also because of her person, of an almost unique specification of the face, which has nothing of the essence left in it, but is constituted by an infinite complexity of morphological functions. As a language, Garbo's singularity was of the order of the concept, that of Audrey Hepburn is of the order of the substance. The face of Garbo is an Idea, that of Hepburn, an Event.

KENNETH TYNAN
GARBO

What, when drunk, one sees in other women, one sees in Garbo
sober. She is woman apprehended with all the pulsating clarity of
one of Aldous Huxley's mescalin jags. To watch her is to achieve
direct, cleansed perception of something which, like a flower or
a fold of silk, is raptly, unassertively, and beautifully itself. Nothing
intrudes between her and the observer except the observer's neu-
roses: her contribution is calm and receptiveness, an absorbent
repose which normally, in women, coexists only with the utmost
vanity. Tranced by the ecstasy of existing, she gives to each onlooker what he needs: her largesse is intarissable. Most actresses in
action live only to look at men, but Garbo looks at flowers,
clouds, and furniture with the same admiring compassion, like Eve
on the morning of creation, and better cast than Mr. Huxley as
Adam. Fame, by insulating her against a multitude of experiences
which we take for granted, has increased rather than diminished her
capacity for wonder. In England two years ago she visited West-
minster Abbey, early one morning when no one was about, and in
this most public of places found a source of enormous private enchantment. A walk along a busy street is for her a semi-mystical
adventure. Like a Martian guest, she questions you about your
everyday life, infecting you with her eagerness, shaming you into
a heightened sensitivity. Conversing with her, you feel like Ramon
Novarro, blinded in *Mata Hari*, to whom she said: "Here are your
eyes," and touched her own.

I half-believed, until I met her, the old hilarious slander which whispered that she was a brilliant Swedish female impersonator who had kept up the pretence too long; behind the dark glasses, it was hinted, beneath the wild brown hair, there lurked the features of a proud Scandinavian diplomat, now proclaiming their masculinity so stridently that exposure to cameras was out of the question. This idle fabrication was demolished within seconds of her entering the room; sidelong, a little tentative, like an animal thrust under a searchlight, she advanced, put out a hand in greeting, murmured something muted and sibilant to express her pleasure, and then, gashing her mouth into a grin, expunged all doubt. This was a girl, all right. It is an indication of the mystery which surrounds her that I felt pleased even to have ascertained her sex.

"Are you all things to all men?" someone asks her in *Two-Faced Woman;* to which the honest reply (I forget the scripted one) would be: "To all men, women, and children." Garbo, Hepburn, and Dietrich are perhaps the only screen personalities for whom such a claim could seriously be made. "She has sex, but no particular gender," I once wrote of Dietrich, "her masculinity appears to women, and her sexuality to men"; which is also true of Hepburn. Yet Garbo transcends both of them. Neither Hepburn nor Dietrich could have played Garbo's scenes with her son in *Anna Karenina;* something predatory in them would have forbidden such selfless maternal raptures. Garbo alone can be intoxicated by innocence. She turns her coevals into her children, taking them under her wing like a great, sailing swan. Her love is thus larger than Hepburn's or Dietrich's, which does not extend beyond the immediately desired object. It was Alistair Cooke who pointed out that in her films she seemed to see life in reverse and, because she was aware of the fate in store for them, offered the shelter of her sympathy to all around her. Through the cellophane *Kitsch* (how it dates!) of the Lubitsch touch she pierced, in *Ninotchka*, to affirm her pity for the human condition. The words were addressed to Melvyn Douglas, but we all knew for whom they were really intended, and glowed in the knowledge: "Bomps will fall, civilizations will crumble—but *not yet. . . . Give us our moment!*" She seemed to be pleading the world's cause, and to be winning, too. Often, during the decade in which she talked to us, she gave signs that she was on the side of life against darkness: they seeped through a series of banal, barrel-scraping scripts like code messages borne through enemy lines. Sometimes, uttering sentences that were plainly designed to speed the end of literature, she could convey her universal charity only in glimpses, such as, for instance, a half-mocking, half-despairing catch in the wine-dark voice. Round the militant bluster of M-G-M dialogue she wrapped a Red Cross bandage of humanity.

It is likely that too many volumes have been read into and written about her, and that every additional adulatory word reinforces the terror I am sure she feels at the thought of having to face us again and measure up to the legend. Possibly we exaggerated her intelligence from the beginning; perhaps she was perfectly happy with the velvet-lung, musk-scented tin lizzies that Salka Viertel and S. N. Behrman (among others) turned out as vehicles for her. Perhaps association with Lewis Stone and Reginald Owen, a stout pair of uncle-substitutes who crop up, variously bewigged, in many of her films, was vitally necessary to inspire her. Recall, too, that Carl Brisson and John Gilbert are known to have been high on her list of ideal men; and that we have no evidence that she has ever read a book. Except physically, we know little more about Garbo than we know about Shakespeare. She looks, in fact, about thirty-four, but her date of birth is disputable; the textbooks oscillate between 1905 and 1906, and one biography ungallantly plumps for 1903, which may, of course, be a wound left by an embittered typesetter. Stockholm cradled her, and like Anna Christie, she was the daughter of an impoverished sailor. She had a brother and two sisters, left school at fourteen, entered the newly expanding Swedish film industry, and was discovered by Mauritz Stiller. After the completion of *Gösta Berling* in 1924, her life is a list of movies, twelve silent, fourteen talking, and a file of newspaper pictures catching her aghast and rain-coated, grey-faced and weirdly hatted, on the gangplanks of ships or the stairways to planes. We often know where she is going, but never why. Occasionally a man is with her, a sort of Kafkaesque guard, employed to escort her to her next inscrutable rendezvous. Baffled, we consult the astrologers, who tell us that those born, as she was, between the end of August and the end of September are almost bound to be perfectionists; but what, we are left sighing, is she perfecting?

She changed her name from Gustaffson to Garbo, the Swedish word for a sprite. I used to think the Spanish "garbo" an insult to her, having heard it applied to matadors whose work seemed to me no more than pretty or neat. A Hispanophile friend has lately corrected me: "garbo," he writes, "is animal grace sublimated—the

571

flaunting of an assured natural charm, poise infected by *joie de vivre*, innate, high-spirited, controlled, the essentially female attribute (even in bullfighters). . . ." In short, "garbo" is Garbo without the melancholy, with no intimations of mortality. The word describes the embryo, the capital letter invests it with a soul. It is the difference between *Gösta Berling* and *Anna Karenina*.

But here again I am acquiescing in the myth of gloom. Long before the fit of hoarse hysterics that convulsed her when Melvyn Douglas fell off his chair, Garbo had laughed, even if it was only "wild laughter in the throat of death," and made us laugh too. She was never wholly austere. Posing as a man in the tavern scene of *Queen Christina*, how blithely she made us smile at her awkwardness when asked to share a bedroom with the Spanish ambassador! A secret half-smile, with the lips drawn back as if bobbing for apples, was always her least resistible weapon. Her gaiety coalesced, to the dismay of academic distinctions, with plangency. Her retirement is unforgivable if only because it means that now we shall never see her as Masha in *The Three Sisters*, a part Chekhov might have written for her. It takes lesser actresses to express a single emotion, mirth or mirthlessness. Garbo's most radiant grins were belied always by the anxiety in the antennae-like eyebrows; and by the angle of her head she could effect a transition, not alone of mood, but of age. When it was tilted back, with the mouth sagging open, she was a child joyously anticipating a sweet; when it was tipped forward, the mouth still agape, she became a parent wide-eyed at her child's newest exploit.

Some of her impact, certainly, was derived from the exoticism of her accent; hers was probably the first Swedish voice that many a million filmgoers had ever heard. Anglo-Saxons are notoriously prone to ascribe messianic characteristics to any stranger with a Slavic, Teutonic, or Nordic intonation; Bergner and Bergman are examples that come to mind, and the history of the London stage is punctuated with shrieks of exultation over long-forgotten soubrettes with names like Marta Kling, Svenda Stellmar, on Ljuba Van Strusi. Garbo was unquestionably assisted by the fact that she had to be cast, more often than not, as an exile: how often, to go about her business of home-wrecking, she arrives by train from afar! The smoke clears, revealing the emissary of fate, hungrily licking her lips. The displaced person always inspires curiosity: who displaced her, what forces drove her from her native land? If it was

572

Garbo's luck to provoke these inquiries, it was her gift which answered them. The impulse behind her voyages was romantic passion. Bergner might have left home to collect Pekes, Bergman to go on a hiking tour: Garbo could only have journeyed to escape or to seek a lover. Which is, as a line in *Ninotchka* has it, "a netchul impulse common to all."

Superficially, she changed very little in the course of her career; a certain solidity in her aspect suggested, at the very end, a spiritualized reworking of Irene Dunne, but that was all. She could still (and often did) fling her head flexibly back at right-angles to her spine, and she kissed as thirstily as ever, cupping her man's head in both hands and seeming very nearly to drink from it. And her appeal never lost its ambiguity. The after-dinner cooch-dance which drives Lionel Barrymore to hit the bottle in *Mata Hari* reveals an oddly androgynous physique, with strong-kneed legs as "capable," in their way, as the spatulate fingers: nothing is here of Herrick's "fleshie Principalities." Pectorally, the eye notes a subsidence hardly distinguishable from concavity: the art that conceals art could scarcely go further. If this undenominational temple-dance is seductive (and, like the swimming-pool sequence in *Two-Faced Woman*, it is), the explanation lies in our awareness that we are watching a real, imperfectly shaped human being, and not a market-fattened glamour-symbol.

I dwell on Garbo's physical attributes because I think the sensual side of acting is too often under-rated: too much is written about how actors feel, too little about how they look. Garbo's looks, and especially her carriage, always set up a marvellous dissonance with what she was saying. The broad ivory yoke of her shoulders belonged to a javelin-thrower; she walked obliquely, seeming to sidle even when she strode, like a middle-weight boxer approaching an opponent: how could this athletic port enshrine so frail and suppliant a spirit? Queen Christina, reputedly her favourite character, is encased for several reels in masculine garb, and when besought by her counsellors to marry, she replies: "I shall die a bachelor!" And think of: "I am Mata Hari—I am my own master!" To lines like these Garbo could impart an enigmatic wit which nobody else could have carried off. Deficient in all the surface frills of femininity, she replaced them with a male directness. Her Marie Walewska was as lion-hearted as Napoleon himself, and I have heard her described as "Charlemagne's Aunt." Her independence (in the last analysis) of either sex is responsible for the cryptic amorality of her performances. In most of the characters she played the only discernible moral imperative is loyalty, an animal rather than a human virtue—that "natural sense of honour" which, as Shaw says, "is nowhere mentioned in the Bible."

"Animal grace sublimated": I return to my correspondent's phrase. If it is true (as I think it is) that none of Garbo's clothes ever appear to be meant for her, much less to fit her, that is because her real state is not in clothes at all. Her costumes hamper her, whether they are stoles or redingotes or (as on one occasion) moiré, sèquinned, principal-boy tights. She implies a nakedness which is bodily as well as spiritual. It is foolish to complain that, basically, she gave but one performance throughout her life. She has only one body, and in this incarnation that is all we can expect.

Through what hoops, when all is said and done, she has been put by Seastrom, Cukor, Clarence Brown, and the rest of her mentors! She has gone blonde for them, danced "La Chica-Choca" for them, played a travesty of Sarah Bernhardt for them, stood straight-faced by for them as Lewis Stone warned her of "a new weapon called The Tank." Can we ask for more self-abnegation? A life of Duse was once mooted for her—what an *éducation sentimentale*, one guesses, she would have supplied for D'Annunzio! Later she hovered over, but did not settle on, a mimed role in Lifar's ballet version of *Phèdre*. And at the last moment, when all seemed fixed, she sidestepped the leading part in Balzac's *La Duchesse de Langeais*. The most recent, least plausible rumour of all insisted that she would film *La Folle de Chaillot*, with Chaplin as the Rag-Picker. . . .

So it looks as if we were never to know whether or not she was a great actress. Do I not find the death scene of *Camille* or the bedroom-stroking scene of *Queen Christina* commensurate with the demands of great acting? On balance, no. The great actress, as G. H. Lewes declared, must show her greatness in the highest reaches of her art; and it must strictly be counted against Garbo that she never attempted Hedda, or Masha, or St Joan, or Medea. We must acclaim a glorious woman who exhibited herself more profoundly to the camera than any of her contemporaries; but the final accolade must, if we are honest, be withheld.

VII

The Film Audience

Theorists have compared viewing a film both with reading a novel and with watching a play. Like the reader of a novel, the viewer of a film, sitting in a darkened hall, enjoys a degree of solitude. Like the viewer of a play, the movie-goer sits in a public place and reacts to humanly significant events in the company of other human beings. André Bazin, who distinguished between the "community" that views a play and the "mass" that watches a film, tries to hold both of these features in balance. But most theorists emphasize one or the other.

For Stanley Cavell, watching a film preserves the modern sense of privacy and anonymity. Man has longed for invisibility and the absence of responsibility it confers and film satisfies precisely this wish. In watching a film we view a magically reproduced world while remaining invisible to it. For Cavell, the experience of film is essentially voyeuristic and even pornographic. It permits the audience a magical sexual contact with the hypnotic Garbos, Dietrichs, and Gables of the screen.

Parker Tyler's view of the film experience is even more explicitly sexual and psychological. For him, the "dark-enshrouded" passivity of the movie house encourages "the daylight dream." In this state the movie screen transcends its role as a mirror of nature, and the viewer's unconscious mind can read the film's images symbolically. Tyler realizes that the Hollywood film (as opposed to the European film) cannot meet the standards of high art. But the resonant images of a Hollywood film mirror mythic cultural values and

575

stimulate our hidden lives. The stars fulfill our need for divinities and gratify our deepest sexual fantasies. This is the argument of a daring essay on the totemic role of the horse in American films, in which Tyler attempts to reveal the buried archetypal-mythological sources of one of the most familiar and popular film genres.

Kracauer likens the film not to the daydream but to the dream itself. The sense of self dissolves, and consciousness drifts into the objects on the screen, even as the subconscious and the unconscious rise within. It is unclear, however, how this resulting stream of unconsciousness which the viewer experiences enables the film to achieve the redemption of physical reality that Kracauer regards as its central aim. If the Hollywood "dream factory" supplies only the escapist needs of the masses, can it be recording and revealing reality? Surely "reality" cannot act like a "drug" to which Kracauer's film-goer is addicted. It is difficult to see how Kracauer reconciles his view of the realist film image with his view of the audience's experience of that image.

Gene Youngblood, the young American critic and disciple of Buckminster Fuller, doesn't think that we dream at Hollywood movies, but he agrees that they put us to sleep. He sympathizes with Ken Kelman's observation that "the spectator is reduced to a *voyeur*—which is, increasingly, the individual's role in society at large." Youngblood believes that films ought to expand the audience's consciousness, as "experimental" films do. Narrative films, and especially the "genre" films of commercial cinema, are "redundant" and tell audiences what they already know. All narratives tell stories based on certain assumptions about human nature and personality that are themselves the opinions of unexpanded men. For Youngblood there is no human nature, no essential human condition (as there is for Parker Tyler). Unexpanded man has simply invented such comforting concepts to mask his ignorance. The only value in even the best narrative films is their "design science" (personal style and technique). They say nothing new, but they say it well.

Youngblood wants to free the audience to create along with the film. Art is "research"; the more information the artist provides the more energy we then have to modify ourselves and to grow, to accept just those responsibilities that Cavell's movie *voyeur* wishes to avoid. Youngblood's view raises many difficult issues about the ends of art and the nature of man, but it is worth observing briefly that he does very little to show that all the films and kinds of film that he classifies as non-commercial (indeed, is *2001: A Space Odyssey* non-commercial?) are actually capable of expanding consciousness. After all, Andy Warhol's audiences probably find most of his "information" about "polymorphous perversity" as redundant as their parents find John Ford's "information" about traditional American values.

Walter Benjamin, the pre-war German Marxist critic, compares films not with an ideal of what works of art might become, but with his sense of what they traditionally have been. In the past, art works have been unique objects, possessing "aura" and traditional "authority." They played a ritual role, contemplated by men who kept a "natural" distance from them. But the contemporary masses want to see things closer, spatially and humanly. They overcome the uniqueness of the work of art by accepting a mechanical reproduction of it as an equivalent. These reproductions are no longer hallowed cult objects but consumer goods sold on the market; rather than absorbing their beholders they are absorbed by them. Reactions to these "works of art" are rarely personal and are almost completely determined by the mass audience to which the individual is subordinated. Indeed, films have now become one of the most powerful agents of mass political movements—in them the mass has for the first time come face to face with itself. In Benjamin's view, the film and the audience's relation to it is so different from all that has gone before that he is inclined to think that photography has transformed the very nature of art.

STANLEY CAVELL
FROM THE WORLD VIEWED

IDEAS OF ORIGIN

It is inevitable that in theorizing about film one at some point speculate about its origins, because despite its recentness, its origin remains obscure. The facts are well enough known about the invention and the inventors of the camera, and about improvements in fixing and then moving the image it captures. The problem is that the invention of the photographic picture is not the same thing as the creation of photography as a medium for making sense. The historical problem is like any other: a chronicle of the facts preceding the appearance of this technology does not explain why it happened when and as it did. Panofsky opens his study of film by remarking, "It was not an artistic urge that gave rise to the discovery and gradual perfection of a new technique; it was a technical invention that gave rise to the discovery and gradual perfection of a new art." We seem to understand this, but do we understand it? Panofsky assumes we know what it is that at any time has "given rise" to a "new art." He mentions an "artistic urge," but that is hardly a candidate to serve as an explanation; it would be about as useful as explaining the rise of modern science by appealing to "a scientific urge." There may be such urges, but they are themselves rather badly in need of explanation. Panofsky cites an artistic urge explicitly as the occasion for a new "technique." But the motion picture is not a new *technique*, any more than the airplane is. (What did we use to do that such a thing enables us to do better?) Yet some idea of flying, and an urge to do it, preceded the mechanical invention of the airplane. What is "given rise to" by such inventions as movable type or the microscope or the steam engine or the pianoforte?

It would be surprising if the history of the establishment of an artistic medium were less complex a problem for the historical understanding than (say) the rise of modern science. I take Bazin to be suggesting this when he reverses the apparent relation between the relevant technology and the idea of cinema, emphasizing that the idea preceded the technology, parts of it by centuries, and that parts of the technology preceded the invention of movies, some of it by centuries. So what has to be explained is not merely how the feat was technically accomplished but, for example, what stood in the way of its happening earlier. Surprisingly, Bazin, in the selection of essays I have read, does not include the contemporary condition of the related arts as a part of the ideological superstructure that elicited the new material basis of film. But it is certainly relevant that the burning issue during the latter half of the nineteenth century, in painting and in the novel and in the theater, was realism. And unless film captured possibilities opened up by the arts themselves, it is hard to imagine that its possibilities as an artistic medium would have shown up as, and as suddenly as, they did.

The idea of and wish for the world re-created in its own image was satisfied *at last* by cinema. Bazin calls this the myth of total cinema. But it had always been one of the myths of art; each of the arts had satisfied it in its own way. The mirror was in various hands held up to nature. In some ways it was more fully satisfied in theater. (Since theater is on the whole not now a major art for us, it on the whole no longer makes contact with its historical and psychological sources; so we are rarely gripped by the trauma we must once have suffered when the leader of the chorus stopped contributing to a narrative or song and turned to face the others, suffering incarnation.)

What is cinema's way of satisfying the myth? Automatically, we said. But what does that mean—mean mythically, as it were? It means satisfying it without *my* having to do anything, satisfying it *by* wishing. In a word, *magically*. I have found myself asking: How could film be art, since all the major arts arise in some way out of religion? Now I can answer: Because movies arise out of magic; from *below* the world.

The better a film, the more it makes contact with this source of its inspiration; it never wholly loses touch with the magic lantern behind it. This suggests why movies of the fantastic (*The Cabinet of Dr. Caligari, Blood of a Poet*) and filmed scenes of magic (say, materialization and dematerialization), while they have provided moods and devices, have never established themselves as cinematic media, however strongly this "possibility" is suggested by the physical medium of film: they are technically and psychologically trivial compared with the medium of magic itself. It is otherwise if the presented magic is itself made technically or physically interesting (*The Invisible Man, Dr. Jekyll and Mr. Hyde, Frankenstein, 2001: A Space Odyssey*), but then that becomes another way of confirming the physicality of our world. Science presents itself, in movies, as magic, which was indeed one source of science. In particular, projected science retains magic's mystery and forbiddenness. Science-fiction films exploit not merely certain obvious aspects of adventure, and of a physicality that special effects specialize in, but also the terrific mumbo-jumbo of hearsay science: "My God, the thing is impervious to the negative beta ray! We must reverse the atom recalcitration spatter, before it's too late!" The dialogue has the surface of those tinbox-and-lever contraptions that were sufficiently convincing in prime *Flash Gordon*. These films are carried by the immediacy of the fantasy that motivates them (say, destruction by lower or higher forms of life, as though the precariousness of human life is due to its biological stage of development); together with the myth of the one way and last chance in which the (external) danger can be averted. And certainly the beauty of forms and motions in Frankenstein's laboratory is essential to the success of *Frankenstein*; computers seem primitive in comparison. It always made more sense to steal from God than to try to outwit him.

How do movies reproduce the world magically? Not by literally presenting us with the world, but by permitting us to view it unseen. This is not a wish for power over creation (as Pygmalion's was), but a wish not to need power, not to have to bear its burdens. It is, in this sense, the reverse of the myth of Faust. And the wish for invisibility is old enough. Gods have profited from it, and Plato tells it at the end of the *Republic* as the Myth of the Ring of Gyges. In viewing films, the sense of invisibility is an expression of modern privacy or anonymity. It is as though the world's projection explains our forms of unknownness and of our ability to know. The explanation is not so much that the world is passing us by, as that we are displaced from our natural habitation within it, placed at a distance from it. The screen overcomes our fixed distance; it makes displacement appear as our natural condition.

PARKER TYLER
FROM MAGIC AND MYTH
OF THE MOVIES

PREFACE

That the movies offer nothing but entertainment is a myth in a sense never used or implied in the following pages. I am not denying that millions of America's movie fans succeed in finding only entertainment in the nation's theaters. Aside from the news-reels and the documentaries given impetus by the war, entertainment remains all that is consciously demanded by those paying rising prices at movie box offices. . . . Patrons of all art media may get more than they demand as well as less, and since the surplus is not precisely expected, it may register vaguely, obliquely, unconsciously. Especially is this true of the movie audience, if only because as a large mass it is critically inarticulate. I hope that my efforts may succeed in giving it some voice on the positive side— movie reviewers take care of its voice on the negative side—and I hope also that for the benefit of students and those hitherto indifferent to the "folk" art of cinema I may further demonstrate that Hollywood is a vital, interesting phenomenon, at least as important to the spiritual climate as daily weather to the physical climate. A myth foisted specifically on the movies proper rather than on the reaction of audiences is furnished by devotees of both stage and novel who scorn movies as below the serious level—as standing in relation to true art somewhat as the circus does to the legitimate stage. But unfortunately these judges, unaware of the ritual importance of the screen, its baroque energy and protean symbolism, are unwarrantably summary, basically uneducated in the movie medium.

. . . The true field of the movies is not *art* but *myth*, between which—in the sense "myth" is invariably used here—there is a perhaps unsuspectedly wide difference. Assuredly a myth is a fiction, and this is its bare link with art, but a myth is specifically a free, unharnessed fiction, a basic, prototypic pattern capable of many variations and distortions, many betrayals and disguises, even though it remains *imaginative* truth. It has one degraded function connected with the idea of entertainment I discussed above, as when the word itself becomes adjectival and is deliberately attached to that pseudonymous Baltic kingdom having no existence saving in fifth-rate novels and in the movies. It is unsound to make a fact such as the existence of the very nation where a story occurs into a fiction, for it is like taking the props out from under a building and assuming it will still stand. No matter how fantastic an action, its background must be firm. It is the status of background that determines the strength of a myth, the status of its perspective in human history.

Essentially the *scene* of imaginative truth, or art, is the mind itself, but in some manner this truth must be objective, capable of projection onto the screen of the world. In a sense man *is* his past, the past of his race, and all the beliefs he ever held. Reality cannot be made up from the material facts of his existence, his immediate sensory reactions; nor can it be fundamentally a world that never was. Certainly man has ceased to believe much he used to believe. "Oh, that is a myth," we say, meaning that even if significant, it is an ideal or an illusion, a thing that has no substance. But psychology has taught us the strange reality of chimeras, their symbolic validity; and comparative mythology has revealed the great persistence of psychic patterns, with special reference to the supernatural, whose continuity in human belief is sometimes surprisingly self-evident. At one time men believed the earth was flat. Today this is a purely ornamental myth; it has died because imagining the earth is flat has no relation to our desires or employments. At one time the pagans believed in Diana as goddess of the moon and the hunt. Today this also might be considered a decorative myth, something in the fairy-tale class. Yet like so many legends it holds a mesmeric appeal for the mind; Diana represents, as a matter of fact, a certain sexual type—the vigorous virgin, the woman resistant to love; and yet according to the legend Endymion made her lose her heart; that is, the man lived who could break down her defenses merely through his physical image. Obviously this sexual pattern is repeated today. The modern belief that the earth is round corresponds to the conditions of our planetary existence insofar as, proceeding on this premise, our astronomical calculations work out. The belief is consistent with *all the facts*. Today the fact that Diana once had for the pagans a reality she does not have for us means merely that the myth lives in another form. It is an ideal archetype, a part of human experience that has its home in the imagination. And yet . . . that which was true once may become true again. What was symbolized by the Diana myth in actual human experience is a permanent legacy of the race. So the essence of myth also has the status of permanent possibility . . . in short, *desires* may have the same power over the mind and behavior, indeed a much greater power, than *facts*.

In the following pages I have occasion to refer specifically to the great researches made in ancient magic by Sir James Frazer. That there are anthropological assumptions contradictory to various of Frazer's own premises is of no importance to the point I am making. In order to explain a single phenomenon, the priest cult of the King of the Wood at Nemi, Frazer accumulated into one work a prodigious array of ancient primitive beliefs and customs suggesting the limitless lineage of the relatively recent cult at Nemi. At this moment, as when his book was written, nobody is a devotee of this cult; nobody believes in the magic of the golden bough that had to be plucked by the aspirant to Diana's priesthood before he was empowered to kill in single combat the incumbent priest. And yet those who do not profoundly know anthropology might be astonished to learn how much of our personal lives is influenced by all the ancient magical and religious beliefs connected with this one cult. The whole history of the decay and fall of gods, the extermination of divine hierarchies, could be told with just the Nemian cult as basis. In discussing in later pages the male comics of the screen who entertained troops all over the world during the war, I show how they may be considered modern medicine men or primitive priests, scapegoats who transferred to themselves the inner fears of the soldier striving to be brave and made cowardice and bravery alike into a kind of joke. Consequently in relation to

585

my argument the myth is not, as a psychological or historical nucleus of fact, necessarily to be judged as true or false, illusory or real, according to its specific labels, its historic status, its literal beliefs. Essentially myths are not factual but symbolic. I assume that movies are essentially likewise.

. . . Briefly movies, similar to much else in life, are seldom what they seem. In this sense—being, to begin with, fiction—movies are dreamlike and fantastic, their fantasy and examples of this are the folk myths of the absent-minded professor, of the efficiency expert, and of the eccentricity of genius. . . .

Naturally when I ally myth with superstition I am taking not only Frazer's view of the profound interrelatedness of myths but also Freud's view that beneath the upper levels of the mind lies a vast human capacity to think in terms of frantic passions and above all in terms of symbols. Even ten years ago it would have been thought impossible by movie moguls that a surrealist artist, Salvador Dali, should be employed to devise images to portray movie dreams, which in turn are subjected to psychoanalysis, a clinical process that provides the solution of the plot. . . .

The fundamental eye trickery that is a genius of the camera—you see the object, yet it isn't there—came to the fore in the movies and ever since then has mocked with its dynamic plasticity the very form from which it developed, the still camera. Today the movie has all the flexibility of the novel as well as the vision and speech of the stage. In striving through imaginative works to create the illusion of reality the movie screen must constantly transcend its own mirror nature of literal reflection. Camera trickery is really camera magic, for illusion can be freely created by the movie camera with more mathematical accuracy and shock value than by sleight-of-hand magic or stage illusion. The very homogeneity of cinema illusion—the images of the actors themselves are illusive, their corporal bodies absent—creates a throwback in the mood of the spectator to the vestiges of those ancient beliefs that I discuss in detail later in the chapter on supernaturalism, such as beliefs in ghosts, secret forces, telepathy, etc.

Moreover, the movie-theater rite corresponds directly to the profoundly primitive responses of the audience; the auditorium is dark, the spectator is relaxed, the movie in front of him requires less sheer mental attention than would a novel or stage play—less attention because all movement seems to exist on the screen; even the background changes easily, quickly; the whole world moves around the spectator, who is a still point. From the capacity of the screen for trick illusion, plus the dark-enshrouded passivity of the spectator, issues a state of daydream, which I termed in my previous book "the daylight dream" because it occurs in the dark: the screen is the focus of light, while the spectator is conscious in a darkness of the bedroom. It is in daydreams that magic seems to operate, in daydreams that things begin to seem rather than to be. "The movie theater," to quote directly from my previous book, "is the psychoanalytic clinic of the average worker's daylight dream." It is likewise in the process of psychoanalysis, where the *part*, truly recognized as symbol, transforms the meaning of the whole. The movie process is a complex myth of sheer synecdoche. People go to the movies merely to see a favorite player, or for the locale or period, or for the genre, or because they are bored almost to death. How, under these conditions, can anyone hope to appreciate the *whole* movie, especially since, to begin with, the movie can hardly be considered a whole?

No longer does man believe in myth or magic. No! For magic has been sifted and reorganized into science and governs only his material world, not the realm of his spirit, while comparative mythology and anthropology merely comprise school subjects. The sects of Christian religion have organized Western man's spiritual beliefs under one heading: the myth of Christ. Yet Christ's myth too can be related to pagan myths. The very fact that for children the Bible itself is but another series of fairy tales, weighted but little by a sense of historical fact, alone demonstrates my point as to the basic importance of myth with regard to popular or folk art. Our imaginary lives as children survive in us as adults and enrich our subsequent natures. So the fairy-tale lives of primitive races, our ancient antecedents, survive in the religions we formally believe in today as well as among those tribes still unassimilated to modern civilization. I do not claim any absolute value for the myth and magic of Hollywood or for those modern vestiges of the old Greek divinities I have dubbed "the gods and goddesses of Hollywood." On the contrary the principle I mean is one of relativity and metamorphosis rather than absolutism and changelessness: just as a word has synonyms and antonyms—so has a myth. In psychoanalytical symbolism, the deepest symbolism of the mind, the identity of objects is established by a complex frame of reference in which an image may represent one of three objects or all three objects at once. If, then, I say that the actors of Hollywood are an enlarged personnel of the realistically anthropomorphic deities of ancient Greece, I do not indulge in a mere bit of verbal humor, satiric or otherwise; on the other hand neither am I proposing or assuming the existence of an unconscious cult of supernatural worship. I feel I am but calling attention to the fact that the glamour actors and actresses of the movie realm are fulfilling an ancient need, unsatisfied by popular religions of contemporary times. Those men and women who perform for us are human, as we are; they have homes, children, love affairs; they suffer and die. And yet a magic barrier cuts across the texture of our mutual humanity; somehow their wealth, fame, and beauty, their apparently unlimited field of worldy pleasure—these conditions tinge them with the supernatural, render them immune to the bitterness of ordinary frustrations. It does not matter if this thought is a mythological exaggeration. It is a *tendency* of the popular imagination. The secret of the power of Hollywood gods and goddesses is that they seem to do everything anyone else does except that when they die—in movies—they die over and over; when they love, they love over and over. Even as the gods do, they undergo continual metamorphoses, never losing their identities, being Rita Hayworth or Glenn Ford no matter what their movie aliases. And like Jupiter in the modern comedy, *Amphitryon 38*, they can condescend, even be ridiculous. All that the public demands is what it always gets— the power to make and break stars—but gods have always led basically mortal lives.

Lastly, in this and my previous book, do I have *a method?* Not in the sense that I am selling ideas, nor above all, is mine a method by which one can test the high or low esthetic content of a given movie. . . . If my method is worthy of a label, it is "psychoanalytic-mythological," often socially angled. I have invented little or nothing. I have merely applied it to new material and formulated in accordance with the reapplication. That I speak metaphorically, in dream symbols, and . . . in terms of my own "hallucination," is a fact I wish not only to admit but to proclaim. Yes, I have made up a collective myth of my own, and I confess that in so doing I have plagiarized Hollywood exhaustively. If I have interpreted many things as dreams are interpreted, I cite as belated authorities recent movies of psychoanalytical themes and dream-symbol material. Indirectly, however, I have only been obeying Hollywood's own law of fluidity, of open and ingenious invention. If I have formulated an element of moviedom to be known as "the supernatural hush" and interpreted it as applicable at once to the hush of a cathedral, the hush of a psychiatrist's clinic, the hush of an isolated lovers' session on Riverside Drive, and the hush of the studio while Jennifer Jones does a scene in *The Song of Bernadette*, I feel that I am defining a quality of the movies as one would classify an acidic combination in the laboratory. And if in one of the magic-lantern metamorphoses internal movie meanings are discussed in terms of doubting the evidence of the senses, I am merely following the technique of psychoanalysis as well as paralleling legal criticism of circumstantial evidence of crimes: *things are not always what they seem*. I hope to have revealed a deeper sort of truth than that to be found on surfaces and at the same time to have assembled here a little mythology, a kind of concordance, showing the frequently unconscious magic employed by Hollywood—a magic of dream creation that far transcends its literal messages.

589

PARKER TYLER
THE HORSE : TOTEM ANIMAL OF MALE POWER–AN ESSAY IN THE STRAIGHT-CAMP STYLE

In that informal realm of civilized thought and action where the vestiges of primitive life survive, the horse and the dog are rivals for fame as American totems. "Civilized" man must have relatively domesticated totems. And it is natural that film, recorder of movement, should be the art pre-eminently glorifying animals. Despite movies as successful as *Lassie* and *Son of Lassie*, the dog must continue to bow, as American totem, to the horse. This ascendency is logical for two reasons. While space was used picturesquely and effectively in Lassie's long journey back home, the range of movement open to what Americans term the "horse opera," and the superiority of the horse as power-symbol, determine the issue of rivalry. After all, the dog is a creature more domesticated than the horse; he gets as close to man as the interior fireside and even his bedroom, whereas, in the living-quarters sense, the horse is more intimate at the open camp fire. Moreover, a dog, especially if small, can be embraced more wholly and is more articulately and aggressively affectionate than the horse. This seemingly superior intimacy between man and his dog, however, is offset by the folk experience of the American cowboy—that experience recorded so voluminously by Hollywood. The cowboy *rides* his animal, and at the same time is more dependent on its power than North American man, below the Artic regions, is on the dog's power. The physical contact between cowboy and horse—an animal bigger than man—provides an emblem, as well as a drama, of mastery that transcends (assuredly in the aesthetic domain) the easier, more urban and commonplace, relations between man and his "best friend," the dog.

Obviously, too, the horse gives the drama of good and evil a more distinctive place in story and legend. As a "wild animal," the horse may be tamed, whereas wild dogs offer men no temptation to tame them. Temperamentally unruly horses, furthermore, yield mysteriously to gifted individuals. In movies, the horse of evil character, which sometimes offsets the docile horse, has a term in American-Spanish lingo also applied to a man: "bad hombry." The best dog movie, in my opinion, came from England, *To the Victor*, which was about sheep dogs. Not only was there the sporting angle (duplicated in the equine domain by racing) but also the drama of blood, moral and immoral. In *To the Victor*, it is not the hero, or totemic, dog who turns out to be the nocturnal sheep-killer, but his rival. This film was excellent precisely because of its moral scope, and because, moreover, this scope subtly reflected the moral struggles in human character. This (like the American-made *The Yearling*, about a fawn) was an extraordinarily *civilized* animal picture. "Horse operas," dedicated to a minimum of sheer violence, are more casual and crass, but highly pertinent, nevertheless, to our national mores. Perennially, horse films tend to be inadvertent legends—invariably, if also unconsciously, totemic in nature.

As England and Europe are more thoughtfully aware than we ourselves, America is the land of, among other things, "the open prairie" and "the lone cowboy"; alone, save for his eternal partner: the horse.* This coupling is a paradigm for the pagan myth-creature, the Centaur. The man-horse becomes a pseudo-organism; a cowboy has a grandeur and a sense of power, with his horse under him, which he could not possibly have afoot. Totemically speaking, this is a merging between the religious-magical image, the clan emblem, and the work animal. But the *personal* relation, with its imaginative reverberation, makes the mythical importance of the American man-horse. The horse is not only a power-symbol as a fleshly engine but as an extension of the man's personal power and, more specifically, of his sexual power. With these considerations,

---

*In latter days, the "spaghetti western" shows just how thoughtful a country Italy is.

one can register more accurately the emotional impact of the film image of a beautiful and powerful horse, mane afloat, rearing against an empty horizon: this is a simple traditional emblem as old as the American film industry itself. A man, traditionally, is seen already on the horse's back; the struggle for mastery has been implicitly won, and this mastery brings American man his power over both equine and bovine herds. In more serious films, the rider-less or yet untamed horse becomes a symbol for man himself—objectively or subjectively, father or son—and sometimes symbol for woman, the woman to be sexually rejected or obtained. The function of the totem animal in the primitive initiation rite for pubescent boys was a parable of birth from the animal itself. This "birth" provided a symbolic origin which the youth could identify as absolute, superseding his mother's womb as scene of his father's fruit; in this way, his incestuous rivalry was replaced by a father-identification, with the sexual element of the mother lacking. "The lone cowboy," in this perspective, is the initiated youth joined to the totemistic father-animal, which, as the horse's rider, he has symbolically vanquished.

Let us take for granted the regulation horse-operas, or Grade B westerns. These have had their human screen idols who embody this totemistic evolution of man-horse in a strictly static sense; actors such as Roy Rogers, Ken Maynard, Bill Elliott and other, lesser, riders. But of highlighted totemic interest are two films, one of which, *The Outlaw*, because of censorship difficulties, was first seen only on the West Coast and at private showings in New York; the other film is *Gallant Bess*. These two movies must be credited with a degree of originality because of their extremism; even if artistically gauche in their lack of consciousness, they are not un-inspired. At the least, they break away from the usual boy-and-girl romance coupled with the winning of big stakes by the boy's or girl's racehorse; a memorable exhibit of this latter type is *Home-stretch*, in which the fate of the romance and the winning of the race are duly dovetailed. Let us not be squeamish about the horse race as a symbolic variety of the sexual act, particularly as we must face an analogous, if more complex, symbolism of this kind in *The Outlaw*. The obsessional temper of racing fans and the emotional build-up to a minutes-long suspense (the race itself) accompanied by the wildest excitement and breathlessly climaxed, are factors of racing that testify to its sexual parallel. Moreover, we are compelled, not only in the light of these two movies, but also in the perspective of traditional legend and ritual, to recognize in horse-operas of a significantly totemic kind the presence of the Oedipus-complex. The anticipated result of the initiation rite previously mentioned was precisely the destruction of this complex. This is true in whatever form it may be found.

As I have written much to signify, the mass unconscious is given free play by the Hollywood habit of catering to the most ancient of popular stereotypes, in which—inevitably—lies a basic substratum of primitive superstition; here the stereotype is the western adventure story. In the *Flicka* pictures, Roddy McDowall portrayed the boy isolated on a farm and striving to establish symbolic power by befriending and mastering a horse; first, a mare and then this mare's son. This was a vestigial, purely individualistic effort to achieve totemic initiation through a horse. Roddy plays a moody youth rebellious towards his father but humoured by his mother. Symbolically, of course, the mare's son is Roddy himself in multiplied power and pitted against the renegade stallion, whom he must succumb to or vanquish. In this way the boy's Oedipus rivalry with his father is displaced to the objective equine drama, made doubly effectual by his ownership of the triumphant stallion; *just because* this plot is a modern vestige, the symbolic totem enters reality and has its drama there. The boy alone is spectator of the crucial fight between the stallions, which takes place in the wilds and which involves, naturally, the leadership of the herd and sovereignty over the mares. Roddy's horse seems to have yielded to domestication, but when his adult power is proven in mortal combat, he takes off to lead the free herd. This anticipates Roddy's own eventual voyage into life beyond his parents' world and virtually proclaims the success of the psychological initiation rite. Another film, *Indiana*, portrayed an adolescent romance in which the boy, by stealth, clandestinely mates two fine racehorses belonging to different stables; not only did this incident provide, in the more obvious sense, a symbolic conjugation with the girl he loved, but also a totemic rite in which the boy could eavesdrop on the parental marriage-bed; by the substitution of the totemic animals, his illicit jealousy is satisfied.

If these symbolic readings of film material appear somewhat

593

exaggerated or overspecial, it is impossible to mistake what is considerably more pointed (deliberately or not) in *Gallant Bess* and *The Outlaw*. The former is straightforwardly—indeed, to the hilt— the story of a youth's obsession with his mare and is the strategic psychic foreshortening of the initiation rite into the struggle to overcome obsession with the maternal sex-image. To summarize the plot: the boy, called to war and enlisting as a Seabee, is parted from Bess, his beloved mare. At camp his pin-up picture is not of a movie queen but of Bess. Hearing that she is about to bear a colt, the boy requests leave to go to her but is denied it until his arrival (from his viewpoint) is too late to save her life in the ordeal. In a kind of delirium, he digs her grave during a violent storm and cannot be persuaded by an old farmhand that "since you love her, you'll always have her." Returning to service, he goes with his outfit to prepare an airfield on a captured Japanese island base. There he has nightmares (how oddly literal!) in which he sees Bess—in "negative"—rearing into space; his tent-pals can't sleep because of his groans and outcries and he is physically chastised by his own buddy (one of those cheerful roughnecks who typically supply humour in American films). Finally, one night, he cannot believe that the insistent, pathetic neighing he hears from the jungle is not that of his dead mare, so he gropes his way into the forest, where he finds on the ground a real horse, seriously wounded; needless to say, a mare. With the connivance of his tent-pals and eventually the toleration of his superior officer (a man whose severity turns to good will, and who obviously is a father-image), the boy revives the new Bess and she is established as a sort of troop mascot. Bess does soldier duty and saves her master's life when a Jap sniper shoots him; she also performs tricks in a little corral, at least one of them (the boy is the ringmaster) being most insinuating. Convalescent from his wounds, the boy is scheduled to leave Bess on the island when his outfit is ordered away, but in an excruciating sequence, Bess breaks leash and swims after the transport, where in defiance of regulations she is allowed to clamber on board: boy and horse are reunited. As a dénouement, Bess (on the American farm) successfully bears a colt. Again, the boy hero is the mating agent, but here no sign of a stallion appears; the boy is clearly master of a totemic birth ritual in which he is both the symbolic stallion and the infant colt.

594

In case anyone believes that this film should be considered innocent of any underlying meaning, I quote verbatim a remark by the boy's wisecracking pal: "Maybe there's something to this love stuff besides *dames*." I submit that my own interpretation is at least free of vulgarity. Furthermore, on the realistic level where such substitutions do take place in the human libido (thus making the film true to life), the story paraphrases in allegory a boy's transference of obsession with his mother (the first Bess) to that with another woman (the second Bess); just so, he might be disconsolate at the death of a beloved mother and then find a girl who would substitute for her. I should add that the emotional tone of the actor taking the youth's role would not have been tolerated had the story been projected in script as about an adolescent crush on a *human* female. In that case, as ironic as the hypothesis is, such an exhibition of masculine emotion would have been condemned as "morbid" and never have been filmed to set before the public!

The Outlaw, as a straight story, is less ingenuous than *Gallant Bess*, although aesthetically, of course, the Howard Hughes production is profoundly inept. The boy (played by a newcomer, Jack Buetel) is a bona-fide outlaw, Billy the Kid himself, second in American legend only, perhaps, to Jesse James, and even more of a lone wolf, since he sets out singly in this movie to avenge his brother's death. A more or less fragile female, apparently, has killed his brother. Let us pass over the more routine innuendoes, as lewd and nude as these are, and turn to what a more sophisticated censorship might have more reasonably, if less needfully, become alarmed at. In its own oafish manner, the movie extends the power-symbol of the horse to an ambivalent and ambiguous sort of homosexual fixation. Here the stallion, frankly termed a "sweetheart" by a rival outlaw (Walter Huston) is a bone of contention between Billy and said rival, whom it seems adequate to identify by his nickname, "Doc," and who is senior crime champion in the story's locale. Originally, the horse had belonged to Billy; stolen, he has been sold to "Doc," in whose possession Billy finds him and from whom, by hook and crook, he wrests him. Billy, by outbraving and outdrawing "Doc" so arouses the latter's admiration that the two enter an ambiguous partnership, half affection and half enmity. The plot of their rivalry for the horse—obviously, as a stallion, the emblem of sexual power—supersedes their rivalry for said

female, and so independently complicated is this major theme that
the stallion symbol assumes a realistic value; i.e., the stallion is
an actual love-object, a co-extended Narcissus image for each male;
certain details indicate that for "Doc" the attractive boy becomes
homosexually symbolic of the horse. At one point, the two males
bargain for either strawberry roan or girl; when Billy chooses the
stallion, dissatisfaction gleams in "Doc's" eyes; the girl forthwith
appears in a doorway and—in the screen's most unladylike manner—shouts at Billy: "What! You'd exchange me for a *horse?*"
This howler was apparently conceived as brutal realism. Throughout, the action gives sadism a big play. This fact is not least evident
in the amusingly exciting climatic sequence of the formal gun-duel
between boy and man to decide by death the parlay-prize of girl
and horse, the survivor to claim both. How ingeniously the sporting atmosphere is preserved! This is curiously pointed out because
twice in the film Billy has been set to shoot the girl, and once he actually gives her the rope-crucifixion—an invention of the Indians—
only to reconsider and come back to release her.

As the rivals face each other for the duel, and the clock gives
the signal to shoot, Billy's guns remain hanging in his holsters. As
"Doc" taunts Billy for cowardice, the former artistically knicks
each of his ears with bullets. Psychologically, Billy's inert passivity
needs explanation; everything, including manly honour, is at stake.
Realistically speaking, something *unconscious* must restrain him.
What can this be—if not subconscious homosexuality—but the
shadow of the Oedipus guilt falling on his trigger finger? He is
faced by a man half of whom is as fond of him as though Billy were
his own son, and half of whom, in the symbolic sense of the paternal sex-rival, is bent on destroying him. In the former role,
"Doc"—true to his nickname—is the paternal medicine man who,
as the rite proceeds, symbolically castrates the initiate by knicking
his ears, and yet, as the father afraid of the usurping son, he is ready
to literally exterminate Billy. This combination of personalities
in "Doc" might well paralyze Billy through sheer bewilderment as
to the proper identification; guilt and innocent faith contend in
his heart. That this scene is saturated with a quasi-homosexual
atmosphere is proven by a sub-plot of the affections—no less than
an old and sentimental friendship between "Doc" and a fourth
character, a rather ridiculous sheriff (Thomas Mitchell) who has
tagged along and finally caught up with the two outlaws. During

the duel, the sheriff (fleeced of his guns) is a helpless bystander, an emasculated figure who raises loud complaint against Billy as cause of his alienation from "Doc" and starts sobbing. One might hazard that this disqualified symbol of law is a masquerade for the wife and mother, whose spirit here interferes with the initiation rite because it is *lethally real*, not a true rite. The girl, although present, is purely negative. Despite the sheriff's wails and his own indecision, Billy at last draws and kills "Doc," thus fulfilling what is to be identified, finally and specifically, as a symbolic Oedipus destiny.

Accordingly, in this film, the virtual totemic rite has fizzled and become *drama*. What appears on the surface as perhaps the most outrageous "fairy tale" of all westerns somehow manages to emerge as the most dramatic and least neatly symbolic of filmdom's masked totemic rites. First, the horse is never in the movie as a dramatic factor: "Doc" himself is a sort of Centaur, a paternal outlaw whose traditional ascendency has been challenged by a stripling novice. Here a mythological parallel is fortunate: Greek myth has it that Chiron, a Centaur, instructed the hero, Achilles, in the arts of peace and war. I suggest Billy's parallel with Achilles also for another reason, for it was Achilles who retired from the Trojan war until he was moved to avenge the death of his bosom friend, Patroclus, and Billy's original motive in the story was simply revenge for his brother's death. Sexual rivalry, however, was automatically thrust on Billy by events. But the significant thing between the two males of *The Outlaw* is that only *one* set of essentials, girl and horse, exists for them. Obviously, the physically desirable female will not suffice either of them: the totemic symbol, the stallion—almost identical with the self—is also necessary. It is the *human* relations, the impersonation of the human father by "Doc," that complicates the boy's totemic imagination. It is as though "Doc" were a medicine man who desired to undermine the ritual totemic release to be considered the boy's traditional right, and this precisely because, perhaps, "Doc's" own totemic release, in terms of modern society, has not been completed, rendered authentic. He himself is to be conceived as a "son" whose initiation once failed, perhaps also became real, violent drama. Are Billy and "Doc," after all, not *outlaws*, traditional bad-men who are paradigms for the rebellious sons of the original horde? We must not fail to note that the "outlaw" is a renegade member of the cowboy clans.

597

Nor must we overlook that, in the trance of the movie theatre, one is inclined to forget too easily that popular fiction represents a vast cultural residue. Yes, movie stories are made up "out of someone's head," but because of this very openness of viewpoint towards the chosen material—that feverish invention so peculiar to Hollywood—what we term "superstition" holds sway. We speak of "romances," of "melodramas," little realizing, as a rule, the religious-magical vestiges that inhere in the integument of these terms as imaginative forms. So it is with the totemic role of the horse in American films. In one sense, the cowboy and his horse (they were once co-starred in American films) are obvious and simple, like a coat-of-arms; in another sense, as in *Gallant Bess*, ancient totemism is fused with modern neuroticism; in still another, as in *The Outlaw*, the horse is present as a sort of totem fantasy: a coveted power-fetish without which the female cannot seem completely desirable—or completely won. After killing "Doc" and mourning at his grave, Billy starts away alone on his roan stallion; a few moments before the movie flashes off, the girl is permitted to jump up behind him and the three go off out of the picture.

SIEGFRIED KRACAUER
FROM THEORY OF FILM

THE SPECTATOR

With the moviegoer, the self as the mainspring of thoughts and decisions relinquishes its power of control. This accounts for a striking difference between him and the theatergoer, which has been repeatedly pointed out by European observers and critics. "In the theater I am always I," a perceptive French woman once told this writer, "but in the cinema I dissolve into all things and beings." Wallon elaborates on the process of dissolution to which she refers: "If the cinema produces its effect, it does so because I identify myself with its images, because I more or less forget myself in what is being displayed on the screen. I am no longer in my own life, I am in the film projected in front of me."

Films, then, tend to weaken the spectator's consciousness. Its withdrawal from the scene may be furthered by the darkness in moviehouses. Darkness automatically reduces our contacts with actuality, depriving us of many environmental data needed for adequate judgments and other mental activities. It lulls the mind. This explains why, from the 'twenties to the present day, the devotees of film and its opponents alike have compared the medium to a sort of drug and have drawn attention to its stupefying effects — incidentally, a sure sign that the spoken word has not changed much. Doping creates dope addicts. It would seem a sound proposition that the cinema has its habitués who frequent it out of an all but physiological urge. They are not prompted by a desire to look at a specific film or to be pleasantly entertained; what they really crave is for once to be released from the grip of consciousness, lose their identity in the dark, and let sink in, with their senses ready to absorb them, the images as they happen to follow each other on the screen. . . .

DREAMING

Lowered consciousness invites dreaming. Gabriel Marcel, for instance, has it that the moviegoer finds himself in a state between waking and sleeping which favors hypnagogic fantasies. Now it is fairly evident that the spectator's condition has something to do with the kind of spectacle he watches. In Lebovici's words: "Film is a dream . . . which makes [one] dream." This immediately raises the question as to what elements of film may be sufficiently dream-like to launch the audience into reveries and perhaps even influence their course.

About the Dream Character of Films

Manufactured Dreams

To the extent that films are mass entertainment they are bound to cater to the alleged desires and daydreams of the public at large. Significantly, Hollywood has been called a "dream factory." Since most commercial films are produced for mass consumption, we are indeed entitled to assume that there exists a certain relationship between their intrigues and such daydreams as seem to be widespread among their patrons; otherwise expressed, the events on the screen can be supposed to bear, somehow, on actual dream patterns, thereby encouraging identifications.

It should be noted in passing that this relationship is necessarily elusive. Because of their vagueness mass dispositions usually admit of diverse interpretations. People are quick to reject things that they do not agree with, while they feel much less sure about the true objects of their leanings and longings. There is, accordingly, a margin left for film producers who aim at satisfying existing mass desires. Pent-up escapist needs, for instance, may be relieved in many different ways. Hence the permanent interaction between mass dreams and film content. Each popular film conforms to popular wants; yet in conforming to them it inevitably does away with their inherent ambiguity. Any such film evolves these wants in a specific direction, confronts them with one among several meanings. Through their very definiteness films thus define the nature of the inarticulate from which they emerge.

However, the daydreams which Hollywood—of course, not Hollywood alone—concocts and markets are beside the point within this particular context. They come true mainly in the intrigue, not in the whole of the film; and more often than not they are imposed upon the medium from without. Much as they may be relevant as indices of subterranean social trends, they offer little interest aesthetically. What matters here is not the sociological functions and implications of the medium as a vehicle of mass entertainment; rather, the problem is whether film as film contains dream-like elements which on their part send the audience dreaming.

Stark Reality

Cinematic films may indeed be said to resemble dreams at intervals—a quality so completely independent of their recurrent excursions into the realms of fantasy and mental imagery that it shows most distinctly in places where they concentrate on real-life phenomena. The documentary shots of Harlem houses and streets in Sidney Meyers's *The Quiet One*, especially its last section, would seem to possess this quality. Women are standing, all but motionless, in house doors, and nondescript characters are seen loitering about. Along with the dingy façades, they might as well be products of our imagination, as kindled by the narrative. To be sure, this is an intended effect, but it is brought about by a clear-cut recording of stark reality. Perhaps films look most like dreams when they overwhelm us with the crude and unnegotiated presence of natural objects—as if the camera had just now extricated them from the womb of physical existence and as if the umbilical cord between image and actuality had not yet been severed. There is something in the abrupt immediacy and shocking veracity of such pictures that justifies their identification as dream images. Certain other communications peculiar to the medium have about the same effect; suffice it to mention the dream-like impressions conveyed by sudden displacements in time and space, shots comprising "reality of another dimension," and passages which render special modes of reality.

601

The Two Directions of Dreaming

Toward the Object

Released from the control of consciousness, the spectator cannot help feeling attracted by the phenomena in front of him. They beckon him to come nearer. They arouse, as Sève puts it, disquiet rather than certainty in the spectator and thus prompt him to embark on an inquiry into the being of the objects they record, an inquiry which does not aim at explaining them but tries to elucidate their secrets. So he drifts toward and into the objects—much like the legendary Chinese painter who, longing for the peace of the landscape he had created, moved into it, walked toward the faraway mountains suggested by his brush strokes, and disappeared in them never to be seen again.

Yet the spectator cannot hope to apprehend, however incompletely, the being of any object that draws him into its orbit unless he meanders, dreamingly, through the maze of its multiple meanings and psychological correspondences. Material existence, as it manifests itself in film, launches the moviegoer into unending pursuits. His is a peculiar brand of sensibility which the Frenchman Michel Dard was perhaps the first to notice. In 1928, when the silents were at the peak, Dard found new sensibility in young people who were haunting the moviehouses; he characterized it in terms which, though exuberant, have all the earmarks of genuine firsthand experience: "Never, in effect, has one seen in France a sensibility of this kind: passive, personal, as little humanistic or humanitarian as possible; diffuse, unorganized, and self-unconscious like an amoeba; deprived of an object or rather, attached to all [of them] like fog, [and] penetrant like rain; heavy to bear, easy to satisfy, impossible to restrain; displaying everywhere, like a roused dream, that contemplation of which Dostoevski speaks and which incessantly hoards without rendering anything. Does the spectator ever succeed in exhausting the objects he contemplates? There is no end to his wanderings. Sometimes, though, it may seem to him that after having probed a thousand possibilities, he is listening, with all his senses strained, to a confused murmur. Images begin to sound, and the sounds are again images. When this indeterminate murmur—the murmur of existence—reaches him, he may be nearest to the unattainable goal.

The Cap Resembling a Leopard

Dreaming processes in the other direction are a product of psychological influences. Once the spectator's organized self has surrendered, his subconscious or unconscious experiences, apprehensions and hopes tend to come out and take over. Owing to their indeterminacy, film shots are particularly fit to function as an ignition spark. Any such shot may touch off chain reactions in the movie-goer—a flight of associations which no longer revolve around their original source but arise from his agitated inner environment. This movement leads the spectator away from the given image into subjective reveries; the image itself recedes after it has mobilized his previously repressed fears or induced him to revel in a prospective wish-fulfillment. Reminiscing about an old film, Blaise Cendrars relates: "The screen showed a crowd, and in this crowd there was a lad with his cap under his arm: suddenly this cap which was like all other caps began, without moving, to assume intense life; you felt it was all set to jump, like a leopard! Why? I don't know. Perhaps the cap transformed itself into a leopard because the sight of it stirred involuntary memories in the narrator (as did the madeleine in Proust)—memories of the senses resuscitating inarticulate childhood days when the little cap under his arms was the carrier of tremendous emotions, which in a mysterious way involved the spotted beast of prey in his picture book.

Interrelation Between the Two Movements

These apparently opposite movements of dreaming are in practice well-nigh inseparable from each other. Trance-like immersion in a shot or a succession of shots may at any moment yield to daydreaming which increasingly disengages itself from the imagery occasioning it. Whenever this happens, the dreaming spectator, who originally concentrated on the psychological correspondences of an image striking his imagination more or less imperceptibly, moves on from them to notions beyond the orbit of that image—notions so remote from what the image itself implies that there would be no meaning in still counting them among its correspondences proper. Conversely, because of his continued exposure to the radiations from the screen, the absentee dreamer can be expected again and again to succumb to the spell of the images he left behind and to persevere in their exploration. He is wavering between self-absorption and self-abandonment.

Together the two intertwined dream processes constitute a veritable stream of consciousness whose contents—cataracts of indistinct fantasies and inchoate thoughts—still bear the imprint of the bodily sensations from which they issue. This stream of consciousness in a measure parallels the "flow of life," one of the main concerns of the medium. Consequently, films featuring that flow are most likely to initiate both movements of dreaming.

GENE YOUNGBLOOD
FROM EXPANDED CINEMA

ART, ENTERTAINMENT, ENTROPY

"It is easier to copy than to think, hence fashion. Besides, a community of originals is not a community."

WALLACE STEVENS

The current generation is engaged in an unprecedented questioning of all that has been held essential. We question traditional concepts of authority, ownership, justice, love, sex, freedom, politics, even tradition itself. But it's significant that we don't question our entertainment. The disenfranchised young man who dropped out of college, burned his draft card, braids his hair, smokes pot, and digs Dylan is standing in line with his girl, who takes the pill, waiting to see *The Graduate* or *Bonnie and Clyde* or *Easy Rider*—and they're reacting to the same formulas of conditioned response that lulled their parents to sleep in the 1930's.

We've seen the urgent need for an expanded cinematic language. I hope to illustrate that profit-motivated commercial entertainment, by its very nature, cannot supply this new vision. Commercial entertainment works against art, exploits the alienation and boredom of the public, by perpetuating a system of conditioned response to formulas. Commercial entertainment not only isn't creative, it actually destroys the audience's ability to appreciate and participate in the creative process. The implications become apparent when we realize that, as leisure time increases, each human will be forced to become a creative, self-sufficient, empirical energy laboratory.

D. H. Lawrence has written: "The business of art is to reveal the relation between man and his circumambient universe at this living moment. As mankind is always struggling in the toil of old relationships, art is always ahead of its 'times,' which themselves are always far in the rear of the living present." Jean-Jacques Lebel stated the same idea in different terms when he described art as "the creation of a new world, never seen before, imperceptibly gaining on reality."

We've seen that man is conditioned by, and reacts to, certain stimuli in the man-made environment. The commercial entertainer is a manipulator of these stimuli. If he employs a certain trigger mechanism, we're guaranteed to react accordingly, like puppets, providing he manipulates the trigger properly. I'm not saying the artist doesn't resort to audience manipulation; we know he often does. The point, however, is the motivation in doing so. If the artist must resort to trigger mechanisms to make himself clear, he will; but it's only a means to his end. In the case of the commercial entertainer, however, it's the end in itself.

Plot, story, and what commonly is known as "drama" are the devices that enable the commercial entertainer to manipulate his audience. The very act of this manipulation, gratifying conditioned needs, is what the films actually are about. The viewer purchases it with his ticket and is understandably annoyed if the film asks him to manipulate himself, to engage in the creative process along with the artist. Our word poetry derives from the Greek root *poiein* meaning "to make" or "to work." The viewer of commercial entertainment cinema does not want to work; he wants to be an object, to be acted upon, to be manipulated. The true subject of commercial entertainment is this little game it plays with its audience.

By perpetuating a destructive habit of unthinking response to formulas, by forcing us to rely ever more frequently on memory, the commercial entertainer encourages an unthinking response to daily life, inhibiting self-awareness. Driven by the profit motive, the commercial entertainer dares not risk alienating us by attempting new language even if he were capable of it. He seeks only to gratify preconditioned needs for formula stimulus. He offers nothing we haven't already conceived, nothing we don't already expect. Art explains; entertainment exploits. Art is freedom from the conditions of memory; entertainment is conditional on a present that is conditioned by the past. Entertainment gives us what we want; art gives us what we don't know we want. To confront a work of art is to confront oneself—but aspects of oneself previously unrecognized.

The extent to which blatant audience manipulation not only is tolerated but extolled is alarming. Alfred Hitchcock, for example, in his interview with François Truffaut, finds merit in his ability to manipulate preconditioned needs for formula stimulus. Speaking of *Psycho*, Hitchcock frankly admits: "It wasn't a message that stirred them, nor was it a great performance, or their enjoyment of the novel . . . they were aroused by the construction of the story, and the way in which it was told caused audiences all over the world to react and become emotional."

It is essential to understand that Hitchcock openly admits that he didn't even try to expand awareness or to communicate some significant message, but only exploited a universal tradition of dramatic manipulation in order to supply his audience with the gratification it paid for. The audience sees itself and its dreams reflected in the film and reacts according to memory, which Krishnamurti has characterized as being always conditioned. "Memory," says Krishnamurti, "is always in the past and is given life in the present by a challenge. Memory has no life in itself; it comes to life in the challenge [preconditioned formula stimulus]. And all memory, whether dormant or active, is conditioned. It is this process that the entertainment industry calls audience identification.

To a healthy mind, anything that is primarily art is also immensely entertaining. It seems obvious that the most important things should be the most entertaining. Where there's a difference between what we "like" and what we know to be vital, we have a condition of schizophrenia, an unnatural and destructive situation. I speak deliberately of a "healthy" mind as one capable of creative thinking. Filmmaker Ken Kelman: "The old cinema removes experience, making us see things along with (or through) a protagonist with whom we identify, and a plot in which we are caught. Such an approach tends toward not only a lack of viewpoint, of definition of *whose* experience it is, but also filters the power of sight into mere habit, dissolves insight into vicariousness. The spectator is reduced to a voyeur—which is, increasingly, the individual's role in society at large."

Minimalist painter David Lee: "When people do not trust their senses they lack confidence in themselves. For the last few centuries people have lacked confidence. They have not trusted their experience to provide a standard for knowing how to act." It is quite obvious that most of us not only don't know much about art, we don't even know what we like. Krishnamurti: "One of the fundamental causes of the disintegration of society is copying, which is the worship of authority."

Imitation is the result of inadequate information. Information results in change. Change requires energy. Energy is the result of adequate information. Energy is directly proportional to the amount of information about the structure of a system. Norbert Wiener: "Information is a name for the content of what is exchanged with the outer world as we adjust to it and make our adjustment felt upon it . . . to live effectively is to live with adequate information." From the cinema we receive conceptual information (ideas) and design information (experiences). In concert they become one phenomenon, which I've described as the experiential information of aesthetic conceptual design. This information is either useful (additive) or redundant. Useful information accelerates change. Redundant information restricts change. If sustained long enough redundant information finally becomes misinformation, which results in negative change.

In communication theory and the laws of thermodynamics the quantity called entropy is the amount of energy reversibly exchanged from one system in the universe to another. Entropy also is the measure of disorder within those systems. It measures the lack of information about the structure of the system. For our purposes "structure of the system" should be taken to mean "the human condition," the universal subject of aesthetic activity. Entropy should be understood as the degree of our ignorance about that condition. Ignorance always increases when a system's messages are redundant. Ignorance is not a state of limbo in which no information exists, but rather a state of increasing chaos due to *mis*information about the structure of the system.

The First Law of Thermodynamics states that energy is constant: it cannot be created or destroyed; its form can change, but not its quantity. The Second Law states that the amount of energy within a local system is naturally entropic—it tends toward disorder, dissipation, incoherence. And since energy is defined as "a capacity to rearrange elemental order," entropy, which runs counter to that capacity, means less potential for change. We've learned from physics that the only anti-entropic force in the universe, or what is called negentropy (negative entropy), results from the process of feedback. Feedback exists between systems that are not closed but rather open and contingent upon other systems. In the strictest sense there are no truly "closed" systems anywhere in the universe; all processes impinge upon and are affected by other processes in some way. However, for most practical purposes, it is enough to say that a system is "closed" when entropy dominates the feedback process, that is, when the measure of energy lost is greater than the measure of energy gained.

The phenomenon of man, or of biological life on earth taken as a process, is negentropic because its subsystems feed energy back into one another and thus are self-enriching, regenerative. Thus energy is wealth, and wealth according to Buckminster Fuller is "the number of forward days a given system is sustainable." Biologist John Bleibtreu arrived at a similar conclusion when he noted that the concept of time can best be viewed as a function of the Second Law of Thermodynamics—that the measure of entropy in a system is a measure of its age, or the passage of time since the system originated. In other words the degree of a system's entropy is equal to redundancy or stasis whereas its negentropy is equal to kinesis or change. So information becomes energy when it contributes to the self-enriching omni-regenerative wealth of the system. When it's not contributing (i.e., redundant) it is allowing the natural entropy to increase.

"It is possible to treat sets of messages as having an entropy like sets of states of the external world . . . in fact, it is possible to interpret the information carried by a message as essentially the negative of its entropy . . . that is, the more probable the message the less information it gives. Clichés, for example, are less illuminating than great poems." Thus the more information concerning the human condition that the artist is able to give us, the more energy we have with which to modify ourselves and grow in accord with the accelerating accelerations of the living present.

Commercial entertainment may be considered a closed system since entropy dominates the feedback process. To satisfy the profit motive the commercial entertainer must give the audience what it expects, which is conditional on what it has been getting, which is conditional on what it previously received, ad infinitum. Inherent in the term "genre," which applies to all entertainment, is that it must be probable. The content of westerns, gangster movies, romances, etc., is probable in that it can be identified and comprehended simply by classification. The phenomenon of drama itself usually is not considered a genre, but is in fact the most universal and archetypical of all genres. Drama, by definition, means conflict, which in turn means suspense. Suspense is requisite on the expectation of known alternatives. One cannot expect the unknown. Therefore expectation, suspense, and drama are all redundant probable qualities and thus are noninformative.

Drama requires a plot that forces the viewer to move from point A to point B to point C along predetermined lines. Plot does not mean "story" (beginning-middle-end). It simply indicates a relatively closed structure in which free association and conscious participation are restricted. Since the viewer remains passive and is acted upon by the experience rather than participating in it with volition, there's no feedback, that vital source of negentropy. Norbert Wiener: "Feedback is a method of controlling a system by reinserting into it the results of its past performance . . . if the information which proceeds backward from the performance is able to change the general method and pattern of performance, we have a process which may well be called learning." Fuller: "Every time man makes a new experiment he always learns more. He cannot learn less."

In the cinema, feedback is possible almost exclusively in what I call the synaesthetic mode, which we'll discuss presently. Because it is entirely personal it rests on no identifiable plot and is not probable. The viewer is forced to create along with the film, to interpret for himself what he is experiencing. If the information (either concept or design) reveals some previously unrecognized aspect of the viewer's relation to the circumambient universe — or provides language with which to conceptualize old realities more effectively — the viewer re-creates that discovery along with the artist, thus feeding back into the environment the existence of more creative potential, which may in turn be used by the artist for messages of still greater eloquence and perception. If the information is redundant, as it must be in commercial entertainment, nothing is learned and change becomes unlikely. The noted authority on communication theory, J. R. Pierce, has demonstrated that an increase in entropy means a decrease in the ability to change. And we have seen that the ability to change is the most urgent need facing twentieth-century man.

The notion of experimental art, therefore, is meaningless. All art is experimental or it isn't art. Art is research, whereas entertainment is a game or conflict. We have learned from cybernetics that in research one's work is governed by one's strongest points, whereas in conflicts or games one's work is governed by its weakest moments. We have defined the difference between art and entertainment in scientific terms and have found entertainment to be inherently entropic, opposed to change, and art to be inherently negentropic, a catalyst to change. The artist is always an anarchist, a revolutionary, a creator of new worlds imperceptibly gaining on reality. He can do this because we live in a cosmos in which there's always something more to be seen. When finally we erase the difference between art and entertainment—as we must to survive—we shall find that our community is no longer a community, and we shall begin to understand radical evolution.

WALTER BENJAMIN
THE WORK OF ART
IN THE AGE OF
MECHANICAL REPRODUCTION

"Our fine arts were developed, their types and uses were estab-
lished, in times very different from the present, by men whose
power of action upon things was insignificant in comparison with
ours. But the amazing growth of our techniques, the adaptability
and precision they have attained, the ideas and habits they are
creating, make it a certainty that profound changes are impending
in the ancient craft of the Beautiful. In all the arts there is a physi-
cal component which can no longer be considered or treated as it
used to be, which cannot remain unaffected by our modern knowl-
edge and power. For the last twenty years neither matter nor space
nor time has been what it was from time immemorial. We must
expect great innovations to transform the entire technique of the
arts, thereby affecting artistic invention itself and perhaps even
bringing about an amazing change in our very notion of art."
—Paul Valéry, PIÈCES SUR L'ART,
"La Conquète de l'ubiquité," Paris.

PREFACE

When Marx undertook his critique of the capitalistic mode of
production, this mode was in its infancy. Marx directed his efforts
in such a way as to give them prognostic value. He went back to
the basic conditions underlying capitalistic production and through
his presentation showed what could be expected of capitalism in

the future. The result was that one could expect it not only to exploit the proletariat with increasing intensity, but ultimately to create conditions which would make it possible to abolish capitalism itself.

The transformation of the superstructure, which takes place far more slowly than that of the substructure, has taken more than half a century to manifest in all areas of culture the change in the conditions of production. Only today can it be indicated what form this has taken. Certain prognostic requirements should be met by these statements. However, theses about the art of the proletariat after its assumption of power or about the art of a classless society would have less bearing on these demands than theses about the developmental tendencies of art under present conditions of production. Their dialectic is no less noticeable in the superstructure than in the economy. It would therefore be wrong to underestimate the value of such theses as a weapon. They brush aside a number of outmoded concepts, such as creativity and genius, eternal value and mystery—concepts whose uncontrolled (and at present almost uncontrollable) application would lead to a processing of data in the Fascist sense. The concepts which are introduced into the theory of art in what follows differ from the more familiar terms in that they are completely useless for the purposes of Fascism. They are, on the other hand, useful for the formulation of revolutionary demands in the politics of art.

I

In principle a work of art has always been reproducible. Man-made artifacts could always be imitated by men. Replicas were made by pupils in practice of their craft, by masters for diffusing their works, and, finally, by third parties in the pursuit of gain. Mechanical reproduction of a work of art, however, represents something new. Historically, it advanced intermittently and in leaps at long intervals, but with accelerated intensity. The Greeks knew only two procedures of technically reproducing works of art: founding and stamping. Bronzes, terra cottas, and coins were the only art works which they could produce in quantity. All others were unique and could not be mechanically reproduced. With the woodcut graphic art became mechanically reproducible for the first time, long before script became reproducible by print. The enormous changes which printing, the mechanical reproduction of writing, has brought about in literature are a familiar story. However, within the phenomenon which we are here examining from the perspective of world history, print is merely a special, though particularly important, case. During the Middle Ages engraving and etching were added to the woodcut; at the beginning of the nineteenth century lithography made its appearance.

With lithography the technique of reproduction reached an essentially new stage. This much more direct process was distinguished by the tracing of the design on a stone rather than its incision on a block of wood or its etching on a copperplate and permitted graphic art for the first time to put its products on the market, not only in large numbers as hitherto, but also in daily changing forms. Lithography enabled graphic art to illustrate everyday life, and it began to keep pace with printing. But only a few decades after its invention, lithography was surpassed by photography. For the first time in the process of pictorial reproduction, photography freed the hand of the most important artistic functions which henceforth devolved only upon the eye looking into a lens. Since the eye perceives more swiftly than the hand can draw, the process of pictorial reproduction was accelerated so enormously that it could keep pace with speech. A film operator shooting a scene in the studio captures the images at the speed of an actor's speech. Just as lithography virtually implied the illustrated newspaper, so did photography foreshadow the sound film. The technical reproduction of sound was tackled at the end of the last century. These convergent endeavors made predictable a situation which Paul Valéry pointed up in this sentence: "Just as water, gas, and electricity are brought into our houses from far off to satisfy our needs in response to a minimal effort, so we shall be supplied with visual or auditory images, which will appear and disappear at a simple movement of the hand, hardly more than a sign." Around 1900 technical reproduction had reached a standard that not only permitted it to reproduce all transmitted works of art and thus to cause the most profound change in their impact upon the public; it also had captured a place of its own among the artistic processes. For the study of this standard nothing is more revealing than the nature of the repercussions that these two different manifestations —the reproduction of works of art and the art of the film—have had on art in its traditional form.

614

II

Even the most perfect reproduction of a work of art is lacking in one element: its presence in time and space, its unique existence at the place where it happens to be. This unique existence of the work of art determined the history to which it was subject throughout the time of its existence. This includes the changes which it may have suffered in physical condition over the years as well as the various changes in its ownership. The traces of the first can be revealed only by chemical or physical analyses which it is impossible to perform on a reproduction; changes of ownership are subject to a tradition which must be traced from the situation of the original.

The presence of the original is the prerequisite to the concept of authenticity. Chemical analyses of the patina of a bronze can help to establish this, as does the proof that a given manuscript of the Middle Ages stems from an archive of the fifteenth century. The whole sphere of authenticity is outside technical—and, of course, not only technical—reproducibility. Confronted with its manual reproduction, which was usually branded as a forgery, the original preserved all its authority; not so *vis à vis* technical reproduction. The reason is twofold. First, process reproduction is more independent of the original than manual reproduction. For example, in photography, process reproduction can bring out those aspects of the original that are unattainable to the naked eye yet accessible to the lens, which is adjustable and chooses its angle at will. And photographic reproduction, with the aid of certain processes, such as enlargement or slow motion, can capture images which escape natural vision. Secondly, technical reproduction can put the copy of the original into situations which would be out of reach for the original itself. Above all, it enables the original to meet the beholder halfway, be it in the form of a photograph or a phonograph record. The cathedral leaves its locale to be received in the studio of a lover of art; the choral production, performed in an auditorium or in the open air, resounds in the drawing room.

The situations into which the product of mechanical reproduction can be brought may not touch the actual work of art, yet the quality of its presence is always depreciated. This holds not only for the art work but also, for instance, for a landscape which passes in review before the spectator in a movie. In the case of the art object, a most sensitive nucleus—namely, its authenticity—is interfered with whereas no natural object is vulnerable on that score. The authenticity of a thing is the essence of all that is transmissible from its beginning, ranging from its substantive duration to its testimony to the history which it has experienced. Since the historical testimony rests on the authenticity, the former, too, is jeopardized by reproduction when substantive duration ceases to matter. And what is really jeopardized when the historical testimony is affected is the authority of the object.

One might subsume the eliminated element in the term "aura" and go on to say: that which withers in the age of mechanical reproduction is the aura of the work of art. This is a symptomatic process whose significance points beyond the realm of art. One might generalize by saying: the technique of reproduction detaches the reproduced object from the domain of tradition. By making many reproductions it substitutes a plurality of copies for a unique existence. And in permitting the reproduction to meet the beholder or listener in his own particular situation, it reactivates the object reproduced. These two processes lead to a tremendous shattering of tradition which is the obverse of the contemporary crisis and renewal of mankind. Both processes are intimately connected with the contemporary mass movements. Their most powerful agent is the film. Its social significance, particularly in its most positive form, is inconceivable without its destructive, cathartic aspect, that is, the liquidation of the traditional value of the cultural heritage. This phenomenon is most palpable in the great historical films. It extends to ever new positions. In 1927 Abel Gance exclaimed enthusiastically: "Shakespeare, Rembrandt, Beethoven will make films . . . all legends, all mythologies and all myths, all founders of religion, and the very religions . . . await their exposed resurrection, and the heroes crowd each other at the gate." Presumably without intending it, he issued an invitation to a far-reaching liquidation.

III

During long periods of history, the mode of human sense perception changes with humanity's entire mode of existence. The manner in which human sense perception is organized, the medium in which it is accomplished, is determined not only by nature but by historical circumstances as well. The fifth century, with its great shifts of population, saw the birth of the late Roman art industry and the Vienna Genesis, and there developed not only an art different from that of antiquity but also a new kind of perception. The scholars of the Viennese school, Riegl and Wickhoff, who resisted the weight of classical tradition under which these later art forms had been buried, were the first to draw conclusions from them concerning the organization of perception at the time. However far-reaching their insight, these scholars limited themselves to showing the significant, formal hallmark which characterized perception in late Roman times. They did not attempt—and, perhaps, saw no way—to show the social transformations expressed by these changes of perception. The conditions for an analogous insight are more favorable in the present. And if changes in the medium of contemporary perception can be comprehended as decay of the aura, it is possible to show its social causes.

The concept of aura which was proposed above with reference to historical objects may usefully be illustrated with reference to the aura of natural ones. We define the aura of the latter as the unique phenomenon of a distance, however close it may be. If, while resting on a summer afternoon, you follow with your eyes a mountain range on the horizon or a branch which casts its shadow over you, you experience the aura of those mountains, of that branch. This image makes it easy to comprehend the social bases of the contemporary decay of the aura. It rests on two circumstances, both of which are related to the increasing significance of the masses in contemporary life. Namely, the desire of contemporary masses to bring things "closer" spatially and humanly, which is just as ardent as their bent toward overcoming the uniqueness of every reality by accepting its reproduction. Every day the urge grows stronger to get hold of an object at very close range by way of its likeness, its reproduction. Unmistakably, reproduction as offered by picture magazines and newsreels differs from the image seen by the unarmed eye. Uniqueness and permanence are as closely linked in the latter as are transitoriness and reproducibility in the former. To pry an object from its shell, to destroy its aura, is the mark of a perception whose "sense of the universal equality of things" has increased to such a degree that it extracts it even from a unique object by means of reproduction. Thus is manifested in the field of perception what in the theoretical sphere

617

is noticeable in the increasing importance of statistics. The adjustment of reality to the masses and of the masses to reality is a process of unlimited scope, as much for thinking as for perception.

IV

The uniqueness of a work of art is inseparable from its being imbedded in the fabric of tradition. This tradition itself is thoroughly alive and extremely changeable. An ancient statue of Venus, for example, stood in a different traditional context with the Greeks, who made it an object of veneration, than with the clerics of the Middle Ages, who viewed it as an ominous idol. Both of them, however, were equally confronted with its uniqueness, that is, its aura. Originally the contextual integration of art in tradition found its expression in the cult. We know that the earliest art works originated in the service of a ritual—first the magical, then the religious kind. It is significant that the existence of the work of art with reference to its aura is never entirely separated from its ritual function. In other words, the unique value of the "authentic" work of art has its basis in ritual, the location of its original use value. This ritualistic basis, however remote, is still recognizable as secularized ritual even in the most profane forms of the cult of beauty. The secular cult of beauty, developed during the Renaissance and prevailing for three centuries, clearly showed that ritualistic basis in its decline and the first deep crisis which befell it. With the advent of the first truly revolutionary means of reproduction, photography, simultaneously with the rise of socialism, art sensed the approaching crisis which has become evident a century later. At the time, art reacted with the doctrine of *l'art pour l'art*, that is, with a theology of art. This gave rise to what might be called a negative theology in the form of the idea of "pure" art, which not only denied any social function of art but also any categorizing by subject matter. (In poetry, Mallarmé was the first to take this position.)

An analysis of art in the age of mechanical reproduction must do justice to these relationships, for they lead us to an all-important insight: for the first time in world history, mechanical reproduction emancipates the work of art from its parasitical dependence on ritual. To an ever greater degree the work of art reproduced becomes the work of art designed for reproducibility. From a photo-

618

graphic negative, for example, one can make any number of prints; to ask for the "authentic" print makes no sense. But the instant the criterion of authenticity ceases to be applicable to artistic production, the total function of art is reversed. Instead of being based on ritual, it begins to be based on another practice — politics.

v

Works of art are received and valued on different planes. Two polar types stand out: with one, the accent is on the cult value; with the other, on the exhibition value of the work. Artistic production begins with ceremonial objects destined to serve in a cult. One may assume that what mattered was their existence, not their being on view. The elk portrayed by the man of the Stone Age on the walls of his cave was an instrument of magic. He did expose it to his fellow men, but in the main it was meant for the spirits. Today the cult value would seem to demand that the work of art remain hidden. Certain statues of gods are accessible only to the priest in the cella; certain Madonnas remain covered nearly all year round; certain sculptures on medieval cathedrals are invisible to the spectator on ground level. With the emancipation of the various art practices from ritual go increasing opportunities for the exhibition of their products. It is easier to exhibit a portrait bust that can be sent here and there than to exhibit the statue of a divinity that has its fixed place in the interior of a temple. The same holds for the painting as against the mosaic or fresco that preceded it. And even though the public presentability of a mass originally may have been just as great as that of a symphony, the latter originated at the moment when its public presentability promised to surpass that of the mass.

With the different methods of technical reproduction of a work of art, its fitness for exhibition increased to such an extent that the quantitative shift between its two poles turned into a qualitative transformation of its nature. This is comparable to the situation of the work of art in prehistoric times when, by the absolute emphasis on its cult value, it was, first and foremost, an instrument of magic. Only later did it come to be recognized as a work of art. In the same way today, by the absolute emphasis on its exhibition value the work of art becomes a creation with entirely new functions, among which the one we are conscious of, the artistic function, later may be recognized as incidental. This much is certain: today photography and the film are the most serviceable exemplifications of this new function.

VI

In photography, exhibition value begins to displace cult value all along the line. But cult value does not give way without resistance. It retires into an ultimate retrenchment: the human countenance. It is no accident that the portrait was the focal point of early photography. The cult of remembrance of loved ones, absent or dead, offers a last refuge for the cult value of the picture. For the last time the aura emanates from the early photographs in the fleeting expression of a human face. This is what constitutes their melancholy, incomparable beauty. But as man withdraws from the photographic image, the exhibition value for the first time shows its superiority to the ritual value. To have pinpointed this new stage constitutes the incomparable significance of Atget, who, around 1900, took photographs of deserted Paris streets. It has quite justly been said of him that he photographed them like scenes of crime. The scene of a crime, too, is deserted; it is photographed for the purpose of establishing evidence. With Atget, photographs become standard evidence for historical occurrences, and acquire a hidden political significance. They demand a specific kind of approach; free-floating contemplation is not appropriate to them. They stir the viewer; he feels challenged by them in a new way. At the same time picture magazines begin to put up signposts for him, right ones or wrong ones, no matter. For the first time, captions have become obligatory. And it is clear that they have an altogether different character than the title of a painting. The directives which the captions give to those looking at pictures in illustrated magazines soon become even more explicit and more imperative in the film where the meaning of each single picture appears to be prescribed by the sequence of all preceding ones.

VII

The nineteenth-century dispute as to the artistic value of painting versus photography today seems devious and confused. This does not diminish its importance, however; if anything, it underlines it. The dispute was in fact the symptom of a historical transformation the universal impact of which was not realized by either of the rivals. When the age of mechanical reproduction separated art from its basis in cult, the semblance of its autonomy disappeared forever. The resulting change in the function of art transcended the perspective of the century; for a long time it even escaped that of the twentieth century, which experienced the development of the film.

Earlier much futile thought had been devoted to the question of whether photography is an art. The primary question—whether the very invention of photography had not transformed the entire nature of art—was not raised. Soon the film theoreticians asked the same ill-considered question with regard to the film. But the difficulties which photography caused traditional aesthetics were mere child's play as compared to those raised by the film. Whence the insensitive and forced character of early theories of the film. Abel Gance, for instance, compares the film with hieroglyphs: "Here, by a remarkable regression, we have come back to the level of expression of the Egyptians. . . . Pictorial language has not yet matured because our eyes have not yet adjusted to it. There is as yet insufficient respect for, insufficient cult of, what it expresses." Or, in the words of Séverin-Mars: "What art has been granted a dream more poetical and more real at the same time! Approached in this fashion the film might represent an incomparable means of expression. Only the most high-minded persons, in the most perfect and mysterious moments of their lives, should be allowed to enter its ambience." Alexandre Arnoux concludes his fantasy about the silent film with the question: "Do not all the bold descriptions we have given amount to the definition of prayer?" It is instructive to note how their desire to class the film among the "arts" forces these theoreticians to read ritual elements into it—with a striking lack of discretion. Yet when these speculations were published, films like L'Opinion publique and The Gold Rush had already appeared. This, however, did not keep Abel Gance from adducing hieroglyphs for purposes of comparison, nor Séverin-Mars from speaking of the film as one might speak of paintings by Fra Angelico. Characteristically, even today ultrareactionary authors give the film a similar contextual significance—if not an outright sacred one, then at least a supernatural one. Commenting on Max Reinhardt's film version of A Midsummer Night's Dream, Werfel states that undoubtedly it was the sterile copying of the exterior world with its streets, interiors, railroad stations, restaurants, motorcars, and beaches which until now had obstructed the elevation of the film to the realm of art. "The film has not yet realized its true meaning, its real possibilities . . . these consist in its unique faculty to express by natural means and with incomparable persuasiveness all that is fairylike, marvelous, supernatural."

VIII

The artistic performance of a stage actor is definitely presented to the public by the actor in person; that of the screen actor, however, is presented by a camera, with a twofold consequence. The camera that presents the performance of the film actor to the public need not respect the performance as an integral whole. Guided by the cameraman, the camera continually changes its position with respect to the performance. The sequence of positional views which the editor composes from the material supplied him constitutes the completed film. It comprises certain factors of movement which are in reality those of the camera, not to mention special camera angles, close-ups, etc. Hence, the performance of the actor is subjected to a series of optical tests. This is the first consequence of the fact that the actor's performance is presented by means of a camera. Also, the film actor lacks the opportunity of the stage actor to adjust to the audience during his performance, since he does not present his performance to the audience in person. This permits the audience to take the position of a critic, without experiencing any personal contact with the actor. The audience's identification with the actor is really an identification with the camera. Consequently the audience takes the position of the camera; its approach is that of testing. This is not the approach to which cult values may be exposed.

IX

For the film, what matters primarily is that the actor represents himself to the public before the camera, rather than representing someone else. One of the first to sense the actor's metamorphosis by this form of testing was Pirandello. Though his remarks on the subject in his novel *Si Gira* were limited to the negative aspects of the question and to the silent film only, this hardly impairs their validity. For in this respect, the sound film did not change anything essential. What matters is that the part is acted not for an audience but for a mechanical contrivance—in the case of the sound film, for two of them. "The film actor," wrote Pirandello, "feels as if in exile—exiled not only from the stage but also from himself. With a vague sense of discomfort he feels inexplicable emptiness: his body loses its corporeality, it evaporates, it is deprived of reality, life, voice, and the noises caused by his moving about, in order to be changed into a mute image, flickering an instant on the screen, then vanishing into silence. . . . The projector will play with his shadow before the public, and he himself must be content to play before the camera." This situation might also be characterized as follows: for the first time—and this is the effect of the film —man has to operate with his whole living person, yet forgoing its aura. For aura is tied to his presence; there can be no replica of it. The aura which, on the stage, emanates from Macbeth, cannot be separated for the spectators from that of the actor. However, the singularity of the shot in the studio is that the camera is substituted for the public. Consequently, the aura that envelops the actor vanishes, and with it the aura of the figure he portrays.

It is not surprising that it should be a dramatist such as Pirandello who, in characterizing the film, inadvertently touches on the very crisis in which we see the theater. Any thorough study proves that there is indeed no greater contrast than that of the stage play to a work of art that is completely subject to or, like the film, founded in, mechanical reproduction. Experts have long recognized that in the film "the greatest effects are almost always obtained by 'acting' as little as possible. . . ." In 1932 Rudolf Arnheim saw "the latest trend . . . in treating the actor as a stage prop chosen for its characteristics and . . . inserted at the proper place." With this idea something else is closely connected. The stage actor identifies himself with the character of his role. The film actor very often is denied this opportunity. His creation is by no means all of a piece; it is composed of many separate performances. Besides certain fortuitous considerations, such as cost of studio, availability of fellow players, décor, etc., there are elementary necessities of equipment that split the actor's work into a series of mountable episodes. In particular, lighting and its installation require the presentation of an event that, on the screen, unfolds as a rapid and unified scene, in a sequence of separate shootings which may take hours at the studio; not to mention more obvious montage. Thus a jump from the window can be shot in the studio as a jump from a scaffold, and the ensuing flight, if need be, can be shot weeks later when outdoor scenes are taken. Far more paradoxical cases can easily be construed. Let us assume that an actor is supposed to be startled by a knock at the door. If his reaction is not satisfactory, the director can resort to an expedient: when the actor happens to be at the studio again he has a shot fired behind him without his being forewarned of it. The frightened reaction can be shot now and be cut into the screen version. Nothing more strikingly shows that art has left the realm of the "beautiful semblance" which, so far, had been taken to be the only sphere where art could thrive.

x

The feeling of strangeness that overcomes the actor before the camera, as Pirandello describes it, is basically of the same kind as the estrangement felt before one's own image in the mirror. But now the reflected image has become separable, transportable. And where is it transported? Before the public. Never for a moment does the screen actor cease to be conscious of this fact. While facing the camera he knows that ultimately he will face the public, the consumers who constitute the market. This market, where he offers not only his labor but also his whole self, his heart and soul, is beyond his reach. During the shooting he has as little contact with it as any article made in a factory. This may contribute to that oppression, that new anxiety which, according to Pirandello, grips the actor before the camera. The film responds to the shriveling of the aura with an artificial build-up of the "personality" outside the studio. The cult of the movie star, fostered by the money of the film industry, preserves not the unique aura of the person but the "spell of the personality," the phony spell of a commodity. So long as the movie-makers' capital sets the fashion, as a rule no other revolutionary merit can be accredited to today's film than the promotion of a revolutionary criticism of traditional concepts of art. We do not deny that in some cases today's films can also promote revolutionary criticism of social conditions, even of the distribution of property. However, our present study is no more specifically concerned with this than is the film production of Western Europe.

It is inherent in the technique of the film as well as that of sports that everybody who witnesses its accomplishments is somewhat of an expert. This is obvious to anyone listening to a group of newspaper boys leaning on their bicycles and discussing the outcome of a bicycle race. It is not for nothing that newspaper publishers arrange races for their delivery boys. These arouse great interest among the participants, for the victor has an opportunity to rise from delivery boy to professional racer. Similarly, the newsreel offers everyone the opportunity to rise from passer-by to movie extra. In this way any man might even find himself part of a work of art, as witness Vertoff's *Three Songs About Lenin* or Ivens' *Borinage*. Any man today can lay claim to being filmed. This claim can best be elucidated by a comparative look at the historical situation of contemporary literature.

For centuries a small number of writers were confronted by many thousands of readers. This changed toward the end of the last century. With the increasing extension of the press, which kept placing new political, religious, scientific, professional, and local organs before the readers, an increasing number of readers became writers—at first, occasional ones. It began with the daily press opening to its readers space for "letters to the editor." And today there is hardly a gainfully employed European who could not, in principle, find an opportunity to publish somewhere or other comments on his work, grievances, documentary reports, or that sort of thing. Thus, the distinction between author and public is about to lose its basic character. The difference becomes merely functional; it may vary from case to case. At any moment the reader is ready to turn into a writer. As expert, which he had to become willy-nilly in an extremely specialized work process, even if only in some minor respect, the reader gains access to authorship. In the Soviet Union work itself is given a voice. To present it verbally is part of a man's ability to perform the work. Literary license is now founded on polytechnic rather than specialized training and thus becomes common property.

All this can easily be applied to the film, where transitions that in literature took centuries have come about in a decade. In cinematic practice, particularly in Russia, this change-over has partially become established reality. Some of the players whom we meet in Russian films are not actors in our sense but people who portray *themselves*—and primarily in their own work process. In Western Europe the capitalistic exploitation of the film denies consideration to modern man's legitimate claim to being reproduced. Under these circumstances the film industry is trying hard to spur the interest of the masses through illusion-promoting spectacles and dubious speculations.

XI

The shooting of a film, especially of a sound film, affords a spectacle unimaginable anywhere at any time before this. It presents a process in which it is impossible to assign to a spectator a viewpoint which would exclude from the actual scene such extraneous accessories as camera equipment, lighting machinery, staff assistants, etc.—unless his eye were on a line parallel with the lens. This circumstance, more than any other, renders superficial and insignificant any possible similarity between a scene in the studio and one on the stage. In the theater one is well aware of the place from which the play cannot immediately be detected as illusionary. There is no such place for the movie scene that is being shot. Its illusionary nature is that of the second degree, the result of cutting. That is to say, in the studio the mechanical equipment has penetrated so deeply into reality that its pure aspect freed from the foreign substance of equipment is the result of a special procedure, namely, the shooting by the specially adjusted camera and the mounting of the shot together with other similar ones. The equipment-free aspect of reality here has become the height of artifice; the sight of immediate reality has become an orchid in the land of technology.

Even more revealing is the comparison of these circumstances, which differ so much from those of the theater, with the situation in painting. Here the question is: How does the cameraman compare with the painter? To answer this we take recourse to an analogy with a surgical operation. The surgeon represents the polar opposite of the magician. The magician heals a sick person by the laying on of hands; the surgeon cuts into the patient's body. The magician maintains the natural distance between the patient and himself; though he reduces it very slightly by the laying on of hands, he greatly increases it by virtue of his authority. The surgeon does exactly the reverse; he greatly diminishes the distance between himself and the patient by penetrating into the patient's body, and increases it but little by the caution with which his hand moves among the organs. In short, in contrast to the magician—who is still hidden in the medical practitioner—the surgeon at the decisive moment abstains from facing the patient man to man; rather, it is through the operation that he penetrates into him.

Magician and surgeon compare to painter and cameraman. The painter maintains in his work a natural distance from reality, the

626

cameraman penetrates deeply into its web. There is a tremendous difference between the pictures they obtain. That of the painter is a total one, that of the cameraman consists of multiple fragments which are assembled under a new law. Thus, for contemporary man the representation of reality by the film is incomparably more significant than that of the painter, since it offers, precisely because of the thoroughgoing permeation of reality with mechanical equipment, an aspect of reality which is free of all equipment. And that is what one is entitled to ask from a work of art.

XII

Mechanical reproduction of art changes the reaction of the masses toward art. The reactionary attitude toward a Picasso painting changes into the progressive reaction toward a Chaplin movie. The progressive reaction is characterized by the direct, intimate fusion of visual and emotional enjoyment with the orientation of the expert. Such fusion is of great social significance. The greater the decrease in the social significance of an art form, the sharper the distinction between criticism and enjoyment by the public. The conventional is uncritically enjoyed, and the truly new is criticized with aversion. With regard to the screen, the critical and the receptive attitudes of the public coincide. The decisive reason for this is that individual reactions are predetermined by the mass audience response they are about to produce, and this is nowhere more pronounced than in the film. The moment these responses become manifest they control each other. Again, the comparison with painting is fruitful. A painting has always had an excellent chance to be viewed by one person or by a few. The simultaneous contemplation of paintings by a large public, such as developed in the nineteenth century, is an early symptom of the crisis of painting, a crisis which was by no means occasioned exclusively by photography but rather in a relatively independent manner by the appeal of art works to the masses.

Painting simply is in no position to present an object for simultaneous collective experience, as it was possible for architecture at all times, for the epic poem in the past, and for the movie today. Although this circumstance in itself should not lead one to conclusions about the social role of painting, it does constitute a serious threat as soon as painting, under special conditions and, as it were, against its nature, is confronted directly by the masses. In the churches and monasteries of the Middle Ages and at the princely courts up to the end of the eighteenth century, a collective reception of paintings did not occur simultaneously, but by graduated and hierarchized mediation. The change that has come about is an expression of the particular conflict in which painting was implicated by the mechanical reproducibility of paintings. Although paintings began to be publicly exhibited in galleries and salons, there was no way for the masses to organize and control themselves in their reception. Thus the same public which responds in a progressive manner toward a grotesque film is bound to respond in a reactionary manner to surrealism.

XIII

The characteristics of the film lie not only in the manner in which man presents himself to mechanical equipment but also in the manner in which, by means of this apparatus, man can represent his environment. A glance at occupational psychology illustrates the testing capacity of the equipment. Psychoanalysis illustrates it in a different perspective. The film has enriched our field of perception with methods which can be illustrated by those of Freudian theory. Fifty years ago, a slip of the tongue passed more or less unnoticed. Only exceptionally may such a slip have revealed dimensions of depth in a conversation which had seemed to be taking its course on the surface. Since the *Psychopathology of Everyday Life* things have changed. This book isolated and made analyzable things which had heretofore floated along unnoticed in the broad stream of perception. For the entire spectrum of optical, and now also acoustical, perception the film has brought about a similar deepening of apperception. It is only an obverse of this fact that behavior items shown in a movie can be analyzed much more precisely and from more points of view than those presented on paintings or on the stage. As compared with painting, filmed behavior lends itself more readily to analysis because of its incomparably more precise statements of the situation. In comparison with the stage scene, the filmed behavior item lends itself more readily to analysis because it can be isolated more easily. This circumstance derives its chief importance from its tendency to promote the mutual penetration of art and science. Actually, of a screened behavior item which is neatly brought out in a certain situation, like a muscle of a body, it is difficult to say which is more fascinating, its artistic value or its value for science. To demonstrate the identity of the artistic and scientific uses of photography which heretofore usually were separated will be one of the revolutionary functions of the film.

By close-ups of the things around us, by focusing on hidden details of familiar objects, by exploring common place milieus under the ingenious guidance of the camera, the film, on the one hand, extends our comprehension of the necessities which rule our lives; on the other hand, it manages to assure us of an immense and unexpected field of action. Our taverns and our metropolitan streets, our offices and furnished rooms, our railroad stations and our factories appeared to have us locked up hopelessly. Then came the film and burst this prison-world asunder by the dynamite of the tenth of a second, so that now, in the midst of its far-flung ruins and debris, we calmly and adventurously go traveling. With the close-up, space expands; with slow motion, movement is extended. The enlargement of a snapshot does not simply render more precise what in any case was visible, though unclear: it reveals entirely new structural formations of the subject. So, too, slow motion not only presents familiar qualities of movement but reveals in them entirely unknown ones "which, far from looking like retarded rapid movements, give the effect of singularly gliding, floating, supernatural motions." Evidently a different nature opens itself to the camera than opens to the naked eye—if only because an unconsciously penetrated space is substituted for a space consciously explored by man. Even if one has a general knowledge of the way people walk, one knows nothing of a person's posture during the fractional second of a stride. The act of reaching for a lighter or a spoon is familiar routine, yet we hardly know what really goes on between hand and metal, not to mention how this fluctuates with our moods. Here the camera intervenes with the resources of its lowerings and liftings, its interruptions and isolations, its extensions and accelerations, its enlargements and reductions. The camera introduces us to unconscious optics as does psychoanalysis to unconscious impulses.

XIV

One of the foremost tasks of art has always been the creation of a demand which could be fully satisfied only later. The history of every art form shows critical epochs in which a certain art form aspires to effects which could be fully obtained only with a changed technical standard, that is to say, in a new art form. The extravagances and crudities of art which thus appear, particularly in the so-called decadent epochs, actually arise from the nucleus of its richest historical energies. In recent years, such barbarisms were abundant in Dadaism. It is only now that its impulse becomes discernible: Dadaism attempted to create by pictorial—and literary—means the effects which the public today seeks in the film.

Every fundamentally new, pioneering creation of demands will carry beyond its goal. Dadaism did so to the extent that it sacrificed the market values which are so characteristic of the film in favor of higher ambitions—though of course it was not conscious of such intentions as here described. The Dadaists attached much less importance to the sales value of their work than to its uselessness for contemplative immersion. The studied degradation of their material was not the least of their means to achieve this uselessness. Their poems are "word salad" containing obscenities and every imaginable waste product of language. The same is true of their paintings, on which they mounted buttons and tickets. What they intended and achieved was a relentless destruction of the aura of their creations, which they branded as reproductions with the very means of production. Before a painting of Arp's or a poem by August Stramm it is impossible to take time for contemplation and evaluation as one would before a canvas of Derain's or a poem by Rilke. In the decline of middle-class society, contemplation became a school for asocial behavior; it was countered by distraction as a variant of social conduct. Dadaistic activities actually assured a rather vehement distraction by making works of art the center of scandal. One requirement was foremost: to outrage the public.

From an alluring appearance or persuasive structure of sound the work of art of the Dadaists became an instrument of ballistics. It hit the spectator like a bullet, it happened to him, thus acquiring a tactile quality. It promoted a demand for the film, the distracting element of which is also primarily tactile, being based on changes of place and focus which periodically assail the spectator. Let us compare the screen on which a film unfolds with the canvas of a painting. The painting invites the spectator to contemplation; before it the spectator can abandon himself to his associations. Before the movie frame he cannot do so. No sooner has his eye grasped a scene than it is already changed. It cannot be arrested. Duhamel, who detests the film and knows nothing of its significance, though something of its structure, notes this circumstance as follows: "I can no longer think what I want to think. My thoughts have been replaced by moving images." The spectator's process of association in view of these images is indeed interrupted by their constant, sudden change. This constitutes the shock effect of the film, which, like all shocks, should be cushioned by heightened presence of mind. By means of its technical structure, the film has taken the physical shock effect out of the wrappers in which Dadaism had, as it were, kept it inside the moral shock effect.

XV

The mass is a matrix from which all traditional behavior toward works of art issues today in a new form. Quantity has been transmuted into quality. The greatly increased mass of participants has produced a change in the mode of participation. The fact that the new mode of participation first appeared in a disreputable form must not confuse the spectator. Yet some people have launched spirited attacks against precisely this superficial aspect. Among these, Duhamel has expressed himself in the most radical manner. What he objects to most is the kind of participation which the movie elicits from the masses. Duhamel calls the movie "a pastime for helots, a diversion for uneducated, wretched, worn-out creatures who are consumed by their worries . . . , a spectacle which requires no concentration and presupposes no intelligence . . . , which kindles no light in the heart and awakens no hope other than the ridiculous one of someday becoming a 'star' in Los Angeles." Clearly, this is at bottom the same ancient lament that the masses seek distraction whereas art demands concentration from the spectator. That is a commonplace. The question remains whether it provides a platform for the analysis of the film. A closer look is needed here. Distraction and concentration form polar opposites which may be stated as follows: A man who concentrates before a work of art is absorbed by it. He enters into this work of art the way legend tells of the Chinese painter when he viewed his finished painting. In contrast, the distracted mass absorbs the work of art. This is most obvious with regard to buildings. Architecture has always represented the prototype of a work of art the reception of which is consummated by a collectivity in a state of distraction. The laws of its reception are most instructive.

Buildings have been man's companions since primeval times.

Many art forms have developed and perished. Tragedy begins with the Greeks, is extinguished with them, and after centuries its "rules" only are revived. The epic poem, which had its origin in the youth of nations, expires in Europe at the end of the Renaissance. Panel painting is a creation of the Middle Ages, and nothing guarantees its uninterrupted existence. But the human need for shelter is lasting. Architecture has never been idle. Its history is more ancient than that of any other art, and its claim to being a living force has significance in every attempt to comprehend the relationship of the masses to art. Buildings are appropriated in a twofold manner: by use and by perception—or rather, by touch and sight. Such appropriation cannot be understood in terms of the attentive concentration of a tourist before a famous building. On the tactile side there is no counterpart to contemplation on the optical side. Tactile appropriation is accomplished not so much by attention as by habit. As regards architecture, habit determines to a large extent even optical reception. The latter, too, occurs much less through rapt attention than by noticing the object in incidental fashion. This mode of appropriation, developed with reference to architecture, in certain circumstances acquires canonical value. For the tasks which face the human apparatus of perception at the turning points of history cannot be solved by optical means, that is, by contemplation, alone. They are mastered gradually by habit, under the guidance of tactile appropriation.

The distracted person, too, can form habits. More, the ability to master certain tasks in a state of distraction proves that their solution has become a matter of habit. Distraction as provided by art presents a covert control of the extent to which new tasks have become soluble by apperception. Since, moreover, individuals are tempted to avoid such tasks, art will tackle the most difficult and most important ones where it is able to mobilize the masses. Today it does so in the film. Reception in a state of distraction, which is increasing noticeably in all fields of art and is symptomatic of profound changes in apperception, finds in the film its true means of exercise. The film with its shock effect meets this mode of reception halfway. The film makes the cult value recede into the background not only by putting the public in the position of the critic, but also by the fact that at the movies this position requires no attention. The public is an examiner, but an absent-minded one.

EPILOGUE

The growing proletarianization of modern man and the increasing formation of masses are two aspects of the same process. Fascism attempts to organize the newly created proletarian masses without affecting the property structure which the masses strive to eliminate. Fascism sees its salvation in giving these masses not their right, but instead a chance to express themselves. The masses have a right to change property relations; Fascism seeks to give them an expression while preserving property. The logical result of Fascism is the introduction of aesthetics into political life. The violation of the masses, whom Fascism, with its *Führer* cult, forces to their knees, has its counterpart in the violation of an apparatus which is pressed into the production of ritual values.

All efforts to render politics aesthetic culminate in one thing: war. War and war only can set a goal for mass movements on the largest scale while respecting the traditional property system. This is the political formula for the situation. The technological formula may be stated as follows: Only war makes it possible to mobilize all of today's technical resources while maintaining the property system. It goes without saying that the Fascist apotheosis of war does not employ such arguments. Still, Marinetti says in his manifesto on the Ethiopian colonial war: "For twenty-seven years we Futurists have rebelled against the branding of war as antiaesthetic . . . . Accordingly we state: . . . War is beautiful because it establishes man's dominion over the subjugated machinery by means of gas masks, terrifying megaphones, flame throwers, and small tanks. War is beautiful because it initiates the dreamt-of metalization of the human body. War is beautiful because it enriches a flowering meadow with the fiery orchids of machine guns. War is beautiful because it combines the gunfire, the cannonades, the cease-fire, the scents, and the stench of putrefaction into a symphony. War is beautiful because it creates new architecture, like that of the big tanks, the geometrical formation flights, the smoke spirals from burning villages, and many others. . . . Poets and artists of Futurism! . . . remember these principles of an aesthetics of war so that your struggle for a new literature and a new graphic art . . . may be illumined by them!"

This manifesto has the virtue of clarity. Its formulations deserve to be accepted by dialecticians. To the latter, the aesthetics of to-day's war appears as follows: If the natural utilization of productive forces is impeded by the property system, the increase in technical devices, in speed, and in the sources of energy will press for an unnatural utilization, and this is found in war. The destructiveness of war furnishes proof that society has not been mature enough to incorporate technology as its organ, that technology has not been sufficiently developed to cope with the elemental forces of society. The horrible features of imperialistic warfare are attributable to the discrepancy between the tremendous means of production and their inadequate utilization in the process of production—in other words, to unemployment and the lack of markets. Imperialistic war is a rebellion of technology which collects, in the form of "human material," the claims to which society has denied its natural material. Instead of draining rivers, society directs a human stream into a bed of trenches; instead of dropping seeds from airplanes, it drops incendiary bombs over cities; and through gas warfare the aura is abolished in a new way.

"Fiat ars—pereat mundus," says Fascism, and, as Marinetti admits, expects war to supply the artistic gratification of a sense perception that has been changed by technology. This is evidently the consummation of *"l'art pour l'art."* Mankind, which in Homer's time was an object of contemplation for the Olympian gods, now is one for itself. Its self-alienation has reached such a degree that it can experience its own destruction as an aesthetic pleasure of the first order. This is the situation of politics which Fascism is rendering aesthetic. Communism responds by politicizing art.

BIBLIOGRAPHY

Agee, James. *Agee on Film: Reviews and Comments*. Boston: Beacon Press, n.d.

Arnheim, Rudolf. *Art and Visual Perception*. Berkeley and Los Angeles: University of California Press, 1954.

————. *Film as Art*. Berkeley and Los Angeles: University of California Press, 1966.

Balázs, Béla. *Theory of the Film: Character and Growth of a New Art*. New York: Dover Publications, 1970.

Barsam, Richard Meran. *Nonfiction Film: A Critical History*. New York: Dutton, 1972.

Barthes, Roland. *Mythologies*. Selected and edited by Annette Laversy. New York: Hill and Wang, 1972.

————. *Semiology of the Cinema*. Boston: Beacon Press, n.d.

Barr, Charles. CinemaScope: Before and After. *Film Quarterly*, XVI, No. 4, Summer 1963.

Battcock, Gregory, ed. *The New American Cinema*. New York: Dutton, 1967.

Bazin, André. *What is Cinema?* Volume I. Berkeley and Los Angeles: University of California Press, 1971.

————. *What is Cinema?* Volume II. Berkeley and Los Angeles: University of California Press, 1971.

Benjamin, Walter. *Illuminations*. Edited and with an introduction by Hannah Arendt. New York: Harcourt Brace, 1968.

Bergson, Henri. Laughter, in *Comedy*. Edited by Wylie Sypher. Garden City, New York: Doubleday Anchor, 1956.

Bluestone, George. *Novels into Film*. Berkeley and Los Angeles: University of California Press, 1966.

635

BIBLIOGRAPHY

Bobker, Lee R. *Elements of Film*. New York: Harcourt Brace, 1969.

Brakhage, Stan. The Art of Vision, in *Film Culture*, No. 30, Fall 1963.

Burch, Noël. *Theory of Film Practice*. Translated by Helen R. Lane and with an Introduction by Annette Michelson. New York: Praeger, 1973.

Cavell, Stanley. *The World Viewed: Reflections on the Ontology of Film*. New York: Viking, 1971.

Cawelti, John. *The Six-Gun Mystique*. Bowling Green, Ohio: Bowling Green Popular Press, n.d.

Cocteau, Jean. *Cocteau on the Film*. Translated by Vera Triall. New York: Roy Publishers.

Cohen-Séat, Gilbert. *Essai sur les principes d'une philosophie du cinéma*. Paris: Presses Universitaires de France, 1958.

———. *Problemes du cinéma et de l'information visuelle*. Paris: Presses Universitaires de France, 1961.

Doesburg, Theo van. Film as Pure Form, in *Form* (Cambridge), No. 1, Summer 1966.

Durgnat, Raymond. *Films and Feelings*. Cambridge, Mass.: The M.I.T. Press, 1967.

Earle, William. Revolt Against Realism in the Films, in *The Journal of Aesthetics and Art Criticism*, XXVII, No. 2, Winter 1968.

Eisenstein, Sergei M. *Film Form*. Edited and translated by Jay Leyda. New York: Harcourt Brace, n.d.

———. *The Film Sense*. Edited and translated by Jay Leyda. New York: Harcourt Brace, n.d.

Faure, Élie. *The Art of Cineplastics*. Boston: Four Seas Company, 1923.

Ferguson, Otis. *The Film Criticism of Otis Ferguson*. Edited and with a preface by Robert Wilson. Foreword by Andrew Sarris. Philadelphia: Temple University Press, 1971.

Film Comment. Hollywood Screenwriters (Special Issue). VI, No. 4, Winter 1970–71.

Film Comment. The Men with the Movie Cameras (Special Issue). June 1972.

Gessner, Robert. *The Moving Image: A Guide to Cinematic Literacy*. New York: Dutton, 1968.

Gouhier, Henri. *L'essence du théâtre*. Paris: Plon, 1948.

———. *Le théâtre et l'existence*. Paris: Auber, 1952.

Grierson, John. *Grierson on Documentary*. Edited by Forsyth Hardy. New York: Harcourt Brace, 1947.

Harrington, John. *The Rhetoric of Film*. New York: Holt, Rinehart, and Winston, 1973.

Hauser, Arnold. *The Social History of Art*. Four volumes. New York: Knopf, n.d.

BIBLIOGRAPHY

Hjelmslev, Louis. *Essais linguistiques*. Copenhague: Nordisk Sprog-og kulturforlag, 1959.

———. *Prolegomena to a Theory of Language*. Bloomington, Ind.: Indiana University Publications in Anthropology and Linguistics, 1953.

Huss, Roy, and Norman Silverstein. *The Film Experience: Elements of Motion Picture Art*. New York: Harper and Row, 1968.

Kauffmann, Stanley. Notes on Theater-and-Film, in *Performance*, Vol. 1, No. 4, October 1972.

Kael, Pauline. *I Lost it at the Movies*. Boston: Little Brown, 1965.

———. Raising Kane, in *The Citizen Kane Book*. Boston: Little Brown, 1971.

Kelman, Ken. The Reality of New Cinema, in *The New American Cinema*, Edited by Battcock. New York: Dutton, 1967.

Kitses, Jim. *Horizons West*. Bloomington, Ind. and London: Indiana University Press, 1970.

Kracauer, Siegfried. *From Caligari to Hitler*. New York: Noonday, 1959.

———. *Theory of Film: The Redemption of Physical Reality*. London, Oxford, New York: Oxford University Press, 1960.

Langer, Susanne K. *Feeling and Form*. New York: Scribner's, 1953.

Lawson, John Howard. *Film: The Creative Process*. New York: Hill and Wang, 1964.

Lebovici, Serge. Psychoanalyse et cinéma, in *Revue internationale de filmologie*, II, No. 5.

Lessing, Gotthold Ephraim. *Laocoon: An Essay Upon the Limits of Painting and Poetry*. New York: Noonday, n.d.

Lévi-Strauss, Claude. Structural Analysis in Linguistics and in Anthropology, in *Structural Anthropology*. New York: Basic Books, 1963.

Lindgren, Ernest. *The Art of the Film*. Revised edition. London: Allen and Unwin, 1963.

Lindsay, Vachel. *The Art of the Moving Picture*. Revised edition. New York: Macmillan, 1922.

Manvell, Roger. *Film*. London: Penguin Books, 1946.

———. *Shakespeare and the Film*. New York: Praeger, 1971.

Marcel, Gabriel. Possibilités et limites de l'art cinématographique, in *Revue internationale de filmologie*, V, Nos. 18–19.

Marinetti, Filippo T. *Selected Writings*. Translated by Arthur A. Coppotelli and R. W. Flint. New York: Noonday, 1972.

Martin, Marcel. *La langage cinématographique*. Paris: Éditions du Cerf, 1955.

Martinet, André. *Elements of General Linguistics*. Translated by Elisabeth Palmer. London: Faber and Faber, 1960.

637

Mast, Gerald. *The Comic Mind: Comedy and the Movies*. New York: Bobbs-Merrill, 1973.

Merleau-Ponty, Maurice. The Film and the New Psychology, in *Sense and Non-sense*. Translated by Hubert L. and Patricia A. Dreyfus. Evanston, Ill: Northwestern University Press, 1964.

Metz, Christian. *Film Language: A Semiotics of the Cinema*. Translated by Michael Taylor. New York: Oxford University Press, 1974.

Meyerhold, Vsevolod. *Meyerhold on Theater*. Edited by Edward Braun. New York: Hill and Wang, 1969.

Mitry, Jean. *Esthétique et psychologie du cinéma*. Two Volumes. Paris: Éditions Universitaires, 1963–65.

Moholy-Nagy, László. *Vision in Motion*. Chicago: University of Chicago, 1947.

Montagu, Ivor. *Film World*. Baltimore: Penguin, 1964.

Morin, Edgar. *Le cinéma; ou, l'homme imaginaire*. Paris: Éditions de Minuit, 1956.

————. *The Stars*. Translated by Richard Howard. New York: Grove Press, 1960.

Münsterberg, Hugo. *The Film: A Psychological Study*. New York: Dover, 1969.

Nicoll, Allardyce. *Film and Theatre*. New York: Thomas Y. Crowell, 1937.

Olson, Elder. *The Theory of Comedy*. Bloomington, Ind., and London: Indiana University Press, 1968.

Orwell, George. Boys' Weeklies, in *Collection of Essays*. New York: Doubleday, 1954.

Panofsky, Erwin. Style and Medium in the Motion Pictures, in *Critique*, I, No. 3, January-February 1947.

Powdermaker, Hortense. *Hollywood, the Dream Factory*. Boston: Little Brown, 1960.

Pudovkin, Vsevolod I. *Film Technique and Film Acting*. Edited and translated by Ivor Montagu. New York: Grove Press, 1960.

Reisz, Karel. *The Technique of Film Editing*. New York: Hastings House, 1968.

Renan, Sheldon. *An Introduction to the American Underground Film*. New York: Dutton, 1967.

Richter, Hans. The Film as an Original Art Form, in *Film Culture*, I, No. 1, January 1955.

Rotha, Paul, Road Sinclair, and Richard Griffith. *Documentary Film*. London: Faber and Faber, 1966.

Sadoul, Georges. *Histoire générale du cinéma*. Five Volumes. Paris: Éditions Denoël, 1946–54.

BIBLIOGRAPHY

Sarris, Andrew. *The American Cinema: Directors and Directions 1929–1968*. New York: Dutton, 1969.

———. Notes on the *Auteur* Theory in 1962, in *Film Culture Reader*. Edited by Sitney. New York: Praeger, 1970.

de Saussure, Ferdinand. *Course in General Linguistics*. Translated by Wade Baskin. New York: McGraw-Hill, 1966.

Schnitzer, Luda and Jean, and Marcel Martin, eds. *Cinema in Revolution: The Heroic Age of the Soviet Film*. New York: Hill and Wang, 1973.

Seldes, Gilbert. *The Great Audience*. New York: Viking, 1950.

———. *The Movies Come From America*. New York: Scribner's, 1937.

———. *The Public Arts*. New York: Simon and Schuster, 1956.

Sitney, P. Adams, ed. *Film Culture Reader*. New York: Praeger, 1970.

Sontag, Susan. *Against Interpretation*. New York: Delta Books, 1966.

———. *Styles of Radical Will*. New York: Farrar, Straus, 1969.

Spottiswode, Raymond. *A Grammar of the Film*. Berkeley and Los Angeles: University of California Press, 1950.

Stephenson, Ralph, and J. R. Debrix. *The Cinema as Art*. Baltimore: Penguin, 1965.

Tyler, Parker. *The Hollywood Hallucination*. New York: Simon and Schuster, 1970.

———. *Magic and Myth of the Movies*. New York: Simon and Schuster, 1970.

———. *Sex Psyche Etcetera in the Film*. Baltimore: Penguin, 1971.

Vorkapich, Slavko. Toward True Cinema, in *Film Culture*, No. 19, March 1959.

Warshow, Robert. *The Immediate Experience*. New York: Doubleday Anchor, 1964.

Wolfenstein, Martha, and Nathan Leites. *Movies, a Psychological Study*. Glencoe: The Free Press, 1950.

Wollen, Peter. *Signs and Meaning in the Cinema*. New and enlarged. Bloomington, Ind., and London: Indiana University Press, 1972.

Youngblood, Gene. *Expanded Cinema*. New York: Dutton, 1970.